AMERICAN GOVERNMENT 97/98

Twenty-Seventh Edition

Editor

Bruce Stinebrickner
DePauw University

Professor Bruce Stinebrickner teaches American politics and chairs the Department of Political Science at DePauw University in Greencastle, Indiana. He has also taught American politics at Lehman College of the City University of New York, at the University of Queensland in Brisbane, Australia, and, for one semester, in a DePauw program for Argentine students in Buenos Aires. He received his Ph.D. from Yale University in 1974. In his courses and publications on American politics, Professor Stinebrickner brings to bear valuable insights gained from living, teaching, and lecturing abroad.

Annual Editions
A Library of Information from the Public Press
Dushkin/McGraw·Hill
Sluice Dock, Guilford, Connecticut 06437

Visit us on the Internet—http://www.dushkin.com

The Annual Editions Series

ANNUAL EDITIONS is a series of over 65 volumes designed to provide the reader with convenient, low-cost access to a wide range of current, carefully selected articles from some of the most important magazines, newspapers, and journals published today. ANNUAL EDITIONS are updated on an annual basis through a continuous monitoring of over 300 periodical sources. All ANNUAL EDITIONS have a number of features that are designed to make them particularly useful, including topic guides, annotated tables of contents, unit overviews, and indexes. For the teacher using ANNUAL EDITIONS in the classroom, an Instructor's Resource Guide with test questions is available for each volume.

VOLUMES AVAILABLE

Abnormal Psychology
Adolescent Psychology
Africa
Aging
American Foreign Policy
American Government
American History, Pre-Civil War
American History, Post-Civil War
American Public Policy
Anthropology
Archaeology
Biopsychology
Business Ethics
Child Growth and Development
China
Comparative Politics
Computers in Education
Computers in Society
Criminal Justice
Criminology
Developing World
Deviant Behavior
Drugs, Society, and Behavior
Dying, Death, and Bereavement

Early Childhood Education
Economics
Educating Exceptional Children
Education
Educational Psychology
Environment
Geography
Global Issues
Health
Human Development
Human Resources
Human Sexuality
India and South Asia
International Business
Japan and the Pacific Rim
Latin America
Life Management
Macroeconomics
Management
Marketing
Marriage and Family
Mass Media
Microeconomics

Middle East and the
   Islamic World
Multicultural Education
Nutrition
Personal Growth and Behavior
Physical Anthropology
Psychology
Public Administration
Race and Ethnic Relations
Russia, the Eurasian Republics,
   and Central/Eastern Europe
Social Problems
Social Psychology
Sociology
State and Local Government
Urban Society
Western Civilization,
   Pre-Reformation
Western Civilization,
   Post-Reformation
Western Europe
World History, Pre-Modern
World History, Modern
World Politics

Cataloging in Publication Data
Main entry under title: Annual Editions: American Government. 1997/98.
   1. U.S.—Politics and government—1945—Periodicals. I. Stinebrickner, Bruce,
comp. II. Title: American Government.
ISBN 0-697-37191-3   320.9'73'0924'05   76-180265
JK1.A7A

Twenty-Seventh Edition

Cover image © 1996 PhotoDisc, Inc.

Printed in the United States of America

Printed on Recycled Paper

Editors/Advisory Board

Staff

To the Reader

In publishing ANNUAL EDITIONS we recognize the enormous role played by the magazines, newspapers, and journals of the *public press* in providing current, first-rate educational information in a broad spectrum of interest areas. Many of these articles are appropriate for students, researchers, and professionals seeking accurate, current material to help bridge the gap between principles and theories and the real world. These articles, however, become more useful for study when those of lasting value are carefully *collected, organized, indexed,* and *reproduced* in a *low-cost format,* which provides easy and permanent access when the material is needed. That is the role played by ANNUAL EDITIONS. Under the direction of each volume's *academic editor,* who is an expert in the subject area, and with the guidance of an *Advisory Board,* each year we seek to provide in each ANNUAL EDITION a current, well-balanced, carefully selected collection of the best of the public press for your study and enjoyment. We think that you will find this volume useful, and we hope that you will take a moment to let us know what you think.

American Government 97/98 is the twenty-seventh edition of a book that has become a mainstay in many introductory courses on American politics. The educational goal is to provide a readable collection of up-to-date articles that are informative, interesting, and stimulating to students beginning their study of the American political system.

In January 1995, for the first time since 1947, a Democratic president faced a Congress in which Republicans controlled a majority of seats in both houses. So-called "divided government"—a situation in which control of the presidency, the House of Representatives, and the Senate is split between Democrats and Republicans—has become commonplace in United States national government since 1969. The usual pattern, however, has been a Republican president facing Democratic control of both houses of Congress. For the first two years of President Clinton's term, party control of American national government was *not* divided between the two major parties: Democrats controlled the presidency as well as both houses of Congress. But the hotly contested congressional elections of November 1994 marked a sharp departure from post–World War II norms. In January 1995, the House of Representatives elected Congressman Newt Gingrich of Georgia to be the first Republican Speaker in 40 years.

The November 1996 elections did little to change the prevailing partisan equation in Washington. President Clinton was reelected by a comfortable margin over Republic Bob Dole, yet Republicans maintained majority control in both houses of Congress. As this book goes to press, another two years of "divided government" have begun. President Clinton's 1997 State of the Union address and proposed budget leave room for accommodation with Republicans in Congress. For their part, Republican congressional leaders have suggested that they are willing to work with the president in seeking to achieve a balanced budget over the next several years. Providing a potentially ominous backdrop for congressional-presidential relations, however, are accusations aimed at Speaker Gingrich and President Clinton. Gingrich was officially censured and fined by the House of Representatives in January 1997, while various real estate and financial dealings involving Bill and Hillary Clinton remain under investigation by the Whitewater special prosecutor and congressional committees. Will these matters affect both men's ability to lead during

the 105th Congress? What will be the effects of Gingrich's smaller Republican majority in the House of Representatives and the style and tactics of Senate majority leader Trent Lott, who succeeded Bob Dole in mid-1996? How will the new group of top officials appointed by President Clinton to replace the Cabinet secretaries and White House staff who left the administration at the end of the president's first term affect the cohesiveness and direction of the second Clinton administration? The selections in this book do not, of course, contain answers to these questions. But they do provide analyses that can help us see connections between such questions and related elements of the American political system.

The systems approach provides a rough organizational framework for this book. The first unit focuses on ideological and constitutional underpinnings of American politics, from both historical and contemporary perspectives. The second unit treats the major institutions of the national government. The third covers the "input" or "linkage" mechanisms of the system—political parties, elections, interest groups, and media. The fourth and concluding unit shifts the focus to policy choices that confront the government in Washington and resulting "outputs" of the political system.

Each year thousands of articles about American politics are published, and deciding which to reprint in a collection of readings such as this is not always easy. Criteria for selecting each article include the topic treated, the approach taken, and the level of analysis used. How well an article stands alone and how well it complements other likely selections are also taken into account. Furthermore, since no position on the political spectrum has a monopoly on truth, articles are chosen with an eye toward providing viewpoints from left, right, and center. More than half of the selections in this book are new to this year's edition.

Next year will bring another opportunity for change, and you, the reader, are invited to participate in the process. Please complete and return the postpaid article rating form on the last page of the book and let us know your reactions and your suggestions for improvement.

Bruce Stinebrickner

Bruce Stinebrickner
Editor

Contents

The concepts in bold italics are developed in the article. For further expansion please refer to the Topic Guide and the Index.

The concepts in bold italics are developed in the article. For further expansion please refer to the Topic Guide and the Index.

UNIT 2

Structures of American Politics

The nineteen articles in this unit examine the structure and present status of the American presidency, Congress, judiciary, and bureaucracy.

The concepts in bold italics are developed in the article. For further expansion please refer to the Topic Guide and the Index.

UNIT 3

Process of American Politics

The seventeen articles in this unit review how political parties, voters, election processes, interest groups, and the media work in the process of American politics.

The concepts in bold italics are developed in the article. For further expansion please refer to the Topic Guide and the Index.

The concepts in bold italics are developed in the article. For further expansion please refer to the Topic Guide and the Index.

UNIT 4

Products of American Politics

The ten selections in this unit examine the domestic, economic, foreign, and defense policies that American government produces.

The concepts in bold italics are developed in the article. For further expansion please refer to the Topic Guide and the Index.

Selected World Wide Web Sites for American Government

(Some Web sites are continually changing their structure and content, so the information listed here may not always be available.)

http://congress.org/ A user-friendly site that is a very effective starting point for Web users in search of Capitol Hill current political information. The site is hot-linked to a wide range of information about the 105th Congress, which began its session on January 7, 1997. The site allows users to access a complete and reliable directory of information about the members of the U.S. House of Representatives and Senate, and it includes a congressional directory, House and Senate committee assignments, and the ability to communicate with specific members.

http://www.c-span.org/ This is the C-Span cable network's Web site, which offers the daily objective gavel-to-gavel coverage of Congress. The site has links to the three branches of government, media organizations, and other Web sites suggested by viewers.

http://www.whitehouse.gov/ This site is a key source for current and historical information about the presidency and the White House. It includes the current president and vice president's accomplishments, their families, and how to reach them via e-mail; an Interactive Citizens' Handbook that is a guide to the federal government; past presidents and their families; a Virtual Library of White House documents; a Briefing Room with today's news releases, hot topics, and the latest federal statistics.

http://www.politicsnow.com/ Supported by the *Los Angeles Times, ABC News, Newsweek,* the *Washington Post,* the *National Journal,* and the daily summary of political news called *Hotline.* This Web site is hot-linked to an enormous amount of Washington resources. These resources include *The Almanac of American Politics,* which offers detailed information about congressional districts and their representatives; *Capitol Source,* the yellow pages for the nation's government; direct access to the National Archives; and access to *The Buzz,* a political gossip column.

http://www.fec.gov/ This Federal Election Commission site offers information on financial standings of candidates, parties, and Political Action Committees; news releases and media advisories; federal elections and voting statistics; and guides for election law.

http://www.fedworld.gov/ Used to access the federal government's on-line information services, this site provides data on Federal Aviation Administration reports, IRS publications, federal job opportunities, access to the Government Information Locator Service, and the World News Connection. (The World News Connection charges a subscription fee, but the service they offer is very valuable—gathering news stories from around the world, translating them into English, and housing them on a database arranged by region and category.)

http://www.rnc.org/ This is the Republican National Committee site that offers the latest GOP information with press releases and audio/video clips.

http://www.democrats.org/ This Democratic National Committee site is hot-linked to other Democratic and liberal organizations.

We highly recommend that you check out our Web site for expanded information and our other product lines. We are continually updating and adding links to our Web site in order to offer you the most usable and useful information that will support and expand the value of your *Annual Edition.* You can reach us at *http://www.dushkin.com*

The concepts in bold italics are developed in the article. For further expansion please refer to the Topic Guide and the Index.

Topic Guide

This topic guide suggests how the selections in this book relate to topics likely to be treated in American politics textbooks and courses. The guide is arranged alphabetically according to topic, and the selections that give substantial coverage to each topic are named. Most of the topics in the topic guide come from the italicized terms in the brief descriptions of each selection that appear in the table of contents.

TOPIC AREA	TREATED IN	TOPIC AREA	TREATED IN
Abortion	15. Our Bodies, Our Souls	Elections and Nominations	18. Racial Gerrymandering 41. What If We Held an Election and Nobody Came? 42. Politics of Money 43. Dirtiest Election Ever 44. Bill's Big Backers 45. Small Change 46. Primary Colours: Nasty, Brutish, and Short? 47. Golden Mean
Affirmative Action	See Race/Racial Discrimination		
Balanced Budget	58. Entitlement Time Bomb 60. Balanced Budget Crusade		
Bureaucracy	13. Can Democratic Government Survive? 36. Still Trying to Reinvent Government 37. Government *Can* Work 38. You Can't Fix It If You Don't Raise the Hood 39. Uncle Sam's Corporate Lawyers	Entitlements	58. Entitlement Time Bomb
		Equality	10. Spiral of Inequality
		Federalism	2. Constitution of the United States, 1787 3. Size and Variety of the Union as a Check on Faction 11. You Say You Want a Devolution
Clinton, Bill	23. Is the President a Waffler? 26. Will Clinton Sing Second-Term Blues? 43. Dirtiest Election Ever 44. Bill's Big Backers 45. Small Change	Foreign and Defense Policy	64. America's Incoherent Foreign Policy 65. Pumping Up the Pentagon: The Domestic Geopolitics of Military Spending 66. Buy the Nukes
Congress	19. Rule by Law 27. Imperial Congress 28. *Too Representative Government* 29. "Outside" Role: A Leadership Challenge 30. It's Not *Mr. Smith Goes to Washington* 51. This Mr. Smith Gets His Way in Washington: Federal Express Chief Twists Some Big Arms	Gender/Gender Discrimination	16. Race and the Constitution
		Interest Groups	3. Size and Variety of the Union as a Check on Faction 48. Demosclerosis 49. Going to Extremes, Losing the Center 50. Cultivating the Grass Roots to Reap Legislative Benefits 51. This Mr. Smith Gets His Way in Washington: Federal Express Chief Twists Some Big Arms 53. Heeding the Call
Conservatism	19. Rule by Law 32. Conservative Case for Judicial Activism		
Constitution	3. Size and Variety of the Union as a Check on Faction 4. Checks and Balances 5. The Judiciary 17. Bill of Rights and the Supreme Court: A Foreigner's View		

TOPIC AREA	TREATED IN	TOPIC AREA	TREATED IN
Historic Perspectives	1. Declaration of Independence, 1776 2. Constitution of the United States, 1787 3. Size and Variety of the Union as a Check on Faction 4. Checks and Balances 5. The Judiciary 27. Imperial Congress 50. Cultivating the Grass Roots to Reap Legislative Benefits 51. This Mr. Smith Gets His Way in Washington: Federal Express Chief Twists Some Big Arms 53. Heeding the Call	**Parties** **Presidency**	44. Bill's Big Backers 47. Golden Mean 21. Do We Ask Too Much of Presidents? 22. Separated System 23. Is the President a Waffler? 24. Agenda at Risk? 25. Rush to Judgment: Picking Presidents 26. Will Clinton Sing Second-Term Blues?
Liberalism	53. Heeding the Call	**Race/Racial Discrimination**	14. Paradox of Integration 16. Race and the Constitution 18. Racial Gerrymandering
Media	46. Primary Colours: Nasty, Brutish, and Short 52. Resisting Pressures on a Free Press 53. Heeding the Call 54. Did You Have a Good Week? 55. 'New' Media and Politics: What Does the Future Hold? 56. Hillary and Us: Rocky Relationship with Media? Not Really, Just No Relationship at All	**Religion** **Rights**	12. The Last Taboo 20. Let Us Pray 14. Paradox of Integration 16. Race and the Constitution 35. In Whose Court?

Foundations of American Politics

- Basic Documents (Articles 1–5)
- Contemporary Views and Values (Articles 6–15)
- Constitutional and Legal Matters (Articles 16–20)

This unit treats some of the less concrete aspects of the American political system—historical ideals, contemporary ideas and values, and constitutional and legal issues. These dimensions of the system are not immune to change. Instead, they interact with the wider political environment in which they exist and are modified accordingly. Usually this interaction is a gradual process, but sometimes events foster more rapid change.

Human beings can be distinguished from other species by their ability to think and reason at relatively high levels of abstraction. In turn, ideas, ideals, values, and principles can and do play important roles in politics. Most Americans value ideas and ideals such as democracy, freedom, equal opportunity, and justice. Yet the precise meanings of these terms and the best ways of implementing them are the subject of much dispute in the political arena. Such ideas and ideals, as well as disputes about their "real" meanings, are important elements in the practice of American politics.

Although the selections in this unit span more than 200 years, they are clearly related to one another. Understanding contemporary political viewpoints is easier if the ideals and principles of the past are also taken into account. In addition, we can better appreciate the significance of historic documents such as the Declaration of Independence and the Constitution if we are familiar with contemporary ideas and perspectives. The interaction of different ideas and values plays an important part in the continuing development of the "foundations" of the American political system.

The first section includes several historic documents from the eighteenth century. The first is the Declaration of Independence. Written in 1776, it proclaims the Founders' views of why independence from England was justified and, in so doing, identifies certain "unalienable" rights that "all men" are said to possess. The second document, the Constitution of 1787, remains in effect to this day. It provides an organizational blueprint for the structure of American national government, outlines the federal relationship between the national government and the states, and expresses limitations on what government can do. Twenty-seven amendments have been added to the original Constitution in two centuries. In addition to the Declaration of Independence and the Constitution, the first section includes three selections from *The Federalist Papers*, a series of newspaper articles written in support of the proposed new Constitution. Appearing in 1787 and 1788, *The Federalist Papers* treated various provisions of the new Constitution and suggested that putting the Constitution into effect would bring about good government.

The second section treats contemporary political ideas and viewpoints. As selections in this section illustrate, efforts to apply or act on political beliefs in the context of concrete circumstances often lead to interesting commentary and debate. "Liberal" and "conservative" are two labels often used in American political discussions, but political views and values are far more complex than these two terms capture.

Selections in the third section show that constitutional and legal issues and interpretations are tied to historic principles as well as to contemporary ideas and values. It has been suggested that, throughout American history, almost every important political question has at one time or another appeared as a constitutional or legal issue.

The historic documents and some other selections in this unit can be more difficult to understand than most articles in other units. Some of them may have to be read and reread carefully to be fully appreciated. But to grapple with the important material treated here is to come to grips with a variety of conceptual blueprints for the American political system. To ignore the theoretical issues raised would be to bypass an important element of American politics today.

Looking Ahead: Challenge Questions

What do you think would surprise the Founding Fathers most about the values and ideals held by Americans today?

Which ideals, ideas, and values seem likely to remain central to American politics, and which seem likely to erode and gradually disappear?

To what rights do you think all Americans are entitled? Do all Americans have these rights now? If not, why not?

What provisions of the U.S. Constitution do you think are particularly wise and desirable? Which provisions, including ones that have been superseded by amendments, seem unwise and undesirable?

What makes constitutional interpretation and reinterpretation necessary in the American political system?

Why, at the same time, do the very words of the Constitution remain a respected foundation of the entire system of government?

What groups seem most likely to become visible, active forces on the American political scene in the way that blacks and women have in the recent past? Why?

Do you consider yourself a conservative, a liberal, a socialist, a reactionary, or what? Why?

The Declaration of Independence

WHEN in the Course of human events, it becomes necessary for one people to dissolve the political bands which have connected them with another, and to assume among the powers of the earth, the separate and equal station to which the Laws of Nature and of Nature's God entitle them, a decent respect to the opinions of mankind requires that they should declare the causes which impel them to the separation.—We hold these truths to be self-evident, that all men are created equal, that they are endowed by their Creator with certain unalienable Rights, that among these are Life, Liberty and the pursuit of Happiness.—That to secure these rights, Governments are instituted among Men, deriving their just powers from the consent of the governed.— That whenever any Form of Government becomes destructive of these ends, it is the Right of the People to alter or to abolish it, and to institute new Government, laying its foundation on such principles and organizing its powers in such form, as to them shall seem most likely to effect their Safety and Happiness. Prudence, indeed, will dictate that Governments long established should not be changed for light and transient causes; and accordingly all experience hath shewn, that mankind are more disposed to suffer, while evils are sufferable, than to right themselves by abolishing the forms to which they are accustomed. But when a long train of abuses and usurpations, pursuing invariably the same Object evinces a design to reduce them under absolute Despotism, it is their right, it is their duty, to throw off such Government, and to provide new Guards for their future security.—Such has been the patient sufferance of these Colonies; and such is now the necessity which constrains them to alter their former Systems of Government. The history of the present King of Great Britain is a history of repeated injuries and usurpations, all having in direct object the establishment of an absolute Tyranny over these States. To prove this, let Facts be submitted to a candid world.—He has refused his Assent to Laws, the most wholesome and necessary for the public good.—He has forbidden his Governors to pass Laws of immediate and pressing importance, unless suspended in their operation till his Assent should be obtained; and when so suspended, he has utterly neglected to attend to them.—He has refused to pass other Laws for the accommodation of large districts of people, unless those people would relinquish the right of Representation in the Legislature, a right inestimable to them and formidable to tyrants only.—He has called together legislative bodies at places unusual, uncomfortable, and distant from the depository of their public Records, for the sole purpose of fatiguing them into compliance with his measures.—He has dissolved Representative Houses repeatedly, for opposing with manly firmness his invasions on the rights of the people.—He has refused for a long time, after such dissolutions, to cause others to be elected; whereby the Legislative powers, incapable of Annihilation, have returned to the People at large for their exercise; the State remaining in the meantime exposed to all the dangers of invasion from without, and convulsions within.—He has endeavoured to prevent the population of these States; for that purpose obstructing the Laws for Naturalization of Foreigners; refusing to pass others to encourage their migrations hither, and raising the conditions of new Appropriations of Lands.—He has obstructed the Administration of Justice, by refusing his Assent to Laws for establishing Judiciary powers.—He has made Judges dependent on his Will alone, for the tenure of their offices, and the amount and payment of their salaries.—He has erected a multitude of New Offices, and sent hither swarms of Officers to harass our people, and eat out their substance. He has kept among us, in times of peace, Standing Armies without the Consent of our legislatures.—He has affected to render the Military independent of and superior to the Civil power.—He has combined with others to subject us to a jurisdiction foreign to our constitution, and unacknowledged by our laws; giving his Assent to their Acts of pretended Legislation:—For quartering large bodies of armed troops among us:—For protecting them, by a mock Trial, from punishment for any Murders which they should commit on the Inhabitants of these States:—For cutting off our Trade with all parts of the world:—For imposing Taxes on us without our Consent:—For depriving us in many cases, of the benefits of Trial by Jury:—For transporting us beyond Seas to be tried for pretended offences:—For abolishing the free System of English Laws in a neighbouring Province, establishing therein an Arbitrary government, and enlarging its Boundaries so as to render it at once an example and fit instrument for introducing the same absolute rule into these Colonies:—For taking away our Charters, abolishing our most valuable Laws and altering fundamentally the Forms of our Governments:—For suspending our own Legislatures, and declaring themselves invested with power to legislate for us in all cases whatsoever.—He has abdicated Government here, by declaring us out of his Protection and waging War against us.—He has plundered our seas, ravaged our Coasts, burnt our towns, and destroyed the lives of our people.—He is at this time transporting large Armies of foreign Mercenaries to compleat the works of death, desolation and tyranny, already begun with circumstances of Cruelty & perfidy scarcely paralleled in the most barbarous ages, and totally unworthy the Head of a civilized nation.—He has constrained our fellow Citizens taken Captive on the high Seas to bear Arms gainst their Country, to become the executioners of their friends and Brethren, or to fall themselves by their Hands.—He has excited domestic insurrections amongst us, and has endeavoured to bring on the inhabitants of our frontiers, the merciless Indian Savages, whose known rule of warfare, is an undistinguished destruction of all ages, sexes and conditions. In every stage of these Oppressions We have Petitioned for Redress in the most humble terms: Our repeated Petitions have been answered only by repeated injury. A Prince, whose character is thus marked by every act which may define a Tyrant, is unfit to be the ruler of a free people. Nor have We been wanting in attentions to our British brethren. We have warned them from time to time of attempts by their legislature to extend an unwarrantable jurisdiction over us. We have reminded them of the circumstances of our emigration and settlement here. We have appealed to their native justice and magnanimity, and we have conjured them by the ties of our common kindred to disavow these usurpations, which would inevitably interrupt our connections and correspondence. They too have been deaf to the voice of justice and of consanguinity. We must, therefore, acquiesce in the necessity, which denounces our Separation, and hold them, as we hold the rest of mankind, Enemies in War, in Peace Friends.—

WE, THEREFORE, the Representatives of the UNITED STATES OF AMERICA, in General Congress, Assembled, appealing to the Supreme Judge of the world for the rectitude of our intentions, do, in the Name, and by Authority of the good People of these Colonies, solemnly publish and declare, That these United Colonies are, and of Right ought to be FREE AND INDEPENDENT STATES; that they are Absolved from all Allegiance to the British Crown, and that all political connection between them and the State of Great Britain, is and ought to be totally dissolved; and that as Free and Independent States, they have full Power to levy War, conclude Peace, contract Alliances, establish Commerce, and to do all other Acts and Things which Independent States may of right do.—And for the support of this Declaration, with a firm reliance on the protection of divine Providence, we mutually pledge to each other our Lives, our Fortunes and our sacred Honor.

The History of The Constitution of the United States

CONSTITUTION OF THE UNITED STATES. The Articles of Confederation did not provide the centralizing force necessary for unity among the new states and were soon found to be so fundamentally weak that a different political structure was vital. Conflicts about money and credit, trade, and suspicions about regional domination were among the concerns when Congress on February 21, 1787, authorized a Constitutional Convention to revise the Articles. The delegates were selected and assembled in Philadelphia about three months after the call. They concluded their work by September.

The delegates agreed and abided to secrecy. Years afterward James Madison supported the secrecy decision writing that "no man felt himself obliged to retain his opinions any longer than he was satisfied of their propriety and truth, and was open to the force of argument." Secrecy was not for all time. Madison, a delegate from Virginia, was a self-appointed but recognized recorder and took notes in the clear view of the members. Published long afterward, Madison's *Journal* gives a good record of the convention.

The delegates began to assemble on May 14, 1787, but a majority did not arrive until May 25. George Washington was elected President of the Convention without opposition. The lag of those few days gave some of the early arrivals, especially Madison, time to make preparations on substantive matters, and Gov. Edmund Jennings Randolph presented a plan early in the proceedings that formed the basis for much of the convention deliberations. The essentials were that there should be a government adequate to prevent foreign invasion, prevent dissension among the states, provide for general national development, and give the national government power enough to make it superior in its realm. The decision was made not merely to revise the articles but to create a new government and a new constitution.

One of the most crucial decisions was the arrangement for representation, a compromise providing that one house would represent the states equally, the other house to be based on popular representation (with some modification due to the slavery question). This arrangement recognized political facts and concessions among men with both theoretical and practical political knowledge.

Basic Features. Oliver Wendell Holmes, Jr., once wrote that the provisions of the Constitution were not mathematical formulas, but "organic living institutions [sic] and its origins and growth were vital to understanding it." The constitution's basic features provide for a supreme law—notwithstanding any other legal document or practice, the Constitution is supreme, as are the laws made in pursuance of it and treaties made under the authority of the United States.

The organizational plan for government is widely known. Foremost is the separation of powers. If the new government were to be limited in its powers, one way to keep it limited would have been executive, legislative, and judicial power to three distinct and non-overlapping branches. A government could not actually function, however, if the separation meant the independence of one branch from the others. The answer was a design to insure cooperation and the sharing of some functions. Among these are the executive veto and the power of the Congress to have its way if it musters a super-majority to override that veto. The direction of foreign affairs and the war power are both dispersed and shared. The appointing power is shared by the Senate and the president; impeaching of officers and financial controls are powers shared by the Senate and the House.

A second major contribution by the convention is the provision for the judiciary, which gave rise to the doctrine of judicial review. There is some doubt that the delegates comprehended this prospect but Alexander Hamilton considered it in *Federalist* No. 78: "The interpretation of the laws is a proper and peculiar province of the Courts. . . . Wherever a particular statute contravenes the Constitution, it will be the duty of the judicial tribunals to adhere to the latter and disregard the former."

Another contribution is the federal system, an evolution from colonial practice and the relations between the colonies and the mother country. This division of authority between the new national government and the states recognized the doctrine of delegated and reserved powers. Only certain authority was to go to the new government; the states were not to be done away with and much of the Constitution is devoted to insuring that they were to be maintained even with the stripping of some of their powers.

It is not surprising, therefore, that the convention has been called a great political reform caucus composed of both revolutionaries and men dedicated to democracy. By eighteenth-century standards the Constitution was a democratic document, but standards change and the Constitution has changed since its adoption.

Change and Adaptation. The authors of the Constitution knew that provision for change was essential and provided for it in Article V, insuring that a majority could amend, but being restrictive enough that changes were not likely for the "light and transient" causes Jefferson warned about in the Declaration of Independence.

During the period immediately following the presentation of the Constitution for ratification, requiring assent of nine states to be effective, some alarm was expressed that there was a major defect: there was no bill of rights. So, many leaders committed themselves to the presentation of constitutional amendments for the purpose. Hamilton argued that the absence of a bill of rights was not a defect; indeed, a bill was not necessary. "Why," he wrote, in the last of *The Federalist Papers,* "declare things that shall not be done which there is no power to do?" Nonetheless, the Bill of Rights was presented in the form of amendments and adopted by the states in 1791.

Since 1791 many proposals have been suggested to amend the Constitution. By 1972 sixteen additional amendments had been adopted. Only one, the Twenty-first, which repealed the Eighteenth, was ratified by state conventions. All the others were ratified by state legislatures.

Even a cursory reading of the later amendments shows they do not alter the fundamentals of limited government, the separation of powers, the federal system, or the political process set in motion originally. The Thirteenth, Fourteenth, Fifteenth, and Nineteenth amendments attempt to insure equality to all and are an extension of the Bill of Rights. The others reaffirm some existing constitutional arrangements, alter some procedures, and at least one, the Sixteenth, states national policy.

Substantial change and adaptation of the Constitution beyond the formal amendments have come from national experience, growth, and development. It has been from the Supreme Court that much of the gradual significant shaping of the Constitution has been done.

Government has remained neither static nor tranquil. Some conflict prevails continually. It may be about the activities of some phase of government or the extent of operations, and whether the arrangement for government can be made responsive to current and prospective needs of society. Conflict is inevitable in a democratic society. Sometimes the conflict is spirited and rises to challenge the continuation of the system. Questions arise whether a fair trial may be possible here or there; legislators are alleged to be indifferent to human problems and pursue distorted public priorities. Presidents are charged with secret actions designed for self-aggrandizement or actions based on half-truths. Voices are heard urging revolution again as the only means of righting alleged wrongs.

The responses continue to demonstrate, however, that the constitutional arrangement for government, the allocation of powers, and the restraints on government all provide the needed flexibility. The Constitution endures.

—Adam C. Breckenridge, *University of Nebraska-Lincoln*

The Constitution of the United States

We the People of the United States, in Order to form a more perfect Union, establish Justice, insure domestic Tranquillity, provide for the common defence, promote the general Welfare, and secure the Blessings of Liberty to ourselves and our Posterity, do ordain and establish this Constitution for the United States of America.

ARTICLE. I.

SECTION. 1. All legislative Powers herein granted shall be vested in a Congress of the United States, which shall consist of a Senate and House of Representatives.

SECTION. 2. The House of Representatives shall be composed of Members chosen every second Year by the People of the several States, and the Electors in each State shall have the Qualifications requisite for Electors of the most numerous Branch of the State Legislature.

No Person shall be a Representative who shall not have attained to the age of twenty five Years, and been seven Years a Citizen of the United States, and who shall not, when elected, be an Inhabitant of that State in which he shall be chosen.

Representatives and direct Taxes shall be apportioned among the several States which may be included within this Union, according to their respective Numbers, which shall be determined by adding to the whole Number of free Persons, including those bound to Service for a Term of Years, and excluding Indians not taxed, three fifths of all other Persons. The actual Enumeration shall be made within three Years after the first Meeting of the Congress of the United States, and within every subsequent Term of ten Years, in such Manner as they shall by Law direct. The Number of Representatives shall not exceed one for every thirty Thousand, but each State shall have at Least one Representative; and until such enumeration shall be made, the State of New Hampshire shall be entitled to chuse three, Massachusetts eight, Rhode-Island and Providence Plantations one, Connecticut five, New-York six, New Jersey four, Pennsylvania eight, Delaware one, Maryland six, Virginia ten, North Carolina five, South Carolina five, and Georgia three.

When vacancies happen in the Representation from any State, the Executive Authority thereof shall issue Writs of Election to fill such Vacancies.

The House of Representatives shall chuse their Speaker and other Officers; and shall have the sole Power of Impeachment

SECTION. 3. The Senate of the United States shall be composed of two Senators from each State, chosen by the Legislature thereof, for six Years; and each Senator shall have one Vote.

Immediately after they shall be assembled in Consequence of the first Election, they shall be divided as equally as may be into three Classes. The Seats of the Senators of the first Class shall be vacated at the Expiration of the second Year, of the second Class at the Expiration of the fourth Year, and of the third Class at the Expiration of the sixth Year, so that one third may be chosen every second Year; and if Vacancies happen by Resignation, or otherwise, during the Recess of the Legislature of any State, the Executive thereof may make temporary Appointments until the next Meeting of the Legislature, which shall then fill such Vacancies.

No Person shall be a Senator who shall not have attained to the Age of thirty Years, and been nine Years a Citizen of the United States, and who shall not, when elected, be an Inhabitant of that State for which he shall be chosen.

The Vice President of the United States shall be President of the Senate, but shall have no Vote, unless they be equally divided.

The Senate shall chuse their other Officers, and also a President pro tempore, in the Absence of the Vice President, or when he shall exercise the Office of President of the United States.

The Senate shall have the sole Power to try all Impeachments. When sitting for that Purpose, they shall be on Oath or Affirmation. When the President of the United States is tried the Chief Justice shall preside: And no Person shall be convicted without the Concurrence of two thirds of the Members present.

Judgment in Cases of Impeachment shall not extend further than to removal from Office, and disqualification to hold and enjoy any Office of honor, Trust or Profit under the United States: but the Party convicted shall nevertheless be liable and subject to Indictment, Trial, Judgment and Punishment, according to Law.

SECTION. 4. The Times, Places and Manner of holding Elections for Senators and Representatives, shall be prescribed in each State by the Legislature thereof; but the Congress may at any time by Law make or alter such Regulations, except as to the Places of chusing Senators.

The Congress shall assemble at least once in every Year, and such Meeting shall be on the first Monday in December, unless they shall by Law appoint a different Day.

SECTION. 5. Each House shall be the Judge of the Elections, Returns and Qualifications of its own Members, and a Majority of each shall constitute a Quorum to do Business; but a smaller Number may adjourn from day to day, and may be authorized to compel the Attendance of absent Members, in such Manner, and under such Penalties as each House may provide.

Each House may determine the Rules of its Proceedings, punish its Members for disorderly Behaviour, and, with the Concurrence of two thirds, expel a Member.

Each House shall keep a Journal of its Proceedings, and from time to time publish the same, excepting such Parts as may in their Judgment require Secrecy; and the Yeas and Nays of the Members of either House on any question shall, at the Desire of one fifth of those Present, be entered on the Journal.

Neither House, during the Session of Congress, shall, without the Consent of the other, adjourn for more than three days, nor to any other Place than that in which the two Houses shall be sitting.

SECTION. 6. The Senators and Representatives shall receive a Compensation for their Services, to be ascertained by Law, and paid out of the Treasury of the United States. They shall in all Cases, except Treason, Felony and Breach of the Peace, be privileged from Arrest during their Attendance at the Session of their respective Houses, and in going to and returning from the same; and for any Speech or Debate in either House, they shall not be questioned in any other Place.

No Senator or Representative shall, during the Time for which he was elected, be appointed to any civil Office under the Authority of the United States, which shall have been created, or the Emoluments whereof shall have been encreased during such time; and no Person holding any Office under the United States, shall be a Member of either House during his Continuance in Office.

SECTION. 7. All Bills for raising Revenue shall originate in the House of Representatives; but the Senate may propose or concur with amendments as on other Bills.

Every Bill which shall have passed the House of Representatives and the Senate, shall, before it become a Law, be presented to the President of the United States; If he approve he shall sign it, but if not he shall return it, with his Objections to that House in which it shall have originated, who shall enter the Objections at large on their Journal, and proceed to reconsider it. If after such Reconsideration two thirds of that House shall agree to pass the Bill, it shall be sent, together with the Objections, to the other House, by which it shall likewise be reconsidered, and if approved by two thirds of that House, it shall become a Law. But in all such Cases the Votes of both Houses shall be determined by yeas and Nays, and the Names of the Persons voting for and against the Bill shall be entered on the Journal of each House respectively. If any Bill shall not be returned by the President within ten Days (Sundays excepted) after it shall have been presented to him, the

Same shall be a Law, in like Manner as if he had signed it, unless the Congress by their Adjournment prevent its Return, in which Case it shall not be a Law.

Every Order, Resolution, or Vote to which the Concurrence of the Senate and House of Representatives may be necessary (except on a question of Adjournment) shall be presented to the President of the United States; and before the Same shall take Effect, shall be approved by him, or being disapproved by him, shall be repassed by two thirds of the Senate and House of Representatives, according to the Rules and Limitations prescribed in the Case of a Bill.

SECTION. 8. The Congress shall have Power To lay and collect Taxes, Duties, Imposts and Excises, to pay the Debts and provide for the common Defence and general Welfare of the United States; but all Duties, Imposts and Excises shall be uniform throughout the United States;

To borrow Money on the credit of the United States;

To regulate Commerce with foreign Nations, and among the several States, and with the Indian Tribes;

To establish an uniform Rule of Naturalization, and uniform Laws on the subject of Bankruptcies throughout the United States;

To coin Money, regulate the Value thereof, and of foreign Coin, and fix the Standard of Weights and Measures;

To provide for the Punishment of counterfeiting the Securities and current Coin of the United States;

To establish Post Offices and post Roads;

To promote the Progress of Science and useful Arts, by securing for limited Times to Authors and Inventors the exclusive Right to their respective Writings and Discoveries;

To constitute Tribunals inferior to the supreme Court;

To define and punish Piracies and Felonies committed on the high Seas, and Offences against the Law of Nations;

To declare War, grant Letters of Marque and Reprisal, and make Rules concerning Captures on Land and Water;

To raise and support Armies, but no Appropriation of Money to that Use shall be for a longer Term than two Years;

To provide and maintain a Navy;

To make Rules for the Government and Regulation of the land and naval Forces;

To provide for calling forth the Militia to execute the Laws of the Union, suppress Insurrections and repel Invasions;

To provide for organizing, arming, and disciplining, the Militia, and for governing such Part of them as may be employed in the Service of the United States, reserving to the States respectively, the Appointment of the Officers, and the Authority of training the Militia according to the discipline prescribed by Congress;

To exercise exclusive Legislation in all Cases whatsoever, over such District (not exceeding ten Miles square) as may, by Cession of Particular States, and the Acceptance of Congress, become the Seat of the Government of the United States, and to exercise like Authority over all Places purchased by the Consent of the Legislature of the State in which the Same shall be, for the Erection of Forts, Magazines, Arsenals, dock-Yards, and other needful Buildings;—And

To make all Laws which shall be necessary and proper for carrying into Execution the foregoing Powers, and all other Powers vested by this Constitution in the Government of the United States, or in any Department or Officer thereof.

SECTION. 9. The Migration or Importation of such Persons as any of the States now existing shall think proper to admit, shall not be prohibited by the Congress prior to the Year one thousand eight hundred and eight, but a Tax or duty may be imposed on such Importation, not exceeding ten dollars for each Person.

The Privilege of the Writ of Habeas Corpus shall not be suspended, unless when in Cases of Rebellion or Invasion the public Safety may require it.

No Bill of Attainder or ex post facto Law shall be passed.

No Capitation, or other direct, Tax shall be laid, unless in Proportion to the Census or Enumeration herein before directed to be taken.

No Tax or Duty shall be laid on Articles exported from any State.

No Preference shall be given by any Regulation of Commerce or Revenue to the Ports of one State over those of another; nor shall Vessels bound to, or from, one State, be obliged to enter, clear or pay Duties in another.

No Money shall be drawn from the Treasury, but in Consequence of Appropriations made by Law; and a regular Statement and Account of the Receipts and Expenditures of all public Money shall be published from time to time.

No Title of Nobility shall be granted by the United States: And no Person holding any Office of Profit or Trust under them, shall, without the Consent of the Congress, accept of any present Emolument, Office, or Title, of any kind whatever, from any King, Prince, or foreign State.

SECTION 10. No State shall enter into any Treaty, Alliance, or Confederation; grant Letters of Marque and Reprisal; coin Money; emit Bills of Credit; make any Thing but gold and silver Coin a Tender in Payment of Debts; pass any Bill of Attainder, ex post facto Law, or Law impairing the Obligation of Contracts, or grant any Title of Nobility.

No State shall, without the Consent of the Congress, lay any Imposts or Duties on Imports or Exports, except what may be absolutely necessary for executing its inspection Laws: and the net Produce of all Duties and Imposts, laid by any State on Imports or Exports, shall be for the Use of the Treasury of the United States; and all such Laws shall be subject to the Revision and Controul of the Congress.

No State shall, without the Consent of Congress, lay any Duty of Tonnage, keep Troops, or Ships of War in time of Peace, enter into any Agreement or Compact with another State, or with a foreign Power, or engage in War, unless actually invaded, or in such imminent Danger as will not admit of delay.

ARTICLE. II.

SECTION. 1. The executive Power shall be vested in a President of the United States of America. He shall hold his Office during the Term of four Years, and, together with the Vice President, chosen for the same Term, be elected, as follows

Each State shall appoint, in such Manner as the Legislature thereof may direct, a Number of Electors, equal to the whole Number of Senators and Representatives to which the State may be entitled in the Congress: but no Senator or Representative, or Person holding an Office of Trust or Profit under the United States, shall be appointed an Elector.

The Electors shall meet in their respective States, and vote by Ballot for two Persons, of whom one at least shall not be an Inhabitant of the same State with themselves. And they shall make a List of all the Persons voted for, and of the Number of Votes for each; which List they shall sign and certify, and transmit sealed to the Seat of the Government of the United States, directed to the President of the Senate. The President of the Senate shall, in the Presence of the Senate and House of Representatives, open all the Certificates, and the Votes shall then be counted. The Person having the greatest Number of Votes shall be the President, if such Number be a Majority of the whole Number of Electors appointed; and if there be more than one who have such Majority, and have an equal Number of Votes, then the House of Representatives shall immediately chuse by Ballot one of them for President; and if no Person have a Majority, then from the five highest on the List the said House shall in like Manner chuse the President. But in chusing the President, the Votes shall be taken by States, the Representation from each State having one Vote; a quorum for this Purpose shall consist of a Member or Members from two thirds of the States, and a Majority of all the States shall be necessary to a Choice. In every Case, after the Choice of the President, the Person having the greatest Number of Votes of the Electors shall be the Vice President. But if there should remain two or more who have equal Votes, the Senate shall chuse from them by Ballot the Vice President.

The Congress may determine the Time of chusing the Electors, and the Day on which they shall give their Votes; which Day shall be the same throughout the United States.

No Person except a natural born Citizen, or a Citizen of the United States, at the time of the Adoption of this Constitution, shall be eligible to the Office of President; neither shall any person be eligible to that Office who shall not have attained to the

1. FOUNDATIONS: Basic Documents

Age of thirty five Years, and been fourteen Years a Resident within the United States.

In Case of the Removal of the President from Office, or of his Death, Resignation, or Inability to discharge the Powers and Duties of the said Office, the Same shall devolve on the Vice President, and the Congress may by Law provide for the Case of Removal, Death, Resignation or Inability, both of the President and Vice President, declaring what Officer shall then act as President, and such Officer shall act accordingly, until the Disability be removed, or a President shall be elected.

The President shall, at stated Times, receive for his Services, a Compensation, which shall neither be encreased nor diminished during the Period for which he shall have been elected, and he shall not receive within that period any other Emolument from the United States, or any of them.

Before he enter on the Execution of his Office, he shall take the following Oath or Affirmation:—"I do solemnly swear (or affirm) that I will faithfully execute the Office of President of the United States, and will to the best of my Ability, preserve, protect and defend the Constitution of the United States."

SECTION. 2. The President shall be Commander in Chief of the Army and Navy of the United States, and of the Militia of the several States, when called into the actual Service of the United States; he may require the Opinion, in writing, of the principal Officer in each of the executive Departments, upon any Subject relating to the Duties of their respective Offices, and he shall have Power to grant Reprieves and Pardons for Offences against the United States, except in Cases of Impeachment.

He shall have Power, by and with the Advice and Consent of the Senate, to make Treaties, provided two thirds of the Senators present concur; and he shall nominate, and by and with the Advice and Consent of the Senate, shall appoint Ambassadors, other public Ministers and Consuls, Judges of the supreme Court, and all other Officers of the United States, whose Appointments are not herein otherwise provided for, and which shall be established by Law: but the Congress may by Law vest the Appointment of such inferior Officers, as they think proper, in the President alone, in the Courts of Law, or in the Heads of Departments.

The President shall have Power to fill up all Vacancies that may happen during the Recess of the Senate, by granting Commissions which shall expire at the End of their next Session.

SECTION. 3. He shall from time to time give to the Congress Information of the State of the Union, and recommend to their Consideration such Measures as he shall judge necessary and expedient; he may, on extraordinary Occasions, convene both Houses, or either of them, and in Case of Disagreement between them, with Respect to the Time of Adjournment, he may adjourn them to such Time as he shall think proper; he shall receive Ambassadors and other public Ministers; he shall take Care that the Laws be faithfully executed, and shall Commission all the Officers of the United States.

SECTION. 4. The President, Vice President and all civil Officers of the United States, shall be removed from Office on Impeachment for, and Conviction of, Treason, Bribery, or other high Crimes and Misdemeanors.

ARTICLE. III.

SECTION. 1. The judicial Power of the United States, shall be vested in one supreme Court, and in such inferior Courts as the Congress may from time to time ordain and establish. The Judges, both of the supreme and inferior Courts, shall hold their Offices during good Behaviour, and shall, at stated Times, receive for their Services, a Compensation, which shall not be diminished during their Continuance in Office.

SECTION. 2. The judicial Power shall extend to all Cases, in Law and Equity, arising under this Constitution, the Laws of the United States, and Treaties made, or which shall be made, under their Authority;—to all Cases affecting Ambassadors, other public Ministers and Consuls;—to all Cases of admiralty and maritime Jurisdiction;—to Controversies to which the United States shall be a Party;—to Controversies between two or more States;—between a State and Citizens of another State;—between Citizens of different States;—between Citizens of the same State claiming Lands under Grants of different States, and between a State, or

the Citizens thereof, and foreign States, Citizens or Subjects.

In all Cases affecting Ambassadors, other public Ministers and Consuls, and those in which a State shall be Party, the supreme Court shall have original Jurisdiction. In all the other Cases before mentioned, the supreme Court shall have appellate Jurisdiction, both as to Law and Fact, with such Exceptions, and under such Regulations as the Congress shall make.

The Trial of all Crimes, except in Cases of Impeachment, shall be by Jury; and such Trial shall be held in the State where the said Crimes shall have been committed; but when not committed within any State, the Trial shall be at such Place or Places as the Congress may by Law have directed.

SECTION. 3. Treason against the United States, shall consist only in levying War against them, or in adhering to their Enemies, giving them Aid and Comfort. No Person shall be convicted of Treason unless on the Testimony of two Witnesses to the same overt Act, or on Confession in open Court.

The Congress shall have Power to declare the Punishment of Treason, but no Attainder of Treason shall work Corruption of Blood, or Forfeiture except during the Life of the Person attainted.

ARTICLE. IV.

SECTION. 1. Full Faith and Credit shall be given in each State to the public Acts, Records, and judicial Proceedings of every other State. And the Congress may by general Laws prescribe the Manner in which such Acts, Record and Proceedings shall be proved, and the Effect thereof.

SECTION. 2. The Citizens of each State shall be entitled to all Privileges and Immunities of Citizens in the several States.

A Person charged in any State with Treason, Felony, or other Crime, who shall flee from Justice, and be found in another State, shall on Demand of the executive Authority of the State from which he fled, be delivered up, to be removed to the State having Jurisdiction of the Crime.

No Person held to Service or Labour in one State, under the Laws thereof, escaping into another, shall, in Consequence of any Law or Regulation therein, be discharged from such Service or Labour, but shall be delivered up on Claim of the Party to whom such Service or Labour may be due.

SECTION. 3. New States may be admitted by the Congress into this Union; but no new State shall be formed or erected within the Jurisdiction of any other State; nor any State be formed by the Junction of two or more States, or Parts of States, without the Consent of the Legislatures of the States concerned as well as of the Congress.

The Congress shall have Power to dispose of and make all needful Rules and Regulations respecting the Territory or other Property belonging to the United States; and nothing in this Constitution shall be so construed as to Prejudice any Claims of the United States, or of any particular State.

SECTION. 4. The United States shall guarantee to every State in this Union a Republican Form of Government, and shall protect each of them against Invasion; and on Application of the Legislature, or of the Executive (when the Legislature cannot be convened) against domestic Violence.

ARTICLE. V.

The Congress, whenever two thirds of both Houses shall deem it necessary, shall propose Amendments to this Constitution, or, on the Application of the Legislature of two thirds of the several States, shall call a Convention for proposing Amendments, which, in either Case, shall be valid to all Intents and Purposes, as Part of this Constitution, when ratified by the Legislatures of three fourths of the several States, or by Conventions in three fourths thereof, as the one or the other Mode of Ratification may be proposed by the Congress; Provided that no Amendment which may be made prior to the Year One thousand eight hundred and eight shall in any Manner affect the first and fourth Clauses in the Ninth Section of the first Article; and that no State, without its Consent, shall be deprived of its equal Suffrage in the Senate.

ARTICLE. VI.

All Debts contracted and Engagements entered into, before the Adoption of this Constitution, shall be as valid against the

United States under this Constitution, as under the Confederation.

This Constitution, and the Laws of the United States which shall be made in Pursuance thereof; and all Treaties made, or which shall be made, under the Authority of the United States, shall be the supreme Law of the Land; and the Judges in every State shall be bound thereby, any Thing in the Constitution or Laws of any State to the Contrary notwithstanding.

The Senators and Representatives before mentioned, and the Members of the several State Legislatures, and all executive and judicial Officers, both of the United States and of the several States, shall be bound by Oath or Affirmation, to support this Constitution; but no religious Test shall ever be required as a Qualification to any Office or public Trust under the United States.

ARTICLE. VII.

The Ratification of the Conventions of nine States, shall be sufficient for the Establishment of this Constitution between the States so ratifying the Same.

done in Convention by the Unanimous Consent of the States present the Seventeenth Day of September in the Year of our Lord one thousand seven hundred and Eighty seven and of the Independence of the United States of America the Twelfth In witness whereof We have hereunto subscribed our Names,

Go. WASHINGTON—Presidt.

and deputy from Virginia

New Hampshire	JOHN LANGDON NICHOLAS GILMAN
Massachusetts	NATHANIEL GORHAM RUFUS KING
Connecticut	Wm. SAML JOHNSON ROGER SHERMAN
New York . . .	ALEXANDER HAMILTON
New Jersey	WIL: LIVINGSTON DAVID BREARLEY: Wm. PATERSON. JONA: DAYTON
Pennsylvania	B FRANKLIN THOMAS MIFFLIN ROBt MORRIS GEO. CLYMER THOs. FITZSIMONS JARED INGERSOLL JAMES WILSON GOUV MORRIS
Delaware	GEO: READ GUNNING BEDFORD jun JOHN DICKINSON RICHARD BASSETT JACO: BROOM
Maryland	JAMES McHENRY DAN OF St THOs. JENIFER DANL CARROLL
Virginia	JOHN BLAIR— JAMES MADISON Jr.
North Carolina	Wm. BLOUNT RICHd. DOBBS SPAIGHT. HU WILLIAMSON
South Carolina	J. RUTLEDGE CHARLES COTESWORTH PINCKNEY CHARLES PINCKNEY PIERCE BUTLER
Georgia	WILLIAM FEW ABR BALDWIN

In Convention Monday, September 17th 1787.

Present

The States of

New Hampshire, Massachusetts, Connecticut, Mr. Hamilton from New York, New Jersey, Pennsylvania, Delaware, Maryland, Virginia, North Carolina, South Carolina and Georgia.

Resolved,

That the preceeding Constitution be laid before the United States in Congress assembled, and that it is the Opinion of this Convention, that it should afterwards be submitted to a Convention of Delegates, chosen in each State by the People thereof, under the Recommendation of its Legislature, for their Assent and Ratification; and that each Convention assenting to, and ratifying the Same, should give Notice thereof to the United States in Congress assembled. Resolved, That it is the Opinion of this Convention, that as soon as the Conventions of nine States shall have ratified this Constitution, the United States in Congress assembled should fix a Day on which Electors should be appointed by the States which shall have ratified the same, and a Day on which the Electors should assemble to vote for the President, and the Time and Place for commencing Proceedings under this Constitution. That after such Publication the Electors should be appointed, and the Senators and Representatives elected: That the Electors should meet on the Day fixed for the Election of the President, and should transmit their Votes certified, signed, sealed and directed, as the Constitution requires, to the Secretary of the United States in Congress assembled, that the Senators and Representatives should convene at the Time and Place assigned; that the Senators should appoint a President of the Senate, for the sole Purpose of receiving, opening and counting the Votes for President; and, that after he shall be chosen, the Congress, together with the President, should, without Delay, proceed to execute this Constitution.

By the Unanimous Order of the Convention

Go. WASHINGTON—Presidt.

W. JACKSON Secretary.

RATIFICATION OF THE CONSTITUTION

State	Date of ratification
Delaware	Dec 7, 1787
Pennsylvania	Dec 12, 1787
New Jersey	Dec 19, 1787
Georgia	Jan 2, 1788
Connecticut	Jan 9, 1788
Massachusetts	Feb 6, 1788
Maryland	Apr 28, 1788
South Carolina	May 23, 1788
New Hampshire	June 21, 1788
Virginia	Jun 25, 1788
New York	Jun 26, 1788
Rhode Island	May 29, 1790
North Carolina	Nov 21, 1789

ARTICLES IN ADDITION TO, AND AMENDMENT OF, THE CONSTITUTION OF THE UNITED STATES OF AMERICA, PROPOSED BY CONGRESS, AND RATIFIED BY THE SEVERAL STATES, PURSUANT TO THE FIFTH ARTICLE OF THE ORIGINAL CONSTITUTION.

AMENDMENT I.

Congress shall make no law respecting an establishment of religion, or prohibiting the free exercise thereof; or abridging the freedom of speech, or of the press; or the right of the people peaceably to assemble, and to petition the Government for a redress of grievances.

AMENDMENT II.

A well regulated Militia, being necessary to the security of a free State, the right of the people to keep and bear Arms, shall not be infringed.

AMENDMENT III.

No Soldier shall, in time of peace be quartered in any house, without the consent of the Owner, nor in time of war, but in a manner to be prescribed by law.

AMENDMENT IV.

The right of the people to be secure in their persons, houses, papers, and effects, against unreasonable searches and seizures, shall not be violated, and no Warrants shall issue, but upon probable cause, supported by Oath or affirmation, and particularly describing the place to be searched, and the persons or things to be seized.

AMENDMENT V.

No person shall be held to answer for a capital, or otherwise infamous crime, unless on a presentment or indictment of a Grand Jury, except in cases arising in the land or naval forces, or in the Militia, when in actual service in time of War or public danger; nor shall any person be subject for the same offence to be twice put in jeopardy of life or limb; nor shall be compelled in any criminal case to be a witness against himself, nor be deprived of life, liberty, or property, without due process of law; nor shall private property be taken for public use, without just compensation.

AMENDMENT VI.

In all criminal prosecutions, the accused shall enjoy the right to a speedy and public trial, by an impartial jury of the State and district wherein the crime shall have been committed, which district shall have been previously ascertained by law, and to be informed of the nature and cause of the accusation; to be confronted with the witnesses against him; to have compulsory process for obtaining witnesses in his favor, and to have the Assistance of Counsel for his defence.

AMENDMENT VII.

In Suits at common law, where the value in controversy shall exceed twenty dollars, the right of trial by jury shall be preserved, and no fact tried by a jury, shall be otherwise re-examined in any Court of the United States, than according to the rules of the common law.

AMENDMENT VIII.

Excessive bail shall not be required, nor excessive fines imposed, nor cruel and unusual punishments inflicted.

AMENDMENT IX.

The enumeration in the Constitution, of certain rights, shall not be construed to deny or disparage others retained by the people.

AMENDMENT X.

The powers not delegated to the United States by the Constitution, nor prohibited by it to the States, are reserved to the States respectively, or to the people.

AMENDMENT XI.
(Adopted Jan. 8, 1798)

The Judicial power of the United States shall not be construed to extend to any suit in law or equity, commenced or prosecuted against one of the United States by Citizens of another State, or by Citizens or Subjects of any Foreign State.

AMENDMENT XII.
(Adopted Sept. 25, 1804)

The Electors shall meet in their respective states and vote by ballot for President and Vice-President, one of whom, at least, shall not be an inhabitant of the same state with themselves; they shall name in their ballots the person voted for as President, and in distinct ballots the person voted for as Vice-President, and they shall make distinct lists of all persons voted for as President, and of all persons voted for as Vice-President, and of the number of votes for each, which lists they shall sign and certify, and transmit sealed to the seat of the government of the United States, directed to the President of the Senate;—The President of the Senate shall, in the presence of the Senate and House of Representatives, open all the certificates and the votes shall then be counted; —The person having the greatest number of votes for President, shall be the President, if such number be a majority of the whole number of Electors appointed; and if no person have such majority, then from the persons having the highest numbers not

exceeding three on the list of those voted for as President, the House of Representatives shall choose immediately, by ballot, the President. But in choosing the President, the votes shall be taken by states, the representation from each state having one vote; a quorum for this purpose shall consist of a member or members from two-thirds of the states, and a majority of all the states shall be necessary to a choice. And if the House of Representatives shall not choose a President whenever the right of choice shall devolve upon them, before the fourth day of March next following, then the Vice-President shall act as President, as in the case of the death or other constitutional disability of the President—The person having the greatest number of votes as Vice-President, shall be the Vice-President, if such number be a majority of the whole number of Electors appointed, and if no person have a majority, then from the two highest numbers on the list, the Senate shall choose the Vice-President; a quorum for the purpose shall consist of two-thirds of the whole number of Senators, and a majority of the whole number shall be necessary to a choice. But no person constitutionally ineligible to the office of President shall be eligible to that of Vice-President of the United States.

AMENDMENT XIII.
(Adopted Dec. 18, 1865)

SECTION 1. Neither slavery nor involuntary servitude, except as a punishment for crime whereof the party shall have been duly convicted, shall exist within the United States, or any place subject to their jurisdiction.

SECTION 2. Congress shall have power to enforce this article by appropriate legislation.

AMENDMENT XIV.
(Adopted July 28, 1868)

SECTION 1. All persons born or naturalized in the United States and subject to the jurisdiction thereof, are citizens of the United States and of the State wherein they reside. No State shall make or enforce any law which shall abridge the privileges or immunities of citizens of the United States; nor shall any State deprive any person of life, liberty, or property, without due process of law; nor deny to any person within its jurisdiction the equal protection of the laws.

SECTION 2. Representatives shall be apportioned among the several States according to their respective numbers, counting the whole number of persons in each State, excluding Indians not taxed. But when the right to vote at any election for the choice of electors for President and Vice President of the United States, Representatives in Congress, the Executive and Judicial officers of a State, or the members of the Legislature thereof, is denied to any of the male inhabitants of such State, being twenty-one years of age, and citizens of the United States, or in any way abridged, except for participation in rebellion, or other crime, the basis of representation therein shall be reduced in the proportion which the number of such male citizens shall bear to the whole number of male citizens twenty-one years of age in such State.

SECTION 3. No person shall be a Senator or Representative in Congress, or elector of President and Vice President, or hold any office, civil or military, under the United States, or under any State, who, having previously taken an oath, as a member of Congress, or as an officer of the United States, or as a member of any State legislature, or as an executive or judicial officer of any State, to support the Constitution of the United States, shall have engaged in insurrection or rebellion against the same, or given aid or comfort to the enemies thereof. But Congress may by a vote of two-thirds of each House, remove such disability.

SECTION 4. The validity of the public debt of the United States, authorized by law, including debts incurred for payment of pensions and bounties for services in suppressing insurrection or rebellion, shall not be questioned. But neither the United States nor any State shall assume or pay any debt or obligation incurred in aid of insurrection or rebellion against the United States, or any claim for the loss or emancipation of any slave; but all such debts, obligations and claims shall be held illegal and void.

SECTION 5. The Congress shall have power to enforce, by appropriate legislation, the provisions of this article.

AMENDMENT XV.
(Adopted March 30, 1870)

SECTION 1. The right of citizens of the United States to

vote shall not be denied or abridged by the United States or by any State on account of race, color, or previous condition of servitude.

SECTION 2. The Congress shall have power to enforce this article by appropriate legislation.

AMENDMENT XVI.
(Adopted Feb. 25, 1913)

The Congress shall have power to lay and collect taxes on incomes, from whatever source derived, without apportionment among the several States, and without regard to any census or enumeration.

AMENDMENT XVII.
(Adopted May 31, 1913)

The Senate of the United States shall be composed of two Senators from each State, elected by the people thereof, for six years; and each Senator shall have one vote. The electors in each State shall have the qualifications requisite for electors of the most numerous branch of the State legislatures.

When vacancies happen in the representation of any State in the Senate, the executive authority of such State shall issue writs of election to fill such vacancies: *Provided,* That the legislature of any State may empower the executive thereof to make temporary appointments until the people fill the vacancies by election as the legislature may direct.

This amendment shall not be so construed as to affect the election or term of any Senator chosen before it becomes valid as part of the Constitution.

AMENDMENT XVIII.
(Adopted Jan. 29, 1919)

SECTION 1. After one year from the ratification of this article the manufacture, sale, or transportation of intoxicating liquors within, the importation thereof into, or the exportation thereof from the United States and all territory subject to the jurisdiction thereof for beverage purposes is hereby prohibited.

SECTION 2. The Congress and the several States shall have concurrent power to enforce this article by appropriate legislation.

SECTION 3. This article shall be inoperative unless it shall have been ratified as an amendment to the Constitution by the legislatures of the several States, as provided in the Constitution, within seven years from the date of the submission hereof to the States by the Congress.

AMENDMENT XIX.
(Adopted Aug. 26, 1920)

The right of citizens of the United States to vote shall not be denied or abridged by the United States or by any State on account of sex.

Congress shall have power to enforce this article by appropriate legislation.

AMENDMENT XX.
(Adopted Feb. 6, 1933)

SECTION 1. The terms of the President and Vice President shall end at noon on the 20th day of January, and the terms of Senators and Representatives at noon on the 3d day of January, of the years in which such terms would have ended if this article had not been ratified; and the terms of their successors shall then begin.

SECTION 2. The Congress shall assemble at least once in every year, and such meeting shall begin at noon on the 3d day of January, unless they shall by law appoint a different day.

SECTION 3. If, at the time fixed for the beginning of the term of the President, the President elect shall have died, the Vice President elect shall become President. If a President shall not have been chosen before the time fixed for the beginning of his term, or if the President elect shall have failed to qualify, then the Vice President elect shall act as President until a President shall have qualified; and the Congress may by law provide for the case wherein neither a President elect nor a Vice President elect shall have qualified, declaring who shall then act as President, or the manner in which one who is to act shall be selected, and such person shall act accordingly until a President or Vice President shall have qualified.

SECTION 4. The Congress may by law provide for the case of the death of any of the persons from whom the House of Representatives may choose a President whenever the right of choice shall have devolved upon them, and for the case of the death of any of the persons from whom the Senate may choose a Vice President whenever the right of choice shall have devolved upon them.

SECTION 5. Sections 1 and 2 shall take effect on the 15th day of October following the ratification of this article.

SECTION 6. This article shall be inoperative unless it shall have been ratified as an amendment to the Constitution by the legislatures of three-fourths of the several States within seven years from the date of its submission.

AMENDMENT XXI.
(Adopted Dec. 5, 1933)

SECTION 1. The eighteenth article of amendment to the Constitution of the United States is hereby repealed.

SECTION 2. The transportation or importation into any State, Territory, or possession of the United States for delivery or use therein of intoxicating liquors, in violation of the laws thereof, is hereby prohibited.

SECTION 3. This article shall be inoperative unless it shall have been ratified as an amendment to the Constitution by conventions in the several States, as provided in the Constitution, within seven years from the date of the submission hereof to the States by the Congress.

AMENDMENT XXII.
(Adopted Feb. 27, 1951)

SECTION 1. No person shall be elected to the office of the President more than twice, and no person who has held the office of President, or acted as President, for more than two years of a term to which some other person was elected President shall be elected to the office of the President more than once. But this Article shall not apply to any person holding the office of President when this Article was proposed by the Congress, and shall not prevent any person who may be holding the office of President, or acting as President, during the term within which this Article becomes operative from holding the office of President or acting as President during the remainder of such term.

SECTION 2. This Article shall be inoperative unless it shall have been ratified as an amendment to the Constitution by the legislatures of three-fourths of the several States within seven years from the date of its submission to the States by the Congress.

AMENDMENT XXIII.
(Adopted Mar. 29, 1961)

SECTION 1. The District constituting the seat of Government of the United States shall appoint in such manner as the Congress may direct:

A number of electors of President and Vice President equal to the whole number of Senators and Representatives in Congress to which·the District would be entitled if it were a State, but in no event more than the least populous State; they shall be in addition to those appointed by the States, but they shall be considered, for the purposes of the election of President and Vice President, to be electors appointed by a State; and they shall meet in the District and perform such duties as provided by the twelfth article of amendment.

SECTION 2. The Congress shall have power to enforce this article by appropriate legislation.

AMENDMENT XXIV.
(Adopted Jan. 23, 1964)

SECTION 1. The right of citizens of the United States to vote in any primary or other election for President or Vice President, for electors for President or Vice President, or for Senator or Representative in Congress, shall not be denied or abridged by the United States or any State by reason of failure to pay any poll tax or other tax.

SECTION 2. The Congress shall have the power to enforce this article by appropriate legislation.

AMENDMENT XXV.
(Adopted Feb. 10, 1967)

SECTION 1. In case of the removal of the President from office or of his death or resignation, the Vice President shall become President.

SECTION 2. Whenever there is a vacancy in the office of the Vice President, the President shall nominate a Vice President who shall take the office upon confirmation by a majority vote of both houses of Congress.

SECTION 3. Whenever the President transmits to the President pro tempore of the Senate and the Speaker of the House of Representatives his written declaration that he is unable to discharge the powers and duties of his office, and until he transmits to them a written declaration to the contrary, such powers and duties shall be discharged by the Vice President as Acting President.

SECTION 4. Whenever the Vice President and a majority of either the principal officers of the executive departments or of such other body as Congress may by law provide, transmit to the President pro tempore of the Senate and the Speaker of the House of Representatives their written declaration that the President is unable to discharge the powers and duties of his office, the Vice President shall immediately assume the powers and duties of the office as Acting President.

Thereafter, when the President transmits to the President pro tempore of the Senate and the Speaker of the House of Representatives his written declaration that no inability exists, he shall resume the powers and duties of his office unless the Vice President and a majority of either the principal officers of the executive department or of such other body as Congress may by law provide, transmit within four days to the President pro tempore of the Senate and the Speaker of the House of Representatives their written declaration that the President is unable to discharge the powers and duties of his office. Thereupon Congress shall decide the issue, assembling within forty-eight hours for that purpose if not in session. If the Congress within twenty-one days after receipt of the latter written declaration, or, if Congress is not in session, within twenty-one days after Congress is required to assemble, determines by two-thirds vote of both Houses that the President is unable to discharge the powers and duties of his office, the Vice President shall continue to discharge the same as Acting President; otherwise, the President shall resume the powers and duties of his office.

AMENDMENT XXVI.
(Adopted June 30, 1971)

SECTION 1. The right of citizens of the United States, who are 18 years of age or older, to vote shall not be denied or abridged by the United States or by any state on account of age.

SECTION 2. The Congress shall have power to enforce this article by appropriate legislation.

AMENDMENT XXVII
(Adopted May 7, 1992)

No law, varying the compensation for the services of the Senators and Representatives, shall take effect, until an election of Representatives shall have intervened.

THE SIZE AND VARIETY OF THE UNION AS A CHECK ON FACTION
THE FEDERALIST NO. 10
(Madison)

To the People of the State of New York:

AMONG the numerous advantages promised by a well-constructed Union, none deserves to be more accurately developed than its tendency to break and control the violence of faction. The friend of popular governments never finds himself so much alarmed for their character and fate, as when he contemplates their propensity to this dangerous vice. He will not fail, therefore, to set a due value on any plan which, without violating the principles to which he is attached, provides a proper cure for it. The instability, injustice, and confusion introduced into the public councils, have, in truth, been the mortal diseases under which popular governments have everywhere perished; as they continue to be the favorite and fruitful topics from which the adversaries to liberty derive their most specious declamations. The valuable improvements made by the American constitutions on the popular models, both ancient and modern, cannot certainly be too much admired; but it would be an unwarrantable partiality, to contend that they have as effectually obviated the danger on this side, as was wished and expected. Complaints are everywhere heard from our most considerate and virtuous citizens, equally the friends of public and private faith, and of public and personal liberty, that our governments are too unstable, that the public good is disregarded in the conflicts of rival parties, and that measures are too often decided, not according to the rules of justice and the rights of the minor party, but by the superior force of an interested and overbearing majority. However anxiously we may wish that these complaints had no foundation, the evidence of known facts will not permit us to deny that they are in some degree true. It will be found, indeed, on a candid review of our situation, that some of the distresses under which we labor have been erroneously charged on the operation of our governments; but it will be found, at the same time, that other causes will not alone account for many of our heaviest misfortunes; and, particularly, for that prevailing and increasing distrust of public engagements, and alarm for private rights, which are echoed from one end of the continent to the other. These must be chiefly, if not wholly, effects of the unsteadiness and injustice with which a factious spirit has tainted our public administrations.

By a faction, I understand a number of citizens, whether amounting to a majority or minority of the whole, who are united and actuated by some common impulse of passion, or of interest, adverse to the rights of other citizens, or to the permanent and aggregate interests of the community.

There are two methods of curing the mischiefs of faction: the one, by removing its causes; the other, by controlling its effects.

There are again two methods of removing the causes of faction: the one, by destroying the liberty which is essential to its existence; the other, by giving to every citizen the same opinions, the same passions, and the same interests.

It could never be more truly said than of the first remedy, that it was worse than the disease. Liberty is to faction what air is to fire, an aliment without which it instantly expires. But it could not be less folly to abolish liberty, which is essential to political life, because it nourishes faction, than it would be to wish the annihilation of air, which is essential to animal life, because it imparts to fire its destructive agency.

The second expedient is as impracticable as the first would be unwise. As long as the reason of man continues fallible, and he is at liberty to exercise it, different opinions will be formed. As long as the connection subsists between his reason and his self-love, his opinions and his passions will have a reciprocal influence on each other; and the former will be objects to which the latter will attach themselves. The diversity in the faculties of men, from which the rights of property originate, is not less an insuperable obstacle to a uniformity of interests. The protection of these faculties is the first object of government. From the protection of different and unequal faculties of acquiring property, the possession of different degrees and kinds of property immediately results; and from the influence of these on the sentiments and views of the respective proprietors, ensues a division of the society into different interests and parties.

The latent causes of faction are thus sown in the nature of man; and we see them everywhere brought into different degrees of activity, according to the different circumstances of civil society. A zeal for different opinions concerning religion, concerning government, and many other points, as well of speculation as of practice; an attachment to different leaders ambitiously contending for pre-eminence and power; or to persons of other descriptions whose fortunes have been interesting to the human passions, have, in turn, divided mankind into parties, inflamed them with mutual animosity, and rendered them much more disposed to vex and oppress each other than to co-operate for their common good. So strong is this propensity of mankind to fall into mutual animosities, that where no substantial occasion presents itself, the most frivolous and fanciful distinctions have been sufficient to kindle their unfriendly passions and excite their most violent conflicts. But the most common and durable source of factions has been the various and unequal distribution of property. Those who hold and those who are without property have ever formed distinct interests in society. Those who are creditors, and those who are debtors, fall under a like discrimination. A landed interest, a manufacturing interest, a mercantile interest, a moneyed interest, with many lesser interests, grow up of necessity in civilized nations, and divide them into different classes, actuated by different sentiments and views. The regulation of these various and interfering interests forms the principal task of modern legislation, and involves the spirit of party and faction in the necessary and ordinary operations of the government.

No man is allowed to be a judge in his own cause, because his interest would certainly bias his judgment, and, not improbably, corrupt his integrity. With equal, nay with greater reason, a body of men are unfit to be both judges and parties at the same time; yet what are many of the most important acts of legislation, but so many judicial determinations, not indeed concerning the rights of single persons, but concerning the rights of large bodies of citizens? And what are the different classes of legislators but advocates and parties to the causes which they determine? Is a law proposed concerning private debts? It is a question to which the creditors are parties on one side and the debtors on the other. Justice ought to hold the balance between them. Yet the parties are, and must be, themselves the judges; and the most numerous party, or, in other words, the most powerful faction must be expected to prevail. Shall domestic manufactures be encouraged, and in what degree, by restrictions on foreign manufactures? are questions which would be differently decided by the landed and the manufacturing classes, and probably by neither with a sole regard to justice and the public good. The apportionment of taxes on the various descriptions of property is an act which seems to require the most exact impartiality; yet there is, perhaps, no legislative act in which greater opportunity and temptation are given to a predominant party to trample on the rules of justice. Every shilling with which they overburden the inferior number, is a shilling saved to their own pockets.

It is in vain to say that enlightened statesmen will be able to adjust these clashing interests, and render them all subservient to the public good. Enlightened statesmen will not always be at the helm. Nor, in many cases, can such an adjustment be made at all without taking into view indirect and remote considerations, which will rarely prevail over the immediate interest which one party may find in disregarding the rights of another or the good of the whole.

The inference to which we are brought is, that the *causes* of faction cannot be removed, and that relief is only to be sought in the means of controlling its *effects*.

If a faction consists of less than a majority, relief is supplied by the republican principle, which enables the majority to defeat its sinister views by regular vote. It may clog the administration, it may convulse the society; but it will be unable to execute and mask its violence under the forms of the Constitution. When a majority is included in a faction, the form of popular government, on the other hand, enables it to sacrifice to its ruling passion or interest both the public good and the rights of other citizens. To secure the public good and private rights against the danger of such a faction, and at the same time to preserve the spirit and the form of popular government, is then the great object to which our inquiries are directed. Let me add that it is the great desideratum by which this form of government can be rescued from the opprobrium under which it has so long labored, and be recommended to the esteem and adoption of mankind.

By what means is this object attainable? Evidently by one of two only. Either the existence of the same passion or interest in a majority at the same time must be prevented, or the majority, having such coexistent passion or interest, must be rendered, by their number and local situation, unable to concert and carry into effect schemes of oppression. If the impulse and the opportunity be suffered to coincide, we well know that neither moral nor religious motives can be relied on as an adequate control. They are not found to be such on the injustice and violence of individuals, and lose their efficacy in proportion to the number combined together, that is, in proportion as their efficacy becomes needful.

From this view of the subject it may be concluded that a pure democracy, by which I mean a society consisting of a small number of citizens, who assemble and administer the government in person, can admit of no cure for the mischiefs of faction. A common passion or interest will, in almost every case, be felt by a majority of the whole; a communication and concert result from the form of government itself; and there is nothing to check the inducements to sacrifice the weaker party or an obnoxious individual. Hence it is that such democracies have ever been spectacles of turbulence and contention; have ever been found incompatible with personal security or the rights of property; and have in general been as short in their lives as they have been violent in their deaths. Theoretic politicians, who have patronized this species of government, have erroneously supposed that by reducing mankind to a perfect equality in their political rights, they would, at the same time, be perfectly equalized and assimilated in their possessions, their opinions, and their passions.

A republic, by which I mean a government in which the scheme of representation takes place, opens a different prospect, and promises the cure for which we are seeking. Let us examine the points in which it varies from pure democracy, and we shall comprehend both the nature of the cure and the efficacy which it must derive from the Union.

The two great points of difference between a democracy and a republic are: first, the delegation of the government, in the latter, to a small number of citizens elected by the rest; secondly, the greater number of citizens, and greater sphere of country, over which the latter may be extended.

The effect of the first difference is, on the one hand, to refine and enlarge the public views, by passing them through the medium of a chosen body of citizens, whose wisdom may best discern the true interest of their country, and whose patriotism and love of justice will be least likely to sacrifice it to temporary or partial considerations. Under such a regulation, it may well happen that the public voice, pronounced by the representatives of the people, will be more consonant to the public good than if pronounced by the people themselves, convened for the purpose. On the other hand, the effect may be inverted. Men of factious tempers, of local prejudices, or of sinister designs, may, by intrigue, by corruption, or by other means, first obtain the suffrages, and then betray the interests, of the people. The question resulting is, whether small or extensive republics are more favorable to the election of proper guardians of the public weal; and it is clearly decided in favor of the latter by two obvious considerations:

In the first place, it is to be remarked that, however small the republic may be, the representatives must be raised to a certain number, in order to guard against the cabals of a few; and that, however large it may be, they must be limited to a certain number, in order to guard against the confusion of a multitude. Hence, the number of representatives in the two cases not being in proportion to that of the two constituents, and being proportionally greater in the small republic, it follows that, if the proportion of fit characters be not less in the large than in the small republic, the former will present a greater option, and consequently a greater probability of a fit choice.

In the next place, as each representative will be chosen by a greater number of citizens in the large than in the small republic, it will be more difficult for unworthy candidates to practise with success the vicious arts by which elections are too often carried; and the suffrages of the people being more free, will be more likely to centre in men who possess the most attractive merit and the most diffusive and established characters.

It must be confessed that in this, as in most other cases, there is a mean, on both sides of which inconveniences will be found to lie. By enlarging too much the number of electors, you render the representative too little acquainted with all their local circumstances and lesser interests; as by reducing it too much, you render him unduly attached to these, and too little fit to comprehend and pursue great and national objects. The federal Constitution forms a happy combination in this respect; the great and aggregate interests being referred to the national, the local and particular to the State legislatures.

The other point of difference is, the greater number of citizens and extent of territory which may be brought within the compass of republican than of democratic government; and it is this circumstance principally which renders factious combinations less to be dreaded in the former than in the latter. The smaller the society, the fewer probably will be the distinct parties and interests composing it; the fewer the distinct parties and interests, the more frequently will a majority be found of the same party; and the smaller the number of individuals composing a majority, and the smaller the compass within which they are placed, the more easily will they concert and execute their plans of oppression. Extend the sphere, and you take in a greater variety of parties and interests; you make it less probable that a majority of the whole will have a common motive to invade the rights of other citizens; or if such a common motive exists, it will be more difficult for all who feel it to discover their own strength, and to act in unison with each other. Besides other impediments, it may be remarked that, where there is a consciousness of unjust or dishonorable purposes, communication is always checked by distrust in proportion to the number whose concurrence is necessary.

Hence, it clearly appears, that the same advantage which a republic has over a democracy, in controlling the effects of faction, is enjoyed by a large over a small republic,—is enjoyed by the Union over the States composing it. Does the advantage consist in the substitution of representatives whose enlightened views and virtuous sentiments render them superior to local prejudices and to schemes of injustice? It will not be denied that the representation of the Union will be most likely to possess these requisite endowments. Does it consist in the greater security afforded by a greater variety of parties, against the event of any one party being able to outnumber and oppress the rest? In an equal degree does the increased variety of parties comprised within the Union, increase this security. Does it, in fine, consist in the greater obstacles opposed to the concert and accomplishment of the secret wishes of an unjust and interested majority? Here, again, the extent of the Union gives it the most palpable advantage.

The influence of factious leaders may kindle a flame within their particular States, but will be unable to spread a general conflagration through the other States. A religious sect may degenerate into a political faction in a part of the Confederacy; but the variety of sects dispersed over the entire face of it must secure the national councils against any danger from that source. A rage for paper money, for an abolition of debts, for an equal division of property, or for any other improper or wicked project, will be less apt to pervade the whole body of the Union than a particular member of it; in the same proportion as such a malady is more likely to taint a particular county or district, than an entire State.

In the extent and proper structure of the Union, therefore, we behold a republican remedy for the diseases most incident to republican government. And according to the degree of pleasure and pride we feel in being republicans, ought to be our zeal in cherishing the spirit and supporting the character of Federalists. PUBLIUS

CHECKS AND BALANCES
THE FEDERALIST NO. 51
(MADISON)

To the People of the State of New York:

To what expedient, then, shall we finally resort, for maintaining in practice the necessary partition of power among the several departments, as laid down in the Constitution? The only answer that can be given is, that as all these exterior provisions are found to be inadequate, the defect must be supplied, by so contriving the interior structure of the government as that its several constituent parts may, by their mutual relations, be the means of keeping each other in their proper places. Without presuming to undertake a full development of this important idea, I will hazard a few general observations, which may perhaps place it in a clearer light, and enable us to form a more correct judgment of the principles and structure of the government planned by the convention.

In order to lay a due foundation for that separate and distinct exercise of the different powers of government, which to a certain extent is admitted on all hands to be essential to the preservation of liberty, it is evident that each department should have a will of its own; and consequently should be so constituted that the members of each should have as little agency as possible in the appointment of the members of the others. Were this principle rigorously adhered to, it would require that all the appointments for the supreme executive, legislative, and judiciary magistracies should be drawn from the same fountain of authority, the people, through channels having no communication whatever with one another. Perhaps such a plan of constructing the several departments would be less difficult in practice than it may in contemplation appear. Some difficulties, however, and some additional expense would attend the execution of it. Some deviations, therefore, from the principle must be admitted. In the constitution of the judiciary department in particular, it might be inexpedient to insist rigorously on the principle: first, because peculiar qualifications being essential in the members, the primary consideration ought to be to select that mode of choice which best secures these qualifications; secondly, because the permanent tenure

by which the appointments are held in that department, must soon destroy all sense of dependence on the authority conferring them.

It is equally evident, that the members of each department should be as little dependent as possible on those of the others, for the emoluments annexed to their offices. Were the executive magistrate, or the judges, not independent of the legislature in this particular, their independence in every other would be merely nominal.

But the great security against a gradual concentration of the several powers in the same department, consists in giving to those who administer each department the necessary constitutional means and personal motives to resist encroachments of the others. The provision for defence must in this, as in all other cases, be made commensurate to the danger of attack. Ambition must be made to counteract ambition. The interest of the man must be connected with the constitutional rights of the place. It may be a reflection on human nature, that such devices should be necessary to control the abuses of government. But what is government itself, but the greatest of all reflections on human nature? If men were angels, no government would be necessary. If angels were to govern men, neither external nor internal controls on government would be necessary. In framing a government which is to be administered by men over men, the great difficulty lies in this: you must first enable the government to control the governed; and in the next place oblige it to control itself. A dependence on the people is, no doubt, the primary control on the government; but experience has taught mankind the necessity of auxiliary precautions.

This policy of supplying, by opposite and rival interests, the defect of better motives, might be traced through the whole system of human affairs, private as well as public. We see it particularly displayed in all the subordinate distributions of power, where the constant aim is to divide and arrange the several offices in such a manner as that each may be a check on the other—that the private interest of every individual may be a sentinel over the public rights. These inventions of prudence cannot be less requisite in the distribution of the supreme powers of the State.

But it is not possible to give to each department an equal power of self-defence. In republican government, the legislative authority necessarily predominates. The remedy for this inconveniency is to divide the legislature into different branches; and to render them, by different modes of election and different principles of action, as little connected with each other as the nature of their common functions and their common dependence on the society will admit. It may even be necessary to guard against dangerous encroachments by still further precautions. As the weight of the legislative authority requires that it should be thus divided, the weakness of the executive may require, on the other hand, that it should be fortified. An absolute negative on the legislature appears, at first view, to be the natural defence with which the executive magistrate should be armed. But perhaps it would be neither altogether safe nor alone sufficient. On ordinary occasions it might not be exerted with the requisite firmness, and on extraordinary occasions it might be perfidiously abused. May not this defect of an absolute negative be supplied by some qualified connection between this weaker department and the weaker branch of the stronger department, by which the latter may be led to support the constitutional rights of the former, without being too much detached from the rights of its own department?

If the principles on which these observations are founded be just, as I persuade myself they are, and they be applied as a criterion to the several State constitutions, and to the federal Constitution, it will be found that if the latter does not perfectly correspond with them, the former are infinitely less able to bear such a test.

There are, moreover, two considerations particularly applicable to the federal system of America, which place that system in a very interesting point of view.

First. In a single republic, all the power surrendered by the people is submitted to the administration of a single government; and the usurpations are guarded against by a division of the government into distinct and separate departments. In the compound republic of America, the power surrendered by the people is first divided between two distinct governments, and then the portion allotted to each subdivided among distinct and separate departments. Hence a double security arises to the rights of the people. The different governments will control each other, at the same time that each will be controlled by itself.

Second. It is of great importance in a republic not only to guard the society against the oppression of its rulers, but to guard one part of the society against the injustice of the other part. Different interests necessarily exist in different classes of citizens. If a majority be united by a common interest, the rights of the minority will be insecure. There are but two methods of providing against this evil: the one by creating a will in the community independent of the majority—that is, of the society itself; the other, by comprehending in the society so many separate descriptions of citizens as will render an unjust combination of a majority of the whole very improbable, if not impracticable. The first method prevails in all governments possessing an hereditary or self-appointed authority. This, at best, is but a precarious security; because a power independent of the society may as well espouse the unjust views of the major, as the rightful interests of the minor party, and may possibly be turned against both parties. The second method will be exemplified in the federal republic of the United States. Whilst all authority in it will be derived from and dependent on the society, the society itself will be broken into so many parts, interests and classes of citizens, that the rights of individuals, or of the minority, will be in little danger from interested combinations of the majority. In a free government the security for civil rights must be the same as that for religious rights. It consists in the one case in the multiplicity of interests, and in the other in the multiplicity of sects. The degree of security in both cases will depend on the number of interests and sects; and this may be presumed to depend on the extent of country and number of people comprehended under the same government. This view of the subject must particularly recommend a proper federal system to all the sincere and considerate friends of republican government, since it shows that in exact proportion as the territory of the Union may be formed into more circumscribed Confederacies, or States, oppressive combinations of a majority will be facilitated; the best security, under the republican forms, for the rights of every class of citizens, will be diminished; and consequently the stability and independence of some member of the government, the only other security, must be proportionally increased. Justice is the end of government. It is the end of civil society. It ever has been and ever will be pursued until it be obtained, or until liberty be lost in the pursuit. In a society under the forms of which the stronger faction can readily unite and oppress the weaker, anarchy may as truly be said to reign as in a state of nature, where the weaker individual is not secured against the violence of the stronger; and as, in the latter state, even the stronger individuals are prompted, by the uncertainty of their condition, to submit to a government which may protect the weak as well as themselves; so, in the former state, will the more powerful factions or parties be gradually induced, by a like motive, to wish for a government which will protect all parties, the weaker as well as the more powerful. It can be little doubted that if the State of Rhode Island was separated from the Confederacy and left to itself, the insecurity of rights under the popular form of government within such narrow limits would be displayed by such reiterated oppressions of factious majorities that some power altogether independent of the people would soon be called for by the voice of the very factions whose misrule had proved the necessity of it. In the extended republic of the United States, and among the great variety of interests, parties, and sects which it embraces, a coalition of a majority of the whole society could seldom take place on any other principles than those of justice and the general good; whilst there being thus less danger to a minor from the will of a major party, there must be less pretext, also, to provide for the security of the former, by introducing into the government a will not dependent on the latter, or, in other words, a will independent of the society itself. It is no less certain than it is important, notwithstanding the contrary opinions which have been entertained, that the larger the society, provided it lie within a particular sphere, the more duly capable it will be of self-government. And happily for the *republican cause,* the practicable sphere may be carried to a very great extent, by a judicious modification and mixture of the *federal principle.*

PUBLIUS

THE JUDICIARY
THE FEDERALIST NO. 78
(HAMILTON)

To the People of the State of New York:

We proceed now to an examination of the judiciary department of the proposed government.

In unfolding the defects of the existing Confederation, the utility and necessity of a federal judicature have been clearly pointed out. It is the less necessary to recapitulate the considerations there urged, as the propriety of the institution in the abstract is not disputed; the only questions which have been raised being relative to the manner of constituting it, and to its extent. To these points, therefore, our observations shall be confined.

The manner of constituting it seems to embrace these several objects: 1st. The mode of appointing the judges. 2d. The tenure by which they are to hold their places. 3d. The partition of the judiciary authority between different courts, and their relations to each other.

First. As to the mode of appointing the judges; this is the same with that of appointing the officers of the Union in general, and has been so fully discussed in the two last numbers, that nothing can be said here which would not be useless repetition.

Second. As to the tenure by which the judges are to hold their places: this chiefly concerns their duration in office; the provisions for their support; the precautions for their responsibility.

According to the plan of the convention, all judges who may be appointed by the United States are to hold their offices *during good behavior;* which is conformable to the most approved of the State constitutions, and among the rest, to that of this State. Its propriety having been drawn into question by the adversaries of that plan, is no light symptom of the rage for objection, which disorders their imaginations and judgments. The standard of good behavior for the continuance in office of the judicial magistracy, is certainly one of the most valuable of the modern improvements in the practice of government. In a monarchy it is an excellent barrier to the despotism of the prince; in a republic it is a no less excellent barrier to the encroachments and oppressions of the representative body. And it is the best expedient which can be devised in any government, to secure a steady, upright, and impartial administration of the laws.

Whoever attentively considers the different departments of power must perceive, that, in a government in which they are separated from each other, the judiciary, from the nature of its functions, will always be the least dangerous to the political rights of the Constitution; because it will be least in a capacity to annoy or injure them. The Executive not only dispenses the honors, but holds the sword of the community. The legislature not only commands the purse, but prescribes the rules by which the duties and rights of every citizen are to be regulated. The judiciary, on the contrary, has no influence over either the sword or the purse; no direction either of the strength or of the wealth of the society; and can take no active resolution whatever. It may truly be said to have neither FORCE NOR WILL, but merely judgment; and must ultimately depend upon the aid of the executive arm even for the efficacy of its judgments.

This simple view of the matter suggests several important consequences. It proves incontestably, that the judiciary is beyond comparison the weakest of the three departments of power*; that it can never attack with success either of the other two; and that all possible care is requisite to enable it to defend itself against their attacks. It equally proves, that though individual oppression may now and then proceed from the courts of justice, the general liberty of the people can never be endangered from that quarter; I mean so long as the judiciary remains truly distinct from both the legislature and the Executive. For I agree, that "there is no liberty, if the power of judging be not separated from the legislative and executive powers."† And it proves, in

---

*The celebrated Montesquieu, speaking of them, says: "Of the three powers above mentioned, the judiciary is next to nothing."—"Spirit of Laws," vol. i., page 186.—PUBLIUS
†*Idem,* page 181.—PUBLIUS

the last place, that as liberty can have nothing to fear from the judiciary alone, but would have every thing to fear from its union with either of the other departments; that as all the effects of such a union must ensue from a dependence of the former on the latter, notwithstanding a nominal and apparent separation; that as, from the natural feebleness of the judiciary, it is in continual jeopardy of being overpowered, awed, or influenced by its coördinate branches; and that as nothing can contribute so much to its firmness and independence as permanency in office, this quality may therefore be justly regarded as an indispensable ingredient in its constitution, and, in a great measure, as the citadel of the public justice and the public security.

The complete independence of the courts of justice is peculiarly essential in a limited Constitution. By a limited Constitution, I understand one which contains certain specified exceptions to the legislative authority; such, for instance, as that it shall pass no bills of attainder, no *ex-post-facto* laws, and the like. Limitations of this kind can be preserved in practice no other way than through the medium of courts of justice, whose duty it must be to declare all acts contrary to the manifest tenor of the Constitution void. Without this, all the reservations of particular rights or privileges would amount to nothing.

Some perplexity respecting the rights of the courts to pronounce legislative acts void, because contrary to the constitution, has arisen from an imagination that the doctrine would imply a superiority of the judiciary to the legislative power. It is urged that the authority which can declare the acts of another void, must necessarily be superior to the one whose acts may be declared void. As this doctrine is of great importance in all the American constitutions, a brief discussion of the ground on which it rests cannot be unacceptable.

There is no position which depends on clearer principles, than that every act of a delegated authority, contrary to the tenor of the commission under which it is exercised, is void. No legislative act, therefore, contrary to the Constitution, can be valid. To deny this, would be to affirm, that the deputy is greater than his principal; that the servant is above his master; that the representatives of the people are superior to the people themselves; that men acting by virtue of powers, may do not only what their powers do not authorize, but what they forbid.

If it be said that the legislative body are themselves the constitutional judges of their own powers, and that the construction they put upon them is conclusive upon the other departments, it may be answered, that this cannot be the natural presumption, where it is not to be collected from any particular provisions in the Constitution. It is not otherwise to be supposed, that the Constitution could intend to enable the representatives of the people to substitute their *will* to that of their constituents. It is far more rational to suppose, that the courts were designed to be an intermediate body

between the people and the legislature, in order, among other things, to keep the latter within the limits assigned to their authority. The interpretation of the laws is the proper and peculiar province of the courts. A constitution is, in fact, and must be regarded by the judges, as a fundamental law. It therefore belongs to them to ascertain its meaning, as well as the meaning of any particular act proceeding from the legislative body. If there should happen to be an irreconcilable variance between the two, that which has the superior obligation and validity ought, of course, to be preferred; or, in other words, the Constitution ought to be preferred to the statute, the intention of the people to the intention of their agents.

Nor does this conclusion by any means suppose a superiority of the judicial to the legislative power. It only supposes that the power of the people is superior to both; and that where the will of the legislature, declared in its statutes, stands in opposition to that of the people, declared in the Constitution, the judges ought to be governed by the latter rather than the former. They ought to regulate their decisions by the fundamental laws, rather than by those which are not fundamental.

This exercise of judicial discretion, in determining between two contradictory laws, is exemplified in a familiar instance. It not uncommonly happens, that there are two statutes existing at one time, clashing in whole or in part with each other, and neither of them containing any repealing clause or expression. In such a case, it is the province of the courts to liquidate and fix their meaning and operation. So far as they can, by any fair construction, be reconciled to each other, reason and law conspire to dictate that this should be done; where this is impracticable, it becomes a matter of necessity to give effect to one, in exclusion of the other. The rule which has obtained in the courts for determining their relative validity is, that the last in order of time shall be preferred to the first. But this is a mere rule of construction, not derived from any positive law, but from the nature and reason of the thing. It is a rule not enjoined upon the courts by legislative provision, but adopted by themselves, as consonant to truth and propriety, for the direction of their conduct as interpreters of the law. They thought it reasonable, that between the interfering acts of an *equal* authority, that which was the last indication of its will should have the preference.

But in regard to the interfering acts of a superior and subordinate authority, of an original and derivative power, the nature and reason of the thing indicate the converse of that rule as proper to be followed. They teach us that the prior act of a superior ought to be preferred to the subsequent act of an inferior and subordinate authority; and that accordingly, whenever a particular statute contravenes the Constitution, it will be the duty of the judicial trubinals to adhere to the latter and disregard the former.

It can be of no weight to say that the courts, on the pretence of a repugnancy, may substitute their own pleasure to the constitutional intentions of the legislature. This might as well happen in the case of two contradictory statutes; or it might as well happen in every adjudication upon any single statute. The courts must declare the sense of the law; and if they should be disposed to exercise WILL instead of JUDGMENT, the consequence would equally be the substitution of their pleasure to that of the legislative body. The observation, if it prove any thing, would prove that there ought to be no judges distinct from that body.

If, then, the courts of justice are to be considered as the bulwarks of a limited Constitution against legislative encroachments, this consideration will afford a strong argument for the permanent tenure of judicial offices, since nothing will contribute so much as this to that independent spirit in the judges which must be essential to the faithful performance of so arduous a duty.

This independence of the judges is equally requisite to guard the Constitution and the rights of individuals from the effects of those ill humors, which the arts of designing men, or the influence of particular conjunctures, sometimes disseminate among the people themselves, and which, though they speedily give place to better information, and more deliberate reflection, have a tendency, in the meantime, to occasion dangerous innovations in the government, and serious oppressions of the minor party in the community. Though I trust the friends of the proposed Constitution will never concur with its enemies,* in questioning that fundamental principle of republican government, which admits the right of the people to alter or abolish the established Constitution, whenever they find it inconsistent with their happiness, yet it is not to be inferred from this principle, that the representatives of the people, whenever a momentary inclination happens to lay hold of a majority of their constituents, incompatible with the provisions in the existing Constitution, would, on that account, be justifiable in a violation of those provisions; or that the courts would be under a greater obligation to connive at infractions in this shape, than when they had proceeded wholly from the cabals of the representative body. Until the people have, by some solemn and authoritative act, annulled or changed the established form, it is binding upon themselves collectively, as well as individually; and no presumption, or even knowledge, of their sentiments, can warrant their representatives in a departure from it, prior to such an act. But it is easy to see, that it would require an uncommon portion of fortitude in the judges to do their duty as faithful guardians of the Constitution, where legislative invasions of it had been instigated by the major voice of the community.

But it is not with a view to infractions of the Constitution only, that the independence of the judges may be an essential safeguard against the effects of occasional ill humors in the society. These sometimes extend no farther than to the injury of the private rights of particular classes of citizens, by unjust and partial laws. Here also the firmness of the judicial magistracy is of vast importance in mitigating the severity and confining the operation of such laws. It not only serves to moderate the immediate mischiefs of those which may have been passed but it operates as a check upon the legislative body in passing them; who, perceiving that obstacles to the success of iniquitous intention are to be expected from the scruples of the courts, are in a manner compelled, by the very motives of the injustice they meditate, to qualify their attempts. This is a circumstance calculated to have more influence upon the character of our governments, than but few may be aware of. The benefits of the integrity and moderation of the judiciary have already been felt in more States than one; and though they may have displeased those whose sinister expectations they may have disappointed, they must have commanded the esteem and applause of all the virtuous and disinterested. Considerate men, of every description, ought to prize whatever will tend to beget or fortify that temper in the courts; as no man can be sure that he may not be to-morrow the victim of a spirit of injustice, by which he may be a gainer to-day. And every man must now feel, that the inevitable tendency of such a spirit is to sap the foundations of public and private confidence, and to introduce in its stead universal distrust and distress.

That inflexible and uniform adherence to the rights of the Constitution, and of individuals, which we perceive to be indispensable in the courts of justice, can certainly not be expected from judges who hold their offices by a temporary commission. Periodical appointments, however regulated, or by whomsoever made, would, in some way or other, be fatal to their necessary independence. If the power of making them was committed either to the Executive or legislature, there would be danger of an improper complaisance to the branch which possessed it; if to both, there would be an unwillingness to hazard the displeasure of either; if to the people, or to persons chosen by them for the special purpose, there would be too great a disposition to consult popularity, to justify a reliance that nothing would be consulted but the Constitution and the laws.

There is yet a further and a weightier reason for the permanency of the judicial offices, which is deducible from the nature of the qualifications they require. It has been frequently remarked, with great propriety, that a voluminous code of laws is one of the incoveniences necessarily connected with the advantages of a free government. To avoid an arbitrary discretion in the courts, it is indispensable that they should be bound down by strict rules and precedents, which serve to define and point out their duty in every particular case that comes before them; and it will readily be conceived from the variety of controversies which grow out of the folly and wickedness of mankind, that the records of

---

*Vide "Protest of the Minority of the Convention of Pennsylvania," Martin's Speech, etc.—PUBLIUS

those precedents must unavoidably swell to a very considerable bulk, and must demand long and laborious study to acquire a competent knowledge of them. Hence it is, that there can be but few men in the society who will have sufficient skill in the laws to qualify them for the stations of judges. And making the proper deductions for the ordinary depravity of human nature, the number must be still smaller of those who unite the requisite integrity with the requisite knowledge. These considerations apprise us, that the government can have no great option between fit character; and that a temporary duration in office, which would naturally discourage such characters from quitting a lucrative line of practice to accept a seat on the bench, would have a tendency to throw the administration of justice into hands less able, and less well qualified, to conduct it with utility and dignity. In the present circumstances of this country, and in those in which it is likely to be for a long time to come, the disadvantages on this score would be greater than they may at first sight appear; but it must be confessed, that they are far inferior to those which present themselves under the other aspects of the subject.

Upon the whole, there can be no room to doubt that the convention acted wisely in copying from the models of those constitutions which have established *good behavior* as the tenure of their judicial offices, in point of duration; and that so far from being blamable on this account, their plan would have been inexcusably defective, if it had wanted this important feature of good government. The experience of Great Britain affords an illustrious comment on the excellence of the institution.
PUBLIUS

The Empty Symbolism of American Politics

by ROBERT A. LEVINE

Seeking a middle ground,
liberal and conservative
politicians alike
propose split-the-difference
"solutions" to our problems
which seem plausible and
pragmatic but do not,
of course, represent solutions
at all. What's missing? The
dimension of reality

IMAGINE a panel of eighteenth-century physicians with a royal patient who has a persistent fever and a hacking cough. Learned doctor Newt Gingrich wants to bleed three pints, learned doctor Richard Gephardt one. Doctors Bill Clinton and Bob Dole want to split the difference at a quart, but they can't decide which of them should make the incision. The next day the patient has acute pneumonia; the following day he dies and the kingdom goes into mourning.

That is what our political debate increasingly resembles. Led by the politics-is-a-game media, we have defined American politics along a single right-to-left dimension. We know that the new conservatives of the House of Representatives are on the right and the old liberals of the Kennedy-Johnson tradition on the left. And the votes are in the middle, so that's where President Clinton and ex-senator Dole have gone. The middle of the road may be mathematically

 From *The Atlantic Monthly*, October 1996, pp. 80-82, 84. © 1996 by Robert A. Levine. Reprinted by permission.

equidistant from the right and the left, but the symbolic middle toward which both candidates have moved is meaningless for making real national policy.

For liberals it is worse than meaningless. It is harmful, because most of the terms defining the political debate are inherently conservative: "less government," "middle-class tax cut," "tough on crime," "abolish welfare as we know it." And for most Americans, who just want solutions to the nation's problems, the symbolic middle is useless, because it provides only symbolic solutions. We need real solutions. The correction of our national problems requires neither right nor left, neither moderation nor extremism. The political debate needs a new dimension: reality.

The issue that best represents the grip of symbolism on the public debate is balancing the budget. There is no difference for Clinton and Dole to split on this issue, because the Administration and the Republican Congress have agreed to balance the budget by 2002. A balanced budget has become the Holy Grail of public policy, a symbol that no politician dares to question. Meanwhile, in the real world of tradeoffs, where rarely do all good things go together, the effort to make that symbol an achieved fact is likely to slow the country's economic growth, increase unemployment, and even trigger a recession.

Other examples of the politics of symbolism can be found in categories from taxes to social programs—categories that are not far apart, since where the money comes from is inextricably linked to where it goes.

Taxes

THE Administration and the Republican Congress agree on the need for a middle-class tax cut. Why? Aside from the excellent politics of handing out money, the tax issue is based on four symbol-clotted myths plus one clear untruth that everyone knows as such and almost no politician mentions:

1. *Tax cuts, balanced by cuts in government expenditures, stimulate economic growth and employment.* Wrong. The supply-side theory is that if you let people keep more of their earnings, they will work harder. That is probably true, but most economists agree that it is a very limited truth—certainly as it applies to small shifts in current low marginal tax rates. Tax cuts do stimulate growth, but primarily on the demand side. People with more after-tax money in their pockets will spend more, and their buying will increase employment. But if the tax cuts are balanced by cuts in government expenditures, the people who were receiving money from the government will have less of it to spend, and that will decrease demand, offsetting the impetus that tax cuts have given demand and thus doing little to increase growth.

2. *The proposed tax cuts are for the middle class.* The middle class approaches motherhood as an American icon, but

at least motherhood is definable. President Clinton has proposed cuts for couples with incomes up to $120,000; the Republicans initially went much higher, although they have now come down. But the middle 50 percent of American families make $15,000 to $50,000 a year; only one family in six has an income above even $75,000.

3. *Federal taxes are being used to equalize incomes.* The debate rages over whether they should or should not be. In fact the redistributive effects of federal taxes are mild at best (or worst). Families with incomes of less than $30,000 pay up to 13 percent of their income in taxes; those above that level do pay significantly more, going above 20 percent, but there is little variation among the groups making more than $30,000.

The alleged leveling effect of taxes calls forth two further myths. The conservative one is that federal taxes are confiscatory, but at an average tax rate that is effectively less than 25 percent for families with incomes higher than $200,000, confiscation is truly mythical. The liberal myth is that a more egalitarian distribution of income can be achieved primarily by playing with income-tax rates. Ronald Reagan's 1986 tax reform reduced progressivity, although loophole-tightening compensated for that to some degree. In focusing on income taxes, however, liberals ignore the really regressive feature of the tax system—Social Security payroll taxes, which are levied only on wages and salaries of less than $62,000, thus exempting not only all pay above that level but also interest, dividends, and capital gains. A truly progressive tax system—that is, one that takes proportionally more from those with higher incomes—would look first at payroll taxes.

4. *Federal "entitlements" and other direct subsidy payments are questionable pieces of pork, whereas federal subsidies provided as tax reductions are rewards for virtue.* This is highly debatable. Entitlements are defined as payments available to all those who meet certain conditions—for example, poverty or willingness not to plant corn. The total cost is determined by the number of applicants and the amount paid to each. That definition of entitlements, however, fits not only direct payments but also most tax deductions—at least as defined by many economists and some tax lawyers. One example of the mythological difference between tax and expenditure subsidies lies in housing. The deductibility of mortgage interest is an entitlement that costs the federal government more than $50 billion a year, and it goes mostly to middle-income homeowners along with better-off owners of expensive or multiple properties. Politically, the mortgage-interest deduction is viewed as almost pure virtue, to be continued even under many proposed "flat tax" plans. It costs twice as much as federal expenditures for public and other low-income housing—popularly considered a dubious subsidy, and one that is

likely to be reduced significantly in the drive toward a balanced budget.

Many other expenditures will also be reduced in the name of budget balancing. Since the deficit is the total of expenditures minus the total of tax revenues, the other way to move toward budget balance would be to increase taxes. What is being proposed, however, by both the budget-balancing Congress and the President, is to cut taxes. The great untruth is that this is somehow consistent with movement toward a balanced budget. It is not, and everybody knows it is not.

Political hypocrisy is hardly unprecedented, but it has seldom before provided the unquestioned basis for national political dialogue. The problem is not that homeownership and other tax entitlements are unjustified, or that tax cuts are a bad way to stimulate economic growth, or that the tax system should be used to redistribute income more efficiently. These are legitimate matters for debate. But they are not being debated. Instead the tax debate in this campaign focuses on which symbolic tax cuts should be given to the symbolic middle class in the symbolic drive to balance the symbolic budget.

Social Programs

THE discussion of "social programs"—federal programs intended to help people rather than, for example, the environment or the physical infrastructure—abounds with myths. At least three of them have to do with entitlements.

1. *All entitlements are social programs.* Incorrect. Many go to business, particularly if we include tax entitlements.

2. *Most entitlements go to the poor and minorities.* Not even close to true. Social Security, federal retirement, and Medicare, all of which go mostly to the middle class, account for 70 percent of total social entitlements. Aid that goes mostly to the poor, including "welfare," food stamps, and Medicaid, constitutes about 25 percent, of which less than one tenth—two percent of total social entitlements—has been for the notorious Aid to Families with Dependent Children (AFDC) program.

3. *Social Security shouldn't be considered a social program because individuals pay for themselves with their contributions.* Never been true. Almost all recipients of Social Security pensions receive much more in benefits than they have ever put in. The difference is federal subsidy.

But it is the symbolic two percent for AFDC—"welfare mothers"—about which the political debate has long raged, with Clinton and the Republicans splitting differences and splitting hairs until Clinton finally accepted an essentially Republican bill, which will phase out AFDC, ending welfare as a federal entitlement. Since AFDC is at the core of what many experts as well as laypeople see as the "welfare syndrome"—the breakdown of the family among the dependent poor—its abolition may be necessary for long-term change, as both Clinton and the Republicans claim. But ending AFDC cannot by itself restore families or heal poor neighborhoods, and children's advocates on the liberal side are surely correct that ending AFDC will cause traumatic short-term suffering for their innocent victims—children in welfare families.

In any case, that is what the debate should be about, not the symbolic two percent of social-entitlement expenditures.

Two Deep Myths

INDEED, the focus on cutting the two percent illustrates one of the two basic myths, one conservative, the other liberal, that distort the debate over federal social programs.

The conservative myth is that spending less is the way to achieve more. AFDC reform provides an example of why that is unlikely. The strong American consensus is that the objective of welfare reform is to move people off the AFDC rolls and into jobs—a reasonable and perhaps realistic goal for most recipients. Two central requirements for such movement are that there be jobs for welfare people to take and that there be child care for the AFDC mothers who are at the heart of the problem. But the economy has seldom made sufficient or sufficiently attractive jobs available at lower levels, particularly in recent years. Pushing welfare recipients off the assistance rolls and into employment will thus necessitate public funding of community jobs as a last resort for those who cannot find employment in the private sector. That will cost public money. So will child care.

Together, these two requisites mean that if welfare reform is to move recipients into jobs, it will take more, not less, money—at least for what may be a very long transitional period. That was recognized in the Family Support Act of 1988, sponsored by Senator Daniel Patrick Moynihan, which was never effective, largely because it was never funded as intended. It is also recognized in the experimental welfare reform of Republican Governor Tommy Thompson, of Wisconsin, embraced by both Clinton and Dole. The essence of the Wisconsin reform—public jobs when private ones are not available, and publicly funded child care—meets the objectives of liberal as well as conservative reformers. Neither Clinton nor Dole, though, has faced up to the fiscal implications of the Wisconsin experiment or of the Republican "reform" bill signed by the President: that federal budgets for the next five years should provide funding increases for welfare reform.

Nor is the spend-less-get-more mythology confined to welfare. In education, for example, conservatives contend that what is needed is structural reform, not "throwing money at the system." Maybe so, but it is generally agreed that small classes work better than large ones, and small classes require more teachers and thus more money. Even more generally agreed is that good education requires good teachers, and as in every other line of economic endeavor, it takes good pay to attract good people (that is certainly what conservatives argue in the case of corporate executives). That, too, takes money.

If spend less, get more is the conservative myth, the liberal one is that we know what would work if we could only get the money to spend. Mostly we don't know. Looking again at jobs, for people on welfare and others, conservatives along with liberals generally accept the wisdom that the key is more training. Unfortunately, almost all the evidence points the other way. At least for welfare recipients and other people with limited skills, training has very little effect on long-term job prospects. Some exceptions exist, but they have proved very difficult to replicate on a large scale.

Similar doubts arise regarding many other social programs, even such a highly touted one as Head Start, for preschool children. Head Start does have immediate effects, but much of the evidence indicates that they fade as children go through the regular school system. The fault is almost certainly with the schools rather than with Head Start, but that criticism carries the dismal implication that everything must work for anything to work.

In fact some programs do work on a stand-alone basis. The food-stamp program, in spite of occasional abuses, has prevented widespread hunger among poor Americans, and its companion school-lunch program has supported child nutrition rather well. In these cases the facts have overcome some negative mythology; fraud certainly exists, for example, but it is hardly rampant. A related program, for nutrition of women, infants, and children (WIC), has never done as well politically, even though it is widely recognized that good pre-natal and postnatal nutrition is crucial to the proper mental and physical development of children.

We should do what we know how to do, but that's limited. One crucial example is that we have no real idea how to keep children in problem families from becoming problem parents starting new problem families. One logical answer would be to remove children at risk from such families at an early age. Newt Gingrich's orphanage scheme was too pat an idea and too easy to caricature, but the issue he raised deserved discussion rather than the dismissal it received as an unacceptable symbol. If the prize of capturing the right symbol—the sainted "middle class"—is often political victory, the price of using the wrong one is as often defeat. Thus is public policy made hostage to public relations.

Abrogation of the opposing myths of spend less, get more and spend on everything could make it possible to spend sufficient money on programs that work while using experimentation and evaluation to invent and search for more. Instead the Republican Congress has been hell-bent on spending less for almost everything (except defense), while the response of the Clinton Administration has been to fight hard for symbolic expenditures for a few more children here, a few more policemen there, and a few volunteers spread around everywhere.

Symbolism has always been a necessary part of political life. But most past symbolic stances, from preserving the Union to defeating the Evil Empire, have been connected with reality. Whether it is the influence of the media or something deeper, the connection is becoming tenuous. So is the ability of the nation to solve its real problems.

Robert A. Levine, a West Coast economic consultant, was a deputy director of the Congressional Budget Office from 1975 to 1979. His article "The Economic Consequences of Mr. Clinton" was part of the cover story in the July *Atlantic*.

What Will Rogers Could Teach the Age of Limbaugh

A voice of selflessness and consensus might sound out of place today, but without one, nothing we need to do will get done

Jon Meacham

No money, no banks, no work, no nothing, but they know they got a man in here who is wise to Congress, wise to our big bankers, and wise to our so-called big men. The whole country is with him. Even if what he does is wrong, they are with him. Just so he does something. If he burned down the Capitol, we would cheer and say, 'Well, at least we got a fire started somehow.'

—Will Rogers on FDR's inauguration, 1933

This no-nonsense but generous welcome to the White House was exactly what Franklin Roosevelt needed. After all, things in the country could hardly have been worse. When a writer for the *Saturday Evening Post* asked John Maynard Keynes if there had ever been anything like the Depression before, he replied, "Yes. It was called the Dark Ages, and it lasted four hundred years."

Of all that was said at the opening of the Roosevelt administration, it's striking that the most sensible words came not from a Brain Truster but from Rogers—a former cowboy rope twirler, star of the *Ziegfeld Follies,* and movie actor. Striking, but not surprising: In the early thirties, Rogers was the nation's most influential popular political and cultural voice, reaching 40 million Americans with his columns and radio commentaries. With wit and common sense, Rogers emphasized pulling together and extending a generous hand to those down on their luck. "These people that you are asked to aid, they are not asking for charity, they are naturally asking for a job. But if you can't give them a job, why the next best thing you can do is see that they

have food and the necessities of life," Rogers said in a 1931 appeal for the unemployed, who then numbered 25 percent of the population. "You know, not a one of us has anything that these people that are without now haven't contributed to what we've got. There is not an unemployed man in the country that hasn't contributed to the wealth of every millionaire in America."

Delivered without sentimentality, this kind of message moved a country deeply skeptical that familiar institutions could work—a world not unlike our own. Americans then were as bewildered by the failure of banks, farms, and the market as we are now by schools, health care, and government itself. What separates us from them is that they pulled themselves out of their ditch and we remain stuck in ours, routinely registering despair with the state of the union. Sixty percent of Americans regularly tell pollsters the country is "on the wrong track."

This is not because there were better ideas or better policies in the past. There are plenty of sound programs around now on health care, entitlements, and education. Yet none seems likely to come about in the current political climate because we are missing what made America work from the thirties to the sixties: a willingness to concede the other side's point and to give up special advantages in order to advance a common good. Without that, all the reforms in the world will come to nothing.

If Rogers' successor as the country's most influential pop political voice—Rush Limbaugh—is any indication, that is exactly the dismal situation Americans now face. Limbaugh's reach is similar to Rogers': a weekly radio audience of 20 million, a nightly television show available to 99.82 percent of the nation's viewing households, and 400,000 subscribers to his monthly newsletter. But Limbaugh's tone and message is a world away from Rogers'—and a world away from generosity of spirit. Limbaugh, for example, greeted the Clinton inauguration on his TV show with an "America Held Hostage" graphic: "We are all imprisoned to the liberal idealism of the hippyish sixties, ladies and gentlemen," Limbaugh warned. "And every night we're going to remind you of it on this show."

The distinction is more than partisan: Rogers stuck up for the little guy and so tended to identify with Democrats, but he hit FDR and his party when they deserved hitting. The signal difference between Rogers and Limbaugh—and between the thirties and the nineties—is one of spirit. Rogers' voice was generous—shrewd, funny, and encouraging. Limbaugh's is childishly ironic—shrewd and funny, to be sure, but uninterested in making anybody do anything except listen to Rush Limbaugh. One was about coming together, the other is about coming apart. Consider:

➤ A year before the 1932 election, Rogers, who had been hard on politically conservative bankers, speculators, and the Harding-Coolidge administrations, said this of Hoover: "I know that [unemployment] is very dear to Mr. Hoover's heart and know that he would rather see the problem of unemployment solved than all the other problems he's got before him combined. . . . He's had a very tough, uphill fight, and this will make him feel good. He's a very human man."

➤ After Clinton opened his Inaugural Address with the phrase "My fellow citizens. . . " Limbaugh ranted: "Wait a minute. Wait a minute. . . 'My fellow citizens'? Whatever happened to 'My fellow Americans'? You think he didn't say Americans by accident? That was on purpose, folks. I guarantee you that's exactly what this administration is all about—their stupid symbolism. You know what the problem with 'Americans' is? Americans is not inclusive enough. No, no, it does not include everybody. It alienates people out there on the fringes whose pain we are all trying to feel. There are a lot of people who aren't proud to be Americans: Native Americans, the people who don't like you to call them Redskins and Braves and all that. This is purposeful. . . He can't just say, 'My fellow Americans.'"

Why is the same nation that idolized Rogers now idolizing Limbaugh? One reason is that we are *not* the same nation anymore. Rogers lived in a time when, because the middle and working classes were basically united, he was

able to urge selflessness on people inclined to be generous. By the sixties, however, that sense of community had frayed. Increasing numbers of upper income parents pulled their children out of public schools, and the draft, which mixed millions of middle class and working class men, ended in 1973. Politically, we have separated as well: As Jonathan Rauch notes in his book *Demosclerosis*, Americans have subdivided into lobbies at an astounding pace since 1956. That year, there were 5,000 associations in Washington; by 1990, there were 20,000. Seventy percent of Americans belong to at least one association; 25 percent belong to four or more. (It's not merely coincidental that Washington, which boasted only three fancy restaurants in the fifties and sixties—Rive Gauche, La Salle du Bois, and the Jockey Club—had a rash of upscale openings in the seventies to meet the demand for lobbyist expense-account meals.) Limbaugh comes out of a selfish world and urges self-absorption on the self-absorbed. In short, FDR could appeal to a nation that had not yet organized itself into chain-link fence manufacturers and mohair farmers; Clinton cannot.

Yet Roosevelt and his successors up to Johnson were not operating in a pastoral world of public selflessness. They too faced a country as potentially susceptible to the politics of self-interest—the politics of Limbaugh—as we are now. But Americans generally overcame their worst tendencies through the New Deal, the Fair Deal, the Eisenhower years, the New Frontier, and much of the Great Society. These were days of rapidly expanding government (from Social Security to Medicare to the Tennessee Valley Authority) with rapidly obvious results (Social Security and Medicare virtually ended poverty among the elderly; TVA brought power to a huge part of the country). The building of the interstate highways and higher top tax rates on the rich (Truman, Eisenhower, and Kennedy, 91 percent; Johnson, 77 percent) were other signs of collective national action, made possible by a national willingness to contribute.

Real reform always means sacrifice—whether it's a well off Social Security recipient taking a means test or a farmer giving up his crop subsidy. Americans were once unselfish enough to make just those kinds of sacrifices. That's what FDR counted on, and he was rewarded with sweeping re-election in 1936. All of which shows that while our problem today—a politics of self-interest—is difficult to solve, it is soluble because we have tilted the margin toward fair play before in difficult times.

A Will to Help

First, a look back. In the mid-thirties, the *New York Sun* wrote, "Will Rogers. . . has a curious national quality. He gives the impression that the country is filled with such sages, wise with years, young in humor and love of life, shrewd yet gentle. He is what Americans think other Americans are like."

Born just 14 years after Appomattox, Rogers traveled by horseback in Oklahoma as a boy and would die in an airplane crash in Alaska in 1935. In the intervening years, American life was rapidly moving from agrarianism to manufacturing. Rogers moved with the times, mastering one medium after another: Wild West shows, vaudeville, radio, newspaper columns, and movies. In the early thirties, Rogers was the most widely read columnist and the number-one box office draw in the nation—a level of popularity in different arenas almost unimaginable today. So it's telling that the public responded so enthusiastically to a man whose public persona resembled that of another figure associated with common sense and the frontier: Huck Finn. Like Huck, Rogers appealed to the best things in the American character—fair play and a throwing off of old class divisions—with a cold eye for hypocrisy and human folly. And this message resonated with people, puzzled as they were by a changing economy and changing times, who took from Rogers the lesson that the decent thing to do was sympathize with those who most needed help.

"You can never have another war in this country unless Will Rogers is for it," an unnamed "Washington statesman" told the popular *American Magazine* in 1930. When newspapers and magazines began calling, only half-jokingly, for a Rogers presidential campaign in 1932, it worried Roosevelt enough that he wrote Rogers, "Don't forget you are a Democrat by birth, training, and tough experience, and I know you won't get mixed up in any fool movement to make the good old Donkey chase his own tail and give the Elephant a chance to win the race." While FDR was right that Rogers' sympathies were basically with the Democrats, his politics, as Ben Yagoda defines them in a landmark 1993 Rogers biography, were more complicated than that:

His main impulse was a broad, neo-Jeffersonian populism tempered by an across-the-board skepticism. He had a general and instinctive distrust of bankers, big business, and Wall Street. . . . Pro-income tax and anti-tariff, he doggedly stuck up for the farmers, whom he (correctly) saw as getting the blunt end of Republican economic policies of the 1920s. He felt that consumer buying on credit and stock-market speculation, both of which reached unprecedented proportions by the end of the decade, were something close to an evil, and he (correctly) felt they would end in disaster. But unlike many populists, Will was no proselytizer.

Rogers wasn't radical in any way. He dismissed Prohibition ("Talking about Prohibition is like whittling used to be—it passes the time but don't get you nowhere") and put no stock in crusaders from William Jennings Bryan to Huey Long to Woodrow Wilson.

Free of partisan baggage, Rogers conceded good points all around: As occasion demanded, he would praise Calvin Coolidge or Al Smith, Hoover or Robert LaFollette. "Suddenly, appearing to be a good sport, a regular guy, had become an important political consideration," writes Yagoda. Rogers' sympathy for right and left pressed the political debate forward and engaged established interests—from Wall Street speculators to new Deal bureaucrats—not just vaguely defined liberal or conservative ones.

Rogers, for example, ebulliently opened the Roosevelt era (remember, after kindly addressing Hoover, who was sometimes threatened with rioters during the '32 campaign), writing in the First Hundred Days, "[Roosevelt] swallowed our depression. He has inhaled fear and exhaled confidence." Two years later, however, Rogers hit both his friend in the White House and big business over the misadministration of FDR's National Recovery Administration (the arm of the New Deal intended to shorten the work week, establish a minimum wage, and let workers organize). Different industries were successfully lobbying for exemptions from the law. "The NRA looked like a good bet at the time, but part of it, in fact maybe over half of it, has proven to be nonpractical. It had all the right ideas but we are still just too selfish to see that exactly the right thing is done for the good of everybody." If we are really all in this together, Rogers said, then we ought to act like it:

Some industry can't come in and say, 'Ours is a special and unique business. You can't judge it by the others.' Well no committee come into Jerusalem looking for Moses and saying 'Ours is a special business.' Moses just went up on the mountain with a letter of credit and some instructions from the Lord, and He just wrote 'em out, and they applied to the steel men, the oil men, the bankers, the farmers, and even the United States Chamber of Commerce. And he said, 'Here they are, Brothers, you can take 'em and live by 'em, or else.'

Instead, Rogers pointed out, industries went to Washington and came back with "24 truckloads" worth of special interest exemptions. The overar-

Limbaugh epitomizes a terrible fact about American life today: Extremism, ego, and irony sell. "Remember this above all else," Limbaugh says, "my success is not determined by who wins elections, my success is determined by how many listeners I have." In other words, as long as he gets his, that's fine.

ching message? Not mindless government-bashing. Rogers never questions the need for action. He was criticizing an institution in a tone—friendly but sharp—that strongly implied the problem ought to be fixed, not just jawed about. Because Rogers talked like this, expressing and reinforcing the basic spirit of the times, it did have an effect. Middle and working class people whose inclination might otherwise have been to turn cynical about Roosevelt gave the president a break in those rocky early days—eventually sending FDR back to the White House in 1936 carrying every state except Maine and Vermont.

The Bum's Rush

Every day at noon, Eastern Time, on 638 radio stations and again late at night on television, a slightly overweight man in flowered ties intones:

Greetings, listeners across the fruited plain, this is Rush Limbaugh, the most dangerous man in America, serving humanity simply by opening my mouth, destined for my own wing in the Museum of Broadcasting, executing everything I do flawlessly with zero mistakes, doing this show with half my brain tied behind my back just to make it fair because I have talent on loan from. . . God. Rush Limbaugh. A man. A legend. A way of life.

Well. The contrast in tone from Rogers—whose signature opening was the self-effacing "All I know is what I read in the papers"—couldn't be greater. Limbaugh's self-promotion, consciously purveyed and heavy with irony, is a prelude to a message of selfishness, the worst element of an otherwise engaging conservatism.

For Limbaugh, on points of policy, is not entirely as antediluvian as his critics make him

out to be. Leaving aside its uncritical adoration of Ronald Reagan, Limbaugh's creed (laid out in two books modestly titled *The Way Things Ought To Be* and *See, I Told You So*) can, at times, get at quite sensible points. For instance:

➤ His critique of government is hardly Know-Nothing: "Sure, I use the public streets and the post office, and if I get a disease someday I may benefit from the government's medical research. . . But the streets cost twice as much as they should and always seem to have potholes. The mail service is twice as slow as it should be. With some diseases the Food and Drug Administration keeps as many lifesaving drugs off the market as it approves."

➤ On the Washington press corps: "The media have covered up Congress' sins for a long time. Many journalists are lazy and they live off snacks of information passed out by congressional staffers. They love prepackaged stories they don't have to work at uncovering themselves. In return, reporters only rarely bite the congressional hand that feeds them."

It goes on: Basically clear-headed assessments of how homelessness is more the result of mental illness, drinking, and drug abuse than of a lack of affordable housing; of how criminals belong in jail; of how kids should be allowed a moment of silence in public schools.

What separates Limbaugh from others who also understand what's wrong with liberalism is that he refuses to acknowledge that polarized debate isn't very useful for the country. In fact, he epitomizes a terrible fact about American life today: Extremism, ego, and irony sell. "Remember this above all else," Limbaugh says, "my success is not determined by who wins elections, my success is determined by how many listeners I have." In other words, as long as he gets his, that's fine—the same view taken, not entirely coincidentally, by other major contemporary political forces like the American Association of Retired Persons or the National Education Association. Limbaugh is the apotheosis of the politics of ego—he is a one man special interest. He thrives on attention, and the less conciliatory he is, the more attention he gets. It's a reversal of the cycle Rogers was part of: Where Rogers was produced by a culture of selflessness and encouraged it, Limbaugh is produced by a culture of selfishness and makes it worse.

Limbaugh, for example, preaches a small-government message to an audience that zealously protects its slices of the federal pie—Social Security, Medicare, home mortgage interest deductions, veterans' benefits, civil service pensions, what have you—that add up to big government. Nevertheless, Limbaugh raves against government without really acknowledging that the people he's talking *to* are the same people he's talking *about:* Limbaugh's beloved middle class, who are "just plain tired and worn out. They get blamed for everything in this country. They are taxed more than ever. . . ." Middle America, put upon by unnamed liberals, is always being asked to pay while the undeserving poor are making off like bandits. "Our inner cities are now collapsing, crime is running rampant, and yet all the money we've poured into those problems hasn't helped." And so on.

Even when Clinton does things Limbaugh agrees with, such as calling on black ministers to stop inner-city violence, Limbaugh fails to give the president credit and instead claims credit for the ideas himself. In November, Limbaugh ran a clip of Clinton's impassioned speech to ministers in Memphis in which the president said, "And then there's some changes we're going to have to make from the inside out, or the others won't matter." Limbaugh then cut to himself (of course, on his TV show, he has to cut to himself; there's one camera, trained on Limbaugh, with rows of his books arrayed behind him), exclaiming, "That's what we've been saying all along. . . And it's the government that's led to the problems that we have. And now he, all of a sudden, is coming to the store, and realizing the problem, and he's being praised for it. I just wanted you to see this, because you know they're Johnny-come-latelies on this, my friends. Got to claim victory. You just have to run around and not let them get away with stealing this issue." There is no building of sentiment for actually doing anything. Great for ratings, bad for the country.

That the ratings are so high proves that a lot of us are buying what Limbaugh is selling. By pressing people to worry only about themselves and their own problems—Clinton's stealing *our* ideas; he's after *our* money—Limbaugh reinforces the increasingly self-absorbed world that has made him a star. "I am now enjoying success in my life," Limbaugh says. "That doesn't mean I don't remember what it was like to struggle. . . . But it would serve no constructive purpose for me to sit around and wring my hands every day over the disadvantaged, the poor, the homeless, the middle class, and others. That would be the liberal thing to do." When you think about what Rogers used to say to a similarly large audience about the same subjects, you can see how far we have traveled from better days.

What would a Rogers say today? That nobody has a monopoly on virtue or the truth, right or left, and

that it's folly to act as if the country's health care, its schools, or its daily life will improve without the willingness to confront uncomfortable truths and to stand aside when it's your stake that stands in the way. That it's a disgrace for 37 million Americans to be without health insurance, for millions more to fear losing coverage, and for reform to be bottled up by those—insurers, hospitals, doctors, and irresponsible patients—who wrecked the system in the first place. That it's a disgrace for public schools to spend so much and fail to educate children, paying more for bureaucrats than for books and teachers. That people who complain about big government and the deficit ought to give up their breaks first. That the poor deserve a hand up—and even public works jobs cost the taxpayer something.

Rereading Rogers, you get the sense that there *is* a similar twang out there today, not from Oklahoma but further south and a little east: from Texarkana's Ross Perot. At first glance, Perot seems to be Rogers' heir in homespun wit: We are cleaning up the barn; Washington is full of alligators in alligator shoes; etc., etc. Rogers was famously generous to drought and Depression victims; Perot did his most humane work in dramatizing the plight of American prisoners of war in Southeast Asia. But Perot built his business processing government contracts by computer, and he was a master at winning special tax breaks from Congress in his business lobbying days.

The great disappointment of Perot's politics in 1992 was that while he talked honestly at first about common sacrifice and offered a tough but fair entitlement-control plan, he quickly shut up about it for fear of alienating voters. He grew content to toss more one-liners around than appeals for national action. And, once Clinton was elected, the Perot egomania that lurked just beneath the surface during the campaign broke out all over and he fell into the Limbaugh trap of criticizing the president without trying to move the country toward a working consensus. Why? Because as polarization increases, so does the audience for polarizers.

What is odd about 1994 is that while most Americans agree things are in a bad way, they register no faith in government—or in themselves—to fix them. But the country did work together once, and it did so against obstacles of selfishness—the rich's hatred of Roosevelt, the sense of lay-that-burden-down immediately after 1945—that we face again today. The country worked when we recognized that while Arcadia was not attainable, the margin could be tilted toward order and fair play—toward a Will Rogers, away from a Rush Limbaugh and a Ross Perot. And that has little to do with policy minutiae and everything to do with how we see ourselves.

The Selfish Decade

THE AUSTRALIAN

The city elders of Hartford, Connecticut, decided that something had to be done. Like so many others in the United States, their city is being transformed by the "white flight" to outer suburbs, leaving behind poorer, gutted neighborhoods.

Along with the rest of the U.S., Hartford is struggling with the widest gulf between rich and poor since the Great Depression. The city elders' answer was simple. They banned the opening of any new welfare centers, even those funded by private charities, for at least six months —on the theory that providing such services simply encourages the demand.

Whole states are now adopting similar logic toward welfare. It is a "not in my back yard" approach to the poor and comes amid other signs of a fundamental change in the way Americans view their responsibilities to each other and the rest of the world.

The U.S. is becoming a more selfish society at precisely the time when other developed nations are becoming more like the U.S. Indeed, if the booming 1980s were labeled the decade of greed, then the 1990s seem to be emerging as a time of more restrained but deliberate selfishness.

One of the U.S.'s most respected sociologists and political scientists, professor Seymour Martin Lipset, believes the "American creed" has always promoted personal responsibility, initiative, and volunteerism. But the flip side has been a latent disregard for communal good and "a particularly virulent strain of greedy behavior."

There is a "worldwide trend" toward a greater emphasis on the rights of the individual rather than the community,

"but we started out much more in that direction," says Lipset. Such a narrow concentration on self-interest can be seen as a logical outcome of aggressive capitalism, he says, as can the U.S.'s crime rates: "The fact that we put more emphasis on individual success than does any other country means people who don't have the means to succeed are pressed by this culture to succeed by hook or by crook."

The pressure to succeed is magnified by the extraordinary disparity in U.S. wealth and income. For the first time since the Great Depression, a five-year-old recovery is producing high corporate layoffs and falling real wages for low- and middle-income earners.

The longtime champion of egalitarianism, the U.S. is now the most economically stratified society in the developed world. The richest society ever seen on Earth, the U.S. in 1996 has child poverty rates four times those of other developed nations. Its poor and lower-income earners are not just falling further behind other Americans—they are lower paid than their counterparts in less successful developed nations and worse off in absolute terms than they were 20 years ago.

Surveys of developed nations find that U.S. citizens are the most politically conservative and the most strongly opposed to government involvement in wage and price controls, in the reduction of the work week, in job creation, and in other forms of regulation. The U.S. is at the bottom among industrialized nations in terms of taxes, public ownership, and spending for entitlements, welfare, and public housing.

The U.S. labor system allows unskilled and temporary workers to receive sig-

nificantly lower wages than those in almost all other developed nations. The upside is the world's strongest job-creation record. Since 1980, the U.S. has added 28 million new jobs, twice the total of all Western European nations. The U.S. jobless rate is just 5.4 percent compared with 10.4 percent in Germany and 11.8 percent in France. The downside is an army of 11 million working poor.

Increases in the rewards for success and the consequences of failure in the U.S. economy have some economists calling it a "plantation" economy in which a small elite dominates the benefits of low inflation, record profits, and equity growth. Others call it a "superstar" economy, as huge rewards flow to those at the top.

Salaries of chief executive officers at U.S. firms rose by 30 percent last year, while average wages went up 2.5 percent. Adjusting for inflation, the salaries of U.S. chief executive officers have tripled since 1974, while the average worker's pay has fallen 13 percent.

The corporations that are so generous to their top executives seem to have less appetite today than they once did to help alleviate poverty through charitable giving, although Americans are still the world's most generous philanthropists. Since 1987, corporate profits have risen 84 percent, but corporate giving has gone up only 11 percent.

Compared with the Reagan era and the altruism involved in leading an expensive cold-war campaign against oppression abroad, Americans and their leaders have a meaner view of the world. Post-cold-war politicians are more ignorant of the outside world than the World War II veterans who preceded them and

From *World Press Review*, September 1996, pp. 34-35. Originally from *The Australian*, May 18–19, 1996. Reprinted by permission.

are highly parochial, determined to put "America first."

One new member of the Senate, Ron Wyden of Oregon, identified Africa when asked by a television interviewer to locate Bosnia on a globe. When a journalist from the satirical magazine *Spy* posed as a radio interviewer and asked some congressmen for their views on "the ethnic cleansing in Freedonia," a frightening number expressed firm opinions about the fictional nation in the Marx Brothers movie *Duck Soup*. "It's coming to the point now that a blind eye to it for the next 10 years is not the answer," argued Washington Democrat Jay Inslee. "I think anything we can do to use the good offices of the U.S. government to assist stopping the killing over there, we should do," said Republican James Talent of Missouri.

According to Lipset, the post-cold-war drive to reduce the U.S.'s active engagement abroad is just part of a broader return to the smaller-government model of earlier times.

The widespread hardship caused by the Great Depression undermined the nation's traditional "leave me alone" brand of freedom. Franklin D. Roosevelt's New Deal reforms introduced a wide range of government services to help the unemployed, and the U.S. witnessed another first, a surge in union membership. World War II and then the cold war cemented Washington's expanded role in U.S. life, and Lyndon Johnson's Great Society of the 1960s saw a further expansion.

Now, the broadly based backlash against government activism suggests that the 60 years of New Deal, world war, and cold-war activism may be a historical aberration. "What the prolonged American prosperity did, in my judgment, was to refurbish the classic American laissez-faire, meritocratic, individualistic values," says Lipset.

But while the current consensus on the need for small government and diminishing state welfare harks back to the pre-New Deal social order, two of the crucial mitigating factors of that era—unusually active civic engagement and the world's broadest public-education system—are under threat. Already

squeezed by ethnic diversity, family decay, and demands to produce a more skillful and competitive work force, public schools are facing heavy funding cuts and waning community support.

The decline in civic engagement is even more worrying. Robert Putnam, the director of the Center for International Affairs at Harvard University, has documented an alarming fall during the past two decades in the participation rate of Americans in community organizations. From 1973 to 1993, the number of Americans who said they had attended "a public meeting on town or school affairs" in the previous year fell by more than one third.

Harvard law professor Mary Ann Glendon agrees with Putnam that more than ever before, the "we" in U.S. society is being replaced by the "me." She traces much of this to a recent tendency to view individual rights as absolute rights, free of social responsibilities and community commitments that were understood by all when the Constitution was written.

Putnam is chairing an international study group to examine whether there has been a similar "withering of public life" in eight other nations.

The challenge, says the group's Australian representative, Eva Cox, is to balance individual rights with a renewed commitment to communities. Perhaps then the problems of the less fortunate will be seen as a shared responsibility rather than a blight to be ignored or shuffled from one community to the next.

—*Peter Wilson, "The Australian"*
(centrist), Sydney, May 18-19, 1996.

Bushbabble to Dolegrowl ⊮THE INDEPENDENT

I've missed George Bush, badly. Not because of anything he ever did in the White House (which, apart from winning the Persian Gulf war, was next to nothing), or because he was the nicest U.S. president in recent memory. The gap in my life has been what he said, or rather the way he said it—in other words, Bushisms.

No one could match Bush in full flow: on the economy ("coming off a pinnacle, so to speak, of low unemployment") or musing about the endangered Pacific spotted owl ("We want to see the little furry-feathery guy protected, and all of that") or the burdens of high office ("Remember Lincoln, going to his knees in times of trial and the Civil War and all that stuff. We are blessed. So don't feel sorry for—don't cry for me, Argentina").

But three and a half years on, happy days are here again. I refer to the dawning era of Dolespeak. If Bush's problem was too many words, half-finished thoughts, and weird nonsequiturs, Dole's is the opposite. The man basically hates talking.

Dole's diction is a law unto itself. Syllables, indeed entire words, are swallowed, lost in truncated phrases fired out in short rasping salvos. What's it all about? He answers, "This election's 'bout 'Merica. It's 'bout the future. Values. Decency. 'Bout makin' 'Merica great again." Often the litany ends with "whatever," Dole's peculiar way of terminating a chain of thought.

But do not be overhasty in writing off Bob Dole in this autumn's presidential debates against the super-smooth, super-articulate Bill Clinton. For one thing, there's Dole's accent. He is an authentic product of the prairies, speaking the "North Midland" dialect of the U.S. heartlands. Language scientists have found that this accent is the one that Americans relate to and trust the most. But to exploit this asset properly, Dole must find something interesting to say. In other words, George Bush's pesky old "vision thing." At which point, a growly shade descends by my ear. "Workin' on it," it mutters. Whatever.

—*Rupert Cornwell, "The Independent" (centrist), London, May 23, 1996.*

MUST WE REMIND YOU THAT GOVERNMENT IS NOT THE ENEMY? WE MUST, ALAS.

A Civics Lesson

BENJAMIN R. BARBER

With the low-flying first debates over and the campaigns in final approach mode, America's increasingly look-alike parties present the country once again with the paradox of swarms of political bureaucrats who have spent most of their lives working for the government in Washington spending the better part of the campaign savaging the Washington governmental bureaucracy. For Bob Dole and Jack Kemp, not to mention Colin Powell, Newt Gingrich, Susan Molinari, Pat Buchanan, George Bush and Alfonse D'Amato, there is the irony of women and men who among them have notched centuries of service in the federal capital wanting us to believe that the very government they have been serving these many years is the enemy of our freedom. "I trust the people, you trust government," Senator Dole admonished the President in the first debate, apparently having forgotten what an earlier Republican President once said about this being a system founded on "government of the people, by the people, for the people."

President Clinton's startling proclamation last winter announcing the "end of the era of big government" can generously be understood as another way of talking about "reinventing government"—reinventing it mean and lean and efficient, the better to accomplish the tasks of progressive democracy. A big, fat, lumbering government can't do for us what we need it to do. But anxious liberals, even if they are neo-, will be forgiven for wondering whether the President is risking his own populist roots in signing on to what has been a libertarian Republican slogan. The

Benjamin R. Barber, director of the Walt Whitman Center and Whitman Professor of Political Science at Rutgers University, is the author, most recently, of Jihad vs. McWorld *(Ballantine).*

week after the President announced the famous "end of," Bill Kristol screamed on the cover of his *Weekly Standard,* "We won!" It makes you think. And it suggests the need for a standard other than Kristol's for judging candidates on both ends of the political spectrum.

Politicians who ask to represent us in Washington by campaigning against the fundamental principles of democratic representation as well as against the city in which they are planning to spend the next four years do not deserve our vote. What they deserve is a basic civics lesson. Something along these lines:

In democracies, representative institutions do not steal our liberties from us, they are the precious medium through which we secure those liberties. Our Founding Fathers understood perfectly well that in the absence of government we get what Thomas Hobbes called the war of all against all: liberty in theory but, in practice, lives that are "nasty, brutish, and short." That is why in the constitutional preamble explaining what they were doing, these same Founders noted that it was precisely in order to "secure the blessings of liberty to ourselves and our posterity" that they were going to "ordain and establish" a constitutional government.

No, they did not say they were going to abolish government to secure liberty, they said they were going to "ordain and establish" government, not just to secure liberty but also to "form a more perfect union" (not downsize it); to "establish justice" (not leave it to the states—that's what the Articles of Confederation had done with such dismal results); and to "insure domestic tranquillity, provide for the common defense, promote the general welfare" (not privatize them in the vain hope that selfish individuals and commercial markets would somehow get the job done).

In time, the successors to our Founders figured out they could not really do all the things they were supposed to do on our behalf without adequate revenue. And so, in the Sixteenth Amendment, they gave Congress the power to "lay and collect taxes on incomes, from whatever source derived." Senator Dole is right: The money does not belong to the government, it belongs to us. But government belongs to us too. "It" does not steal from "us," we pool resources so we can act on behalf of the commonweal—the weal (well-being) common to us. If we do not like how our government spends what it collects on our common behalf, we should change the government, not deprive it of resources to do the job it does for us. Taxes are not tithes imposed by tyrants, they are self-imposed duties that permit our government to discharge our common purposes.

To cry, "Give Americans back their hard-earned tax dollars!" is a disingenuous way of saying, "To hell with establishing justice, promoting welfare and securing the blessings of liberty!" It's nothing more than a cynical bribe to citizens calling on them to give up on one another and go it alone. That may work for the rich and privileged but it's something most of us can ill afford. Big government—or let's call it strong democracy—is for the little guy; it's how he and his neighbors can take on the big bullies in the private sector. Naturally, the bullies resent the competition and make war on "big government," ostensibly on behalf of the little guy.

Bashing Washington in favor of Russell, Kansas, is just another way of bashing democracy. Russell, Kansas—and Hope, Arkansas, too—are a couple of small towns where politicians who now live and work in Washington once came from—a very long time ago—and where they still go every few years when they are running for office in a city they want to pretend they are not really from. The irony is not the hypocrisy—that's just politics, folks—but the unreality. For America is much more like Washington, D.C., than like Russell, Kansas, or Hope, Arkansas. In fact, it is precisely the passing of small-town life and the neighborly amenities and common assets it once afforded that necessitates governmental remedies for local problems. It is in large urban/suburban metropolises beset by problems of education, safety, transportation, health, housing, welfare and poverty that the greater part of America's sovereign people live, and they need government badly. Russell may represent a memory of someone's vanished youth and may once have helped heal Bob Dole's war wounds, but Houston, New York, Los Angeles, Atlanta, Chicago and, yes, Washington, D.C., along with the sprawling suburbs that surround them, define, for better or worse, the American present on the threshold of this new century, and politicians who affect to serve us need to start thinking about them instead of talking about the vanished magic of village life.

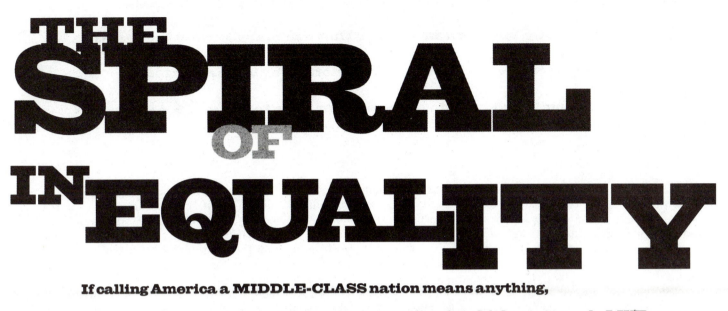

THE SPIRAL OF INEQUALITY

If calling America a MIDDLE-CLASS nation means anything,

it means that we are a society in which most people LIVE more or

less the same kind of life. In 1970 we were that kind of society. Today

we are not, and we become less like one with each PASSING year.

PAUL KRUGMAN

EVER SINCE THE ELECTION OF RONALD REAGAN, RIGHT-WING RADICALS have insisted that they started a revolution in America. They are half right. If by a revolution we mean a change in politics, economics, and society that is so large as to transform the character of the nation, then there is indeed a revolution in progress. The radical right did not make this revolution, although it has done its best to help it along. If anything, we might say that the revolution created the new right. But whatever the cause, it has become urgent that we appreciate the depth and significance of this new American revolution—and try to stop it before it becomes irreversible.

The consequences of the revolution are obvious in cities across the nation. Since I know the area well, let me take you on a walk down University Avenue in Palo Alto, California.

Palo Alto is the de facto village green of Silicon Valley, a tree-lined refuge from the valley's freeways and shopping malls. People want to live here despite the cost—rumor has it that a modest three-bedroom house sold recently for $1.6 million—and walking along University you can see why. Attractive, casually dressed people stroll past trendy boutiques and restaurants; you can see a cooking class in progress at the fancy new kitchenware store. It's a cheerful scene, even if you have to detour around the people sleeping in doorways and have to avoid eye contact with the beggars. (The town council plans to crack down on street people, so they probably won't be here next year, anyway.)

If you tire of the shopping district and want to wander further afield, you might continue down University Avenue, past the houses with their well-tended lawns and flower beds—usually there are a couple of pickup trucks full of Hispanic gardeners in sight. But don't wander too far. When University crosses Highway 101, it enters the grim environs of East Palo Alto. Though it has progressed in the past few years, as recently as 1992 East Palo Alto was the murder capital of the nation and had an unemployment rate hovering around 40 percent. Luckily, near the boundary, where there is a cluster of liquor stores and check-cashing outlets, you can find two or three police cruisers keeping an eye on the scene—and, not incidentally, serving as a thin blue line protecting the nice neighborhood behind them.

Nor do you want to head down 101 to the south, to "Dilbert Country" with its ranks of low-rise apartments, the tenements of the modern proletariat—the places from which hordes of lower-level white-collar workers drive to sit in their cubicles by day and to which they return to watch their VCRs by night.

No. Better to head up into the hills. The "estates" brochure at Coldwell Banker real estate describes the mid-Peninsula as "an area of intense equestrian character," and when you ascend to Woodside-Atherton, which the *New York Times* has recently called one of "America's born-again Newports," there are indeed plenty of horses, as well as some pretty imposing houses. If you look hard enough, you might catch a glimpse of one of the new $10 million-plus mansions that are going up in growing numbers.

What few people realize is that this vast gap between the affluent few and the bulk of ordinary Americans is a relatively new fixture on our social landscape. People believe these scenes are nothing new, even that it is utopian to imagine it could be otherwise.

But it has not always been thus—at least not to the same extent. I didn't see Palo Alto in 1970, but longtime residents report that it was a mixed town in which not only executives

Foreign trade and advances in technology are part of the SPIRAL of inequality, but only a small part. They don't fully explain the DISPARITY between the HAVES and the have-nots. Why is it harder today for most people to make a living but easier for a few to make a KILLING?

and speculators but schoolteachers, mailmen, and sheet-metal workers could afford to live. At the time, I lived on Long Island, not far from the old *Great Gatsby* area on the North Shore. Few of the great mansions were still private homes then (who could afford the servants?); they had been converted into junior colleges and nursing homes, or deeded to the state as historic monuments. Like Palo Alto, the towns contained a mix of occupations and education levels—no surprise, given that skilled blue-collar workers often made as much as, or more than, white-collar middle managers.

Now, of course, Gatsby is back. New mansions, grander than the old, are rising by the score; keeping servants, it seems, is no longer a problem. A couple of years ago I had dinner with a group of New York investment bankers. After the business was concluded, the talk turned to their weekend homes in the Hamptons. Naively, I asked whether that wasn't a long drive; after a moment of confused silence, the answer came back: "But the helicopter only takes half an hour."

You can confirm what your eyes see, in Palo Alto or in any American community, with dozens of statistics. The most straightforward are those on income shares supplied by the Bureau of the Census, whose statistics are among the most rigorously apolitical. In 1970, according to the bureau, the bottom 20 percent of U.S. families received only 5.4 percent of the income, while the top 5 percent received 15.6 percent. By 1994, the bottom fifth had only 4.2 percent, while the top 5 percent had increased its share to 20.1 percent. That means that in 1994, the average income among the top 5 percent of families was more than 19 times that of the bottom 20 percent of families. In 1970, it had been only about 11.5 times as much. (Incidentally, while the change in distribution is most visible at the top and bottom, families in the middle have also lost: The income share of the middle 20 percent of families has fallen from 17.6 to 15.7 percent). These are not abstract numbers. They are the statistical signature of a seismic shift in the character of our society.

The American notion of what constitutes the middle class has always been a bit strange, because both people who are quite poor and those who are objectively way up the scale tend to think of themselves as being in the middle. But if calling America a middle-class nation means anything, it means that we are a society in which most people live more or less the same kind of life.

In 1970 we were that kind of society. Today we are not, and we become less like one with each passing year. As politicians compete over who really stands for middle-class values, what the public should be asking them is, *What* middle class? How can we have common "middle-class" values if whole segments of society live in vastly different economic universes?

If this election was really about what the candidates claim, it would be devoted to two questions: Why has America ceased to be the middle-class nation? And, more important, what can be done to make it a middle-class nation again?

The Sources of Inequality

Most economists who study wages and income in the United States agree about the radical increase in inequality—only the hired guns of the right still try to claim it is a statistical illusion. But not all agree about why it has happened.

Imports from low-wage countries—a popular villain—are part of the story, but only a fraction of it. The numbers just aren't big enough. We invest billions in low-wage countries—but we invest trillions at home. What we spend on manufactured goods from the Third World represents just 2 percent of our income. Even if we shut out imports from low-wage countries (cutting off the only source of hope for the people who work in those factories), most estimates suggest it would raise the wages of low-skill workers here by only 1 or 2 percent.

IRREVERENT ECONOMIST

Paul Krugman has been examining and debunking the popular economic theories of the era he's called "the age of diminished expectations" for over half his life. The 43-year-old MIT and former Stanford professor's criticisms of trade protectionism— as well as his bipartisan and sometimes personal criticisms of prominent Washington policy wonks—has made him anathema to some. But Krugman's work, which includes 16 books and more than 100 articles, earned him the prestigious John Bates Clark Medal in 1991 and recently led *Newsweek* to describe him as "Nobel-bound."

Much to the horror of conservatives everywhere, Krugman's unusual-for-an-economist ability to convey his ideas in layman's terms has earned his books, like his 1994 national bestseller, *Peddling Prosperity*, their place on college syllabi everywhere. What's next? Krugman says he's working on a textbook about basic economic principles. "It's something I'm doing because I thought the basics were not getting through," Krugman says. "But I also needed the money."

We should not IDEALIZE unions. Occasionally they were corrupt, and sometimes they ENFORCED inefficiency. But they helped keep us a middle-class society because they provided a COUNTERWEIGHT to the power of wealthy INDIVIDUALS and corporations.

Information technology is a more plausible villain. Technological advance doesn't always favor elite workers, but since 1970 there has been clear evidence of a general "skill bias" toward technological change. Companies began to replace low-skill workers with smaller numbers of high-skill ones, and they continue to do so even though low-skill workers have gotten cheaper and high-skill workers more expensive.

These forces, while easily measurable, don't fully explain the disparity between the haves and the have-nots. Globalization and technology may explain why a college degree makes more difference now than it did 20 years ago. But schoolteachers and corporate CEOs typically have about the same amount of formal education. Why, then, have teachers' salaries remained flat while those of CEOs have increased fivefold? The impact of technology and of foreign trade do not answer why it is harder today for most people to make a living but easier for a few to make a killing. Something else is going on.

Values, Power, and Wages

In 1970 the CEO of a typical Fortune 500 corporation earned about 35 times as much as the average manufacturing employee. It would have been unthinkable to pay him 150 times the average, as is now common, and downright outrageous to do so while announcing mass layoffs and cutting the real earnings of many of the company's workers, especially those who were paid the least to start with. So how did the unthinkable become first thinkable, then doable, and finally—if we believe the CEOs—unavoidable?

The answer is that values changed—not the middle-class values politicians keep talking about, but the kind of values that helped to sustain the middle-class society we have lost.

Twenty-five years ago, prosperous companies could have paid their janitors minimum wage and still could have found people to do the work. They didn't, because it would have been bad for company morale. Then, as now, CEOs were in a position to arrange for very high salaries for themselves, whatever their performance, but corporate boards restrained such excesses, knowing that too great a disparity between the top man and the ordinary worker would cause problems. In short, though America was a society with large disparities between economic classes, it had an egalitarian ethic that limited those disparities. That ethic is gone.

One reason for the change is a sort of herd behavior: When most companies hesitated to pay huge salaries at the top and minimum wage at the bottom, any company that did so would have stood out as an example of greed; when everyone does it, the stigma disappears.

There is also the matter of power. In 1970 a company that appeared too greedy risked real trouble with other powerful forces in society. It would have had problems with its union if it had one, or faced the threat of union organizers if it didn't. And its actions would have created difficulties with the government in a way that is now unthinkable. (Can anyone imagine a current president confronting a major industry over price increases, the way John F. Kennedy did the steel industry?)

Those restraining forces have largely disappeared. The union movement is a shadow of its former self, lucky to hold its ground in a defensive battle now and then. The idea that a company would be punished by the government for paying its CEO too much and its workers too little is laughable today: since the election of Ronald Reagan the CEO would more likely be invited to a White House dinner.

In brief, much of the polarization of American society can be explained in terms of power and politics. But why has the tide run so strongly in favor of the rich that it continues regardless of who is in the White House and who controls the Congress?

The Decline of Labor

The decline of the labor movement in the United States is both a major cause of growing inequality and an illustration of the larger process under way in our society. Unions now represent less than 12 percent of the private workforce, and their power has declined dramatically. In 1970 some 2.5 million workers participated in some form of labor stoppage; in 1993, fewer than 200,000 did. Because unions are rarely able or willing to strike, being a union member no longer carries much of a payoff in higher wages.

There are a number of reasons for the decline of organized labor: the shift from manufacturing to services and from blue-collar to white-collar work, growing international competition, and deregulation. But these factors can't explain the extent or the suddenness of labor's decline.

The best explanation seems to be that the union movement fell below critical mass. Unions are good for unions: In a nation with a powerful labor movement, workers have a sense of solidarity, one union can support another during a strike, and politicians take union interests seriously. America's union movement just got too small, and it imploded.

We should not idealize the unions. When they played a powerful role in America, they often did so to bad effect. Occasionally they were corrupt, often they extracted higher wages at the consumer's expense, sometimes they opposed new technologies and enforced inefficient practices. But unions helped keep us a middle-class society—not only because they forced greater equality within companies, but because they provided a counterweight to the power of wealthy individuals and corporations. The loss of that counterweight is clearly bad for society.

The point is that a major force that kept America a more or less unified society went into a tailspin. Our whole society is now well into a similar downward spiral, in which growing inequality creates the political and economic conditions that lead to even more inequality.

The Polarizing Spiral

Textbook political science predicts that in a two-party democracy like the United States, the parties will compete to serve the interests of the median voter—the voter in the middle, richer than half the voters but poorer than the other half. And since ordinary workers are more likely to lose their jobs than strike it rich, the interests of the median voter should include protecting the poor. You might expect, then, the public to demand that government work against the growing divide by taxing the rich more heavily and by increasing benefits for lower-paid workers and the unemployed.

In fact, we have done just the opposite. Tax rates on the wealthy—even with Clinton's modest increase of 1993—are far lower now than in the 1960s. We have allowed public schools and other services that are crucial for middle-income families to deteriorate. Despite the recent increase, the minimum wage has fallen steadily compared with both average wages and the cost of living. And programs for the poor have been savaged: Even before the recent bipartisan gutting of welfare, AFDC payments for a typical family had fallen by a third in real terms since the 1960s.

The reason why government policy has reinforced rather than opposed this growing inequality is obvious: Well-off people have disproportionate political weight. They are more likely to vote—the median voter has a much higher income than the median family—and far more likely to provide the campaign contributions that are so essential in a TV age.

The political center of gravity in this country is therefore not at the median family, with its annual income of $40,000, but way up the scale. With decreasing voter participation and with the decline both of unions and of traditional political machines, the focus of political attention is further up the income ladder than it has been for generations. So never mind what politicians say; political parties are competing to serve the interests of families near the 90th percentile or higher, families that mostly earn $100,000 or more per year.

Because the poles of our society have become so much more unequal, the interests of this political elite diverge increasingly from those of the typical family. A family at the 95th percentile pays a lot more in taxes than a family at the 50th, but it does not receive a correspondingly higher benefit from public services, such as education. The greater the income gap, the greater the disparity in interests. This translates, because of the clout of the elite, into a constant pressure for lower taxes and reduced public services.

Consider the issue of school vouchers. Many conservatives and even a few liberals are in favor of issuing educational vouchers and allowing parents to choose among competing schools. Let's leave aside the question of what this might do to education and ask what its political implications might be.

Initially, we might imagine, the government would prohibit parents from "topping up" vouchers to buy higher-priced edu-

cation. But once the program was established, conservatives would insist such a restriction is unfair, maybe even unconstitutional, arguing that parents should have the freedom to spend their money as they wish. Thus, a voucher would become a ticket you could supplement freely. Upper-income families would realize that a reduction in the voucher is to their benefit: They will save more in lowered taxes than they will lose in a decreased education subsidy. So they will press to reduce public spending on education, leading to ever-deteriorating quality for those who cannot afford to spend extra. In the end, the quintessential American tradition of public education for all could collapse.

School vouchers hold another potential that, doubtless, makes them attractive to the conservative elite: They offer a way to break the power of the American union movement in its last remaining stronghold, the public sector. Not by accident did Bob Dole, in his acceptance speech at the Republican National Convention, pause in his evocation of Norman Rockwell values to take a swipe at teachers' unions. The leaders of the radical right want privatization of schools, of public sanitation—of anything else they can think of—because they know such privatization undermines what remaining opposition exists to their program.

If public schools and other services are left to deteriorate, so will the skills and prospects of those who depend on them, reinforcing the growing inequality of incomes and creating an even greater disparity between the interests of the elite and those of the majority.

Does this sound like America in the '90s? Of course it does. And it doesn't take much imagination to envision what our society will be like if this process continues for another 15 or 20 years. We know all about it from TV, movies, and bestselling novels. While politicians speak of recapturing the virtues of small-town America (which never really existed), the public—extrapolating from the trends it already sees—imagines a *Blade Runner*-style dystopia, in which a few people live in luxury while the majority grovel in Third World living standards.

Strategies for the Future

There is no purely economic reason why we cannot reduce inequality in America. If we were willing to spend even a few percent of national income on an enlarged version of the Earned Income Tax Credit, which supplements the earnings of low-wage workers, we could make a dramatic impact on both incomes and job opportunities for the poor and near-poor—bringing a greater number of Americans into the middle class. Nor is the money for such policies lacking: America is by far the least heavily taxed of Western nations and could easily find the resources to pay for a major expansion of programs aimed at limiting inequality.

But of course neither party advanced such proposals during the electoral campaign. The Democrats sounded like Republicans, knowing that in a society with few counterweights to the power of money, any program that even hints at redistribution is political poison. It's no surprise that Bill Clinton's repudiation of his own tax increase took place in front of an audience of wealthy campaign contributors. In this political environment, what politician would talk of taxing the well-off to help the low-wage worker?

And so, while the agenda of the GOP would surely accelerate the polarizing trend, even Democratic programs now amount only to a delaying action. To get back to the kind of society we had, we need to rebuild the institutions and values that made a middle-class nation possible.

The relatively decent society we had a generation ago was largely the creation of a brief, crucial period in American history: the presidency of Franklin Roosevelt, during the New Deal and especially during the war. That created what economic historian Claudia Goldin called the Great Compression—an era in which a powerful government, reinforced by and in turn reinforcing a newly powerful labor movement, drastically narrowed the gap in income levels through taxes, benefits, minimum wages, and collective bargaining. In effect, Roosevelt created a new, middle-class America, which lasted for more than a generation. We have lost that America, and it will take another Roosevelt, and perhaps the moral equivalent of another war, to get it back.

Until then, however, we can try to reverse some of the damage. To do so requires more than just supporting certain causes. It means thinking strategically—asking whether a policy is not only good in itself but how it will affect the political balance in the future. If a policy change promises to raise average income by a tenth of a percentage point, but will widen the wedge between the interests of the elite and those of the rest, it should be opposed. If a law reduces average income a bit but enhances the power of ordinary workers, it should be supported.

In particular, we also need to apply strategic thinking to the union movement. Union leaders and liberal intellectuals often don't like each other very much, and union victories are often of dubious value to the economy. Nonetheless, if you are worried about the cycle of polarization in this country, you should support policies that make unions stronger, and vociferously oppose those that weaken them. There are some stirrings of life in the union movement—a new, younger leadership with its roots in the service sector has replaced the manufacturing-based old guard, and has won a few political victories. They must be supported, almost regardless of the merits of their particular case. Unions are one of the few *political* counterweights to the power of wealth.

Of course, even to talk about such things causes the right to accuse us of fomenting "class warfare." They want us to believe we are all members of a broad, more or less homogeneous, middle class. But the notion of a middle-class nation was always a stretch. Unless we are prepared to fight the trend toward inequality, it will become a grim joke.

You Say You Want a Devolution

BY NOAM CHOMSKY

Imagine yourself in the office of a public-relations firm trying to turn people into ideal, manipulatable atoms of consumption who are going to devote their energies to buying things they don't want because you tell them they want those things. They're never going to get together to challenge anything, and they won't have a thought in their heads except doing what they're told. A utopia.

Suppose you're trying to do that. What you do is get them to hate and fear the government, fear the bigness of the government, but not look at the Fortune 500, nor even medium-sized businesses, not ask how they work. You don't want people to see that. You want them to worry about the one thing they might get involved in and that might protect them from the depredations of private power. So you develop a mood of anti-politics.

That's what has happened in America. People hate the government, fear the government, are worried about the bureaucrats.

Take, say, health care. There's a lot of concern that the government bureaucrats will be controlling it, yet there are many more bureaucrats in insurance offices who are already in control. But that's not what people worry about. It's not those pointy-headed bureaucrats in insurance offices who are making us fill out these forms and telling us what to do, and we've got to pay for their lunches and their advertising while they propagandize us. That's not what people's anger is focused on. What it's focused on, after a very conscious manipulation and a perfectly rational design, is this dangerous federal bureaucracy.

What's going on now with the attempt at devolution—the effort to reduce decision-making to the state level—makes great sense if you believe in tyranny. Devolution could be a step toward democracy, but not when you've got private tyrannies around.

General Electric is not influenceable by the population except very indirectly through regulatory mechanisms, which are very weak and which they mostly control anyhow. But you can't vote to decide what GE ought to do, and you can't participate in those decisions.

When you've got private tyrannies around, the only institution that at least in part reflects public involvement, that can cope with them, is the federal government.

Let's say you send block grants down to the states. Even middle-sized businesses have all kinds of ways of pressuring states to make sure that this money ends up in their pockets and not in the pockets of hungry children. Devolution under these circumstances is a great way to increase tyranny and to decrease the threat of democracy as well as to shift resources even more dramatically toward the rich and away from the poor. That's the obvious consequence of the current devolution.

But I've never seen it discussed in the mainstream. What's discussed are complete irrelevancies, like whether we can trust the governors to care for the poor.

What's that got to do with anything? It's totally meaningless. But that kind of absurdity is what's discussed, not the obvious, overwhelming fact that distributing governmental resources to the lower levels will simply make them more susceptible to the influence and control of private power. That's the major fact. And it's part of the same anti-politics: to weaken the federal government.

But not all of the federal government is being weakened. It's just being changed.

The security system is expanding, not only the Pentagon, but even the internal

This article was excerpted from a two-hour interview with David Barsamian. For information about obtaining cassette copies or transcripts, write to David Barsamian, P.O. Box 551, Boulder, Colorado 80306, or call 1-800-444-1977. Barsamian has a forthcoming book of Chomsky interviews, including this one, called "Class Warfare" (Common Courage). Noam Chomsky, professor of linguistics at MIT, is the author of many books on U.S. politics, foreign policy, and the media.

security system—jails, etc. That's not just for control, although it's partly for that. It's also a way of transferring resources to the rich, which is virtually never discussed.

In fact, this manipulation is almost off the agenda, unless you read the business press. But it's overwhelmingly significant. It ought to be a front-page article every day.

By now the sham is so obvious it's hard to miss. The Russians are gone. The Pentagon's budget stays the same; in fact, it's even going up.

It's there for the same reason it always was. How else are Newt Gingrich's rich constituents going to stay rich? You obviously can't subject them to market discipline. They'll be out selling rags! They wouldn't know what it means to exist in a market.

What they know is, the government puts money in their pockets, and the main way it does so is through the whole Pentagon system. In fact, the criminal security system is beginning to take on this character. It's reached, if not the scale of the Pentagon, a sufficient scale so that the big investment firms and even the high-tech industry, the defense industry, are getting intrigued by the prospects of feeding off another public cash cow. So it's not that the government is getting weaker.

But the long and very successful effort over many, many years to get people to focus their fears and angers and hatreds on the government has had its effect.

We all know there's plenty to be upset about. The primary thing to be upset about is that the government is not under popular influence. It is under the influence of private powers. But then to deal with that by giving private, unaccountable interests even more power is just beyond absurdity. It's a real achievement of doctrinal managers to have been able to carry this off.

The new Republicans represent a kind of proto-fascism. There's a real sadism. They want to go for the jugular. Anybody who doesn't meet their standards, they want to kill, not just oppose, but destroy. They are quite willing to try to engender fear and hatred against immigrants and poor people. They are very happy to do that. Their attitudes are extremely vicious. You can see it all over.

Take the governor of Massachusetts, William Weld, who's supposed to be a moderate, nice-guy type. Just last week every day in the newspapers there was another headline about forcing people out of homeless shelters if he didn't like the way they lived.

Some mother took a day off to take care of a mentally retarded child. OK, out of the homeless shelter. He doesn't like

that. He thinks she should work, not take care of her child.

Some disabled veteran didn't want to move into a well-known drug den. OK, out in the street.

That's one day. The next day he says state social services have to report to the INS if they think somebody may be an illegal immigrant. Then that person gets deported. Which means that person's child gets deported. The child could well be an American citizen. So American citizens have to be deported, according to the governor, if he doesn't like their parents being here.

This is day after day. Pure sadism. Very self-conscious.

Weld is not a fool. And he's trying to build public support for it by building up fear and hatred. The idea is, there are these teenage kids who are black by implication (although you don't say that in a liberal state) who are just ripping us off by having lots and lots of babies. We don't want to let them do that. So let's hate them and let's kick them in the face. That's real fascism.

And that's the liberal side. It's not the Gingrich shock troops. That's the liberal, moderate, educated side. This aggression runs across the spectrum.

In the long term, I think the centralized political power ought to be eliminated and dissolved and turned down ultimately to the local level, finally, with federalism and associations and so on. On the other hand, right now, I'd like to strengthen the federal government. The reason is, we live in this world, not some other world. And in this world there happen to be huge concentrations of private power that are as close to tyranny and as close to totalitarian as anything humans have devised.

There's only one way of defending rights that have been attained, or of extending their scope in the face of these private powers, and that's to maintain the one form of illegitimate power that happens to be somewhat responsible to the public and which the public can indeed influence.

So you end up supporting centralized state power even though you oppose it.

I would propose a system that is democratic, and you don't have democracy unless people are in control of the major decisions.

And the major decisions, as has long been understood, are fundamentally investment decisions: What do you do with the money? What happens in the country? What's produced? How is it produced? What are working conditions like? Where does it go? How is it distributed?

Where is it sold?

Unless that range of decisions is under democratic control, you have one or another form of tyranny. That is as old as the hills and as American as apple pie. You don't have to go to Marxism or anything else. It's straight out of the mainstream American tradition.

That means total dismantling of all the totalitarian systems. The corporations are just as totalitarian as Bolshevism and fascism. They come out of the same intellectual roots, in the early Twentieth Century. So just like other forms of totalitarianism have to go, private tyrannies have to go. And they have to be put under public control.

Then you look at the modalities of public control. Should it be workers' councils, or community organizations, or some integration of them? What kind of federal structure should there be?

At this point you're beginning to think about how a free and democratic society might look and operate. That's worth a lot of thought. But we're a long way from that.

The first thing you've got to do is to recognize the forms of oppression that exist. If slaves don't recognize that slavery is oppression, it doesn't make much sense to ask them why they don't live in a free society. They think they do. This is not a joke.

Take women. Overwhelmingly, and for a long time, they may have sensed oppression, but they didn't see it as oppression. They saw it as life. The fact that you don't see it as oppression doesn't mean that you don't know it at some level. The way in which you know it can take very harmful forms for yourself and everyone else. That's true of every system of oppression.

But unless you sense it, identify it, understand it, you cannot proceed to the next step, which is: How can we change the system?

I think you can figure out how to change the system by reading the newspapers that were produced by twenty-year-old young women in Lowell, Massachusetts, 150 years ago, who came off the farms and were working in the factories. They knew how to change the system. They were strongly opposed to what they called "the new spirit of the age: gain wealth, forgetting all but self." They wanted to retain the high culture they already had, the solidarity, the sympathy, the control. They didn't want to be slaves. They thought that the Civil War was fought to end slavery, not to institute it.

All of these things are perfectly common perceptions, perfectly correct. You can turn them into ways in which a much more free society can function.

Why America needs atheism.

THE LAST TABOO

Wendy Kaminer

It was King Kong who put the fear of God in me, when I was 8 or 9 years old. Blessed with irreligious parents and excused from attending Sunday school or weekly services, I had relatively little contact with imaginary, omnipotent authority figures until the Million Dollar Movie brought *King Kong* to our living room TV. Tyrannical and invincible (I never found his capture and enslavement believable), he awakened my superstitions. Watching Kong terrorize the locals, I imagined being prey to an irrational, supernatural brute whom I could never outrun or outsmart. I couldn't argue with him, so my only hope was to grovel and propitiate him with sacrifices. Looking nothing like Fay Wray, I doubted I could charm him; besides, his love was as arbitrary and unpredictable as his wrath.

For the next several years, like the natives in the movie, I clung to rituals aimed at keeping him at bay. (I can only analyze my rituals with hindsight; at the time, I was immersed in them unthinkingly.) Instead of human sacrifices, I offered him neatness, a perfectly ordered room. Every night before going to bed, I straightened all the stuff on my desk and bureau, arranged my stuffed animals in rectangular tableaus and made sure all doors and drawers were tightly shut. I started at one end of the room and worked my way around, counterclockwise; when I finished, I started all over again, checking and rechecking my work three, four or five times.

Going to bed became an ordeal. I hated my rituals; they were tedious and time-consuming and very embarrassing. I knew they were stupid and always kept them secret until, eventually, I grew out of them. I still harbor superstitions, of course, but with less shame and more humor; I find them considerably less compelling.

If I were to mock religious belief as childish, if I were to suggest that worshiping a supernatural deity, convinced that it cares about your welfare, is like worrying about monsters in the closet who find you tasty enough to eat, if I were to describe God as our creation, likening him to a mechanical gorilla, I'd violate the norms of civility and religious correctness. I'd be excoriated as an example of the cynical, liberal elite responsible for America's moral decline. I'd be pitied for my spiritual blindness; some people would try to enlighten and convert me. I'd receive hate mail. Atheists generate about as much sympathy as pedophiles. But, while pedophilia may at least be characterized as a disease, atheism is a choice, a willful rejection of beliefs to which vast majorities of people cling.

Yet conventional wisdom holds that we suffer from an excess of secularism. Virtuecrats from Hillary Clinton to William Bennett to Patrick Buchanan blame America's moral decay on our lack of religious belief. "The great malady of the 20th century" is "'loss of soul,'" bestselling author Thomas Moore declares, complaining that "we don't believe in the soul." Of course, if that were true, there'd be no buyers for his books. In fact, almost all Americans (95 percent) profess belief in God or some universal spirit, according to a 1994 survey by *U.S. News and World Report.* Seventy-six percent imagine God as a heavenly father who actually pays attention to their prayers. Gallup reports that 44 percent believe in the biblical account of creation and that 36 percent of all Americans describe themselves as "born-again."

Adherence to mainstream religions is supplemented by experimentation with an eclectic collection of New Age beliefs and practices. Roughly half of all Catholics and Protestants surveyed by Gallup in 1991 believed in ESP; nearly as many believed in psychic healing. Fifty-three percent of Catholics and 40 percent of Protestants professed belief in UFOs, and about one-quarter put their faith in astrology. Nearly one-third of all American teenagers believe in reincarnation. Once I heard Shirley MacLaine explain the principles of reincarnation on the "Donahue" show. "Can you come back as a bird?" one woman asked. "No," MacLaine replied, secure in her convictions. "You only come back as a higher life form." No one asked her how she knew.

In this climate—with belief in guardian angels and creationism becoming commonplace—making fun of religion is as risky as burning a flag in an American Legion hall. But, by admitting that they're fighting a winning battle, advocates of renewed religiosity would lose the benefits of appearing besieged. Like liberal rights organizations that attract more money when conservative authoritarians are in power, religious groups inspire more believers when secularism is said to hold sway. So editors at *The Wall Street Journal* protest an "ardent hostility toward religion" in this country, claiming that religious people are "suspect." When forced by facts to acknowledge that God enjoys unshakable, non-partisan, majoritarian support, religion's proselytizers charge that our country is nonetheless controlled by liberal intellectual elites who disdain religious belief and have denied it a respected public role.

Educated professionals tend to be embarrassed by belief, Yale Law Professor Stephen Carter opined in *The Culture of Disbelief*, a best-selling complaint about the fabled denigration of religion in public life. Carter acknowledges that belief is widespread but argues that it has been trivialized by the rationalist biases of elites and their insistence on keeping religion out of the public sphere. Carter's thesis is echoed regularly by conservative commentators. Another recent *Wall Street Journal* editorial asserted that religious indoctrination is one of the most effective forms of drug treatment and wondered at the "prejudice against religion by much of our judicial and media elites." Newt Gingrich has attacked the "secular, anti-religious view of the left."

No evidence is adduced to substantiate these charges of liberal irreligiosity run rampant. No faithless liberals are named, no influential periodicals or articles cited—perhaps because they're chimeras. Review the list of prominent left-of-center opinion makers and public intellectuals. Who among them mocks religion? Several have gained or increased their prominence partly through their embrace of belief. Harvard Professor Cornel West is a part-time preacher; Michael Lerner came into public view as Hillary Clinton's guru; Gloria Steinem greatly expanded her mainstream appeal by writing about spirituality. Bill Moyers, who introduced New Age holy men Joseph Campbell and Robert Bly to the American public, regularly pays homage to faith in traditional and alternative forms in television specials. Popular spirituality authors, like Thomas Moore, are regarded as public intellectuals in spite or because of their pontifications about faith. Even secular political theorists, preoccupied with civic virtue, are overly solicitous of religion and religious communities.

The supposedly liberal, mainstream press offers unprecedented coverage of religion, taking pains not to offend the faithful. An op-ed piece on popular spirituality that I wrote for *The New York Times* this past summer was carefully cleansed by my editors of any irreverence toward established religion (although I was invited to mock New Age). I was not allowed to observe that, while Hillary Clinton was criticized for conversing with Eleanor Roosevelt, millions of Americans regularly talk to Jesus, long deceased, and that many people believe that God talks to them, unbidden. Nor was I permitted to point out that, to an atheist, the sacraments are as silly as a seance. These remarks and others were excised because they were deemed "offensive."

Indeed, what's striking about American intellectuals today, liberal and conservative alike, is not their Voltairean skepticism but their deference to belief and their utter failure to criticize, much less satirize, America's romance with God. They've abandoned the tradition of caustic secularism that once provided refuge for the faithless: people "are all insane," Mark Twain remarked in *Letters from the Earth*. "Man is a marvelous curiosity ... he thinks he is the Creator's pet ... he even believes the Creator loves him; has a passion for him; sits up nights to admire him; yes and watch over him and keep him out of trouble. He prays to him and thinks He listens. Isn't it a quaint idea." No prominent liberal thinker writes like that anymore.

Religion is "so absurd that it comes close to imbecility," H.L. Mencken declared in *Treatise on the Gods*. "The priest, realistically considered, is the most immoral of men, for he is always willing to sacrifice every other sort of good to the one good of his arcanum—the vague body of mysteries that he calls the truth."

Mencken was equally scornful of the organized church: "Since the early days, [it] has thrown itself violently against every effort to liberate the body and mind of man. It has been, at all times and everywhere, the habitual and incorrigible defender of bad governments, bad laws, bad social theories, bad institutions. It was, for centuries, an apologist for slavery, as it was an apologist for the divine right of kings." Mencken was not entirely unsympathetic to the wishful thinking behind virtually all religion—the belief that we needn't die, that the universe isn't arbitrary and indifferent to our plight, that we are governed by a supernatural being whom we might induce to favor us. Still, while a staunch defender of the right to say or think virtually anything, he singled out as "the most curious social convention of the great age in which we live" the notion that religious opinions themselves (not just the right to harbor them) "should be respected." Name one widely published intellectual today who would dare to write that.

Mencken would have been deeply dismayed by contemporary public policy discussions: left and right, they are suffused with piety. The rise of virtue talk—which generally takes the form of communitarianism on the left and nostalgia for Victorianism on the right—has resulted in a striking re-moralization of public policy debates. Today, it's rare to hear a non-normative analysis of social problems, one that doesn't focus on failings of individual character or collective virtue: discussions of structural unemployment have given way to jeremiads about the work ethic; approaches to juvenile crime focus on the amorality of America's youth, not the harsh deprivations that shape them. Among academic and media elites, as well as politicians, there is considerable agreement that social pathologies such as crime, drug abuse, teenage pregnancy and chronic welfare dependency are, at least in part, symptomatic of spiritual malaise—loss of faith in God or a more generalized anomie. (Some blame TV.) Try to imagine an avowed atheist running successfully for public office; it's hard enough for politicians to oppose prayer in school.

Today, proposals for silent school prayer promise to bring spirituality into the classroom, avoiding religious sectarianism. "Spirituality," a term frequently used to describe the vaguest intimations of supernatural realities, is popularly considered a mark of virtue and is as hostile to atheism as religious belief. Spirituality, after all, is simply religion deinstitutionalized and shorn of any exclusionary doctrines. In a pluralistic marketplace, it has considerable appeal. Spirituality embraces traditional religious and New Age practices, as well as forays into pop psychology and a devotion to capitalism. Exercises in self-esteem and recovery from various addictions are presented as spiritual endeavors by codependency experts ranging from John Bradshaw to Gloria Steinem. The generation of wealth is spiritualized by best-selling personal development gurus such as Deepak Chopra, author of *The Seven Spiritual Laws of Success*, which offers "the ability to create unlimited wealth with effortless ease." (Some sixty years ago, Napoleon Hill's best-selling *Think and Grow Rich* made readers a similar promise.)

Spirituality discourages you from passing judgment on any of these endeavors: it's egalitarian, ranking no one religion over another, and doesn't require people to choose between faiths. You can claim to be a spiritual person without professing loyalty to a particular dogma or even understanding it. Spirituality makes no intellectual demands on you; all it requires is a general belief in immaterialism (which can be used to increase your material possessions).

In our supposedly secular culture, atheists, like Madelyn Murray O'Hare, are demonized more than renegade believers, like Jimmy Swaggart. Indeed, popular Christian theology suggests that repentant sinners on their way to Heaven will look down upon ethical atheists bound for Hell. Popular spirituality authors, who tend to deny the existence of Hell, and evil, suggest that atheists and other skeptics are doomed to spiritual stasis (the worst fate they can imagine). You might pity such faithless souls, but you wouldn't trust them.

You might not even extend equal rights to them. America's pluralistic ideal does not protect atheism; public support for different belief systems is matched by intolerance of disbelief. According to surveys published in the early 1980s, before today's pre-millennial religious revivalism, nearly 70 percent of all Americans agreed that the freedom to worship "applies to all religious groups, regardless of how extreme their beliefs are"; but only 26 percent agreed that the freedom of atheists to make fun of God and religion "should be legally protected no matter who might be offended." Seventy-one percent held that atheists "who preach against God and religion" should not be permitted to use civic auditoriums. Intolerance for atheism was stronger even than intolerance of homosexuality.

Like heterosexuality, faith in immaterial realities is popularly considered essential to individual morality. When politicians proclaim their belief in God, regardless of their religion, they are signaling their trustworthiness and adherence to traditional moral codes of behavior, as well as their humility. Belief in God levels human hierarchies while offering infallible systems of right and wrong. By declaring your belief, you imply that an omnipotent, omniscient (and benign) force is the source of your values and ideas. You appropriate the rightness of divinity.

It's not surprising that belief makes so many people sanctimonious. Whether or not it makes them good is impossible to know. Considering its history, you can safely call organized religion a mixed blessing. Apart from its obvious atrocities—the Crusades or the Salem witch trials—religion is a fount of quotidian oppressions, as anyone who's ever lost a job because of sexual orientation might attest. Of course, religion has been a force of liberation, as well. The civil rights movement demonstrated Christianity's power to inspire and maintain a struggle against injustice. Today, churches provide moral leadership in the fight to maintain social welfare programs, and in recent history, whether opposing Star Wars or providing sanctuary to Salvadoran refugees, church leaders have lent their moral authority to war resistance. Over time, the clergy may have opposed as many wars as they started.

It is as difficult to try to quantify the effect of organized religion on human welfare as it is to generalize about the character, behavior and beliefs of all religious people. Religion is probably less a source for good or evil in people than a vehicle for them. "Religion is only good for good people," Mary McCarthy wrote, in the days when liberal intellectuals may have deserved a reputation for skepticism.

It's equally difficult to generalize about the character of non-believers. Indeed, the disdain for self-righteousness that atheism and agnosticism tend to encourage make them particularly difficult to defend. How do you make the case for not believing in God without falling into the pit of moral certainty squirming with believers? You can't accurately claim that atheists are particularly virtuous or intelligent or even courageous: some are just resigned to their existential terrors.

Of course, whether or not atheists are in general better or worse citizens than believers, neither the formation of individual character nor religious belief is the business of government. Government is neither competent nor empowered to ease our existential anxieties; its jurisdiction is the material world of hardship and injustice. It can and should make life a little more fair, and, in order to do so, it necessarily enforces some majoritarian notions of moral behavior—outlawing discrimination, for example, or a range of violent assaults. But, in a state that respects individual privacy, law can only address bad behavior, not bad thoughts, and cannot require adherence to what are considered good thoughts—like love of God. Government can help make people comfortable, ensuring access to health care, housing, education and the workplace. But government cannot make people good.

Champions of more religion in public life are hard put to reconcile the prevailing mistrust of government's ability to manage mundane human affairs—like material poverty—with the demand that it address metaphysical problems, like poverty of spirit. It is becoming increasingly popular to argue, for example, that welfare recipients should be deprived of government largess for their own good, to defeat the "culture of dependency," while middle-class believers receive government subsidies (vouchers) to finance the private, religious education of their kids.

Even those "judicial elites" scorned by *Wall Street Journal* editorial writers for their hostility to religion are increasingly apt to favor state support for private religious activities. In a remarkable recent decision, *Rosenberger v. University of Virginia,* the Supreme Court held that private religious groups are entitled to direct public funding. Rosenberger involved a Christian student newspaper at the University of Virginia that was denied funding provided to other student groups because of its religiosity. A state-run institution, the university is subject to the First Amendment strictures imposed on any governmental entity. Reflecting obvious concern about state entanglement in the exercise of religion, the school's funding guidelines prohibited the distribution of student activities funds to religious groups. The guidelines did not discriminate against any particular religion or viewpoint; funds were withheld from any group that "primarily promotes or manifests a particular belief in or about a deity or an ultimate reality." The student paper at issue in the case was actively engaged in proselytizing.

Arguing that the University of Virginia had an obligation to pay for the publication of this paper, as it paid for other student activities, editors of the newspaper, *Wide Awake,* sued the school and ultimately prevailed in the Supreme Court, which, like other "elitist" institutions, has become more protective of religion than concerned about its establishment by the state. In a five to four decision, authored by Justice Anthony Kennedy, the Court held that the denial of funding to *Wide Awake* constituted "viewpoint discrimination." Religion was not "excluded as a subject matter" from fundable student discussions, the Court observed; instead funding guidelines excluded discussions of secular issues shaped by "student journalistic efforts with religious editorial viewpoints."

It is one of the ironies of the church/state debate that the equation of Christianity (and other sects) with worldly ideologies, such as Marxism, supply-side economics, theories of white supremacy, agnosticism or feminism, has been championed by the religious right. Those inclined to worship, who believe that their sect offers access to Heaven, are the last people you'd expect to argue that religion is just another product vying for shelf space in the marketplace, entitled to the same treatment as its competitors. You wouldn't expect critics of secularism to suggest that devout Christians are merely additional claimants of individual rights: religion is more often extolled by virtuecrats as an antidote to untrammeled individualism. But new Christian advocacy groups, modeled after advocacy groups

on the left, are increasingly portraying practicing Christians as citizens oppressed by secularism and are seeking judicial protection. The American Center for Law and Justice (ACLJ), founded by Pat Robertson, is one of the leaders in this movement, borrowing not just most of the acronym but the tactics of the American Civil Liberties Union in a fight for religious "rights."

It's worth noting that, in this battle over rights, science—religion's frequent nemesis—is often reduced to a mere viewpoint as well. Evolution is just a "theory," or point of view, fundamentalist champions of creationism assert; they demand equal time for the teaching of "creation science," which is described as an alternative theory, or viewpoint, about the origin of the universe. "If evolution is true, then it has nothing to fear from some other theory being taught," one Tennessee state senator declared, using liberal faith in the open marketplace of ideas to rationalize the teaching of creationism.

So far, the Supreme Court has rejected this view of creationism as an alternative scientific theory, and intellectual elites who are hostile to secularism but who champion religion's role in public life generally oppose the teaching of "creation science"; they are likely to ground their opposition in creationism's dubious scientific credibility, not its religiosity. Stephen Carter argues that the religious motivations of creationists are irrelevant; the religious underpinnings of laws prohibiting murder do not invalidate them, he observes.

Carter is right to suggest that legislation is often based in religion (which makes you wonder why he complains about secularism). You'd be hard-pressed to find a period in American history when majoritarian religious beliefs did not influence law and custom. From the nineteenth century through the twentieth, anti-vice campaigns—against alcohol, pornography and extramarital or premarital sex—have been overtly religious, fueled by sectarian notions of sin. Domestic relations laws long reflected particular religious ideas about gender roles (which some believe are divinely ordained). But religion's impact on law is usually recognized and deemed problematic only in cases involving minority religious views: Christian ideas about marriage are incorporated into law while the Mormon practice of polygamy is prohibited.

I'm not suggesting that religious people should confine their beliefs to the home or that religion, like sex, does not belong in the street. The First Amendment does not give you a right to fornicate in public, but it does protect your right to preach. Secularists are often wrongly accused of trying to purge religious ideals from public discourse. We simply want to deny them public sponsorship. Religious beliefs are essentially private prerogatives, which means that individuals are free to invoke them in conducting their public lives—and that public officials are not empowered to endorse or adopt them. How could our opinions about political issues not be influenced by our personal ideals?

Obviously, people carry their faith in God, Satan,

crystals or UFOs into town meetings, community organizations and voting booths. Obviously, a core belief in the supernatural is not severable from beliefs about the natural world and the social order. It is the inevitable effect of religion on public policy that makes it a matter of public concern. Advocates of religiosity extol the virtues or moral habits that religion is supposed to instill in us. But we should be equally concerned with the intellectual habits it discourages.

Religions, of course, have their own demanding intellectual traditions, as Jesuits and Talmudic scholars might attest. Smart people do believe in Gods and devote themselves to uncovering Their truths. But, in its less rigorous, popular forms, religion is about as intellectually challenging as the average self-help book. (Like personal development literature, mass market books about spirituality and religion celebrate emotionalism and denigrate reason. They elevate the "truths" of myths and parables over empiricism.) In its more authoritarian forms, religion punishes questioning and rewards gullibility. Faith is not a function of stupidity but a frequent cause of it.

The magical thinking encouraged by any belief in the supernatural, combined with the vilification of rationality and skepticism, is more conducive to conspiracy theories than it is to productive political debate. Conspiratorial thinking abounds during this period of spiritual and religious revivalism. And, if only small minorities of Americans ascribe to the most outrageous theories in circulation these days—that a cabal of Jewish bankers run the world, that AIDS was invented in a laboratory by a mad white scientist intent on racial genocide—consider the number who take at face value claims that Satanists are conspiring to abuse America's children. According to a 1994 survey by *Redbook*, 70 percent of Americans believed in the existence of Satanic cults engaged in ritual abuse; nearly one-third believed that the FBI and local police were purposefully ignoring their crimes.

(They would probably not be convinced by a recent FBI report finding no evidence to substantiate widespread rumors of Satanic abuse.) As Debbie Nathan and Michael Snedeker report in *Satan's Silence*, these beliefs infect public life in the form of baseless prosecutions and convictions. If religion engenders civic virtue, by imparting "good" values, it also encourages public hysteria by sanctifying bad thinking.

Skepticism about claims of abuse involving Satanism or recovered memories would serve the public interest, not to mention the interests of those wrongly accused, much more than eagerness to believe and avenge all self-proclaimed victims. Skepticism is essential to criminal justice: guilt is supposed to be proven, not assumed. Skepticism, even cynicism, should play an equally important role in political campaigns, particularly today, when it is in such disrepute. Politicians have learned to accuse anyone who questions or opposes them of "cynicism," a popular term of opprobrium associated with spiritual stasis or soullessness. If "cynic" is a synonym for "critic," it's a label any thoughtful person might embrace, even at the risk of damnation.

This is not an apology for generalized mistrust of government. Blind mistrust merely mirrors blind faith and makes people equally gullible. Would a resurgence of skepticism and rationality make us smarter? Not exactly, but it would balance supernaturalism and the habit of belief with respect for empirical realities, which should influence the formulation of public policy more than faith. Rationalism would be an antidote to prejudice, which is, after all, a form of faith. Think, to cite one example, of people whose unreasoned faith in the moral degeneracy of homosexuals leads them to accept unquestioningly the claim that gay teachers are likely to molest their students. Faith denies facts, and that is not always a virtue.

WENDY KAMINER is a Public Policy Fellow at Radcliffe College and author most recently of *True Love Waits: Essays and Criticism* (Addison Wesley).

SLOUCHING TOWARDS GOMORRAH

Can Democratic Government Survive?

Although Americans still invest a great deal of time and energy in the electoral process, the country is in fact governed by unelected institutions—and they are changing the very nature of our society.

ROBERT H. BORK

SIR Henry Maine made the point that, looking back, we are amazed at the blindness of the privileged classes in France to the approach of the Revolution that was to overwhelm them. Yet Maine finds "the blindness of the French nobility and clergy eminently pardonable. The Monarchy . . . appeared to have roots deeper in the past than any existing European institution." In his own place and time, men looked upon popular government and the democratic principle as destined to last forever. Maine asked whether the confidence of the French upper classes just before the Revolution "conveys a caution to other generations than theirs." In the following century, of course, nations that had adopted the democratic principle, in whole or in part, rejected it for totalitarian systems.

Yet we seem at least as sanguine about the prospects for democratic government as were Maine's contemporaries. The democratic principle is in rhetorical ascendancy everywhere, and yet it is worth asking whether in actuality, as a matter of practice rather than declamation, it is not in retreat, particularly in what had been its strongest bastion, the United States. Unlike the sudden cataclysm that overtook the French monarchy, ours appears to be a slow crisis, a hollowing out of democracy from within, that gives ample warning of the unhappy condition toward which matters tend.

Modern liberalism is fundamentally at odds with democratic government because it demands results that ordinary people would not freely choose. Liberals must govern, therefore, through institutions that are largely insulated from the popular will.

In his First Inaugural Address, Abraham Lincoln asserted: "The candid citizen must confess that if the policy of the Government upon vital questions affecting the whole people is to be irrevocably fixed by decisions of the Supreme Court . . . the people will have ceased to be their own rulers, having to that extent practically resigned their Government into the hands of that eminent tribunal." Lincoln was thinking of *Dred Scott*, the infamous decision that created a constitutional right, good against the Federal Government, to own slaves. Today, however, his observation is even more pertinent, as we have resigned into the hands of the federal judiciary ever more vital questions affecting the whole people.

There seems no possibility of retrieving democratic government from the grasp of the Supreme Court, which now governs us in the name of the Constitution in ways not remotely contemplated by the framers and ratifiers of that Constitution. Professor Lino Graglia concludes:

The hope that this situation can be changed by shifts in personnel on the Court has been shown to be futile. Eleven consecutive appointments to the Court by Republican Presidents pledged to change the Court's direction have not resulted in the overruling of a single major ACLU victory or even halting the flow of ACLU victories. . . . The Court will continue to

(*A substantially different version of this chapter originally appeared in* Aspects of American Liberty: Philosophical, Material, and Political [*American Philosophical Society, 1977*].)

serve as the mirror, mouthpiece, and enacting arm of a cultural elite that is radically alienated from and to the left of the ordinary citizen. . . .

The only practical way of reining in the Supreme Court is a constitutional amendment making its rulings subject to democratic review. As matters now stand, the Court's assumption of complete governing power is intolerable, and yet, absent a constitutional amendment, we have no way of refusing to tolerate it.

The question is not only one of the illegitimacy of the

The Court's assumption of complete governing power is intolerable, and yet, absent a constitutional amendment, we have no way of refusing to tolerate it

---

Court's performance in usurping powers that belong to the people and their elected representatives. The judiciary is slowly disintegrating the basis for our social unity.

We too often forget that the liberties guaranteed by our Constitution were not based on legalisms or moral theorizing but upon the historical experience of being governed by the British Crown. Our Constitution, and most particularly our Bill of Rights, were designed to prevent the Federal Government from becoming as oppressive as British rule was perceived to be. But as the historical meaning of the Constitution fades from memory, or is regarded as irrelevant, its guarantees begin to change. We have a student who can say, with no sense of incongruity, that speech should not be free unless it is also correct.

As it departs from the constitutional text and history that give our rights life, rootedness, and meaning, and substitutes abstractions reflecting modern liberalism's agenda, the Supreme Court brings itself and the entire concept of the rule of law into disrepute. It expends a dwindling moral capital and weakens both political authority and the possibility of a common culture. The increasing legalization of our culture is a sign of the fracturing of that culture, the continuing disappearance of the vestiges of unity. Professor John Gray, after discussing the fragmentation of British culture, noted:

> We may see the same somber development occurring on a vast scale in the United States, which appears to be sliding inexorably away from being a civil society whose institutions express a common cultural inheritance to being an enfeebled polity whose institutions are captured by a host of warring minorities, having in common only the dwindling capital of an unquestioned legalism to sustain them. . . . The idea that political authority could ever be solely or mainly formal or abstract arose in times when a common cultural identity could be taken for granted. For . . . the framers of the Declaration of Independence, that common cultural identity was that of European Christendom. In so far as this cultural identity is depleted or fragmented, political authority will be attenuated.

As the courts recklessly squander our common cultural inheritance in the names of radical individualism and radical egalitarianism, they necessarily offer themselves and their authority over law as the only institution capable of holding our turbulent society together. But that task will prove beyond the capabilities of the courts. It takes more than legalisms, abstractions, and judicial diktats to hold a community together. Indeed, by its emphasis on individual and group rights—rights it had invented—against those of the larger community, the Court denigrates the idea that there is value in community, the idea that the collectivity should exert a centripetal force. What the Court is doing is forcing the libertarian-egalitarian philosophy of our cultural elites upon the rest of us.

We head toward constitutional nihilism. No one knows what will happen if Americans see the judiciary for what it is, an organ of power without legitimacy either in democratic theory or in the Constitution. Perhaps we will simply accept the fact that the courts are our governing bodies. Perhaps, though it is highly unlikely, we will amend the Constitution to reassert ultimate democratic control. There does not seem to be a third choice except civil disobedience by legislatures and executives. The most likely outcome seems, at the moment, to be passive acceptance of the ukases of the Court.

THE other institution that may seem to hold the prospect of unifying a multi-ethnic and increasingly contentious society is the federal bureaucracies. Bureaucracies tend to be leveling institutions. A strong egalitarian philosophy implies extensive regulation of individuals by law (because equality of condition does not come about naturally) and a depreciation of the value of democratic processes.

If equality is the ultimate and most profound political good, there is really very little to vote about. Only a society with a profusion of competing values, all regarded as legitimate, needs to vote. In such a society, there being no way of saying that one outcome is *a priori* better than another, it is the legitimacy of the process that validates the result; not, as in a thoroughly egalitarian society, the morality of the result that validates the process. There is thus a built-in tension between the ideal of equality of condition and the ideal of democracy. That tension is not merely philosophical, which is how it has just been stated, but exists as well at the level of practical governance.

A modern society whose predominant value is equality necessarily displays three related symptoms: a strong sense of guilt; a consequent feeling of personal insecurity; and, as a direct result of the first two, the spread of an oppressive and excessive legalism throughout the social body.

A society whose morality is egalitarian but whose structure is inevitably hierarchical, a society that feels there are unjustifiable inequalities throughout its social, political, and economic order, is a society that feels guilty. It may seem odd that people who understand that a complex, vital society is necessarily hierarchical can simultaneously feel that the existence of hierarchies is somehow immoral. Yet it is plain that many of us do feel that way. Bad social conscience is taught to the young as dogma. Randall Jarrell wrote of a fictional but not untypical New England college that could have carved on an administration building: *Ye shall know the truth, and the truth shall make you feel guilty.* In certain academic circles, with which I was once familiar, a sense of guilt became as essential to good standing as proper manners used to be.

It is also true that at a time when we have achieved greater personal security than ever before in recorded history, we have become increasingly anxious. The demand that all should be insulated from risk is an egalitarian response to the prospect of varying individual fortunes.

SECURITY has become a religion. We demand it not only from government but from schools and employers, we demand it not only from major catastrophe but from minor inconvenience; not only, to take health plans as an example, from the financial disaster of major surgery and prolonged hospitalization but also from having to pay for a medical checkup—and we demand it as a right. David Riesman's picture of university students some forty years ago seems a passingly accurate description of our society now.

Riesman had his students read about the cultures of the Pueblo and Kwakiutl Indians, and asked which most closely resembled the culture of the United States. The Pueblo were described as a peaceable, cooperative, relatively unemotional society, in which no one wishes to be thought a great man and everyone wishes to be thought a good fellow. Kwakiutl society, on the other hand, was pictured as intensely rivalrous, marked by conspicuous consumption, competition for status, and power drives. The great majority of the students questioned saw American society as essentially Kwakiutl.

Only modern liberalism, which was on the way when Riesman's students responded, could persuade anyone that our relatively safe and cooperative society is actually egomaniacal and ruthless. The students made their assessment before the violence of the underclass had exploded. People who regard mainstream American culture as comparable to Kwakiutl are obviously highly insecure.

A society whose members feel insecure and guilty seeks the antidotes of security and expiation by trying to legislate equality. Our legislatures, our bureaucracies, and our courts are attempting to guarantee every right, major or minor or merely symbolic, that people think they ought ideally to possess. There is no reason to suppose that we will achieve equality of condition. We will not. In saying that we are necessarily a hierarchical society, I mean simply to state the obvious: any big, complex society must depend upon differential rewards of some kind to operate effectively. There is, as has been remarked, a "natural tyranny of the bell-shaped curve" in the distribution of the world's goods. Because of the inefficiency the effort to achieve equality imposes, it may, as in Communist countries, result in everybody having less, but what there is will still be distributed unequally.

But the enormous profusion of egalitarian regulations is incompatible with democratic processes in still another way. As government spreads, bureaucracies get beyond the power of the elected representatives to control. Government is too big, too complicated, there are too many decisions continually to be made. The staffs of both the President and Congress have been so enlarged in the effort to cope with the workload that both institutions have become bureaucratized.

Democratic processes become increasingly irrelevant. And there is increasing acceptance of this condition, in part because egalitarians do not care greatly about process. That is why they prefer an activist Supreme Court as a means of displacing democratic choice by moral principle. That was the reason for the Equal Rights Amendment, which provided that it should be primarily the function of the judiciary to define and enforce equality between the sexes. The amendment, we were assured, did not mean that no distinctions whatever may be made between men and women, that women must, for instance, be conscripted for combat duty or that unisex bathrooms are required. Yet it was proposed that the Supreme Court rather than Congress or the state legislatures make the necessary detailed and sensitive political choices to write a gender code for the nation. In that sense, the amendment represented less a revolution in sexual equality than a revolution in our attitudes about constitutional methods of government.

This episode is characteristic. When a controversial proposition is put to the nation for an up-or-down vote, an effective political leader—like Phyllis Schlafly, in the case of the ERA—can rally the electorate and their representatives to stop a departure from democratic governance. But the issue is rarely put that way. There was nothing Mrs. Schlafly or anyone else could do to stop the judicial enactment of the ERA (through new interpretations of the Equal Protection clause) or the judicial approval of homosexual marriages. The political rejection of the ERA by the American people hardly seems to have mattered to how we are governed in the matter. Still less is it possible to mount effective opposition across the board to myriad bureaucratic usurpations of democratic control. With scores of agencies all churning out regulations, it is apparent that the bureaucracies make most of the law by which we are governed. Regulations issued in 1994 took up nearly 65,000 pages in the *Federal Register*; in 1995, the number was 67,518.

It is true that Congress can alter the decisions made by bureaucracies, but that is by no means an adequate answer. So much law is made by bureaucracies that no legislature can focus on more than a small fraction of the choices made. Moreover, the bureaucracies develop rather small but intense constituencies, which often have more political influence than an electorate aggrieved by the total amount of regulation but rarely unified in opposition to any one regulation.

The prospect, then, is the increasing irrelevance of democratic government. What replaces it is bureaucratic and judicial government, which may be benign and well intentioned, and may respond somewhat to popular desires, though by no means always, but cannot by definition be democratic.

Tocqueville, it will be remembered, warned of a soft form of despotism that would suffuse society with small complicated rules that would soften and guide the will of man to acceptance of a "servitude of the regular, quiet, and gentle kind." That, he saw, was not at all incompatible with the sovereignty of the people; it is just that sovereignty, the ability to elect representatives from time to time, becomes less and less important.

It does not seem far-fetched to think there may be a connection between the rise of egalitarian bureaucracies, the proliferation of "small complicated rules," our sense of guilt, the paramountcy of security among our domestic gods, and the symptoms of enervation and loss of self-confidence that seem to afflict all Western democracies, in domestic matters as well as international. That there is a decline in self-confidence seems plain. It takes confidence in your values to punish for crime, and yet punishment rates in the United States and all of the Western world have declined even as crime rates soared. It takes assurance to enforce community standards of behavior, but, though most of us do not like the fact, pornography has become a national plague.

If there is a connection, as seems highly likely, then something very ominous and perhaps irreversible is happening to us as a people and as a community. It is disturbing in many respects but in none more so than in relation to the prospects for democratic government. A people without energy and self-confidence runs a greater risk of tyranny, albeit of the soft variety.

This does not necessarily suggest that the relatively mild and well-intentioned, though insistent, reign of the bureaucracies will be stable. If it is true that bureaucratic

> *That kind of society—anxious, insecure, irritated, bored, the people an undifferentiated mass— may be vulnerable to one or another form of authoritarianism*

egalitarianism suffocates the spirit and weakens the morale and self-confidence of the community while it saps the strength of intermediate institutions, then it leaves society as an aggregation of individual particles ranged against the state. That kind of society—anxious, insecure, irritated, bored, the people an undifferentiated mass— may perhaps more easily be swept by mass movements joined to populist rhetoric and transcendental principles. Such movements create excitement and a sense of purpose; they promise the restoration of the lost but longed-for sense of community. In a word, a society so reduced is more vulnerable to one or another form of authoritarianism.

Rule of Non-Law

THE first time I heard Judge Bork speak was at the Philadelphia Society in 1987. He was like a Hebrew prophet excoriating a faithless band of rulers, the judges who had perverted our Constitution. But he held out hope, in the wave of conservative legal theorists even then rising in the academy and on the bench. Nine years later, Judge Bork's essay above implies that it may take divine intervention to save our country.

Something very like that was the consensus of this year's Philadelphia Society meeting. The theme was "Is There Still a Legal Order?" and the short answer was: No. The longer answers explored the many ways in which our current jurisprudence is a through-the-looking-glass distortion of traditional Anglo-American legal theory and practice.

Lawyer jokes are nothing new—

Miss Bridges, NR's managing editor, is co-author of The Art of Persuasion.

Shakespeare gave Dick the Butcher the line, "The first thing we do, let's kill all the lawyers"—but the theory used to be, as Father Robert Sirico reminded us, that legal proceedings were in some sense a search for truth.

While that search was never disinterested—a lawyer, having accepted a case, was bound to do his best even for a guilty client—the assumption was that the truth would out. But today, Judge Stephen Markman pointed out, the legal establishment says quite openly that it cares not about the truth, but about "procedural safeguards." If the arresting policeman made the slightest slip in collecting evidence, the evidence is withheld from the jury: "The fact-finder [in a trial] must be misled concerning the facts." Worse yet, Professor David Forte remarked, is the corrupting effect on the police: "Police lie all the time, and they lie because the truth is not available to them." The one good thing Judge Markman saw in the O. J. Simpson trial

is that the corruption of the criminal-justice system was exposed to public view, "and the American people did not like what they saw."

A parallel corruption has taken place in civil law. By now it is not only conservatives and insurance executives who complain about the huge awards given to plaintiffs. But the problem goes much deeper than that, Professor Michael Krauss explained. It is that human beings are no longer regarded as moral agents in American law. Tort and contract law used to be the "twin pillars" of the "private ordering" of affairs, with government merely providing a framework within which people could make their own agreements and settle their disputes. Now, however, the courts have transmuted both tort and contract law from a framework for private ordering into a vehicle of public policy. If an injury has occurred, the courts have decided, someone with deep pockets must be held responsible. The idea that someone who the court agrees acted blamelessly could nonetheless be held liable would have seemed to our ancestors not merely a perversion of justice but an impossibility; and yet that is what happens in virtually all successful product-liability suits. Likewise, a contract is no longer a

Perversely enough, the spread of secondary and higher education, along with the extension of the suffrage, has reinforced these trends. The complexity of institutions and relationships in our society was never well understood, and the freedom and power of those institutions and relationships rested in no small measure on an unreasoned, awed acceptance of them. The spread of education, particularly university education, has served to decrease that awe without increasing, in the same proportions, the reality of understanding. We are left unhappily in between; respect founded in ignorance is lost but is not fully replaced with respect founded in sophistication.

Democratic government requires something that democratic government has badly damaged in the past half century and continues to damage today—civil society. By that is meant the institutions that serve public (as well as private) purposes but are not government—neighborhoods, families, churches, and voluntary associations, to name the ones discussed by Peter L. Berger and Richard John Neuhaus in their influential pamphlet *To Empower People*. What we are talking about is institutions that shape and maintain values; the bridge club is not on the list. These are also institutions that assist people who need assistance, giving charity or advice or consolation or companionship.

One of the most important aspects of these institutions—Berger and Neuhaus call them "mediating structures"; Robert Nisbet calls them "intermediate associations"—is that they stand as buffers between the individual and the state. They do that, in part, by performing functions for individuals that the state would otherwise perform. The difficulty is that, ever since the New Deal, the state has increasingly ousted the institutions of civil society and taken over their functions or controlled them.

It is proposed to attempt to restore these intermediate institutions, but it may be quite difficult to do so. In the first place, if government attempts the restoration, the result is likely to be more bureaucratic interference and hence damage to civil society. In the second place, churches are among the most important of the intermediate institutions and should lead in the restoration of other institutions and in the maintenance of values. The difficulty is that if government were to try to cooperate with or assist churches in their efforts, the courts, which have made a mess of the religion clauses of the Constitution, might well intervene to stop the effort.

Modern liberals will continue to try to govern through the judiciary and the bureaucracies. To the degree they have already succeeded, democratic government has not survived. As the behavior of modern liberal politicians, the courts, and the bureaucrats demonstrates, they have no intention of relinquishing any of their power to the popular will.

---

contract if one party wants out, and if the contract contravenes the judiciary's current social thinking.

This is partly, Judge Markman summarized, a matter of government taking on "frivolous responsibilities" (such as micromanaging "diversity") and neglecting its real ones (such as protecting law-abiding people from criminals); and we see another, vivid manifestation in the field of constitutional law. In short, as Michael Uhlmann of the Ethics and Public Policy Center put it, the Supreme Court has been transmogrified from an institution meant to limit the activity of government into one taking control of "the minutest details of human life."

And totally without warrant. Lino Graglia made a point that he has also made in these pages: Constitutional law as it is taught and practiced today has nothing to do with the Constitution. It is derived almost entirely "from four words of one clause of one amendment": "due process" and "equal protection." And you can bet, he added, that the Justices "do not reach their decisions by pondering those four words." As a result of the public policies that they impose in the course of their "interpretation," Professor Ellis Sandoz added, we should be "less worried about whether we have a Constitution than about whether we have a country." "Civic consciousness" is not faring well in today's society, where group is set against group and every wrong is thought to have a government-imposed remedy.

However, Roger Pilon of the Cato Institute took issue with the view expressed by Professor Graglia that our representative institutions would govern more in accordance with the Constitution if the courts could be stopped from interfering. It was not the courts, Mr. Pilon reminded us, but the President and the Congress that—in the Progressive Era, in the New Deal, in the Great Society, and even under Republican Administrations since then—have given us the welfare state. (Mr. Pilon suggested that the Supreme Court has actually been far too restrained: it should be striking down any act of Congress that is not explicitly permitted by Article I of the Constitution.)

Another point of disagreement was over the extent to which natural law should be brought into the discussion. Forrest McDonald pointed out that through the many centuries of Western Civilization, it is only recently that anyone has argued against the notion of the *jus gentium*—the "assumption that there is a concept of what is right, and that the rational person has the ability to discover what this is." (Even our cultural elites, while arguing against an "imposed morality," are busily imposing a counter-morality of their own.) But invoking a higher law—whether in terms of the *jus gentium* or of natural law—has its risks, as Stan Evans put it, for Justices Brennan and Douglas would have said that *they* were applying a higher law.

But sometimes, David Forte called, they don't even bother to do that. In *Roe* v. *Wade*, "the *only* legitimacy Justice Blackmun asserted for the creation of that new right was that, in his words, 'The members of the Court *feel* it is a liberty of the Fourteenth Amendment.'" Blackmun, like so many other post–New Deal Justices, had "forgotten the difference between authority and power." Authority "limits the exercise of power to only those who have the legitimate right to exercise it."

What can be done to recall judges to a recognition of that difference?

Work to elect Republicans who will appoint and confirm better judges, suggested Ed Meese.

"Prayer and fasting," suggested Mike Uhlmann.

—Linda Bridges

THE PARADOX OF INTEGRATION

Orlando Patterson

ORLANDO PATTERSON is John Cowles professor of sociology at Harvard University and the author of a forthcoming book on black Americans.

The traumas of the Million Man March and the O.J. Simpson verdict have forced America to focus its gaze once again on its lingering racial crisis. In sharpening our focus, they have done at least one good. By casting too bright a light on the realities of our unfinished racial agenda, they have scrambled the sordid use of coded and covert racial rhetoric by conventional politicians. We must now call a spade a spade, and, while it is good old American politics to fan racial division while pretending the opposite, it is far too risky to appear clearly to be doing so. But what exactly is the crisis upon which we again gaze?

For African Americans, these are genuinely the best and worst of times, at least since the ending of formal Jim Crow laws. What is odd, however, is that, in the current rhetoric of race, the pain completely dominates the gain. "Pain and predicament is driving this march," cried Jesse Jackson in a by now familiar African American refrain. The orthodox view among blacks at nearly all points on the political spectrum is that relations between the races are disastrous, whether it is the left, focusing on the political neglect of the devastated ghettos, or the right, condemning the abuses of affirmative action and failed government policies. Paradoxically, it is precisely the considerable success of America's experiment in integration that makes it almost impossible for black Americans to recognize what they have achieved. This perceived lack of gratitude in turn fuels white resentment and gives public discourse on race today the bewildering quality of a dialogue of the deaf.

On the one hand, there is no denying the fact that, in absolute terms, African Americans, on average, are better off now than at any other time in their history. The civil rights movement effectively abolished the culture of post-juridical slavery, which, reinforced by racism and legalized segregation, had denied black people the basic rights of citizenship in the land of their birth. They are now very much a part of the nation's political life, occupying positions in numbers and importance that go well beyond mere ethnic representation or tokenism. Quite apart from the thousands of local and appointed offices around the country (including mayorships of some of the nation's largest cities), blacks have occupied positions of major national importance in what is now the dominant power in the world—as governors, senators and powerful members of Congress chairing major congressional committees, and as appointed officials filling some of the most important offices in the nation, including that of the head of the most powerful military machine on earth.

Even as I write, the Colin Powell phenomenon bedazzles. For the first time, a black man is being seriously considered for the nation's highest office, with his strongest support coming from people with conservative views on race. It would be ridiculous to dismiss these developments as mere tokens. What they demonstrate, beyond a doubt, is that being black is no longer a significant obstacle to participation in the public life of the nation.

What is more, blacks have also become full members of what may be called the nation's moral community and cultural life. They are no longer in the basement of moral discourse in American life, as was the case up to about thirty or forty years ago. Until then blacks were "invisible men" in the nation's consciousness, a truly debased ex-slave people. America was assumed to be a white country. The public media, the literary and artistic community, the great national debates about major issues, even those concerning poverty, simply excluded blacks from consideration. Even a liberal thinker like John Kenneth Galbraith could write a major discourse on the affluent society without much thought to their plight.

No longer. The enormity of the achievement of the last forty years in American race relations cannot be overstated. The black presence in American life and thought is today pervasive. A mere 13 percent of the population, they dominate the nation's popular culture: its music, its dance, its talk, its sports, its youths' fashion; and they are a powerful force in its popular and elite literatures. A black music, jazz, is the nation's classical voice, defining, audibly, its entire civilizational style. So powerful and unavoidable is the black popular influence that it is now not uncommon to find persons who, while remaining racists in personal relations and attitudes, nonetheless have surrendered their tastes, and their viewing and listening habits, to black entertainers, talk-show hosts and sit-com stars. The typical Oprah Winfrey viewer is a conservative, white lower-middle-class housewife; the typical rap fan, an upper-middle-class white suburban youth. The cultural influence of so small and disadvantaged a minority on the wider society that has so harshly abused it finds few parallels in the history of civilization.

Closely related to the achievement of full political and cultural citizenship has been another great success of the post-war years: the desegregation of the military between 1948 and 1965. The extraordinary progress made in eliminating all formal discrimination, and a good deal of informal prejudice in promotions, has made the military, especially the Army, a model of successful race relations for the civilian community. With more than 30 percent of Army recruits and 10 percent of its officer corps black, the Army, and to a lesser extent the other services, stands out in American society as the only arena in which blacks routinely exercise authority over whites.

Most of these developments were helped along by another revolution in black life: the rapid growth in school enrollment and achievement at all levels. In 1940 there was a four-year gap in median years of schooling between whites and blacks; by 1991 this gap had been reduced to a few months. During the same period, the proportion of blacks aged 25 to 34 completing high school almost caught up with that of whites: 84 percent compared to 87 percent.

The record is far more mixed, and indeed troubling, in the case of higher education. After rapid growth in college completion during the '70s, the numbers fell off considerably during the '80s, especially for black men. The long-term effect has been that, while the proportion of blacks completing college has grown from less than 2 percent in 1940 to almost 12.8 percent in 1994, this is still only about half the white completion rate of almost 25 percent.

Even so, a six-fold increase in college completion is nothing to sniff at. It is great absolute progress and, compared to white populations elsewhere, great relative progress. African Americans, from a condition of mass illiteracy fifty years ago, are now among the most educated persons in the world, with median years of schooling and college completion rates higher than those of most Western Europeans. The average reader might find this statement a shocking overstatement. It is not. It only sounds like an overstatement when considered in light of the relentless insistence of the advocacy community that the miseducation of black Americans is the major source of their present dilemmas.

The rise of a genuine black middle class over the past quarter of a century is another cause for celebration, although no group of persons is less likely to celebrate it than the black establishment itself. The term "black middle class" once referred dismissively to those black persons who happened to be at the top of the bottom rung: Pullman porters, head waiters, successful barbers and street-front preachers, small-time funeral parlor owners and the like. Today the term "black middle class" means that segment of the nation's middle class which happens to be black, and it is no longer dependent on a segregated economy. These are without doubt the best of times for middle-class African Americans, who own more

businesses and control a greater share of the national wealth than at any other period. At the most conservative estimate, they are between a quarter and a third of the black population, which means anywhere between 8 and 10 million persons. It is a mistake to overemphasize their shaky economic base, as is routinely done. Almost all new middle classes in the history of capitalism have had precarious economic starts. Seen from a long-term perspective, the important thing to note is that the children they produce will be second- and third-generation burghers with all the confidence, educational resources and, most of all, cultural capital to find a more secure place in the nation's economy.

And yet it is also no exaggeration to say that, both subjectively and by certain objective standards, these are among the worst of times, since the ending of Jim Crow, for the African American population.

Put in the starkest terms, the bottom third of the African American population—some 10 million persons—live in dire poverty, while the bottom 10 percent or so—the so-called underclass—exist in an advanced stage of social, economic and moral disintegration. The grim statistics are now familiar to anyone who pays even the most cursory attention to the news.

Thirty-one percent of all black families (in contrast with only 8 percent of non-Hispanic whites), comprising nearly a third of all African Americans, live in poverty. This is worse than in 1969. Children disproportionately bear the brunt of impoverishment. In 1994, 46 percent of all black children lived in poverty, nearly three times that of white children, and the situation is likely to get worse. Their parents and other adult caretakers experience Depression-level unemployment. The overall unemployment rate for blacks is 14 percent, more than twice that of whites (6 percent). But this obscures the fact that unemployment is concentrated in certain areas and among the young, where it tops 40 percent.

These figures tell only part of the plight of poor children. The other, grimmer aspect of the dilemma is the growing number of children born to female children with little or no social or economic support from the biological fathers or any other man, for that matter. The resulting abusive, mal-socialization of children by mothers who were themselves abused and mal-socialized is at the heart of the social and moral chaos in what is called the underclass. The situation is one of complete social anarchy and moral nihilism, reflected in the casual devaluation of human life. Kids and young adults kill for sneakers, leather jackets, cheap jewelry and drugs; worse, they kill for no other reason than having been dissed by a wrong look or misstatement. Linked to this social and moral catastrophe are the other well-known pathologies: the high drop-out rate in inner-city high schools, the epidemic of drugs and crime resulting in a horrendous incarceration rate wherein one in three of all black men aged 25 to 29 are under the supervision of the criminal justice system. Although government action is needed, solving these problems will take considerably more than changes in government policy. Clearly, the message of the Million Man March was long overdue.

There is undoubtedly much to outrage our sense of justice, but the condition of the bottom third should not obscure the extraordinary achievements of the upper two-thirds of the black population or the progress made in race relations over the past forty years. Black leaders' near-complete disregard of these hard-won achievements is obtuse and counterproductive.

This strange tendency to more loudly lament the black predicament the better it gets can be understood as a paradox of desegregation. When blacks and whites were segregated from each other there was little opportunity for conflict. The two groups lived in largely separate worlds, and when they did come in contact their interactions were highly structured by the perverse etiquette of racial relations. The system may have worked well in minimizing conflict, as long as both groups played by the rules, but it was clearly a pernicious arrangement for blacks since it condemned them to inferior status and excluded them from participation in the political life of their society and from nearly all the more desirable opportunities for economic advancement.

Desegregation meant partial access to the far superior facilities and opportunities open previously only to whites. Hence, it entailed a great improvement in the condition and dignity of blacks. All this should be terribly obvious, but it must be spelled out because it is precisely this obvious improvement that is so often implicitly denied when we acknowledge one of the inevitable consequences of desegregation: namely that, as individuals in both groups meet more and more, the possibility for conflict is bound to increase.

Whites outnumber blacks eight to one, and this simple demographic fact has an enormous social significance often unnoticed by whites. Numerous polls have shown tremendous change in white attitudes toward blacks over the last thirty years. For example, the number of whites who hold racist beliefs, measured by unfavorable attitudes toward miscegenation, integrated housing and job equality, has declined from a majority in the '50s to a quarter of the total population today. For whites this is real progress, however one may wish to quibble over the meaning of the survey data. But, even with only a quarter of all whites holding racist beliefs, it remains the case that for every black person there are two white racists.

Furthermore, the vast majority of blacks will rarely come in contact with the 75 percent of whites who are tolerant, for simple socioeconomic reasons. More educated, more prosperous and more suburban, the tolerant three-quarters tend to live exactly where blacks are least likely to be found: in the expensive suburbs. On the other hand, it is the least educated and most prejudiced whites who tend to be in closest proximity to blacks.

Further, the behavior of the tolerant three quarters of whites, and their attempts to improve the condition of blacks, tends to intensify racist feelings among the whites most likely to come in contact with blacks. The cost of racial change is disproportionately borne by those whites who have traditionally been most hostile to blacks. Black improvement is invariably perceived as competition in the once-protected economic preserves of working-class whites. Hence, not only do racist whites continue to outnumber blacks but their racist behavior also finds more frequent and intense outlets.

Of special concern here is the behavior of law-enforcement agencies. The typical big-city police officer is the white person with whom the typical lower- and working-class black person is most likely to come in contact outside the workplace. Unfortunately, white police officers tend to come from precisely the working-class urban communities most likely to be hostile to blacks. And there is also abundant psychological evidence that they tend to conform to the authoritarian personality type which most closely correlates with racist behavior. At the same time, their profession brings them into contact with the most lawless members of the black community, continuously reinforcing their prejudices.

The result is that the typical white police officer holds all blacks in suspicion and treats them in a manner that constantly threatens their dignity and most basic rights. In some urban communities this amounts to life under a virtual police state for many law-abiding working-class and poor black Americans. Middle-class status makes some difference, but only in well-defined social situations. It can sometimes even be a disadvantage. The Mark Fuhrman tapes revealed what every bourgeois black person already knew: that in unprotected contexts—driving on the highway, visiting a white suburban friend or caught in some minor traffic or other infraction—they are likely to find themselves specially targeted by white police officers and detectives who resent their success and take malignant pleasure in harassing them, especially if they are in mixed relationships.

In this context, the speedy decision of the jury in the O.J. Simpson trial makes perfect sense. The type of lower-middle and working-class black people who sat on the jury have every reason to believe that white police officers are racists only too willing to plant evidence and lie in court. All this is in direct contrast to the experience of the typical white person, who views the police officer either as a friend or acquaintance from the neighborhood or as a protector and guardian of the suburban peace.

What exists, then, is a serious mismatch in racial perception of change. Most middle-class whites feel, correctly, that things have gotten much better not only in the objective socioeconomic condition of blacks but in their improved attitude toward blacks. The typical black person perceives and experiences the situation as either having not changed or having gotten worse.

The experience of Massachusetts is typical. By all objective criteria this is one of most racially liberal areas of America. Not only was it the first state to elect a black U.S. senator since Reconstruction, but its current two senators are among the most liberal and pro-black in the Senate. And yet, among blacks of all classes, the Boston area has the unenviable reputation of being one of the most racist parts of the country. Many African Americans, put off by its racist image, still refuse to move to the area. The fears of blacks are legitimate; but so is the bewilderment of whites in middle-class Boston or in neighboring cities such as Cambridge (arguably one of the most racially liberal cities in the nation) when black colleagues insist they would rather go back South than settle anywhere near Boston. The sad truth is that, even as the number of tolerant whites rapidly increased between the '60s and '70s, the amount of contact between blacks and racist working-class whites also increased, as did the racial animosity of these whites, expressed most notoriously in the anti-busing violence of South Boston.

To make matters worse, the hostile reaction of a small proportion of whites not only hurts a large proportion of blacks; but, given the adversarial and litigious nature of the culture, and the tendency of the media to highlight the exceptional, a small but active number of whites can disproportionately influence the perception of all whites, with consequences deleterious to blacks. The current political hostility to affirmative action is a perfect case in point.

Only a small proportion of whites—7 percent, according to recent opinion-poll data—claim to have been personally affected in any way by affirmative action. Yet the point of affirmative action is to bring blacks into greater contact with whites at the workplace and other sites where they were traditionally excluded. Aggrieved whites who feel they have been passed over in preference for blacks react sharply to this experience, which in turn colors the views of many whites who are in no way influenced by the policy. The result is the "angry white male" syndrome: increased hostility toward what are perceived as unreasonable black demands, and the conviction that the vast majority of whites are being hurt—78 percent of whites think so—when, in fact, only 7 percent can actually attest to such injuries from their own experience.

The experiential mismatch between blacks and whites is made still worse by what may be called the outrage of liberation. A formerly oppressed group's sense of outrage at what has been done to it increases the more equal it becomes with its former oppressors. In part, this is simply a case of relative deprivation; in part, it is the result of having a greater voice—more literate and vocal leadership, more access to the media and so on. But it also stems from the formerly deprived group's increased sense of dignity and, ironically, its embrace of the formerly oppressive Other within its moral universe.

The slave, the sharecropping serf, the black person living under Jim Crow laws administered by vicious white police officers and prejudiced judges, were all obliged, for reasons of sheer survival, to accommodate somehow to the system. One form of accommodation was to expect and demand less from the racist oppressors. To do so was in no way to lessen one's contempt, even hatred and loathing, for them. Indeed, one's diminished expectations may even have been a reflection of one's contempt.

It has often been observed that one of racism's worst consequences is the denial of the black person's human-ity. What often goes unnoticed is the other side of this twisted coin: that it left most blacks persuaded that whites were less than human. Technically clever yes, powerful, well-armed and prolific, to be sure, but without an ounce of basic human decency. No one whose community of memory was etched with the vision of lynched, barbecued ancestors, no black person who has seen the flash of greedy, obsessive hatred in the fish-blue stare of a cracker's cocked eyes, could help but question his inherent humanness. Most blacks, whatever their outward style of interaction with whites, genuinely believed, as did the mother of Henry Louis Gates, that most whites were inherently filthy and evil, or as the poet Sterling Brown once wrote, that there was no place in heaven for "Whuffolks ... being so onery," that, indeed, for most of them "hell would be good enough—if big enough."

Integration, however partially, began to change all that. By dis-alienating the Other, the members of each group came, however reluctantly, to accept each other's humanness. But that acceptance comes at a price: for whites, it is the growing sense of disbelief at what the nightly news brings in relentless detail from the inner cities. For blacks, it is the sense of outrage that someone truly human could have done what the evidence of more than three and a half centuries makes painfully clear. Like a woman chased and held down in a pitch-dark night who discovers, first to her relief, then to her disbelief, that the stranger recoiling from her in the horror of recognition had been her own brother, the moral embrace of integration is a liberation with a double take: outrage verging on incomprehension.

Increasingly exposed to the conflicts that result from integration, whites may rebel against affirmative action and other programs that bring them face to face with black anger. But resegregation is neither plausible nor desirable. Instead, whites, who dominate America's powerful institutions, must address the roots of black rage by committing to black America's socioeconomic advancement.

But, despite this imperative, a painful truth (one seemingly recognized by the participants in last week's march) emerges from the comparative sociology of group relations: except for those now-rare cases in which a minority constitutes the elite, the burden of racial and ethnic change always rests on a minority group. Although both whites and blacks have strong mutual interests in solving their racial problem, though the solution must eventually come from both, blacks must play the major role in achieving this objective—not only because they have more to gain from it but also because whites have far less to lose from doing nothing. It is blacks who must take the initiative, suffer the greater pain, define and offer the more creative solutions, persevere in the face of obstacles and paradoxical outcomes, insist that improvements are possible and maintain a climate of optimism concerning the eventual outcome. Or, to paraphrase Martin Luther King, it is they, and often they alone, who must keep the dream of a racially liberated America alive.

OUR BODIES, OUR SOULS

Naomi Wolf

NAOMI WOLF is the author of *Fire with Fire: The New Female Power and How It Will Change the 21st Century* (Ballantine).

> I had an abortion when I was a single mother and my daughter was 2 years old. I would do it again. But you know how in the Greek myths when you kill a relative you are pursued by furies? For months, it was as if baby furies were pursuing me.

These are not the words of a benighted, superstition-ridden teenager lost in America's cultural backwaters. They are the words of a Cornell-educated, urban-dwelling, Democratic-voting 40-year-old cardiologist—I'll call her Clare. Clare is exactly the kind of person for whom being pro-choice is an unshakeable conviction. If there were a core constituent of the movement to secure abortion rights, Clare would be it. And yet: her words are exactly the words to which the pro-choice movement is not listening.

At its best, feminism defends its moral high ground by being simply faithful to the truth: to women's real-life experiences. But, to its own ethical and political detriment, the pro-choice movement has relinquished the moral frame around the issue of abortion. It has ceded the language of right and wrong to abortion foes. The movement's abandonment of what Americans have always, and rightly, demanded of their movements—an ethical core—and its reliance instead on a political rhetoric in which the fetus means nothing are proving fatal.

The effects of this abandonment can be measured in two ways. First of all, such a position causes us to lose political ground. By refusing to look at abortion within a moral framework, we lose the millions of Americans who want to support abortion as a legal right but still need to condemn it as a moral iniquity. Their ethical allegiances are then addressed by the pro-life movement, which is willing to speak about good and evil.

But we are also in danger of losing something more important than votes; we stand in jeopardy of losing what can only be called our souls. Clinging to a rhetoric about abortion in which there is no life and no death, we entangle our beliefs in a series of self-delusions, fibs and evasions. And we risk becoming precisely what our critics charge us with being: callous, selfish and casually destructive men and women who share a cheapened view of human life.

In the following pages, I will argue for a radical shift in the pro-choice movement's rhetoric and consciousness about abortion: I will maintain that we need to contextualize the fight to defend abortion rights within a moral framework that admits that the death of a fetus is a real death; that there are degrees of culpability, judgment and responsibility involved in the decision to abort a pregnancy; that the best understanding of feminism involves holding women as well as men to the responsibilities that are inseparable from their rights; and that we need to be strong enough to acknowledge that this country's high rate of abortion—which ends more than a quarter of all pregnancies—can only be rightly understood as what Dr. Henry Foster was brave enough to call it: "a failure."

Any doubt that our current pro-choice rhetoric leads to disaster should be dispelled by the famous recent defection of the woman who had been Jane Roe. What happened to Norma McCorvey? To judge by her characterization in the elite media and by some prominent pro-choice feminists, nothing very important. Her change of heart about abortion was relentlessly "explained away" as having everything to do with the girlish motivations of insecurity, fickleness and the need for attention, and little to do with any actual moral agency.

This dismissive (and, not incidentally, sexist and classist) interpretation was so highly colored by subjective impressions offered up by the very institutions that define objectivity that it bore all the hallmarks of an exculpatory cultural myth: poor Norma—she just needed stroking. She was never very stable, the old dear—first she was a chess-piece for the pro-choice movement ("just some anonymous person who suddenly emerges," in the words of one NOW member) and then a codependent of the Bible-thumpers. Low self-esteem, a history of substance abuse, ignorance—these and other personal weaknesses explained her turnaround.

To me, the first commandment of real feminism is: when in doubt, listen to women. What if we were to truly, respectfully listen to this woman who began her political life as, in her words, just "some little old Texas girl who got in trouble"? We would have to hear this: perhaps Norma McCorvey actually had a revelation that she could no longer live as the symbol of a belief system she increasingly repudiated.

Norma McCorvey should be seen as an object lesson

   From *The New Republic*, October 16, 1995, pp. 26, 28-29, 32-35.

for the pro-choice movement—a call to us to search our souls and take another, humbler look at how we go about what we are doing. For McCorvey is in fact an American Everywoman: she is the lost middle of the abortion debate, the woman whose allegiance we forfeit by our refusal to use a darker and sterner and more honest moral rhetoric.

McCorvey is more astute than her critics; she seems to understand better than the pro-choice activists she worked with just what the woman-in-the-middle believes: "I believe in the woman's right to choose. I'm like a lot of people. I'm in the mushy middle," she said. McCorvey still supports abortion rights through the first trimester—but is horrified by the brutality of abortion as it manifests more obviously further into a pregnancy. She does not respect the black-and-white ideology on either side and insists on referring instead, as I understand her explanation, to her conscience. What McCorvey and other Americans want and deserve is an abortion-rights movement willing publicly to mourn the evil—necessary evil though it may be—that is abortion. We must have a movement that acts with moral accountability and without euphemism.

With the pro-choice rhetoric we use now, we incur three destructive consequences—two ethical, one strategic: hardness of heart, lying and political failure.

Because of the implications of a Constitution that defines rights according to the legal idea of "a person," the abortion debate has tended to focus on the question of "personhood" of the fetus. Many pro-choice advocates developed a language to assert that the fetus isn't a person, and this, over the years, has developed into a lexicon of dehumanization. Laura Kaplan's *The Story of Jane*, an important forthcoming account of a pre-*Roe* underground abortion service, inadvertently sheds light on the origins of some of this rhetoric: service staffers referred to the fetus—well into the fourth month—as "material" (as in "the amount of material that had to be removed..."). The activists felt exhilaration at learning to perform abortions themselves instead of relying on male doctors: "When [a staffer] removed the speculum and said, 'There, all done,' the room exploded in excitement." In an era when women were dying of illegal abortions, this was the understandable exhilaration of an underground resistance movement.

Unfortunately, though, this cool and congratulatory rhetoric lingers into a very different present. In one woman's account of her chemical abortion, in the January/February 1994 issue of *Mother Jones*, for example, the doctor says, "By Sunday you won't see on the monitor *what we call the heartbeat*" (my italics). The author of the article, D. Redman, explains that one of the drugs the doctor administered would "end the growth of the fetal tissue." And we all remember Dr. Joycelyn Elders's remark, hailed by some as refreshingly frank and pro-woman, but which I found remarkably brutal: that "We really need to get over this love affair with the fetus...."

How did we arrive at this point? In the early 1970s, Second Wave feminism adopted this rhetoric in response to the reigning ideology in which motherhood was invoked as an excuse to deny women legal and social equality. In a climate in which women risked being defined as mere vessels while their fetuses were given "personhood" at their expense, it made sense that women's advocates would fight back by depersonalizing the fetus.

The feminist complaint about the pro-life movement's dehumanization of the pregnant woman in relation to the humanized fetus is familiar and often quite valid: pro-choice commentators note that the pro-life film *The Silent Scream* portrayed the woman as "a vessel"; Ellen Frankfort's *Vaginal Politics*, the influential feminist text, complained that the fetus is treated like an astronaut in a spaceship.

But, say what you will, pregnancy confounds Western philosophy's idea of the autonomous self: the pregnant woman is in fact both a person in her body and a vessel. Rather than seeing both beings as alive and interdependent—seeing life within life—and acknowledging that sometimes, nonetheless, the woman must choose her life over the fetus's, Second Wave feminists reacted to the dehumanization of women by dehumanizing the creatures within them. In the death-struggle to wrest what Simone de Beauvoir called transcendence out of biological immanence, some feminists developed a rhetoric that defined the unwanted fetus as at best valueless; at worst an adversary, a "mass of dependent protoplasm."

Yet that has left us with a bitter legacy. For when we defend abortion rights by emptying the act of moral gravity we find ourselves cultivating a hardness of heart.

Having become pregnant through her partner's and her own failure to use a condom, Redman remarks that her friend Judith, who has been trying to find a child to adopt, begs her to carry the pregnancy to term. Judith offers Redman almost every condition a birth-mother could want: "'Let me have the baby,'" she quotes her friend pleading. "'You could visit her anytime, and if you ever wanted her back, I promise I would let her go.'" Redman does not mention considering this possibility. Thinking, rather, about the difficulty of keeping the child—"My time consumed by the tedious, daily activities that I've always done my best to avoid. Three meals a day. Unwashed laundry..."—she schedules her chemical abortion.

The procedure is experimental, and the author feels "almost heroic," thinking of how she is blazing a trail for other women. After the abortion process is underway, the story reaches its perverse epiphany: Redman is on a Women's Day march when the blood from the abortion first appears. She exults at this: "'Our bodies, our lives, our right to decide.' ... My life feels luxuriant with possibility. For one precious moment, I believe that we have the power to dismantle this system. I finish the march, borne along by the women. . . .'" As for the pleading Judith, with everything she was ready to offer a child, and the phantom baby? They are both off-stage, silent in this chilling drama of "feminist" triumphalism.

And why should we expect otherwise? In this essay, the fetus (as the author writes, "the now-inert material from my womb") is little more than a form of speech: a vehicle to assert the author's identity and autonomy.

The pro-life warning about the potential of widespread abortion to degrade reverence for life does have a nugget of truth: a free-market rhetoric about abortion can, indeed, contribute to the eerie situation we are now facing, wherein the culture seems increasingly to see babies not as creatures to whom parents devote their lives but as accoutrements to enhance parental quality of life. Day by day, babies seem to have less value in themselves, in a matrix of the sacred, than they do as products with a value dictated by a market economy.

Stories surface regularly about "worthless" babies left naked on gratings or casually dropped out of windows, while "valuable," genetically correct babies are created at vast expense and with intricate medical assistance for infertile couples. If we fail to treat abortion with grief and reverence, we risk forgetting that, when it comes to the children we choose to bear, we are here to serve them—whomever they are; they are not here to serve us.

Too often our rhetoric leads us to tell untruths. What Norma McCorvey wants, it seems, is for abortion-rights advocates to face, really face, what we are doing: "Have you ever seen a second-trimester abortion?" she asks. "It's a baby. It's got a face and a body, and they put him in a freezer and a little container."

Well, so it does; and so they do.

The pro-choice movement often treats with contempt the pro-lifers' practice of holding up to our faces their disturbing graphics. We revile their placards showing an enlarged scene of the aftermath of a D & C abortion; we are disgusted by their lapel pins with the little feet, crafted in gold, of a 10-week-old fetus; we mock the sensationalism of *The Silent Scream*. We look with pity and horror at someone who would brandish a fetus in formaldehyde—and we are quick to say that they are lying: "Those are stillbirths, anyway," we tell ourselves.

To many pro-choice advocates, the imagery is revolting propaganda. There is a sense among us, let us be frank, that the gruesomeness of the imagery *belongs* to the pro-lifers; that it emerges from the dark, frightening minds of fanatics; that it represents the violence of imaginations that would, given half a chance, turn our world into a scary, repressive place. "People like us" see such material as the pornography of the pro-life movement.

But feminism at its best is based on what is simply true. While pro-lifers have not been beyond dishonesty, distortion and the doctoring of images (preferring, for example, to highlight the results of very late, very rare abortions), many of those photographs are in fact photographs of actual D & Cs; those footprints are in fact the footprints of a 10-week-old fetus; the pro-life slogan, "Abortion stops a beating heart," is incontrovertibly true. While images of violent fetal death work magnificently for pro-lifers as political polemic, the pictures are not polemical in themselves: they are biological facts.

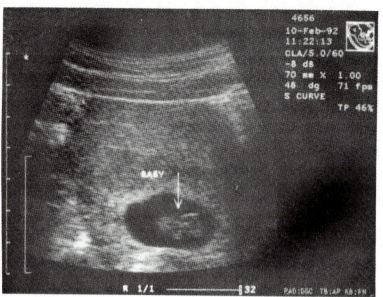

ULTRASONOGRAPHIC IMAGE OF A FETUS
AT APPROXIMATELY SEVEN WEEKS GESTATION

We know this.

Since abortion became legal nearly a quarter-century ago, the fields of embryology and perinatology have been revolutionized—but the pro-choice view of the contested fetus has remained static. This has led to a bizarre bifurcation in the way we who are pro-choice tend to think about wanted as opposed to unwanted fetuses; the unwanted ones are still seen in schematic black-and-white drawings while the wanted ones have metamorphosed into vivid and moving color. Even while Elders spoke of our need to "get over" our love affair with the unwelcome fetus, an entire growth industry—Mozart for your belly; framed sonogram photos; home fetal-heartbeat stethoscopes—is devoted to sparking fetal love affairs in other circumstances, and aimed especially at the hearts of overscheduled yuppies. If we avidly cultivate love for the ones we bring to term, and "get over" our love for the ones we don't, do we not risk developing a hydroponic view of babies—and turn them into a product we can cull for our convenience?

Any happy couple with a wanted pregnancy and a copy of *What to Expect When You're Expecting* can see the cute, detailed drawings of the fetus whom the book's owner presumably is not going to abort, and can read the excited descriptions of what that fetus can do and feel, month by month. Anyone who has had a sonogram during pregnancy knows perfectly well that the 4-month-old fetus responds to outside stimulus—"Let's get him to look this way," the technician will say, poking gently at the belly of a delighted mother-to-be. *The Well Baby Book*, the kind of whole-grain, holistic guide to pregnancy and childbirth that would find its audience among the very demographic that is most solidly pro-choice reminds us that: "Increasing knowledge is increasing the awe and respect we have for the unborn baby and is causing us to regard the unborn baby as a real person long before birth...."

So, what will it be: Wanted fetuses are charming, complex, REM-dreaming little beings whose profile on the sonogram looks just like Daddy, but unwanted ones are mere "uterine material"? How can we charge that it is vile and repulsive for pro-lifers to brandish vile and repulsive images if the images are real? To insist that the truth is in poor taste is the very height of hypocrisy. Besides, if these images *are* often the facts of the matter, and if we then claim that it is offensive for pro-choice women to be confronted by them, then we are making the judgment that women are too inherently weak to face a truth about which they have to make a grave decision. This view of women is unworthy of feminism. Free women must be strong women, too; and strong women, presumably, do not seek to cloak their most important decisions in euphemism.

Other lies are not lies to others, but to ourselves. An abortion-clinic doctor, Elizabeth Karlin, who wrote a recent "Hers" column in *The New York Times,* declared that "There is only one reason I've ever heard for having an abortion: the desire to be a good mother."

While that may well be true for many poor and working-class women—and indeed research shows that poor women are three times more likely to have abortions than are better-off women—the elite, who are the most vociferous in their morally unambiguous pro-choice language, should know perfectly well how untrue that statement often is in their own lives. All abortions occupy a spectrum, from full lack of alternatives to full moral accountability. Karlin and many other pro-choice activists try to situate all women equally at the extreme endpoint of that spectrum, and it just isn't so. Many women, including middle-class women, do have abortions because, as one such woman put it, "They have a notion of what a good mother is and don't feel they can be that kind of mother at this phase of their lives." In many cases, that is still a morally defensible place on the spectrum; but it is not the place of absolute absolution that Dr. Karlin claims it to be. It is, rather, a place of moral struggle, of self-interest mixed with selflessness, of wished-for good intermingled with necessary evil.

Other abortions occupy places on the spectrum that are far more culpable. Of the abortions I know of, these were some of the reasons: to find out if the woman could get pregnant; to force a boy or man to take a relationship more seriously; and, again and again, to enact a rite of passage for affluent teenage girls. In my high school, the abortion drama was used to test a boyfriend's character. Seeing if he would accompany the girl to the operation or, better yet, come up with the money for the abortion could almost have been the 1970s Bay Area equivalent of the '50s fraternity pin.

The affluent teenage couples who conceive because they can and then erase the consequences—and the affluent men and women who choose abortion because they were careless or in a hurry or didn't like the feel of latex—are not the moral equivalent of the impoverished mother who responsibly, even selflessly, acknowledges she already has too many mouths to feed. Feminist rights include feminist responsibilities; the right to obtain an abortion brings with it the responsibility to

contracept. Fifty-seven percent of unintended pregnancies come about because the parents used no contraception at all. Those millions certainly include women and men too poor to buy contraception, girls and boys too young and ill-informed to know where to get it, and countless instances of marital rape, coerced sex, incest and couplings in which the man refused to let the woman use protection.

But they also include millions of college students, professional men and women, and middle- and upper-middle-class people (11 percent of abortions are obtained by people in households with incomes of higher than $50,000)—who have no excuse whatsoever for their carelessness. "There is only one reason I've ever heard for having an abortion: the desire to be a good mother"—this is a falsehood that condescends to women struggling to be true agents of their own souls, even as it dishonors through hypocrisy the terminations that are the writer's subject.

Not to judge other men and women without judging myself, I know this assertion to be false from my own experience. Once, I made the choice to take a morning-after pill. The heavily pregnant doctor looked at me, as she dispensed it, as if I were the scum of the earth.

If what was going on in my mind had been mostly about the well-being of the possible baby, that pill would never have been swallowed. For that potential baby, brought to term, would have had two sets of loving middle-income grandparents, an adult mother with an education and even, as I discovered later, the beginning of diaper money for its first two years of life (the graduate fellowship I was on forbade marriage but, frozen in time before women were its beneficiaries, said nothing about unwed motherhood). Because of the baby's skin color, even if I chose not to rear the child, a roster of eager adoptive parents awaited him or her. If I had been thinking only or even primarily about the baby's life, I would have had to decide to bring the pregnancy, had there been one, to term.

No: there were two columns in my mind—"Me" and "Baby"—and the first won out. And what was in it looked something like this: unwelcome intensity in the relationship with the father; desire to continue to "develop as a person" before "real" parenthood; wish to encounter my eventual life partner without the off-putting encumbrance of a child; resistance to curtailing the nature of the time remaining to me in Europe. Essentially, this column came down to: I am not done being responsive only to myself yet.

At even the possibility that the cosmos was calling my name, I cowered and stepped aside. I was not so unlike those young louts who father children and run from the specter of responsibility. Except that my refusal to be involved with this potential creature was as definitive as a refusal can be.

Stepping aside in this way is analogous to draft evasion; there are good and altruistic reasons to evade the draft, and then there are self-preserving reasons. In that moment, feminism came to one of its logical if less-than-inspiring moments of fruition: I chose to sidestep biology; I acted—and was free to act—as if I were in control of my destiny, the way men more often than women have let themselves act. I chose myself on my own terms over a possible someone else, for self-absorbed reasons. But "to be a better mother"? *Dulce et decorum est...*"? Nonsense.

Now, freedom means that women must be free to choose self or to choose selfishly. Certainly for a woman with fewer economic and social choices than I had—for instance, a woman struggling to finish her higher education, without which she would have little hope of a life worthy of her talents—there can indeed be an *obligation* to choose self. And the defense of some level of abortion rights as fundamental to women's integrity and equality has been made fully by others, including, quite effectively, Ruth Bader Ginsberg. There is no easy way to deny the powerful argument that a woman's equality in society must give her some irreducible rights unique to her biology, including the right to take the life within her life.

But we don't have to lie to ourselves about what we are doing at such a moment. Let us at least look with clarity at what that means and not whitewash self-interest with the language of self-sacrifice. The landscape of many such decisions looks more like Marin County than Verdun. Let us certainly not be fools enough to present such spiritually limited moments to the world with a flourish of pride, pretending that we are somehow pioneers and heroines and even martyrs to have snatched the self, with its aims and pleasures, from the pressure of biology.

That decision was not my finest moment. The least I can do, in honor of the being that might have been, is simply to know that.

Using amoral rhetoric, we weaken ourselves politically because we lose the center. To draw an inexact parallel, many people support the choice to limit the medical prolongation of life. But, if a movement arose that spoke of our "getting over our love affair" with the terminally ill, those same people would recoil into a vociferous interventionist position as a way to assert their moral values. We would be impoverished by a rhetoric about the end of life that speaks of the ill and the dying as if they were meaningless and of doing away with them as if it were a bracing demonstration of our personal independence.

Similarly, many people support necessary acts of warfare (Catholics for a Free Choice makes the analogy between abortion rights and such warfare). There are legal mechanisms that allow us to bring into the world the evil of war. But imagine how quickly public opinion would turn against a president who waged war while asserting that our sons and daughters were nothing but cannon fodder. Grief and respect are the proper tones for all discussions about choosing to endanger or destroy a manifestation of life.

War is legal; it is sometimes even necessary. Letting the dying die in peace is often legal and sometimes even necessary. Abortion should be legal; it is sometimes even necessary. Sometimes the mother must be able to decide that the fetus, in its full humanity, must die. But it is never right or necessary to minimize the value of the lives involved or the sacrifice incurred in letting them go. Only if we uphold abortion rights within a matrix of individual conscience, atonement and responsibility can we both correct the logical and ethical absurdity in our position—and consolidate the support of the center.

Many others, of course, have wrestled with this issue: Camille Paglia, who has criticized the "convoluted casuistry" of some pro-choice language; Roger Rosenblatt, who has urged us to permit but discourage abortion; Laurence Tribe, who has noted that we place the fetus in shadow in order to advance the pro-choice argument. But we have yet to make room for this conversation at the table of mainstream feminism.

And we can't wait much longer. Historical changes—from the imminent availability of cheap chemical abortifacients to the ascendancy of the religious right to Norma McCorvey's defection—make the need for a new abortion-rights language all the more pressing.

In a time of retrenchment, how can I be so sure that a more honest and moral rhetoric about abortion will consolidate rather than scuttle abortion rights? Look at what Americans themselves say. When a recent *Newsweek* poll asked about support for abortion using the rare phrasing, "It's a matter between a woman, her doctor, her family, her conscience and her God," a remarkable 72 percent of the respondents called that formulation "about right." This represents a gain of thirty points over the abortion-rights support registered in the latest Gallup poll, which asked about abortion without using the words "God" or "conscience." When participants in the Gallup poll were asked if they supported abortion "under any circumstances" only 32 percent agreed; only 9 percent more supported it under "most" circumstances. Clearly, abortion rights are safest when we are willing to submit them to a morality beyond just our bodies and our selves.

But how, one might ask, can I square a recognition of the humanity of the fetus, and the moral gravity of destroying it, with a pro-choice position? The answer can only be found in the context of a paradigm abandoned by the left and misused by the right: the paradigm of sin and redemption.

It was when I was four months pregnant, sick as a dog, and in the middle of an argument, that I realized I could no longer tolerate the fetus-is-nothing paradigm of the pro-choice movement. I was being interrogated by a conservative, and the subject of abortion rights came up. "You're four months pregnant," he said. "Are you going to tell me that's not a baby you're carrying?"

The accepted pro-choice response at such a moment in the conversation is to evade: to move as swiftly as possible to a discussion of "privacy" and "difficult personal decisions" and "choice." Had I not been so nauseated and so cranky and so weighed down with the physical gravity of what was going on inside me, I might not have told what is the truth for me. "Of course it's a baby," I snapped. And went rashly on: "And if I found myself in circumstances in which I had to make the terrible decision to end this life, then that would be between myself and God."

Startlingly to me, two things happened: the conservative was quiet; I had said something that actually made sense to him. And I felt the great relief that is the grace of long-delayed honesty.

Now, the G-word is certainly a problematic element to introduce into the debate. And yet "God" or "soul"—or, if you are secular and prefer it, "conscience"—is precisely what is missing from pro-choice discourse. There is a crucial difference between "myself and my God" or "my conscience"—terms that imply moral accountability—and "myself and my doctor," the phrasing that Justice Harry Blackmun's wording in *Roe* ("inherently, and primarily, a medical decision") has tended to promote in the pro-choice movement. And that's not even to mention "between myself and myself" (Elders: "It's not anybody's business if I went for an abortion"), which implies just the relativistic relationship to abortion that our critics accuse us of sustaining.

The language we use to make our case limits the way we let ourselves think about abortion. As a result of the precedents in *Roe* (including *Griswold* v. *Connecticut* and *Eisenstadt* v. *Baird*), which based a woman's right to an abortion on the Ninth and Fourteenth Amendments' implied right to personal privacy, other unhelpful terms are also current in our discourse. Pro-choice advocates tend to cast an abortion as "an intensely personal decision." To which we can say, No: one's choice of *carpeting* is an intensely personal decision. One's struggles with a life-and-death issue must be understood as a matter of personal conscience. There is a world of difference between the two, and it's the difference a moral frame makes.

Stephen L. Carter has pointed out that spiritual discussion has been robbed of a place in American public life. As a consequence we tend—often disastrously—to use legislation to work out right and wrong. That puts many in the position of having to advocate against abortion rights in order to proclaim their conviction that our high rate of avoidable abortion (one of the highest in developed countries, five times that of the Netherlands, for example) is a social evil; and, conversely, many must pretend that abortion is not a transgression of any kind if we wish to champion abortion rights. We have no ground on which to say that abortion is a necessary evil that should be faced and opposed in the realm of conscience and action and even soul; yet remain legal.

But American society is struggling to find its way forward to a discourse of right and wrong that binds together a common ethic for the secular and the religious. When we do that, we create a moral discourse that can exist in its own right independent of legislation, and we can find ground to stand upon.

Norma McCorvey explained what happened to her in terms of good and evil: she woke in the middle of the night and felt a presence pushing violently down on her.

"I denounce you, Satan," she announced. This way of talking about evil is one of the chief class divisions in America: working-class people talk about Satan, and those whom Paul Fussell calls "the X group"—those who run the country—talk instead about neurotic guilt. While the elite scoff at research that shows that most Americans maintain a belief in the embodiment of evil—"the devil"—they miss something profound about the human need to make moral order out of chaos. After all, the only real difference between the experience described by Clare, the Cornell-educated pro-choicer, and McCorvey, the uneducated ex-alcoholic, is a classical allusion.

There is a hunger for a moral framework that we pro-choicers must reckon with. In the Karlin "Hers" column, the author announced proudly that pregnant women are asked by the counselor in the office, "So, how long have you been pro-choice?" Dr. Karlin writes that "Laughter and the answer, 'About ten minutes,' is the healthiest response. 'I still don't believe in abortion,' some women say, unaware that refusal to take responsibility for the decision means that I won't do the procedure."

How is this "feminist" ideological coercion any different from the worst of pro-life shaming and coercion? The women who come to a clinic that is truly feminist—that respects women—are entitled not only to their abortions but also to their sense of sin.

To use the term "sin" in this context does not necessarily mean, as Dr. Karlin believes, that a woman thinks she must go to hell because she is having an abortion. It may mean that she thinks she must face the realization that she has fallen short of who she should be; and that she needs to ask forgiveness for that, and atone for it. As I understand such a woman's response, she *is* trying to take responsibility for the decision.

We on the left tend to twitch with discomfort at that word "sin." Too often we have become religiously illiterate, and so we deeply misunderstand the word. But in all of the great religious traditions, our recognition of sin, and then our atonement for it, brings on God's compassion and our redemption. In many faiths, justice is linked, as it is in medieval Judaism and in Buddhism, to compassion. From Yom Kippur and the Ash Wednesday-to-Easter cycle to the Hindu idea of karma, the individual's confrontation with her or his own culpability is the first step toward ways to create and receive more light.

How could one live with a conscious view that abortion is an evil and still be pro-choice? Through acts of redemption, or what the Jewish mystical tradition calls *tikkun*; or "mending." Laurence Tribe, in *Abortion: The Clash of Absolutes*, notes that "Memorial services for the souls of aborted fetuses are fairly common in contemporary Japan," where abortions are both legal and readily available. Shinto doctrine holds that women should make offerings to the fetus to help it rest in peace; Buddhists once erected statues of the spirit guardian of children to honor aborted fetuses (called "water children" or "unseeing children"). If one believes that abortion is killing and yet is still pro-choice, one could try to use contraception for every single sex act; if one had to undergo an abortion, one could then work to provide contraception, or jobs, or other choices to young girls; one could give money to programs that provide prenatal care to poor women; if one is a mother or father, one can remember the aborted child every time one is tempted to be less than loving—and give renewed love to the living child. And so on: *tikkun.*

But when you insist, as the "Hers" column writer did, on stripping people of their sense of sin, they react with a wholesale backing-away into a rigid morality that reimposes order: hence, the ascendancy of the religious right.

Just look at the ill-fated nomination of Dr. Henry Foster for Surgeon General. The Republicans said "abortion," and the discussion was over. The Democrats, had they worked out a moral framework for progressivism, could have responded: "Yes: our abortion rate is a terrible social evil. Here is a man who can help put a moral framework around the chaos of a million and a half abortions a year. He can bring that rate of evil down. And whichever senator among you has ever prevented an unplanned pregnancy—and Dr. Foster has—let him ask the first question."

Who gets blamed for our abortion rate? The ancient Hebrews had a ritual of sending a "scapegoat" into the desert with the community's sins projected upon it. Abortion doctors are our contemporary scapegoats. The pro-lifers obviously scapegoat them in one way: if pro-lifers did to women what they do to abortion doctors—harassed and targeted them in their homes and workplaces—public opinion would rapidly turn against them; for the movement would soon find itself harassing the teachers and waitresses, housewives and younger sisters of their own communities. The pro-life movement would have to address the often all-too-pressing good reasons that lead good people to abort. That would be intolerable, a tactical defeat for the pro-life movement, and as sure to lose it "the mushy middle" as the pro-choice movement's tendency toward rhetorical coldness loses it the same constituency.

But pro-choicers, too, scapegoat the doctors and clinic workers. By resisting a moral framework in which to view abortion we who are pro-abortion-rights leave the doctors in the front lines, with blood on their hands: the blood of the repeat abortions—at least 43 percent of the total; the suburban summer country-club rite-of-passage abortions; the "I don't know what came over me, it was such good Chardonnay" abortions; as well as the blood of the desperate and the unpreventable and accidental and the medically necessary and the violently

conceived abortions. This is blood that the doctors and clinic workers often see clearly, and that they heroically rinse and cause to flow and rinse again. And they take all our sins, the pro-choice as well as the pro-life among us, upon themselves.

And we who are pro-choice compound their isolation by declaring that that blood is not there.

As the world changes and women, however incrementally, become more free and more powerful, the language in which we phrase the goals of feminism must change as well. As a result of the bad old days before the Second Wave of feminism, we tend to understand abortion as a desperately needed exit from near-total male control of our reproductive lives. This scenario posits an unambiguous chain of power and powerlessness in which men control women and women, in order to survive, must have unquestioned control over fetuses. It is this worldview, all too real in its initial conceptualization, that has led to the dread among many pro-choice women of departing from a model of woman-equals-human-life, fetus-equals-not-much.

This model of reality may have been necessary in an unrelenting patriarchy. But today, in what should be, as women continue to consolidate political power, a patriarchy crumbling in spite of itself, it can become obsolete.

Now: try to imagine real gender equality. Actually, try to imagine an America that is female-dominated, since a true working democracy in this country would reflect our 54-46 voting advantage.

Now imagine such a democracy, in which women would be valued so very highly, as a world that is accepting and responsible about human sexuality; in which there is no coerced sex without serious jailtime; in which there are affordable, safe contraceptives available for the taking in every public health building; in which there is economic parity for women—and basic economic subsistence for every baby born; and in which every young American woman knows about and understands her natural desire as a treasure to cherish, and responsibly, when the time is right, on her own terms, to share.

In such a world, in which the idea of gender as a barrier has become a dusty artifact, we would probably use a very different language about what would be—then—the rare and doubtless traumatic event of abortion. That language would probably call upon respect and responsibility, grief and mourning. In that world we might well describe the unborn and the never-to-be-born with the honest words of life.

And in that world, passionate feminists might well hold candlelight vigils at abortion clinics, standing shoulder to shoulder with the doctors who work there, commemorating and saying goodbye to the dead.

Race and the Constitution

Thurgood Marshall

THURGOOD MARSHALL is Associate Justice of the U.S. Supreme Court.* This article is adapted from a presentation given at the Annual Seminar of the San Francisco Patent and Trademark Law Association, in Maui, Hawaii, May 6, 1987.

1987 marks the 200th anniversary of the United States Constitution. A commission has been established to coordinate the celebration. The official meetings, essay contests, and festivities have begun.

The planned commemoration will span three years, and I am told 1987 is "dedicated to the memory of the Founders and the document they drafted in Philadelphia."[1] We are to "recall the achievements of our Founders and the knowledge and experience that inspired them, the nature of the government they established, its origins, its character, and its ends, and the rights and privileges of citizenship, as well as its attendant responsibilities."[2]

Like many anniversary celebrations, the plan for 1987 takes particular events and holds them up as the source of all the very best that has followed. Patriotic feelings will surely swell, prompting proud proclamations of the wisdom, foresight, and sense of justice shared by the Framers and reflected in a written document now yellowed with age.

[*Marshall, the first African American justice ever to have served on the Supreme Court, was appointed by President Lyndon B. Johnson in 1967. He resigned in 1991 because of declining health, and he died in January 1993. Ed.]

This is unfortunate—not the patriotism itself, but the tendency for the celebration to oversimplify and overlook the many other events that have been instrumental to our achievements as a nation. The focus of this celebration invites a complacent belief that the vision of those who debated and compromised in Philadelphia yielded the "more perfect Union" it is said we now enjoy.

I cannot accept this invitation, for I do not believe that the meaning of the Constitution was forever "fixed" at the Philadelphia Convention. Nor do I find the wisdom, foresight, and sense of justice exhibited by the Framers particularly profound. To the contrary, the government they devised was defective from the start, requiring several amendments, a civil war, and momentous social transformation to attain the system of constitutional government, and its respect for the individual freedoms and human rights, we hold as fundamental today. When contemporary Americans cite "The Constitution," they invoke a concept that is vastly different from what the Framers barely began to construct two centuries ago.

For a sense of the evolving nature of the Constitution we need look no further than the first three words of the

document's preamble: "We the People." When the Founding Fathers used this phrase in 1787, they did not have in mind the majority of America's citizens. "We the People" included, in the words of the Framers, "the whole Number of free Persons" (art. I, sec. 2). On a matter so basic as the right to vote, for example, Negro slaves were excluded, although they were counted for representational purposes—at three-fifths each. Women did not gain the right to vote for over 130 years, until the 19th Amendment was ratified in 1920.

These omissions were intentional. The record of the Framers' debates on the slave question is especially clear: The Southern states acceded to the demands of the New England states for giving Congress broad power to regulate commerce, in exchange for the right to continue the slave trade. The economic interests of the regions coalesced: New Englanders engaged in the "carrying trade" would profit from transporting slaves from Africa as well as goods produced in America by slave labor. The perpetuation of slavery ensured the primary source of wealth in the Southern states.

Despite this clear understanding of the role slavery would play in the new republic, use of the words "slaves" and

From *Social Policy,* Summer 1987, pp. 29–31. This article is adapted from a presentation at the annual seminar of the San Francisco Patent and Trademark Law Association, May 6, 1987.

67

"slavery" was carefully avoided in the original document. Political representation in the lower House of Congress was to be based on the population of "free Persons" in each state, plus three-fifths of all "other Persons" (art. I, sec. 2). Moral principles against slavery, for those who had them, were compromised, with no explanation of the conflicting principles for which the American Revolution had ostensibly been fought: the self-evident truths "that all men are created equal, that they are endowed by their Creator with certain unalienable Rights, that among these are Life, Liberty and the pursuit of Happiness."

It was not the first such compromise. Even these ringing phrases from the Declaration of Independence are filled with irony, for an early draft of what became that Declaration assailed the King of England for suppressing legislative attempts to end the slave trade and for encouraging slave rebellions. The final draft adopted in 1776 did not contain this criticism. And so again at the Constitutional Convention eloquent objections to the institution of slavery went unheeded, and its opponents eventually consented to a document that laid a foundation for the tragic events that were to follow.

Pennsylvania's Gouverneur Morris provides an example. He opposed slavery and the counting of slaves in determining the basis for representation in Congress. At the Convention he objected that:

> the inhabitant of Georgia [or] South Carolina who goes to the coast of Africa, and in defiance of the most sacred laws of humanity tears away his fellow creatures from their dearest connections and damns them to the most cruel bondages, shall have more votes in a Government instituted for protection of the rights of mankind, than the Citizen of Pennsylvania or New Jersey who views with a laudable horror, so nefarious a practice.[3]

And yet Gouverneur Morris eventually accepted the three-fifths accommodation. In fact, he wrote the final draft of the Constitution, the very document the bicentennial will commemorate.

As a result of compromise, the right of the Southern states to continue importing slaves was extended, officially, at least until 1808. We know that it

actually lasted a good deal longer, as the Framers possessed no monopoly on the ability to trade moral principles for self-interest. But they nevertheless set an unfortunate example. Slaves could be imported, if the commercial interests of the North were protected. To make the compromise even more palatable, customs duties would be imposed at up to ten dollars per slave as a means of raising public revenues (art. I, sec. 9).

No doubt it will be said, when the unpleasant truth of the history of slavery in America is mentioned during this bicentennial year, that the Constitution was a product of its times, and embodied a compromise that, under other circumstances, would not have been made. But the effects of the Framers' compromise have remained for generations. They arose from the contradiction between guaranteeing liberty and justice to all, and denying both to Negroes.

The original intent of the phrase, "We the People," was far too clear for any ameliorating construction. Writing for the Supreme Court in 1857, Chief Justice Taney penned the following passage in the *Dred Scott* case,[4] on the issue whether, in the eyes of the Framers, slaves were "constituent members of the sovereignty," and were to be included among "We the People":

> We think they are not, and that they are not included, and were not intended to be included. . . . They had for more than a century before been regarded as beings of an inferior order, and altogether unfit to associate with the white race . . . ; and so far inferior, that they had no rights which the white man was bound to respect; and that the negro might justly and lawfully be reduced to slavery for his benefit. . . . [A]ccordingly, a negro of the African race was regarded . . . as an article of property, and held and bought and sold as such. . . . [N]o one seems to have doubted the correctness of the prevailing opinion of the time.

And so, nearly seven decades after the Constitutional Convention, the Supreme Court reaffirmed the prevailing opinion of the Framers regarding the rights of Negroes in America. It took a bloody civil war before the 13th Amendment could be adopted to abolish slavery, though not the conse-

quences slavery would have for future Americans.

While the Union survived the Civil War, the Constitution did not. In its place arose a new, more promising basis for justice and equality, the 14th Amendment, ensuring protection of the life, liberty, and property of *all* persons against deprivations without due process, and guaranteeing equal protection of the laws. And yet almost another century would pass before any significant recognition was obtained of the rights of Black Americans to share

---

What is striking is the role legal principles have played throughout America's history in determining the condition of Negroes. They were enslaved by law, emancipated by law, disenfranchised and segregated by law, and, finally, they have begun to win equality by law.

---

equally even in such basic opportunities as education, housing, and employment, and to have their votes counted, and counted equally. In the meantime, Blacks joined America's military to fight its wars and invested untold hours working in its factories and on its farms, contributing to the development of this country's magnificent wealth and waiting to share in its prosperity.

What is striking is the role legal principles have played throughout America's history in determining the condition of Negroes. They were enslaved by law, emancipated by law, disenfranchised and segregated by law; and, finally, they have begun to win equality by law. Along the way, new constitutional principles have emerged to meet the challenges of a changing society. The progress has been dramatic, and it will continue.

The men who gathered in Philadelphia in 1787 could not have envisioned these changes. They could not have imagined, nor would they have accepted, that the document they were drafting would one day be construed by a Supreme Court to which had been appointed a woman and the descendent of an African slave. "We the People" no longer enslave, but the credit does not belong to the Framers. It belongs to those who refused to acquiesce in outdated notions of "liberty," "justice," and "equality," and who strived to better them.

And so we must be careful, when focusing on the events that took place in Philadelphia two centuries ago, that we not overlook the momentous events which followed, and thereby lose our proper sense of perspective. Otherwise, the odds are that for many Americans the bicentennial celebration will be little more than a blind pilgrimage to the shrine of the original document now stored in a vault in the National Archives. If we seek, instead, a sensitive understanding of the Constitution's inherent defects, and its promising evolution through 200 years of history, the celebration of the "Miracle at Philadelphia"[5] will, in my view, be a far more meaningful and humbling experience. We will see that the true miracle was not the birth of the Constitution, but its life, a life nurtured through two turbulent centuries of our own making, and a life embodying much good fortune that was not.

Thus, in this bicentennial year, we may not all participate in the festivities with flag-waving fervor. Some may more quietly commemorate the suffering, struggle, and sacrifice that has triumphed over much of what was wrong with the original document, and observe the anniversary with hopes not realized and promises not fulfilled. I plan to celebrate the bicentennial of the Constitution as a living document, including the Bill of Rights and the other amendments protecting individual freedoms and human rights.

NOTES

[1] Commission on the Bicentennial of the United States Constitution, *First Full Year's Report* (Sept. 1986), p. 7.

[2] Commission on the Bicentennial of the United States Constitution, *First Report* (Sept. 1985), p. 6.

[3] Max Farrand (ed.), *The Records of the Federal Convention of 1787*, vol. 2 (New Haven: Yale University Press, 1911), p. 222.

[4] 19 How. (60 U.S.) 393, 405, 407–408 (1857).

[5] Catherine D. Bowen, *Miracle at Philadelphia: The Story of the Constitutional Convention, May to September 1787* (Boston: Little, Brown, 1966).

The United States has left the balancing of rights and interests to judges, who have developed techniques to avoid balancing anything.

The Bill of Rights and the Supreme Court:
A Foreigner's View

By FRANK BRENNAN

APPROACHING THE FIRST centenary of our Constitution in the year 2001, we Australians are wondering whether we should have a bill of rights. We do not now have one. I came to the United States mildly attracted to a bill of rights. I am returning to Australia thinking we can probably continue to get by without one. I have been surprised at the interest Americans have in foreigners' reflections on such hallowed national icons as the Bill of Rights. So let me explain my reservations in the perhaps vain hope that they may contribute to constructive political discourse about the law, rights and the Constitution in the United States.

The Problem: Balancing Individual Rights Against the Public Interest.

In both countries, 1996 is an election year. Recently I have been obliged to vote. Yes, voting is compulsory in Australia. It is not just a right; it is a duty. Such an imposition by the state on the citizen is thought to be very undemocratic in the United States. In Australia most citizens unquestioningly accept compulsory voting as a good thing for themselves and democracy. If the United States is said to be the land of freedom, Australia is the land of the "fair go." Whereas individual liberty is the hallmark of public argument in the United States, in Australia the discussion is more likely to focus on equality—what is good for everyone.

American individualism produces a sharp divide

FRANK BRENNAN, S.J., is an attorney based at Uniya, the Australian Jesuit Social Justice Center. He was recently the first Visiting Research Fellow at the Center for Australian and New Zealand Studies at Georgetown University.

between the public and private; it encourages initiative, and in most instances of conflict individual rights trump all other claims. The presumption is that there are many things the state cannot and should not do, even in the public interest. It is for individuals to determine for themselves what the public interest is, how they want to contribute to it and the extent to which they are willing to forego their liberty in the interest of others. Political liberals accept that there can be no useful discussion about the common good. People of good will confronting new social problems are limited as to how far they can impinge on the private realm, even if they are legislators or judges. The separation of powers is considered almost sacred—and gridlock is accepted as its inevitable cost.

I have sympathy with many of these limits. But I have been surprised at how complex, incomprehensible and unworkable these limits have become in the U.S. constitutional framework. Of course, it is not for a foreigner to argue that Americans should not have a bill of rights. I cannot imagine the United States without one. But it is another question whether other societies, even those committed to freedom and equality, would want to adopt a U.S.-style bill of rights now that it has become so homegrown and on its face insufficient to resolve the issues of the age. The contentious issues of abortion, gay rights, women's rights, free speech on cable television and the Internet, commercial free speech and electoral redistricting all require judges to balance conflicting interests that rest on essentially political, value-laden scales. The present Supreme Court, ideologically very divided, has had to wrestle with all these questions.

To avoid such an overtly political role, judges try to set up barriers to fence themselves off from contested public questions that they as unelected officials trying to apply a transparent judicial process are ill-equipped to resolve. Or else, when they simply must make a decision, they design tests like "undue burden" to disguise their own value judgments. The result? Where it is urgent that someone balance the conflicting claims of public versus private interests, legislators are banned by the judges, and judges proceed to place restrictions on themselves. The balancing process is left incomplete, and the only result is that by default individual rights prevail over the interests of all.

Coming from a country without a bill of rights, I was eager to experience its benefits and come to understand its operation, especially the ways judges place limits on rights and on their own powers. Countries like Canada and South Africa, which have only recently constitutionalized a bill of rights, have set down a catalogue of rights but then expressly conceded the power of the elected legislators to limit the exercise of those rights in a manner that is reasonable and justifiable in an open and democratic society based on freedom and equality. To lawyers in the United States, these words of qualification seem to take away with one hand what was given with the other. The courts of these other countries, of course, have always looked to U.S. jurisprudence for guidance in the interpretation of key rights and their limits. American judges rarely look elsewhere.

Though the U.S. Constitution does not contain any similar words of permissive limitation on the rights and liberties set down, the Supreme Court has long accepted that the ban on deprivation of life, liberty or property *without due process* requires the judges to strike a balance between individual liberty and the demands of organized society. They say the balance is struck by honoring the traditions from which the country developed as well as the traditions from which it broke. This has meant that elected legislators have not had the last say in striking the balance. It has instead been the prerogative of unelected judges, who are free to determine the relative weight of entrenched and broken traditions in defining the national ethos, once they have been chosen by a President and run the gauntlet of Senate confirmation hearings. But what is weighed on the other side of the balance to individual liberty? Political liberalism in contemporary America dictates that there can be no thick notion of the good. There can be no agreement on the common good. The public interest, it often seems, is a figment of the collectivist imagination.

Weighing a Thin Public Good—in Practice.

What then are the demands of organized society? How does the Supreme Court determine the values of a society that has both maintained and broken traditions throughout its history? There is never any evidence of these historic traditions that can be put before the court, but only bold assertions. For example, when the Court was reconsider-

Not Just an Academic Question

AT A RECEPTION celebrating aboriginal poetry and music held at the Australian Embassy in Washington, D.C., last Nov. 2, Frank Brennan, S.J., was inducted as an officer of the Order of Australia. The honor came to him at the urging of Aborigine groups, for whose cause he has worked tirelessly for the last 15 years. Understand, then, that when Father Brennan raises the question of whether Australia would be wise to adopt a U.S.-style bill of rights into its Constitution—

whose centenary will occur in 2001—the ramifications are immediate and very down-to-earth. This is not an academic matter.

What the Civil Rights movement was to the United States in the 1960's, the movement for aboriginal rights has been to Australia in the 1980's and 90's. Some historical background is in order. Ever since Governor Phillip landed at Sidney Cove in 1788 and claimed what is now known as the eastern state of Queensland for the British Crown, Australia's Aborigines have been a dispossessed people in their own land. Unlike Native Americans, Aborigines have no treaties to go on; no Crown Government ever respected them enough to make one with them. They were invisible non-persons, legal "nobodies." As recently as 1971, Sir Richard Blackburn, a Supreme Court judge of the Northern Territory

where mining and ranching interests have always dominated, could nullify all aboriginal claims to land title by serenely asserting that, prior to the colonial period, Australia was a *terra nullius*—"a land of nobody."

The Blackburn decision, however, turned out to be the last gasp of an old, unquestioned order that was already giving way under the pressure of an emergent Green party and new activism on the part of indigenous groups. In 1975 the Australian Federal Parliament passed a strong anti-racial discrimination act. By 1987 polls showed that 58 percent of the Australian population supported the idea of a treaty with Aborigines. (The latest poll puts that support at 65 percent.) But the decisive turn came with the celebrated Mabo case in 1992, in which the Federal High Court exploded the myth of *terra nullius* and ruled that, despite

(continued)

ing Roe v. Wade four years ago, the attorney for Planned Parenthood said the judges had to "look very generally at whether the nation's history and tradition has respected interests of bodily integrity and autonomy and whether there has been a tradition of respect of equality of women." The attorney insisted that guidance in determining the scope of liberty was not to be obtained by looking at whether or not abortion was lawful at the time of the adoption of the 14th Amendment.

In trying to weigh the balance without articulating what is on the other scale of the balance, judges have tried to convert questions of substantive content into questions of judicial procedure using content-neutral categories or, worse, indeterminate value judgments. It all depends on whether the right in question is "fundamental" or whether the petitioner is from a "suspect class" (for example, a classification based on race). In redistricting cases, the courts are now required to scrutinize computer-drawn, octopus-shaped electoral boundaries to see whether in constructing minority-majority electorates the state has drawn the boundaries with their "customary districting principles." In one recent case the bench, puzzling over how the boundaries became so contorted, was reminded by counsel: "You must remember that politics is a contact sport." So it has always customarily been.

In scrutinising the abortion codes of the various states, the Court now attempts to determine if the law places an "undue burden" on the woman making her decision. There is no agreement among the Justices as to what constitutes an undue burden. When Justice Blackmun, the author of Roe v. Wade, said, "Roe's requirement of strict scrutiny as implemented through a trimester framework should not be disturbed," he lost out. The plurality of Justices O'Connor, Kennedy and Souter—whose thinking determines the outcome of any split decision on the present court—insisted: "The trimester framework no doubt was erected to ensure that the woman's right to choose not become so subordinate to the State's interest in promoting fetal life that her choice exists in theory but not in fact. We do not agree, however, that the trimester approach is necessary to accomplish this objective." No wonder the conservatives on the court, led by Chief Justice Rehnquist, responded, "Roe continues to exist, but only in the way a store front on a western movie set exists: a mere facade to give the illusion of reality."

The deeper illusion is that the U.S. Supreme Court can strike a balance between the woman's right to choose and the state's interest in promoting fetal life. The criterion of "undue burden" masks one of two things: either a political decision or the personal preference of the individual judge. In Planned Parenthood v. Casey (1992), the middle votes of the present Court sought to consolidate the Court's task by inviting "the contending sides of a national con-

Crown sovereignty, aboriginal land title survived and was legally enforceable under the Commonwealth common law tradition.

The shock waves of the Mabo decision, whose majority opinion was written by Justice Brennan (now Chief Justice and, incidentally, Frank Brennan's father), have yet to subside in Australian society. For a while, industry panicked, fearing that all its property titles stood in jeopardy. Not so. In December 1993, after much heated controversy, the Federal Parliament passed a Native Titles Bill that sets down procedures for adjudicating aboriginal claims to land. But as the nation anticipates the centenary (and possible revisions) of its Constitution in the year 2001, weighty questions remain unresolved.

What does the Aborigine majority want? Some Aborigines proudly see themselves as part of an Australian nation and seek to negotiate a "fair go." Others, asserting a sovereignty never voluntarily ceded, refuse to be party to any process that presumes them to be Australian citizens. Does the nation owe Aborigines a treaty? Given the tragic history, what is morally called for here? The term "treaty" is anathema to many Australians and, in fact, implies a uniformity in Aborigine situations and culture that does not exist. A compact or "instrument of reconciliation" setting forth Aborigine rights and entitlements is clearly in order.

But what is politically achievable? After closely studying the snares and trials surrounding the U.S. Bill of Rights, Father Brennan returns home believing that, at least for Australians, there is another way to go—by appealing to his country's sense of fairness and to international law.

On his visit to Australia in 1986, Pope John Paul II issued a challenge to all Australians when he told Aborigines gathered at Alice Springs, "The church herself in Australia will not be fully the church that Jesus wants her to be until you have made your contribution to her life and until that contribution has been joyfully received by others." In 1990, the Australian Catholic bishops, whom Frank Brennan advises on these matters, spoke out strongly, calling for "a secure land base for dispossessed Aboriginal communities...a just process for the resolution of conflicting claims to the land and its use," "an assured place for powerless Aborigines in our political processes" and "a guaranteed future for Aboriginal culture and tradition."

In brief, in the eyes of God—if not in those of big landowners—Aborigines are somebodies.   D.S.T.

*Judges have
tried to convert
questions of substantive
content into
questions of
judicial procedure.*

troversy to end their national division by accepting a common mandate rooted in the Constitution." And this in a country that remains the most politically polarized over abortion of any country in the world! As a foreigner privileged to sit and watch the Court in action over some months, I have no doubt this was not judicial conceit; it was a humble, failed attempt to discharge a mandate that can never be performed by unelected persons in a pluralistic, democratic society. Whatever the rights and wrongs of abortion may be, its legally permissible limits have been further politicized and rendered unresolvable in the United States precisely because the issue has been made a constitutional one.

Commencing his epic decision in Roe v. Wade, Justice Blackmun said, "Our task, of course, is to resolve the issue by constitutional measurement, free of emotion and predilection." The spectacular failure of this effort is found in Justice Blackmun's last judicial utterance on the matter two decades later: "A woman's right to reproductive choice is one of those fundamental liberties. Accordingly that liberty need not seek refuge at the ballot box.... I am 83 years old. I cannot remain on this Court forever, and when I do step down, the confirmation process of my successor well may focus on the issue before us today." There is more than a dose of emotion and predilection in all that. The limits of the fundamental liberty depend not on the ballot box directly but on the view of the judge chosen and confirmed by those who do face the ballot box.

The Fallacy of Constitutionalizing an Issue.

It is a bold step to assume that by constitutionalizing an issue, everyone gains: the judges by becoming more important to the national life, the legislators by being able to sidestep the hard decisions, the unpopular and powerless

by making gains across the board nationally that could not be achieved locally, and the citizenry generally by being assured that there is a sphere of personal conduct immune to invasion by the state. But there are other ways that can be less costly for all parties. And when the issue affects all, it may be an overly one-dimensional view of the human person to portray the issue as a conflict between the individual David and the Goliath state.

The most prominent case this last term has been the gay rights case from Colorado, Romer v. Evans. After three cities in Colorado enacted policies outlawing discrimination against gays, a statewide referendum was carried in the name of putting an end to special rights for special groups. The legal problem was that the citizen-initiated referendum inserted a very broad provision into the state constitution banning any branch of government from adopting a policy whereby sexual orientation could be the basis for a claim of discrimination. If gays were a "suspect class" or if "fundamental rights" were in question, the Court would apply "strict scrutiny" to the state law, which inevitably has fatal consequences for such law. Colorado argued that gays are not a suspect class and therefore the state need only show that there is a rational basis for the law, such as maintaining uniform statewide laws for the protection of marriage or for discouraging homosexual activity. The gay rights groups argued that the issue was not one of special rights or special protection, but the right of every person to be free of arbitrary discrimination. Justice Scalia, in argument, put it as a case of reversing special laws that gave favored treatment to those engaging in homosexual activity.

Given that the Supreme Court in the 1986 case Bowers v. Hardwick decided that the state could criminalize homosexual activity conducted in private by consenting adults, Justice Scalia asked, "Why can a State not take a step short of that and say, 'We're not going to make it criminal, but on the other hand, we certainly don't want to encourage it, and therefore we will neither have a State law giving special protection, nor will we allow any municipalities to give it special protection'?" Counsel was asked specifically, "Are you asking us to overrule Bowers v. Hardwick?" She replied, "No, I am not." This shows just how fickle is the present law of privacy in the United States: A woman exercising her right to privacy can abort a fetus in which the state has an interest, but homosexuals engaged consensually in private sexual behavior have no similar right to privacy. And in the first gay rights case before the Supreme Court in 10 years, the Court, even when it asks, is not being invited to extend the right to privacy to gays by overruling Bowers v. Hardwick.

The majority in that case once again constitutionalized the issue with breathtaking particularity: "The issue presented is whether the Federal Constitution confers a fundamental right upon homosexuals to engage in sodomy." They found there is "in constitutional terms, no such thing as a fundamental right to commit homosexual sodomy." There is a constitutional right to abortion but not to consensual sodomy. In his strong dissent Justice Blackmun said the Court had refused to recognize "the fundamental interest all individuals have in controlling the nature of their intimate associations with others." For him, the Constitution has sheltered certain rights associated with family "not because they contribute, in some direct and material way, to the general public welfare, but because they form so central a part of an individual's life."

The Supreme Court doesn't know which way to turn in these controverted matters. Consider another case: In 1992 Senator Jesse Helms introduced at the last minute an amendment to the Cable Television Consumer Protection and Competition Act aimed at restricting the amount of indecent material carried on leased access channels and public access channels. The cable operators were required to ban or block indecent material, which could then be unscrambled only on written request from the consumer. In February the Supreme Court heard argument against the law. The free speech petitioners argued that the Government's calculus ignored the crucial right of adult cable viewers to have access to a variety of ideas and experiences.

> *I fear the Bill of Rights ethos inculcates the notion that rights are protected only because they form so central a part of an individual's life.*

As for the protection of children, the petitioners claimed that the decision should lie with parents and not with government. They claimed strong, uncontroverted evidence that lock boxes offer the cable subscriber an easy method of avoiding unwanted programming. The choice being between the state and parents barring child access, the argument was that free speech could be protected by leaving the decision to the parents. The Justices questioned whether they could presume there was some parental inertia in this regard or whether they would require evidence of a lack of parental supervision. The next day the Montgomery County District Court heard evidence of an 11-year-old boy raping a 5-year-old girl. He had learned about having sex from watching the porno

cable channel in his parents' home. But in the United States the parents of both children will be guaranteed the right to watch what they want.

Judicial Gridlock vs. Legislative Responsibility.

Throughout the Court's jurisprudence, as it has developed within this straitjacket of individual rights, is the notion that the person belongs only to himself and not to others or to society as a whole. By constitutionalizing individual rights and declining to qualify such rights in the interests of others, the United States has left the balancing of rights and interests increasingly to judges—while the judges have developed techniques to avoid balancing anything. It is a sustained gridlock. If a right is fundamental or if the law affects a suspect class, the individual's claim is trump. But how does a judge determine if a right is fundamental or if the person is a member of a suspect class? There is no definitive test. It is a matter of judicial preference.

Women have the fundamental right to make the ultimate decision about termination of pregnancy before viability. Homosexuals do not have the fundamental right to conduct intimate relationships in the privacy of their own homes. If it ever comes to balancing competing rights or interests, the best the Supreme Court has been able to do is to ask whether an undue burden or substantial obstacle has been placed in the way of the individual. Having constitutionalized the questions, the Court has failed to provide a judicial method for balancing the incommensurable interests of the citizen as an independent individual and the citizen as a member of a society, each contributing well or adversely to the life of the other and to the common good.

There can be no getting away from a balancing of interests. Who best to do the weighing, the legislators elected by all or the judges nominated by the few? If I felt the United States was the freest possible place to live in, I would hold my peace. But here, freedom and security depend very much on individual initiative and personal wealth. I fear the Bill of Rights ethos not only quashes any sustained public discussion of the common good. It also inculcates the notion that rights are protected not because they contribute to the general public welfare but only "because they form so central a part of an individual's life," as Justice Blackmun put it.

One Australian state has also retained anti-sodomy laws. Though it has no bill of rights, Australia is a signatory to the First Optional Protocol of the International Covenant on Civil and Political Rights, which permits citizens who have exhausted all domestic remedies to communicate with the Human Rights Committee of the United Nations in Geneva. In 1994 the committee found that the prohibition by law of consensual homosexual acts in private was a violation of the right to privacy in the international covenant. The covenant says, "No one shall be subjected to arbitrary or unlawful interference with his privacy" and "Everyone has a right to the protection of law against such interference." Responding to the committee's finding, the Australian Federal Parliament passed a law that sexual conduct involving only consenting adults in private is not to be subject to any arbitrary interference with privacy. So homosexuals in Australia are guaranteed their privacy without judges having to constitutionalize the question. Politicians can weigh notions of individual liberties and public welfare and strike a balance. Judges are on thin ice when they try. In the United States, they are required to try very often.

Over time the American Bill of Rights has probably given politicians greater license to pass the buck to the Justices. It has allowed the legislative process to be more loose and inconsistent. Politicians can pass laws for the public display of the Ten Commandments knowing they will be struck down. They can wildly promise to ban abortion even in cases of rape, knowing that the courts will not permit it. Meanwhile they have satisfied their more fundamentalist constituents.

I return to Australia without any passionate desire to see the complex issues of the day constitutionalized, taken out of the hands of politicians and reserved to judges who will go to great lengths in judicial reasoning to avoid simply having to apply their own values in weighing the conflicting claims. I am delighted that the United States has a robust tradition for debating the issues from an individual rights perspective. In Australia,

we do not have capital punishment. We do not interfere with the privacy of gays. We accord much the same level of protection to the fetus *and* the woman's choice. We do not have judges as the final arbiters of abortion codes and redistricting maps. We allow government to restrict indecent material on television, and I do not lose too much sleep over that.

When under greatest pressure, the U.S. system, as Justice Blackmun admits, depends on just one vote. So too in Australia—only there the person with the one vote is elected and voting is compulsory. As ever, I will continue to look to the U.S. Supreme Court for a jurisprudence of individual rights. Your system can correct those of us with a parliamentary system that places more trust and accountability in the elected lawmakers who have to face all the people who come to the polling booth not just to exercise their right, but to perform their lawful duty. *Vive la différence*. Thank you, America, for the chance to learn from a different tradition in which the results are so often the same, reached by different routes. Your robust ideas on rights and freedom are an antidote to our populist notions of equality and the common good, all of which are needed for the healthy enjoyment of liberty in an organized society.

Racial gerrymandering

MARK F. BERNSTEIN

MARK F. BERNSTEIN is a lawyer with Hoyle, Morris & Kerr in Philadelphia.

WHEN the 102nd Congress convened in January 1991, the Georgia House delegation was comprised of nine Democrats and one Republican— Newt Gingrich. Eight of the Democrats were white (as, of course, is the Republican) and one was black. But more than a quarter of Georgia's citizens are black, and, in order to comply with the Voting Rights Act following the 1990 census, two more black-majority districts had to be drawn.

Finding blacks around whom to draw those districts proved challenging. But, under pressure from the U.S. Justice Department, the legislature adopted what was known as the "max-black" plan, which stretched the new Eleventh District for 260 miles, snaking block by block through neighborhoods from Atlanta to Savannah in order to collect enough blacks to form a majority. Just over four years later, Newt Gingrich is Speaker of the House, and the only Democrats in the state's delegation are the three representing the black-majority districts. All the other Georgia congressmen are white Republicans.

If Georgia is the most extreme example of Democratic decline following the creation of black-majority districts, it is by no means the only one. Within the last four years, while the Democratic share of the southern black vote has increased to a near-unanimous 91 percent, its share of the white vote has declined to just 35 percent, which has cost the party seats in Alabama, Arkansas, Florida, Mississippi, North Carolina, and South Carolina. For the first time since Reconstruction, Republicans hold a majority of southern House seats.

However, if the purpose of the redistricting was to increase black representation in Congress, the Voting Rights Act has actually been a great success. Every one of the newly created black-majority districts elected a black congressman, all of them Democrats. Six southern states elected their first black congressmen since the Hayes administration. And increased numbers have brought increased clout; before Republicans took control of the House, the Congressional Black Caucus influenced national policy on issues ranging from the crime bill to the use of military force in Haiti.

Last summer, however, the Supreme Court ruled in *Miller v. Johnson* that the Georgia reapportionment plan unconstitutionally classified citizens according to race. A year earlier, North Carolina's plan, which had also gerrymandered black districts, was called into question and will be reviewed again in the coming term, along with plans from Texas and perhaps Louisiana, as well. More such challenges surely are on the way.

The debate over racial gerrymandering has bred exaggerations on both sides. Cynthia McKinney, elected from Georgia's max-black Eleventh District, warns direly that the Supreme Court's decision will revive segregation. Justice Sandra Day O'Connor suggests that the drawing of black-majority districts smacks of apartheid, overlooking the fact that most of those districts are no more than 55 percent to 65 percent black and, by that measure, are actually among the most integrated in the country. Republicans contend that racial gerrymandering had little to do with their recent electoral success, ignoring cases where it clearly made the difference. Democrats blame racial gerrymandering for their loss of the House, which was, however, too broad not to have had other causes.

Yet the fact is that the aggressive drawing of black-majority congressional districts has coincided almost exactly with Democratic decline in the House. With the Supreme Court possibly forcing almost a dozen states to draw reapportionment plans from scratch, it is worth assessing to what extent racial gerrymandering actually has contributed to Democratic electoral losses in Congress, in the South, and in the nation as a whole. Can the collapse of the Democratic party's majorities be blamed on racial gerrymandering? Or, to put the question more bluntly, are black electoral success and Democratic electoral success incompatible?

Into the "political thicket"

Gerrymandering has been practiced for as long as there has been apportionment. The term itself mocks a Massachusetts assembly district approved by Governor Elbridge Gerry in 1812, which, it was said, resembled a salamander. Nothing in the Constitution, however, requires that congressmen be elected by districts; that was not required by federal statute until 1842, at which time almost one-third of the states still elected all their representatives at large. Given, however, that representatives are elected by district, the unbreakable rule of apportionment is that congressional districts within a state must have an equal number of people. This is the "one-person, one-vote" requirement. Numerical equality, however, is not the same as political equality, for it is easy to draw the lines in a discriminatory way yet still make the numbers balance.

The Voting Rights Act, the history of which neatly parallels the history of the civil-rights movement in general over the last 30 years, was enacted in 1965 to ensure blacks the right

Reprinted with permission of the author and *The Public Interest,* Winter 1996, pp. 59-69. © 1996 by National Affairs, Inc.

to vote in elections. But, in 1982, Congress amended Section 2 of the Voting Rights Act to prohibit election laws that had the effect of reducing minority voting power. It thus became a vehicle for guaranteeing blacks the right to win elections, though, due to pressure from Republicans, the 1982 amendments stated explicitly that they did not require proportional representation according to race.

As a practical matter, though, it is hard to prohibit practices weakening minority voting strength without effectively guaranteeing minorities a certain minimum number of seats; in other words, proportional representation. Interpreting the 1982 amendments in the 1986 case of *Thornburg v. Gingles,* the Supreme Court conceded that the Voting Rights Act not only now permitted but even required that race be taken into consideration during reapportionment in order to prevent the dilution of minority votes.

Minority votes are diluted, the Court reasoned, if three circumstances exist: first, there must be a minority group "sufficiently large and geographically compact" to constitute a majority in the district. In other words, one can't sue New York for failing to create an Aleut-majority congressional district, because there aren't enough Eskimos in the state to comprise one. Second, the minority group must be "politically cohesive," i.e., it must be determined that they tend to vote alike. Third, the minority's preferred candidate must usually be defeated by white bloc voting. Wherever a large, cohesive minority group existed, but could not elect the candidates of its choice because of unified white opposition, the solution was to create districts in which the minority could be a majority.

Gingles, although circumvented by the Court's decision in the Georgia reapportionment case last June, turned the Voting Rights Act in a new direction for the next round of reapportionment. If a redistricting plan could be successfully challenged because it had the effect of keeping minority representation below where it demographically could be—even if that effect was unintentional—the safer course was to draw boundaries that gave minorities something approximating proportional representation. As the 1990 census approached, minority interest groups, which had successfully fought for the Voting Rights amendments, found an unlikely ally in the Bush Justice Department. Having failed to defeat the 1982 amendments, many Republicans came to recognize the opportunity the amendments created.

Strange bedfellows

Population had continued to shift during the 1980s away from the Rust Belt and toward the South and West. California, for example, would gain seven seats as a consequence of redistricting, Florida, five, and Texas, three. Fortuitously, the areas that were gaining seats were also areas that tended to vote Republican, while the states losing seats—e.g., New York, Pennsylvania, and Illinois—tended to vote Democratic. Several Southern and Western states also now had Republican governors who could influence the redistricting process. More fed-

eral judges, who would hear challenges to reapportionment plans, had been appointed by Republican presidents, giving the party another intangible advantage that it had not enjoyed in previous years. The Republican governor of Alabama, for one, refused to call the Democratic legislature into special session to adopt a reapportionment plan, preferring to take his chances in federal court.

The Bush administration decided to enforce the 1982 Voting Rights amendments aggressively, siding with those Republicans who had concluded that the creation of black-majority districts could actually benefit the party by drawing black voters out of suburban districts whose white voters overwhelmingly voted Republican. As Benjamin Ginsburg, former chief counsel for the Republican National Committee, remarked after the 1994 elections, "Look at the results. . . . We'd be nuts to want to see these districts abolished."

An alliance of sorts was created between black Democrats and white Republicans, usually only tacit but occasionally more open. In 1989, the Republican National Committee and conservative groups formed a tax-exempt organization called Fairness For The '90s, which offered computer redistricting software packages, worth almost $360,000 apiece, to black groups in order to help them draw reapportionment plans.

In fact, the new technology was crucial to the new wave of reapportionment. Master reapportioners of the past, such as California's Phil Burton, had aggressively sought to maximize the number of safe Democratic seats and had used such computer technology as existed at the time to help them. What changed after the 1990 census was that the software to do this sort of work became widely available. Without computers, partisan redistricting was unavoidably ham-handed. In addition to a tradition in most states against splitting all except the most populous counties between districts, few plans were drawn that divided actual neighborhoods because it was not possible to do so accurately. By 1990, it was.

The software program used by the Texas legislature to design its reapportionment plan (known as REDAPPL), for example, could provide racial and ethnic information down to the block level, making it possible for line drawers to wend their way through neighborhoods, sorting black streets into one district and white streets into another. Moreover, REDAPPL could *only* show racial breakdowns; it lacked the capacity to show party affiliation or previous voting patterns at the block level. As the computer technician for the Texas legislature later explained, "The problem is when you draw on this computer, it tells you the population data, racial data. Every time you make a move, it tabulates right there on the screen. You can't ignore it."

Racial gerrymandering's political cost

In the two elections since the last round of reapportionment, racial gerrymandering has directly cost the Democrats about a dozen seats in the House; i.e., about one-fifth of their total losses, but half of their losses in the South. Clearly, drawing the most loyal part of the Democratic constituency out of a district will make it harder for the Democrats to hold the district. Two examples from Alabama demonstrate how this has happened.

When Democrat Ben Erdreich was reelected without opposition in 1990, the Sixth District consisted of the eastern half of Jefferson County: Birmingham and its suburbs. Erdreich, who is white, had a moderate voting record among southern congressman and had always run well in the black neighborhoods of his district. The neighboring Seventh District, which also was represented by a white Democrat, Claude Harris, had included the black-majority counties in western Alabama. In order to satisfy the Voting Rights Act, the Seventh District was converted into a black-majority district by dropping three white-majority counties and adding two long arms, one taking in the black areas around Montgomery, in the Second District, and the other reaching into Erdreich's district to take all the black areas around Birmingham. The new plan split Jefferson and Montgomery Counties cleanly along racial lines.

Because so many voters were drawn out of the Sixth and Second Districts, new ones had to be drawn in. Erdreich's district was expanded to include all of Shelby and part of Tuscaloosa County, areas that are predominantly white, transforming a district that had been 37 percent black when Erdreich ran in 1990 to one that was only 9 percent black when he ran in 1992. So obvious was it that reapportionment had made this a Republican seat that Erdreich, despite his earlier landslide victory, almost decided not to seek reelection. As it was, he lost the seat narrowly.

Reapportionment cost the Democrats the Second District, as well. To replace the black sections of Montgomery County, two counties that are almost 80 percent white were added. This had been a competitive district, giving Republican Bill Dickinson a bare majority in 1990. When Dickinson retired, the Republicans nominated Terry Everett, a local real-estate developer. Everett's Democratic opponent was George Wallace, Jr., son of the former governor and bearer of one of the most famous names in Alabama politics. Despite the senior Wallace's reputation as a segregationist, he had won a respectable share of black votes in his later gubernatorial campaigns, and his son was endorsed by several black political groups.

Everett beat Wallace by only 3,571 votes. Except for the white neighborhoods of Montgomery and the towns of Dothan and Enterprise, Wallace carried the district easily, but these were enough to make the difference. Had the boundaries been where they were before reapportionment, Wallace would have won, 48 percent to 46 percent.

Claude Harris, in contrast, chose not to run in the newly configured Seventh District. Black state senator Earl Hilliard stepped in and trounced the Republican candidate, gaining two-thirds of his majority in the black neighborhoods around Birmingham and Montgomery.

The effect of reapportionment on the Democratic party has been more than just seats lost, but seats weakened, as well. There are many more examples of districts, such as Charlie Rose's in North Carolina or William Lipinski's in Illinois, that the Democrats still hold, but with much narrower majorities. According to David I. Lublin of the University of South Caro-

lina, racial redistricting has also endangered Democrats outside the South, such as Jane Harman in California and Sander Levin of Michigan, both of whom were barely reelected after Hispanic and black voters were drawn into neighboring districts. Effects have also been felt in districts that once were competitive but now are unassailably Republican.

But racial gerrymandering is not the only cause of Democratic decline. What has cost the Democrats so many seats has been the loss of southern white support, a fact of life in southern politics for a generation, but one laid bare at the congressional level only after the last round of reapportionment. No Democratic presidential candidate has won the southern white vote since 1964, not even when a Southerner has been on the ticket. Strong white support has also enabled the Republicans to claim several southern governorships and control of assembly chambers in North Carolina, South Carolina, and Florida.

Two things enabled the Democratic party to delay the electoral impact of their weakness in the South. The first was control of the state legislatures, where most apportionment still is initiated. By manipulating the boundary lines, it had been possible to keep the Democratic share of House seats higher than the party's share of the total congressional vote would have suggested. But as Democratic control of the legislatures slips, so too will this advantage. With courts and Republicans now doing much of the reapportioning, the percentage of Democratic seats in the House is close to the overall percentage of Democratic votes in House elections. The second factor delaying their decline in the South was the strength of incumbency. Yet, as popular Democratic incumbents have retired, the party has been unable to hold the open seats.

Color-blind ambition

It is easy to oversimplify the influence of racialist thinking on the Democratic party. The way districts were drawn depended considerably upon how individual political careers would be affected. Ambitions must be accommodated, both the ambitions of minority politicians and those of incumbents. Courts draw a lot of reapportionment plans not because the ones the legislatures adopt are unconstitutional but because the legislature either can't (or won't) reach agreement at all. The Illinois legislature, for instance, has not enacted a redistricting plan since 1961.

Thus a large part of the reapportionment debate turned not so much on whether, but how, to draw minority districts. Often, black-majority districts could have been drawn more compactly but for the need to serve other interests. Georgia's reapportionment plan was designed by Assembly Speaker Tom Murphy in order to unseat Gingrich—a plan that obviously backfired. The black-majority Fourth District of Maryland was drawn in order to pull enough blacks out of Democrat Steny Hoyer's district to prevent a primary challenge. Part of the debate in Illinois concerned in which of two black districts to put the Second Ward, a decision that was believed to affect the career of the ward's alderman.

Republicans were as adept as Democrats at playing this game. The reapportionment plan proposed by Florida Republican Andy Ireland had the same racial allocation as the one drawn by the NAACP, except that one of Ireland's black-majority districts would have covered parts of 17 counties and three television markets. North Carolina Republicans pressed for the creation of one black-majority district, which would in places have been only a single precinct wide.

It is also a mistake to view the reapportionment struggle as one solely between minorities and whites. In Texas and Florida, among other places, the struggle was as much between different minorities seeking to divide the racial pie. They also sometimes served as proxies in a larger battle between the major political parties. For example, Florida's Hispanics, who tend to vote Republican, argued that, because their numbers were increasing more rapidly, they deserved an extra minority district. But blacks, who are strongly Democratic, cited past discrimination as justifying special protection. Those who blithely assume the existence of a "rainbow" coalition overlook such divisions.

The desire of legislators to protect incumbents, as well as to boost minority representation, makes it difficult in some cases to decide whom to blame for the loss of a seat. Democrats might have defeated Republican Clay Shaw in Florida's 22nd District in 1992; they lost by only 36,771 votes, almost all of them in Broward County, which was divided between four congressional districts. One can attribute defeat here to the loss of votes to black Democrat Alcee Hastings, who won the new 23rd District in a landslide, but one could just as easily blame white Democrats Peter Deutsch and Harry Johnston, who also won comfortably and could have spared voters in Broward County. As Lublin observes, Joan Kelly Horn might have held her seat in Missouri had not both Richard Gephardt and black congressman William Clay taken strong Democratic neighborhoods to pad their own majorities.

Finally, one should recognize that black-majority districts sometimes were drawn in order to further the personal political interests of the black legislators who proposed them. It is no accident that several of the architects of minority-majority plans—Eddie Bernice Johnson in Texas, Earl Hilliard in Alabama, Cynthia McKinney in Georgia, Cleo Fields in Louisiana, Luis Gutierrez in Illinois—now represent the districts they helped draw.

The end of biracial coalitions?

If racial gerrymandering has been bad for Democrats, has it been good for minorities? The reason for creating black-majority districts, as the Supreme Court recognized in *Gingles,* was that black candidates can rarely win outside a black-majority district since whites will not vote for them. With very few exceptions, that has not changed. Black candidates who do win white-majority districts don't do so with much of the white vote. But then, neither do white Democrats.

The Court managed to strike down the Georgia reapportionment plan without repudiating *Gingles,* but consider this: Only two of the 41 black members of Congress were elected from white-majority districts. If the Court is serious about eliminating race as a predominant factor in reapportionment, Congress would probably again become an almost all-white institution. Given that likely outcome, is it really so bad to extend the lines a bit in order to allow black candidates to win?

Well, yes. Black participation in Congress may be at an all-time high, but are black interests better represented this year under Republican control than they were last year? Loss of the House cost the Congressional Black Caucus three full committee and 17 subcommittee chairmanships. As David A. Bositis of the Joint Center for Political and Economic Studies notes, blacks feel the loss of House control more severely than do whites because black political fortunes are inseparable from those of the Democratic party. True, the Black Caucus does now exercise proportionately more influence within the Democratic caucus, but gaining a larger share of a shrinking pie is not a formula for success.

A compromise might be reached if the lines were softened. Every congressional district in the country that is more than 30 percent black, 46 in all, has a Democratic congressman, all but three of them black or Hispanic. The gerrymandered districts do not need so many black voters to be safely Democratic, but they probably do need that many to be safely black. Reducing the percentages a little would sacrifice some minority representation in exchange for more Democratic representation. This is coalition politics, which usually translates into black voters supporting white candidates. The Black Caucus responds that blacks are better off as representatives than as constituents. Black *representatives* are certainly better off— it's their jobs that are at stake—but are blacks in general?

And what about the political system as a whole? It is hard to look at something as tortured and as obviously over-extended as Louisiana's "Zorro" District or North Carolina's "I-85" District and not feel some qualms. It cannot be good for our politics to split neighborhoods street by street so that black residents are weeded out or, for that matter, weeded in. But, because of the alliance between racialists who want to see more blacks elected to Congress and conservatives who want to see more Republicans elected to Congress, some form of racial apportionment will likely survive the Supreme Court's attempt to eradicate it. Some have begun to advocate scrapping geographically based apportionment altogether in favor of an unabashed system of proportional representation such as Lani Guinier proposes. Georgia Congresswoman McKinney has already introduced such legislation.

We enter unexplored territory. Cynical as their tactics might be, the Republicans seem to have succeeded where the Democrats failed—in forging a political alliance that enables both blacks and whites to win election. Unless the Democratic party can devise something better, it will continue to suffer.

Rule by Law

*Conservatives yearning to rein in the courts
have a long-neglected tool ready at hand.*

ROBERT P. GEORGE & RAMESH PONNURU

Mr. George is a professor of politics at Princeton. Mr. Ponnuru is NR's national reporter.

CONGRESSIONAL conservatives have an ambitious agenda: limiting government, promoting economic growth, reforming social policy. Fighting the considerable resistance to that agenda has occupied most of their time and energies. It's understandable, then, that until recently another important conservative goal has not received much attention. That long-term project is nothing less than the restoration of America's constitutional order.

Judging from this year's paeans to the Tenth Amendment, Republicans recognize the troubling divergence between current governmental practice and sound constitutional principle. But the Tenth Amendment is hardly the only part of the Constitution that has fallen into desuetude; and the federal judiciary bears the main responsibility for this state of affairs. Courts have repeatedly imposed liberals' pet policies on everything from abortion to welfare, in defiance both of their constitutional mandate and of public opinion. In so doing, they have not only frequently enacted unjust and counterproductive policies.

They have also narrowed the scope of democracy in American life.

Conservatives need, therefore, to devise a strategy for reining in the courts. It's important, of course, for Congress to block the appointment of judges who confuse themselves with legislators; and the next Republican President, one hopes, will appoint judges who understand their proper role. But the disappointing performance of several Reagan and Bush appointees to the Supreme Court testifies to the limitations of that strategy. External restraints are also necessary.

To his credit, Pat Buchanan has incorporated this idea into his presidential campaign. Speaking before the Heritage Foundation in late January, he proposed a series of judicial reforms, including: an end to lifetime tenure for federal judges; voter recall of judges; congressional restrictions on the Supreme Court's jurisdiction; and national referenda on major Supreme Court decisions. Many of these proposals, whatever their merits, would require constitutional amendments. But one of them, as Buchanan noted, is an unwisely neglected provision already in the Constitution.

UNDER Article III, Section 2 of the Constitution, the Congress has the power to make exceptions to and regulate the appellate jurisdiction of the Supreme Court. When the Justices overstep their bounds, Congress can strip them of jurisdiction. Since the "inferior" federal courts are created by Congress, their jurisdiction is also subject to congressional limitation. Congress has largely failed to perform this regulatory duty. But a Congress that is serious about reclaiming the Constitution could rehabilitate Article III, Section 2 by regulating the federal judiciary's jurisdiction in three strategic areas: prison management, school prayer, and term limitation.

Prison management is perhaps the easiest place to start limiting judicial power. Many judges now realize that even if they had a constitutional mandate to micromanage prisons, they lack the capacity to do so intelligently. And they have a bad conscience over the mess they have made in this area. As well they should: in Philadelphia alone, over one hundred people have been murdered by criminals set free by court-ordered prison population caps. Re-

From *National Review*, February 26, 1996, pp. 54-55, 68. © 1996 by National Review, Inc., 150 East 35th Street, New York, NY 10016. Reprinted by permission.

sponding to justified public outrage over such travesties, House Republicans have proposed limiting the remedies available to the courts in prison-related cases. They should go further, and stipulate what conditions and policies of prisons should be beyond the review of the courts.

Republicans in Congress who support a constitutional amendment allowing school prayer should consider using Article III, Section 2 to achieve the same result. The political argument for this method is simple: stripping the courts of the ability to review state and local policies on school prayer requires a simple statutory majority, whereas a constitutional amendment requires a two-thirds majority and ratification by three-quarters of state legislatures. Conservatives have a more important reason to prefer the statutory approach: they have never believed that the First Amendment, properly construed, prohibits states, localities, and school districts from permitting school prayer. It would violate a principle of economy to amend the Constitution to put back something that is already there. Indeed, to do so could be construed to concede that the Supreme Court was right in its interpretation of the Constitution as it stands.

Removing the courts' jurisdiction over state term limits would reverse the Supreme Court's disappointing decision on that issue and thereby affirm American federalism. It is abundantly clear that term limits do not enjoy two-thirds support in the current Congress; no constitutional amendment on the subject, however watered down, is going to pass. Republicans committed to the idea should therefore content themselves with establishing the legality of those limits already put in place by the voters of various states. Even Republicans with reservations about the wisdom of term limits might come on board, in deference to the popular will. And while any defense of term limits will be a tough sell to some Republican incumbents, all Republicans should realize that the movement for term limitation is large, it is energetic, and it is not going to fade away. Because of the Supreme Court's decision, the cause of term limits is in a worse position now than it was before the Republican Congress convened. And that Congress has already defeated a term-limits measure. True, 85 per cent of Republicans supported that bill. But the GOP Congress will bear the brunt of many voters' wrath anyway—unless it takes action now.

Any attempt to resurrect Article III, Section 2 will provoke liberals' opposition. They will call it an assault on the Constitution and the rights it protects. A common misunderstanding of the distribution of constitutional duties will reinforce their view: decades of judicial imperialism without effective legislative response have obscured the truth that the Constitution was never meant to be enforced primarily by the judiciary. In particular, liberal piety toward the Supreme Court lasting more than a generation has given the public an inflated view of its sacrality. Republicans will have to meet this criticism head-on. They should remind the public that congressmen take an oath to uphold the Constitution no less faithfully than judges, and have as great a responsibility to prevent violations. Clarifying this point would in itself be no small service to the cause of constitutionalism.

The course outlined here is not for the faint of heart. But Republicans need not be timorous. Even if Congress ultimately refrains from action in these areas, the mere prospect may inhibit the courts from defying Congress in other areas, like welfare reform. Moreover, proposals for term limits, voluntary school prayer, and prison reform enjoy broad public support. If these ideas were not so popular, after all, liberals would not be forced to run to the courts to prevent the American people from adopting them.

LET US PRAY

School-prayer advocates are fighting the Supreme Court on the ground of religious freedom, but that is exactly what the Court protects.

STEPHEN L. CARTER

NOT every legal funeral leads to a political burial. Three decades ago, the Supreme Court held that organized classroom prayer in the public schools violates the First Amendment, and today most constitutional scholars believe that school prayer is a dead issue. Yet seven out of ten Americans continue to say that they favor it, and the politicians who serve them are finding increasingly sophisticated ways of giving the public what it wants. Several states and the District of Columbia are considering measures to restore some form of school prayer, and Georgia's Representative Newt Gingrich, who is slated to become the Speaker of the House in January, has called for a vote by July 4th on a constitutional amendment that would do just that. Two weeks ago, President Bill Clinton stunned many Democrats when he suggested that a properly crafted measure might gain his support.

Even though some White House officials quickly backed away from that possibility, the school-prayer issue does not divide Democrats and Republicans in quite the way that the political posturing of recent years might suggest. Senator Jim Sasser, a Tennessee Democrat, ran a commercial touting his support of school prayer during his 1994 reëlection campaign; he lost anyhow. During this summer's Democratic mayoral-primary race in Washington, the three

candidates—liberal African-Americans all—endorsed school prayer or a moment of silence as a way of conveying values to troubled young people. Around the same time, the Clinton Administration, acting under a 1984 federal law, sided with a group of California high-school students who had been told that their prayer club could not meet during the lunch hour, when other student groups held meetings on virtually every subject under the sun; the school, the Justice Department argued in its brief, must not be allowed to "discriminate against religion," a phrase that was once a conservative patent.

The Supreme Court has remained steadfast, issuing firm edicts against a variety of forms of what could be described as school prayer no fewer than five times in the past thirty-two years. Such public-advocacy and litigation heavyweights as the American Civil Liberties Union and People for the American Way have worked to root out the practice whenever it has found fertile soil.

These battles create heroes. A Mississippi high-school principal with the marvellously ironic name of Bishop Knox is disciplined for allowing students to read a prayer over the public-address system and becomes an instant martyr. A Louisiana high-school valedictorian, told by her principal that she cannot address the graduating class on the subject

she wants—the role of Jesus Christ in her life, complete with a prayer—becomes a symbol. (When she sues, a federal magistrate explains that the school was "compelled to censor" her remarks, the sort of language that feeds the fears of some conservative evangelists, who make the astonishing claim that America has "declared war" on Christianity.)

Indeed, although classroom prayer gets the headlines—and the promises of political action—prayer at graduation is, at the moment, a hotter issue, and one that was endorsed by the President early in his term. In its 1992 decision in a case called *Lee v. Weisman*, the Supreme Court ruled that a Rhode Island public school had violated the First Amendment by allowing a rabbi to read a prayer at its commencement. The same year, however, a federal appellate court permitted what it called a "nonsectarian and nonproselytizing" prayer at a high-school graduation, as long as it was initiated by a student and approved by a majority of the graduating class. The Supreme Court declined to review that decision, leaving school authorities all over the country in a quandary, for in nearly every school district there will be those students and parents who want a graduation prayer and those who do not.

The number of young people who want organized school prayer in some form may be growing. This fall, more than a million students across the country took part in a "pray-in" around school flagpoles. Their parents seem to want prayer, too: a 1993 Gallup survey for Phi Delta Kappa, an organization of educators, revealed that eighty-two per cent of Protestants and seventy-two per cent of Roman Catholics wanted Lee v. Weisman overturned. And they may be getting what they want, even without any legislative action. More than seventy per cent of public high schools surveyed by Phi Delta Kappa in 1993 either permitted student-led prayer at formal graduations or offered seniors a baccalaureate service—that is, a graduation ceremony with prayer.

Most controversial Supreme Court decisions settle into the nation's moral and political consciousness within a few decades, as long as the Justices are steadfast. It is no longer possible, for example, to run a national electoral campaign on a promise to overturn Brown v. Board of Education, and so we forget that it was once criticized by serious politicians as the handiwork of an overreaching judiciary. The Supreme Court's decision on "one person, one vote," the focus of considerable public rage just thirty years ago, has become so much a part of the culture that most Americans seem to assume that the rule is actually laid down somewhere in the Constitution. A substantial majority of voters have even come to support at least a limited form of the abortion right proclaimed in Roe v. Wade.

But prayer is evidently different. The matter of whether children should pray in school touches some fundament of the spirit, some wellspring of emotion and commitment, that other controversial decisions have not. One need not think public-school prayer a particularly good idea (I certainly don't) in order to realize how practicing religion—and passing it on to children—might be more relevant to the day-to-day lives of tens of millions of Americans than race, abortion, and other questions we often treat as more central. Besides, as polls and casual conversation quickly reveal, most parents believe that the public schools must do more to strengthen basic values in the young. So it is perhaps not so hard to understand why, no matter how many court decisions and

public-policy arguments say that school prayer is forbidden, most Americans say that they want it.

The rejections by the courts—and the schools—almost always cite, quite properly, the principle commonly known as the separation of church and state. Indeed, that doctrine is cited so often that some religious activists have chosen it as an object of disdain, implying that, because the phrase does not appear in the Constitution, the courts must have made it up. But the "wall of separation" metaphor, which appears in the work of Roger Williams and Thomas Jefferson, has a strong footing in the First Amendment. It was developed, and must be preserved, for the protection not of the state but of religions.

THE best place to start trying to understand precisely what is wrong with classroom prayer is with the Supreme Court's original classroom-prayer decisions, for they are among the most cited and least understood pronouncements in the Court's history. The two facts most commonly misapprehended are these: first, contrary to the extravagant rhetoric of some opponents of school prayer (and the strange rhetoric of a few federal judges), the Justices have never said that prayer is bad for children or that all vestiges of religion must be banished from public schools; second, contrary to the outlandish claims of some supporters of school prayer, the Justices have never put God "out of the classroom" and have never prohibited students from praying by themselves. Furthermore, there were conservative Justices as well as liberals in the majority in the original, 1962 school-prayer case.

This last point matters, because one cannot appreciate the nuanced jurisprudence of the original school-prayer cases without recognizing that they represented a cause that many conservatives found themselves—then and now—able to support. In 1962, the Justices struck down the daily recitation of a prayer written by the New York State Board of Regents: "Almighty God, we acknowledge our dependence upon Thee, and we beg Thy blessings upon us, our parents, our teachers, and our Country." The Court was confronting a nation that had not so long before won a shoot-

ing war against forces of religious hatred and exclusion, and one that, in the civil-rights struggle, was just beginning to acknowledge the tragedy of its own history.

The nation was changing religiously as well. It is true, as supporters of school prayer point out, that American children prayed in school for most of the nation's history, but it is also true that America was less religiously diverse—or, at least, less interested in preserving its religious diversity—than it had become by the sixties. Many historians believe that the great wave of Roman Catholic and Jewish private religious schools established in this century came in direct response to a sense on the part of parents that the public schools, in the process of trying to "Americanize" the immigrant children, were also trying to "Protestantize" them. Perhaps this history is what the Court had in mind in 1963, when it struck down the practices of reciting the Lord's Prayer and reading aloud sections of the Bible for religious purposes in school, and one Justice wrote, "Today the Nation is far more heterogeneous religiously. . . . Practices which may have been objectionable to no one in the time of Jefferson and Madison may today be highly offensive to many persons, the deeply devout and the nonbelievers alike."

In each of the Supreme Court's school-prayer cases, the Justices have been trying to avoid, at the minimum, official coercion of children to be religious or endorsement by the state of particular religious practices. If the state writes a prayer, selects a prayer, approves a prayer, or (through a teacher or a principal) leads a prayer, the message that it sends to impressionable children is that it is better if they pray than if they do not. Of course, the great majority of Americans believe precisely that, and, as one conservative activist told me earlier this year, in obvious irritation, "no one is forced to pray, and nobody is harmed by prayer." As a Christian, I quite agree that prayer is not harmful; indeed, my wife and I consider it essential, and want our children to grow up surrounded by it, and partly for that reason they attend a private religious school. But what the Supreme Court has recognized, and school-prayer advocates sometimes miss, is that the ideal of religious freedom means that the state should not express a view on how anyone should pray.

THAT much is hornbook constitutional law, and few serious scholars argue with it. But legal argument alone will not cause either worried parents or committed activists to change their view. The case pressed by advocates of school prayer has basically two parts: first, that the act of praying in school will help infuse much needed positive values into the educational enterprise, and hence into the students themselves; and, second, that the opening prayer (or the increasingly popular moment of silence) can lend the school day an aura of sobriety that it otherwise lacks.

On its face, the moral argument for classroom prayer has a certain appeal. Unfortunately, school-prayer supporters overlook—or omit—some important facts. First, no reliable data support the claim that more prayer in public schools would lead to more morally upstanding children. In place of evidence, supporters offer a *post hoc, ergo propter hoc* argument: the rates of teen pregnancy, youth violence, and drug use have increased rapidly in the years since school prayer was banned, and therefore the ban must be the cause. This is reminiscent of the charming but statistically naïve point somebody came up with years ago: television viewership and lung cancer were both increasing, so one must cause the other. Second, throughout much of that often-cited period of American history in which children did pray in the public schools, we as a nation countenanced slavery, Jim Crow, lynchings, child labor, the oppression of women, and much more; that is, there are important ways in which our national morality has improved, not declined, in recent decades. To be sure, intensely religious people were in the forefront of the movements to end these and most other serious abuses and oppressions in our history. But there is no reason to suppose that they were motivated by the classroom prayers of their youth.

The argument that prayer leads to a supportive school atmosphere can perhaps be made most strongly in a setting that the news media, in the absence of violent crime to report, too frequently ignore: the inner cities. Although opponents of school prayer like to present as

the image of the movement the white-male face of the Reverend Pat Robertson (or now Newt Gingrich), surveys paint a different picture: support for classroom prayer is higher among women than among men and is stronger in the black and Hispanic communities than in the white community. And although some opponents casually and offensively dismiss these apparently unexpected supporters as dupes of the "religious right," it is surely more sensible, and more helpful, to try to figure out why this support exists.

After giving an address at a meeting of a nationwide religious organization several months ago, I was approached by two black Christians from Washington, D.C., where the murder rate exceeds that of Northern Ireland. They had heard me explain why the Supreme Court was correct to rule organized classroom prayer unconstitutional, and wanted to know what I could offer in its place: school prayer, they argued, would help children understand the solemnity of the educational enterprise and would provide a vital step toward helping young people regain the strong positive values that they needed in order to resist the lure of easy sex, easy drugs, easy guns, and easy death.

The two men were not conservatives in the usual sense, but their message was one that conservatives are comfortable with. The night before that lecture, I had met two white Christians who run an organization often identified in the press as part of the religious right. They, too, talked of prayer as helping children begin the day in a centered way—centered on important rather than frivolous things—and as a tool for inculcating positive values to help children resist the many immoral temptations of secular culture. Their organization, they said, was rapidly gaining members from the black community, especially from the inner city.

In recent years, organizations of religious conservatives have worked hard to increase their black membership. The media tend to be skeptical of their motives, and so do many black leaders, who understandably cry foul. Where were conservatives, Eleanor Holmes Norton (among others) has asked in angry rebuttal, during the struggle for basic civil rights? The answer, of course, is that

conservatives were on the wrong side of history, and this is a fact that black people are unlikely to forget. At the same time, it must be recognized that the religious activists at work among African-Americans are tapping into a genuine conservative sentiment. Walk into an inner-city Christian bookstore and run your fingers along the racks in the nonfiction section, and you may well find books by Pat Robertson right next to books by Carl Rowan. Black Americans, although they nearly always vote for liberal Democrats—for sensible historical and political reasons—are on many of our most divisive cultural issues quite conservative. To take just one example, opposition to gay rights unfortunately seems to run higher in the black community than in the nation as a whole, with many reserving special scorn for the claim that the struggle of homosexuals mirrors the struggle of African-Americans.

This cultural conservatism has deeply religious roots; it currently finds few political outlets, and, for the historical reasons cited by Norton, it is unlikely to find one among the activists of conservative Christianity. Yet even if one disputes, as I do, most of the particular political conclusions that this conservative strain among African-Americans would dictate, one must recognize its reality. It represents the voice of a community crying out desperately for a stable set of values to pass on to the next generation, which is seriously at risk; among black Christians, as among evangelicals generally, there are few moral relativists.

None of this should come as a surprise. Any other group with the religious demography of black America—overwhelmingly Protestant, and, within Protestantism, heavily evangelical and deeply imbued with the spirit of Biblical literalism—would be expected to come out strongly for classroom prayer, and most of them have.

AFRICAN-AMERICAN parents are not alone in believing that school prayer will help their children learn a better set of values. Indeed, public-school parents as a group are more supportive of school prayer than private-school parents. The fact that the Supreme Court has necessarily turned a deaf ear to their appeals may help explain why increasing numbers of parents seem inclined to opt out of the public-school system altogether: roughly twelve per cent of the nation's fifty million schoolchildren attend private schools. More than half of the nation's public-school parents say they would send their children to private school if they could afford it, and most of those parents would probably choose a religious school.

But alternatives to public school are often expensive, and, with private-school-voucher programs defeated wherever they've been put on the ballot, parents who believe that religion is necessary to set the proper moral tone in public schools are pressing a variety of other proposals, which include providing instruction in the role of religion in American history and life, excusing students from classes (especially sex-education classes) to which their parents have religious objections, and regulating the curriculum. The most prominent example of this last proposal involves the teaching of the theory of evolution, which some states banned for decades, on the ground that it interfered with the effort by parents to teach their children the Biblical version of creation. The Supreme Court struck down those restrictions in 1968, but some states responded by mandating the teaching of what has come to be called "scientific creationism"—the presentation of scientific evidence in support of the concept of a deliberate creation. In 1987, the Justices put a stop to that, too. As each effort to control what goes on in the public schools fails, worried parents and the activists who support them keep coming back to classroom prayer.

Still, the trend is not all one way. In 1984, Congress passed the Equal Access Act, which requires public schools to grant student religious groups the same meeting privileges that they grant to others. The Supreme Court sustained the constitutionality of the act in 1990. An increasingly popular way of making an end run around all the school-prayer cases is to require children to open the school day by sharing a moment of silence, which could be used for meditation or prayer, or even a quick nap. President Clinton has explicitly endorsed the idea, even though in 1985

the Supreme Court upheld a federal appellate-court ruling that struck down an Alabama law allowing teachers to require a moment of silence, "for meditation or voluntary prayer," in the state's public schools. The Justices reasoned that the law endorsed religion as a "favored practice." But the Court, by resting its decision on the presence of the word "prayer" in a law, badly misapprehended its own jurisprudence on prayer in public schools. The evil that the original school-prayer decisions sought to avoid was not prayer or religion but government endorsement of particular religious practices.

The Court's implicit conclusion that the rights of some children are violated when children who want to pray silently are given an opportunity to do so puts one in mind of a famous story about Aron Nimzowitsch, the Baltic chess genius of the early twentieth century. In 1927, he sat down at an important tournament to play a game against the Slovenian master Milan Vidmar, who immediately lit up a cigar. Distracted by the fumes, Nimzowitsch complained to the tournament director, who asked Vidmar to put the cigar out. Vidmar good-naturedly did so, and the game resumed.

A few minutes later, Nimzowitsch stood once more before the puzzled tournament director. "Your opponent isn't smoking," the official pointed out.

"Yes, I know," Nimzowitsch said, "but he looks as if he wants to!"

OF course, when conservative activists call for classroom prayer, they have in mind nothing as neutral as a moment of silent reflection. But—assuming that no constitutional amendment is actually forthcoming—the movement must still reckon with the Supreme Court, which just last June, in the case of Board of Education of Kiryas Joel v. Grumet, issued another stern warning about mixing religion and public education. In Grumet, the Justices struck down the law under which the school district of Kiryas Joel was created. The village, situated about fifty-five miles north of New York City, is inhabited only by Satmar Hasidim. Nearly all the community's children attend private religious schools, where they learn to follow the strict rules of their faith. Kiryas Joel operates only a single public

school, which serves about two hundred special-education students. According to the Justices, the very existence of the Kiryas Joel school district was a special favor that the State Legislature had bestowed upon a religious group. The evidence was in the village's demographics.

The residents of Kiryas Joel had sought their own district in 1989, a few years after the adjoining local district, citing constitutional concerns, stopped sending publicly paid special-education instructors into the private religious schools; a brief experiment of sending the special-education students to nearby public schools ended when the children suffered what parents called "panic, fear, and trauma." But the Court was not persuaded. "The fundamental source of constitutional concern here," Justice David Souter wrote for the majority, "is that the legislature itself may fail to exercise governmental authority in a religiously neutral way." In other words, special treatment for the Satmar community (as the Court designated it) might grant one religious group a special privilege that others, religious and non-religious, were denied.

Of course, one might quarrel with the notion that the special accommodation for the Satmar constituted a threat to the religious freedom of others. One might point out, as the Stanford law professor Kathleen M. Sullivan has done, that, once one moves beyond our urban areas, the nation is full of religiously homogeneous school districts; presumably, children do not make fun of the accents or traditions or clothing of other children in such districts. It is difficult to imagine, moreover, that the Satmar Hasidim really are the special favorites of the law. But, once one accepts the majority's characterization of the facts (the dissent, naturally, had a different view), acceptance of the decision becomes quite easy. The message to worried parents seems to be that the Court will not look kindly on efforts to infuse public education with religious values.

BUT is that the only way to look at the villagers of Kiryas Joel—as a religious group that obtained a special favor from the state? A community's desire to preserve its values and traditions, even if they have a religious base, is not obviously the same as the desire to promote their religion. In other words, the people of Kiryas Joel could have had many concerns other than religious chauvinism to explain their desire to control the atmosphere in which their children would learn. And in this they would have been like most of the nation's parents.

The simple truth is that millions of parents, of all races, creeds, and economic strata, want their children's education to reflect the deep religiosity that permeates their own lives. One need not agree that prayer is the answer—again, there are no reliable data in support of the claim—in order to understand and share the concern that children learn strong, positive values, and also to recognize the commonalities between the black parents in Washington who demand classroom prayer and the Hasidic parents in Kiryas Joel who demand a safe and nurturing public school for their children. Both sets of parents want to send their children to schools that reinforce the moral teachings they offer at home instead of trivializing, ignoring, or actually opposing them.

In a community without religious dissenters, school prayer might actually work. One can readily imagine tiny, religiously homogeneous communities, perhaps along the Bible Belt or in the vast spaces of the West, in which the schools *do* reinforce the values that the parents teach, and prayer *is* a part of the school day, and nobody sues, because nobody minds. But the number of such communities must be vanishingly small, and the message of the Supreme Court's Kiryas Joel decision is that the state cannot intentionally create one.

Some culturally distinctive groups have indeed been preserved, such as the Old Order Amish, whose tightly knit communities, largely devoid of modern technology, are mainly found in Pennsylvania and several Midwestern states. In its 1972 decision in a case called Wisconsin v. Yoder, the Supreme Court ruled that the Amish may keep their children home from school after the eighth grade, in defiance of compulsory-attendance laws that the state applies to everybody else—a type of ruling that is called in the legal parlance an "accommodation" of religious beliefs. Without

that parental freedom, the Amish way of life would likely have collapsed. But, as the Justices seemed to recognize, the Amish hold a peculiar place in American iconography: they are viewed less as a religious group than as a tourist attraction. "The Amish community has been a highly successful social unit within our society," the Court wrote, "even if apart from the conventional 'mainstream.'" The Amish, according to the Justices, prefer "informal learning-through-doing [and] wisdom, rather than technical knowledge; community welfare, rather than competition," and their children need just enough education "to read the Bible" and "to be good farmers and citizens." Reading Yoder today, the word "quaint" comes constantly to mind. And, indeed, when one travels through what has come to be called Pennsylvania Dutch country, and stops for ice cream at a shop where non-Amish teenagers behind the counter dress in cheap, kitschy imitations of the determinedly plain Amish garb, one sees the ultimate in trivialization of a religious community. The State of Pennsylvania might as well erect a sign: "Welcome to Amishland."

But that, perhaps, is the risk that a community accepts when it struggles hard to build a nurturing world for its children by preserving its differences from the mainstream. The separateness of the Amish community must have been the key to the Court's decision, because just about every other group that has sought a similar freedom since then has lost. The parents of Kiryas Joel, hoping to turn the tide, sought similar freedom and were evidently prepared to make a similar sacrifice. (One suspects that most Americans find the Hasidim as peculiar as they do the Amish.) This, however, the Justices would not allow. Indeed, now that the Satmar Hasidim of Kiryas Joel have lost their case, one has to wonder whether Yoder would be decided the same way today.

Many liberals cheered the Kiryas Joel decision as a paean to the cherished separation of church and state, but several religious organizations, concerned about preserving the ability of parents to bring up their children to follow religious rather than secular rules, were crushingly disappointed. It was left, oddly, to the conservative polemicist and

sometime political candidate Patrick Buchanan to point to the contemporary liberal ideal of diversity, which so often seems to vanish when the issue is religion. "What, after all, is America all about, if not the freedom of people to be different?" Buchanan demanded in his syndicated column. Certainly it is true that the nation's culture is a composite of America's rich variety of variously assimilated groups, and although it is becoming increasingly hard for groups who wish to preserve their distinctiveness to do so, accomplishing that feat can be vital if they want to pass down traditions to their children. And children, it is often said, are precisely who one has religion for.

But the issue of teaching children is one in which cultural differences seem to be accorded less respect than in almost any other sphere. Perhaps the widespread demand for prayer in the public schools is best viewed as a metaphor for the same need that the Amish and the villagers of Kiryas Joel are seeking to fulfill: the desire to preserve for their children a core set of values and traditions in an increasingly complex and, to many religious parents, an increasingly hostile culture.

Small wonder that such sentiment is especially widespread among African-American parents, for although all children in America face risks and temptations that their parents did not, the calamities befalling young people in the inner cities are particularly acute. When the leading mayoral candidates in Washington call for prayer or moments of silence, this desire to instill values is surely the sentiment they are tapping. Many parental objections to the school curriculum can be viewed in the same way. "It doesn't seem right that the objection of one child should be able to stop everybody else from praying," one Christian activist said to me. She went on to compare prayer with sex education: why, then, she asked, shouldn't the objection of one child be able to stop everybody else from studying homosexuality as an alternative life style?

Classroom prayer, of course, is banned by the First Amendment, not by one child's objection. But a religious parent's objection should be sufficient to excuse her child from learning subjects, whether sex education or evolution or an American history from which religion is absent; otherwise, the schools will play into the hands of those religious conservatives who argue that the implicit message of contemporary public education is that religion is not important, whereas these other matters—biology, sex education—are.

Here, again, what links concerns about prayer to concerns about sex education (and other parts of the curriculum) may be less a desire for schools that teach the parents' religion than a yearning for schools that teach the parents' values. This, in turn, suggests that the way for educators to deal seriously with the concerns of parents without introducing religious indoctrination in the public schools is to find ways of putting explicit instruction in values—in right and wrong—into the curriculum. In this way, worried parents might come to see the schools as their allies rather than their enemies in the project of the moral education of their children.

But will we be able to find values to agree on? Surprisingly, the evidence is that we can. According to a 1993 Gallup survey, more than ninety per cent of American adults believe that the public schools should teach honesty, racial tolerance, belief in democracy, and the Golden Rule. Two-thirds believe that the curriculum should preach sexual abstinence outside marriage. So, even though we as a nation quite famously have trouble agreeing on some issues, there are basic values on which there is a broad consensus. The idea of using the

public schools as tools to educate for good character frightens many activists on the right and the left alike, since each side is desperately afraid that the other side would turn out to have more votes. But reinforcing strong, positive values need not mean immersing grade-school children in every contemporary controversy, and although many an interest group would have a curricular wish list, such wishes, in general, should not be granted. Education for values should stick to the points where the society has reached consensus; otherwise, when religious (or nonreligious) parents complain that the schools are trying to wean their children from them they will be right.

The idea of explicit education in morality in the public schools has the support of such figures as William Bennett, on the right, and such groups as People for the American Way, on the left. Several publishers are preparing textbooks, betting that the increasing public support will lead to curricular changes. And, despite the worries of some activists, nobody denies that the public schools are already in the values-teaching business: the only question is whether to make rigorous and explicit what is now often hazy and indirect. The teaching of shared values in the public schools might even draw the teeth of the school-prayer movement, for it would accomplish what the great majority of the parents who support that movement seem to want most, without abandoning the precious separation of church and state.

As for the villagers of Kiryas Joel, the New York Legislature worked

out a response that would allow any autonomous village fulfilling certain requirements to establish a school district of its own—a possibility that Justice Sandra Day O'Connor pointed to in her very sensible concurring opinion on Grumet. The Satmar Hasidim would qualify, but so would other groups; religiosity would not be required. The response could, of course, still face legal challenge, and if it is struck down—one hopes that the courts will show better sense—another is available: the state could decide to allow special-education teachers paid with state funds to teach at parochial schools, exactly what it allowed before all the controversy. O'Connor correctly pointed out that nothing about the practice offends the Constitution: "If the government provides this education on-site at public schools and at nonsectarian private schools, it is only fair that it provide it on-site at sectarian schools as well."

Compromises of this kind would protect the Satmar Hasidim in their effort to rear their children in accordance with their values and traditions. But that is probably as far as a respect for religious freedom allows the schools to go. So it may be time for the seventy per cent or so of American adults who support classroom prayer to heed the remarks of Queen Elizabeth II, who commented during the celebration of America's bicentennial on what Britain learned from the Revolutionary War: it is important to know, Her Majesty said, "the right time, and the manner, of yielding that which it is impossible to keep."

Structures of American Politics

- The Presidency (Articles 21–26)
- Congress (Articles 27–30)
- Judiciary (Articles 31–35)
- Bureaucracy (Articles 36–39)

James Madison, one of the primary architects of the American system of government, observed that the three-branch structure of government created at the Constitutional Convention of 1787 pitted the ambitions of some individuals against the ambitions of others. Nearly 2 centuries later, contemporary political scientist Richard Neustadt wrote that the structure of American national government is one of "separated" institutions sharing powers. These two eminent

students of American politics suggest an important proposition: the very design of American national government contributes to the struggles that occur among government officials who have different institutional loyalties and potentially competing goals.

This unit is divided into four sections. The first three treat the three traditional branches of American government and the last one treats the bureaucracy. One point to remember when studying these institutions is that the Constitution provides only the barest skeleton of the workings of the American political system. The flesh and blood of the presidency, Congress, judiciary, and bureaucracy, are derived from decades of experience and the shared expectations of today's political actors. A second point to keep in mind is that the way a particular institution functions is partly determined by those who occupy relevant offices. The presidency operates differently with Bill Clinton in the White House than it did when George Bush was president. Similarly, Congress and the Supreme Court also operate differently, according to who are serving as members and who hold leadership positions within the institutions. There have been significant changes in the House of Representatives since Republican Newt Gingrich succeeded Democrat Tom Foley as Speaker of the House in 1995, and somewhat lesser changes in the Senate since Trent Lott replaced fellow Republican Bob Dole as majority leader in mid-1996.

The first section contains articles on the presidency. After 12 straight years of Republican presidents (Ronald Reagan and George Bush), Democrat Bill Clinton assumed the presidency in 1993. For the first 2 years of his presidency, the Democrats also held a majority of seats in the House of Representatives and Senate. But in the 1994 and 1996 congressional elections, Republicans won control of the House and Senate, a development that has led to changes in the way Clinton has functioned as president. An important point to remember is that neither the presidency nor any other institution operates in isolation from the other institutions of American national government.

The second section addresses Congress. The legislative branch underwent substantial changes in recent decades under mostly Democratic control. Reforms to the seniority system and the budgetary process in the 1970s brought an unprecedented degree of decentralization and, some would say, chaos to Capitol Hill. In addition, during the 1970s and 1980s both the number of staff and special-interest caucuses in Congress increased. The Republican takeover of the House of Representatives as a result of the November 1994 elections has brought even more changes to that body. Compared with his Democratic predecessors of the past few decades, Republican Speaker Newt Gingrich has consolidated power within the House and become a prominent figure on the national scene. Whether these developments will raise the American public's low appraisal of Congress as an institution remains to be seen.

The Supreme Court sits at the top of the court system and is the main topic of the third section on the structures of American politics. The Court is not merely a legal institution; it is a policymaker whose decisions can affect the lives of millions of citizens. Like all people in high government offices, Supreme Court justices have policy views of their own, and observers of the Court pay careful attention to the way the nine justices interact with one another in shaping decisions of the Court.

The bureaucracy of the national government, the subject of the fourth and last section in this unit, is responsible for carrying out policies determined by top-ranking officials. The bureaucracy is not merely a neutral administrative instrument, and bureaucratic waste and inefficiency often seem excessive. On the other hand, government bureaucracies also share credit for many of the accomplishments of American government. Most presidents claim that they will make the bureaucracy perform more efficiently, and President Clinton is no exception in this regard. Vice President Al Gore's National Performance Review of the federal bureaucracy is one of the subjects treated in the fourth section of this unit.

For many readers, the selections in this unit will probably rank among the most enjoyable in the book. Not surprisingly, most of us are more comfortable on familiar territory, and the separate branches of government are likely to be familiar from earlier study in school or from media coverage of politics. Nevertheless, the selections in this unit should provide additional and more sophisticated insights into how the institutions of American national government actually work.

Looking Ahead: Challenge Questions

Read Articles I, II, and III of the United States Constitution to get a picture of the legislative, executive, and judicial branches as intended by the words of the Founding Fathers. How does that picture compare with the reality of the three branches as they operate today?

How might the presidency and Congress change in the next 100 years?

What advantages and disadvantages do each of the following have for getting things done: The president? The vice president? A cabinet member? The Speaker of the House of Representatives? The Senate majority leader? The chief justice? A top-ranking bureaucrat in an executive branch agency? A congressional aide?

Which position in American government would you most like to hold? Why?

Do you think George Bush was a successful president in getting things done? A *good* president? Why, or why not? Similarly, what is your evaluation of Bill Clinton?

Do you think it makes sense for a president to emphasize economic and domestic concerns over foreign policy, as Bill Clinton promised during his 1992 campaign?

How well do you think Congressman Newt Gingrich and Senator Trent Lott have performed as Speaker of the House of Representatives and majority leader of the Senate, respectively?

Do We Ask Too Much of PRESIDENTS?

BURT SOLOMON

ichard M. Nixon is dead. Jacqueline Kennedy Onassis is dead. George W. Ball is dead. A generation of American leaders is passing, as another has arrived. A generation that was forged in the clarity of World War II is being supplanted by one that was molded by the muddled lessons of the war in Vietnam.

Twenty-five years ago, when *National Journal* entered the scene, Nixon had just taken office and the world—in many ways—was a harsher but a clearer place. As the pages of this silver anniversary issue will attest, a lot has happened since then. The nation's demographics have shifted, its economic dynamics have been rearranged and its political processes are nastier and less forgiving than they were. The nation has become a harder place to govern than it used to be. It isn't likely to get any easier.

If evidence is needed, consider the past quarter-century's string of failed Presidents. Franklin D. Roosevelt, Harry S Truman and Dwight D. Eisenhower served seven terms, all told, and by most measures proved successful Presidents. It took twice as many Presidents to serve out the next seven terms—and that doesn't even count the two since.

Neither the voters nor the historians have been wowed. Only Ronald Reagan, who stuck to his guns and persuaded the public to accept his version of reality, was permitted to serve out a second term. But historians rank him between Zachary Taylor and John Tyler as below-average Presidents, according to Tim H. Blessing, a co-author of *Greatness in the White House: Rating the Presidents From George Washington Through Ronald Reagan* (Pennsylvania State University Press, 1994). The five or six Presidents who preceded the most recent five or six "will rank much higher in the verdicts of history," retired Williams College professor James M. Burns, a noted political historian, predicted.

This isn't the first time the country has suffered a run of mediocre Presidents. From the 1840s to the 1890s, only Abraham Lincoln was an obvious success. And even he had "the good luck to get himself shot," Blessing, an American history professor at Alvernia College in Reading, Pa., said in an interview. "The problem of Reconstruction was probably unresolvable."

WHEN TALENT'S NOT ENOUGH

One school of thought is that America has encountered a run of bad luck. "Basically coincidence," Everett Carll Ladd, the president of the Roper Center for Public Opinion Research Inc. at the University of Connecticut (Storrs), said of the succession of Presidents who've been found wanting. He portrayed Nixon as psychologically unsuited, Gerald R. Ford as an accident, Jimmy Carter as untested, George Bush as inattentive to the public's economic anxieties and Bill Clinton as "poorly situated" because of deficiencies in character.

But more likely, the problem hasn't been them so much as us. The particulars of the individuals who've entered the White House have paled beside the increasing demands that the public has piled on them. "There's been a lot of cranking up of expectations," Fred I. Greenstein, an expert on the presidency at Princeton University, said. Problems are expected to be solved overnight. Stephen J. Wayne, a presidential scholar at Georgetown University, reasoned that the complexity of government, along with "the recognition that certain problems are too big not to have government involvement," have combined to push more and more of the nation's troubles onto the President's desk.

Recent Presidents, by and large, have been politically and intellectually talented men. But that isn't enough anymore. "Flexible, pragmatic, capable of compromise—also firm, decisive, principled," Hedley Donovan, who'd been a White House counselor to Carter, wrote in *Time* magazine in 1982, listing 31 attributes that a President needs. "To be a 'good' President in the 1980s," he wrote, "may be even harder than to be a

Reagan served a full eight years . . .

. . . But Carter was denied reelection . . .

'great' President in the days of Antietam or Pearl Harbor."

And the criteria by which Presidents are judged—and damned—keep proliferating. Presidents must also be telegenically talented, delicately balanced in personality and pristine in private life. Thomas Jefferson, with his squeaky voice and his Deist beliefs, probably couldn't succeed in politics now. Lincoln, so prone to melancholia that he supposedly wouldn't carry a penknife, might not be trusted with his finger on the button. The wealthy FDR might be prey to a nanny problem.

More than ever, interest groups want what they want and will fight to get it, meaning that a President must mobilize unwieldy coalitions to get things done. This political task has been made harder by the social fragmentation that has turned communities with common interests—in the United States, as in the rest of the world—into competing enclaves. The political parties, internally torn, are unreliable as sources of support for an embattled President. (Ask Bush.) James David Barber of Duke University, a specialist in the presidency, noted that a President faces so many different pressures nowadays that he can't satisfy them all.

TRYING TIMES

A lot else about the times has conspired to ruin presidency after presidency. Recent Presidents haven't been fortunate in the nature of the national afflictions they've faced. "All the problems tend to run together," Henry F. Graff, a retired professor of history at Columbia University, noted. They may not be as critical as a war or an economic depression. But that only deprives the President of the extra authority and moral certitude that urgency brings. Witness the current debate over health care, which has the White House proclaiming a crisis and its opposition denying it. "The more severe the problem," Georgetown's Wayne noted, "the easier it is for a President to deal with it."

It's always been hard to govern, but now it's "super-difficult," Burns said. "Government is just much more difficult today than it used to be."

At best, technology has proved a mixed political blessing. Television, on balance, has probably bolstered presidential power. (It did for Reagan.) But having so much of what a President says stored on tape—audio or video—contributed to Nixon's downfall and has undermined his successors' chances of denying their promises and screwups. Since the Watergate scandal, when investigative reporters became the journalistic elite, the press has been prone to build up Presidents

and then tear them down—a good story both times.

The advent of the media age has also turned the President into a celebrity. Stardom is tempting for a President, especially one who feels underappreciated—that is, all of them. But it's dangerous. By making Presidents so familiar, television has helped to relieve the office of its mystique. Had the public known that FDR was crippled, it would have "made him a less dramatic figure," A. James Reichley, the author of a recent book on political parties, said. He noted that the press at the time felt obliged to sustain the stature of the presidency.

Presidents have ushered the process along. Carter carried his own garment bag as part of his political strategy in reaction to Nixon's imperial pretensions. Ford toasted English muffins. Clinton, with his penchant for Big Macs and his willingness to describe his underwear, has further shrunk the President into Everyman. The recent discussion in public about Clinton's genitals smacked of the earlier talk about Michael Jackson's and may have evoked as uncomfortable a public response. No longer do Presidents grow to fit the job; they've started to seem smaller than life just as the electorate's standards have inflated.

It's no wonder that the distrust of government—and of all institutions—has climbed so much. Candidates promise more and more to get elected and seem like hypocrites all the faster when they don't deliver. The pessimism of an increasingly cynical electorate has become self-fulfilling. If people expect a one-term President, Burns said, "the prospect of presidential authority evaporates."

There's precious little reason to think that these dynamics will turn around any time soon. Expectations that the White House should try to fix whatever ails the nation aren't likely to diminish much if at all. The public's titillation with the President's personal life and its eagerness to cast judgments aren't likely to fade. The conundrums that the country faces at home and abroad aren't about to get any simpler or more susceptible to being managed one at a time. A long period of prosperity might suffice to prompt voters to ease up on their leaders, but that won't happen in a hurry.

Neither Clinton nor his successors during the next quarter-century, that is, have any reason to expect an easy time of it. "We'll continue to have vexed presidencies," Columbia's Graff prophesied. Their surest hope for success may depend on the problems they face getting worse. That way, at least, they might be given a shovel worthy of the hole they're in. History shows that it takes a great crisis, after all, to make a great leader.

. . . And Bush was similarly rejected.

Which predecessor will Clinton emulate?

Photos by Richard A. Bloom

The Separated System*

Charles O. Jones

Charles O. Jones is Hawkins Professor of Political Science, University of Wisconsin–Madison. A former president of the American Political Science Association, he is author of The Presidency in a Separated System. *In the fall 1995 he delivered the Rothbaum Lectures on Representative Government at the University of Oklahoma.*

Shortly after his inauguration, President Bill Clinton reiterated an extravagant campaign promise, accompanied by a dramatic announcement:

> As a first step in responding to the demands of literally millions of Americans, today I am announcing the formation of the President's Task Force on National Health Reform. Although the issue is complex, the task force's mission is simple: Build on the work of the campaign and the transition, listen to all parties, and prepare health care reform legislation to be submitted to Congress *within 100 days of our taking office.* This task force will be chaired by the First Lady, Hillary Rodham Clinton.

The effect was to draw accountability clearly and unmistakably to the White House, indeed, into the residence itself. The president and his partner by marriage would be held directly accountable for what happened. Yet as political scientist Hugh Heclo observed, "Never in the modern history of major social reform efforts had a president with so few political resources tried to do so much."

Ours is not a unified political and governmental system. Setting ambitious goals, promising swift action, and assuming complete management for dramatic change, taken together, represent a huge political gamble for a leader in a government of truly separated institutions. To do so having won 43 percent of the popular vote is surely an instance of derring-do. By drawing accountability to himself, Clinton accentuated a problem inherent in a separated system. A prime challenge to presidents is to manage the often-lavish expectations of their accountability under conditions of distributed power. A necessary background for my assessment of the Clinton presidency, therefore, is an understanding of the diffused accountability inherent in our system.

Accountability in a Separated System

Though a government of separated institutions sharing or competing for powers has many virtues, *focused responsibility is not one of them*. Accountability is highly diffused by dint of the dispersal that is characteristic of separationism. And though some observers argue that to have accountability everywhere is to have it nowhere, that is not so. A system like ours has substantial *individual accountability* but limited *collective accountability*. The reasons why are clear enough to those familiar with constitutional history.

Operationally, formal accountability for presidents is primarily rhetorical. Presidents speak of representing the public. The media often act as enforcers, holding presidents accountable to an inexact public-interest standard. Presidents are held answerable for actions within the government, and yet the precise manner of holding them to account is rather indistinct. This real-

---

*Forum essays are slightly revised versions used by permission from the Spring 1996 issue of *Extensions*, a copyrighted publication of the Carl Albert Congressional Research and Studies Center, University of Oklahoma. Charles O. Jones's essay is a version of his discourse in the 1995 Julian J. Rothbaum Distinguished Lecture in Representative Government.

ity is central to the governing strategy of modern presidents. They should be aware that they will be held responsible for that over which they have only limited control. At the very least, they must avoid contributing further to this tendency by guaranteeing grand results.

In brief, the White House cannot depend for support on what happened in the last election but must account for how the members' policy preferences relate to the next election. The president must develop and redevelop policy strategies that acknowledge the ever-shifting coalitional base. Serious and continuous in-party and cross-party coalition building thus typifies policy making in the separated system.

The defining challenge for a new president is to capitalize on his freshness without elevating further the lofty expectations of his position. The president is well advised to resist the efforts by others, or himself, to assign him the heady charge of being the commander of government.

Managing High Expectations

Imagine that the fires of ambition burn so strongly that sleep is your enemy. Success by most measures comes easily, but it does not provide solace. The need to do more is all-consuming. There is no reward great enough; an obstacle overcome is less valued than the identification of a new challenge.

Conceive, if you can, the challenge involved in making everyone happy, then in getting credit for having done so and you will understand why there is little time or patience for sleep. Meet Bill Clinton, "first in his class"; bound to be president.

Bill Clinton's ambition is for a kind of greatness that is defined by approval. He wants to do good things for many people. He is a talker, engaged in a gamelike process of exploration. As such, he is puzzled by listeners who hear the talk as commitment. Talkers find satisfaction in the immediate response. They are unlikely to make a strong distinction between campaigning and governing. Nor are they likely to be intrigued by the intricacies of the lawmaking process. Bill Clinton is the quintessential campaigner as president. He most assuredly is not a lawmaker president in the Lyndon Johnson mold; had he been so, he may have had a more successful first two years. What follows, then, is a description and analysis of a presidency increasingly at risk, one persistently "on the edge," as Elizabeth Drew entitled her book on the Clinton administration, yet one prepared as few have been to seek reelection.

The 1992 campaign and election were bound to encourage a parliamentary-style accounting. A new-generation Democrat won after twelve years of Republican dominance of the White House. He promised to work hardest at economic recovery, as well as acting on a number of other issues generally acknowledged to form the contemporary agenda. One party would now be in charge of both ends of Pennsylvania Avenue. The gridlock that was presumed by many to have prevented the proper functioning of government was judged to be over.

Additionally, there was the sheer energy and excitement conveyed by the youthful Clinton-Gore team. It would require a substantial degree of self-discipline to ensure that postelection enthusiasm did not overreach and contribute to inflated expectations as to what could be achieved by the 103rd Congress.

Bill Clinton's ambition is for a kind of greatness that is defined by approval. He wants to do good things for many people.

Contributing to high expectations were political analysts, especially those who adhere to the perspective on national elections that I term "unitarian" (as opposed to "separationist"). At root, the unitarians disagree with the separation of powers concept. They propose reforms designed to ensure one-party government so as to achieve collective accountability. For the unitarian the best possible election result is that in which one political party wins the White House and majority control of both houses of Congress. That party is then expected to display unity on policy issues and to produce a record for which it can be held responsible at the next election. Though I cannot produce an exact count, I would wager that most political analysts are unitarians.

In contrast, the general voting public and most members of Congress are practicing "separationists." For the separationist the best possible election result is one that reinforces the legitimacy of independent participation by each branch. Party leaders, including presidents, are then expected to build cross-partisan support within and between the elected branches whether or not one party has majorities in Congress and a president in the White House. A separationist perspective of the 1992 election would have stressed the rejection of George Bush without identifying a mandate for Clinton. By this view, voters continued to split their tickets, albeit in new and interesting ways, making it difficult to spot a "mandate."

Evidence for this separationist interpretation abounds. There is the substantial vote garnered by Ross Perot, the most for an independent or third-party candidate since

Theodore Roosevelt ran in 1912. A president won in a three-way contest by designating a credible agenda and projecting a sufficiently moderate policy posture as to be reassuring to just over half of the Ronald Reagan (1984) and Bush (1988) voters who were disillusioned with the Bush presidency. Clinton's campaign strategy was, by William Schneider's view, to "convince middle-class voters that Democrats could work within the Reagan-Bush consensus." Moreover, House Republicans had a net gain of ten seats and received 46 percent of the national vote for the House, compared to Bush's 37 percent of the national vote for president.

Perhaps most stunning as a measure of political mismanagement was the fact that by raising expectations, inviting responsibility, and yet failing to produce, the president and his leaders in Congress deflected criticism of Republicans for having obstructed much of the president's legislative program.

It follows from these assertions that a partisan, unitarian approach was unlikely to succeed. Yet that is the approach Clinton employed. Not only that, but Clinton's activist style drew accountability to himself. A book of promises, entitled *Putting People First*, was published during the campaign; it was bound to raise hopes while defining awesome challenges and providing a scorecard for the media. In reading from this text of pledges, little was to be left untouched by a Clinton-Gore administration—it included 35 proposals for the "national economic strategy" and 577 proposals for "other crucial issues."

Lacking was an understanding of how ours is truly the most elaborated lawmaking system in the world. It does not submit to enthusiasm alone. Effective leadership starts with knowing how the system works. The 1992 election produced exceptionally challenging conditions for lawmaking, requiring extraordinarily sensitive strategies for producing cross-party majorities on Capitol Hill. Bill Clinton lacked the skills for devising these strategies and therefore had to learn them or, like Reagan, rely on those who did have that competence.

It is with the understanding of the centrist underpinnings of Clinton's electoral and preinaugural support that one comes to understand the problems the new president faced during the first two years of his presidency. For the actions that could be taken early in order to demonstrate momentum—executive orders regarding abortions performed in military hospitals, federal funding of fetal tissue transplant research, the importation of abortion pill RU-486, and ending the ban on gays in the military—were likely to project a substantially more liberal cast than could be justified by public opinion as expressed either in the election or in subsequent polls.

Moreover, actions that were more moderate-to-conservative in nature—reducing the federal workforce, terminating advisory committees, seeking to make government more efficient—were overshadowed at the start by the more liberal actions cited above. Why? They were noncontroversial, not newsworthy, and therefore unavailable as ballast to the liberal tilt on controversial issues.

As if these developments were not sufficient to ensure Republican unity, Democrats in the House of Representatives used the rules of that chamber to prevent Republicans from effective participation in the amending process. Senate Republicans were in a substantially stronger position than their colleagues in the House due to the fact that they had sufficient numbers to prevent the closing of debates, an advantage used early against the president's economic stimulus package and late in 1994 to kill much of the president's program.

With all of these problems and miscalculations, Clinton's first year was moderately productive under contentious political circumstances in which partisan lines hardened substantially. Several bills vetoed by Bush were passed again and signed by the president, a deficit-reduction package was enacted by Vice President Gore's tie-breaking vote in the Senate and two votes in the House, NAFTA was approved with the crucial support of Republicans, and the president got a modified version of his National Service Program.

However, many of the most contentious issues were carried over to the second session. As a result, the second year was among the least productive of major legislation in the post–World War II period. Of the ten presidential priorities mentioned in the State of the Union Message, four became law—the GATT (again with Republican support in a special session), Goals 2000, an anticrime package, and community development loans. Each was important, but none was as important for the president as the proposal to reform the health care system—a matter that dominated the politics of the year. "We will make history by reforming the health-care system," was the president's promise in his January 1994 State of the Union Address. Yet by September 26, 1994, Senate Majority Leader George Mitchell had issued the last rites.

Perhaps most stunning as a measure of political mismanagement was the fact that by raising expectations, inviting responsibility, and yet failing to produce, the president and his leaders in Congress deflected criticism of Republicans for having obstructed much of the president's legislative program. As was noted in a *New York Times* editorial, Republican cooperation "was never part of the original promise." Democratic leaders had informed the president that they could deliver without Republican support. Republicans were content to be excluded. In the end it permitted them to avoid the accountability that was solicited by the administration.

Clinton's personal strengths are many. He is a superb campaigner—an effective and empathetic communicator with the public and a man with an "upbeat personality." He is, unquestionably, highly intelligent, possessed of an extraordinary capacity to identify and explore public policy issues. We also know from David Maraniss's fine biography, *First in His Class*, that he knows how to cram for an exam—a characteristic displayed in playing his role in lawmaking, as he often waits to the last minute to engage the issue to the extent of making a choice.

The Midterm Earthquake

But Bill Clinton also has a number of weaknesses. He had never held a position in the federal government. While governor, he worked with a Democratic legislature, seldom having to take Republicans into account or to display the kind of lawmaking prowess of a governor from a state with a more competitive two-party government. As with most governors, he lacked direct experience in foreign and national security policy. He is an admitted "policy talk wonk" who finds it difficult to concentrate on a limited agenda. And there is ample evidence that Bill Clinton lacks direct experience in forming and accommodating to an effective staff. Clinton's strengths are more intellectual than managerial.

Moreover, instead of compensating for his weaknesses, Clinton preferred to capitalize on his strengths. He sought to govern by campaigning, not lawmaking, virtually melding the two in his own mind and in his behavior. In his first two years the president visited 194 places, making 264 appearances (excluding foreign travel, visits to Arkansas, and vacations). Bill Clinton is the most traveled president in history, exceeding even President George Bush. One effect was to reinforce the distorted view of the president as the government, with the effect of holding him accountable for what is and has ever been a separated system of diffused accountability. As a consequence, Bill

Clinton became a major issue in the midterm election. The result was to produce a very different presidency for his second two years in office.

Bill Clinton has a number of weaknesses. He had never held a position in the federal government. While governor, he worked with a Democratic legislature, seldom having to take Republicans into account or to display the kind of lawmaking prowess of a governor from a state with a more competitive two-party government.

It is standard wisdom that congressional elections are state and local events, albeit with important national effects. In 1994, however, there were two bids to nationalize the midterm elections: one by the president, who seemingly could not resist joining the fray, and one by Newt Gingrich, the House Republican Leader in waiting, who had national, crusadelike ambitions.

As the election approached, the president might well have followed the advice given Harry Truman by the Democratic National Committee Chairman in 1946—that is, stay out of midterm politics! Truman, whose standing in the polls was at 40 percent, accepted this advice. "He kept silent on politics." Few, if any, Democratic candidates invoked his name.

Clinton was in a similar situation, with approximately the same poll results. And in fact his pollster, Stanley Greenberg, issued a memorandum to Democratic candidates advising that they run on their own accomplishments, not on those of the president. "There is no reason to highlight these as Clinton or Democratic proposals. Voters want to know that you are fighting to get things done for them, not that you are advancing some national agenda."

A flurry of foreign and national security policy decisions on North Korea, Haiti, and Iraq—all judged to be successful—resulted in a boost in the president's approval rating to 50 percent, exceeding his disapproval rating for the first time in six months. That was the good news; the bad news was that the good news encouraged him to reenter the campaign. He launched a last-minute, furious schedule of appearances, drawing attention to his record and attacking the Republican "Contract *on* America," as he called it. By campaigning so energetically in the last week, the president naturally attracted press attention to himself as an issue. The effect was to ensure that dramatic Republican gains would be interpreted as a rejection of Clinton's presidency, whether or not that conclusion was merited in terms of actual voting behavior.

The other half, or more, of the nationalization of the 1994 elections is explained by what the Republicans did. As political scientist Gary C. Jacobson pointed out: "All politics was *not* local in 1994. Republicans succeeded in framing the local choice in national terms, making taxes, social discipline, big government, and the Clinton presidency the dominant issues." The Republicans tied "congressional Democrats to Clinton, a discredited government establishment, and a deplorable status quo."

Bill Clinton was still president, but he was not leader of the Democrats in any serious or meaningful sense.

Gingrich, too, deserves notice for his daring strategy of committing Republican candidates to a bold midterm party platform, the "Contract with America." It is true that most voters knew little or nothing about the contract. But the act of getting over three hundred Republican candidates to commit themselves in a media show at the Capitol on September 27 had profound effects on how the election results would then be interpreted.

The new Republican leaders were also not in the least bothered by Democratic claims that the contract tied "Republican candidates back into their congressional leadership." That was precisely the point. Gingrich and company would be strengthened in their effort to establish firm control of the agenda if the new members supported them. Meanwhile, the Democrats were in considerable disarray. Bill Clinton was still president, but he was not leader of the Democrats in any serious or meaningful sense. One study concluded that "the more the Democratic incumbent voted to support the president's policies, the more likely he or she was to be defeated."

Justified or not in terms of what the voters actually wanted, a new agenda had been created. "Change isn't Bill Clinton's friend anymore," is how two reporters put it. A *Washington Post* editorial referred to a "sea change," pointing out that "this was not just an 'anti-incumbent' vote. The incumbents who were defeated this year were Democrats—and in particular Democrats in Congress.... the change called for went almost uniformly in one direction, and that was against liberalism and toward the right." A mandate had been declared, centered in just one of the three elected branches—the House of Representatives. Meanwhile, defeated or not, Bill Clinton remained in office, now freed from the responsibilities of leading Congress, for which he seemed ill-suited anyway.

Reclaiming Leadership

How then did this policy-ambitious president—one who wanted government to do more, not less, and to do it better, not worse—how did he respond to dramatically new political conditions? I have made the point that Bill Clinton is not a lawmaker president. Yet there are functions that cannot be avoided, choices that have to be made—notably whether to sign or to veto a bill, to let it become law or to let it die without his signature. How did the president cope? He altered his governing style from that of a *campaigner* to that of a *prospector*, searching for a role compatible with the unusual politics of the time. The strategy devised in 1995 contained these tenets:

• Associate the president with the change seemingly demanded by the voters.

• Remind the public that the president was there first with many of the issues in the Contract with America.

• Argue that the Republicans are going too far. It is not necessary to destroy programs to improve government. Be the voice of moderation against the extremist Republicans. "I'm for that, but not so much."

• Search for high-profile issues subject to executive order, pushing the limits of that power (as with the anti–teenage smoking measures and barring government contracts with firms replacing strikers).

• Await the completion of lawmaking, then exercise the veto while imploring Republicans to meet on "common ground." Avoid specifics in favor of a "no, that's not it" response.

• Travel, taking your presidency to the people, posturing as the voice of reason, the interpreter of change, the preserver of values.

• Take full advantage of the uniquely presidential status in foreign and national security issues and disasters.

Taken as a whole, this strategy was defensible and rational given the president's political status. It permitted him to turn full attention to raising money and creating an organization for reelection while Republicans were absorbed with the difficult and often unrewarding exercises of balancing the budget and reforming social programs. Lacking an opponent, the president was able to rise above the fray, even calling for a moratorium on politics as usual. Republicans, on the other hand, were engaged in a hotly contested nomination battle in the early months of 1996, with the winner, Bob Dole, then held responsible for leading the Congress that was taken from the president in 1994. Until he announced his resignation from the Senate, Dole found himself battling surrogate campaigners—Tom Daschle, Ted Kennedy, and Chris Dodd—rather than the president.

Clinton in Historical Perspective

Bill Clinton joins others whose presidencies have been at risk. Indeed, the imbalance between expectations and authority perpetuates political peril for presidents.

I stressed earlier that Bill Clinton amplified the inherent risk for the president by raising expectations despite weak political advantages. He invited accountability for the failures that, given the overreaching that characterized his early months in office, were likely to come. A dramatically new politics was created as a result.

Freed from the exacting demands of his original ambitious agenda by the 1994 elections, the president settled into the role of moderating the striking, even threatening, policy changes proposed by Republicans. Though not a leadership role, it is a mode that becomes him. As the nation's moderator in the serious policy debates at hand, he can justify the travel and public exposure that he finds personally and intellectually rewarding. He displayed patience in 1995, permitting Republicans to dominate the agenda and awaiting the time when his veto power would inevitably attract their lawmaking efforts—inexorably drawing them into the public arena where he excels. At last the campaigner could reinsert himself into the policy process. But having been more an observer than participant during the active congressional session, it was no simple matter for President Clinton to reconnect with the lawmaking process. Therefore, negotiations with congressional leaders have been protracted and disorderly, with the Republicans of the 104th Congress having drawn to themselves precisely the large measure of accountability that the White House invited in the 103rd Congress. Given his experience, President Clinton was more than

happy to oblige in holding Republicans responsible for, among other things, shutting down the government.

The reports of his political demise were premature. Once more, Bill Clinton demonstrated his capacity for political regeneration.

Control of his political destiny was taken from the president in the 1994 elections, and so he positioned himself to take advantage of what others did or failed to do. The reports of his political demise were premature. Once more, Bill Clinton demonstrated his capacity for political regeneration. Perhaps even he would agree, however, that the separated system works best when success is measured less by recovery than by effective participation by the president throughout. It is exceptional to be the "Come Back Kid" over and over again. Yet it is substantially more imposing as president not to require recuperation.

SUGGESTED FURTHER READING

David W. Brady, John F. Cogan, and Douglas Rivers. "How the Republicans Captured the House: An Assessment of the 1994 Midterm Elections." Stanford, Calif.: Hoover Institution, Stanford University, 1995.

Bill Clinton and Al Gore. *Putting People First: How We Can All Change America.* New York: Times Books, 1992.

Elizabeth Drew. *On the Edge: The Clinton Presidency.* New York: Simon & Schuster, 1994.

Gary C. Jacobson. "The 1994 House Elections in Perspective." In *Midterm: The Elections of 1994 in Context*, Philip Klinker, ed. Boulder, Colo.: Westview Press, 1996.

David Maraniss. *First in His Class: A Biography of Bill Clinton.* New York: Simon & Schuster, 1995.

Is the President a Waffler?

In some cases, yes. But part of the reason is that he shuns the easy answers of both right and left. Often, he ends up just where he should be

BY JEREMY PAUL

Though Bill Clinton has surely been delighted by the venomous brawl for the Republican nomination, that venom will soon be aimed squarely at the President himself. Republicans will call him a big government, tax-and-spend, pro-abortion liberal. And, of course, they'll brand him an inveterate waffler. "Bill Clinton," says Haley Barbour, chairman of the Republican National Committee, "shares with the hummingbird the incredible ability to turn 180 degrees in a split second."

This image has dogged Clinton from early in his presidency. A number of prominent campaign promises—to enact a middle-class tax cut, for example—were quickly abandoned. In 1995, the President suddenly supported balancing the budget in seven years. Even die-hard supporters threw up their hands in frustration when Clinton told a crowd of wealthy supporters in Houston, "You think I raised your taxes too much [in 1993]. It might surprise you to know that I think I raised them too much, too."

Reversals like these give Americans reason to doubt Clinton's sincerity. But if he deserves partial blame for his weak-kneed image, so does the narrow-minded press, the cynical opposition, and the contradictory wishes of the American people. It is crucial to discern where Clinton has truly "waffled" and where he's smartly compromised; where he's retreated in cowardice, and where he's changed course in the face of new information; where he refuses to take a stand out of political opportunism, and where his ambivalence reflects the ambivalence of the country. In 1996, many Americans are insisting on a leader who speaks for the sensible center. But Clinton's record of being punched in the nose for breaking with ideological extremes raises the question: Can we really handle a truly moderate president?

Imagine the scenario of two parents with a difficult teenage son. He doesn't do his schoolwork or chores; at times, he is openly defiant. One parent, call him the "conservative" father, offers a clear solution. "We're just not being tough enough. We have to have clear rules and impose swift, immediate punishment when they're violated." The other parent, call her the "liberal" mother, is equally certain. "Our problem," she says, "is that we aren't encouraging enough. We need to love and support him no matter what he does."

Broadly speaking, each parent represents an extreme ideological position. Conservatives want to be

Jeremy Paul is a professor of law at the University of Connecticut. Research assistance was provided by Christopher Stratton.

tough and demanding. Liberals want to be generous and forgiving. But most of us realize that neither position makes sense in all cases. Children need both understanding *and* a firm hand. With only the latter, they'll likely grow hostile and detached. With only the former, they may quit trying.

This is as true for stubborn questions of policy as it is for child-rearing. On welfare, for example, it doesn't make sense to offer the underclass only Horatio Alger tales and stern exhortations to "get a job." Without training and child-care, welfare mothers are likely to have a hard time surviving in the workplace. On the other hand, it is equally true that unlimited compassion—without any demands or expectations—can sap individual initiative and lead to permanent dependence. On this issue, as well as many others, Bill Clinton has smartly claimed the middle ground, proposing to limit welfare payments but also offer training and child-care. He also champions the positive role of government, but insists that it be more efficient and less expensive. On issue after issue, Clinton resists the formulaic approaches of both left and right, instead looking for reasonable solutions.

It shouldn't surprise us much that neither conservatives nor rabid liberals have much affection for this administration. But shouldn't a largely moderate nation cheer Clinton's efforts to steer a middle ground? Now that America seems convinced that government runs things poorly, the left's old love-affair with government programs is out of step with the country. Conservatives, meanwhile, want to return to laissez-faire capitalism and eviscerate environmental protection. Shouldn't most of us line up behind a President seeking a "third way"?

Much of the problem is that the press corps, while paying lip service to the country's desire for a centrist, still insists on viewing leaders through a prism of ideology. When Clinton emphasizes a theme associated with the left or right, he's often incorrectly portrayed as "lurching" in that direction or being chronically indecisive. He's "a President who wakes up every day on both sides of the street," Maureen Dowd writes in *The New York Times*. He is constantly "zigzagging from left to right," opines Paul Gigot of *The Wall Street Journal*. Thomas Friedman says "Clinton changes political identities with each season." It's not that these pundits are 100 percent wrong. They are merely simplistic and unhelpful. Clinton has at times embraced both traditionally conservative positions (the death penalty and more cops on the streets) and liberal positions (gun control and rehabilitation). But building a program that draws on both liberal and conservative mainstays is not being "indecisive." It's being a smart policymaker.

On some issues, Clinton has in fact changed his mind. On the budget, a program of modest deficit reduction gave away to a radical budget balancing. But a strong case can be made that Clinton was intelligently, and properly, reacting to what the people seemed to want. Voters in 1994 gave control of Congress to a Republican party that was promising a balanced budget. Shouldn't the President take that into consideration?

A president shouldn't be a slave to public opinion. Sometimes it is his duty to *shape* that opinion. President Clinton hasn't always struck the perfect balance between exercising leadership and obeying the polls. But much of the flak he draws from pundits is due to their own cynicism and simplicity, not his equivocating. Consider just one example occurring soon after the 1994 congressional elections. Newt Gingrich announced his plan to push a constitutional amendment authorizing voluntary school prayer. During a press conference in Indonesia, Clinton was asked if he could support such an amendment. Here is his full reply:

Well, what I think the country needs and what I think the schools need is a sense that there are certain basic values of citizenship, including valuing the right of people to have and express their faith, which can be advocated without crossing the line of the separation of church and state, and without in any way undermining the fabric of our society. Indeed, the schools, perhaps today more than ever before, need to be the instrument by which we transfer important values of citizenship.

One of the things that was in the Elementary and Secondary Education Act that I signed, that passed with strong bipartisan support, but was little noticed, was the advocacy of basically the teaching of civic values in the schools. Now, on the school prayer thing, I can only tell you what my personal opinion is about that. I have always supported voluntary prayer in the schools. I have always thought that the question was, when does voluntary prayer really become coercive to people who have different religious views from those that are in the majority in any particular classroom. So that, for example, I personally did not believe that it was coercive to have a prayer at an outdoor sporting event or at a graduation event because I don't believe that is coercive to people who don't participate in it. So I think there is room for that.

Obviously, I want to reserve judgment. I want to see the specifics. But I think this whole values debate will go forward and will intensify in the next year. And, again, I would say, this ought to be something that unites the American people, not something that divides us. This ought not to be a partisan debate. The American people do not want us to be partisan, but they do want us to proceed in a way that is consistent with their values and that communicates those values to our children. So let's just—I'll be glad to discuss it with them. I want to see what the details are. I certainly wouldn't rule it out. It depends on what it says.

These comments drew immediate, harsh reaction. Clinton had opposed a school prayer amendment during the 1992 campaign and his refusal now to "rule it out" was portrayed by the media as a typical flip-flop. On the talk show circuit—"This Week with David Brinkley," the "MacNeil-Lehrer News-Hour," and CNN's "Capital Gang," to name just a few—the school prayer remarks were the subject of lengthy conversation. But these shows quoted only the final paragraph of the President's Indonesia comments and perhaps one additional sentence. Based on this narrow slice of his extensive comments, Clinton was tried and convicted of waffling. Margaret Carlson found him "too ready to compromise." William Schneider of CNN awarded Newt Gingrich the political play of the week award for having drawn Clinton into this "wishy-washy" position. Look at Clinton's comments, however, and decide for yourself if he's "wishy-washy." Quite the contrary. He reveals an extraordinarily subtle understanding of the issues at stake. He articulates what he sees as the key distinction between voluntary prayer, which he supports, and coercive prayer, which he does not. He explains the problem that merely proclaiming something voluntary does not make it so. And, he takes a controversial position within his own political party, disagreeing with existing Supreme Court cases involving prayer at graduations and sports events. Then, he says he won't categorically rule out a position deeply held by many in the opposing political party who have just won a major election.

The Mushy Middle

Al Hunt was revealing when he quoted with approval a Democratic strategist's complaint that "voters are looking ... to be able to place [Clinton] on a map." But Hunt and his colleagues use a map with only two poles. Everything else is the "mushy middle," as it was put in a recent *Newsweek* story on the differences between Robert Rubin and Robert Reich. "Characteristically, Clinton is waffling," Bill Turque wrote. " ... For Big Bob and Little Bob, it's a typical response from Big Bill, who's lodged squarely in the mushy middle."

Indeed, the portrait of Clinton as indecisive has been particularly resonant on economic issues. Just 16 months into the administration, Bob Woodward published *The Agenda,* an insider's account of a tug-of-war between deficit hawks (such as Rubin) and investment-oriented neo-liberals (such as Reich). The book sketches a President who is enamored of long meetings, but never able to come to decisions. "Mr. Clinton," Andrew Sullivan wrote in *The New York Times Book Review*, "seems to agree with everything anybody says."

Well, anybody who reads *The Agenda* can see that Clinton was genuinely torn. But he also faced the extraordinary challenge of both imposing fiscal discipline on an economy wracked by huge deficits, and finding money for neglected investments such as infrastructure, education, and job training. In a revealing moment, Woodward records the reaction of Clinton aide Bob Boorstin to a memo that explained this conflict to the President: *"You have inherited a two-part challenge of historic proportions,* he read. In other words, he thought, you've been f___ed."

Boorstin was right. Perhaps a better man than Clinton would have juggled this set of economic and political knives more gracefully, without cutting himself in the process. What matters, though, is that Clinton in the end wrote—and passed—an economic plan that was the model of smart centrism with modest tax increases on the rich and new investments to create jobs.

Now, I have plenty of criticism for Clinton on the economy. But it's one thing to differ on the substance. It's another to defiantly ignore outcomes in order to sock it to him on process. Consider the nomination of Ruth Bader Ginsburg to the Supreme Court in 1993. At the Rose Garden ceremony announcing Ginsburg's selection, Brit Hume complained of a "certain zig-zag quality in the decision-making process."

Well, yes. Clinton had considered dozens of candidates seriously for the Court vacancy—choosing in the end between Ginsburg and Stephen Breyer. The selection of a Supreme Court justice, however, is among the most important and far-reaching of presidential decisions. Hume's niggling flew in the face of powerful evidence that Clinton had just chosen extremely well. Both Ginsburg and Breyer, who Clinton was also later to name to the Court, are judges, intellectuals, and citizens of the highest order.

Clinton has also been charged with chronic indecisiveness on foreign policy. But isn't it fair to say that he stood with most Americans when he hesitated to send U.S. soldiers to Bosnia and Haiti? Isn't it also true that his strategies now look like they have a good chance of working? We'd have much more reason to worry if Clinton continually failed to appreciate the need for action or unduly rushed to commit American forces.

Where the President truly suffers is in the perception that he has no core beliefs, that he's someone, as Steve Forbes puts it, who "gets up each day and figures out by looking at the polls what he's supposed to believe that day, with no coherence, no vision for moving America forward." To take one of a thousand examples: Last April, Clinton was lambasted for his remark, in a discussion of affirmative action, that "this is psychologically a difficult time for a lot of white males, the so-called angry white males." "What the country needs from Clinton," Colbert King wrote in *The Washington Post*, "is less Hamlet and political sweet talk and more of what it paid for: a president who will take a stand."

But what clearer stand does King want? Clinton has pledged full support for the principle of affirmative action, while calling for a curb on programs that overreach. It's no betrayal of affirmative action to concede that such policies have winners and losers. His refusal to embrace two undesirable extremes—ending all programs to remedy past injustice or uncritically supporting them—isn't at all the same thing as refusing to take a stand. And in pushing those on the far left toward the center—this speech was given to hard-core Democratic activists—he's not just talking the talk of common ground, but working towards its realization.

On affirmative action as well as any number of issues, many Americans would prefer to dump Clinton in favor of a take-charge leader such as Colin Powell. But Powell's popularity reveals a stark contradiction among the public: Americans want their leaders to be decisive, but they also tend to punish decisions that they judge to be contrary to their own interests. Powell seems perfect because he has the aura of moral center and resolution but hasn't offended any interest groups.

It's not just the press, then, that contributes to the misunderstanding of Bill Clinton, but also the contradictory impulses of the public—the impulses that led to Powell-mania. And politicians who delight in collapsing the nuances of their opponents' positions don't help, either. Witness the constant, simplistic jabs at Clinton as a "big government" liberal. Or consider Bill Bradley, who explained in his retirement speech that "Republicans are infatuated with the 'magic' of the private sector and reflexively criticize government as the enemy of freedom, and the Democrats distrust the market, preach government as the answer to our problems and prefer the bureaucrat they know to the consumer they can't control."

Where has Bradley been the last three years? Was Bill Clinton's health-care plan—which fully embraced private insurers—the work of a man who distrusts the market? Has the President given a single major speech without emphasizing the importance of entrepreneurs and job creation? When Bradley parrots the media's familiar categories he reinforces the ideological divide he purports to be criticizing.

Clinton's problem is that pressure to adhere to a strictly leftist or right-wing agenda—or be derided as a "waffler"—shows no signs of easing. His task, then, is to articulate his vision in terms that can be readily communicated and understood. In actions, as in tone, Clinton has already established a powerful theme for a post-ideological presidency: He will defend average citizens who play by the rules, but who are threatened by economic insecurity, intolerance, and the inevitable bouts of misfortune or bad luck. Whether through tax cuts for the working poor or beefed up law enforcement or job-training, the President has already shown he means business. And for the future, this theme cuts across virtually every challenge the country faces.

Both for the election and for a potential second term, Clinton must frame those challenges, explain the choices, and work to persuade the public on which way to go. At times, he has played this role brilliantly. Clinton was initially reluctant to endorse the NAFTA trade agreement, for example. But when he did support the treaty, he threw the full weight of the presidency into explaining to the country the choice between open markets and closed borders, and the benefits that would accrue with the former. The treaty was ratified by a wide margin and, despite continuing economic pain caused by plant closings, it still seems clear that Clinton did the right thing for the country's future.

Part of Clinton's task is to not simply walk fine lines on questions of race, welfare, and the economy, but to pose new questions for the country: Does global competition mean we have to give businesses absolute power over the rules of the marketplace, or does government have a role in shaping market rules to serve the public interest? Is government merely a tax drain on household finances or does a democratic allocation of funds sometimes serve us better than the self-interested decisions of profit-seekers? Will a few examples of regulatory excess sway us from strong bipartisan efforts to improve our environment, or will we sacrifice short-term gain for the hope of a greener future?

When all is said and done, we know that Bill Clinton has the right answers to these questions—even if working out the details will inevitably involve some indecision. Those who disagree with him have every reason to oppose his re-election. But the majority of us who agree should sign on for another bumpy ride.

An Agenda at Risk?

Bert A. Rockman

Bert A. Rockman, author of The Leadership Question: The Presidency and the American System *(1984), is the University Professor of Political Science at the University of Pittsburgh, where he also holds appointments in the Graduate School of Public and International Affairs and as research professor in the University Center for International Studies.*

Is the Clinton presidency at risk? Yes, but that is inherent to holding political office in a democracy. There are, however, two areas of risk for the Clinton presidency: The first is obviously its own political survival. The second is its policy agenda.

From the standpoint of the first of these, namely, getting reelected, it is certainly the case that Bill Clinton's prospects look surprisingly promising when contrasted with his political condition after the Republican sweep of 1994. At that point Clinton may well have bottomed out. The Republican capture of Congress and the party's clear policy stance, particularly in the House of Representatives, gave the Republicans a triumphant glow. By contrast, the Democrats were sent reeling, many of them blaming Clinton for the losses. In turn, Clinton himself seemed befuddled, uncertain of direction, and caught between his instincts to look reasonable, his political need to make the opposition look unreasonable, and his own party's core constituencies, whose advocates ironically were strengthened by the results of the 1994 election largely because of the contraction of the Democratic base.

But as House Republicans, especially the large freshman class, overplayed their hand, the inevitable action-reaction cycle of politics took over. Clinton and his fellow Democrats mostly have had to just say no to the sharp policy departures being proposed by the congressional (especially House) Republicans. Talking big change may be the ticket to Washington these days, but trying to do it may produce a one-way ticket back home. Big change sounds good until it changes people's lives, which it frequently does for the worse. Moreover, this one word—"no"—has brought a substantial degree of harmony between the White House and its party in Congress. It turns out to be a much less complicated word than "yes". "Yes" requires one to do things, to extract agreements and build coalitions, to commit to changes that will not satisfy all and, indeed, are guaranteed to displease and mobilize some. Republicans in Congress have been learning this, especially during the past year. Even so, their party unity, for the most part, continued to be impressive and their unstinting commitment to their goals perhaps perversely admirable. Like other true believers, they seemed convinced that time was on their side. Matters have not turned out that way, and consequently Clinton will probably renew his lease on the presidency while the Republicans may lose theirs in the House of Representatives.

This brings me to the second and more formidable area of risk for Clinton's presidency. For even in the sunniest scenario for Clinton and his party, the programmatic initiatives with which he began his presidency on inauguration day of 1993 have been lost. In this regard, Clinton and the freshman Republicans will have had in common the experience of seeing most of their fondest wishes significantly stymied. A 1997 model of the Clinton presidency will inevitably look different from the 1993 model. The difference might be analogized to the ways in which automobiles are

From *Society*, September/October 1996, pp. 24-27. © 1996 by Transaction Publishers. All rights reserved. Reprinted by permission.

marketed. A Porsche, for example, is marketed to emphasize its performance features, especially how fast and how firmly it can take you where you want to go. By contrast, a Volvo, let us say, is marketed to stress its safety characteristics and its ability to keep disastrous things from happening. The 1993 Clinton came into office promising big performance, but a 1997 version will feature much more defensive governing skills—not what he can do but what he can by his presence make others not do.

In consequence, while the Clinton presidency may be at less political risk than we would have imagined not so long ago, the Clinton program is beyond risk—it is, in fact, largely dead, at least that part of it that connects to the Democratic Party. The question, of course, is: Why?

A Stalemated Polity?

Three reasons come to mind why the Clinton agenda has come undone. The first and most obvious, which also accounts for why the Republicans are also finding policy success to be more complicated than policy rhetoric, is institutional, particularly the phenomenon of divided government. Divided government is what is presently standing in the way of the Republican quest to remake government for the twenty-first century, just as it impeded Ronald Reagan's dreams to be all he could be. If Clinton is returned to office in the 1996 election, at the very least it is likely that the Republicans will retain control of the Senate, given their present edge and the number of retiring Democrats. Of course, Clinton did not face a divided government in his first two years. How successful he was is debatable. While Barbara Sinclair has shown that Clinton's legislative success record was indeed very high during those two years, Charles Jones notes that Clinton fared badly when it came to important pieces of legislation. Divided government is a big part, but by no means all, of the answer.

A second explanation has to do with the changed nature of the policy environment and the altered character of the governing problem in a generation's time. Simply put, initiatives that cost money are out. The cumulative effect of government's past programs and, above all, expenditure commitments constrain existing degrees of freedom in the absence of a commensurate commitment to raise taxes. The rising tide of mandated entitlement expenditures minus equivalent revenues to match has resulted, by U.S. standards of the last half century, in rapidly accumulating deficits. This, in turn, means that deficit financing itself becomes a big part of the federal budget, and also that the ratio between mandated and discretionary expenditures has changed dramatically, resulting in a squeeze of programs subject to annual appropriations. It also means that entitlements themselves are now being targeted for cuts simply because there is no other realistic way to achieve significant spending reductions.

What the appropriate level of deficit is and what can be managed is in small part a question of public finance and in large part a question of politics. What the appropriate rate of taxation is in absolute terms is inherently a value question, and thus a political one. How the tax bite is distributed is equally laden with political meaning. Among countries of comparable wealth and development, U.S. taxes are relatively low. Also, the nature of taxation shifted quite a bit beginning in the 1980s from income-based to payroll-based taxes, thus resulting in a more regressive tax structure.

Thus, the dilemma for the Democrats is that raising taxes is politically costly, while the dilemma for the Republicans is that cutting benefits to the middle class may be deleterious to their political health.

Regardless, Republicans had articulated the antitax theme with great success well before the 1994 election. The Democrats, in opposition to the Reagan policies of large and deficit-inducing tax cuts, had emphasized eliminating the structural side of the budget deficit mainly by raising taxes, especially on income and wealth. In so doing, they painted themselves into a political corner. It was evident to Clinton that new programs costing money would have to be self-financing, meaning that they would need new taxes or some mechanism for controlling expenditures through regulations such as those embodied in Clinton's managed-competition health care program. Desperate to avoid—as matters turned out unsuccessfully—the Republicans' "tax and spend" label, Clinton and his "New Democrats" in presenting the administration's health care proposal fudged real costs and created extravagantly complicated mechanisms to control costs without having to directly raise taxes. Having been painted into a political corner as the "tax" party, the Democrats, in their "new" version, proceeded to paint themselves into a policy corner by generating new public commitments based on purely conjectural assumptions about expenditure control backed up by coercive regulations should those assumptions not be met. The policy corner that Clinton's "New Democrats" trapped themselves into was to create proposals of monumental complexity in an effort to avoid direct governmental responsibility for raising the revenues necessary to run such programs.

Thus, the dilemma for the Democrats is that raising taxes is politically costly, while the dilemma for the Republicans is that cutting benefits to the middle class may be deleterious to their political health. In the meantime, certainly in health care, the private sector is doing what the public sector could not—namely controlling costs by rationing care.

The Democrat's ideas for rationalizing the welfare state with programs such as universal health care coverage, welfare reform tied to labor market policies, and so on are nonsynchronous with what Stephen Skowronek calls "political time." All of these programs would cost more, at least in the short run. They would add to the budget deficit or necessitate tax increases—a political Hobson's Choice. These options are not presently a good way to dominate political debates or win the hearts of voters. The problem for the Democrats is that they have to figure out a way to do what they would like to do by avoiding taxing and spending and by thus regulating the private sector to do what they would like it to do. That was essentially the idea behind the Clinton managed-competition health care proposal. The problem with such nostrums, of course, is that those who would bear greater costs, face higher risks, or have their discretion constrained are apt to oppose policy proposals that threaten to do that to them. Such was the fate of Clinton's scheme.

The policy environment has made the cost of policy action more expensive. But one of the reasons for that has to do with the Republicans' success in dominating the symbols of political rhetoric. By dominating the terms of political discourse, it is the Republican agenda that has largely set the parameters of the present policy debate. The election results of 1994, from this perspective, were no mere short-term deviation; rather, they were a culmination of a longer-term set of political trends. Thus the third explanation for the Democrats' programmatic frustration may well have to do with the fact that, for the most part, the electorate has realigned to favor the Republicans. This conclusion, at least until recently, has generally been at odds with the conventional wisdom rampant among political scientists. That conventional wisdom emphasized politically volatile electorates that produced inconclusive outcomes, usually resulting in a divided government of Republican executives and Democratic congressional majorities.

As any given election is, the 1994 election was several stories in one. One of those stories obviously was short term and had a lot to do with turnout and politi-

cal mobilization. Particular groups closely identified with Republicans, such as National Rifle Association (NRA) supporters and fundamentalist Christians, turned out in droves, partly in response to their dislike of Clinton and his agenda. Much of the outcome can be explained in these terms. Yet the 1994 election particularly solidified the realignment thesis, especially in the South and Southwest. These regions now had become as solidly Republican as generations ago they had been Democratic. This has been true for some time in most presidential elections.

The changed political tide now was running deeper, though, as it became clear that the Democratic Party in the South was essentially a party of racial minorities, labor unions, and other voices of the party's increasingly dominant liberal wing, made even more dominant by redistricting decisions designed to maximize the number of districts represented by blacks. The Southern realignment had been partly masked by the powers of incumbency that Democrats in the House had enjoyed and by the party's showings in areas that two generations ago had not been fertile territory. Over this time span, New England, the mid-Atlantic, the Midwest (especially the Great Lakes region), and the West Coast all looked better for congressional Democrats while the South and Southwest looked worse. But in 1994, short-term forces were running powerfully in the Republicans' direction in most of these areas as well. Perhaps the 1996 results will speak with the same measure of clarity inferred from the 1994 election, in which case one or the other of the party contestants will claim a mandate. That, however, is probably a perilous bet, and the standoff will probably continue.

The American Political System at Risk?

The question that eclipses whether or not Clinton's presidency is at risk is the more vital one of whether or not the U.S. political order is at risk. Our system of separated powers was designed to frustrate those with crystalline political visions. Elections in our system rarely produce straightforward policy outcomes. Bargaining is required to get anywhere. The structure of the U.S. political system is such that alternate and fundamentally opposed visions of the world can collide with one another, and when that happens they are likely to create a lot of political sound and fury, if not necessarily much in the way of definitive outcome. Such passionate collisions of opposite perspectives have happened in the U.S. past, more often in the nineteenth than in the twentieth century. Those of us of a certain age, however, can easily recall, with some irony, the frequent complaint that the U.S. party system was failing to create clear and robust alternatives.

Indeed, one argument about the nature of U.S. political institutions is that they create powerful incentives for compromise, mainly because pure political domination is so hard to come by. Such incentives are powerful, though, only when politicians want to accomplish something and when their visions of the world are not fundamentally at odds. The first of these matters deals in motives and thus cannot be known. The second, unfortunately, is known, and what is known about it is that the competing visions of our political parties have come to rest on clear-cut ideologies maintained and nurtured by party clienteles of pure-bred ideologues.

More issues have become politicized over time, dominated by powerful sectors within each of the parties. The liberal-conservative dimension of cultural issues has become a far more powerful component of party politics than it was a generation ago. In addition, the regulatory reach of the state and its responsibilities for ensuring public health and safety, civil rights, and environmental integrity have become more salient as the economic and social costs of regulation increase and its benefits become less certain. Above all, the growing conflict over the social welfare state between, on the one hand, the social democratic ("liberal" in U.S. parlance) and conservative but ameliorist conceptions (such as those of the Roman Catholic hierarchy) and, on the other, the liberal ("conservative" in U.S. parlance) laissez-faire conception has come to the fore in a fashion not articulated so clearly since the 1930s. Politicization has widened the spectrum of issues subject to interparty conflict while intensifying older cleavages.

Can compromise be expected in the presence of such powerfully disparate views? Perhaps. But for now that would constitute the triumph of hope over experience. In fact, the center is not holding; it is collapsing. Politicians of moderate temperament are leaving public office in droves. Indicators, from the growing use of filibusters and holds in the Senate to an increased incivility in political discourse, to the growing disgruntlement of the citizenry toward its government suggest that our government is not working well. In fact, twice

within a year it literally did not work at all. Much attention has been focused on the management of government and on its reinvention. But the problem is not fundamentally with its administration. Rather, the problem lies more fundamentally in the political class and in the lost arts of political compromise. Politics is now harder to do precisely because governing is harder to do. This requires more searching for acceptable solutions, not less.

Bill Clinton's dilemma is that he accepts compromise in a political culture that increasingly scorns it and that finds virtues in term limits and the inevitable incompetence and intolerance that a legislature full of inexperienced legislators breeds. Learning to live with others with whom one does not agree is an acquired skill, not a natural trait. In fact, it is an unnatural trait. Bob Dole may find out what Clinton already has: that compromise is becoming the art of the impossible. After 1994, Clinton has sailed with the prevailing winds, buying into the Republican agenda on the budget and welfare reform when he apparently concluded that could not be resisted. Whether that will do him any good is at least questionable. On the larger questions of universal entitlements that directly affect the mass of voters' interests, the Republican agenda has proven to be profoundly unpopular. Clinton, not surprisingly, has found it easier here to say no. The great irony may well be that Clinton will risk his hold on the presidency less merely by standing fast and saying no, while the longer-term risk to the political system rises.

SUGGESTED FURTHER READINGS

Charles O. Jones. "Campaigning to Govern: The Clinton Style." In *The Clinton Presidency: First Appraisals*, Colin Campbell and Bert Rockman, eds. Chatham, N.J.: Chatham House, 1996.

Barbara Sinclair. "Trying to Govern Positively in a Negative Era: Clinton and the 103rd Congress." In *The Clinton Presidency*.

Stephen Skowronek. *The Politics Presidents Make: Leadership from John Adams to George Bush*. Cambridge, Mass.: Belknap, Harvard University Press, 1993.

RUSH TO JUDGMENT: PICKING PRESIDENTS

JAMES A. BARNES

If Bill Clinton had been elected President in 1968, could he have won approval of a sweeping free-trade treaty with a majority of congressional Republicans on his side and a majority of Democrats in the opposition?

To pass health care reform, would he have had to campaign around the country, sometimes almost nonstop for a week, to sell his plan?

In all likelihood, no.

A little more than 25 years ago, the route to a presidential nomination and to election still ran through the political party's key constituent groups and power brokers. Once elected, the President governed through that coalition.

In 1969, Clinton, owing his nomination and election in large part to organized labor, wouldn't have pushed a free-trade agreement that unions couldn't support. And on health care, he would have been talking to just a few key congressional committee chairmen, not to people gathered for televised town hall meetings.

Although the social revolution of the 1960s was beginning to reshape American politics, the presidential nominating system held some of those changes back. When Democratic Party reformers in the late 1960s and early 1970s pushed through revamped rules for nominating presidential candidates, they "took the brake off," said Byron E. Shafer, the Andrew W. Mellon professor of American government at Oxford University.

Those electoral reforms have posed challenges for presidential candidates and Presidents alike.

THE WAY IT WAS

In the pre-reform era, less than a fourth of the national convention delegates in either party were selected in so-called candidate primaries, where the popular vote for presidential candidates determined the composition of a state's delegation.

Almost three-fourths of the delegates to the national conventions were selected at state party conventions and caucuses or in primaries where voters cast their ballots directly for convention delegates instead of for candidates. The press found it much harder to make sense of these contests than of true candidate primaries.

At caucuses and state conventions, the process of selecting delegates could take months or might be brokered by party pols in back rooms. And even delegates who were directly elected were often pledged to a favorite-son candidate or ran uncommitted to any candidate. These delegates took orders from local and state party leaders, and often they wouldn't know which candidate they would end up supporting until shortly before the convention opened.

That is not to say that candidates in the pre-reform era couldn't build political momentum by winning primaries. By capturing such states as Wisconsin and West Virginia in 1960, John F. Kennedy was able to demonstrate his vote-getting ability in places where a Catholic candidate was not expected to fare well; his victories there reassured party leaders that his religion would not doom his candidacy in the fall.

Kennedy's momentum going into the nominating convention was less the product of newspaper and television headlines that trumpeted his victories than it was the consequence of the endorsements of party leaders who reasoned from his primary victories that he could appeal to a broad coalition of voters.

All that changed by 1976, when almost two-thirds of the delegates to the Democratic and Republican National Conventions were selected in candidate primaries. Now the momentum came directly from the voters, as interpreted by the news media.

The number of states that hold primary or caucus elections in the early stages of the preconvention season has also increased dramatically. In 1972, only about a fifth of Democratic National Convention delegates came from states that had primaries or caucuses in February or March. In 1996, at least two-thirds of Republican National Convention dele-

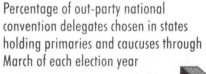
Percentage of out-party national convention delegates chosen in states holding primaries and caucuses through March of each election year

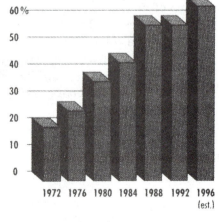

gates will come from states that have held their primaries or caucuses by the end of March. *(See chart)*

THE PRESS'S ROLE

Political scientists have argued that these and other reforms have allowed candidates to make critical strides toward winning nomination by energizing only a fraction of voters and party activists who have participated in the primaries and caucuses rather than being compelled to mobilize a broad political coalition within the party. At the very least, an increasing number of candidates are able to launch their campaigns with the support of a relatively small slice of the electorate.

The rush to the starting line—what the political pros call front-loading—only amplifies the role of the news media and the importance of momentum for many White House hopefuls. A candidate who wins an early primary or caucus reaps a bounty of generally favorable press coverage, which becomes a strong asset for a campaign that must run in multistate primaries every Tuesday in March.

But the media can also confer "big mo" to a candidate who does better than the political press corps expects. Although they're often wrong, reporters don't hesitate to set political expectations. Because it's such an easy way to write about presidential elections, and because the expectations game is taken so seriously in Washington, it has also become one of the ways that the press covers Washington after the campaign and the election are over.

"The media now plays the same role during the presidency that it does during the campaign," said Oxford University's Shafer. "In some sense, press behavior is less different before and after the election."

The current health care debate is a good example. The news media established the expectation early in the game that Congress would pass some sort of health care reform bill before the midterm elections. That perception has clearly affected the legislative strategies and posturing on Capitol Hill. Had the expectation been that no bill would be approved this year, Republican lawmakers, particularly conservative Republicans, would probably not be pressing their own brands of health care legislation. Likewise, the current expectation that Clinton's proposal will not pass without substantial revisions has spawned a variety of Democratic alternatives.

In the 1960s, when entrenched committee chairmen still had the ability to control the flow and shape of legislation, they set the agenda, not the news media.

Recent campaign reforms mean that presidential candidates, to win nomination, are no longer compelled to mobilize a broad political coalition within the party.

The modern news media, particularly television, present a President with tremendous opportunities for public persuasion, but their polls confound him.

But that changed as the institutional powers of congressional leaders eroded and as the number of actors on and off Capitol Hill who had a role in crafting legislation multiplied.

"So many people have a piece of the action that expectations are more central [to the legislative process] and that is largely the media's game," Shafer said.

POLLING BINGE

The changes in the presidential nominating process during the past quarter-century coincided with another democratizing development in post-reform politics: the increase in the number and frequency of media-sponsored public opinion polls. To be sure, improvements in survey research techniques were a major factor in this growth, most notably the use of the telephone to conduct interviews. In the 1960s, the more-expensive and time-consuming in-person interviews were the generally accepted method for taking the public's pulse.

Reporters had always attempted to get a handle on public opinion by talking to professional politicians. But in an era of growing cynicism about government and politics, the press decided that it was important for it to develop its own tools to find out what people were thinking. Opinion surveys became a staple of reporting on presidential campaigns, fertilizing the "horse race" coverage of the candidates.

As election-year polling proliferated, the news media borrowed some of the techniques that the campaigns were using. Now it's not uncommon for one of the television network news divisions to produce nightly tracking polls in the days leading up to the first-in-the-nation New Hampshire primary to measure the electorate's leanings on a daily basis and pick up late-breaking shifts in voters' opinions. The same technique is used during the closing week of the presidential race in the fall.

But the press's polling binges no longer stop on Election Day. During Clinton's first four months in office, a new poll by a major media outlet measuring his job approval rating was conducted every three days, on average. And ABC News conducted a virtual tracking poll on the North American Free Trade Agreement (NAFTA) last year, with three seperate readings on the public's attitudes about the treaty in the week before the House voted.

"The election model is now the governmental model," Kathleen A. Franko-

vic, director of surveys for CBS News, said. Polling has become "a fundamental part of how you look at an election and, later, how you look at the President and, after that, how you look at policy. It's a piece of everything."

That puts a premium on Presidents who can maintain their popularity in the polls and rally public opinion behind their initiatives.

"Their behavior now is much more similar to what they have to do as a campaigner," Princeton University political scientist Larry M. Bartels said. "So much of being President involves keeping your poll numbers up. If nothing else, it makes the policy-making process more sporadic."

Indeed, the occupant of the Oval Office now governs in the context of a horse race presidency. Instead of facing a challenge from another candidate, Presidents run against their own approval ratings in the opinion polls, statistics that are constantly being monitored by the news media. In fact, both the press and Members of Congress rely on the ratings as a key barometer for judging the President's political health—and thus his ability to rally the nation behind his initiatives.

The modern media, particularly television, present a President with tremendous opportunities for public persuasion. On the other hand, Presidents "can be embarrassed" by polls that constantly

check on how well they're doing selling their programs, said Everett Carll Ladd, president of the Roper Center for Public Opinion Research Inc. at the University of Connecticut (Storrs). Earlier Presidents, he said, "weren't getting hit in the face by a slide in their poll numbers."

OUT OF THE BOTTLE

Many scholars say that it's been a long downhill slide since the presidential nominating rules were changed and the press became such a dominant participant in elections. Chief among their complaints is that the political parties have been weakened.

But is that such a bad thing? A strong party system might have denied Clinton his victory on the NAFTA vote. When polls show that a majority of Americans support such an agreement, the country may be better off if a President has a chance to assemble a bipartisan congressional coalition.

Campaigning for public opinion is nothing new for Presidents. Woodrow Wilson hit the stump for the League of Nations. Today, however, Presidents have to wage their battles on a daily, sustained basis.

Whether the changes that have accompanied the new political order have made for better or worse Presidents is an academic question. Like the genie, they are not going back into the bottle.

WILL CLINTON SING SECOND-TERM BLUES?

WILLIAM SCHNEIDER

For Presidents who have been reelected, their second terms have rarely been as successful as their first. Call it the "second-term blues."

President Clinton is well aware of the problem. "I'm very mindful of history's difficulties," he said at his postelection news conference, "and I'm going to try to beat them."

Look at the record of second terms in this century.

After World War I, Woodrow Wilson couldn't persuade the Senate to approve the Versailles Treaty and let the United States become a League of Nations member. He made internationalism the defining issue of the 1920 election. The Democrats lost in a landslide. Wilson's presidency ended in failure, compounded by the President's tragic disability.

The greatest defeats of Franklin D. Roosevelt's presidency came during his second term. Congress refused to support his plan to expand the Supreme Court. FDR failed to persuade voters to purge anti-New Deal Democrats in the 1938 midterm elections.

After Harry S Truman's come-from-behind victory in 1948, voters turned against him because of the military stalemate in Korea, his firing of Gen. Douglas MacArthur and charges of corruption and Communist subversion.

Dwight D. Eisenhower's second term was marred by periods of illness and a series of Cold War crises. When the Soviet Union in 1957 launched *Sputnik*, the first space satellite, Americans became alarmed over what they saw as the nation's military and technological deficiencies. The Administration suffered another embarrassing setback in 1960, when the Soviets shot down a U-2 reconnaissance plane.

Lyndon B. Johnson's second-term domestic achievements—voting rights, medicare, the war on poverty—were offset by the crisis in the country over racial violence, student protests and the war in Vietnam.

Richard M. Nixon's second term? One word: Watergate.

Much of Ronald Reagan's second term was consumed by the Iran-contra scandal. Reagan recovered his popularity, and he had some achievements, such as tax reform. But the scandal was a painful diversion.

At his news conference, Clinton cited a recent book by Alfred J. Zacher, *Trial and Triumph: Presidential Power in the Second Term*. Zacher concludes that "Presidents who experienced diminished effectiveness or failure were those who lost control of Congress."

That happened to Wilson, FDR and Reagan during their second terms. It also happened to Truman and Johnson, especially when their public support collapsed as a result of unpopular Asian wars. Clinton intends to heed that lesson. "We understand the American people want us to work together with the Republicans, and that we have to build a vital center," he said on Nov. 8.

The biggest reason for the second-term blues? Presidents who get too ambitious and overreach their mandate. Wilson, Johnson and even FDR all made that mistake—and paid for it. Clinton is aware of that problem, too. "Sometimes a President thinks he has more of a mandate than he does and tries to do too much in the absence of cooperation," he observed.

Can the President avoid that mistake? After all, he didn't get much of a mandate on Nov. 5. No majority. No coattails. No Congress. And no big agenda. Just small-scale initiatives. What some have labeled, "the Nouvelle Deal."

But Clinton believes he *did* run on a big agenda. "I went out of my way at the Democratic National Convention to make a very long list of specific things I wanted to do," he said on Nov. 8, "because I wanted an agenda to organize the attention, the spirits and the energies of people."

> **President Clinton's "second-term blues" came in his first term, and he's acquired the skills he needs to cope if they strike again.**

"We do have a big agenda. We have a driving agenda. We know what we have to do," Clinton insisted. Uh-oh. That's where the trouble usually starts.

Consider some surprising results from a poll that the Pew Research Center for The People & The Press conducted the weekend after the election. The election produced a divided result. So which party has the mandate?

The poll asked people, "Are you happy or unhappy that the Republican Party maintained control of the U.S. Congress?" Sixty-five per cent said they were happy with that outcome. By comparison, only 53 per cent said they were happy that Clinton got reelected.

In fact, nearly 4 in 10 Clinton voters said they were happy to see the GOP keep control of Congress. So Republicans may have received just as big a mandate as Clinton has. Maybe bigger.

Presidents typically use their second terms to create a legacy. After all, they can't (or in the past, usually didn't) run for reelection. So the temptation is to put politics aside and play to history. The problem is that a lame-duck President rapidly loses political clout. If he puts politics aside, he runs the risk of becoming politically irrelevant. He may not run for reelection, but he needs support from a lot of people who will. And they must decide whether supporting him is a winning or losing proposition.

Clinton is in an especially difficult situation. The voters want him to govern in partnership with Republicans in Congress, but that will curb his ambition and force him to share credit for his legacy.

Not to mention the possibility of a debilitating scandal. The danger keeps growing. Independent counsel Kenneth W. Starr's Whitewater investigation. *(See National Journal, November 23, 1996, p. 2558.)* Allegations of improper fund-raising practices by the Democratic Party. A possible influence-peddling relationship between the President and former Commerce Department official and Democratic Party operative John Huang.

One thing always damages Presidents in their second term: The party that controls the White House suffers a big loss in the midterm elections, and that turns Congress against the President in his final two years. In Clinton's case, however, it already happened—in 1994. That could be an advantage for him in his second term. He's already learned how to govern with a hostile Congress. Clinton's second-term blues came early, and he's acquired the skills he needs to cope if it happens again.

IMPERIAL CONGRESS

JOSEPH A. CALIFANO JR.

Joseph A. Califano Jr., an attorney, is chairman and president of the Center on Addiction and Substance Abuse at Columbia University. He was President Lyndon Johnson's top assistant for domestic affairs and Secretary of Health, Education and Welfare under President Jimmy Carter.

ongress has become the King Cong of Washington's political jungle, dominating an executive branch that can no longer claim the coequal status that the Founding Fathers saw as crucial. Those who blame Bill Clinton for this sorry imbalance of power fail to take into account the stunning ascendancy of Congressional clout since the years of Lyndon Johnson.*

In the 1960's, Democratic members of Congress not only depended on Lyndon Johnson. Many owed their seats to him. The 89th Congress of 1965-66 — the only time in this century when a liberal majority ruled both House and Senate — was a tribute to Johnson's walloping 61-to-39-percent margin over Barry Goldwater. Johnson never let those young Senators and Representatives forget that he had carried their states and districts by margins wider than their own.

Even members who didn't owe their victories to L. B. J. needed him to raise money for their campaigns. Johnson was quick to accommodate those who supported his programs with appearances at fundraising events and donations from his own political bankroll.

*This article first appeared almost a year before the Republicans' startling takeover of both houses of Congress in the November 1994 elections. The author served in two Democratic administrations (Lyndon Johnson and Jimmy Carter) during which Democrats were also in majority control of both houses of Congress. Since President Johnson left office in 1969, however, there have usually been Republican presidents (Richard Nixon, Gerald Ford, Ronald Reagan, and George Bush) at the same time Democrats controlled both houses of Congress. In 1995 and 1996, the reverse has been true: Democratic President Bill Clinton will have to contend with Republican majorities in both houses of Congress. Under these new circumstances, it should be particularly interesting to observe the shape and direction of congressional-presidential power relations and to consider whether Califano's notion of an "imperial Congress" remains valid. **Editor**

Members of Congress also needed Johnson for political patronage. In those days the President controlled jobs even as menial as that of local postmaster and had discretion to decide where to build roads, sewerage systems, hospitals and courthouses.

The executive branch had the staff to draft legislation, and Congressional committees depended on executive departments to write their bills. We in the Johnson Administration were happy to oblige; that way we could provide plenty of room for executive action.

When we wanted to close post offices, consolidate regional centers or shut down military bases, we did it. L. B. J. stiff-armed Congressional attempts to trim our efforts, vetoing legislation to limit his power to close bases as an unconstitutional intrusion on Presidental prerogatives. When Johnson wanted to step up military action in Vietnam, he had Congress pass the sweeping Gulf of Tonkin Resolution which he (and later Richard Nixon) used as authority to wage a full-scale war without asking Congress to declare one.

But the next 20 years saw a steady erosion of

executive power as Congress moved to center stage. The triple hit — escalation of the Vietnam War, the Watergate scandal and President Nixon's refusal to carry out civil rights laws and spend money appropriated for Great Society programs — bred in the Congress a profound distrust of the Executive that persists to this day. As a result, Congress began writing laws in excruciating detail on the premise that the executive branch would try to circumvent them.

BY THE 1990'S, CONGRESS HAD NOT only knocked the crown off the imperial Presidency. It had legislated itself into a position of independent power, shedding its reliance on the White House.

First and foremost, members no longer need the President to raise money for them. Congress has given itself the power to raise its own campaign funds by legalizing political action committees and by creating enough committees and subcommittees (more than 100 in the Senate; almost 150 in the House) so that virtually every Senator and most Representatives can have a senior position. Congressional leaders can assign members to committees that oversee well-heeled private interests. Committee chairmen can provide funds to a junior member's re-election campaign out of war chests they amass from their perches of power.

Nor do members any longer need the President to dole out patronage. Congress has increased its work force from about 22,000 in 1960 to 37,000 today, giving each member plenty of jobs to fill. Personal staffs of House members have jumped from 2,500 in 1960 to more than 7,000 in 1992; in the Senate personal staffs have more than tripled, from 1,200 in 1960 to more than 4,000 in 1992.

A new President goes to Washington, as Clinton did, with only a handful of loyal aides. He usually has his cabinet and key members of his White House staff on board within a week of his inauguration. But it takes more than a year to choose most remaining Presidential appointees. Many of them, new to the ways of political Washington, face off against a Congress that is already well staffed with experienced institutional partisans. While the President struggles to find hundreds of appointees to fill the geographic, ethnic and political commitments of his campaign, Congress is already moving *its* agenda forward.

Not content with its own patronage positions, Congress has assumed greater control over executive branch personnel. In 1960, there were 149 Presidential appointments that required Senate confirmation. Today there are 310. And the Senate has abandoned the deference accorded Presidential nominations in the 1960's.

At the flood tide of Great Society legislation in 1965-66, Congress passed laws totaling 2,912 statute book pages. Most observers thought the nation would never again see such a flurry of Congressional activity. But Senators and Representatives have come to revel in the power of patronage gained from a prolific legislative pen. Despite numerous vetoes by President George Bush, in 1991-92 the Congress enacted laws, totaling 7,544 pages.

Such laws claim for Congress a host of powers that are truly executive. The tax committees legislate in such detail that lawyers go to staffers on the Senate Finance and House Ways and Means Committees with matters that, 20 years ago, they could have resolved only with the Internal Revenue Service. In fiscal 1993, Congress earmarked $763 million — triple the 1988 amount — for specific projects on more than 200 college campuses, like a $76,000 University of Georgia study of urban pests. Congress has legislated that the Interior Department maintain 23 positions in the Wilkes-Barre, Pa., office of anthracite reclamation and that the Secretary of Health and Human Services hire "six medium sedans" for transportation. This trespassing occurs in lengthy reconciliation and appropriations bills that the President must veto in their entirety if he wants to challenge the intrusion.

As a result, King Congress has become the throne

It has tripled its own payroll, abandoned its deference to the President and tilted, alarmingly, the scales of constitutional power.

before which most governors and mayors plead for Federal bounty. Congress has learned that it's better to give out the goodies directly than to let the President get the credit. State and local officials who once prowled the corridors of executive departments and the White House now crowd the anterooms of representatives and senators.

WHEN I REORGANIZED the Department of Health, Education and Welfare in 1977, Congress made it more difficult for my successors to take similar actions. When President Clinton lifted the ban on gay soldiers, Congress legislated a narrower change, assuring that any future moves would require legislation rather than simply executive action. The foreign policy ax of Congress has chopped off Presidential moves in Bosnia, Haiti and Somalia.

Democratic members of Congress, confident of perpetual control of the legislative branch, are not as concerned about who sits in the Oval Office as they were a generation ago. The barons of Capital Hill make it clear to any incoming Administration where the true power resides. Cabinet officers and agency heads spend far more time testifying before Congressional committees and visiting their members and staffs than they do with the President, while their subordinates prepare the battery of reports Congress demands of them—some 5,000 last year.

Clinton's situation is aggravated by the fact that he was elected with only 43 percent of the popular vote, less than the margins by which incumbent Representatives and Senators carried their districts and states. When the President submitted his stimulus package, these members ridiculed and killed it. When he proposed his deficit reductions, Congress returned essentially the same budget cuts it had shipped to George Bush the year before, knowing that this President had to take whatever they sent him and declare victory.

Health care reform offers a quintessential example of the fundamental shift of power in the capital. The President has spoken in broad principles, assuming the role of cheerleader to arouse the citizenry. When he finally sent Congress draft legislative language, he stressed his willingness to compromise on just about everything. Clinton knows that Congress will draft the reforms in detail unthinkable even for executive branch regulations 25 years ago. Congress knows that the President will, again, have to sign whatever it sends him and, again, declare victory.

It won't be easy to reset the scales of constitutional power, but it is as critical to try today as it was to bring the imperial Presidency down to size in the early 1970's. Congress has enormous difficulty making coherent policies (conservative or liberal) that complex problems like economic development and urban decay require. Individual members tend to ricochet from the demands of their constituents to the interests served by their committees and caucuses.

Congressional muscle is most easily flexed in obstructionist ways. The members' ability to fudge individual accountability licenses them to play political games—sending President Bush a campaign reform bill they knew he'd veto; refusing to send President Clinton the same bill because they know he'll sign it.

Where Congress takes the initiative, it tends to write laws with a little bit for everyone who has votes to barter or bucks to donate, at the expense of a focused national policy. Thus, it pours money into tobacco, sugar and dairy subsidies as it promotes free trade and tries to cut health care spending. A proposal to test a model program in a few cities quickly becomes a national undertaking with something for every state and enough Congressional districts to muster a House majority.

The Nafta battle underscores this point. While no President in this century has lost a legislative contest over trade, none had to pay so much in the way of tribute to Congress: hundreds of millions in subsidies for fruits and nuts, lower cigarette tax increases and barrels of other pork.

To help put Congress back in its constitutional place will require significant campaign finance reform with public financing, and a Presidential line-item veto. Campaign finance reform is critical to give the President more power to assert the national interest over the special interests that prevail on Capitol Hill. The line-item veto is essential to end the Congressional blackmail contained in lengthy bills the President is forced to sign in order to keep Government functioning.

Such steps are only a beginning. But they can help a President, even one elected by a minority, reclaim coequal status as the Founding Fathers intended.

Too Representative Government

Why is Congress held in such low esteem? One reason is that as it has become more truly representative, it has tried to solve more and more problems, including many that no one knows how to solve—thus raising expectations and frequently disappointing them. Quick-fix reforms aren't likely to make the public any happier with the legislative branch

STEVEN STARK

Steven Stark writes frequently about politics and popular culture and is a commentator on National Public Radio and on Cable News Network. He is completing a book about the most influential programs in the history of television.

"SUPPOSE you were an idiot," Mark Twain wrote during the Gilded Age. "And suppose you were a member of Congress. But I repeat myself." "Do you pray for the senators?" someone asked the chaplain of the Senate in 1903. "No, I look at the senators and pray for the country," he replied.

The more things change, the more they remain the same. The 104th Congress began work in January, and talk of institutional revolution is once again in the air. It's not just that the Republicans—finally in control of both Houses for the first time in four decades—have begun reforming the least popular branch by taking such measures as applying all federal employment laws to Congress, cutting House committee staffs by a third, and requiring a 60 percent majority in the House to approve tax increases. Many critics, such as Kevin Phillips and Lamar Alexander, have discussed a number of rather radical proposals for recasting the institution—everything from term limits to increasing the size of Congress to cutting the length of the session in half to instituting national referenda.

One might argue that some of these changes would make Congress more effective, as would a few of the currently popular (but unlikely to pass) proposals for campaign-finance overhaul and restrictions on lobbying.

A number of scholars, former members of Congress, and other observers suggest, however, that even far-reaching reforms—not to mention the recent election results—are unlikely to quell the public's considerable discontent with Congress for long. In its attempts to lay the blame for that discontent at the feet of the Democrats, the new Republican majority is ignoring a fundamental reality that has come into being over the past generation: owing largely to the changing nature of representation, the expanding role of the federal government, and the influence of television, the public has arrived at new and often contradictory expectations of how Congress should act and what it should do. Until these contradictions are resolved, Congress is doomed to unpopularity and ineffectiveness, no matter who controls it.

There is, after all, an inevitable tension in any legislative system between deliberation and action, discretion and responsiveness. The job of a legislature is not only to get things done but also to air points of view and ensure the legitimacy of governmental action. These goals often conflict—as do the objectives of representing a constituency while exercising independent judgment, or looking out for both the national and the local interest. Throughout American history the pendulum has swung back and forth as legislators have tried to come to terms with these tensions. Today, however, voters apparently believe that the pendulum can be made to stop. In much the same way as the public seems to want a welfare state without picking up the tab, it wants the advantages of a legislative system without any of the costs.

Even if Congress adopts all the most ambitious reforms, this cannot be achieved. No matter how noble the goal, virtually any reform that seeks to change the makeup of Congress (such as term limits) or encourage debate or make members rely less on staff, so that they will draft their own bills and read those of others, will lead the institution to be even more dependent on special interests or to get less done. Almost any proposal that increases the institution's ability to act quickly, such as eliminating the filibuster or making it easier to "fast track" legislation, will tend to alienate those in the minority and cause some attempts at lawmaking to be less judicious and acceptable to the masses. Attempts to limit the length of the session will inevitably narrow the range of concerns that Congress can tackle. Although many of the current Republican proposals for institutional reform have surface appeal, chances are that they will eventually end up antagonizing at least as many voters as they please. And Congress will end up just as unpopular as it was when the Republicans took over, if not more so.

The Wired Congress

For the first four decades of the Republic, congressmen actually spent very little time in Washington. For the next century or so they had little contact with their districts once they were in Washington. (Senators, of course, were not even popularly elected until early in this century.) Theorists from Thomas Hobbes to Edmund Burke had debated the extent to which representatives should directly reflect the desires of their constituents, but that debate took place in a world in which a lot of groups couldn't vote, news was hard to come by, and no one really knew how to measure public opinion other than in an election. The difficulty of travel and the irregularity of mail delivery made communication between constituents and Congress problematic. Thus members inevitably had to exercise independent judgment on most issues, no matter where they stood philosophically on the representation question.

Today things have swung to the opposite extreme, and not just because the infamous lobbyists surround congressmen and senators. Daily polling, E-mail, 800 numbers, and call-in shows have exponentially increased the contact that representatives have with their constituents. "Many days I felt like nothing more than the end of a computer terminal," Elliott Levitas, a former representative from Georgia, told me in an interview. The danger today is not that representatives know too little about what the electorate feels but that they know too much. Like body temperature, public opinion can shift hourly without consequence. "The cooling-off process that used to exist isn't there any more," Dennis Eckart, a former representative from Ohio, says. "As a lover of democracy, I can appreciate that, but there was an advantage to having an electorate that couldn't figure out what was in a tax bill." What's more, polls are often misleading—in part because they can be manipulated, and in part because many issues are so complex that the public holds conflicting views of what it wants, and expects its representatives magically to resolve the conflict.

"Ultimately, there's very little clarity to all those poll numbers, even though a lot of analysts attach great significance to them," says Peter Smith, formerly a representative from Vermont and now the founding president of California State University at Monterey Bay. "Health care and welfare reform are abstractions, no matter what a poll says. People favor something in general. When you get down to specifics, however, they often don't." The debate last session over President Bill Clinton's health-care bill illustrated that principle once again.

The rise of constituency politics has also led the public to view legislators simply as instruments of its will. The political scientist David Mayhew, of Yale University, is not alone in having observed that the job of a federal legislator changed dramatically with the rise of New Deal and Great Society programs. Now an increasing number of constituents look to their legislator not only to obtain valuable pork-barrel projects for their state or district but also to help them obtain personal benefits from the government and its bureaucracies.

This development has been exacerbated by the fact that representatives have to serve more constituents today than they did in the past. Sixty-five representatives served four million Americans in the first Congress—a ratio of approximately 1:60,000. Today, with 435 representatives serving a population of more than 260 million, the ratio is approximately 1:600,000. Offices in home states have proliferated, and legislative aides have increasingly been transformed into caseworkers, thereby accounting for a healthy proportion of the increase in the size of those vilified congressional staffs. (The Republican reforms haven't even touched House and Senate personal-staff members, almost 40 percent of whom now work in district or state offices.) It should be no surprise, then, that voters increasingly view their legislators almost as personal therapists—a perspective that hardly encourages representatives to show any independence from the will of their districts, or to act in the national interest when it conflicts with local concerns. If legislators now seem excessively parochial and preoccupied with day-to-day responsiveness, that is what they are hearing the public demand.

While these changes have been occurring, Congress has also been attracting members of a different kind, whether Republican or Democrat. Virtually everyone agrees that today's representatives tend to be far better educated and informed, more professional, and less graft-ridden than their predecessors. Yet many also believe that something is missing from this generation in Congress—even from the new Republicans. "What happened is that as the quality of the legislature went up, its performance went down," says Theodore Lowi, a professor of government at Cornell University. "These people are much more individual entrepreneurs; they have far less respect for party institutions and hierarchy." Or, as the former representative Al Swift, of Washington, puts it, "We'd be better off with four hundred and ten followers and twenty-five leaders than the other way around."

The new entrepreneurial style is blamed in part for the lack of collegiality in Congress and the proliferation of committee and subcommittee assignments on the Hill, which have increased for senators and nearly doubled for representatives since the 1950s. (The number of committees and subcommittees has actually shrunk, owing to reorganizations; the Republican Contract With America has consolidated even more committees.) It also helps account, Lowi says, for the fact that Congress has become so sensitive to short-term public opinion: "They don't have the party to hide behind anymore. Because they're more individually accountable, they feel much more vulnerable and they react accordingly."

Circular Cures

REVERSING the trend toward a professional class of legislators is the goal of the term-limits movement. Mark Petracca, a political scientist at the University of California at Irvine, has written that legislative professionalization runs counter to the basic values of representative government, because "a profession entails a set of role relationships between 'experts' and 'clients'" which are fundamentally at odds with the way Congress is supposed to work. Yet the desire for a "citizen legislature," embodied in the term-limits movement, may be as quixotic as the search for a doctor who still makes house calls. "Sure, Congress has changed, but so has the country," says Ronald Peters, the director of the Carl Albert Congressional Research and Studies Center, at the University of Oklahoma. "Things have become less hierarchical than they once were almost everywhere. Part of this is generational, but a lot of it is just the way we've changed as a people. Legislators are more autonomous, but so is everyone else in the culture. This institution may be more professional, but all disciplines are becoming more professionalized. This is all part of a larger pattern, which in one sense couldn't be more representative."

The current cultural preoccupation with inclusion has also had important effects. Opening up the process to everyone—by such means as expansion of voting rights, more primaries and referenda, and encouraging access to government services—could be characterized as the major theme of our politics over the past third of a century, and there's obviously a lot to be said for it. The congressional response to Watergate, for example, often focused on the process of government, not its substance: lawmakers passed "sunshine laws" to force government to be more open and ethical, and in a spasm of reform wiped out many seniority privileges to make Congress more egalitarian. Even today, when complaints about Congress focus on how process reforms have still failed to address the institution's underlying problems, many of the popular ideas about how to change Congress—such as term limits and more referenda—continue to focus on process. The problems caused by being more democratic and process-oriented, both Republicans and Democrats seem to be saying, can be solved by being even more democratic and process-oriented.

The more a system values giving everyone a voice, however, the less it can value speed and effectiveness. All those voices have to be heard, and frequently they have to be accommodated. The correlate of enabling more women and members of minorities to be part of the legislature—a laudable goal—is that their concerns must be addressed, even though some of these concerns have traditionally been ignored by most legislatures. Irwin Gertzog, in his book *Congressional Women,* finds that women in Congress are far likelier than their male colleagues to stress such issues as the treatment of rape victims, the problems of displaced homemakers, and funding for diagnostic tests for breast cancer. "Congress succeeds much better as a representative body than it used to," says Michael Mezey, a professor of political science at DePaul University, "which means it's probably somewhat less successful as a lawmaking body."

Democratizing the internal rules of Congress has also made it harder to accomplish anything substantive. The more a culture moves toward democracy, however, the more it empowers those forces that have the ability to manipulate public opinion or provide access. The rise in the importance of media consultants, the press, and special-interest money is directly proportional to the growth of democracy in the culture and in Congress over the past thirty years. Read the polls or listen to talk radio and you will find that the complaints today are as much about these new forces and what they have done to the process as about anything else. The urge to destroy elites has simply created another class of them; the solution has become the problem. And the Republicans are doing next to nothing to stop that.

The Buck
Stops Nowhere

CONGRESS once tended to pass relatively concrete, simple laws in relatively few areas, which meant that the results of any lawmaking were far easier to assess. For our first 140 years it dealt with economic issues primarily through tariffs and focused on the country's expansion, wars, and treaties. There was little money to spend, and the Constitution had been interpreted as allowing far less federal intrusion into the workings of the states than we know today. "Nineteenth-century Congresses actually worked better," Theodore Lowi says. "They just passed very limited, piecemeal laws." At the turn of the century the House had no staff members and the Senate only a few. (By 1991 the personal staffs of the two houses together numbered more than 11,000, and nearly another 3,500 people worked for the committees.)

The passage of a federal income tax early in this century was the first step toward the creation of the welfare state. Still, the concept of dealing with complicated economic and social-welfare problems on a systematic national basis really arose during the crisis presented by the Great Depression and then the Second World War. Congress's response in the 1930s and the three decades that followed was to cede to the executive branch (which had drafted most of the laws in the first place) the authority to solve most of these problems—and the creation of administrative agencies, along with the enlargement of administrators' responsibilities, was often part of the solution. The idea was that many problems were too complex or technical for a legislature and that a specialized agency such as the Federal Communications Commission, or an administrator such as the Secretary of Agriculture, could do a better job of solving them. These agencies were also created in an era when there was much intellectual support for the notion that decisions should be taken away from legislatures and given to experts, who knew better.

The typical congressional grant of authority to do this was quite brief, simple, and vague: "[to regulate] interstate and foreign commerce in communication by wire and radio"; to make agricultural marketing "orderly." In theory, Congress would strictly oversee the agency's performance. In reality, representatives were usually happy to pass the buck to someone else and leave the agency alone, except when they needed a favor. As it happened, legislators soon discovered that such a setup also allowed them to claim credit for a program and then, if things went awry, "run against the bureaucracy"—a bureaucracy they had created, to avoid having to deal with problems themselves. The buck stopped nowhere.

The Supreme Court put a stop to elements of Roosevelt's New Deal, on the grounds that the Constitution simply did not allow the federal government to act in many areas. Support for a further expansion of federal power, however, took hold in the public imagination in the 1950s and 1960s, with the civil-rights revolution, which ended up discrediting intellectual and legal arguments about "states' rights." Nelson Polsby, an expert on Congress and a professor of political science at the University of California at Berkeley, says, "It became an article of faith among liberals that you can't trust Mississippi, so you have to nationalize these things."

60,000 Pages

FOR Lyndon Johnson's Great Society programs, in the mid-sixties, Congress was still using the New Deal agency as a model—with important differences. First, the traditional division between federal and state authority having been obliterated, Congress began moving into substantive areas, such as crime and housing, that had traditionally been beyond the purview of the federal government except in extreme emergencies. The early civil-rights laws were working, after all, and many of the nation's problems seemed rooted in its troubled racial past; a federal takeover seemed justified. Once involved in those areas, however, Congress kept expanding its grasp, eventually dictating to states on traditionally local questions—speed limits, for example. The result is that today Congress routinely passes laws dealing with local matters—crime, homelessness, education—and nobody even blinks at the loss of local control, which was once a cornerstone of our Jeffersonian public philosophy. As the former representative Al Swift puts it, "We've kind of blurred the distinction between a county sheriff and a congressman."

That's a recent and radical turn in our history, and one— "devolution" rhetoric to the contrary—that the Republicans show little sign of undoing. It is not simply that Speaker of the House Newt Gingrich may be misreading last year's election returns when he maintains that the public agrees it is time to dismantle much of the Great Society, or return programs to the states. The Contract With America, for example, promised a tougher anti-crime package, "strengthening rights of parents in their children's education," stronger child-pornography laws, and new rules to reform the welfare system, tort law, and product liability—efforts in many areas beyond what was seen as the purview of Congress when the Republicans last held both houses.

The 1960s blizzard of legislation came during an era when belief in the possibilities of governmental power may have been at a peak. In the 1965–1966 session alone nearly 20,000 bills were introduced. (The number in recent years has averaged fewer than 10,000 a session.) "If we can put a man on the moon, we can [fill in the blank]" seemed to characterize almost every politician's stump speech. Every problem, it seemed, had an effective legislative solution. Alan Ehrenhalt, the author of *The United States of Ambition*, finds that legislators of both parties still hold this belief. "Legislators are used to solving problems," he says. "Government tends to attract people who think government can solve problems. But once you get into things like crime, welfare, and education, you're trying to change human behavior, and that's much tougher to do. The New Deal was small potatoes compared to most of this stuff."

"Several things happen when the government gets into these areas," says James Q. Wilson, a professor of management and public policy at the University of California at Los Angeles. "First, no one really knows how to solve these problems. Second, the public itself is deeply conflicted about most of these issues; you rarely have a consensus from which to act. Third, these issues tend to be so complex that they overwhelm the process. And finally, when these measures fail to do much to solve something like crime—which is what inevitably happens—they greatly reinforce the general disillusionment with government. There's something to be said for sticking with what you know how to do."

During that legislative blizzard Congress was no longer just distributing money or dealing with problems in discrete areas (how to regulate the airwaves, or how to provide a supplemental income to senior citizens), and the grand problems it confronted, like poverty and crime, seemed to require a variety of coordinated strategies. "That was a key mistake," Theodore Lowi says. "Health and welfare are not holistic things; they're a collection of problems. The bills collapse of their own weight." Such bills also tend to be so elaborate that voters have difficulty understanding them—which means, at a minimum, that opponents have an easy time raising fears about them. Unsurprisingly, the public becomes more engaged when Congress is debating a seemingly straightforward issue like the Gulf War, in which voters can understand what is at stake.

Nonetheless, over time congressmen on both sides of the aisle began drafting longer, more comprehensive bills; the number of pages of law entered into the statute books during the relatively uneventful 1991–1992 session was two and a half times the number entered by the 1965–1966 Great Society Congress. With many legislators continually preoccupied by issues of openness and equal availability of services, access and due process became legislative focuses. That translated into greatly increased complexity and bureaucracy, not to mention a drain on the courts as litigants attempted to enforce their new rights. In 1936 there were 2,355 pages of regulations amplifying federal laws published in the Federal Register. By 1969 the number had risen to 20,464 pages; in the 1990s the register has been averaging about 60,000 pages a year.

No Amendments
Wanted

TRYING to solve a national megaproblem with one huge bill is still an American obsession, as the recent health-care debate showed. Still, by the late 1960s the old model of legislating had begun to fall out of favor, at least in one respect. The criticism, advanced by Ralph Nader and others, was that administrative agencies such as the Interstate Commerce Commission and the Federal Communications Commission inevitably became controlled by the forces they were supposed to regulate. Moreover, distrust of authority was expanding along with voting rights, and there was a corresponding lack of trust in the opinions of experts vis-à-vis "the people." As David Schoenbrod, a professor at New York Law School, has related in *Power Without Responsibility* (1993), what followed was a series of congressional statutes (beginning with the Clean Air Act, in 1970), passed with bipartisan support, that started to abandon the concept of open-ended delegation to independent agencies. Instead these laws essentially ordered the agency in question to take action and gave "elaborate instructions about the goals that it should achieve and the procedures for promulgating them." These instructions often placed administrative obligations on the states, while Congress took credit for the benefits of the legislation.

As a result of this legislative model statutes not only became lengthier and more complicated but also began running up hidden costs, while parochial and elite interests inevitably asserted their influence with help from both sides of the aisle: it was Alaska's Republican senator Ted Stevens, after all, who got grant money for Alaska to try to convert the aurora borealis into electricity. (As Congress-watchers point out, by the past session Congress was appropriating money for a University of Georgia study of city pests, ordering the Department of Health and Human Services to hire "six medium sedans" for transport, and adding what amounted to a gang-rehabilitation program to a flood-relief bill.) And over time Congress confronted many scientific or technical questions—such as how to clean the air—that were far beyond the expertise of most congressmen. So legislators of both parties hired more staff members to deal with these questions, and stopped reading much of their own legislation. Because members needed to rely on experts to draft these extensive and specific statutes, they also became increasingly reliant on "special interests"—if not to write the bills, then at least to tell them what the bills said before a vote. Cutting committee staff, as the Republicans have done, will hardly solve this problem, particularly for newer members, who tend to know less about technical problems than their more experienced colleagues.

The effect of an interstate-highway-building program or a Voting Rights Act—two legislative success stories from the 1950s and 1960s—can be assessed fairly easily. But, as Bruce Ackerman and Susan Rose-Ackerman, professors at Yale Law School, ask in *The Uncertain Search for Environmental Quality*, how does a deliberative body measure precisely the relationship between clean water and public health, let alone determine whether clean water could be had more cheaply by another method? What's more, even if a given approach makes sense now, things change over time. Once a bill gains a constituency—and all those that are enacted do, if only for economic reasons—it becomes very difficult to shift course.

The result has been a proliferation of vague or increasingly unworkable laws that judges cannot revise under current theories of statutory interpretation. (The same is not true of the common law.) These laws can also bankrupt the country, as the laws become ever more complex and costs mount. The Clean Air Act of 1970, complex as it was, filled forty-seven pages in the United States Code. The revision twenty years later filled more than 200 in the denser Congressional Record.

Having so many more constituents and areas of responsibility than it had in the past has also stymied Congress and shifted the way it operates. Besides muscling its way into areas once left to the states, Congress has spent an increasing amount of time over the past two decades on budgetary matters: the number of roll calls on budget questions in the House was almost six times as great in 1991 as it was in 1955—yet another trend that seems unlikely to change with Republican control. "The change in work load has affected the way Congress acts, which in turn has affected public perceptions," says Bruce I. Oppenheimer, a professor of political science at Vanderbilt University, who studies Congress. "In a time-constrained environment the opposition gains power. The filibuster wasn't used much before 1970, because it wasn't a very effective weapon. Who cared if you wasted time? Congress never ran out of time." In a legislative world where time is scarce, democratic values also tend to collapse and mistakes to become more common. One of the purposes of deliberation, after all, is to achieve consensus and avoid error. Tellingly, bills for many of the major legislative achievements of the past sixty years, though contentious, ended up passing with large majorities. For example, the Social Security Act passed in 1935 with seventy-seven votes in the Senate; the Civil Rights Act in 1964 won seventy-three.

Yet one of the distinguishing characteristics of recent sessions, particularly in the House, is that what little deliberation did once occur has been virtually eliminated. That, in turn, has increased partisanship. In recent years a bill has had about half the chance of passage that it had fifty years ago. In part to speed things up—which is, after all, what the public says it wants—bills introduced on the floor increasingly restrict amendments. Although the Republicans have promised to address that, so far there has been no significant change. Debates now typically take place with no one listening in the chamber, as anyone who has ever watched C-SPAN knows. Even the much-praised Senate and House exchanges before passage of the Gulf War resolution, in January of 1991, consisted primarily of members' rising to deliver prepared speeches to a body in which virtually every mind was already made up. And this year? The Republicans have added many new wrinkles to Congress, but careful deliberation does not appear to be among them.

The Camera and Congress

A DIFFERENT kind of congressional persona tends to flourish in the television age. Fifteen years ago Michael J. Robinson, a professor at Catholic University, wrote, "The increasingly greater reliance on the media for nomination, election, status in the Congress, and reelection is one sign of a new congressional character—one more dynamic, egocentric, immoderate, and, perhaps, intemperate." These telegenic figures, according to one source Robinson cited, were often more concerned with getting on television than with legislative mechanics—yet another reason for the lack of consensus, the emphasis on the illusion of results, and the expansion of staff to deal with the institution's real missions.

Because of its inherent biases, television has also subtly altered the way the public perceives Congress. C-SPAN, of course, has opened up the daily workings of Congress, but its effect is quite limited. C-SPAN's typical audience is minuscule compared with the audience that receives news about Congress from the major networks—which have greatly influenced the way print sources cover Congress.

The communications theorist Ernest Bormann once wrote that "television news coverage is, in many respects, an exercise in creative dramatics in which a cast of familiar characters assembles . . . and improvises a drama according to a stock scenario depending on the news event." By now the scenario involving Congress is very familiar. Because television is drawn to strong characters, it elevates the importance of the President and the speaker of the House vis-à-vis the institution of Congress. Because the medium is drawn to conflict, it denigrates the value of compromise, upon which legislatures depend, and plays up scandal or contentiousness. A recent study by S. Robert Lichter and Daniel R. Amundson, of the Center for Media and Public Affairs, has found that from 1972 to 1992 the proportion of network news stories concerning ethical lapses in Congress more than quadrupled, and the proportion of those portraying conflict between members nearly tripled from 1987 to 1992 (though, to be fair, conflict is up). Television is wedded to the dramatic gesture, and legislative bodies when legislating rarely act in a theatrical fashion. What's more, the legislative process is often messy and difficult; its lack of clear lines and packaging violates the whole spirit of scripted entertainment that has come to dominate the culture. The workings of Congress are complex and thus time-consuming to explain, and time is something that network television apparently cannot afford.

Changing the voters as much as the candidates, television creates a passive audience of viewer-voters who demand instant gratification and no loose ends. In a world where advertisers constantly proclaim, "You can have it all!" and "Just Do

It!" voters have come to see government institutions as ones that should provide it all and just do it, Ross Perot–style. Commercial television also offers an implicit vision of the world in which it's not community or belief in an abiding principle that offers happiness but the acquisition of goods. No wonder, then, that as television became pervasive and the postwar consumer culture took root, voters came increasingly to view the purpose of Congress—if not of government—as guaranteeing their right to that happiness.

With Congress thus increasingly frustrated in its primary responsibility to develop and pass good laws, its members have turned to other tasks, many of them nurtured by television. Here, too, the Republicans have been no different from the Democrats. The memorable moments of the past three decades in Congress have naturally tended to come in front of the cameras—from the McCarthy hearings to Watergate to the Anita Hill–Clarence Thomas confrontation. Congress has been conducting investigations since the 1790s. Yet it is undeniable that congressional investigations have flourished in the television age, thereby appropriating more of Congress's time and attention. Unlike the typical lawmaking process, these hearings offer the broadcast media drama and compelling characters in a stately scene. And, as Daniel Boorstin pointed out nearly thirty-five years ago, in his book *The Image*, the real purpose of hearings is often difficult to discern. "In many cases," Boorstin wrote, "these committees have virtually no legislative impulse, and sometimes no intelligible legislative assignment."

And there is the confirmation process—another area that consumes increasing amounts of the Senate's energy, if only because the number of posts that require confirmation has risen from 149 to 310 since 1960. Confirmation fights are also part of our history, but dramatic confirmation *hearings* are mostly a media-age phenomenon. Here, too, the consensus is that the cameras have contorted the process into great TV drama but something of a well-documented travesty. In foreign policy, a stage that Presidents have long dominated, Congress has tried to share the television spotlight in recent decades, with the same mixed results and a commensurate loss of time to spend in other areas. In *War and Responsibility* (1993) the Stanford University law professor John Hart Ely argues that while Congress has appeared to try to take more responsibility for military action in recent decades, it has in fact happily abdicated to the President most of its powers in this area. This has allowed many members to claim credit when military ventures go well, but to hold accusatory hearings and press conferences before the cameras when they don't.

Congressional actions in the television age have thus come to join the category that Boorstin called "pseudo-events"—in which the illusion of results becomes far more significant in the culture than the results themselves. In legislative hearings that don't really look at legislation, in crime bills that almost everyone privately admits will do next to nothing to reduce crime, the appearance and the drama of the action overshadow the importance of the action itself. Pseudo-events, Boorstin said, are usually more interesting than real actions, and they therefore seem more compelling and often more real. He wrote,

> Once we have tasted the charm of pseudo-events, we are tempted to believe they are the only important events. . . . And the poison tastes so sweet that it spoils our appetite for plain fact. Our seeming ability to satisfy our exaggerated expectations makes us forget that they are exaggerated.

Tainted Prescriptions

IN the end it is always easy to romanticize the past, just as it is tempting to exaggerate how much a shift in control will change Congress. A fifty-two-seat shift in the House is unusual in modern times, but it may mean only that the country is returning to the electoral patterns of a century ago, when party control of Congress often shifted back and forth by large margins, while the body drew its share of criticism. "There was no golden age of legislation," says the Yale political scientist David Mayhew.

Agreement is almost universal that Congress could take a number of steps both to purge itself of the effects of special-interest money and to make the legislative process operate more efficiently. After last November there is a perception of hope that the new majority will at least try to do the latter. (The Republican Party has never been enthusiastic about campaign-finance or lobbying reform.) But the Republicans, while in some ways addressing the expanding role of the federal government, appear only slightly more aware than the Democrats before them of the real polarities of sentiment that will have to be addressed before Congress can truly be reformed.

Few of the proposed structural reforms, moreover, would have the effect their proponents suggest. The notion, for example, that a national referendum would be any less susceptible than the legislative process to special-interest influence is ludicrous; and studies on term limits suggest that imposing a twelve-year limit would increase the mean turnover rate in the House by all of one percent per election (though it might, for better or worse, change the type of person elected to Congress). Sending Congress home for six months a year, or cutting down on staff, means that legislators would do less, more slowly; eliminating the filibuster and instituting referenda would be designed to get more or different laws on the books more quickly.

These reforms would not solve "the problem" with Congress, because voters and their representatives are terribly confused about what that is. Voters say they want less government at lower cost, but they apparently want it to do much of what it now does—or more. Polls tell us that among the major complaints about Congress are that it doesn't represent the voters well enough and that it becomes gridlocked—failing to solve the nation's lingering problems, such as health care and welfare reform. Yet over the past two generations Congress has become far more representative and responsive than it used to be, and it now addresses issues that previous legislatures never dreamed of. Nevertheless, as public disillusionment increases, the impulse has been to become even more closely tied to public opinion and to find new legislative ways of attacking megaproblems more quickly and efficiently. The Republicans don't propose to turn all of crime control or tort-law reform over to the states; they propose to enact many of the sweeping reforms themselves, and do it better and faster than the Democrats. So the demands and the contradictions spiral on, out of control. The solutions are manifestations of the problem.

Ironically, what Congress may need is not more democracy but less, and the will to address not bigger problems faster but smaller ones in more-measured ways. Admittedly, much of the civil-rights legislation of the 1960s changed the country profoundly for the better, and subsequent efforts toward greater democracy and openness were implemented in good faith. Now it is time to declare these efforts a success—we have democratized the process!—and move on to developing a public philosophy to address some of the problems we have acquired from encouraging access to national government.

In the populist rush to extend the spirit of democracy that, as Alexis de Tocqueville reminded us 150 years ago, is part of the American character, today's voters and leaders often forget that this is, in the end, a republic. The founders feared the power of the mob and provided distance between the rulers and the ruled, so that our representatives could deliberate much like a jury and exercise collective judgment and even wisdom. Their job, in the words of *The Federalist Papers*, was to "refine and enlarge" the popular will. It is a hierarchical relationship; they are entrusted with power. No parents or teachers worth their salt poll their children or pupils constantly and then give in at the first sign of discontent—just as no legislators in their right minds would cut taxes while keeping government benefits the same. Yet that's what pure representation will do for us a lot of the time. Paradoxically, giving legislators the freedom to forget about public opinion once in a while would do much to restore the voters' faith in the integrity of their representatives. Similarly, few would quarrel with the success of much of the New Deal—and even some of the Great Society—and many of our problems do require national solutions. But they don't necessarily demand complicated, comprehensive solutions.

"If I could get legislators to do just one thing, it would be to take a political Hippocratic oath," the author Alan Ehrenhalt says. "First, do no harm. Just attack things you can do something about." Theodore Lowi concurs. "Congress should narrow its agenda to a few things it knows how to do," he says. "And it should quit writing these large bills which pretend to address a problem but really don't, and create unforeseen problems in their wake."

Those steps alone, it seems, would require a shift in sentiment, in both parties and in the nation at large, not simply because they might mean the passage of fewer complicated entitlement programs for the middle class, but also because they would spell the end of the notion that there can somehow be a risk-free society with a government solution to every problem. The public and the press would also be required to reevaluate whether a buzz of legislative activity really constitutes a "golden age," and whether gridlock—which often means doing nothing because nothing can be done or because we don't know what to do—is always such a terrible thing. Yet such a change would even benefit liberalism. Congress would do less, but might well do better what it did, thereby increasing confidence in the national government generally. And the body might then have the will, occasionally, to act in the national interest by expanding government, even if that meant temporarily rejecting public opinion.

The "Outside" Role:
A Leadership Challenge

Joe S. Foote
Southern Illinois University

Joe Foote is dean of the College of Mass Communication and Media Arts at Southern Illinois University at Carbondale. He served as press secretary to Speaker Carl Albert.

Leaders of Congress have traditionally been considered strictly "inside" figures, fully consumed by the cloistered environment of Capitol Hill. The "outside" figure has always been the president, consistently attentive to the media and the winds of public opinion. Yet, the last two years have shown that a congressional leader can be just as visible as a president and can be just as effective in influencing public opinion. In Newt Gingrich, the congress finally has a television-age leader who values the external role more than any other twentieth century congressional leader. Some would argue that the outside role has already eclipsed the internal role in the Gingrich regime.

Speaker Gingrich is not only a disciple of an aggressive public strategy, but is a product of it. If it weren't for his unrelenting external presence, carefully calculated and executed over the past decade, Newt Gingrich would not be speaker today. As he told *Vanity Fair* in 1979, "If you're not in the *Washington Post,* every day, you might as well not exist." Abetted by C-SPAN and gifted with a knack for surfing the waves of media attention, Speaker Gingrich has already established himself as the House's most visible leader ever.

This is quite a contract to Speaker Sam Rayburn fifty years earlier who worked hard to avoid being quoted in the *Washington Post* every day. Speaker Rayburn routinely turned down interview opportunities that senators would die for. He ensured that all House proceedings, including committees, would be off limits to television cameras. Speaker Rayburn was making no idle comparison when he separated members into "showhorses" and "workhorses." In Rayburn's mind, the roles were mutually exclusive; there could be no successful leader of the House with obvious showhorse tendencies. Making headlines was a temptation, not an opportunity.

The contrasts between the styles of Rayburn and Gingrich—Mr. Inside and Mr. Outside—are clear. One methodically climbed the ladder to leadership; the other pole-vaulted over it. One built a career on personal relationships; the other built a career in spite of them. One quietly molded his life around protecting the House as an institution; the other boldly and visibly built a career fighting against it. One saw the media as a force to fear; the other, a force to embrace.

While Speakers Rayburn and Gingrich stand out in the panorama of important congressional figures who influenced media coverage in the twentieth century, the sea change in attitude between the two speakerships occurred incrementally over a generation. Speaker Gingrich accelerated an evolutionary process that began in the years after Sam Rayburn's death and steadily grew during the succeeding forty years in the House of Representatives.

Sam Rayburn left a strong philosophical legacy that affected a whole generation of his successors. McCormack, Albert, O'Neill, Wright, and Foley all had Rayburn's stamp on them in one degree or another. Yet, each of these legislative leaders made a mark that paved the way for an externally-oriented leader like Gingrich to emerge.

Legislative leaders following Rayburn had little choice but to pay closer attention to their external roles. During the 1960s and 1970s, the president's public opinion ascendance through television was extraordinary, leaving Congress deep in the media backwaters. The huge gap created by the ascendance of the presidency was so wide that the media became its own self-appointed, de facto "loyal opposition" to the president. Americans became accustomed to seeing a network commentator rather than a congressional leader rebut the president. Congressional leaders were invisible on the national stage. Only years later, with the iron grip of the networks on audiences loosened and the leadership more attuned to the media, did the Congress make headway.

While there was public criticism of the leadership for its obvious publicity shortcomings vis-á-vis the White House, the real impetus for change came from within the House itself. After the "Watergate" class of Democrats was elected in 1974, a sizable group of activist backbenchers questioned the Rayburn legacy of strictly inside leadership. The freshmen quickly seized on the inability of the leadership to communicate effectively to an external audience and pressured them to play a more aggressive external role. Newer members who had clawed their way to victory in closely-contested districts by running media-savvy campaigns saw disaster approaching for leaders who did not strive for exposure.

This internal discontent over external matters was the first sign that Rayburn's showhorse/workhorse dichotomy was breaking down. A new generation of House members already had press secretaries and advocated a proactive, aggressive use of the mass media on behalf of their party and the institution. In response to the freshmen's demands, Speaker Albert appointed a Task Force on Information within the Democratic Caucus headed by Majority Whip John Brademas of Indiana, a House member well-attuned to the concerns of the freshmen. The goal was to improve congressional Democrats' ability to communicate. This was a forerunner of the efforts by Speakers Wright and Foley to craft a message of the day and develop a cohesive leadership communication strategy.

Speaker O'Neill faced similar pressures from the rank-and-file when the leadership appeared incapable of mounting a stand to Ronald Reagan's bold economic assault in the early 1980s. As the Democratic point man facing off with the "great communicator," Speaker O'Neill had to rachet up the profile of his office. He switched from a press secretary known for his keen legislative prowess to one known strictly for his ability to lead a partisan publicity charge. Former Carter speechwriter Chris Matthews established a presidential style press operation in the Speaker's office and spoke directly to the media on behalf of the leadership, breaking a longstanding taboo that leadership staff should be invisible. This combative, proactive media stance was designed to grab headlines, not avoid them. By the time this new press operation had been fully implemented, the Speaker was grabbing headlines and sound bites comparable to the president. In one personnel change, the Rayburn media legacy had taken a huge dive.

entire Congress; the majority of coverage went to a handful of members. With the televising of the House, however, backbench members started to eat away at the leadership's exclusive franchise on media attention. Many new opportunities for exposure appeared, especially at the regional and local level.

Newt Gingrich and some of his minority colleagues quickly proved that being noticed on C-SPAN by a few thousand of the right citizens and by the Washington media could be a springboard for national exposure. The Republicans' clever and consistent use of the obscure Special Orders prerogative at the end of the House day proved a more effective communication tool than any traditional media the minority leader had used. Within a few years, the minority House leadership was scrambling to keep up with the publicity machine created by minority backbenchers.

Having seen the success of their home-grown publicity machine, younger minority members became less tolerant of their leadership's Rayburn-mold passivity, placing the same kind of pressure on Minority Leader Bob Michel as the Democrats had on Albert and O'Neill. When Gingrich was elected minority whip in 1989, the Republican leadership's "outside" role escalated. Republican guerilla media attacks, now

even members, became much more conversant with the floor proceedings and committee hearings through the monitors in their offices. With internal communication coming from sources other than the leadership, both the majority and minority leaders had to devise higher profile communication with their constituencies. Increasingly, cues from the leadership to members and staff came from a mass media backdrop.

After a decade of televised House proceedings, the leadership, as well as younger members, were becoming comfortable with the American public looking over their shoulders. By getting a seven-year headstart on the Senate, the House charged ahead of its showhorse counterpart in gaining media exposure, forcing senators to race to catch up. C-SPAN attracted a small, but loyal, following. The national broadcast media gravitated toward the real time coverage of the House floor. Local television stations around the nation found it much easier and cheaper to pick up a sound bite from their representative on the House floor than to arrange a special interview with a senator. When a major legislative issue came to Congress, C-SPAN captured the drama of the moment in the House, making the previously reclusive body more appealing. By the time C-SPAN II started covering the Senate, channel space on local cable systems was very tight, leaving the House coverage on the dominant channel.

DURING THE 1960s AMERICANS BECAME ACCUSTOMED TO SEEING A NETWORK COMMENTATOR RATHER THAN A CONGRESSIONAL LEADER REBUT THE PRESIDENT.

Outside the leadership, only a handful of House members gained national television exposure though many sought it. Some of my research showed that the majority of House members never received any network exposure during an

an official part of the leadership arsenal, became a constant distraction for the majority leadership and a great morale builder for the minority.

Televising of the House also had an effect within the institution. Staff, and

By the beginning of the Bush administration, the leadership had come a long way from the Rayburn media legacy. There had been significant changes in the leadership's attitudes towards media exposure and the entire external role. Professional press operations became the norm. Coordinated leadership initiatives designed to sway public opinion were mounted. The broadcast media found new doors open to them. The stage was set for a leader born in the television age who could consolidate these evolutionary forces and frame a new model for congressional leadership communication.

Speaker Gingrich met that challenge. He charged into his speakership fully mindful of the importance of the external role and determined to move the leadership toward a more competitive position with the White House than it had ever known. Within a few months, Speaker Gingrich had focused an unprecedented amount of attention on the majority leadership; for a few weeks, the Speaker was more visible than the president. Yet, there was a downside risk to this high profile strategy. More publicity was not always good publicity. Just a few months into his speakership, Speaker Gingrich cancelled his daily news briefing, a tradition that his "inside" predecessors had adhered to religiously for more than half a century. A year later when polls showed the Speaker's negative ratings among the public were high, he virtually disappeared from the media radar screen.

Because confrontation was a key ingredient in Speaker Gingrich's recipe for publicity, he ran the risk that his "outside" strategy could negatively influence his "inside" strategy. In the end, congressional leaders are measured more by their success in passing legislation and their success in dealing with colleagues than in the publicity they generate. The same members of Congress who grouse about leaders failing to mount an external offensive might be the first to criticize a leader for being unfair or overly partisan during their particular moment of need. Ultimately, Speakers must satisfy their internal constituency. Traditionally, members have placed great value on having a Speaker whom they respect who can arbitrate their conflicts, preside over the institution fairly, and be responsive to their needs.

We are now at a point where the "inside" and "outside" roles of the congressional leadership, previously only remotely connected, are highly interrelated. The House can afford neither to squander opportunities to compete forcefully in the public arena nor to let a compulsive quest for publicity diminish its internal cohesiveness or legislative effectiveness. The challenge for Speaker Gingrich and all congressional leaders is to strike the right balance between the internal and external elements of their jobs. Yet, to do both simultaneously in an institution where the "inside" role is more firmly anchored may prove elusive.

It's Not *Mr. Smith Goes to Washington*

The Senate filibuster ain't what it used to be

BY BILL DAUSTER

THE LADY VANISHED. . . . "I OBJECT," was all she said before she turned and strode through the swinging doors. Senate Democratic Leader Tom Daschle called out to the lady, Senator Kay Bailey Hutchison: "Would the senator from Texas wish to state her reason for the objection? Mr. President, could we get the attention of the senator from Texas?" But she was gone.

Such is the fashion of the filibuster in the modern Senate. No longer does a senator hold the floor in long, impassioned debate, as in the film *Mr. Smith Goes to Washington*. Now legislators log their filibusters with the leadership, and the Senate pretends to hold them. A senator doesn't even need to attend her own filibuster. Her party handles it for her.

It used to be more like the movies. Senators delivered seemingly interminable speeches. They taxed their stamina to the limit. They employed clever means to sustain themselves for long periods during which they could neither eat nor withdraw to answer nature's call.

BILL DAUSTER *is the Senate Budget Committee's Democratic Chief of Staff.*

The indefatigable Senator Strom Thurmond holds the record. In August 1957, he addressed the Senate for 24 hours and 18 minutes in an effort to halt the advance of civil rights for African Americans. Running a close second, Senator Wayne Morse held the floor for over 22 hours fighting the Tidelands oil bill in 1953. Senator Robert La Follette Sr. spent almost 19 hours on his feet battling the Aldrich-Vreeland currency bill in 1908.

These somnolent soliloquies earned the Senate a reputation as a tiring place. Former Dean of the House of Representatives Jamie Whitten told how, in the wee hours of the morning, Senator Homer Ferguson once confessed, "Jamie, there are only two ways our Senate can act, either by unanimous consent or exhaustion."

The record for the longest speech of recent years belongs to Senator Alfonse D'Amato of New York, who held up a tax bill in October 1992 in a vain bid to save jobs at a Cortland, N. Y., typewriter factory. But Senator D'Amato's election-year filibuster had more to do with showmanship than legislation. His performance included singing selections from "Deep in the Heart of Texas" (for the benefit of Finance Committee Chairman Lloyd Bentsen, who just wanted to finish his tax bill) and "South of the Border" (where the typewriter jobs seemed headed). Alessandra Stanley of _The New York Times_ placed it "somewhere between Jimmy Stewart taking on the capital and the final moments of the 'Jerry Lewis Telethon.'"

Senator D'Amato's musical revue was the exception to the modern rule. More and more frequently, senators are forgoing the traditional practice of personally holding the floor to delay a vote. Now, senators simply register with their party leader, usually by letter, their objections to the Senate's proceeding to a matter. This objection—called "a hold"—implies the threat of a filibuster should the Senate take up the disputed matter. With the leadership honoring her hold, a senator can be assured that action on the disputed matter will be slowed—even in the senator's absence. The majority leader reserves the right to force a senator to come down to the Senate floor and object in person, as Majority Leader Trent Lott obliged Senator Hutchison to do on the occasion just related. But once Senator Hutchison registered her objection, she felt entirely secure exiting the chamber, relying on her leader to protect her rights—in this instance, to block the confirmation of a district court judge in Minnesota.

Of course, by choosing not to hold the floor themselves, senators lose some of their influence over the process. In honoring a hold, the party leadership agrees to slow a disputed matter from coming to the floor, but its overriding concerns remain to advance the party's general interests and to prevent the legislative process from grinding to a halt. (In Hutchison's case, the Senate went on to confirm the nominee.) If the disputed matter affects only one region or interest group, the party may not do much to protect an individual senator. In such instances, the affected legislators may have to resort to a full-fledged fili-

No longer does a senator hold the floor in a long, impassioned debate. Now they log their filibusters with the leadership, and the Senate pretends to hold them.

buster, as Senators Harry Reid and Richard Bryan of Nevada did in opposing legislation to locate a nuclear waste dump in their state. Still, more and more frequently, senators seem content to sacrifice a little control for convenience.

Stand and Deliver

When senators felt compelled to stand and deliver their demurrals, they tended to reserve the fili-

buster for a deeply held belief. But the modern filibuster, what Senate Parliamentarian Bob Dove calls "the gentleman's filibuster," involves so little inconvenience to individual senators that they use it for everything. Now, minor policy disputes readily escalate into filibusters requiring a vote of cloture, creating what Dove calls the "60-vote Senate": Any matter about which senators hold any feelings winds up requiring a supermajority of votes. As then-Senator Dan Quayle complained to _Congressional Quarterly_ in 1987, the Senate has "trivialized" the filibuster.

Ending debate by a vote of cloture has also become less cumbersome. To make the trains run on time, in 1975, then-Majority Whip Robert Byrd pushed through a change in the filibuster rule, reducing the two-thirds vote requirement to a vote of 60 senators. Not surprisingly, the leadership began invoking cloture more frequently. Whereas the Senate conducted 45 roll-call votes on cloture in the entire half-century from 1919 to 1969, it conducted 99 in the 1970s and 138 in the 1980s. Already, 168 have been conducted in the 1990s. This increase has not gone unnoticed by legislators. Back in 1984, a select committee on procedure chaired by then-Senator Quayle concluded: "Cloture is not only invoked too often, it is invoked too soon."

At this point, the Senate rarely even bothers with the formal cloture procedure, which allows debate on a disputed bill to continue for 30 hours after the cloture is invoked. Instead, the Senate usually agrees by unanimous consent to hold the final vote at the time convenient to the largest number of senators. Why debate all night when you cannot debate and say you did?

This no-fuss objection process has become a favorite tool for partisan disruption. This summer, the minimum wage bill, a gas-tax repeal, the health insurance bill, and a small-business tax cut bill were all locked together for a time like so many scorpions in a death grip of objections. During the previous Congress, Republicans successfully employed filibusters to block several Clinton initiatives, notably campaign finance and health care reform. Democrats tried the same in the 1980s.

This being an election year, the threat of filibusters has been especially popular in putting the brakes on the confirmation of judges and other appointed officials. No majority leader wants to spend the several days that calling a senator's bluff—or enduring an actual filibuster—would take simply to confirm a judge, especially one nominated by the president of another party. In effect, the Senate has raised the bar for appointment to many high offices to near unanimous approval from a club that includes—truth to tell—at least a few eccentric members. To his credit, Majority Leader Lott tried to march the Senate through a number of nominations, but occasionally ran into resistance, as with Senator Hutchison.

The ever-present threat of a filibuster does have an upside. At times, the intimation of such a delay is enough to get people talking. This summer, Senator Ted Kennedy used the threat of a filibuster to alter the Kennedy-Kassebaum health insurance bill. Making only a few explanatory speeches of reasonable length, and with the cooperation of his party's leadership, Senator Kennedy held up the appointment of conferees in order to negotiate differences between the House and Senate bills. He thus extracted from the Republican leadership a commitment that the final bill would contain a much more modest experiment on tax-subsidized medical savings accounts than Republicans wanted.

Still, the filibuster madness often frustrates senators. In mid-July, Majority Leader Lott complained bitterly at his news briefings of "slow-rolling gridlock" and "absolute gridlock." This increased frustration further erodes the Senate's storied comity. Perceiving less comity, a senator is more likely to throw a filibuster into the works of another senator's legislative dream. And so the Senate descends into a spiral of bitterness.

Frequent filibustering also frustrates voters. The 60-vote Senate has sapped the effectiveness of even relatively strong majority leaders like Bob Dole, Robert Byrd, and George Mitchell. When the Senate cannot enact the majority party's legislative agenda, the public questions the majority's competence or—worse yet—its sincere desire to get anything done. Without the accompanying oratories of explanation, the delays caused by gentleman's filibusters can seem pointlessly disruptive to the general public, and the Senate's workings become even less understandable to observers (which, thanks to C-Span, constitute more and more Americans). The public's cynicism grows because of the incomprehensible nature of the legislative process.

Cloture Clots

Several legislators have proposed changing the system. Senator Ron Wyden has made the modest proposal that senators be required to publicly acknowledge the holds they place. Majority Leader Lott is considering the proposal, but don't hold your breath.

Senator Quayle's 1984 committee recommended making it possible to end a filibuster simply on the motion to proceed. The 1993 Joint Committee on the Organization of Congress endorsed the proposal, but it went nowhere.

Calling filibusters "a process that is out of control," Senator Tom Harkin of Iowa proposed a sliding-scale cloture rule not unlike the pricing practices at clothing stores. The longer the Senate stayed on a matter, the fewer votes cloture would require. The Senate rejected Senator Harkin's amendment by a 76-to-19 vote.

The change most likely to curb the filibuster is the expansion of the budget process. Early in the 1980s and again this year, the majority stretched the budget process—which has time limits and thus immunity from filibustering—to cover nonbudgetary matters. That's how Congress enacted a Republican-leaning welfare reform bill this year. And this year's budget blueprint contemplated using the fast-track budget process for tax cuts.

While aimed at curbing abuses, these incursions on the filibuster threaten an important tool. For all its inconveniences, the filibuster serves useful purposes. Most significantly, it empowers organized minority parties and coalitions. Senator Byrd, who has stood on both the giving and receiving end of many a filibuster, writes in his Senate history:

> The Senate is the only forum in the government where the perfection of laws may be unhurried and where controversial decisions may be hammered out on the anvil of lengthy debate. The liberties of a free people will always be safe where a forum exists in which open and unlimited debate is allowed.

Maybe what we need is more debate, not less. Bring the decision making out of the back rooms and onto the Senate floor. Let the public see what all the deliberations and delays are about. Senators should be compelled once more to stand up, literally, for their convictions. Organized minorities certainly deserve a forum for objections, but the process should not be so simple it invites abuse. As with any freedom, misuse will lead to frustration and anger, resulting in misguided "reforms" that endanger the freedom itself. And senators' freedom to filibuster may at times preserve freedoms for us all.

The case against strict constructionism.

WHAT AM I? A POTTED PLANT?

RICHARD A. POSNER

Richard A. Posner is a judge on the U.S. Court of Appeals for the Seventh Circuit and a senior lecturer at the University of Chicago Law School.

MANY PEOPLE, not all of conservative bent, believe that modern American courts are too aggressive, too "activist," too prone to substitute their own policy preferences for those of the elected branches of government. This may well be true. But some who complain of judicial activism espouse a view of law that is too narrow. And a good cause will not hallow a bad argument.

This point of view often is called "strict constructionism." A more precise term would be "legal formalism." A forceful polemic by Walter Berns in the June 1987 issue of *Commentary*—"Government by Lawyers and Judges"—summarizes the formalist view well. Issues of the "public good" can "be decided legitimately only with the consent of the governed." Judges have no legitimate say about these issues. Their business is to address issues of private rights, that is, "to decide whether the right exists—in the Constitution or in a statute—and, if so, what it is; but at that point inquiry ceases." The judge may not use "discretion and the weighing of consequences" to arrive at his decisions and he may not create new rights. The Constitution is a source of rights, but only to the extent that it embodies "fundamental and clearly articulated principles of government." There must be no judicial creativity or "policy-making."

In short, there is a political sphere, where the people rule, and there is a domain of fixed rights, administered but not created or altered by judges. The first is the sphere of discretion, the second of application. Legislators make the law; judges find and apply it.

There has never been a time when the courts of the United States, state or federal, behaved consistently in accordance with this idea. Nor could they, for reasons rooted in the nature of law and legal institutions, in the limitations of human knowledge, and in the character of a political system.

"Questions about the public good" and "questions about private rights" are inseparable. The private right is conferred in order to promote the public good. So in deciding how broadly the right shall be interpreted, the court must consider the implications of its interpretation for the public good. For example, should an heir who murders his benefactor have a right to inherit from his victim? The answer depends, in part anyway, on the public good that results from discouraging murders. Almost the whole of so-called private law, such as property, contract, and tort law, is instrumental to the public end of obtaining the social advantages of free markets. Furthermore, most private law is common law—that is, law made by judges rather than by legislators or by constitution-framers. Judges have been entrusted with making policy from the start.

Often when deciding difficult questions of private rights courts have to weigh policy considerations. If a locomotive spews sparks that set a farmer's crops afire, has the railroad invaded the farmer's property right or does the railroad's ownership of its right of way implicitly include the right to emit sparks? If the railroad has such a right, shall it be conditioned on the railroad's taking reasonable precautions to minimize the danger of fire? If, instead, the farmer has the right, shall it be conditioned on his taking reasonable precautions? Such questions cannot be answered sensibly without considering the social consequences of alternative answers.

A second problem is that when a constitutional convention, a legislature, or a court promulgates a rule of law, it necessarily does so without full knowledge of the circumstances in which the rule might be invoked in the future. When the unforeseen circumstance arises—it might be the advent of the motor vehicle or of electronic surveillance, or a change in attitudes toward religion, race, and sexual propriety—a court asked to apply the rule must decide, in light of information not available to the promulgators of the rule, what the rule should mean in its new setting. That is a creative decision, involving discretion, the weighing of consequences, and, in short, a kind of legislative judgment—though, properly, one more confined than if the decision were being made by a real legislature. A court that decides, say, that copyright protection extends to the coloring of old black-and-white movies is making a creative decision, because the copyright laws do not mention colorization. It is not being lawless or usurpative merely because it is weighing consequences and exercising discretion.

Or if a court decides (as the Supreme Court has done in one of its less controversial modern rulings) that the Fourth Amendment's prohibition against unreasonable searches and seizures shall apply to wiretapping, even though no trespass is committed by wiretapping and hence no property right is invaded, the court is creating a new right and making policy. But in a situation not foreseen and expressly provided for by the Framers of the Constitution, a simple reading out of a policy judgment made by the Framers is impossible.

EVEN THE MOST carefully drafted legislation has gaps. The Constitution, for example, does not say that the federal government has sovereign immunity—the right, traditionally enjoyed by all sovereign governments, not to be sued without its consent. Nevertheless the Supreme Court held that the federal government has sovereign immunity. Is this interpolation usurpative? The Federal Tort Claims Act, a law waiving sovereign immunity so citizens can sue the government, makes no exception for suits by members of the armed services who are injured through the negligence of their superiors. Nevertheless the Supreme Court has held that the act was not intended to provide soldiers with a remedy. The decision may be right or wrong, but it is not wrong just because it is creative. The 11th Amendment to the Constitution forbids a citizen of one state to sue "another" state in federal court without the consent of the defendant state. Does this mean that you can sue your own state in federal court without the state's consent? That's what the words seem to imply, but the Supreme Court has held that the 11th Amendment was intended to preserve the sovereign immunity of the states more broadly. The Court thought this was implied by the federalist system that the Constitution created. Again the Court may have been right or wrong, but it was not wrong just because it was creative.

Opposite the unrealistic picture of judges who apply law but never make it, Walter Berns hangs an unrealistic picture of a populist legislature that acts only "with the consent of the governed." Speaking for myself, I find that many of the political candidates whom I have voted for have failed to be elected and that those who have been elected have then proceeded to enact much legislation that did not have my consent. Given the effectiveness of interest groups in the political process, much of this legislation probably didn't have the consent of a majority of citizens. Politically, I feel more governed than self-governing. In considering whether to reduce constitutional safeguards to slight dimensions, we should be sure to have a realistic, not an idealized, picture of the legislative and executive branches of government, which would thereby be made more powerful than they are today.

To banish all discretion from the judicial process would indeed reduce the scope of constitutional rights. The framers of a constitution who want to make it a charter of liberties and not just a set of constitutive rules face a difficult choice. They can write specific provisions, and thereby doom their work to rapid obsolescence or irrelevance; or they can write general provisions, thereby delegating substantial discretion to the authoritative interpreters, who in our system are the judges. The U.S. Constitution is a mixture of specific and general provisions. Many of the specific provisions have stood the test of time amazingly well or have been amended without any great fuss. This is especially true of the rules establishing the structure and procedures of Congress. Most of the specific provisions creating rights, however, have fared poorly. Some have proved irksomely anachronistic—for example, the right to a jury trial in federal court in all cases at law if the stakes exceed $20. Others have become dangerously anachronistic, such as the right to bear arms. Some have even turned topsy-turvy, such as the provision for indictment by grand jury. The grand jury has become an instrument of prosecutorial investigation rather than a protection for the criminal suspect. If the Bill of Rights had consisted entirely of specific provisions, it would have aged very rapidly and would no longer be a significant constraint on the behavior of government officials.

MANY PROVISIONS of the Constitution, however, are drafted in general terms. This creates flexibility in the face of unforeseen changes, but it also creates the possibility of multiple interpretations, and this possibility is an embarrassment for a theory of judicial legitimacy that denies that judges have any right to exercise discretion. A choice among semantically plausible interpretations of a text, in circumstances remote from those contemplated by its drafters, requires the exercise of discretion and the weighing of consequences. Reading is not a form of deduction; understanding requires a consideration of consequences. If I say, "I'll eat my hat," one reason that my listeners will "decode" this in non-literal fashion is that I couldn't eat a hat if I tried. The broader principle, which applies to the Constitution as much as to a spoken utterance, is that if one possible interpretation of an ambiguous statement would entail absurd or terrible results, that is a good reason to adopt an alternative interpretation.

Even the decision to read the Constitution narrowly, and thereby "restrain" judicial interpretation, is not a decision that can be read directly from the text. The Constitution does not say, "Read me broadly," or, "Read me narrowly." That decision must be made as a matter of political theory, and will depend on such things as one's view of the springs of judicial legitimacy and of the relative competence of courts and legislatures in dealing with particular types of issues.

Consider the provision in the Sixth Amendment that "in all criminal prosecutions, the accused shall enjoy the right . . . to have the Assistance of Counsel for his defense." Read narrowly, this just means that the defendant can't be forbidden to retain counsel; if he can't afford counsel, or competent counsel, he is out of luck. Read broadly, it guarantees even the indigent the effective assistance of counsel; it becomes not just a negative right to be allowed to hire a lawyer but a positive right to demand the help of the government in financing one's defense. Either reading is compatible with the semantics of the provision, but the first better captures the specific intent of the Framers. At the time the Sixth Amendment was written, English law forbade a criminal defendant to have the assistance of counsel unless abstruse questions of law arose in his case. The Framers wanted to do away with this prohibition. But, more broadly, they wanted to give criminal defendants protection against being railroaded. When they wrote, government could not afford, or at least did not think it could afford, to hire lawyers for indigent criminal defendants. Moreover, criminal trials were short and simple, so it was not ridiculous to expect a person to defend himself without a lawyer if he couldn't afford to hire one. Today the situation is different. Not only can the society easily afford to supply lawyers to poor people charged with crimes, but modern criminal law and procedure are so complicated that an unrepresented defendant will usually be at a great disadvantage.

I DO NOT KNOW whether Professor Berns thinks the Supreme Court was usurping legislative power when it held in the *Gideon* case that a poor person has a right to the assistance of counsel at the state's expense. But his article does make clear his view that the Supreme Court should not have invalidated racial segregation in public schools. Reading the words of the 14th Amendment in the narrowest possible manner in order to minimize judicial discretion, and noting the absence of evidence that the Framers wanted to eliminate segregation, Berns argues that "equal protection of the laws" just means non-discriminatory enforcement of whatever laws are enacted, even if the laws themselves are discriminatory. He calls the plausible empirical proposition that "separate educational facilities are inherently unequal" "a logical absurdity."

On Berns's reading, the promulgation of the equal protection clause was a trivial gesture at giving the recently freed slaves (and other blacks, whose status at the time was little better than that of serfs) political equality with whites, since the clause in his view forbids the denial of that equality only by executive officers. The state may not withdraw police protection from blacks (unless by legislation?) but it may forbid them to sit next to whites on buses. This is a possible reading of the 14th Amendment but not an inevitable one, unless judges must always interpret the Constitution as denying them the power to exercise judgment.

No one really believes this. Everyone professionally connected with law knows that, in Oliver Wendell Holmes's famous expression, judges legislate "interstitially," which is to say they make law, only more cau-

tiously, more slowly, and in more principled, less partisan, fashion than legislators. The attempt to deny this truism entangles "strict constructionists" in contradictions. Berns says both that judges can enforce only "clearly articulated principles" and that they may invalidate unconstitutional laws. But the power to do this is not "articulated" in the Constitution; it is merely implicit in it. He believes that the courts have been wrong to interpret the First Amendment as protecting the publication of foul language in school newspapers, yet the words "freedom of speech, or of the press" do not appear to exclude foul language in school newspapers. Berns says he deduces his conclusion from the principle that expression, to be within the scope of the First Amendment, must be related to representative government. Where did he get that principle from? He didn't read it in the Constitution.

THE FIRST AMENDMENT also forbids Congress to make laws "respecting an establishment of religion." Berns says this doesn't mean that Congress "must be neutral between religion and irreligion." But the words will bear that meaning, so how does he decide they should be given a different meaning? By appealing to Tocqueville's opinion of the importance of religion in a democratic society. In short, the correct basis for decision is the consequence of the decision for democracy. Yet consequences are not—in the strict constructionist view—a fit thing for courts to consider. Berns even expresses regret that the modern Supreme Court is oblivious to Tocqueville's opinion "of the importance of the woman . . . whose chastity as a young girl is protected not only by religion but by an education that limits her 'imagination.'" A court that took such opinions into account would be engaged in aggressively consequentialist thinking rather than in strict construction.

The liberal judicial activists may be imprudent and misguided in their efforts to enact the liberal political agenda into constitutional law, but it is no use pretending that what they are doing is not interpretation but "deconstruction," not law but politics, because it involves the exercise of discretion and a concern with consequences and because it reaches results not foreseen 200 years ago. It may be bad law because it lacks firm moorings in constitutional text, or structure, or history, or consensus, or other legitimate sources of constitutional law, or because it is reckless of consequences, or because it oversimplifies difficult moral and political questions. But it is not bad law, or no law, just because it violates the tenets of strict construction.

A Conservative Case for Judicial Activism

David P. Bryden

David P. Bryden is professor of law at the University of Minnesota.

Conservatives sometimes remark that liberals would be less enamored of judicial activism if it were employed on behalf of conservative causes. A powerful polemical point, surely, but not one that has caused much insomnia in Cambridge.

For the premise of the argument—that conservative Justices might fashion an array of novel "conservative rights"—is known to be an almost entirely empty threat. Most conservatives reject that sort of activism, and so does the Rehnquist Court. When conservatives fault the Court, it is not for failing to create conservative rights, but for occasionally reaffirming liberal rights such as the right to abortion.

I have much sympathy for this view. I agree that the Court's role should, ideally, be narrowly circumscribed. In defending this ideal, however, conservatives have neglected to ask whether it is attainable—a curious omission for those who habitually accuse liberals of wishful thinking.

I will offer here some friendly criticisms of conventional conservative jurisprudence. My purpose is to acknowledge the political realities of constitutional adjudication, without sacrificing what is authentic and valuable in the concepts of neutral principles and the rule of law.

FRAMING THE QUESTION

Scholars of all political creeds have assumed that the basic question in constitutional jurisprudence is: How should the Supreme Court interpret the Constitution? We do not ask how an individual Justice should interpret the Constitution, but rather how "the Court" should do so. There are obvious reasons for this. Judicial decisions are usually the product of at least some collective deliberation, and are handed down not as the edicts of individuals, nor even of a dominant majority, but rather in the name of the court. Yet the question of how a "court" should decide cases is—in an important sense—unrealistic. Courts don't think; individuals do. Even when Justices act in concert, their collective decisions require antecedent individual decisions.

Of course, in most legal contexts the convention that leads us to discuss what "a court" ought to do, rather than what an individual judge should do, is convenient and harmless. There is no important difference between the two. If we know how a court" should decide an issue of contract law, then we know how an individual judge should decide the same issue. In the field of constitutional law, I will suggest, this is far less true. In constitutional law, unlike most other branches of law, there is no judicial consensus on the ground rules and aims of the enterprise. In constitutional law, liberal and conservative judges are not always playing by the same rules.

Mainstream conservatives believe that the most fundamental norm of constitutional adjudication is "judicial restraint." This is a loose term that I will define as a court's refusal, for principled reasons, to exceed its proper authority and role. Conservatives justify judicial restraint chiefly on two grounds. First, they argue that restraint is often required by the Justices' obligation to apply the original meaning of the Constitution ("originalism"), rather than engage in "result-oriented" judging. And second, conservatives believe that by confining the role of courts, judicial restraint preserves federalism and democracy.

These are the standard justifications for judicial restraint. My question is this: Do these justifications lose validity, for any individual Justice, if he or she discovers that most other Justices do not accept them?

RIGHT, WRONG, AND IN-BETWEEN

In everyday life we commonly distinguish between courses of action that are right regardless of how others behave, and those that are right only if many or most others follow them. It is wrong, for example, for a prison guard to treat prisoners brutally. Such conduct does not cease to be wrong if all the other guards are brutal. It is also wrong to steal, even if you live in a neighborhood where theft is rampant. But often the propriety of conduct is affected by the practices of others, especially of one's competitors:

- A professor may believe that, ideally, teachers should devote most of their time to teaching, and far less to research. After observing his colleagues' behavior, however, he may reverse these priorities in order to maintain his standing in the profession.

I am most grateful to Michael Zuckert, John Cound, Larry Alexander, Stanley Brubaker, Robert Nagel, Paul Meehl, John Dolan, Richard Morgan, and Linda Shimmin.

- Assume the same professor is a conservative in a department dominated by leftists. For many years, they have discriminated against conservatives in hiring decisions. The professor may decide to oppose the hiring of leftist candidates, even though he believes that ideally professors should be hired without regard to their political views.
- A corporation that wishes to do business in a country where bribes are necessary to obtain the requisite permits, may engage in bribery even though the company's directors and officers deplore the custom and would abolish it if they could.
- A senator who opposes filibusters in principle, but observes that the other party has filibustered against bills he favors, may decide to filibuster against some of the other party's bills.
- Just Cause, a public interest group, may believe that ideally no politician should obtain money from a political action committee. But since such committees are lawful, and have been formed by other groups that compete for politicians' favors, the members of Just Cause may decide to form their own political action committee.

Each of these choices is debatable, but in practice most people make the kinds of decisions that I have suggested because they are unwilling to place themselves or their causes at a competitive disadvantage.

The question for conservative jurists is this: Is the wrong of judicial activism absolute, like the wrong of brutality toward a prisoner, or is it more like one of these other hypothetical cases? Surprisingly, discussions of constitutional interpretation regularly ignore this fundamental question. All major constitutional theorists seem to assume that a justice should interpret the Constitution in whatever fashion—originalist or nonoriginalist, activist or restraintist—the theorist believes to be proper for the Court as a whole, without considering the contrary practices of other Justices. If a theorist believes, as conservatives commonly do, that most twentieth-century justices have rejected his theory, he concludes that the nation needs new Justices, not that he himself needs a new theory.

Is it true that the obligation of a Justice to interpret the Constitution properly is unconditional? Let us consider two hypothetical cases.

JUSTICE NEW'S DILEMMA

Justice New has recently joined the Supreme Court. He is, we will assume, a man of conservative political opinions. Concerning jurisprudential theories, however, he is unusually open-minded.

Case One. In the first case that comes before Justice New, the petitioner is a liberal Democrat who has been fined for violating an ordinance that prohibits the distribution of "scurrilous literature." The petitioner handed out a pamphlet that denounced Republicans as "white-collar racists" and urged voters to elect a Democratic town council.

This is about as easy as a constitutional case can be. Despite his political differences with the pamphleteer, our Justice will doubtless vote to reverse the conviction. Why? The obvious reasons are freedom of speech, fidelity to precedent, and the rule of law. But there is another reason. Justice New knows that liberal judges will vote to protect conservatives' speech in analogous cases, and he prefers a society in which both parties observe this rule to one in which they lawlessly fight, case by case, to establish a one-party reign of censorship. He believes in a "neutral principle" of freedom of speech, but his commitment to that principle may be, at bottom, conditional. In a society where the opposing party's judges did not respect his party's right to speak, he might not respect theirs.

Justice New also knows that by and large other Justices of every political persuasion apply all rules of law—not just freedom of speech—impartially to political friends and foes, to men and women, to whites and blacks. He gladly joins this tradition, preferring it to a dog-eat-dog struggle for absolute power. Again, he is subscribing to a neutral principle, but his adherence to that principle may again be conditional. If his political opponents were to reject the principle with sufficient consistency, duration, and consequence, he might reciprocate.

Case Two. Justice New's next case is more difficult. Mary and John O'Brien have asked the Court to invalidate a school financing system that requires them to pay taxes to support free public schools, but that does not compensate them for the cost of the parochial school education they prefer for their children. The O'Briens allege that this system deprives them of liberty and property without due process of law, infringes the reserved rights of the people under the Ninth Amendment, and violates the free exercise of religion clause.

At least as a matter of legislative policy, Justice New agrees with the O'Briens. He knows that few rights are more fundamental than the right to shape one's children's education, and he believes that religious parents should have the right to choose a religious school without having to pay the state for the secular education that they reject. He believes, moreover, that competition improves education just as it does other services; by subsidizing public schools the government reduces educational quality. Therefore, New favors school voucher systems that compensate parents for the cost of private schooling. But he is doubtful that the Constitution dictates this result.

One of Justice New's clerks points out that several precedents lend some support to the O'Briens' constitutional argument. Although none of the cases is squarely on point, they are about as pertinent as *Griswold v. Connecticut* was in *Roe v. Wade*.

New believes *Roe* and *Griswold* were activist decisions that lacked any solid constitutional foundation. Yet both decisions have recently been reaffirmed. The Court has assumed the power to act without clear constitutional warrant, New observes, and there seems to be no prospect that it will abandon that power. What bearing does this have on New's vote in the *O'Brien* case?

To answer this question, we need to consider the major arguments for judicial restraint (rule of law and deference to democracy), and whether Justice New should feel bound by them even in situations where most liberals do not.

THE RULE OF LAW

By their very nature, purely legal reasons for judicial restraint lose much of their force unless most judges obey them, or can eventually be persuaded to do so. The rule of law requires a critical mass, a threshold below which some of its values cannot even partially be achieved.

Equal treatment of litigants, avoidance of arbitrariness, predictable decisions—all of these goals require a high degree of judicial consensus. A Court on which only three of the Justices were influenced by a particular type of legal authority (such as the Framers' intentions) would probably not be one-third as predictable as one on which all nine Justices followed that authority. Indeed, a Court that was one-third originalist might be more erratic in some fields than one whose decisions were based solely on the well-known prejudices of nine politician-lawyers.

Insofar as his goal is to maintain the rule of law, Justice New needs to know not just whether the Court ought to practice originalism, but whether it actually does. Ironically, the more he accepts the conservative charge that liberal Justices have repeatedly ignored the original meaning of the Constitution, the more he must reject the conservative assumption that Justices are required by the rule of law to be faithful to that meaning.

Constitutional thinkers seem to agree that some of the Justices are originalists. Clashes between originalists and nonoriginalists, we are given to understand, occur regularly on the Court, and not merely in the law schools.

But who are these originalists? Few scholars have paused to draw up a list. To do so, one should distinguish—as scholars hardly ever do—between votes that were in all likelihood determined by an originalist approach to judging, on the one hand, and votes that were merely coincidentally originalist, on the other. If all it takes to be an originalist is a vote that coincides with the Framers' intentions, then all Justices are at least part-time originalists.

A true originalist, however, feels bound by the original meaning even when he disagrees with it. For this reason, one cannot cite Chief Justice Rehnquist's votes in capital cases as examples of his "following" or "adhering to" the Framers' intentions. Since Rehnquist is a devoted conservative, we would expect him to uphold capital punishment even if he were a thoroughgoing legal realist who rejected any obligation to follow the Constitution. We have no reason, in such cases, to applaud Rehnquist's "judicial restraint." His restraint is not tested.

By the same token, it would be misleading to cite the Marshall Court as an exemplar of originalism. If the decisions of the Marshall Court were more in accord with the Framers' intentions than were those of the Warren Court, it does not follow that Marshall and his brethren were more restrained. Their "originalism" may have been due to the fact that they held socioeconomic views that coincided with the Framers' (or because they had a much smaller corpus of anti-originalist precedents to deal with), and not because they exercised greater self-restraint in interpreting the Constitution.

In order to conclude that authentic originalism exists, we need to find Justices who seem to have voted against their personal political convictions, not out of a sense of prudence, nor even out of fidelity to precedent or democracy, but out of a sense of duty to enforce the original meaning of the Constitution.

In cases where the text of the Constitution is clear, there is a great deal of evidence that the Court's decisions have at least sometimes been affected by the wishes of the Framers. Nobody ever argues, for example, that the Court should "adapt the Constitution to modern conditions" by holding that the president's term is now eight years. Where the text is unclear, however—as it is in our *O'Brien* case—I see no evidence that more than an occasional Justice has been swayed by research into the Framers' imperfectly expressed intentions. Indeed, it is difficult to think of a single major case in the entire history of the Court in which the Framers' ambiguously expressed intentions seem to have been decisive.

But resolving all doubts as generously as possible, let us assume that of today's Justices, Rehnquist, Scalia, and Thomas are all consistent, authentic originalists. That strikes me as insufficient originalism to supply the requisite critical mass. Lacking that (and, in many cases, lacking consensus even among originalists), the argument that originalism promotes consistent, predictable decisions is weak. Therefore, Justice New should not feel obligated by the rule of law to cast his vote in accordance with the original meaning of the Constitution, even if he can ascertain its meaning for this case.

DEMOCRATIC VALUES

In most constitutional cases, the best arguments against judicial intervention are based not on the rule of law, but on democratic values. Justice New dislikes judicial activism because even when it is lawful it usually detracts, however slightly, from self-government. New believes that the Court has too often intruded on the proper spheres of elected legislators. He believes that ideally local legislatures, close to local problems and answerable to local people, should be left to devise their own remedies for educational dilemmas such as school funding.

As Justice New muses, however, it occurs to him that a liberal Justice would probably feel fewer compunctions about compromising federalism and democracy, provided that judicial intervention served liberal political ends such as abortion rights, procedural rights for criminal defendants, and so forth.

In such cases, liberals typically invoke one of two arguments. The more activist liberals urge the Court to enforce the evolving "fundamental values" of America, regardless of whether those values are stated in the text of the Constitution. The goal is to keep the Constitution in tune with "the changing aspirations and needs of the people." Unfortunately for this theory, opinion polls reveal that the values of average Americans differ from those of professorial and judicial elites. On most cultural questions, ordinary folk are more conservative. According to the polls, most Americans favor school prayer, oppose affirmative action, and are prepared to crack down on dissidents and criminals without much regard for legal niceties. Those who advocate "adapting the Constitution to the evolving needs and values of our times" don't have *these* fundamental values in mind. Liberal scholars never say that the horrendous new problems of drugs and inner-city crime justify reinterpreting the Fourth and Fifth Amendments so as to narrow their scope, nor do they Argue that the failures of our public schools justify a constitutional right to a school voucher system. As Professor John Hart Ely has observed, "the fundamental values of the American people," as that phrase is used by constitutional jurisprudents, is a euphemism for the fundamental values of the *New York Review of Books*.

Liberals also justify activism on the ground that it rectifies prejudices against "out groups" that are inadequately represented in the political process. Like other theories of judicial review, this is a highly manipulable concept, usually invoked to justify decisions that are also desired on ordinary political grounds. When we ask whether some class of citizens is unduly disadvantaged in the political arena, it is almost impossible to avoid smuggling normative, political judgments into this ostensibly factual investigation. Not surprisingly, liberal Justices never find that conservatives such as the O'Briens (or Bakke) suffer from unfair political disadvantages.

BALANCING THE INTERESTS

Justice New may well conclude that parents seeking good schooling for their children are as politically disadvantaged as "the liberal interest groups." Nevertheless, he may reasonably decide not to imitate liberal activism. The argument for restraint based on democratic values, unlike the argument based on the rule of law, does not presuppose a judicial consensus. Democracy, like fiscal responsibility or prudence in foreign affairs, is valuable in any quantity. If it is desirable for educational issues to be fought out in the political arena, and our Justice can help to achieve that result by voting against the O'Briens, he should do so. *Pro tanto*, democracy will be served.

Unfortunately, the problem is not quite so simple. There are other considerations. Suppose that several conservative Justices who value judicial restraint on

"democratic values" grounds are able to form a majority in many cases that come before the Court. They can block liberal activism, and they can also prevent the revival of conservative activism. So far, so good. But they also know that liberals will eventually regain control of the Court. What they must then decide is whether to practice restraint when they are a majority, even if they do not expect liberals to show similar restraint when their time comes.

What should they do? A crucial factor, of course, is just how unrestrained liberal Justices have been and are likely to be in the future. New may believe that liberal activist creations like the right of privacy, although grave errors, are somewhat aberrational. Liberal activism has not been as uniform and monolithic as polemicists often imply. Even the least principled, most activist Justice feels certain constraints. Just as liberals have exaggerated the conservatism of the Rehnquist Court, so conservatives have exaggerated the liberalism of the Warren Court. However true it may be that liberal activists have gone too far, it is also true that, for one reason or another, they have not created many of the rights that one might expect from a wholly unconstrained liberal Court: for example, constitutional rights to welfare, to "due care for the environment," and so forth.

LAW OR POLITICS?

Returning to the *O'Brien* case, let us assume that Justice New concludes that a decision in the O'Briens' favor would not require a degree of activism greater than that exercised by most liberal Justices. According to standard conservative jurisprudence, liberals' practices are relevant only as illustrations of bad judging. But in contexts that are at least arguably analogous, most conservatives would weigh the behavior of liberals in determining what course to follow. Consider three cases:

- Senator Bright believes that it violates sound principles of federalism for Congress to provide the states with grants, for example highway construction funds, that are conditioned on compliance with federal rules concerning unrelated matters. But such conditions are now common. Should Senator Bright vote against a conditional grant bill today, even if he approves of the cause served by the conditions?
- A Supreme Court decision has liberalized standing rules, thus permitting the federal courts to resolve disputes that Writ, a conservative public interest lawyer, believes should be left to the politicians. When a case arises that would advance a conservative cause, but that can only be brought by taking advantage of the liberalized standing rules, should Writ decline to take the case? (Assume that this would not violate Writ's duty to any client.)
- Green, an ultra-liberal lawyer with impressive credentials, has been nominated to the Supreme Court by President Clinton. Knutsen, a conservative senator, must decide how to vote. Knutsen believes that ideally

nominees should be evaluated solely on the basis of their credentials, without regard to the popularity of their constitutional positions, and without the oversimplifications of television "attack ads." He also believes, however, that liberals have rejected and will continue to reject that view of the process whenever they care strongly about the result.

Knutsen believes that Green would be an extraordinarily bad Justice, though not for reasons that have sufficient mass appeal to carry the day. Knutsen is aware, however, that from time to time Green has taken unpopular stands that make him vulnerable to an all-out political attack of the sort that liberals mounted against Judge Robert Bork. Should Knutsen decline to participate in this sort of political maneuvering to defeat the nomination?

I believe that in all three of these situations most conservatives would give decisive weight to the behavior of liberals.

Can these situations be distinguished from *O'Brien*? The most obvious distinction is that *O'Brien* arises in a judicial context, where we do not ordinarily think it appropriate to speak of how "political opponents" behave, much less to imitate their "mistakes." We think of judges as umpires, not players. But this legal mode of thought assumes a degree of professional consensus that is lacking in constitutional law.

In other branches of law, a "mistaken" decision is commonly perceived as a lapse that will eventually be overruled, or at least rejected by most other courts. But constitutional law, as perceived by most conservatives, does not conform to this paradigm: The major liberal-activist decisions have not been overruled even by a conservative" Court; they more closely resemble sacrosanct entitlements like farm subsidies than mistaken common-law decisions. In this unique environment, political analogies are more apt than legal ones.

CONVERTING LIBERALS

Conceivably, liberal opinion will eventually veer back to the restraintist views that were popular early in this century. But what might generate such a reversal? This subject is never discussed; yet unless liberals are somehow converted, the long-term effect of conservative restraint is not to make "the Court" restrained, but only to create lulls between eras of liberal activism.

One possibility, of course, is that conservative Justices will win converts by their example of restraint. But this hope is wildly unrealistic. When conservative restraint serves conservative political causes, liberals quite reasonably perceive it as political conservatism, not principled judging. When conservative restraint does not serve conservative political causes, as in the field of property rights, liberals regard this not as a fair exchange for liberal restraint in sociocultural fields, but as an entirely different

matter. The great majority of liberals believe that the case for activism is strong on the merits in fields where activism produces results liberals favor. They believe, with equal passion, that the case for activism is weak in fields where it would serve conservative ends. The fact that conservatives agree with them on activism in property rights is certainly not going to lead liberals to change their views on activism in other spheres.

The paradox of judicial restraint is that, insofar as it can be inculcated at all, it can only be inculcated by judicial activism. It was conservative activism, prior to 1937, that bred moderately restraintist liberal Justices like Frankfurter and Black. And it was the liberal activists of the Warren and Burger Court eras who transformed judicial restraint into the tenet of conservative orthodoxy it is today.

Conservatives complain constantly about the self-serving apologies for judicial activism that flow out of the liberal law schools. In a sense, I wholeheartedly agree. But on another level such criticisms are naive: If for fifty years the French had been the only people who were willing to go to war, then *of course* the Sorbonne's faculty would take a relatively expansive view of the circumstances in which war is morally legitimate.

Superficially the Supreme Court, like the presidency, alternates between liberal and conservative eras, giving both factions' theoreticians an incentive to fashion a politically neutral constitutional jurisprudence. In practice, however, the major prerogative of the Court—rights-creation—-has been exercised almost exclusively by liberals for over half a century. Even today the "conservative" Court creates very few conservative rights. Absent a credible threat of broad-scale conservative activism, judicial restraint is contrary to the substantive political interests of liberals, and will remain, in their view, misguided.

The liberal restraintists of the New Deal generation are now a dying breed. Today, even the most moderate of liberal constitutional scholars are activists, at least by conservative standards, as is the current generation of liberal law students—the pool from which Democratic Justices will be drawn thirty years hence. The central strategic fact is that, in the long run, conservatives lack the power to determine whether "the Court" is restrained. They have only the power to determine whether *they* are restrained. Mainstream conservative jurisprudence, which ignores this reality, is utopian.

The dilemma of conservative jurisprudence, then, is that we must sacrifice either our commitment to judicial restraint or our right to equal power on the Supreme Court. If, with his eyes open, Justice New chooses to sacrifice equal power, I cannot confidently assert that he is mistaken. But he should not do so under the illusion that he has no ethical alternative. He does.

THE REHNQUIST REINS

The Chief Justice has brought order to the Court and won striking support for judicial restraint. But Anthony Kennedy turns out to be the decisive voice.

David J. Garrow

David J. Garrow is the author of "Liberty and Sexuality" and "Bearing the Cross," which won the Pulitzer Prize in 1987. He wrote about Justice David H. Souter for the Magazine in 1994.

WHEN THE SUPREME COURT RECONVENES TOMORROW morning, William H. Rehnquist will mark his 10th anniversary as the 16th Chief Justice of the United States. The Rehnquist Court's first decade may best be remembered for such surprisingly "liberal" decisions as the 1992 reaffirmation of Roe v. Wade and this year's vindication of gay rights in a case from Colorado. In both exceptional cases, Rehnquist was in dissent on the losing sides, but those outcomes are unrepresentative of his winning record in crucial, if less publicized, areas of the law.

Rehnquist's most far-reaching triumphs have come in cases raising fundamental questions of federalism, involving the distribution of power between the Federal Government and the states. One year ago, in United States v. Lopez, for the first time in 58 years a court majority restricted Congress's ability to expand Federal authority after it enacted an anti-gun-possession law. This June, in the otherwise unsung death penalty case of Felker v. Turpin, Rehnquist ratified a significant victory in a longstanding war over the power of Federal courts to review and potentially reverse state inmates' criminal convictions. This seemingly abstruse battle over greatly truncating Federal courts' habeas corpus jurisdiction demonstrates how successfully Rehnquist has extended his own staunchly conservative, lifelong beliefs into a judicial agenda that has significantly remade major portions of American law.

But as decisions like Romer v. Evans, the Colorado gay rights case, and 1992's reaffirmation of Roe in Planned Parenthood of Southeastern Pennsylvania v. Casey exemplify, the "Rehnquist Court" is only sometimes the Rehnquist Court. That's true only when the Chief Justice is able to win the determinative fifth vote of the one crucial Justice who most oftentimes is the deciding voice whenever the Court is split 5 to 4—Anthony Kennedy. When he chooses to side with the High Court's four moderates, the "Rehnquist Court" is turned into the "Kennedy Court." In the meantime, Rehnquist will no doubt continue his drive to shrink the influence of Federal courts in American life.

MONDAY MORNING, JUNE 3, 1996, MARKED A POTENTIALLY culminating moment for the 72-year-old Chief Justice.

Just as it will be tomorrow, the court's magisterial courtroom is packed to capacity. United States Senators and members of the House sit toward the front. Former clerks to several Justices have come from as far away as California just to watch; senior members of the Court's press corps squeeze into two tightly packed wooden benches on the left. Members of the marshal's staff shush tourists in the rear of the intimate chamber.

At precisely 10 A.M., a marshal brings the courtroom to its feet as the nine Justices emerge from behind the velvet curtain to take their seats on the elevated bench. Chief Justice Rehnquist declares that several decisions are ready for announcement, and in quick succession the authors of the majority opinions offer brief summaries of the new holdings.

Only at 10:28 A.M. does Rehnquist reach the event the capacity crowd has come to see. "We'll hear argument now in No. 95-8836, Ellis Wayne

Felker v. Tony Turpin." The Chief Justice, too, has been waiting for this opportunity for a long time.

The Court's regular argument calendar ended more than five weeks earlier, on April 24; for all of May and June, the Justices normally would have devoted themselves simply to finishing up their opinions in cases that had been argued during the standard October-through-April schedule. However, on that very same April 24, President Clinton signed into law a new statute awkwardly titled the Antiterrorism and Effective Death Penalty Act of 1996.

Long under consideration by Congress, the new law includes a host of provisions intended to reduce and hasten Federal court review of criminal offenders' challenges to the finality of their state court convictions—including challenges by convicted murderers sentenced to death. Prisoners have an initial right to appellate court review; those who fail can pursue subsequent challenges by filing petitions for writs of habeas corpus—literally "you have the body" but in essence a Federal court order overturning a state court conviction. The new law imposes stringent limits on *any* Federal court consideration of a *second* or additional habeas petition from a convict. Death-row prisoners often file petition after petition, thereby delaying their executions even if their sentences are never overturned; some noncapital felons file such papers year after year.

Opponents of the new law argued that, if allowed to stand, it would eventually open the floodgates to speedier executions of the 3,153 prisoners now on death row nationwide. For Rehnquist, however, the limiting of Federal habeas corpus reflects not some sort of personal blood lust for the death penalty. It instead bespeaks his commitment to a federalism-centered view of American politics and government, which encompasses many other issues in addition to Federal court respect for the finality of state court criminal convictions. "The core" of Rehnquist's theory, one scholar has written, "is the idea of state sovereignty," above and beyond Federal Government control.

Testifying at his 1986 confirmation hearings for promotion to Chief Justice, Rehnquist acknowledged that "my personal preference has always been for the feeling that if it can be done at the local level, do it there. If it cannot be done at the local level, try it at the state level, and if it cannot be done at the state level, then you go to the national level."

Rehnquist strongly opposed an expansive habeas role for the Federal courts even long before President Richard M. Nixon nominated him to the Supreme Court in the fall of 1971. Then a 47-year-old Assistant Attorney General, Rehnquist had joined the Justice Department in 1969 at the behest of his fellow Arizonan, Deputy Attorney General Richard G. Kleindienst, whom he had come to know during 15 years of law practice in Phoenix. But 1969 hadn't marked Rehnquist's first job in Washington, for way back in 1952 and 1953—just after he had graduated first in his class from Stanford Law School—young Rehnquist had served for 18 months as one of two law clerks to the highly regarded Supreme Court Justice Robert H. Jackson. Rehnquist had enjoyed his clerkship immensely, but when he himself was nominated to the High Court in 1971, his work for Jackson generated a major controversy when a Rehnquist memorandum arguing *against* any Supreme Court voiding of segregated schools and *for* a continued endorsement of the old doctrine of "separate but equal" was discovered in Jackson's file on Brown v. Board of Education. Rehnquist unpersuasively insisted—as he would again during his 1986 confirmation hearings for Chief Justice—that the memo represented an articulation of *Jackson's* views rather than his own. The Senate nonetheless confirmed him on a vote of 68 to 26.

Jackson's papers also contain a Rehnquist memo with a minority view on *another* Brown case, Brown v. Allen, a 1953 ruling little known to the general public but justly famous among criminal law practitioners as the modern fount of an expansive approach to Federal courts' habeas jurisdiction. In that memo, Rehnquist argued that Federal courts should not grant habeas petitions involving any issue that had been considered by a state court unless the defendant had been denied the right to counsel. In 1953, that recommendation had no more impact than did Rehnquist's advice in the other Brown case, but three decades later, once he sat on the High Court in his own right, habeas excesses reappeared as a subject of his special concern. In a 1981 opinion involving a death-row petitioner, Coleman v. Balkcom, Rehnquist complained that in light of habeas's "increasing tendency to postpone or delay" death-penalty enforcement, "stronger measures are called for" beyond the Court's simple denial of repeated death-row appeals.

Reminded of his Jackson clerkship memos in a 1985 interview with this Magazine—the last such interview Rehnquist has granted—he frankly acknowledged that "I don't know that my views have changed much from that time." Four years later, Chief Justice Rehnquist vented his continuing anger at repetitive filings in a 5-4 majority opinion rebuffing an application from an ostensibly penniless petitioner named Jessie McDonald. "Since 1971," Rehnquist observed, McDonald "has made 73 separate filings with the Court, not including this petition, which is his eighth so far this term." Rejecting the solicitude of four dissenters who objected to the majority's order instructing the clerk's office to reject any further unpaid filings from

McDonald, Rehnquist emphasized that "every paper filed with the clerk of this Court, no matter how repetitive or frivolous, requires some portion of the institution's limited resources."

A few months later, Rehnquist took up his capital habeas cudgel in his role as head of the Judicial Conference, the administrative arm of the Federal judiciary. Failing in an effort to obtain majority support for a recommendation calling upon Congress to limit Federal habeas jurisdiction, Rehnquist nonetheless forwarded a report to the Senate Judiciary Committee. In an unprecedented public letter, 14 of the conference's 26 other members objected to the Chief Justice's action. Rehnquist refused to back down.

Congress did not act, but in April 1991 Rehnquist achieved much of his legislative goal *judicially* in a 6-3 court ruling that starkly limited successive habeas petitions and vindicated his 1981 call for action in Coleman. Decrying "the abusive petitions that in recent years have threatened to undermine the integrity of the habeas corpus process," the majority stressed that "perpetual disrespect for the finality of convictions disparages the entire criminal justice system."

But even that ruling in McCleskey v. Zant did not set as high a hurdle to successive petitions as Rehnquist sought. Warning that America cannot afford "the luxury of state and Federal courts that work at cross purposes or irrationally duplicate" each others' efforts, the Chief Justice continued to emphasize that "capital habeas corpus still cries out for reform." Come April 1996, after 24 years on the court and 10 years as Chief Justice, it seemed with the Felker case that Rehnquist's wish had finally come true.

WHEN REHNQUIST WAS NOMINATED TO SUCCEED THE retiring Warren E. Burger as Chief Justice by President Ronald Reagan in 1986, his colleagues were unanimously pleased and supportive. Fourteen years of working together had built good personal relations even between Rehnquist and his ideological opposites, William J. Brennan and Thurgood Marshall. Brennan startled one acquaintance by informing him that "Bill Rehnquist is my best friend up here," and a Washington attorney, John D. Lane, who privately interviewed all seven other Justices on behalf of the American Bar Association's Committee on the Federal Judiciary, informed the Senate Judiciary Committee that Rehnquist's nomination was met with "genuine enthusiasm on the part of not only his colleagues on the Court but others who served the Court in a staff capacity and some of the relatively lowly paid individuals at the Court. There was almost a unanimous feeling of joy."

Rehnquist's colleagues looked forward to his installation as "Chief" in part because they welcomed the departure of his overbearing, manipulative and less-than-brilliant predecessor, Burger, who had succeeded the legendary Earl Warren 17 years earlier. Reporters always stressed that Burger *looked* the part of Chief Justice of the United States, but among his fellow Justices there was virtually unanimous agreement that his skills at leading the Conference—the Justices' own name for their group of nine—had been woefully lacking. John Lane told the Judiciary Committee that one Justice said that "he looks for a tremendous improvement in the functioning of this Court" under Rehnquist. Based upon all the Justices' comments, Lane reported, "I came away with a very strong opinion that Justice Rehnquist will make an excellent Chief Justice."

Much of the 1986 debate over Rehnquist's promotion focused upon newly augmented allegations that 20-odd years earlier he had taken part in Republican Party efforts to intimidate black voters at Phoenix polling places. The charges were not provable, but the final Senate confirmation vote of 65 to 33 was closer than Rehnquist's backers had expected and in its wake the new Chief Justice privately told friends that he felt the Judiciary Committee hearings had treated him very badly. "He took it somewhat personally," one acquaintance remembered, but within the Court there was immediate agreement that Rehnquist was far superior to Burger in leading the Conference's discussion of cases.

Ten years before, in a 1976 law review essay on "Chief Justices I Never Knew," Rehnquist had stressed the importance of firmly run sessions in which each Justice, speaking in order of seniority, stated his views succinctly and without interruption: "A give and take discussion between nine normal human beings, in which each participates equally, is not feasible." He also acknowledged how a "Chief Justice has a notable advantage over his brethren: he states the case first and analyzes the law governing it first. If he cannot, with this advantage, maximize the impact of his views, subsequent interruptions of colleagues or digressions on his part or by others will not succeed either." Citing Harlan Fiske Stone and Felix Frankfurter as brilliant Justices of the past whose efforts to influence their colleagues had generally failed, Rehnquist added that "the power of persuasion is a subtle skill, dependent on quality rather than quantity."

In his 1987 book, "The Supreme Court," Rehnquist gently noted that "I have tried to make my opening presentation of a case somewhat shorter than Chief Justice Burger made his." Justice Harry A. Blackmun often disagreed substantively with Rehnquist, but he was quick to praise Rehnquist's management skills. "The Chief in conference is a splendid administrator," he told one semiprivate gathering. Unlike the Burger years, "we get through in a hurry. If there's anything to be criticized about it, he gets through it in too much of a hurry at times."

Warren Burger was seen by his colleagues as a Chief who often abused his power to assign the writing of majority opinions whenever he was not in dissent. One Rehnquist clerk from the mid-1970's still recalls how Burger, unhappy with the political humor of a Rehnquist-produced skit at the Court's 1975 Christmas party, the next month assigned Rehnquist only one opinion, in an Indian tax case. Most Justices expected Rehnquist to eschew such gamesmanship, and the record of the past decade generally bears that out. Some former clerks contend in private that in recent years Anthony Kennedy has fared far better in receiving important assignments from Rehnquist than other Justices, but Rehnquist as Chief is far more concerned with maximizing the speed and efficiency of the Court's opinion-writing than with playing favorites.

In a 1989 memo to his colleagues, Rehnquist divulged that "the principal rule I have followed in assigning opinions is to give everyone approximately the same number of assignments of opinions for the Court during any one term." But, he warned, any Justice who failed to circulate a first draft of a majority opinion within four weeks or who failed to circulate the first draft of an anticipated dissent within four weeks of the majority opinion or who had not voted in any case in which both majority and dissenting opinions had circulated would now be looked upon less favorably. "It only makes sense," he asserted, "to give some preference to those who are 'current' with respect to past work."

Rehnquist's announcement provoked an immediate objection from John Paul Stevens, now the second-most-senior Justice to the Chief himself. An iconoclastic and generally liberal thinker, Stevens in recent years has outpaced all of his colleagues in his number of individual dissents and concurrences. Reminding Rehnquist that "too much emphasis on speed can have an adverse effect on quality," Stevens warned that it "may be unwise to rely too heavily" on rigid deadlines, especially when a Justice's investment in a major dissent, or a handful of dissents, might create a lag. "I do not think a Justice's share of majority opinions should be reduced because he is temporarily preoccupied with such an opinion, or because he is out of step with the majority in a large number of cases." Rehnquist remained largely unmoved, chiding his colleagues just a few weeks later about several de-

cisions that were running behind schedule. "I suggest that we make a genuine effort to get these cases down 'with all deliberate speed.' "

EIGHT DAYS AFTER PRESIDENT CLINTON SIGNED THE NEW HABEAS legislation into law, a three-judge panel of the Court of Appeals for the 11th Circuit applied the statute in denying a request from a Georgia death-row inmate, Ellis Wayne Felker, to file a successive petition. Convicted 13 years earlier of murdering a 19-year-old woman soon after being released from prison on a prior felony conviction, Felker now was finally facing actual execution; three times before, the Supreme Court had turned aside appeals. Later that very same day, May 2, Felker's attorneys asked the High Court to review how the new law prohibited Felker from appealing the circuit court's refusal.

Less than 24 hours later, the Supreme Court granted Felker's request for a hearing and set oral argument on his challenge to the new law for exactly one month later. The Court's swift action—the first such accelerated hearing in six years and the fastest grant of review since the famous Pentagon Papers case, New York Times Co. v. United States, a quarter-century earlier—brought a cry of protest from the four least conservative Justices, John Paul Stevens, David H. Souter, Ruth Bader Ginsburg and Stephen G. Breyer. Formally dissenting, they called the majority's action "both unnecessary and profoundly unwise" and declared that review of the new law "surely should be undertaken with the utmost deliberation, rather than unseemly haste."

One question posed by Felker was whether the new limits on appeals involving second or successive habeas petitions represented a Congressional diminution of the Supreme Court's own appellate jurisdiction. That would be a constitutional issue of the highest order; not since the Civil War era had the Court directly confronted it. Felker's lawyers, focusing on an avenue Congress had failed to address, noted in their brief that the new law did not expressly affect the Court's authority to consider "original" habeas petitions filed directly with it. Conceding that the High Court's use of "original habeas" would be "exceptional and discretionary," Felker's attorneys nonetheless acknowledged that "no unconstitutional interference with this Court's appellate jurisdiction exists if Congress merely eliminates one procedure for review but leaves in place an equally efficacious alternative."

Henry P. Monaghan, a Columbia University law professor and an experienced Supreme Court advocate, spoke for Felker when oral argument got under way on June 3. The present-day Rehnquist Court is as vocal and energetic a nine-member bench as any attorney could imagine confronting (only Justice Clarence Thomas is usually silent, but the liberal icons William Brennan and Thurgood Marshall were likewise generally quiet), and Rehnquist himself—along with Justices Souter, Breyer, Ginsburg and Antonin Scalia—is an outspoken questioner, as both Monaghan and his opponent, Senior Assistant Attorney General Susan V. Boleyn of Georgia, soon found. "Why shouldn't we just try to apply the statute as written?" asked Rehnquist with some exasperation. "I mean, rather than trying

to torture some meaning out of it that's not there?" Monaghan tried to demur, but drolly conceded that "this statute passed by Congress with respect to second petitions is not the work of Attila the Hun."

Susan Boleyn, however, faced a far tougher grilling. "That's not a very specific position, Ms. Boleyn," the Chief Justice interjected before she had uttered her fourth sentence. Peppering her with questions, Rehnquist asked how she would distinguish a 19th-century decision, Ex Parte Yer-

ONE ANGRY MAN

Antonin Scalia's Decade

William Rehnquist's 10th anniversary as Chief Justice is also Antonin (Nino) Scalia's 10th anniversary as an Associate Justice. Nominated to Rehnquist's seat when Rehnquist was promoted to replace Warren Burger, Scalia—a four-year veteran of the United States Court of Appeals for the District of Columbia Circuit—faced no opposition. He was confirmed, 98-0, after less than five minutes of Senate floor discussion.

During Scalia's first few years on the Court, commentators wondered whether his combination of intelligence and gregariousness would make him into the Rehnquist Court's real intellectual leader. As Laurence H. Tribe, a Harvard law professor, told The Boston Globe in 1990: "There is no question Scalia is brilliant. What remains to be seen is if he is wise."

Six years later, the verdict is all but unanimous: Scalia is rash, impulsive and imprudent, a Justice who in case after case would rather insult his colleagues' intelligence than appeal to them. Judge Alex Kozinski, a conservative member of the United States Court of Appeals for the Ninth Circuit, pronounced his judgment as early as 1992: "Commentators said, 'This is the guy who, through his charm and intellect, will forge a conservative consensus.' He hasn't done it." The New Republic's Jeffrey Rosen, contending that Scalia "has intellectual contempt for most of his colleagues," suggests that the relatively young Justice—Scalia is now 60—calls to mind the sad career of another brilliant judicial failure, Felix Frankfurter.

One former Scalia clerk insists that the Justice is "100 percent impervious" to public criticism. But Scalia is hardly ignorant of his bad-boy reputation; three years ago, he insisted to one Washington audience that "I am not a nut." In comments to the Supreme Court Historical Society, Scalia observed that dissenting opinions "do not, or at least need not, produce animosity and bitterness among the members of the Court." But even more revealing was a statement Justice Sandra Day O'Connor made to a Ninth Circuit judicial conference. Reminding her audience of the old saying that "sticks and stones will break my bones but words will never hurt me," O'Connor added, "That probably isn't true."

A colleague confirms that O'Connor has been "deeply wounded" by the insults Scalia has sent her way, starting in 1989 in the abortion case Webster v. Reproductive Health Services. O'Connor analysis, Scalia wrote there, "cannot be taken seriously."

A former Scalia clerk acknowledges that Scalia "completely alienated" O'Connor and "lost her forever," and a former Rehnquist clerk notes how O'Connor's "personality is in many ways just the opposite of Justice Scalia's. She's very willing to build consensus on opinions." But Scalia, says another ex-clerk, is not only "in love with his own language," he also believes that "what he's doing is a matter of principle. He knows how right he is."

On the next-to-last day of the 1995–96 term, Scalia turned his rhetorical guns on Rehnquist, who

had committed the grievous sin of concurring with the Court's 7-1 majority in striking down the Virginia Military Institute's exclusion of women from a state institution. In his lonely, splenetic dissent, Scalia called the majority's equal protection analysis "irresponsible" and mocked Rehnquist's separate views as "more moderate than the Court's but only at the expense of being even more implausible." Saying Rehnquist erroneously suggested that Virginia "should have known . . . what this Court expected of it" because of an earlier Court ruling, Scalia truculently asserted that "any lawyer who gave that advice to the Commonwealth ought to have been either disbarred or committed."

Scalia's characterization of the Chief Justice's views represented the first time in memory that one member of the Court had suggested that another might be better situated in a nonjudicial institution, but virtually nothing that Scalia might say could worsen the reputation he has made for himself among students of the Court. Harvard's Laurence Tribe decries Scalia's "extreme stridency and disrespect for opposing views." Another well-known law professor, far less liberal than Tribe and a social colleague of several Justices, ruefully looks back on the Senate's 1987 rejection of Supreme Court nominee Robert H. Bork and concludes that Bork would have been "more civil and more broad-minded than Scalia by a long shot." Indeed, Scalia, he contends, "has become precisely what the Bork opponents thought Bork would be."

—D.J.G.

ger. Boleyn struggled. "Well, I think that this Court has recognized exceptions to its jurisdiction both in the constitutional venue under Article III—." An unhappy Rehnquist cut her off. "Are you familiar with the Yerger case?" "Yes, Your Honor, but I'm not familiar with what exactly you're asking me to respond to."

It only got worse. Breyer, telling her, "I'm sorry, I don't understand," asked Boleyn a fast-paced hypothetical and demanded an answer. "Do we have jurisdiction to hear it? Yes or no." Boleyn said no, but Breyer objected: "I thought from your brief the answer was yes."

Asked in 1992 by C-span's Brian Lamb whether he could tell if attorneys are nervous during oral argument, Rehnquist jocularly replied that "I assume they're all nervous—they should be." Occasionally—most often in the months before his wife's slow death from cancer in October 1991—Rehnquist has rebuked or snapped at lawyers who have been unprepared or who have committed the tiny but grievous sin of calling him Judge rather than Chief Justice.

The day after the Felker argument, the Justices met in private conference to discuss the case. The substance of that meeting isn't likely to be known for a long time; accounts of conference discussions generally become available only years after the event, with release of the handwritten notes of one or more Justices. Even then, some Justices' papers—Thurgood Marshall's are the most recent example—shed next to no light on conference discussions, for not all Justices take notes. Those of William O. Douglas and Brennan offer reliable guides to the 1960's, 70's and 80's, but every modern Court scholar knows full well that the ultimate treasure trove for the years 1970 through 1994 will, in time, be the conference notes of now-retired Justice Blackmun.

In his own chambers, Rehnquist instructs each of his three clerks to have their first drafts of his opinions ready for his review within 10 to 14 days. Some wags insist that Rehnquist has three clerks—seven other Justices now have four, Stevens has three—primarily to ease the arrangements for his weekly tennis-match doubles, but Rehnquist treats his young aides in a warm, low-key manner. He revises their drafts by orally dictating amended wording into a recorder, and he volunteered in his 1987 book that "I go through the draft with a view to shortening it, simplifying it and clarifying it."

In Rehnquist's first 15 years on the Court, commentators praised his writing as "clear, lucid, brief and mercifully free of bureaucratese." One commended "the somewhat peculiar references to history, the classics and gamesmanship with which Rehnquist likes to sprinkle his opinions"—this June a Rehnquist concurrence included a passing reference to "Grover Cleveland's second inaugural address"—but since 1986 such acclaim has gradually diminished, with critics noting "the characteristic terseness of a Rehnquist opinion" and journalists labeling his prose "dry and to the point."

Rehnquist's June 28 opinion announcing the Court's *unanimous*—including the four Justices who had protested the accelerated hearing—resolution of Felker v. Turpin manifested all these traits. Back in 1987, Rehnquist acknowledged how "the Chief Justice is expected to retain for himself some opinions that he regards as of great significance," but Rehnquist traditionally has written a disproportionate number of criminal law rulings. The 12½-page Felker decision had been written, edited and circulated for other Justices' comments and agreement in little more than three weeks' time, and the substance of Rehnquist's—and the Court's—holding followed closely from the implications of the questions Rehnquist had put to Monaghan and Boleyn back on June 3.

Not long after Ellis Wayne Felker finally goes to the electric chair, the pace of death-row executions across America will pick up substantial speed. Rehnquist's victory may not yet be 100 percent complete; his triumph nonetheless is impressive, and still growing.

The new statute "makes no mention of our authority to hear habeas petitions filed as original matters in this Court" and thus, fully in keeping with Ex Parte Yerger, it "has not repealed our authority to entertain" such petitions. Therefore, Rehnquist held, "there can be no plausible argument that the Act has deprived this Court of appellate jurisdiction in violation of Article III." No constitutional collision thereby occurred, and the new statutory restrictions on Federal court consideration of successive habeas petitions could remain fully in place. Convicts and death-row prisoners *could* send "original" petitions directly to the High Court, but—just as Felker's lawyers had conceded in their brief—only in a rare instance of "exceptional circumstances" would such an appeal be granted.

Felker's own habeas request was denied; Georgia has not yet set a new date for Felker's execution.

Some habeas specialists, pointing back to Rehnquist's earlier 1991 judicial breakthrough in McCleskey, dismiss Felker's actual holding as "relatively insignificant." They emphasize that several pending challenges to other particular provisions of the new law, including Lindh v. Murphy, a case that was decided by the Court of Appeals for the Seventh Circuit in Chicago in late September, are likely to force Rehnquist and his colleagues to revisit the habeas battlefield sometime in 1997.

But such characterizations unintentionally minimize the extent and scale of Rehnquist's long-term agenda and long-term victory. Federal habeas jurisdiction is now only a shadow of what it was when Rehnquist first joined the Supreme Court, and what in 1981 in Coleman was a lonely individual call for action has now won decisive support from a solid Court majority and from bipartisan majorities in both houses of Congress as well as an ostensibly liberal Democratic President. Not long after Ellis Wayne Felker finally goes to the electric chair, the entire pace of death-row executions all across America will pick up substantial speed as one habeas petition after another is quickly cast aside by the courts. Rehnquist's victory may not yet be 100 percent complete; his triumph nonetheless is remarkably impressive and still growing.

F ELKER IS THE LATEST IN A LINE OF FEDERALISM CASES that for Rehnquist began with a 1975 solo dissent in Fry v. United States, an opinion that directly foreshadowed the landmark 5-4 majority victory he would win exactly 20 years later in United States v. Lopez. In 1975, writing only for himself, Rehnquist had advocated "a concept of constitutional federalism which should . . . limit federal power under the Commerce Clause." In Lopez, writing on behalf of a 5-vote majority, Rehnquist dismissed the Justice Department's defense of the Federal anti-gun-possession law and declared that "if we were to accept the Government's arguments, we are hard-pressed to posit any activity by an individual that Congress is without power to regulate."

As early as 1982, a Yale Law Journal analysis of Rehnquist's jurisprudence by H. Jefferson Powell (now a high-ranking Clinton Justice Department appointee) cogently identified "federalism's role as the organizing principle in Rehnquist's work" and persuasively concluded that "Rehnquist's federalism does form a consistent constitutional theory."

In 1986, Rehnquist had volunteered that a one-third decline in the Court's annual caseload from 150 to 100 would be 'unseemly,' but by the 10th anniversary of his statement, the Court had reduced its annual workload by more than half—from 151 to 75.

More than 10 years later, in one of the three most important decisions of the 1995–96 term, Seminole Tribe of Florida v. Florida, another 5-vote Rehnquist majority forthrightly declared that "each State is a sovereign entity in our Federal system." Dissenting vigorously, Justice Souter protested how Rehnquist was deciding "for the first time since the founding of the Republic that Congress has no authority to subject a State to the jurisdiction of a Federal court at the behest of an individual asserting a Federal right." Souter's objection brought him a harsh rebuke from the Chief: the dissent's "undocumented and highly speculative extralegal explanation . . . is a disservice to the Court's traditional method of adjudication."

One core principle of Rehnquist's federalism, as the habeas battle has reflected, is a firm belief in a modest—some would say *excessively* modest—political and supervisory role for the Federal courts. Back in the early 1980's, the annual docket of the Supreme Court itself—the number of cases it chooses to hear, not the thousands upon thousands it turns aside—had grown to a peak of 151. Many voices, including both Burger and Rehnquist's, called unsuccessfully for the creation of a new, nationwide court of appeals to ease the pressure on the High Court's docket, but the idea died aborning and in recent years has completely vanished from both public—and private—discussion.

At his 1986 confirmation hearings, Rehnquist told the Senate Judiciary Committee that "I think the 150 cases that we have turned out quite regularly over a period of 10 or 15 years is just about where we should be at." Addressing whether that load might be too great and noting how the caseloads of Federal district and appellate courts were increasing rapidly, Rehnquist said that "my own feeling is that all the courts are so much busier today than they have been in the past, that there would be something almost unseemly about the Supreme Court saying, you know, everybody else is deciding twice as many cases as they ever have before, but we are going to go back to two-thirds as many as we did before."

A year later, in his 1987 book, Rehnquist cited the 150 figure and observed that "we are stretched quite thin trying to do what we ought to do." Privately, inside the Court, Rehnquist brooded about the annual "June crunch" of backlogged decisions awaiting finished opinions and suggested to his colleagues the "desirability of cutting down the number of cases set for argument in April," toward the end of the Court's year. But year by year the Court's annual caseload has shrunk further and further: from 132 cases in 1988–89 to 129 in 1989–90, to 112 in 1990–91, to 108 in 1991–92, to 107 in 1992–93, markedly to 84 in 1993–94, then to 82 in 1994–95 and finally to 75 in the just-completed term of 1995–96.

In 1986, Rehnquist had volunteered that a one-third decline in the Court's annual caseload from 150 to 100 would be "unseemly," but on the 10th anniversary of his statement, the Court had reduced its annual workload by *more than half*—from 151 to 75. Granted, a 1988 statute had virtually eliminated some mandatory appeals that the Court previously had been obligated to hear, whether or not a minimum of four Justices voted to accept the case, but the issue of the "incredible shrinking docket"—what Court watchers call it—has been one of the most striking developments of the Rehnquist years.

The Court, of course, issues no explanations for even so momentous a trend, but in April 1995, at the Third Circuit's annual dicial conference in White Sulphur Springs, W.Va., Justice Souter spoke extemporaneously about the docket shrinkage in remarks that were virtually unprecedented in their public frankness. Referring back to the early 1980's, when he was still an obscure New Hampshire state judge, Souter recalled that in reading Supreme Court opinions at the time, it "seemed to me . . . some of those opinions had the indicia of rush and hurriedness about them." Now he realized, given the caseloads of those years, that those shortcomings "could not have been otherwise and the remarkable thing is that the number of really fine things that came down in that period was as high as it was."

Souter said he was "amazed" that the docket annually had continued to shrink throughout the 1990's, but he stressed that "nobody sets a quota; nobody sits at the conference table and says: 'We've taken too much. We must pull back.' . . . It simply has happened." Identifying a host of contributing factors, Souter noted the "diminishing supply" of new Federal statutes in the late 1980's and early 1990's, and how "not much antitrust work" and "not much civil rights" work, beyond voting cases, had been generated by the Reagan and Bush Administrations' Justice Department. In the criminal area, "drug prosecution does not make for Supreme Court cases these days" because of how Fourth Amendment search-and-seizure standards have "been pretty much raked over. . . . The basic law, the basic standards which have been governing and do govern most of the appeals that people want to bring to us are products of the 60's and the 70's and the 80's. There hasn't been an awful lot for us to take."

In addition, Souter added, according to a comprehensive account of his remarks in the Pennsylvania Law Weekly, 12 years of Reagan-Bush judicial nominations had produced "a relative homogeneity" and "a diminished level of philosophical division within the Federal courts." But, he emphasized, "I know of no one on my court who thinks that we're turning away cases which by traditional standards . . . we should be taking. In fact, it's just the contrary."

Once, he confessed, when the numbers were declining, "I said out loud as well as to myself that if that continued, I was going to start voting to take interesting Federal questions whether there was a conflict [among lower Federal courts] or not." However, Souter went on, "those were rash words," for "as it turned out, I didn't have to make good on that" because more cases began attracting 4 or more affirmative votes. "About 100 a year is about right," Souter concluded, and the number for the upcoming 1996–97 term seems destined to rise from this past year's remarkable minimum of 75.

With a total caseload of 75 (34 of which were decided unanimously), there are not all that many opinions to spread out over nine months of work for nine Justices—and 34 law clerks. The image of clerks working seven-day-a-week, 12-hour-a-day jobs is a polite fiction of the past, and—though it is considered rude to mention it—many Court observers know that a typical at-the-office workday for the Chief Justice of the United States often stretches from about 9:10 A.M. to 2:30 P.M. Some Justices—Souter, Kennedy and Stevens among them—work decidedly longer hours, but Rehnquist's crusade to shrink the role and responsibilities of the Federal courts has definitely born fruit right at home.

Rehnquist has certainly registered historic doctrinal achievements—in habeas law, in United States v. Lopez, in Seminole Tribe and in the 1994 "takings clause" decision in Dolan v. City of Tigard, but there is no denying Rehnquist has been on the losing side in the two most important, highly visible constitutional holdings of the last five years: 1992's vindication of abortion rights in Planned Parenthood v. Casey and, just a few months ago, the remarkable voiding of a homophobic, antigay Colorado state constitutional amendment in Romer v. Evans. The 6-3 Romer ruling, in which two swing Justices, Anthony Kennedy and Sandra Day O'Connor, sided with the "liberal" foursome of Stevens, Souter, Ginsburg and Breyer rather than with Rehnquist, Scalia and Thomas, was without doubt the most important and symbolically momentous decision of the 1995–96 term.

Romer's majority opinion, written by Kennedy, featured a rhetorical verve rare for the High Court. The Colorado amendment "seems inexplicable by anything but animus toward the class that it affects," Kennedy explained, and "disqualification of a class of persons from the right to seek specific protection from the law is unprecedented in our jurisprudence." Declaring that "it is not within our constitutional tradition to enact laws of this sort," Kennedy pointed out that a statute "declaring that in general it shall be more difficult for one group of citizens than for all others to seek aid from the government is itself a denial of equal protection of the laws in the most literal sense." The state amendment "classifies homosexuals not to further a proper legislative end but to make them unequal to everyone else. This Colorado cannot do. A State cannot so deem a class of persons a stranger to its laws."

In a style and tone to which his colleagues have become all too well accustomed, Scalia angrily and vituperatively dissented. Joined by both Rehnquist and Thomas, Scalia protested that the majority's holding "places the prestige of this institution behind the proposition that opposition to homosexuality is as reprehensible as racial or religious bias." Avowing that his fellow Justices have "no business imposing upon all Americans the resolution favored by the elite class from which the Members of this institution are selected," Scalia alleged that "our constitutional jurisprudence has achieved terminal silliness" and complained of how Kennedy's opinion was "so long on emotive utterance and so short on relevant legal citation." Declaring that Colorado's action was "eminently reasonable" since citizens are "entitled to be hostile toward homosexual conduct," Scalia maintained that "the degree of hostility reflected by" the state enactment was "the smallest conceivable." His final blast was explicitly contemptuous: "Today's opinion has no foundation in American constitutional law, and barely pretends to."

BUT THE MOST IMPORTANT JUSTICE ON the 1996 Rehnquist court is not the angry Antonin Scalia; it's the man who ascended to the Court in the wake of Robert H. Bork's rejection:

Anthony Kennedy. A quiet and thoughtful Californian, Kennedy throughout his eight-year tenure has been both the crucial fifth vote for virtually all of Rehnquist's major victories *and* the decisive vote and voice when Rehnquist has suffered historic defeats in cases like Casey and Romer. Occasionally apologetic in tone ("sometimes we must make decisions we do not like," Kennedy volunteered in the 1989 flag-burning decision, Texas v. Johnson), Kennedy term after term has been the balance wheel of the Rehnquist Court. Early on, in 1988–89, when Rehnquist and the now-retired William Brennan disagreed in *every one* of that year's 31 5-4 outcomes, Kennedy was with Rehnquist 29 times. (Johnson was one of the two exceptions.) In 1991–92, when Kennedy dissented from only 8 of the term's 108 decisions, his crucial "liberal" votes in both Casey and an important school prayer decision, Lee v. Weisman, drew intense flack from conservative critics.

The following term, 1992–93, Kennedy dissented in only 5 of 107 cases, and the year after that, when he was in the majority in *every one* of the term's 14 5-4 decisions, he again dissented in only 5 cases out of 84. In 1994–95, Kennedy was in the majority in 13 of the term's 16 5-4 cases, including both Lopez and the highly publicized Congressional term limits decision, and in the just-completed 1995–96 term, Kennedy again was the Court's least frequent dissenter (in just 5 of 75 cases) and was in the majority in 9 of the 12 5-4 outcomes.

Now Kennedy is again under fire from extreme conservatives for his memorable majority opinion in Romer (National Review magazine labels him "the dimmest of the Court's intellectual lights"), but among serious Court watchers the impression is growing that Kennedy has more than found his footing. David O'Brien of the University of Virginia calls Kennedy "more principled, less of a pragmatist" than other Justices. Peter J. Rubin, a Washington attorney and a former two-year High Court clerk, points out that Kennedy "understands the moment of what he's doing" and stresses how there can be "no question after Romer about his integrity and courage."

Legal historians sometimes wonder whether the "Brennan Court" and the "Powell Court" might actually be more accurate monikers for the 1960's, 70's and early 80's than the "Warren Court" and the "Burger Court." And in that same spirit, Peter Rubin readily agrees that, yes, "it's the Kennedy Court." But, Romer and Casey notwithstanding, in most other particulars the court of 1996 is indeed the "Rehnquist Court," and it is likely to stay the Rehnquist Court for longer than most commentators now think.

Prior to the death of his wife, Nan, in October 1991, most people who knew Rehnquist expected him to step down as Chief Justice sooner rather than later. In July 1991, Rehnquist apologetically turned down the newly retired Thurgood Marshall's request for home-to-office transportation in a court car, while adding that "in all probability I will be in the same boat you are within a couple of years." Eleven months later, Rehnquist told C-Span's Brian Lamb that while he enjoyed his job, "I wouldn't want to hold it forever." In September 1995, when he underwent major back surgery to remedy a long-festering problem that had suddenly mushroomed into crippling pain, what Tony Mauro of Legal Times called Rehnquist's "rumored plan for retiring from the Court after the next Presidential election" looked all the more certain.

But a wide sample of former Rehnquist clerks say "not so" and predict against any Rehnquist retirement in the summer of 1997, especially—as some of them hesitantly volunteer—if Bill Clinton is re-elected this November. The Wall Street Journal columnist Paul Gigot has slyly pronounced

Rehnquist's scheduled departure, but a former clerk says the Chief already has begun hiring the clerks who will join him next summer.

"I think he's too committed and too interested in winning the battles he's been fighting to retire during the Presidency of a Democrat," says one Court insider with a high personal opinion of Rehnquist. He adds, with emphasis, that the Chief is "extraordinarily politically savvy" and that Bill Rehnquist "plays for the long, long, long run," as his entire career consistently demonstrates.

"He's more inclined to stay," says another former Rehnquist clerk who keeps in regular touch and who feels that the Chief does not want to leave during a Democratic Presidency but "would never say it."

"He enjoys his work," this clerk states. "He never expected to be in the majority as much as he is now," and the ongoing victories—like Lopez and Seminole Tribe on federalism, and in the habeas arena with cases like Felker—all incline him to stay, not retire. "He's fully in stride right now."

Illiberal Court

The United States Supreme Court is engaged in the process of undermining democracy.

DAVID FORTE

Mr. Forte is a professor of law at Cleveland State University.

SOME people simply cannot mind their manners. Jeremiah was roundly despised for proclaiming the infidelity of Israel. The little boy of Hans Christian Andersen exclaimed at the nakedness of the emperor. And Justice Antonin Scalia has the effrontery to expose the oligarchic agenda of his brethren.

Justice Scalia has long used his acerbic style to disassemble the jerry-built logic of Supreme Court opinions. In the *Romer* case this last term, for example, he declared that in the Court's current view of the equal-protection clause, "our constitutional jurisprudence has achieved terminal silliness."

Scalia has paid a political price for his temerity. Truthfully, his disparagement of his colleagues' views has sometimes verged on the personal insult. It is doubtful that his style has won many votes from his fellow Justices.

Yet he will not be turned aside. In the just-completed 1995–96 term of the Supreme Court, he went further than he has ever done before. Taking a cue from academia, Scalia spiritedly "deconstructed" the arguments of the Court in a

> *The elite has 'embarked on a course of inscribing one after another' of its current preferences into the Constitution*

number of significant decisions, and revealed where he thought the majority's political agenda lay. Scalia is no longer content with taking apart a badly constructed argument. He sees something much more dangerous afoot, and has decided to confront it.

Scalia believes that the nation's "law-trained elite" and its social prejudices have gained control of the Constitution-making machinery of government. That elite, he says, has "embarked on a course of inscribing one after another" of its current preferences into the Constitution. He decries the Court as elitist, "illiberal," and intolerant of the democratic process. He bitterly confesses to being profoundly disturbed by the Court's changing of long-standing political practices overnight, especially

since this is being done "by an institution whose conviction of what the Constitution means is so fickle."

Despite his ire, the 1995-96 term of the Supreme Court was not as radical as either Justice Scalia or the press depicted it. The largest group of significant cases was in the area of criminal procedure. There, the tradition of the Rehnquist Court continued, in incrementally strengthening law enforcement as well as in limiting repetitive appeals by convicted felons. The Court decided many of those cases, however, by a fragile one-vote margin.

The Court continued to strike down race-conscious redistricting, in North Carolina and Texas (again by vulnerable 5 to 4 votes), and let stand a ban against a racially preferential admissions program at the University of Texas Law School. Two cases modestly improved the position of the states, one requiring federal courts to enforce New York State's revision of punitive-damage awards, and another preventing Congress from authorizing suits by Indians against the states.

The Court continued to enforce a rigorous interpretation of the First Amendment. It struck down a Rhode Island ban on liquor-price advertising. It also voided a state law that limited the right of a political party to campaign expenditures. Even in the face of community values, the Court voided a congressional act that would have limited "indecent" visual and verbal expression coming into the home via cable.

Little progress came, however, in the protection of property interests. An innocent owner of an automobile used in a criminal activity by her husband (engaging a prostitute) had her interest forfeited with no recourse. In cases dealing with labor disputes, the Court leaned on the side of the labor unions over the employer. And the Court showed little inclination to help the states protect the unborn, even within the narrow confines of the 1992 *Casey* decision. It did remand a decision of a federal Circuit Court to determine whether Utah's restriction of abortions after the 20th week of pregnancy was constitutional. On the other hand, the Court refused to grant certiorari to a questionable decision out of South Dakota in which a parental-notification law had been struck down on its face.

It was in the area of moral concern and community mores, however, that the Court demonstrated most clearly the kind of attitude that Justice Scalia finds so biased and objectionable.

In two of the most controversial cases, dealing with gay rights in Colorado and male-only military education in Virginia, Justice Scalia discerned a consistently pursued agenda by a privileged elite to impose its moral views. Once the Court had implanted those views into the Constitution, he argued, they became permanent bars to the social values long and deeply held by the people. These cases provoked his most bitter and vehement denunciations to date.

In *Romer* v. *Evans*, the Supreme Court struck down a Colorado constitutional provision passed by the state's voters directed at repealing existing laws and prohibiting future laws that would grant preferred status to homosexuals. The Court's majority could find no reasonable purpose in such a provision, and attributed it to hatred and animus against homosexuals by the Colorado electorate in violation of the equal-pro-

tection clause of the Fourteenth Amendment. The Court stated a blanket rule that a law that makes it more difficult for one group to obtain government aid than others is by definition a denial of equal protection.

In reply, Justice Scalia (joined by Chief Justice Rehnquist and Justice Thomas) ticked off a number of what he thought were quite obvious propositions.

—Since the Supreme Court itself has declared that a state may criminalize homosexual conduct, it logically follows that the state can deny those who engage in it benefits in its civil law.

—Colorado's disapproval of homosexual conduct is in fact unusually mild. It was one of the earliest states to repeal its criminal prohibitions against homosexual conduct. Its non-discrimination laws protect homosexuals now and would continue to do so. All the state wanted to do was to limit the opportunity for homosexuals as a group to achieve additional benefits in the law.

—In the political and moral battle over homosexuality, gay partisans, who tend to be well educated, well financed, and concentrated in particular areas, achieved political victory in certain political districts. Their opponents took the battle to a higher level of democratic decision-making and won. This has happened countless times before and is normal in a hierarchical democratic regime.

What the Court has really done, Justice Scalia declares, is to take sides in the culture war and write its preferences into the Constitution. The principles of the majority opinion are not in the Constitution, but only reflect the "views and values of the lawyer class from which the Court's members are drawn." He cites the rules of the American Association of Law Schools that prohibit potential employers access to campus if their firms do not disavow discrimination based on sexual orientation.

There is an irony in Scalia's analysis. The Supreme Court struck down the attempt of Colorado to remove the issue of the legitimacy of homosexual conduct from the local political process and lodge it in the state constitution. But in doing so, the Supreme Court itself went far to

remove the issue from most of the political process altogether.

Justice Scalia's accusations against the Court were even more biting in the VMI case. In the Court's decision that voided the Virginia Military Institute's exclusion of female cadets, Scalia stood completely alone (Justice Thomas did not participate in the case).

For him, the question of whether there was any real benefit to single-sex public education should be left to the political process. True, he admits, previous generations were biased against women's education. Nevertheless, democracy "enables the people, over time, to be persuaded that what they took for granted is not so, and to change their laws accordingly." At least our biased ancestors "left us free to change," he said. But if the "smug assurances" of any age—of this age, of this elite—are written into the Constitution, the democratic process is necessarily destroyed.

Justice Scalia has moved beyond a critique of the reasoning process of the opinions of the Court. It is clear that he believes that political and social objectives are corrupting the constitutional enterprise itself. His rhetoric has never been as alarmist.

What good does Antonin Scalia's jeremiad do? It has attracted few admirers on the Court. Even Chief Justice Rehnquist veered away from Scalia in a number of cases this term. His effect on lower-court judges is necessarily attenuated, and any effect on law schools will not be seen until far into the future at best.

The prophetic role of Justice Scalia is to speak to the age, as is the role of all prophets. He speaks less to his own—the courts and the legal fraternity—and more to those in other parts of our political system. He casts up a dire warning that not only has the Supreme Court in many ways removed the Constitution from the Framers, it is also removing the democratic process from the people and their representatives. His words are on the edge of the apocalyptic: If the Republic is to stand, the Republic must take heed.

In Whose Court?

State courts have increasingly blunted the impact of recent Supreme Court decisions. And Congress is under continuing pressure to overturn unfavorable high court rulings.

W. JOHN MOORE

At the Naked i cabaret, a seedy club in Boston's shrinking Combat Zone, a woman pirouettes on the runway bar, oblivious to the clusters of men sipping Budweisers and watching her performance. The dancer twirls to 20-year-old disco music, shedding pasties first and, finally, her G-string.

"Look, bub," the cabaret manager growled in a brief telephone interview. "In this club, naked means completely nude."

The manager may talk more like a stevedore than a legal scholar, but he knows his state constitutional law. "In Massachusetts, the show does go on," said Boston attorney David R. Kerrigan, who represents the cabaret.

Such a display of the ecdysiast's art might shock U.S. Supreme Court-watchers as much as it would any Puritans left in Boston. The high court earlier this year ruled (in *Barnes v. Glen Theatre Inc.*) that nude go-go dancing was not protected as free expression under the 1st Amendment to the Constitution. Any such constitutional protection for nude dancing, Chief Justice William H. Rehnquist wrote, was outweighed by "the substantial governmental interest in protecting order and morality."

Critics of the decisions decried the Court's deference to majoritarian morality. State and local officials cheered the ruling as giving them the authority to shut down tacky strip joints. Both sides ignored the fact that in Massachusetts, at least, nude dancing has been a constitutionally protected activity since a State Judicial Supreme Court ruling in 1984.

The sight of a woman displaying her naked body to a gang of inebriated men may not hit everyone as the ultimate vindication of 1st Amendment freedoms. But Massachusetts's protection of nude dancing is just one example of how state courts have increasingly blunted the impact of recent Supreme Court decisions.

In some areas of the law, state court decisions appear like liberal oases in a vast desert of conservative high court rulings. "They are little Warren Courts," Ronald K.L. Collins, a visiting associate professor at Catholic University of America Law School, said. "The state courts are keeping the legacy of the Warren Court alive."

The Supreme Court has indirectly accelerated this trend by taking an increasingly expansive view of federalism, leaving many issues to be resolved by the states. As a result, the Court has occasionally relinquished its role as the ultimate arbiter of all legal questions.

On the other hand, state courts have sometimes simply ignored Supreme Court rulings, relying on the language of their states' constitutions to carve out exceptions to high court dogma. State courts, for example, have increasingly recognized rights that the Supreme Court has rejected, including abortion rights, criminal rights, 1st Amendment protections and gay rights, as well as a requirement for redistribution of state education funds from wealthy school districts to poorer ones. According to Collins, there are more than 750 state court opinions that go beyond federal minimum standards on individual-rights issues. *(See map.)*

On many issues, the nine Supreme Court Justices are making a judgment call, said Robert F. Williams, a professor at Rutgers Law School and the author of a textbook on state constitutional law. "Is that necessarily any better than a call made by five or six judges in Trenton, N.J., or Hartford, Conn.?"

Gay-rights activists, for example, learned in 1986 that the Court was no ally when it upheld (in *Bowers v. Hardwick*) a Georgia sodomy statute that had been interpreted to outlaw sexual relations between consenting adults of the same sex. "From the gay movement's perspective, the federal courts have been blocked since *Hardwick*, which really was the nail in the coffin," Urvashi Vaid, executive director of the National Gay and Lesbian Task Force in Washington, said.

On the other hand, state courts and legislatures have been more receptive to a whole host of gay-rights issues, ranging from the repeal of sodomy laws and changes in discriminatory family law to new antidiscrimination laws protecting gays. New York and Pennsylvania courts were the first that eliminated sodomy laws under privacy provisions of their state constitutions. In 1990, lower state courts in Kentucky, Michigan and Texas, citing state constitutional protections, also moved to strike down laws forbidding sodomy.

Other activist groups are also revising their strategies as the Supreme Court becomes increasingly conservative. At a briefing on the Court's forthcoming term, American Civil Liberties Union (ACLU) lawyers acknowledged the need for new strategies and tactics beyond litigation in federal courts.

But legal experts emphasized that a state-court strategy has significant drawbacks. A major success in one state leaves citizens in other states without those same rights. As a result, geography is destiny when it comes to what some believe are fundamental rights.

The other problem with the balkanization of rights is that defenders of those rights must proceed state by state instead of dealing with the issue once and for all before the Supreme Court. "If I had my druthers, I would rather go to the Supreme Court and liberate every single state in the union," said Thomas B. Stoddard, executive director of the Lambda Legal Defense and Education Fund, a gay-rights group based in New York City.

COURT AND CONGRESS

But with the Supreme Court seen as more of a problem than a solution, activist groups and business organizations are instead asking Congress to overturn unfavorable Supreme Court decisions. Some of these efforts are major league squabbles between competing business interests—for example, the securities industry-small investors dispute over a recent ruling on securities law. Others are far more-controversial efforts to deal with fundamental issues.

"The Court and the Congress have gotten out of sync," Johnny H. Killian, a senior specialist in constitutional law at the Congressional Research Service, added. (See box.)

The ideological nature of the dispute distinguishes the recent attempts to override Supreme Court decisions, Georgetown University Law Center professor William N. Eskridge Jr. said. Although Congress has overturned an average of 10 Court rulings per session since 1967, he said, recent congressional efforts demonstrated the widening political differences. "When a divided Court issues an opinion, Congress tends to override the conservative decisions. That is a major change in the post-New Deal, post-World War II era," he said.

Legal scholars are divided over the meaning of this trend. Some, such as Cass R. Sunstein, a professor at the University of Chicago Law School, argue that Congress, not the courts, should make the controversial policy decisions. He praised, for example, Congress's enact-

ment of the 1990 Americans With Disabilities Act after the Court declined to cover the handicapped under existing civil rights statutes.

But Sunstein and other scholars don't believe Congress should be forced to reconsider statutes enacted years ago. The Court's recent *Rust v. Sullivan* ruling, for example, which upheld a federal regulation barring doctors employed by a clinic receiving federal money from discussing abortion with patients, was attacked by those who argued that it ran counter to the intent of a 1970 law. Legislation to reverse the decision was immediately introduced.

In fact, Supreme Court decisions in the abortion and civil rights areas have set off such intense debate on Capitol Hill that there are growing concerns that the Court now sets much of Congress's agenda. In some instances, lawmakers complained, a Court controlled by Republican appointees has forced a Congress with a Democratic majority to revisit issues it had thought were settled.

Problems arise when the Court forces Congress to reexamine its earlier policy determinations, particularly on such sensitive subjects as civil rights and abortion. At a time of ideological conflict between the three branches of government, the Court can swing the balance to the President by overturning statutes. And Congress, if it attempts to reverse the Court, may have to muster a two-thirds majority to cope with a potential presidential veto.

Winning isn't easy. Witness the still-unresolved two-year struggle over a civil rights bill that would overturn 10 Court decisions. And some critics don't like the idea of having key individual rights decided by a legislative body. "When it's a privacy right or the rights of criminal defendants, ideally you want an anti-majoritarian institution, the judiciary, protecting those rights. You want to safeguard rights from majoritarian pressure," University of Southern California law professor Erwin Chemerinsky said.

CLASHING COURTS

Nobody suggests that the Supreme Court's enormous clout has been jeopardized by its clashes with Congress or by the rise of more-liberal state courts.

"The Supreme Court will remain enormously influential," said Rodney A. Smolla, director of the College of William and Mary's Institute of Bill of Rights Law. "To say that personnel changes means the Court is no longer the place where the action is means you're trapped in the liberal agenda of the last five years."

Rights activists concede that their options are limited, at best, when the Court is hostile. "The victories tend to be

very small and the losses tend to be very large," ACLU legal director John A. Powell worried.

Legal scholars emphasize that the Court will continue to be a major force in both the legal and policy-making arenas and is unlikely to shrink into obscurity. For liberals, the great fear is that the Court will shift from powerful friend to formidable foe. "I think the Court will continue to be extremely important, but in a very different way," said Elliot Mincberg, legal director of People for the American Way, a liberal public-interest group. "In years past, the Court could be depended on to defend and advance civil liberties. Now the Court finds itself, for the most part, going in an opposite direction."

But liberal groups such as the ACLU and even conservative organizations such as the National Rifle Association intend to circumvent unfriendly high court rulings with more-favorable results in the state courts. Such a trend would have been unthinkable 20 years ago, when the federal courts, especially in the civil rights areas, seemed determined to overturn the most conservative state court rulings.

But legal scholars note that state courts and constitutions have always been powerful allies of progressives. The original Constitution and Bill of Rights, said Rutgers law professor Williams, was largely the brainchild of such statesmen as James Madison, who lifted many of its sections from the Virginia constitution, which he had drafted earlier.

In 1977, no less a liberal than then-Supreme Court Justice William J. Brennan Jr., who is hardly viewed as an ardent fan of federalism or states' rights, urged state courts in a *Harvard Law Review* article to protect individual rights. In the same decade, Hans J. Linde, an Oregon Supreme Court justice, told lawyers that they should initiate their cases in state courts, relying on state constitutional protections, before proceeding to the federal courts. In his speeches, Linde, who is now retired, took the then-unpopular view that state constitutions often provided specific guarantees of individual rights that were addressed only vaguely in the U.S. Constitution.

Linde now looks like a prophet. Numerous state courts are now viewed as friendlier venues than the federal courts for bringing many types of cases involving individual rights. This is the reverse of the earlier situation, when the federal courts were regarded as progressive arenas and state courts as conservative backwaters. "If judicial activism is your concern, you see it in the most striking form at the state courts," Catholic University Law School's Collins said.

WHEN THE STATES GO BEYOND THE SUPREME COURT

As the U.S. Supreme Court increasingly becomes a less activist body, interests as different as the abortion-rights movement and the National Rifle Association are looking to state courts and state constitutions for help. In many instances, the states have obliged by going beyond Supreme Court rulings. Here are some examples.

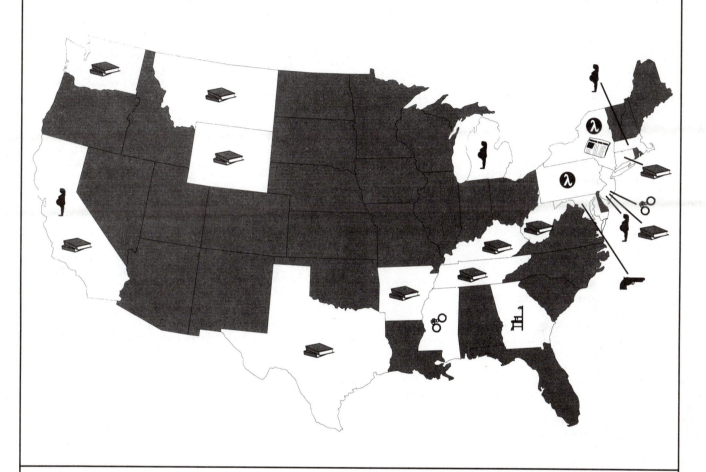

 Abortion: allowed state medicaid financing of abortions

 Criminal law: rejected good-faith exception to the exclusionary rule

 Death penalty: barred execution of the mentally incompetent

Education: requires equal spending in all school districts

 Freedom of the press: held that opinion is protected from libel suits under state constitution

 Gay rights: overturned state sodomy statutes*

 Gun control: found a constitutional right to own a handgun

*20 other states have done the same through legislation

TAKING ON THE SUPREME COURT

More and more frequently, Congress is taking up legislation that would overturn U.S. Supreme Court decisions. Here are some of its recent attempts.

DECISION	STATUS
Boutillier v. U.S. (1967) Held that immigration laws barred entry of bisexuals, gays and lesbians into the United States	Overturned 1990
Druro v. Reina (1990) Barred an Indian tribe from using its courts to try non-tribal Indians	Pending
Employment Division v. Smith (1990) Outlawed use of peyote during Native American religious ritual; has raised broad freedom of religion issues	Pending
Johnson v. Texas (1989) Found flag-burning protected by 1st Amendment	Overturned 1989 Reversed Congress in *U.S. v. Eichman* in 1990
Sawyer v. Smith (1990) This and eight other cases limited the number of habeas corpus appeals to the federal courts by individual state prisoners	Dropped in House-Senate conference
Wards Cove Packing Co. v. Atonio (1989) This and nine other civil rights rulings narrowed interpretation of employment discrimination provisions of 1964 Civil Rights Act	Pending

The Supreme Court, for example, issued a decision in the past term that limits its review of death penalty cases. The New Jersey Supreme Court, on the other hand, has overturned 30 of the past 31 death penalty rulings.

New Jersey, in fact, is one of the leaders in what has been called the "new judicial federalism." In 1987, the New Jersey court, rejecting an earlier Supreme Court ruling, held that prosecutors could not use evidence obtained during an illegal search even if police gathered it in "good faith." In a series of rulings at odds with federal decisions, the New Jersey court has struck down zoning ordinances used to block low-income housing, allowed a terminally ill patient to refuse treatment, struck down a law barring medicaid funds for abortion and held that unequal spending in the state's school districts was unconstitutional. Because virtually all of these decisions were based on the court's interpretation of the state constitution, the rulings can't easily be challenged in federal court.

New York's highest court, the Court of Appeals, also has a reputation for protecting individual rights, particularly in the free speech area. In 1989, for example, it overturned a state anti-harassment law. In a 1986 decision, Chief Judge Sol Wachtler used language that could be considered a manifesto for state court judges. "The Supreme Court's role in construing the federal Bill of Rights is to establish minimal standards for individual rights applicable throughout the nation," he wrote. "The function of the comparable provisions of the state constitution, if they are not to be considered purely redundant, is to supplement those rights to meet the needs and expectations of the particular state."

It's not surprising that the New York and New Jersey state courts are activist bodies. Their judges are appointed by the governor, not elected, and that offers them some protection from irate voters. But many legal experts have been surprised when some other state courts have issued major rulings. Georgia's Supreme Court in 1989 cited the state's constitution in barring the execution of the mentally retarded. "To think back only 10 years ago that the prohibition on cruel and unusual punishment in the Georgia constitution was broader than in the U.S. Constitution would just be a joke. Yet today, that is a fact," Stephen B. Bright, director of the Southern Center for Human Rights in Atlanta, marveled.

The Florida Supreme Court recently permitted adoption by homosexual couples. Earlier, the same court ruled that language in its state constitution establishing a privacy right also gave a woman the right to have an abortion.

EXPANDING RIGHTS

State court decisions have somewhat emboldened abortion-rights organizations. For 10 years, these groups have waged a guerrilla war through the state courts in an effort to make medicaid money available for abortions.

"This is a very promising avenue for us," said Eve W. Paul, vice president and general counsel of the Planned Parenthood Federation of America Inc. in New York City, noting the movement's success in five states since 1981. The abortion-rights groups have increasingly gone to state courts to challenge parental consent laws for minors seeking abortions, Paul added.

Liberal and conservative activists have increasingly relied on state court remedies. The effort to provide equal financing for all school districts in a state has gone hand in hand with a revolution in state court rulings. The fact that those rulings are based on the state constitutions has an added benefit, liberal activists point out: The increasingly unfriendly Supreme Court has only limited authority to review decisions based on state constitutional language.

In fact, Catholic University professor Collins urged, those seeking protection of their rights should push for rulings on state constitutional grounds. Of the state Supreme Court rulings that reached the U.S. Supreme Court last term, Collins said, 61 per cent were reversed. "If you are concerned about civil liberties and the protections of the 4th, 5th and 6th Amendments," he added, "then your objective should be to keep those cases out of the Supreme Court. If the state court affirms a right based on a reading of federal law, then you can expect to feel the claws of the Rehnquist Court."

Despite the growing reliance on state courts to offset the Supreme Court, some legal experts and scholars cautioned against viewing this tactic as a panacea. On criminal law issues, for instance, state courts have issued more-liberal criminal rulings only about a third of the time, said Barry Latzer, a government professor at City University of New York's John Jay College of Criminal Justice.

Most of the time, state courts copy what the U.S. Supreme Court has ruled, he added.

Another problem is that in many states, Supreme Court judges remain vulnerable to political pressures, which sometimes result in judges' rejection at the next election and other times in the prompt overturning of unpopular decisions by state legislatures. Unlike federal judges, "there are political restraints on elected judges," Atlanta civil rights lawyer Bright said. In North Carolina, for example, the death penalty is a hot issue in the reelection campaign this year of a state Supreme Court justice, he added.

But the biggest problem in relying on state court decrees is that justice becomes, to some extent, unequal around the nation even if most states now meet the minimum federal standards established by the Supreme Court.

On such issues as abortion, a state-by-state approach is often considered unsatisfactory. "However important it is to wage this fight at the state level and to develop state constitutional theories to protect women, the only ultimate protection is a national policy, which means going to Congress," said Kathryn Kolbert, state coordinating counsel for the ACLU's Reproductive Freedom Project in New York City.

"Congress is increasingly asked to look at these issues because there is nobody else," said Leslie A. Harris, the ACLU's chief legislative counsel in Washington. "It is now the court of last resort."

CONGRESS V. THE COURT

Asking Congress for help when the Court has already ruled is nothing new. According to Georgetown's Eskridge, Congress has overturned approximately 120 Court rulings since 1967.

Numerous recent Court rulings have moved quickly to Congress. For example, the Court last year, in *Employment Division v. Smith*, upheld an Oregon law that criminalized the use of peyote even during religious ceremonies. In so doing, the Court antagonized not only Native Americans who used the drug during religious rites but also mainstream religious groups

who feared the ruling's impact on the Constitution's free exercise of religion clause.

A coalition that includes evangelical Christians and People for the American Way have spearheaded the legislative effort to overturn the decision.

Native American groups also want to overturn another 1990 decision (*Druro v. Reina*) they view as a direct threat to Indian sovereignty. The decision said that Native American tribes had no jurisdiction over members of another tribe who allegedly committed a crime on the reservation. It was hardly a high-profile case—except to Native Americans. Lawyers for Native American groups have learned that Congress is barely an acceptable substitute as a forum to ensure their rights. "The Supreme Court used to represent the Native Americans' best chance of getting a fair decision based on the law," said Henry Sockbeson, an attorney with the Native American Rights Fund in Washington. "If you go to Congress, it is policy, not the principle of law, that is important."

What has ignited the hottest battles is the perception on Capitol Hill and among some legal experts that the Court is not only conservative but activist as well in rejecting Congress's interpretation of statutes, especially civil rights laws.

"Congress is very uncomfortable doing judicial work. It is simply not the grist of the legislative mill ordinarily. But the Court has forced the issue," Chief Judge Abner J. Mikva of the U.S. Court of Appeals for the District of Columbia Circuit and a former House Democrat from Illinois, said in an interview.

"An important question for the 1990s is whether the Court will curtail its activism. If it does not, Congress might reduce the Court's role in civil rights cases by imposing new procedural requirements on the Court and by shifting interpretive power from the Court to alternative fora," Eskridge wrote in the May issue of the *California Law Review*.

The harshest critics of the Court's activism cite what they call its narrow reading of civil rights statutes and laws governing whether doctors may advise

patients about abortion as examples of the Court's willingness to thwart congressional intent.

But criticizing the Court's rulings is one thing; getting Congress to overturn them is another matter. First, Congress needs a two-thirds majority in many instances to overcome promised presidential vetoes. And that skews the legislative process, according to some critics. "It sets up a very nasty political fight in which the President can set the terms," Herman Schwartz, a professor at the American University's Washington College of Law, said.

Equally annoying to critics is that the Supreme Court in effect helps establish the congressional agenda through its rulings. "To the extent Congress spends time overruling Supreme Court decisions, it deters Congress from a positive agenda," People for the American Way's Mincberg said.

In any event, Congress is not always ready to overturn Court rulings. Earlier this year, the Court restricted the number of appeals to the federal courts by state prisoners on death row. But Congress is not eager to get involved in this issue (or to stand in opposition to the death penalty), fearing political fallout for appearing to be sympathetic to criminals. Last year, the House dropped provisions in the crime bill that would have overruled recent Court rulings restricting prisoners' rights.

The issue demonstrates the difficulties that exist when an unpopular minority with little legislative influence tries to overturn popular Court opinions. "There is a real danger in separating the rights of death-sentence prisoners from the rights of all of us," warned Michael A. Kroll, executive director of the Death Penalty Information Center in Washington.

Other legal experts also raise doubts about the prospects of life without the Supreme Court. The ACLU's over-all strategy, according to legal director Powell, is to bring cases in the state courts. The states will then develop a track record. After there is body of law developed based on state rulings, the ACLU will then go back into federal court.

"We can't," Powell said, "avoid the federal courts forever."

STILL TRYING TO REINVENT GOVERNMENT

ELIZA NEWLIN CARNEY

Ever since Thomas Jefferson in 1801 sang the praises of "a wise and frugal government," the promise of a waste-free federal bureaucracy has enticed and eluded the third President's successors in the Oval Office.

Franklin Delano Roosevelt pledged to struggle "against confusion, against ineffectiveness, against waste, against inefficiency." Richard M. Nixon hailed a "New Federalism" that would bring government closer to the people. Jimmy Carter tackled big spending with "zero-base budgeting." Ronald Reagan promised to root out waste, fraud and abuse.

Perhaps most ambitious of all, President Clinton's National Performance Review aims, in his words, "to redesign, to reinvent, to reinvigorate the entire national government." Championed by Vice President Albert Gore Jr., the Administration's vision is lofty: to modernize government with new management techniques, cut red tape and treat each citizen like a valued customer.

Certain factors set the Clinton initiative apart from past reform efforts: It has top executive support, it was crafted in close cooperation with career civil servants and it promotes some radical notions about the way government should work.

At bottom, however, this most recent push to reinvent government suffers from the same problems that have stymied reform efforts over the past quarter-century and more. These include the lack of institutional follow-through, an obsession with public relations at the expense of meaningful investment and disregard for an essential government player—Congress.

A TOUGHER TASK?

Clinton arguably faces a tougher task than any of his predecessors. Far from trimming the federal bureaucracy, this century's political leaders have added layers with a ballooning array of programs and regulations. Early reorganization efforts, including Roosevelt's Brownlow

From *National Journal,* June 18, 1994, pp. 1442-1444. © 1994 by National Journal, Inc. All rights reserved. Reprinted by permission.

Richard A. Bloom

The bureaucracy has increased in complexity.

Committee and the two Hoover Commissions under Presidents Truman and Eisenhower, recognized the boom in federal programs and the need for a powerful bureaucracy to implement them.

Nixon's reform effort struggled to control this bureaucratic growth, which was accelerated by Lyndon B. Johnson's Great Society. Nixon's Advisory Council on Government Organization, known as the Ash Council (for its chairman, businessman Roy Ash), pledged to streamline management by consolidating government into four "super-Cabinet" departments.

Like previous reform efforts, the Ash Council also set out to shore up and consolidate presidential authority. Nixon succeeded in converting the old Budget Bureau into a new Office of Management and Budget and in giving OMB's director more clout.

But Congress rejected Nixon's sweeping Cabinet reorganization, and his reform plans unraveled quickly under the weight of the Watergate scandal. This failure points up an inherent problem with presidential reorganizations: Although genuine institutional reform takes a decade or more to implement, management analysts say, Presidents often last no more than four years.

Carter was equally determined to put his own stamp on government management. Reflecting the growth in popular antigovernment sentiment, Carter campaigned as an outsider and promised to reorganize the government completely. Once in office, he assigned about 300 people to work on a reorganization project housed in OMB and detailed another 160 to reform the civil service through his personnel management project.

Ironically, Carter's myriad study groups and poorly publicized recommendations reflected the very organizational problems that he said were plaguing big government. His reorganization team toiled for years but produced no public report.

Some concrete changes emerged: the creation of the Energy and Education Departments and professionalization of the civil service. Over all, however, Carter's reforms fell far short of their original promise.

Reagan accomplished even less with his Private Sector Survey on Cost Control, better known as the Grace Commission after its chairman, businessman J. Peter Grace. The Reagan reforms, long on public relations but short on actual savings, amplified the antigovernment rhetoric of the 1980s' tax revolt.

Like Clinton's National Performance Review, Reagan's reorganization promised to save the government big dollars—about $424 billion over three years. Unlike Clinton, however, Reagan stacked his commission with outsiders from the business world who had little experience dealing with federal departments.

PROMISES, PROMISES

Clinton has made the most of this contrast, noting that when the Grace Commission disbanded, its chairman went back to New York City, but that when Gore's group ended its task, the Vice President simply went back to his office down the hall.

Yet Gore's September report, "From Red Tape to Results: Creating a Government that Works Better & Costs Less," echoes the promises of previous reform proposals. As the Grace Commission did, it touts enormous savings: $108 billion from fiscal 1995-99.

It also builds on the popular theme that government is broken and needs to

2. STRUCTURES: Bureaucracy

Changing philosophies of government management

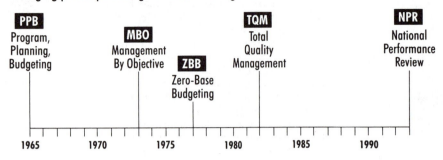

| PPB Program, Planning, Budgeting | MBO Management By Objective | ZBB Zero-Base Budgeting | TQM Total Quality Management | NPR National Performance Review |

1965   1970   1975   1980   1985   1990

be fixed. Government programs "are being undermined by an inefficient and outdated bureaucracy," Clinton declared when he unveiled the National Performance Review; government's culture is one of "complacency and entitlement."

This focus on the culture of government—the way managers function day-in and day-out—distinguishes the Performance Review from earlier efforts that emphasized reorganization.

The political climate is also very favorable to reform. A recent ABC News-*Washington Post* poll found that 68 per cent of Americans are "dissatisfied or angry" with the way government works.

At the same time, budget pressures are forcing Congress and the executive to pare programs to the bone. With little or no resources to launch government initia-

tives, the pressure to shrink the bureaucracy is at a peak.

The key to achieving more with less, according to the Gore model, is new technology. Just as private companies are tightening their belts to compete in a global economy, the Gore report says, government needs to modernize. The buzzword for this decade's reforms is Total Quality Management—the philosophy of nonhierarchical management style, employee "empowerment" and customer satisfaction popularized by the late W. Edwards Deming.

The problem with this "entrepreneurial" model of government, its critics say, is that government is not and should not function like a business. Businesses respond to the bottom line; government is supposed to respond to laws written in the public interest.

The Gore report has also rung alarm bells with its promise to cut about 252,000 federal employees over the next five years, including many middle managers. (Congress has upped the ante to 270,000.) Employee cuts without structural reforms could leave government more dysfunctional than ever, perpetuating what some analysts have dubbed "hollow government."

WHERE'S THE FOLLOW-THROUGH?

For all Gore's involvement, some government management experts say, the Clinton Administration is ill-equipped to follow through on its recommendations because of changes in OMB.

By merging management and budget functions, director Leon E. Panetta has taken the "M" out of OMB, some critics say. Some of them are calling for a separate Office of Federal Management to carry out management reforms.

By giving big play to staff cuts and dollar savings, the Gore report may perpetuate a false notion that reorganization alone can realize major savings. If anything, genuine reform requires serious, long-term investment, such as on upgrading arcane data collection systems.

The National Performance Review's real Achilles' heel, some analysts say, is that it largely overlooked Congress's role. To really save money and streamline government, they say, the Administration will have to work closely with Congress to rewrite the laws that built the bureaucracy in the first place. That means going after big programs—medicare and social security, to name just two—that the public will fight hard to keep.

President Nixon names George P. Shultz to be OMB's first director (1970 photo).

White House

Government *Can* Work

Where it got us in the past and how to get it back on track

Nicholas Lemann

Nicholas Lemann, an editor of The Washington Monthly *from 1976 to 1978, is a national correspondent for* The Atlantic Monthly.

I had my job interview at *The Washington Monthly* in February 1976. Everything went extremely well. In those days most of the life of the magazine took place in three locations, none of which exists anymore: the La Salle Building, a combination cheap residential hotel and office building, where the actual office was; the old Sholl's Colonial Cafeteria, with its constant low hum of people talking to themselves, where the staff hung out; and the Safari Lounge, where Charles Peters, the editor-in-chief, lunched every day amid mounted heads of big game (unless someone else was paying, in which case he went to Jean-Pierre). I moved progressively through the office, Sholl's, and the Safari Lounge without incurring any major damage, and I was beginning to allow myself to luxuriate in a feeling of new membership.

But when I returned to the office with Charlie after lunch, I saw something that sent an icy stab of anxiety through me. While we were out, the latest issue of the magazine had arrived from the printer; on the cover, in giant-sized letters, was the headline CRIMINALS BELONG IN JAIL.

It's surprisingly difficult to reconstruct the standard contents of a young liberal's mind back then. It wasn't exactly that I, and the people at the *Monthly* who had argued heatedly against using that headline on the cover, believed that criminals belonged *out* of jail; it was more that we believed you just couldn't say things like that. Why not? Because the information might fall into the wrong hands. Because you felt that most of the people who believed that criminals belong in jail believed it for the wrong reasons, and you didn't want to be in league with them. Because liberals should present a united front. Because to want criminals in jail was somehow also to want to abandon all attempts to alleviate poverty. It put you on the wrong side.

Much of the early history of this magazine can be understood as a struggle to get liberals to stop blindly clinging to the weak ideas in liberalism. The feeling wasn't so much of convincing people to change their minds about things; it was of overcoming the sense of "that may be true, but you just can't say it" that pervaded liberalism at the time. One of the main taboo subjects—probably *the* main one, in terms of the energy the magazine expended on it—was the inefficiency of government bureaucracies. This subject was considered the province of diehard anti-New Dealers and Taftites, people who either hadn't been able to come to terms with the realities of a modern industrial society or who were using a stated concern about government inefficiency as a polite cover for opposition to the basic health, education, and welfare provisions of the modern welfare state. Even among Republicans, ominous rhetoric about "big government" was considered faintly embarrassing—the kind of thing that one doled out for Nebraskans at fundraisers but didn't really mean—until about 1978. It wasn't, again, that everyone didn't know bureaucracies tended toward inefficiency, it was that the idea seemed to be disreputable and not to lead anywhere useful. Frustration with bureaucracy had been almost an overriding theme of American life during World War II, for example, but nobody would have suggested that we not fight because of it.

No change in the general climate of political thought over the last 10 or 15 years has been as dramatic as the one in the attitude toward government: We've gone from intellectual dishonesty about the genuine issue of inefficiency all the way over to a prevailing conviction of government's complete inefficiency. In the 1970s, Pandora's Box arguments were often thrown at *The Washington Monthly:* If you open up certain subjects for discussion, unimaginable disaster will result. That wasn't what happened in this case, though. The great and surprising political success of Ronald Reagan, first of all, demonstrated that running against the very idea of government could be a big winner, and in politics the intellectual climate often follows electoral trends rather than leading them. Also, a strain of thinking on the left that glorifies grassroots community activity and mistrusts large centralized efforts has been growing steadily stronger since the late 1950s, and it makes the anti-government attitude look bipartisan rather than merely right wing. Over the last generation, the American leadership class has shifted its base away from big organizations and now tends to be employed in various elite advising, commenting, and deal-making roles; this has made hostility to big organizations a respectable prejudice. And, of course, there have been plenty of spectacular government failures to feed the attitude.

The result is that today the mission of *The Washington Monthly* is quite different from what it was in the seventies. The old pervasive liberal fear of discussing issues like crime and bureaucracy has almost completely disappeared—partly under the press of political expediency, since it became clear that liberals would almost always lose unless they gave up the luxury of refusing to confront tough questions, and partly thanks to the good work done by liberal rethinkers. Today there isn't the sense that an enormous struggle must be waged to induce liberals to confront the real issues facing the country: The level of agreement about what our problems are is vastly higher than it was in the seventies. The main difficulty now is that discussions of the mechanism for solving these problems have taken on a facile, unreal quality. One can now confidently assert, without fear of being challenged, that central government can *never* successfully address any problem, and that everything can be solved from the bottom up, and without the participation of public agencies.

DESERT STORMING

Now we have to break this attitude down, and develop a body of real thinking, instead of an unthinking pose, about what makes government work and not work. The reason this is such a pressing need is simple and obvious, though to state it in the current climate is to risk becoming the kind of person friends nervously edge away from: Government is the best means of accomplishing a good many basic tasks in American society, so if government can't be invoked in political discourse, we can't discuss a great deal of what we need to do.

The area where just about the right attitude toward government prevails is military affairs: Everybody who has spent time around the military knows that bureaucratic inefficiency is a constantly looming danger, but nobody (except truly purist libertarians and disarmers) argues that there's any choice but to use a government agency to defend the country. Our military history is full of examples that could be used to support the proposition that government programs don't work—think of Pearl Harbor, the Bay of Pigs, Desert One, and the Beirut barracks bombing. Instead, in our better moments at least, we respond to such disasters by devising ways to make the military bureaucracy perform better, such as the unified field command that kept interservice rivalry from dominating Desert Storm.

But in domestic affairs, the leap from particular failures to a general dismissal of government is made all the time. It's probably made most often in the area of anti-poverty programs—the $2 billion a year War on Poverty has been used to drag down the whole concept of active government. By now, though, the idea that government by its nature never works hovers behind the discussion of almost every domestic issue.

It's partly responsible, surely, for the decision of President Clinton (who seems to believe deep in his heart that government *can* work) to steer clear of a single-payer health care system, and even the conservative-sounding option he did choose is regularly attacked in terms like this one, from a *New York Times* headline: HEART OF CLINTON HEALTH PLAN: A SURLY BUREAUCRAT OR A PUBLIC SERVANT?

Clinton's "reinventing government" plan, which in public relations terms is meant to appeal to people who are skeptical about government, was attacked in *The Washington Times* by Thomas DiLorenzo for "its failure to acknowledge the fundamental fact that government is by nature wasteful, bureaucratic, and inefficient." The distrust of government also helps explain why by far the most expensive new social initiative Clinton has passed to date so far is a tax incentive (the expansion of the Earned Income Tax Credit—a good idea, by the way), not a service-providing program. It's already clear that the big problem with the next major item on the domestic agenda after health care, welfare reform, is people's unwillingness to believe that government social services can help get people off the dole—hence there is a lot of support for new welfare time limits but not much for new work programs that would get the people kicked off the rolls ready for steady employment.

Imagine yourself at a dinner table remarking, "The federal government could really improve inner-city public schools." At this moment in history, the reaction would be like that of Margaret Dumont in a Marx Brothers movie (jaw dropping in disbelief, eyes widening in horror).

There is a cognitive dissonance in discussions of all these issues. On the one hand, the idea of actually eliminating most of the existing big government bureaucracies is unthinkable, either because, as in the case of the military, everyone assumes they're a necessary evil, or, in the case of agencies like the Post Office and the Social Security Administration, because they matter so much to ordinary people that they're politically inviolable. On the other hand, influential people in American society—who themselves don't depend much on government services because they use private schools, private pensions, private police protection, private mail delivery (that is, messengers, faxes, and Federal Express)—have come to use as a starting point for consideration of new problems the idea that government never works, and business almost always works. Imagine yourself, dear reader, to be at a dinner table and to make a remark like, "The federal government could really improve inner-city public schools," or, "Government can build decent, safe housing for the poor." At this moment in history, the reaction to your comment would be like that of Margaret Dumont in a Marx Brothers movie (jaw dropping in disbelief, eyes widening in horror), wouldn't it?

Countervailing the anti-romance of big government is, currently, a romance of the private sector and of small local organizations. To say what's wrong with these attitudes is to state the obvious, but it has to be done. Business is sufficiently capable of bureaucratic inefficiency that it can't simply be assumed that it will always deliver and government never will. Examples like the automobile companies and the steel companies have become too familiar to have much impact; an example that may have more power to change minds comes from personal computers.

IBM, the traditional giant of the industry, for decades "worked" so well that it would be held up as the exemplar of the modern corporation. Then it notably didn't invent the personal computer. But what's interesting is the intermittent leadership of IBM. Garage inventors beat it to the PC; then, in the early eighties, IBM's outside-the-bureaucracy Entry Systems Division became the leader in the industry; then the head of the division died in a plane crash and IBM became a laughingstock; and in the last couple of years IBM has pulled itself together and become the leader in notebook computers. The lesson is that all bureaucracies, public and private, sometimes work and sometimes don't, depending on how they're organized and who leads them. Conversely, small organizations simply can't deliver everything an advanced society needs. Going back to the personal computer case, little Apple made it on the basis of technology appropriated from big Xerox; Microsoft made it by getting a crucial contract from IBM; and so on.

Government is actually full of examples of organizations that worked once or that work now. Public education is now one of the most often held up examples of a failed government program, even though, as one of the most localized government functions, it should according to the prevailing theory escape the iron law of bureaucratic failure. But what about the state universities? With exceptions, they clearly "work" in the sense that people from all over the world are clamoring to be admitted to them, even though they are run by big state bureaucracies with heavy federal involvement. (Even conservatives don't claim that the problems of higher education, such as tenure abuse and overpricing, are characteristic of the public system but not the private.)

The Post Office is generally acknowledged to work better now than it did in the 1970s. NASA worked magnificently well in the sixties, terribly in the eighties, and now seems to be getting its act together again. During the Depression, the Works Progress Administration, the Civilian Conservation Corps, and the Tennessee Valley Authority all worked, at least in the early going. During World War II, the Office of Price Administration did the theoretically impossible by keeping prices steady at a time of shortages and rapidly rising incomes. The military quickly developed such effective equipment as the P-51 fighter plane and the amphibious troop-transport boat. After the war, the interstate highway program may have been unpopular with liberal planners, but it worked. In the sixties, the military medical system in Vietnam did such a good job that it inspired a revolution in the practice of civilian emergency medicine. Today, probably the category of agency with the highest reputation inside government is the small monitoring or evaluating organization: Examples, not well known to the general public, are the Office of Technology Assessment, the National Highway Traffic Safety Administration, the Congressional Budget Office, and the General Accounting Office. Our system for ensuring the safety of prescription drugs, though often questioned on ideological grounds, is efficient.

FREE AGENCIES

The skepticism about government bureaucracies—indeed, all bureaucracies—that *The Washington Monthly* has been trying to engender for a quarter century is not supposed to lead to a turning away from government and large organizations. Quite the opposite: It's supposed to lead to an obsession with them that will produce a clear sense of the difference between, and the causes of, good and bad performance. At the moment, because this obsession doesn't yet exist, it's possible only to suggest what the ground rules are that determine bureaucratic quality (which might replace the current ground rule, "Nothing government does can ever work").

Every agency has a constituency of clients—the people it theoretically exists to serve—and a constituency of employees and contractors. As believers in the virtues of the spoils system, we don't think government, to work, must focus wholly on the former groups and ignore the latter. But when the employees are more powerful in society than the clients, it sets the stage for inefficiency. For example, local police forces have a large employee constituency of lower-middle-class people, and a client constituency of poor people (the class from which most crime victims and criminals come)—so they tend toward corruption and inefficiency. The same goes for inner-city public school systems, which employ vast armies of teachers and custodians while serving the powerless. On the other hand, for government employees in charge of processing millionaires' tax returns, or making sure private jets land safely, not much inefficiency will be tolerated.

Agencies with a fresh, urgent sense of mission tend to work; so do agencies with super-capable directors. As the urgency fades and directors begin to fossilize, watch out—think of the FBI, or Robert Moses's Triborough Bridge Authority in New York. Agencies that attract bright non-lifers who know their performance will be closely watched—for competence, not complaisance—by the institutions where their economic future rests have a built-in advantage: The Securities and Exchange Commission and the White House staff are examples. Smaller agencies work better than bigger agencies. Agencies whose output is highly public and easy to evaluate (the air traffic control system or the Secret Service, for example) work better than agencies that operate in a fog. Agencies whose foul-ups lead directly to complaints being made to members of Congress (the Social Security Administration) have a built-in spur toward efficiency, too.

Of course these conditions are not obtainable in every case. Sometimes they're only temporary, and sometimes (as in the case of inner-city schools) they hardly ever exist; in other words, there are cases when institutions simply can't be made to work on autopilot. So it's absolutely essential that the society pay closer attention to institutional performance. The role of the press here is especially important, and currently especially shameful. Even the biggest news organizations typically ignore the entire federal bureaucracy except in times of scandal or other crisis, while, by contrast, wildly overcovering national politics. Do you know who runs the Medicaid program? Neither do I. Imagine what a difference it would make if people like that, and the person who runs the Chapter One programs for poor elementary school kids, or the regulators who were supposed to monitor the savings and loans in the eighties, received one-tenth the intense scrutiny from the press that the likes of Ed Rollins and James Carville get. Reporters and editors ought to be ashamed of themselves for knowing so little about the consequences of the campaigns whose consequentiality they're always reminding us of.

Government bureaucracies exist in the first place for two reasons, one practical and one moral. The practical reason is that in modern industrial society, not everything can be accomplished by small local organizations. The moral reason is that

Do you know who runs the Medicaid program? Neither do I. Imagine what a difference it would make if people like that, or the regulators who monitored the S&Ls in the 1980s, received one-tenth the scrutiny from the press that the likes of Ed Rollins and James Carville get.

communities and private business don't necessarily protect the interests of everybody in society—especially those who lack money, influence, education, and the life-stability that active citizenship requires. Government will work, some of the time, for some people: the people government can't afford to cross. Where it won't work is where it doesn't work now (and where the private sector doesn't, either), in the inner cities and other venues where bureaucratic failure is tolerated. Only one thing will make government perform in those places: attention.

You Can't Fix It If You Don't Raise the Hood

*Before we cut or reinvent
government, we need to know
more about what it is really
doing and think more about
what it should do*

AMY WALDMAN

The Republican chopping block is overflowing. The Department of Energy can certainly go. Commerce, too, is dispensable. Education? We'll be better off without it, they say. For good measure, throw in Housing and Urban Development. Top it off with scores of smaller offices and programs. Government is big and inefficient, the argument goes, so slice away.

But do you have any idea what the agencies that are poised on the block—let alone the ones that aren't—actually do, or whether they do a good job? When did you last read an article that told you? If your answers are "No" and "A long time ago," don't feel bad: Nobody—including the most ardent of the Republican axe-wielders—knows enough about what these places do. Without that information, how can they make intelligent decisions about what to cut, and how to improve what remains?

Occasionally, it's true, a high-profile screw-up prompts the press to unearth important information about a government agency. Last year's American Eagle crash in Roselawn, Illinois, for example, prompted *The New York Times* and *The Washington Post* to run excellent investigations of the Federal Aviation Administration, highlighting the agency's poor track record in responding to safety concerns and the bureaucratic culture responsible. "A review of five years of FAA documents, plus interviews with dozens of officials, paints a picture of an agency that talks a lot about [how to handle different weather conditions] but doesn't get much done about it," the *Post* wrote. Yet this kind of article—a useful analysis of how government actually works—is far too rare.

What's truly mind-boggling, though, is that the government itself doesn't do much better. For any endeavor to work well, it must be regularly examined to make sure it's on the right track. Yet nobody examines, in a sustained and comprehensive way, how America's largest endeavor—the federal government—is doing.

The agencies themselves have little sense of what's going on either within their walls or out in the field, a problem that worsened in the eighties when Ronald Reagan whacked agency evaluation budgets. Since 1978, 33 agencies have established an Office of the Inspector General (IG)—but the IGs focus on policing administrative waste and fraud, bounding from one mini-crisis to another. The General Accounting Office (GAO), Congress's investigative arm, does valuable evaluative work. But because it mostly responds to specific Congressional requests, the light the GAO sheds on government operations is spotty. Thumb through a catalogue of GAO reports on, say, HUD, and you'll find a lot of fragmented evaluation of lead-based paint standards or management of the Buffalo Municipal Housing Authority, but very little on the big picture. The GAO lacks the mandate to monitor agencies comprehensively from year to year.

Congress, the institution that spends the taxpayers' money, is also supposed to oversee how all that money is used. But when Congressional hearings do occur, they are usually anecdotal duels between Kafkaesque tales of constituents victimized by the government's bureaucracy and fuzzy stories of those touched by the government's munificence.

The Office of Management and Budget (OMB), which is supposed to keep track of how well the government is being managed, instead spends most of its time number-crunching. It's also horribly understaffed: Just 201 examiners oversee an executive branch with $500 billion worth of programs.

The government, then, is flying blind, and the public knows almost nothing about what it is paying for. And so before anything can be fixed, somebody needs to start getting answers to these essential questions: What is a department doing? What is it trying to do? How well is it doing that job? And, most importantly, what *should* it be doing? Until we know, the biggest chopping block in the world isn't going to make government work any better.

Take the most basic of the questions: What is the agency actually doing? Federal evaluators rarely comb the halls of their targets and talk to government workers about what they're doing and what they're not. When Alice Rivlin became the director of the OMB, she asked a researcher to collect newspaper and magazine clips on the agencies. What greater testament is there to both the failure of government evaluation and the illuminative powers of old-fashioned reporting?

When the press descends into an agency's bowels to see what's happening, its revelations can be striking. "So What Do People At Energy Do All Day Long?" asked a December story in *The Wall Street Journal* by Timothy Noah. By poking around the agency and talking to the secretary, mid-level bureaucrats, and employees in the field, Noah found an awful lot of wheel-spin-

ning going on. People seemed to spend more time writing memos and performing nebulous tasks to improve "quality" than actually accomplishing anything for the country.

A 1981 *Monthly* article detailed a similar trip to the Labor Department to investigate a program called "flexitime," which gave workers greater flexibility in their hours and working conditions. Flexibility proved to be an understatement: Ringing phones were going unanswered as radios blared. Secretaries were reading novels and knitting. A woman padded toward her office in fuzzy bedroom slippers. Nine phone calls to department employees found all of them "out of the office." How could anyone try to evaluate the Labor or Energy Departments without these kinds of simple observations?

Unfortunately, the social scientist mindset that only pure statistics make research respectable has rubbed off on government evaluators. For years, the Department of Education evaluated its largest elementary and secondary student assistance program for disadvantaged children by quantifying how many dollars reached how many children, and how many extra minutes of instruction that meant (about 15 minutes per day).

But what the department's numbers failed to uncover was that the program's structure closeted poor children in classes with low standards and terrible teachers. That fact emerged only after an independent commission made up of people who had seen the program in action sat down and compiled their observations.

The Department of Defense has carefully designed and thoroughly analyzed a series of tests, known as the Armed Services Vocational Aptitude Battery, which are given to soldiers. But no one from the DoD has ever gone into the field to see if higher scorers actually do a better job. Numbers are concrete and respectable, but they don't necessarily tell you all you need to know.

The only government agency that does this type of reportorial evaluation with any regularity is the Office of Technology Assessment (OTA). To study airline safety, for example, one analyst worked shifts in air traffic control centers. The OTA is also unique among government evaluators in writing reports in readable, example-laden, and often engaging prose. In contrast, on the rare occasions when other evaluators venture out to see what people do all day, their discoveries are usually buried in "bureaucratese." One Inspector General reported on an office that "was not properly organized or staffed and was not always performing appropriate functions or conducting its work efficiently and effectively.... [It] had more personnel than necessary, unclear missions, and staffing imbalances." Why couch such observations in abstractions?

It's the Mission, Stupid

The next question evaluators should be asking—of the biggest cabinet department and the tiniest job training program—is equally basic: What are you *trying* to do?

The *Monthly* asked this very question of Secretary of Education Richard Riley, whose department is one of those on the Republican hit list. At first, he seemed a bit taken aback. The department's mission, he finally said, is "to be a person for the importance of education in this country ... [to run] our department in an efficient and effective way [and to run] all of the education programs."

Increasing efficiency is certainly a noble cause, but it is a means to an end, not a mission. "You can have," notes Charles Bowsher, head of the GAO, "an efficient program that is totally ineffective." The mission of the department, Riley might have answered, is to make sure all Americans have equal opportunity to get an education. Or to use education to make our citizens better able to compete in a changing economy. The shallowness of his answer suggests that he isn't trying to guide his department's efforts by this crucial question.

Apparently, Riley is not alone. What exactly is Commerce's mission? *The Wall Street Journal*'s Helene Cooper recently asked. "We are at the intersection of a variety of significant policy areas that spur economic growth," replied Jonathan Sallet, the department's policy director. What does it mean to be "at the intersection?" Does that involve actually doing anything? As the *Journal* noted, that "intersection" includes everything from trade talks with Japan to scientific research on the zebra mussel.

Similar confusion reigns elsewhere. The federal government spends more than $200 billion annually contracting out government services. So it's worrisome, to say the least, that the State Department had such a hard time figuring out what it wanted its contractors to do that it had to hire another contractor to help it decide.

The GAO has occasionally tackled the mission question—what is this government agency trying to accomplish?—most notably in its 1992 transition reports for the incoming White House. But these reports didn't try to answer the question; they just encouraged departments to do so.

One of the reasons the "what are you trying to do" question doesn't get asked more often is that the answer might reveal why congressmen pass many programs in the first place—to get their names on programs or to send dollars to their districts, rather than to accomplish something meaningful. And so Congress has adopted a "kill the messenger" approach—if the GAO points out that no one knows why we're conducting a certain program, Congress accuses it of overstepping its bounds and getting into "policy analysis." As a result, the GAO's ability to evaluate mission is hamstrung by the very institution—Congress—that needs to know the most.

The Education Department, for example, has been funding a vocational education program for years to train people for work in fields such as cosmetology. Two hundred thousand aspiring cosmetologists sign up for the program every year. Just one problem: The country already has a surplus of one million cosmetologists, and that means there aren't many nail parlors hanging "Help Wanted" signs. The question no one's asking: Is this program meant to train people or to give them a way to earn a living?

With a mission clearly in mind, the evaluators could then truly determine the answer to the third question: *How well* are the agencies doing what they are doing? Are they achieving their missions? Here, too, the government fails miserably. In 1991, the GAO surveyed the 103 agencies that spent 76 percent of the $1.3 trillion in federal outlays that year. Of those, only nine could claim that they were evaluating their programs based on information that legitimately measured progress.

Once again, the Energy Department provides a perfect example. Oddly buried in the department is a program meant to bolster pre-college science and math education. The Energy Department, the GAO wrote, "had not evaluated almost half of its 17 resource-intensive projects." (We assume "resource-intensive" means they cost a lot of money.) In other words, the department had no idea what, if anything, it was getting for its—that is, your—money. Yet it substantially increased funding for most of these projects—in one case by over 1,700 percent. The reason? "The department did not emphasize effectiveness evaluations because program expansion was its primary objective," the GAO report tersely stated.

Similarly, Health and Human Services gave public recognition awards to "promising" drug abuse prevention programs without knowing whether any of them actually prevented drug abuse. And while the government has been running an unseemly number of job training programs—more than 160 at last count—the GAO found that none of the administering agencies knew whether they were helping people find jobs.

The understaffed OMB, overwhelmed with spreadsheet configurations and reconfigurations, spends very little of its time looking into whether programs actually work. The IGs are little more than bean counters, checking to see whether minute regulations have been followed, or policing mini-scandals while the bigger issues boil right under their noses. The Department of Energy's IG, for example, revealed last year that—alert the media!—"the Parking Committee [for the department] had not been formally established or defined and that there were no formal guidelines for its activities." Part of the problem is that Congress measures IGs' success by the number of dollars they save their departments, and that means busting bad administration—not badly conceived or implemented programs.

To be sure, government should take care that contractors are not ripping the taxpayer off—that the Pentagon or General Services Administration isn't paying hundreds of dollars for a legal pad. IGs play an important role in uncovering the costly abuses which can undermine the public's faith in government. But which is the greater fraud, the contractor skimming $10,000 off a government contract or the job training program that costs $100 million but isn't providing anyone jobs?

Look Before You Chop

If, by chance, agencies do successfully evaluate how well they've fulfilled their mission, they believe that their duties end there. On the contrary: Each agency needs to go one step further and ask what precisely its mission *should* be.

When this question doesn't get asked, the government runs on autopilot, and that can waste an awful lot of gas. There's no better example of this than the Rural Electrification Administration (REA), which was created at the height of the Great Depression to bring electricity, and later telephones, to farms and isolated areas. It was a noble mission, and one well-served. But by 1953, more than 90 percent of farms had electricity. By 1975, 90 percent had phones. Yet even today, the REA marches on.

The Clinton Administration has begun to examine, agency by agency, just what line of business the federal government should be in, as part of the National Performance Review's (NPR) second phase. (The first phase looked at improving efficiency.) The idea holds promise. But some of NPR's vaunted successes don't hold up to much scrutiny. Bruce Babbitt has made much of his plan to eliminate the Interior Department's Office of Territorial and International Affairs, but, as the department's own spokesperson says, the office "has been downsizing for years. The staff was extremely small." There is a simple reason for such

small-potato sacrifices: NPR relies on agency employees to say what they don't need to be doing, and that's the same as asking them to put themselves or their co-workers out of business.

Eager to toe the downsizing line, NPR and all the other evaluators generally miss another essential point. It is not enough to eliminate programs that have outlived their usefulness. To truly transform government, they must also ask whether agencies need a more active vision of their role.

The results can be astounding. As Daniel Franklin details. . . , the Federal Emergency Management Agency languished for years as one of the government's least effective agencies until it stepped back to ask what its mission *should* be. Instead of seeing itself as an agency that responded—slowly—to state request for aid, the agency recast itself. When disasters hit, it resolved, it would do all it could to help. Now it is one of government's success stories.

For years, the Coast Guard has inspected towing vessels for leaks, measuring success by the number of inspections conducted. But what the Coast Guard really wanted, it finally realized, was to reduce sea fatalities. Some two-thirds of accidents at sea result from human error; far fewer are the result of leaky vessels. So now the Coast Guard puts more of its energy into training people not to make mistakes. And to measure success, it doesn't count the number of training programs—it counts fatalities, which have already begun to drop.

The Coast Guard's new thinking was prompted by a law Congress passed in 1993, the Government Performance and Results Act (GPRA), which orders agencies to define what they're trying to accomplish and find ways to measure whether they actually meet their goals. The GAO and OMB are beginning to help agencies answer these questions, and by 1999 the performance reports are scheduled to become part of the budget.

But GPRA will work only if Congress takes an interest in it. Otherwise, it will become just one more set of numbers dutifully reported, and dutifully ignored. And there's another reason Congress needs to pay close attention. As President Johnson's Programming-Planning-and-Budgeting System showed, agencies asked to cough up numbers to show results can exhibit extraordinary amounts of ingenuity—not devoted to improving performance, but to doctoring the numbers to make it look like they have.

But at least the GPRA is trying to move in the right direction. The Republican abolitionists, unfortunately, are not. Even as they argue that the government's hand is clumsy, they are sure to make it clumsier by cutting back on the very agencies that uncover wasteful programs and suggest better ways of carrying out others. The Republicans have announced plans to reduce the staff of the GAO—which has been getting better and better at evaluating government over the last 15 years—by a quarter, leaving it with about 4,000 employees. Even more amazing, they plan to eliminate the entire 143-person Office of Technology Assessment, with its blunt and literate reports on program effectiveness.

If anything, this should be a time to *expand* the government's evaluators—they're our best tool for cutting the budget intelligently. We ought to give them broader mandates—the GAO, for example, should be required to do regular, comprehensive reviews of every agency at least every three years. The IGs ought to be encouraged to look more at what's working and what's not in their agency. They need to be reminded that the biggest perpetrators of waste, fraud, and abuse are programs that spend money and accomplish nothing.

And the OMB, which is supposed to be making sure that these programs are managed properly, needs some serious beefing up. The Clinton Administration has moved to make one important reform: joining together the budget and management functions, which were separated for two decades. By combining them, the same person who has the power of the purse will have leverage to make sure the money is well spent. And the person who is evaluating the agency will be a real expert in its workings, rather than a management guru spouting 10-step abstractions.

But no amount of reform will do much good until the OMB gets the people it needs to do its job properly. In 1955, OMB had 450 staffers for a federal budget of $68.4 billion. Today, OMB has 550 people—for a federal budget of more than $1 trillion. "The chances of us spending significant time doing independent reviews across the board are not great," concedes John Koskinen, OMB's Deputy Director for Management.Yet the White House doesn't ask for more people because it's afraid that it will be beaten up in the press for expanding its own staff while demanding that the rest of the government slim down.

If the press were doing its job correctly, the White House would be more afraid of the stories detailing where government fails. The press should be conducting regular, top-to-bottom analyses of what agencies are doing, what they're trying to do, how well they're doing it, and whether it's the right thing to be doing at all. Now, such

stories are far too rare—reporters rely on an agency's critics and defenders for evaluation, as in a recent *Washington Post* story on the National Oceanic Atmospheric Administration (NOAA). The reporter simply parroted a Commerce official's warnings of dire consequences if even a single dollar were cut. Cutting fisheries' resources, the official said, would make it impossible to set quotas and make predictions about fish populations. "Make the wrong decision," he warned, "and you can destroy a billion-dollar resource in just a couple of days."

That may be true, but how are we to know? And if the reporter had bothered to pick up the latest Commerce IG's report, he would have found half a dozen examples of where NOAA could stand some slimming—like its plan to "consolidate" into a new building with room for 100 extra employees, or its plan to spend $16.5 million constructing and equipping a facility "that has not been justified and may not be needed."

If the press did annual reviews of each agency—as a public service the major papers could divide the major departments among themselves—agency heads might be scared into trying to answer the important basic questions. Reporters, of course, require incentive too, so why not add a Pulitzer Prize category for this kind of reporting on government?

With a vigilant press, Congress and the White House would be encouraged to hear about—and hopefully do something about—problems, rather than just idly hoping they'll go away. The Space Shuttle Challenger disaster probably would not have happened, for example, if top officials at NASA had not in effect said that they did not want to hear from Morton-Thiokol engineers who knew the O-ring could fail in cold weather. As it is, a highly placed White House official once confessed that nobody in the White House even looks at GAO reports.

These aren't the issues the Republicans are raising, though, even as they speak of razing departments. Instead, they're leading a debate full of sound and fury—but few facts. And they know it: "I don't doubt we're going to discover we did something here we shouldn't have and have to go back and fix it," says Kansas Representative Sam Brownback, one of the freshmen leading the GOP charge. Why not try to make those discoveries now? Regardless of political bent, we should be able to agree that unless we know more about what government does and how well it does it, we can't figure out how to fix it.

Uncle Sam's Corporate Lawyers

And you thought welfare was a waste of your tax dollars

By Ralph Nader
and Wesley J. Smith

T HOUSANDS OF LAWYERS WORK IN-HOUSE at the various agencies and departments of the U.S. government. So it may surprise you to learn that more than 120 government agencies are permitted by law to hire outside lawyers and that, each year, the government pays approximately $600 million to those lawyers for representation in litigation or other legal services. This figure happens to be more than twice the amount the government gives the federally chartered Legal Services Corporation to provide basic legal representation to millions of low-income people.

And it gets worse. The government actually pays the legal bills of its outside contractors who run into legal trouble in the course of their work, even when that legal trouble is defending themselves against employees who blow the whistle on their illegal or unsafe activities. At the Department of Energy (DOE), the largest civilian user of private contractors in the executive branch, this indemnification scheme costs taxpayers approximately $30 million in legal fees and costs each year.

The DOE's own regulations require workers to report unsafe conditions. But when they do, DOE contractors can—and often do—use federal funds to battle those same workers. How can this be? To attract private sector companies to run its nuclear weapons programs, the DOE enters into deals that specifically

RALPH NADER *is a national consumer activist.*

WESLEY J. SMITH *is an attorney, consumer advocate, and author.*

protect contract companies from certain liabilities. This means that in addition to paying these companies' legal fees, the government may be responsible for money damages arising from their improper operations. The DOE accepts such a bad deal in part because it fears that, if contractors were responsible for their own legal costs and liabilities, they might frequently sue the government, claiming that government negligence or misconduct caused the harms alleged. By assuming the costs up front, DOE hopes to maintain greater control of litigation decisions.

Unfortunately, the real-life result is that the DOE allows its contractors to decide whether to defend a case, to choose the lawyers (subject to approval by the DOE), and to exert tremendous influence over decisions such as whether to settle or go to trial. Then, the government rubber-stamps the company's legal bills. This often forces whistleblowers into protracted litigation, fighting companies that want to beat them into the ground and that have little incentive to quit since taxpayers are paying the bills. Meanwhile, whistleblowers frequently must pay their own legal fees, even as they risk losing their jobs.

Just ask Ed Bricker. In 1977, he went to work at the Hanford Nuclear Reservation, a federal facility in Washington State that processes plutonium for nuclear weapons for the DOE. Under contract with the government, Rockwell International Corporation operated portions of Hanford from 1977 until 1987, when Westinghouse Electric Corporation took over the contracts. That same year, Bricker reported what he thought were safety deficiencies that could have exposed workers directly to plutonium, one of the most dangerous carcinogens known to humankind.

Bricker first noticed that alarms in his work area had been shut off because they were malfunctioning. That meant workers exposed to unsafe levels of radiation would not be aware of the contamination. Bricker also noticed leaks at the "hood windows," through which workers observed plutonium processing and used insulated gloves to reach into sealed processing areas.

There was more. Bricker realized that the original schematic drawings of the plant had not been updated over the previous 30 years, even though the layout of the plant had changed. That meant there was no accurate map to safe and unsafe areas. The last straw came one day when Bricker walked into the plant control room and found no plant operator at the controls—only an engineer who clearly didn't know what to do in an emergency. "It was as if the whole plant was on autopilot. That was when I decided to nail my 'Ten Theses' to the church door."

Bricker complained about the safety deficiencies he had observed. He got nowhere going up the chain of command, so he took his complaints to *The Seattle*

The DOE paid two law firms more than $1 million to fight its own worker. He had offered to settle for $65,000.

Times, which reported them. That, he says, "is when the campaign of harassment began."

"I was called a nitpicker and a troublemaker. I was called a 'government mole.' I was told that if I didn't stop complaining, the facility would be shut down and everyone would lose their jobs. I began to receive poor work performances. I was threatened. Petitions were circulated with management's active involvement stating that I had mental health problems. The icing on the cake came when my air equipment was sabotaged that allowed me to go safely into contaminated areas. I held my breath and ran out of the facility and passed out."

Bricker filed a formal complaint against Rockwell and Westinghouse with the Department of Labor, contending he was being harassed on the job because he had engaged in legally protected whistleblowing activities. After an extensive investigation, the Labor Department's Occupational Safety and Health Administration (OSHA) concluded that Rockwell Hanford had retaliated against Bricker for making the complaints,

but that Westinghouse seemed to have attempted to correct the problem after taking over.

But Bricker contends even though the Labor Department report led to an agreement by Westinghouse Hanford officials to cease all harassment, the intimidation continued unabated. "The company was thumbing its nose at the Department of Labor and sending the message to other workers that it did not pay to blow the whistle because the government could not protect you," Bricker says.

Finally, after suffering years of abuse, Bricker gave the officials of Hanford what they so dearly wanted: He quit and took a job working for the state of Washington. Fittingly, he now is a state regulator overseeing some of Hanford's health and safety practices.

In August 1990, Bricker brought a lawsuit in the Yakima, Wash., federal district court against both Rockwell and Westinghouse, alleging that the companies had waged a campaign of illegal harassment because he blew the whistle. Despite the OSHA finding in his favor, and despite substantial reporting by the media on Hanford's harassment campaign, Rockwell and Westinghouse, with the support of the DOE, denied the charges and fought Bricker every step of the way.

Here's where the corporate lawyers come in. According to material supplied by the DOE under the Freedom of Information Act, the agency paid two Seattle law firms, Helsell, Fetterman, Martin, Todd & Hokanson and Davis Wright Tremain, more than $1 million in taxpayer dollars for legal fees and expenses to fight Bricker's claim. What makes that figure especially outrageous is that Bricker offered to settle his entire dispute with the companies for $65,000, which would have done little more than cover his legal fees. The DOE rejected this offer, according to Bricker's lawyer, as "outrageously high"!

How could these law firms spend so much money? First, Westinghouse and Rockwell appear to have authorized, and the DOE appears to have approved, a full-bore, all-out, spare-no-expense litigation. Then, the company representatives merely sent the legal bills on to the general counsel at the Richland, Wash., DOE office for rubber-stamp approval, after which the DOE accommodatingly wrote a check.

We reviewed the lawyer billing sheets charged in the Bricker litigation. They reveal that each month, the two Seattle firms billed the taxpayers (through Westinghouse or Rockwell) between $18,000 and $45,000. Thus, two or three months' worth of lawyering more than equaled the entire amount for which Bricker had been willing to settle his case. The bills show how many hours corporate lawyers, billing at high hourly rates, are willing to devote to cases, with tremendous amounts of time spent on reviewing records, pleadings, correspondence, deposition notices, responses to discovery, writing memoranda, revising memoranda, conferring, telephoning, and so on.

Legal expenditures on the Bricker case achieved their desired effect: stalling a final resolution of Bricker's claims. In September 1991, Hanford lawyers convinced the federal trial judge that Hanford employees, who worked for a private company rather than the government, had no right under federal law to recover damages for whistleblower harassment. Because all of Bricker's other claims arose under state law, the federal judge ruled that he had no jurisdiction to hear the case. Two years later, the U.S. Court of Appeals for the Ninth Circuit affirmed that decision, and in October 1994 the U.S. Supreme Court refused to review the lower court rulings. Bricker would have to start all over again, with fewer legal claims, in state court.

The DOE approved the settlement of these remaining state law claims against Rockwell and Westinghouse in December 1994. Bricker got $200,000. As late as August 1994, the DOE Richland Field Office had offered only $25,000. Bricker's lawyer, Tom Carpenter, reports, "It was only through Washington headquarters' intervention that a reasonable settlement figure was offered." (The DOE's contractors admitted no wrongdoing. Officials at the DOE Richland office did not make themselves available for comment.)

Meanwhile, the government had spent more than $1 million on outside attorneys' fees and costs in resisting Bricker's legitimate claim—plus costs incurred by assigning the DOE's own in-house lawyers to the matter. Only the corporate lawyers, who received fat fees for throwing legal obstacles in the way of a clearly meritorious case, suffered no adverse consequences from the litigation.

Government payouts of taxpayers' money to corporate lawyers representing private interests are in no way limited to controversies involving the DOE. For example, when health care corporations are denied Medicare benefits for services rendered, the government pays their legal fees, win or lose. Indeed, as a recent General Accounting Office report showed, 11.1 percent of one company's Medicare payments were reimbursed legal fees. (The company's name was kept confidential by the GAO.) The average proportion of legal fees to total Medicare payouts to providers was 3.3 percent. That represents many millions of dollars that could be better spent on citizens in need of health care than on lawyers representing corporations, sometimes against the very government that is paying their bills.

Power Billing

If you think it's bad that the government is paying for high-priced lawyers, how would you feel if you knew it was overpaying them? In too many cases, that's just what's happening. It's actually not that surprising: When government agencies retain outside lawyers, they usually turn to the same large firms that represent the country's major corporations. Many of those corporations have long been taken for a ride by power law firms. Why should the government get treated any differently?

Consider just one case that has come to light, involving the two agencies responsible for by far the most hiring of outside lawyers: the Resolution Trust Corporation (RTC) and the Federal Deposit Insurance Corporation (FDIC), both of which have had key responsibilities for regulating the country's financial institutions. (The RTC, which was established to clean up the savings and loan debacle, has subsequently fulfilled its mandate and been shut down.)

When the RTC and FDIC contended that the investment banking firm Drexel Burnham Lambert and its employee Michael Milken had fraudulently rigged the market for high-risk junk bonds—resulting in, among other things, the collapse of 45 federally insured savings and loans—Drexel and Milken were already in deep, documented trouble. The agencies were alleging more than $2 billion in damages, and they sought to recover $6.8 billion from Milken and other Drexel and savings and loan executives. They hired Cravath, Swaine & Moore and its top litigators, Thomas Barr and David Boies. In March 1992, Cravath concluded a settlement that resulted in a $500 million payment from Drexel and Milken to the government— only 25 percent of the claimed damages.

The government's agreement with Cravath guaranteed the firm's senior partners a $300 hourly billing rate and other partners $250 per hour, with a major bonus built in: If the Cravath lawyers obtained $200 million or more for the government in the case, senior partner fees would double to $600 per hour, partner fees would increase to $425 per hour, associate fees to $270 per hour, and paralegal fees to $85. Tallying up all its efforts, Cravath submitted a bill for about $40 million.

Considering its rather high hourly rates, Cravath might have been satisfied with a straightforward accounting of reasonable time and necessary expenses. But it wasn't, as an investigation by the RTC's inspector general (the office in charge of RTC internal investigations) made clear. The investigation spot-checked the overall bill. Although the inspector general's office concluded that Cravath "typically verified through supporting documentation" that expenses billed were accurate and related to the case, it questioned many of the charges. For the three months—out of a 17-month representation—that were closely reviewed, the inspector general challenged or found improper $379,000 in fees and expenses. The inspector general also questioned $165,069 in "overhead" charges over the entire 17 months, as well as $60,000 for five months' worth of undocumented photocopying charges. The report added that "a detailed review of charges relating to other months would undoubtedly reveal additional unallowable charges."

Included in the disputed $165,069 for "overhead expenses" were charges for use of Cravath's in-house computer systems ($58,494), office supplies ($57,314), transmitting document facsimiles ($1 per page for all outgoing transmissions, totaling $45,924), and binding documents ($3,337). According to the report, Cravath had billed the government in the same manner it billed its corporate clients, despite restrictions in the retention agreement with the government prohibiting such charges. Cravath also charged the federal agencies for a New York hotel room for a lawyer who lived in the New York area and for a weekend hotel stay for a lawyer not working on government matters over that weekend. Out of $43,526 claimed for three months' travel expenses by Cravath, the RTC inspector general disallowed $10,763 and recommended that Cravath's $308,081, 17-month travel claim be subjected to further auditing.

The inspector general also found that Cravath had overbilled hours. One energetic Cravath attorney had charged for a 26-hour day. In that instance, the inspector general reduced the allowable hours by two, allowing a 24-hour billed day despite "serious reservations about the effectiveness of individuals working these type of hours." Cravath had also charged $22,095 for "learning curve costs" and $9,639, according to the report, "for services rendered by employees who were on vacation or sick leave."

Cravath eventually agreed to reduce its payment, although we have been unable to confirm the amount it ultimately received. The RTC advised us that it has performed no further audits of the Cravath bill. Cravath declined to respond to repeated requests for comment.

Process of American Politics

- Voters, Parties, and Elections (Articles 40–47)
- Interest Groups (Articles 48–51)
- Media (Articles 52–56)

According to many political scientists, what distinguishes *more* democratic political systems from *less* democratic ones is the degree of control that citizens exercise over government. This section focuses on the institutions, groups, and processes that are supposed to serve as links between Americans and their government.

Political parties, elections, pressure groups, and news media are all thought to play important roles in communications between people and government in the American political system. Changes that are occurring today in some of these areas may affect American politics for decades to come, and these changes are the focus of many of the readings in this section.

The first section focuses on voters, parties, and elections. One of the legacies of the Watergate scandal of the early 1970s was the passage of new laws to regulate campaign financing, followed by extensive debate about the impact of the reforms. Violence and controversy relating to the 1968 Democratic nominating convention led to a series of changes in the procedures that both parties use to select their candidates. In the 1980s, candidates increasingly used focus groups, political consultants, and public opinion polling to shape expensive advertising campaigns, and many observers thought that negative television ads played a particularly prominent role in the 1988 presidential campaign. In 1992 more changes in campaign tactics and techniques appeared, including numerous appearances by presidential candidates on television talk shows and a half dozen or so 30-minute paid "infomercials" by Ross Perot. In the 1994 congressional elections, Republicans were generally successful in "nationalizing" the competition for 435 House and 30-odd Senate seats, apparently belying the adage that "all politics is local" and winning control of both houses of Congress for the first time since 1954. In 1996, apparently unprecedented amounts of "soft" money from allegedly questionable sources fueled President Clinton's reelection campaign. All these developments and more underlie the selections in the section.

The second section treats the roles of interest groups in the American political process and their impact on what government can and cannot do. While "gridlock" is a term usually applied to inaction resulting from "divided government" in which neither major party controls the presidency and both houses of Congress, it seems clear that "gridlock" also results from the interaction of interest groups and various government policymakers. The relative weakness of parties is almost certainly responsible for the great strength of interest groups in the American political system, and one can wonder whether a possible new era of stronger, more disciplined parties in government will contribute to weakening interest groups.

The third section addresses news media, which probably play a more active role in the American political system than their counterparts do in any political system in the world. Television news broadcasts and newspapers are not merely passive transmitters of information. They inevitably shape—or distort—what they report to their audiences. They also greatly affect the behavior of people and organizations in politics. As previously noted, in recent years, especially during the 1992 presidential campaign, less traditional media forums have begun to play bigger roles in politics. Radio and television talk shows and 30-minute paid advertisements sometimes known as "infomercials" entered the political landscape with considerable effect. Selections in the third section provide coverage of how media can shape or distort political communication and the behavior of political actors.

Looking Ahead: Challenge Questions

How "democratic" is the American political system compared with others?

Do the Republican and Democratic parties offer the American people alternatives that amount to a meaningful choice?

How do the political views of young people compare and contrast with those of their parents?

If you were running for office, would you use public opinion polls? Focus groups? Talk radio? If so, how?

Do American citizens have satisfactory ways of getting information about their government that do not involve news media?

What effects do you think running for and holding political office have on the individuals involved?

Who do you think are likely to be major candidates for the presidency in the next election and thereafter? Do you think that the kinds of backgrounds from which future presidential candidates come will be much different from those of recent candidates? Why or why not?

Do you think that our current procedures for choosing the president are good ones? Why or why not?

WHY AMERICANS DON'T VOTE

And what to do about it.

ROBERT KUTTNER

THE UNIVERSAL vote is both the essence of political democracy and its most jarringly radical aspect. When people from all economic walks of life have an equal say in governance, ordinary power relationships are transformed. Some people, by dint of wealth, education, or position, normally enjoy more influence than others. Yet in the electoral realm, these deep economic and social inequalities are supposedly neutralized by the egalitarian logic of one person-one vote.

Not surprisingly, modern democracies experience a tension between these two sets of logic—the economic and the political. The tension is evident whenever campaign contributions buy votes, whenever family fortunes win elections, whenever the political power of have-nots takes something of economic value from the haves, or whenever wide differences in voting participation exist between different races or social classes. The tension is especially acute in the United States, which is both the most durably democratic of nations and the most fiercely capitalist of the democracies. Ours is also the democracy where the fewest citizens bother to vote. In the 1986 election, voting turnout as a fraction of the adult population, about 38 percent, was the lowest since the wartime election of 1942.* In states outside the South, it was the lowest since 1798.

One of the most consistent findings of voting research in America is that when voting participation falls off, it is the poorer, less educated people who stop voting, and that the inclination of low-status people to stay home has much to do with their greater cynicism about whether civic participation can make much difference in their lives. Among the wealthiest fifth of citizens, about 75 percent of eligible voters turned out in recent presidential elections. Among the poorest fifth, less than 40 percent voted. In effect, upper-middle-class and well-educated Americans still turn out to vote at near-European levels. The decay in our civic culture has been mainly at the bottom.

As a matter of practice, most politicians do not care very much about the general level of political participation. They care about getting their own likely supporters to the polls. And most well-educated and affluent Americans seem to harbor an intuitive belief that if poorly educated, lower-class people (who are probably not well informed on the issues anyway) do not bother to vote, that is a kind of

---

* There have been two mid-term congressional elections since 1986. In 1990 the turnout was a record low of 36.4 percent. In 1994 the figure was 38.7 percent. The turnout rates in the two most recent presidential elections were 50.2 percent (1988) and 55.9 percent (1992). In summary, the relatively low rate at which Americans turn out to vote has continued into the 1990s. **Editor**

natural purgative. "Voting ought to be a little bit difficult" is an axiomatic rejoinder to those who call for easier registration and more nearly universal voting. People with the purest of democratic souls catch themselves saying words to the effect of: voting is a privilege, not a right.

In a democracy, of course, voting is a right—even for the unwashed, the ill-informed, and the mean-spirited. Though it may seem counterintuitive, it is the political participation of all social classes that helps build political community and social cohesion. But the narrowing of the franchise makes it easier for the inegalitarian market to coexist with the egalitarian polity, because it reduces the political influence of the less well-off. This phenomenon is especially vivid in the United States, despite our deeply democratic origins as a nation of scant class differences and our liberty-loving spirit.

The Founding Fathers, after all, gave us a Republic. A republic is generally defined as an indirect and qualified democracy. The early Federalists worried as much about the tyranny of majorities as the tyranny of elites, putting all kinds of constraints into their Constitution, including the well-known checks and balances, as well as the indirect election of presidents and senators. Most of the fathers of the federal Republic also presumed a fairly limited franchise. Though states determined the eligibility of voters, property qualifications were then the norm. In elections of the late 18th century, less than five percent of adults constituted the typical electorate.

It was only in the populist Jacksonian era that the somewhat patrician Republic began evolving into a more universalist and raucous Democracy. Gradually property qualifications fell, and "universal manhood suffrage" was the cry of the early populists. According to Walter Dean Burnham of MIT, the leading student of voting participation and social class, voting participation began rising dramatically in the 1820s. By the 1830s it was already higher than it is in most states today. Between 1848 and 1896, roughly 75 percent of eligible voters voted.

But as participation increased, so did epic voting fraud, especially in large cities. As the rabble was drawn into partisan politics, electoral abuse became flagrant. According to the historian Joseph P. Harris, in a charming 1929 volume recapitulating earlier histories of voting, "Hoodlums were rounded up and lodged for a night or so in various lodging houses or cheap hotels and then registered from all of them. On the day of the election, gangs of 'repeaters' were hauled from precinct to precinct and voted under different names. Sometimes the same persons would vote several times at each precinct, changing coats and hats between times."

The system responded with a variety of restraints, such as literacy requirements and voter registration systems. Some of these had only the most purely civic intentions. Often, however, the evident purpose was not only to eliminate fraud but to restore the narrower franchise of the earlier Republic. By the 1880s most states had some form of voter registration. The Civil War gave Southern states one more good reason to erect barriers to voting. Complex

"literacy" requirements, poll taxes, grandfather clauses, and the like became normal in much of the South, to restrict the Negro vote. Elsewhere there were tighter residency restrictions and repeated re-registration requirements, with periodic "purges" to rid the rolls of dead people (and also people who had moved, or had failed to vote in the last election). In this cumbersome and politically unique legacy, civic purpose and patrician purpose are hard to disentangle. But by the turn of the 20th century, populist America paradoxically had erected a series of subtle and overt barriers that gradually reduced the voting participation of society's lower classes.

RESTORING BROADER voting participation, as a civic goal or even as a partisan one, strikes many citizens as a ho-hum, League of Women Voters sort of issue. Jimmy Carter's proposal for easier voter registration roused little support. The last time voter registration pervaded the national consciousness was during the civil rights struggles of the 1960s, and then only as a racial equity issue. By 1984 black and white voting turnout rates were very nearly equal, while participation among poorer people of both races continued to decline.

In recent years a number of liberal and social reform groups have perceived a connection between low voting turnout of lower-class voters and the current conservative tilt of recent American politics. But among most politicians enthusiasm for broader voter registration efforts has remained lukewarm, even among partisan and liberal Democrats. Linda Davidoff, the director of one such voter-mobilization group called Human-SERVE (Human Service Employees' Voter Registration and Education), says, "The [national] Democratic Party wants the working class to vote, but not necessarily in this election in my district. A lot of elected officials cannot stand the idea of people being allowed to register on election day, for example, because that means a whole bunch of new voters coming out of the woodwork. And if people up in Harlem vote, then you have to go up there and campaign at them, on their issues. If they don't vote, you can stay in more familiar territory."

HUMAN-SERVE was formed in 1983, the brainchild of two activist-scholars, Frances Fox Piven and Richard Cloward, who have spent two decades working on welfare rights movements and similar efforts to increase the political organization and participation of the poor. They arrived, finally, at the most fundamental political act of all: voting. Their initial plan was that the voting participation of the poor might be increased dramatically if workers at human service agencies, such as welfare and food stamp offices, were put in the business of voter registration. The idea was unveiled before the 1984 election, endorsed by 30 organizations of human-service professionals, as well as the National League of Cities, representing mayors. A few venturesome governors—in Texas, Ohio,

New York, and New Mexico, among others—issued orders permitting registration at welfare offices, but did so reluctantly. For the plan seemed to confirm the most lurid conservative stereotypes of a symbiosis between the welfare state and its dependent clients. Welfare workers, in this view, were the modern counterpart of Professor Harris's corrupt ward heelers. Welfare recipients were the modern "hoodlums," being "voted" by those with a partisan interest in electing tax-and-spend liberals. Even worse, the whole scheme reinforced the awkward image of the Democratic Party as an alliance between professional do-gooders and the undeserving, dependent poor.

The 1984 voter registration drive by Human-SERVE and by several groups sponsored by liberal foundations, was a modest success, registering millions of new voters, mostly minority and poor. After 1984 Human-SERVE moved to a higher and more sophisticated ground, operating as a national lobby to reduce systematically barriers to voting, and leaving mobilization and direct organizing to others. The group promotes a shrewd concept, pioneered more than a decade ago in Michigan, dubbed "Motor-Voter." The idea is that you should get certified as a voter at the same time that you get certified to drive a car. This nicely takes the pro-welfare sting out of the project; and in fact driving as a function of social class is slightly skewed away from the urban poor, though far less skewed than current voting proclivities. "What could be more American than driving a car?" asks Davidoff.

Well, voting could be. Motor-Voter has recently been adopted by Arizona, Iowa, Minnesota, Nevada, and Colorado. Under the Nevada and the Colorado versions, which took effect in 1985, it is not even necessary for the applicant to fill out a separate form. The driver simply checks off a box on the license application or renewal form, indicating that he or she wishes to be enlisted as a qualified voter. In its first year motor-voter was credited with adding 140,000 new voters to Colorado's rolls, increasing the number of registered voters by 11 percent. Elsewhere Human-SERVE has sought to promote postcard registration (now in effect in 23 states) and election day registration, long established in Wisconsin, Maine, and Minnesota.

California Senator Alan Cranston has proposed legislation to establish minimal federal standards for state election systems, which would include public agency registration programs such as Motor-Voter, mail-in registration, and election day registration. The proposed federal law would also prohibit certain practices, such as automatically purging citizens from the rolls when they skip an election.**

** In May 1993, President Bill Clinton signed the National Voter Registration Act into law after President George Bush had vetoed similar legislation in 1992. The so-called "motor-voter" part of the Act required states, effective January 1, 1995, to allow citizens to register to vote when applying for driver's licenses. Other provisions of the Act required states to allow voter registration by mail and to facilitate voter registration at military recruitment stations and welfare and disability benefits offices. Whether making voter registration easier will significantly increase voter turnout in the United States remains to be seen. **Editor**

Though working-class voters, especially white voters, have not seemed especially liberal in recent years, it turns out that the perceived "liberalism" or "conservatism" of lower-income voters depends largely on the issue. Survey data and focus group research generally confirm that even socially conservative white working-class voters (when they vote) are reliably liberal on economic issues, in the sense that they welcome activist government interventions on their behalf. Historically, the Democratic Party has been ascendant when its ability to deliver economic benefits to a working- and middle-class base stimulated broad voting turnout, built secure political loyalties, and purchased some running room for the party's more cosmopolitan views on social questions, which otherwise alienate many working-class voters.

Exit polls on Election Day 1986 (asking voters of different backgrounds how they voted) generally revealed that the historic correlation between class and party persists. Richer people still generally support Republicans, poorer ones Democrats. In Georgia, for example, the incumbent Republican senator, Mack Mattingly, swept the white upper-income vote, by a margin of 72 to 28. But Democratic challenger Wyche Fowler was able to gain the votes of 46 percent of whites from households earning $25,000 or less, plus a healthy majority of blacks, and to win the election. The tendency to vote for the progressive candidate goes up as income goes down—but the tendency to vote at all goes down.

THREE FACTORS explain low American voter turnouts. The first is the characteristically American fear of the State. In other democracies, where the state routinely keeps a roster of citizens, their addresses, occupations, and so on, there is no such thing as "registration" to vote. Despite the fact that several federal agencies keep rosters of citizens, including the IRS, the Social Security Administration, Selective Service, and the Census Bureau, the idea of a federal responsibility for a universal registry of voters seems to frighten libertarian Americans, or to evoke more ghosts of Tammany. This is ironic, of course, since it would be the surest remedy to concerns about hoodlums and voter fraud that are ostensibly the reason behind the archaic registration systems.

The second reason has to do with social class and political party. It is a staple of political science literature that parties are essential mechanisms for mobilizing lower-status citizens to participate politically. Parties deliver benefits and identities to voters, and deliver voters to polls. The American version of this tradition departs dramatically from the European. The United States, in the famous phrase of the historian Louis Hartz, was "born free," with democratic institutions and relatively scant differences of social class. Much of Europe, on the other hand, fought for basic republican principles and greater class equality almost simultaneously. It understandably developed stronger institutions of class representation, such as trade unions and labor parties, which do a more systematic job of mobilizing lower status voters.

Finally, most of the other democracies have some form of proportional representation in their parliaments. Proportional representation has many variations, but the common idea is to divide parliamentary representation according to the total nationwide vote. One effect is to assure all voters that their vote will "count," even if they happen to live in jurisdictions dominated by another party. Many Americans live in virtually one-party states, or are represented by hopelessly safe incumbents. If you happen to live in such a place, voting can seem futile. Even so, elimination of registration barriers could probably increase our voting turnout to the 75 percent range typical of the United States in the 19th century, and of Britain and Canada today.

The decay of civic participation is a circular problem. People stop voting because they feel they can't make a difference, and then the entire political system seems somebody else's property. Frustrations build up outside the system, and the system needn't respond to them because they are not being articulated politically. Though it seems just as well that the ill-informed and the poorly motivated stay home, in fact a better informed citizenry is probably as much the product of a more active electorate as a precondition. A narrow base of political participation, by definition, corrodes democracy itself. The idea that everybody, credentialed or not, gets to participate is the most wonderful and audacious thing about democracy.

The populist aspect of America's heritage is often only latent, but it can ignite in surprising ways. The revival of tax reform produced the deathbed conversion of one special interest politician after another, and the collapse of the special interests themselves. Taxpayers vote. Anyway, some of them do, and it would be very salutary for American democracy if more of us did.

What If We Held an Election and Nobody Came?

*Voter turnout is
plummeting.
How vote-by-mail
reverses the trend*

BY PHIL KEISLING

Whether the "Republican Revolution" made you cheer or want to move to Canada, it's hard to take solace in the final scorecard for November 1994: 20 percent support for Republican congressional candidates, 18 percent for Democrats, and 62 percent for none of the above.

Just 56 percent of registered voters in America actually cast ballots in that election. Considering those who weren't even registered, just 38 percent of America's adults voted. Nearly 80 percent of twentysomethings just said "no" to voting.

Politicians and highly partisan voters may not really mind chronic low turnout. But declining participation is perilous for the country. It means public officials are accountable to only a relative handful of voters, and special interests have an easier time manipulating money and voting blocs to drive the political process.

Some of the reasons for low turnout—negative advertising, vacuous political rhetoric, excessive partisanship, and a loss of faith in government —are profound, so the solutions are elusive. But one step in the right direction involves nothing more complicated than a 32-cent postage stamp.

In Oregon, we're not holding our breath for another century, waiting for Congress to adopt European-style voting on weekends or holidays. For 15 years, Oregon's 1.8 million registered voters have voted by mail in special elections on everything from road levies to amendments to the state Constitution. Our success has been dramatic.

On January 30, Oregon conducted the first vote-by-mail election for a U.S. Senate seat, electing Rep. Ron Wyden to succeed Bob Packwood in a razor-close election. Almost 66 percent of registered voters cast ballots, a new record for special elections in Oregon. The last time a special election occurred to fill a U.S. Senate vacancy—the June 1993 Texas election in which Kay Bailey Hutchison succeeded Lloyd Bentsen—turnout of registered voters was less than 21 percent.

The logistics of vote-by-mail are straightforward. Voters receive their ballots in the mail about two-and-a-half weeks before Election Day. They can fill them out on their own time, even at 10 p.m. after the kids are in bed. Ballots can be mailed or dropped off (for free) at any of 160 sites. Fraud is minimized by checking the signature on

Phil Keisling is Oregon's secretary of state and a contributing editor of The Washington Monthly.

the ballot envelope against the original on the voter registration card. In 15 years of elections involving tens of millions of ballots, there's been just one documented case of vote-by-mail fraud here.

Given the reality of minority government in today's America—a situation bemoaned by prestigious foundations, editorial writers, and elected officials alike—you'd think this simple but compelling reform would be sweeping America. Not so. To date, vote-by-mail has only a tenuous foothold in about a dozen states. No state explicitly allows it in regular primary or general elections. And the opposition is fierce.

The debate over vote-by-mail reveals some deeper truths about what's wrong with our democratic process. For one thing, vote-by-mail has illuminated the yawning gap between the priorities of some members of the intellectual and political elite who shape public discourse, and those who have to punch a time clock or work two jobs to support their families.

Here's American Enterprise Institute scholar Norman Ornstein inveighing against vote-by-mail in a *USA Today* column: "Standing in line, getting a ballot, going in the private booth, filling it out and then putting it in a box—all express the highest value of democracy."

Standing in line may be the "highest value" of democracy for a resident scholar at a prestigious Washington, D.C. think tank. But for many Americans, standing in line also means finding a parking space, arranging and paying for a baby-sitter, getting off work early, or braving bad weather. What ought to matter is not whether you stand in line to vote, but whether you vote at all.

The visceral opposition to vote-by-mail by others is even more revealing. Oregon's record-breaking vote-by-mail turnout uncorked this tirade from *Boston Globe* columnist Jeff Jacoby: "Somehow the delusion has taken hold that a commitment to democratic self-rule means coaxing apathetic numbskulls into voting…By now, we have so degraded the franchise that the vote of an illiterate, unemployed, unstable high school drop-out couch potato is deemed no less valuable than that of the president of Columbia [University]."

Delusion? Jacoby ought to reread the first paragraph of the Declaration of Independence.

American history for the last two centuries reflects a continuing effort to make the reality of the voting franchise more closely conform with the rhetoric "all men are created equal"— which implies that no vote is worth more than another. In the process, we've struck down requirements that citizens must own property, be men, speak English, pass literacy tests, or pay poll taxes in order to vote. Polling stations clearly aren't on par with the barriers mentioned above. But the mechanics of how we vote *are* an obstacle to a growing number of citizens.

Remember all the Republicans in high dudgeon over "motor voter" laws, which allow citizens to register to vote when they get their driver's licenses? How ironic, then, that so far Democrats have been more hostile to vote-by-mail. Donald Fowler, chairman of the Democratic National Committee, and other national Democrats urged Oregon Gov. John Kitzhaber to veto an Oregon bill passed by the legislature last year that would have made all our elections vote-by-mail. A fellow Democrat and former congressman called me personally to proclaim that vote-by-mail would be the "death of the Democratic Party in Oregon." Even political operatives in the Clinton White House weighed in. Imagine their surprise when a Democrat won an Oregon Senate seat for the first time in 33 years through a vote-by-mail election.

Perhaps the most resonant argument against vote-by-mail is that it will further fray the bonds of community. Indeed, this worry helped sway me to vote against a vote-by-mail bill when I was a legislator in 1989. I enjoy taking my two small children to the polling place, and I felt pangs at the thought of its passing. But now this argument strikes me as misplaced nostalgia, confusing a particular ritual of democracy with its essence —participation.

Yes, our sense of shared community is in trouble. Yes, we need to dedicate ourselves to reinvigorating civic institutions. But the illusion that biennial visits to the polling place will make any substantial difference seriously *under*estimates the peril our shared sense of community is in. In the short term, we need to bring more people back into the processes of democracy. Then we should turn our attention to the larger issues driving so many Americans to cast their vote for "none of the above."

DO CANDIDATES AND THEIR FINANCIAL BACKERS REFLECT PUBLIC OPINION? A DISTURBING POLL.

The Politics of Money

ROBERT L. BOROSAGE and RUY TEIXEIRA

When money talks in politics, it doesn't sound like the American people. A new survey sponsored by *The Nation* and the Institute for America's Future shows that those who pay for the parties differ with most Americans on what's wrong with government, what's wrong with the economy and what needs to be done to make things better. The voice of money is more supportive of free trade and big business and more opposed to government spending and regulation than the public. Both big political donors and the public are cynical about politicians and special interests, but fat cats are far more likely to worry about the influence of labor than is the public, and are far less likely to be concerned about the influence of business. Not surprisingly, the conservative bipartisan consensus on economic policy that dominates politics reflects the views of big donors rather than majority opinion.*

Two Views of the Economy

The press has highlighted a growing optimism about the economy, now in what economists count as the sixth year of recovery. But the *Nation–America's Future* poll reveals that more Americans view today's economy as one of increasing instability, not one of increasing opportunity. A remarkable 83 percent agree (almost three-fifths strongly) that "average working families have less economic security today, because corporations have become too greedy and care more about their profits than about being fair and loyal to their employees." Only 15 percent disagree at all with the statement.

---

*These conclusions are documented in a survey sponsored by *The Nation* and the Institute for America's Future and undertaken by Lake Research in July. The survey compares the opinions of major donors to the federal political candidates with those of a nationally representative sample of citizens. Public views were drawn from a survey of 1,007 adults, donor views from a random-sample survey of 200 contributors who gave $5,000 or more to federal candidates between November 1993 and March 1996, according to records kept by the Federal Election Commission—100 from each major party.

Robert L. Borosage is co-director of the Campaign for America's Future. Ruy Teixeira is director of the politics and public opinion program of the Economic Policy Institute.

On the other hand, a majority of large contributors disagree, and 34 percent disagree strongly. Big-check writers are also more likely to see an economy of increasing opportunity rather than increasing instability.

Big donors believe "government spends too much, taxes too much and interferes too much in things better left to individuals and businesses." By nearly a 2-to-1 margin, they embrace that view over the more populist proposition that "government is too concerned with what big corporations and wealthy special interests want, and does not do enough to help working families." In contrast, Americans generally are more likely to agree with the latter statement, while barely a third think that government spending is the greater problem.

A similar divide occurs on views about trade, an issue central to the conservative economic consensus of both political parties. Most Americans see free-trade agreements with other countries as job losers, rather than job creators (59 to 25 percent). But big donors disagree, viewing free-trade accords as creating jobs by a 65-to-24-percent margin, with Democratic Party fat cats even more positive than Republican donors.

With different views about the economy, it is not surprising that moneyed interests and the public think differently about what should be done. By 53 to 38 percent, the public believes "we need to make government regulations tougher in order to stop companies from moving jobs overseas, polluting here at home and treating their workers badly" rather than thinking that "most government regulations go too far now, making it too difficult for companies to grow and create jobs, and costing consumers money." Big contributors have the reverse view, endorsing the "government regulations go too far" argument by 58 to 31 percent.

So on question after question, the public demonstrates a far more populist viewpoint about what's wrong with the economy, why the government isn't doing much about it and what should be done to set things straight. And among the overwhelming majority of the public that is not affluent (makes less than $75,000 per year in household income) or not well educated (lacks a four-year college degree), the strength of the populist viewpoint and the contrast with big donors are even more notable.

Money Doesn't Whisper

Candidates who expect to be standing at the finish line better have more money than God.

—Frank Luntz, Republican pollster

These differences are important because money talks louder than ever in the political game. This year, experts predict that a record $1.6 billion will be raised and spent on national elections. In the 1994 elections, the Center for Responsive Politics reports, the average victor spent more than $500,000 for a House seat and about $4.5 million for a place in the Senate. As Jamin Raskin has argued, there is now a "money primary"—the ability to raise significant sums of money early in the election cycle separates the serious candidates from the dreamers before voters even learn their names.

Large individual donors—those giving a candidate more than $200—make up less than one-third of 1 percent of all Americans yet provide more than a third of all money for federal campaigns. (Political action committees provide another fourth, and small donors and the candidates themselves most of the rest.) Large donors are vital to challengers, who have a harder time collecting PAC money from corporations than incumbents do.

Indeed, with corporations and conservative special interests dominating PAC money, one might hope that individual donors would provide an alternative source of money for liberal or progressive candidates. The *Nation*–America's Future poll shows that big Democratic Party donors agree with the public that working families have less economic security these days. They are split more or less evenly on whether regulation of corporations should be tougher, whether government interferes too much, whether business has too much influence. Republican donors are true representatives of the corporate conservative view—three out of four believe business regulation goes too far, reject the idea that corporate greed means less economic security for working families, and think government interferes too much. They don't believe business has too much influence.

But whatever their partisan differences, in both parties, the big-ticket donors are notably more pro-business and more anti-populist than the voters. This includes Democratic Party donors and is especially notable when the opinions of those donors are compared with those of rank-and-file Democrats.

Money and Politics: A Realistic Cynicism

People say it's not the money, it's the principle, but when you hear people say that, it's the money.

—Senator Bob Kerrey,
chairman, Democratic Senatorial Campaign Committee

While donors and citizens differ on economic policy, they tend to share cynical—or realistic—views about the role of money in politics. Asked who has the most control in Washington, both big donors and citizens are more likely to name "special interests and lobbyists" than either the President or Congress. Both identify "business and corporations" as the primary special interest. Strong majorities of both donors (61 percent) and citizens (71 percent) believe that, half the time or more, members of Congress decide what to do based on what their political contributors want rather than on what they believe to be right.

But put a populist edge on these views and once again donors and citizens disagree. For example, more than two-thirds of the public believe that business exercises too much influence in Washington, while a majority of big donors think business influence is just about right or insufficient. (Here partisan differences are notable. While a small majority of big Democratic Party donors think business has too much influence, fully two-thirds of Republican big donors think business has insufficient or only adequate amounts of influence. Pat Buchanan is likely to have more success among voters than among donors on the Republican side.)

Similarly, large-check writers are more likely than ordinary citizens to worry about the influence of labor unions. When the public is asked to name "special interests" with great influence in Washington, unions are rarely mentioned. When big donors think about powerful special interests, 17 percent name labor unions. This may explain why pro-labor measures have met such resistance on the Hill, despite widespread agreement that the decline in labor unions has contributed to sagging wages and growing inequality.

Political contributors are modest—one might suggest self-effacing—in assessing their own influence. For example, half the public believe that people contribute to candidates to buy influence. In contrast, only a third of large donors admit that people buy influence, while half (and three-fifths of Republican donors) attribute contributions to belief in the candidate's politics. Of course, donors are likely to support candidates whose views reflect their own.

When asked whether Dole or Clinton was more likely to base his decisions on the influence of lobbyists, partisan differences hit their height, with a majority of Republican donors certain that Clinton is easier to influence and a majority of Democratic donors sure that Dole has rounder heels.

Women Count

The gender gap that pollsters say now benefits Democratic candidates is mirrored in attitudes of both big donors and the public. Female donors' views are markedly closer to overall public opinions than are those of male donors. Women are less positive toward business, more concerned about economic security and more willing to regulate corporations.

Some of the poll results were counterintuitive. For example, the more education citizens have and the more income they earn, the more cynical they seem to be about the political process. College graduates and high-income earners are far more likely to think special interests (by which they are more likely to mean business and corporations) control Washington than do high school dropouts or low-income earners. The well-educated and affluent are more likely to think members of Congress make decisions based not on what they believe but on what their donors tell them to do. This pattern contrasts with economic views, where the less educated and less affluent are more likely to see corporate interests and corporate greed as a problem than are their upscale counterparts.

The Limits of the Acceptable

Over the past two decades, writes M.I.T. economist Lester Thurow, the United States has witnessed a wrenching redistribution of income and wealth upward, of a magnitude usually reserved for war or revolution. Inequality is at levels not witnessed since before the Great Depression. Census Bureau data show wages and earnings, despite last year's gains, in a twenty-year trajectory of decline. Yet neither political party has a coherent argument or agenda to deal with this fundamental dynamic. Many factors contribute to this default—globalization's reinforcement of market ideology, skepticism of large government programs, and the influence of corporate lobbies and PACs among them.

The *Nation*–America's Future survey reveals a dramatic divide between the economic policy views of citizens and the perspectives of those who pay for the parties. A majority of voters are open to a policy that is more nationalist, more assertive, more willing to regulate business and stand with citizens. Yet these views are relegated to the fringe of the bipartisan consensus that suffocates debate in both major parties. Donors are not the sole source of this consensus; their views reflect those of many other elites. It is clear that the boundaries of the acceptable adhere rather closely to the conservative, business-oriented views of the country's political donors.

So when the pundits decry "class warfare" and suggest that economic populism just doesn't "sell" in the United States, we should ask who is buying. While a majority of Americans are open to populist prescriptions, a majority of big donors are not. Their opinion, reinforced by the dominance of corporate and conservative special-interest PACs, makes avoiding populism the better part of valor.

Revealingly, it has mostly been in presidential primaries—where public financing provides matching money and public attention insures that major candidates get significant free media—that economic populism has gotten any hearing in the major parties. In each case, the message has been carried by non-traditional candidates, like Jesse Jackson and Pat Buchanan, who have not been neutered by the money primaries that career politicians must survive.

Clearly, the need to raise hundreds of thousands of dollars tends, as Samuel Johnson said of the prospect of being hanged, to concentrate the mind. Successful politicians will tend to be receptive to the boundaries of acceptable opinion among the small circles of wealthy contributors, particularly on economic policy. Populist perspectives and assertive government solutions are likely to be particularly alien to those circles, and less likely to be heard as a result. A system that relies on private campaign financing tends to produce candidates who reflect the views and values of those who have the money. And in an economy of growing inequality, in which a few make out like bandits while the many struggle to survive, the views of those who pay for the parties are likely to be increasingly divorced from those expected to vote for them.

The Dirtiest Election Ever

The campaign finance abuses of 1996 should finally shame us into reform

Fred Wertheimer

Fred Wertheimer is a longtime advocate of campaign finance reform and the former president of Common Cause.

In 25 years of following political money, I have seen campaign finance abuses, and I have seen campaign finance abuses. And I say without hesitation that this election will go down as the worst in modern times, if not in our history. In important ways, the abuses involving hundreds of millions of dollars are worse even than the illegal contributions gathered by Richard Nixon's men during the Watergate era.

This year we've seen a record-shattering $200 million in contributions made outside the federal law, mostly from business interests. We've seen huge amounts of foreign money raised by the elusive Democratic operative John Huang from an Indonesian conglomerate and others, hundreds of six-figure checks from corporations and business executives to Democrats and Republicans, a first-ever $20-million-plus advertising blitz funded by union dues to win back Democratic control of Congress, Sen. Dole's finance vice chairman convicted for laundering contributions, President Clinton personally involved in a $35 million ad campaign circumventing the campaign finance laws, Philip Morris contributing more than $3 million primarily to Republicans to help protect its tobacco interests, and even the spectacle of Vice President Gore participating in a fund-raiser at a Buddhist temple.

When you add it all up—the illegality, the cheating, the evasion, as well as the arrogance and cynicism—what we have is a collapse of the system on a scale we simply haven't seen before. It is a collapse that tainted the results of last Tuesday's presidential and congressional elections.

Put simply, we've seen that the attitude of our national leaders when it comes to campaign laws is no different than that of tax evaders, deadbeat dads and welfare cheats. The most powerful people in the country have proved in the 1996 political season that they do not believe the law applies to them.

The abuses involve the Democratic president and his Republican challenger; the Democratic and Republican national party committees; Democrats and Republicans running for Congress; labor unions, corporations, wealthy individuals and foreign-based interests. Special mention must be made of the incumbent president, who has led the way in setting the tone and unleasing an escalating money war that resembles the Cold War arms race.

As a result, in 1996 the campaign finance system put in place following the Watergate scandals has been washed away. Though still on the books, campaign finance laws have been replaced by the law of the jungle. The abuses may well have seriously tilted the election results. And who knows what they will do to the integrity of the political process.

Some will no doubt argue that this proves that campaign finance laws to limit corruption and the appearance of corruption cannot work. They will argue that court decisions on free speech, and the impossibility of closing loopholes in the law, show that you cannot stem the tide of huge corrupting contributions. The ugly reality, however, belies this argument. The key to understanding much of what has happened in 1996 is not loopholes, it's law breaking. There are laws that matter, but people are breaking them. And no one's doing anything about it.

Whatever else we do, we have to start enforcing the laws we have. Attorney General Janet Reno, for example, should appoint an independent counsel to investigate whether the Clinton and Dole campaigns engaged in massive violations. If people are guilty of criminal conduct, they should be prosecuted and punished. That's what happened during Watergate, and it had a very sobering effect on potential lawbreakers for years afterward.

The Watergate analogy is one we should keep in mind, both for its abuses and the reforms it spurred. Watergate remains our nation's greatest political scandal and involved a lot more than campaign money. It involved obstruction of justice, criminal convictions of the top officials in the White House and two men who served as attorney general, as well as the resignation of the president. But while the campaign finance abuses of Watergate were momentous and contemptible, what has happened this year is actually larger in scope and impact. The shady dealings by Nixon's Committee to Re-Elect the President (CREEP), which included secret slush funds and cash-stuffed envelopes solicited from businessmen, focused only on one officeholder.

In 1974, following Watergate, a new system of public financing and spending limits was established for presidential elections. Limits also were imposed in all federal elections for contributions from individuals and political action committees, to go with the longstanding ban on corporate and labor union money.

A fundamental purpose of the laws was to prevent contributions from buying, or appearing to buy influence over presidential and congressional decisions. And at least for presidential elections, the system worked well until 1988 when the "soft money" scam was used by both the Michael Dukakis and George Bush campaigns to bring huge money back into politics. When all efforts to fix this problem and the similarly dangerous problem of special interest money in congressional campaigns, were blocked in Congress or by a presidential veto, the stage was set for this year's fiasco.

SEVERAL THINGS WERE DIFFERENT THIS TIME. FIRST, all the political players approached the 1996 election as if it were World War III—that is to say, each side felt that if the other side won full control of the White House and Congress, American civilization would come to an end. Under these circumstances, they concluded, anything goes.

Second, everyone decided there were no real consequences to behavior that might break the law. While this view has been growing for years because of the failure of the Federal Election Commission (FEC) to seriously enforce the law, in 1996 a collective judgment was reached that if you break the law no one will do anything about it, and even if they do it will simply result in some fine being imposed literally in the next century.

Third, the person who kicked off this ethical race to the bottom was none other than the president of the United States. In the summer of 1995, Bill Clinton and his political operatives designed what turned out to be an unprecedented $35 million advertising campaign, using money that the law said should not have been in his control, to promote the president's reelection.

There followed in quick succession all sorts of people bending and/or breaking the laws for their own ends, including the AFL-CIO's massive television buy, Al D'Amato's evasive National Republican Senate Committee schemes to pump extra money into Senate races and Dole's $17 million ad campaign after he had reached his spending limit.

Much of what I believe to be illegal conduct centers on so-called soft money, since 1988 a legal fiction that has served as cover for injecting tens of millions of dollars improperly into the presidential campaigns (and now congressional races as well). The fiction, tragically blessed and thereby given the aura of legitimacy by the FEC, is the claim that these funds were being raised and used for political party-building activities. The reality is that they are used to support the presidential campaigns. The impact of this has been to bring back into presidential campaigns huge contributions of $100,000 or more from corporations, labor unions and wealthy individuals that have been barred from federal elections, in some cases—such as corporations—since the turn of the century.

SOFT MONEY HAS BEEN A SCAM FROM THE BEGINning. This year it ended up being a $200 million scam. Here's how: The Clinton and Dole campaigns each used millions of dollars in soft money to help finance TV ad campaigns

that promoted their candidacies and attacked their opponents. Using their political parties as conduits, they prepared, directed and controlled the ad campaigns, raised the money for them, and targeted them to presidential battleground states. These expenditures were beyond the spending limits that Clinton and Dole had agreed to abide by in return for receiving public funds to help finance their elections.

In Clinton's case, flouting the law may well have had a major impact on the race. Much of his early ad burst ran last fall and winter at a time when he had the airwaves to himself. It allowed him to frame the national debate to his liking for the entire campaign year that followed. This may have affected not just the presidential race but the context in which the congressional races were run as well.

For the first time, the Republican and Democratic national party committees used millions of dollars in soft money contributions to finance TV ad campaigns that attacked and promoted congressional candidates by name.

The parties have been using as a fig leaf the notion that since the ads did not say "vote for" or "vote against" the candidate, these are "issue ads" and not subject to federal limits. This is a ludicrous argument on its face. A political party running ads that attack or support a specific named federal candidate cannot seriously claim that these are just issue ads. And they cannot use soft money to finance such ads.

Beyond soft money to the political parties, interest groups, led by the AFL-CIO, also made unprecedented expenditures on TV ad campaigns to attack and promote congressional candidates. The Supreme Court has ruled in the case of independent groups that ads require express advocacy such as "vote for" or "vote against" in order to be treated as ads covered by the campaign finance laws rather than issue ads. The AFL-CIO decided to use this ruling as a license to cheat, running its $20-million-plus TV and radio ad campaign with the stated intention of defeating Republicans in selected House districts.

The Republicans have filed complaints with the FEC charging that the ads, financed by union dues, which cannot be used to support or oppose a federal candidate, constitute multimillion-dollar illegal campaign expenditures. Once again we see a situation where dubious conduct could have an impact on the balance of power in American politics.

None of this, of course, even takes into account the corrupting impact that all of these contributions and expenditures may have on government decisions affecting all of us, now that the elections are over. A relatively few powerful people and groups have put a lot of money on the table. What do they expect in return? What will they get?

IF THERE IS ANYTHING GOOD IN ALL THIS, IT'S THE realizations, which should be clear to all by now, that the system is "broke" and has to be "fixed." It can be done. We do not lack for solutions. It is a question of having the political will to implement them. Here are five steps to take to achieve real reform:

■ *Move quickly.* Beware of politicians bearing a "commission" to examine the problems and propose the solution. Delay has always been a principal weapon in killing campaign finance reform. And a commission means serious delay. It also means commissioners appointed by political leaders who for the most part have no credibility when it comes to a demonstrated commitment to real reform. A campaign finance reform bill should be the first one acted on in the new Congress, otherwise members will soon turn their attention to the business of financing their next election.

■ *Fix the enforcement system.* No new laws will work unless they're seriously enforced. The terms of four of the six FEC commissioners will be up by next May. Appoint nonpartisan commissioners, such as retired federal judges, who see their job as representing the public, not the politicians. Change the commission structure to eliminate deadlocks. Provide the commission with adequate and permanent funding. Give the commission powers to act during an election, not just years afterward.

■ *Ban soft money.* Prohibit national parties and federal candidates and officeholders from raising or spending money that cannot legally be used to directly support a federal candidate. Legislative measures to accomplish this already exist. They are contained in the campaign finance bills sponsored in the last Congress by Republican Sen. John McCain of Arizona and Democratic Sen. Russell Feingold of Wisconsin and Republican Reps. Chris Shays of Connecticut and Linda Smith of Washington and Democratic Rep. Martin Meehan of Massachusetts. Enact new rules to ensure that campaign ads can't masquerade as issue ads.

■ *Provide new sources of "clean" funds.* We have to replace the interested money that pervades the system. Provide public funds and free and low-cost TV and mailings for those willing to participate in a new system for financing congressional elections.

■ *Eliminate the Washington-based professional fund-raising circuit.* The PAC/lobbyist/special interest money machine dominates congressional campaign financing. Place tough new restrictions on contributions from these sources. Develop legislative measures and new congressional rules to minimize fund-raising activities in Washington.

This year's extraordinary and unprecedented abuses, ironically, have provided us with the best chance since Watergate to fundamentally reform the nation's campaign finance laws. Every American who cares about democratic values should join in this battle. The only thing at stake is our democracy in the 21st century.

BILL'S BIG BACKER$

by THOMAS FERGUSON

IF ONE LOOKS BENEATH THE SURGING POLITICAL business cycle that—along with the simple fact that the president is not Newt Gingrich—has brought Bill Clinton back from the dead, signs of a remarkable and ominous new turn in American public life are visible everywhere. It is not just that both major party candidates now embrace the orthodoxy that we must eliminate the deficit and balance the budget (despite their noisy differences over how far taxes should be cut at the same time). Or that earlier this year Clinton renominated Republican Alan Greenspan as head of the Federal Reserve Board, without any opposition from Bob Dole.

What is extraordinary is that only months after Pat Buchanan shocked the political establishment by prying open the Pandora's box of slow growth, wage stagnation, globalization, and increasing inequality, the lid is back on again. All the Republicans want to talk about is cutting taxes and government. Clinton downplays questions of wage stagnation in favor of breathless encomia to the (cyclical) strength of the economy. And billionaire Ross Perot's "Reform Party" campaigns at public expense for even bigger budget cuts. The whole spectrum of policy debate is right back where it was before Buchanan's rebellion.

How to account for this miraculous inversion? Surely not by attributing it to the voters' will. The disdain that millions of them feel for all three candidates is apparent, as is their palpable frustration with the political system's continuing refusal to confront the economic uncertainties facing most Americans.

A much more compelling explanation is the power of money, or more precisely, what I call the "investment" theory of political parties. This view holds that in countries like the United States, where most voters are unorganized, desperately pressed for both time and money, and minimally informed or interested in politics, a political party's real market is defined by major political investors, who generally have good and clear reasons for giving money to control the state. Accordingly, in analyzing an election, the place to begin is with a systematic study of blocs of large investors. This requires a clear break with the usual media fixation on gross spending totals—however stunning—in favor of more subtle efforts to identify and dissect coalitions in politically significant terms. Like my other efforts to trace the workings of the "golden rule" in American elections, this essay relies extensively on my own analysis of Federal Election Commission data covering "early money" (i.e., all of 1995 and early 1996) in this year's presidential election.

BACKDROP: THE 1994 GOP LANDSLIDE

The 1996 Clinton campaign was constructed almost entirely from the wreckage of the 1994 debacle, when the Democrats lost control of both houses of Congress for the first time in

Though CLINTON'S contributions from Wall Street were lower than expected, other industries—notably oil and defense—took up some of the slack. But the best-kept secret of the election is that it was the telecommunications industry that rescued Bill Clinton.

four decades. The road to comprehending 1996, therefore, begins by retracing the path to the 1994 disaster.

Polls taken shortly before the 1994 off-year elections suggested that as many as half of all voters were unable to name a single achievement of the Clinton administration. Even worse, the administration faced a dual squeeze on its supply of campaign financing.

On the one hand, the long-running battle over health care, regulatory skirmishes over the environment, and talk of raising the minimum wage were prompting anxious businesses to send enormous streams of money to the GOP. For example, tabulations for the 1993-94 election cycle published by the FEC (which omit the vast amounts of money paid for "issue-oriented" advertising by pharmaceuticals, insurers, and medical instrument companies) indicate that total spending in congressional races amounted to the record-breaking sum of $725 million, "with increased activity by Republican candidates...entirely responsible for the growth." Spending by the national political parties, which the FEC tallies separately, was equally astronomical, amounting to more than $385.5 million—well above the $304 million reported in the 1989-90 off-year election cycle—again, with a heavy GOP tilt.

On the other hand, while the administration's opponents anted up at a breakneck pace, some of Clinton's most impor-

tant allies were closing their checkbooks. Wall Street, which in 1992—as in many other presidential elections—had provided a plenary share of funds for the Democratic candidate, was now abandoning the party. After more than half a century, the tectonic plates of American political life were shifting.

This process (which is only in its initial stages, and might still reverse itself) has long-term roots. But two new developments brought matters to a head in early 1994. The first was the administration's running battle to roll back the Japanese trade surplus and open Japanese markets to American producers. Exasperated by what they regarded as Japanese stonewalling, the Clinton economic team began trying to "talk down the dollar" (i.e., talk up the yen) in February 1994. The idea, which was immensely appealing to American producers of automobiles, semiconductors, telecommunications, and other tradable goods, was to make Japanese wares so expensive in the U.S. market that Japan would have to open up out of sheer self-preservation.

This strategy, however, implied a sharp drop, at least for a time, in the international value of the dollar. In New York financial circles, notions of this sort are pure poison. No matter how clever and intricate arguments from pure economic theory may occasionally be, international financial centers are generally unwilling to risk sustained declines in their currencies. Too many asset holders and traders start shifting out, with the perceived risk of the currency's irrevocable decline rising sharply the longer such episodes continue and the more frequent they become.

That the administration's shift caught much of Wall Street off-guard added fuel to the fire. Some houses that had bet the wrong way briefly endured spectacular losses and sold out of bonds they had bought on credit. After central banks around the world began raising interest rates (or, as in the case of the Bundesbank, signaled an unwillingness to continue lowering them), havoc spread to many other bond markets.

The second factor in Wall Street's estrangement from the Clinton administration grew out of the search for scapegoats that followed the turmoil in world financial markets. With some encouragement from rival financial concerns and from international and domestic regulatory authorities, congressional Democrats briefly held hearings into so-called hedge funds (off-shore vehicles for wealthy investors, which frequently augment their own very considerable resources by borrowing). While this effort, like the push to talk down the dollar, was soon abandoned, the damage was done. Importuned to open their wallets by Democratic National Committee (DNC) officials, Wall Street's Masters of the Universe nearly all refused. Some even walked out of earlier six-figure pledges. The immediate result was a sharp drop in the pace of DNC soft money receipts at precisely the moment they should have been rising.

COMEBACK KID II
Though virtually no one noticed, Bill Clinton began his long climb out of the crypt by breaking the hold the Republicans had tried to estab-

---

THE GOLDEN RULE

Thomas Ferguson is a professor of political science at the University of Massachusetts, Boston, and a *Mother Jones* contributing writer. He is the author of many scholarly studies into money and politics, including *Golden Rule: The Investment Theory of Political Parties and the Logic of Money-Driven Political Systems* (Chicago: University of Chicago Press, 1995).

The sample of large investors and statistical methods used in this article follow the discussion in chapters 4 and 6 of *Golden Rule*. The sample includes firms and large private investors at the top of the American economic pyramid—specifically, the 400 largest firms listed in the Fortune 500; equally large, privately held firms; large Wall Street firms; and *Forbes* magazine's 400 richest Americans. In contrast to many studies of campaign spending, this study looks at the individual contributions of the top officers of all the firms, as well as "soft money" and political action committee (PAC) donations.

NOTE: This chart shows the percentages of companies in Ferguson's sample that gave "early money" to Clinton's presidential campaign. The sample contains a total of 774 firms/investors, including 13 defense contractors, 56 telecommunications firms, 45 oil and gas companies, and 35 investment banks. The results for telecommunications, defense, and oil and gas are all statistically significant at the .05 level or better, regardless of which significance tests one prefers, or precisely how one calculates the level of contributions. By contrast, the lower results for the investment bankers are always statistically borderline (.10 or worse)—a warning that this industry's rate of early support for the Clinton campaign might not really differ from the low (20 percent) average of the sample as a whole. (All data comes from the Federal Election Commission.)

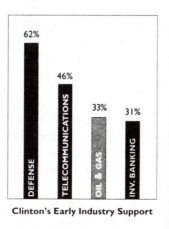

62% DEFENSE
46% TELECOMMUNICATIONS
33% OIL & GAS
31% INV. BANKING

Clinton's Early Industry Support

lish over two powerful constituencies: defense and oil.

A few weeks after the 1994 election, as pundits vied with one another to write off his chances for re-election, the president surprised everyone by declaring himself in favor of increased defense spending. With the United States already spending more on defense than the next six countries in the world combined, and polls showing that the public ranked military spending at the very bottom of its list of new spending priorities, this step made little sense in electoral terms. Brushing aside doubts expressed by the foreign policy establishment and the military, the administration also loudly advertised its devotion to rapid NATO expansion—an issue of burning interest to defense contractors, whose increasingly vital export business cannot hope to flourish in countries where links to former Soviet military suppliers remain strong.

Leapfrogging over congressional Republicans, who had begun to tout the former Soviet Republic of Georgia as a vital U.S. interest, the administration also threw its weight behind American multinationals involved in the titanic struggle now raging for control of Transcaucasian oil. While constrained by its strong commitment to the Yeltsin regime, the Clinton team moved on several fronts at once. The United States intensified its already close relationship with Turkey, which potentially holds a key position in the region. Clinton also personally telephoned the president of Azerbaijan to win support for a pipeline leading down through Georgia and, eventually, through Turkey, instead of one running only through Russian-controlled territory. American diplomats also backed Chevron in its struggle over a mammoth oil concession in Kazakhstan.

By mid-1995, this "multinational pork barrel" strategy was bringing some real advantages to the president. Though he continued to languish in the polls, Clinton and his advisers

BOB'$ BEST BUDDIES

DOLE won his party's nomination by developing a much wider base of contributors than his Republican opponents—and using it to wear them down, one by one.

BECAUSE OF THE "FRONT-LOADED" CHARACTER OF THE PRIMARY system, which forces candidates to purchase enormous amounts of media time early in the race, a well-heeled candidate can sometimes literally win by losing, in the durable style of the old Russian army: Just pile up resources, and keep hanging in there until everyone else has to drop out.

As a senator from Kansas, a major supporter of farm exports, and a longtime member of the Senate Finance Committee (which functions rather like a high tribunal of tolls, taxes, and levies), Bob Dole commanded the GOP's equivalent of the Russian army. Until recently a champion of fiscal orthodoxy, he had many friends on Wall Street, in houses such as Smith Barney and Merrill Lynch. While essentially a free trader, he had—like Clinton, but unlike his GOP rivals Lamar Alexander, Steve Forbes, or Phil Gramm—moved to accommodate big business' increasing demand to pursue American commercial interests more aggressively. This flexibility paid big dividends: Despite a long courtship from the Clinton administration, top officials of all three automakers ended up contributing to Dole's campaign.

Pat Buchanan's presidential campaign, like Steve Forbes', reflected the concerns of one SUPERDONOR.

Deeply involved in the revision of telecommunications law, Dole garnered far more contributions from this sector than any other GOP candidate. (Most of the regional Bells were ringing for him; broadcasters proved much chillier.) Dole was also as committed to defense spending as anyone in the GOP, and his refusal to bring minimum wage legislation to a vote in the Senate endeared him to retailers and wholesalers. Although some holes existed in Dole's network (the computer industry, for instance, which did not go especially heavily for Clinton either), his base was much wider than any other GOP primary candidate's.

Steve Forbes did not lack for money—his own, and that of supporters in the chemical and pharmaceutical industries and a surprisingly wide swath of Wall Street. But his concentration on the flat tax made him vulnerable to well-financed counterattacks, once real estate (which feared for its tax concessions), defense (which feared that flatter taxes implied flatter defense spending), and more orthodox financiers woke up to the challenge. Forbes' aggressive support of Taiwan (a stance he shared with Buchanan) also drove a wedge between him and multinational businesses desperate to capture the Chinese market. After the Dole machine chewed him up in the Deep South and New York (where Forbes had to spend a small fortune merely to get on the ballot), Forbes thriftily withdrew.

had taken an initiative away from Gingrich and the GOP in a way that paid off in a modest number of campaign contributions and applause—at first grudging, but more recently, much warmer—from foreign policy elites.

Foreign policy efforts like these, however, hardly sufficed to secure Clinton's re-election. Two additional steps were required. First, the president needed to amass a much larger war chest to scare off potential Democratic challengers and to pay for an advertising blitz as the general election approached. Second, Clinton needed some way to highlight his differences with the Republicans without frightening off potential campaign investors.

In 1995, reconciling these two contradictory imperatives was an even taller order than usual. As one Democratic strategist confessed to the *Philadelphia Inquirer* in August 1995, "Lately we've been cowed into the position of not sticking up for working people, because we've been looking increasingly to wealthy interests in order to fund our campaigns. You end up spending time with wealthy people who say, 'Let's not make this a class thing.'"

MICKEY MOUSE TO THE RESCUE

After the president called off the automobile war with Japan in 1995, his economic team regularly proclaimed that the United States would welcome a stronger dollar. But my survey of early campaign contributions to Clinton's re-election campaign indicates that neither this belated profession of faith, nor even the Mexican bailout, sufficed to bring Wall Street around. Wall Street contributions were only modestly above the generally low average (20 percent) contributed by business as a whole (see sidebar "The Golden Rule").

Industries the White House was courting, notably oil and defense, took up some of the slack. More money also came from trial lawyers, particularly as Clinton made up his mind

At first glance, **Pat Buchanan**'s campaign looks like the polar opposite of Forbes'. But it, too, reflected the preoccupations of one superdonor, Roger Milliken. The textile magnate—an opponent of NAFTA, U.S. trade policy with China, and unions—reportedly contributed at least $250,000 to The American Cause, the nonprofit controlled by Buchanan and his sister before Buchanan entered the race. Milliken also reportedly donated almost $2 million to the Coalition for the American Cause, which lobbied on trade issues and appears to have had close ties to The American Cause. He also contributed to Buchanan's campaign, along with some rather small textile companies and a couple of sizable chemical concerns.

By concentrating his resources in a few early states (notably New Hampshire) and appealing to the religious right, Buchanan managed to reach just enough donors to create a splash. After tiny New Hampshire, however, his inability to resist playing to stereotype, along with a lack of resources and a hostile media, spelled doom.

Lamar Alexander came from the opposite end of the GOP spectrum, with very close ties to multinational businesses. His problem was that his rivals (Dole, Forbes, Phil Gramm, and even Richard Lugar) all had equally plausible claims to be considered free traders. Consequently, Alexander raised respectable, but not overwhelming, amounts of money from the traditional citadels of free trade: Wall Street, commercial banks, foreign multinationals (including Nissan, whose entry into Tennessee Alexander had spearheaded as governor). He raised similarly modest amounts from some of the usual GOP suspects (health care and chemical companies) and from cable companies, including giant TCI, which has a substantial presence in Tennessee.

At the crucial moment, as Alexander closed in on Bob Dole and Buchanan in the last weekend before the New Hampshire primary, he simply did not have the resources to blanket the airwaves with ads. Bob Dole, however, did. His campaign, far more concerned with Alexander in the long run than with Buchanan, focused its early attacks on the Tennessean, spending hundreds of thousands of dollars on ads branding him a "tax-and-spend liberal." According to the *Boston Globe*, before the ads ran, 44 percent of voters considered Alexander "conservative"; five days later, only 22 percent did. In the New Hampshire primary, this proved lethal. Facing giant, multistate media buyouts to stay in the race, Alexander briefly staggered on before folding his campaign. When Forbes checked out a few weeks later, the nomination became Dole's by default. No one else had any money left.—*T.F.*

IN 1995, Clinton needed some way to highlight his differences with the GOP without scaring off campaign donors. "Lately," said one Democratic strategist, "we've been cowed into not sticking up for working people, because we've been looking to wealthy interests in order to fund our campaigns."

$ $

to veto legislation curbing lawsuits. A small amount arrived from unions. (Note that union contributions are likely to bulk considerably larger in this year's congressional campaigns, and that the AFL-CIO is also waging a sizable national campaign focusing on "issues" nominally unconnected to the election.)

In the end, however, the best-kept secret of the 1996 election is that, more than any other single bloc, it was the telecommunications sector that rescued Bill Clinton. In my sample of large firms, this staggeringly profitable sector (which I treat as distinct from both the computer and software industries) stands out in its support for Clinton: Forty-six percent of the firms in my sample contributed to the president's re-election campaign through either individual contributions from top executives or soft money to the Democratic Party.

This is a level matched by no other comparably large industry. And the amounts given by individual companies are sometimes remarkable. Over the course of 1995, for example, Miramax, a Disney subsidiary, contributed more than $250,000 in soft money to the Democrats, while several Disney executives also made personal donations to the Clinton campaign.

The reason why isn't complicated. For years, Hollywood, network and cable television, book publishers, news concerns, radio stations, computer and software makers, and phone companies had all been making vast sums of money as separate entities. By 1993, however, changes in technology and regulatory practice were bringing these industries together at an explosive pace, and almost everyone wanted legal rights to get into everyone else's business.

The initial charge for what became the Telecommunications Act of 1996 was led mostly by congressional Republicans, on behalf of the regional Bells and a few other companies responsible for local telephone service (see "Channel Surfer," *Mother Jones*, September/October). After the cable companies won a promise of rate deregulation, they, too, mostly fell in behind the proposed legislation.

But these early, largely Republican, versions of the bill alarmed many producers of "content"—Hollywood, the major networks, and media companies whose core businesses include generating programs and gathering news. These content producers were acutely sensitive to the possibility that the Bells and cable companies, which already had lines to local customers in place, might end up dominating the channels leading to their customers. Like the long-distance companies, such as Sprint and AT&T, they were also apprehensive that the regional Bells would only grudgingly open up their systems to rivals, and would use the huge cash flows from their regulated "captive" local phone customers to subsidize their new business ventures.

With campaign contributions pouring in from all sides, the Clinton administration finally tilted in favor of Hollywood, the networks, and the newspapers. In part thanks to White House efforts, the final bill was much kinder to the content providers, though virtually all the companies won some outcome important to them, and the Bells and GTE were widely regarded—perhaps prematurely—as having come off best of all.

The Clinton administration has recently proposed another bill that appeals to content providers. This legislation would vastly tighten enforcement of copyrights on the Internet as well as over the air, and would sharply cut back traditional "fair use" rights. The bill could also make owners of online systems responsible for copyright abuses by network users. And, of course, for the content producers, but for no one else, the administration was willing to go to the wall—the Great Wall—and threaten sanctions on the Chinese if they did not stop pirating that sector's products (videotapes, CDs, etc.).

STANDING FIRM ON THE BUDGET

Within the Democratic Party, the Clinton strategy of winning through intimidation worked very well. With contributions racing far ahead of the president's standing in the polls, potential Democratic challengers first paused and assayed their wallets. Then they thought better of the whole idea.

Unlike Democratic challengers, however, the Republicans were never going to run out of money. What turned the tide toward the White House in the general election was a dual strategy. First the president broad-jumped to the right and endorsed the Republican goal of balancing the budget.

Then, brushing aside the gigantic cuts that his own budget plan entailed after the 1996 election, the president spotlighted areas where his budget priorities clashed with the GOP's: health, education, Medicare and Medicaid, the environment. This sudden willingness to stand "firm" was not motivated purely by moral principle: Reductions in Medicare and Medicaid involve not just patients, but the medical industrial complex, which was willing to fight (and help pay) to defend the programs. Fearful that the White House might fold completely, lobbyists for the National Education Association (whose organizational network probably matters more in presidential campaigns that its money) also warned the White House not to take its support for granted.

THE BUDGET SQUEEZE

In committing themselves to balancing the budget by 2002, Clinton and the Republicans resemble the characters in children's cartoons who run far out over the edge of the cliff before they suddenly wake up and discover that they are trotting on air. Right after the election, however, the winner is going to have to stop running (in more than one sense) and deliver, or face massive bombardment from the media, financial markets, and

ALAS, there is nothing in either President Clinton's or the Republicans' economic proposals that seriously addresses the question of declining wages. In contrast to his 1992 campaign, Clinton is hardly even talking about the problem.

$$$$$$$$$$$$$$$$$$$$$$$$$$$$$$$$$

any number of (often subsidized) economists. The Federal Reserve Board is also sure to intensify the pressure: In all probability, it will be nudging rates up anyway and will again be superbly positioned to offer the fool's bargain of restraint on rate rises in exchange for "meaningful" budget cuts.

What will the lucky White House winner do? Many optimistic progressives, and not a few pessimistic financial analysts, essentially assume that neither candidate would dare persist with his projected cuts. But in the last few years economic austerity packages unimaginable a few decades ago have been implemented around the world—in, for example, Canada, Britain, France, Sweden, and, most recently, Germany.

Signs are everywhere that the American climate may also be right for yet another triumph of the bond market. The publicity afforded Perot's calls for far deeper budget cuts, the budding campaign to privatize Social Security, and the Senate's all-but-unanimous confirmation of Alan Greenspan as chair of the Federal Reserve (Democratic Sen. Daniel Patrick Moynihan of New York even saluted him as a "national treasure") are three of the most obvious. So, I think, are the "indexed bonds" that the Treasury is now planning to issue. These bonds, indexed for inflation, are the debt market's equivalent of a constitutional amendment for a balanced budget: They relieve their holders of all inflation risk by transferring it to taxpayers, who are contractually obliged to make up any loss of purchasing power, no matter how huge. Once issued in substantial amounts, such securities hold future administrations hostage to rapid rises in tax liabilities, straitjacketing both monetary policy and expenditures.

But there are more telling indicators as well. Both the European Community's drive to introduce a common currency and the increasing cooperation among Asian central banks enhance possibilities for long-run substitution out of the dollar. Competition from other currencies will reinforce the Fed's emphasis on controlling inflation rather than ensuring job growth. Not accidentally, the next president is likely to have to make up his mind whether to sign a bill repealing language in the Humphrey-Hawkins amendment to the Federal Reserve Act that requires the Fed to report periodically on its success in combating employment. Such a repeal would essentially make price stability the only legal goal of the central bank.

Alas, there is nothing in either the GOP's or Clinton's economic proposals that seriously addresses the question of declining wages. In contrast to 1992, Clinton is hardly even talking about the problem. Dole, as all the world knows, didn't have a clue that the issue even existed as late as the New Hampshire primary. And as increasing numbers of elites are openly saying in the media, the conventional wisdom is that nothing much can really be done about the problem anyway.

This is an inherently unstable set of affairs, made to order for another round of divide-and-conquer after the election, as Congress and the president finally have to deal with the budget. If, as seems increasingly likely amid the turmoil in the Near East, the new tremors in Mexico, and the everlasting Balkan wars, one or more of the White House's many ventures in foreign stabilization ends up as a severe case of imperial overextension, all sorts of political pathologies are likely to flourish. In a money-driven political system that none of the major candidates shows any real interest in reforming, this is a recipe for real disaster.

Small Change

In the end, President Clinton won an unimpressive victory. Voters rewarded him for his economic performance. But they didn't come to trust him, and they didn't give him much of a mandate.

BY WILLIAM SCHNEIDER

It was a status quo election. The voters weren't angry. There was no frenzy for change, comparable to that of 1992. Incumbents did extremely well. And not much changed.

You can see a mood of satisfaction in the exit poll that Voter News Service conducted on behalf of five television networks and the Associated Press. Only 20 per cent of voters reported that their family's financial situation had worsened since 1992. Most voters described the nation's economy as excellent or good. And a majority described things in the country today as "generally going in the right direction."

So what happened? The voters reelected just about everybody. The Democratic President. The Republican Senate. The Republican House. Governors running for another term.

President Clinton carried almost all of the states he carried in 1992 and picked up two additional states—Arizona and Florida—that President Bush had carried four years ago. They are the two states with the highest proportion of elderly voters. That looks suspiciously like a medicare backlash vote. With those two exceptions, all the Bush states went to Robert Dole.

It was not a historic landslide. Voters split just about 50-50 over Clinton's reelection. What made his victory decisive was the fact that the anti-Clinton vote was split, 41 per cent for Dole and 8 per cent for Ross Perot.

Perot was quick to point out on election night that he couldn't be blamed for Dole's defeat. The Reform Party's candidate said that he took votes equally from both major parties.

He was right. When his voters were asked whom they would have supported if Perot had not been on the ballot, just 29 per cent of them said Dole. About the same number, 31 per cent, said Clinton. A plurality (36 per cent) of Perot's voters said they would not have voted had he not been on the ballot.

If the strong message of 1992 was "change," the equally powerful message of 1996 was "not much change." Democrats made small gains in the House, enough to narrow, not overturn, the GOP majority. Republicans enlarged their majority slightly in the Senate. Democrats lost one governor and Republicans lost one.

Clinton had no noticeable coattails. The Democrats even lost a Senate seat in his home state of Arkansas.

It was hard to find any ideological shift in this election. *(See tables.)* Most voters (52 per cent) endorsed the view that "government is doing too many things that should be left to businesses and individuals," as opposed to the view (held by 42 per cent) that "government should do more to solve problems."

Conservatives continue to outnumber liberals, 33-20 per cent. But Clinton captured the moderates—nearly half the voters—by almost 2-1. His carefully planned strategy of moving to the center worked.

The gender gap was also decisive—and bigger than ever. Men couldn't make up their minds. They split their vote between Clinton and Dole. Women reelected Clinton. They gave him a 16-percentage-point lead over Dole.

The No. 1 issue? The economy and jobs. Just as in 1992. Only this time, it worked for the incumbent. Those who cited the economy as the issue that decided their vote went for Clinton by better than 2-1.

The story of the election is captured by one question in the Nov. 5 exit poll: "Compared to four years ago, is your family's financial situation better, worse or about the same?" A plurality of voters (44 per cent) said "about the same." And they split their vote just about equally between Clinton and Dole. Those who said "worse" went strongly for Dole. Those who said "better" went strongly for Clinton. The bottom line: More voters said "better " (33 per cent) than "worse" (20 per cent).

If Americans are worried about the economy, it's not because of their own bad economic experiences. It's because of all the stories they read in the press about corporate layoffs and downsizing.

Sure enough, the stories died with

WHO VOTED FOR CLINTON, DOLE AND PEROT

	CLINTON	1996 DOLE	PEROT	CLINTON	1992 BUSH	PEROT
All (100%)	50%	42%	8%	44%	37%	19%
Men (48)	44	44	10	41	37	21
Women (52)	54	38	7	47	36	17
Whites (83)	44	45	9	40	39	21
Blacks (10)	84	12	4	83	11	7
Hispanics (5)	73	20	5	62	24	14
Didn't complete high school (6)	60	28	11	56	27	18
High school graduate (23)	52	35	13	44	36	21
Some college (27)	49	39	10	43	36	21
College graduate (26)	44	46	7	41	39	20
Postgraduate (17)	52	39	5	50	35	15
Age						
18-29 (17)	53	34	10	47	31	22
30-44 (33)	49	41	9	41	35	24
45-59 (26)	49	41	9	42	38	21
60+ (23)	49	43	7	44	37	19
Family income*:						
Less than $15,000 (11)	60	27	11	59	22	19
$15,000-29,999 (23)	54	36	9	46	34	20
$30,000-49,999 (27)	49	40	10	42	37	21
$50,000-74,999 (21)	47	44	7	41	41	18
$75,000 or more (18)	42	50	7	38	46	16
Protestants (55)	43	47	9	34	45	21
Catholics (29)	54	37	9	42	37	21
Jews (3)	78	16	3	78	10	11
Family financial situation compared with four years ago:						
Better (33)	67	26	6	25	60	15
Worse (20)	28	57	13	62	13	25
About the same (44)	46	44	8	42	41	18
Democrats (40)	84	10	5	78	10	13
Republicans (34)	13	80	6	11	72	18
Independents (26)	43	35	17	39	31	30
Liberals (20)	78	11	7	69	13	18
Moderates (47)	57	32	9	49	30	21
Conservatives (33)	20	71	8	18	64	17
1992 votes:						
Clinton (44)	85	9	4	—	—	—
Bush (34)	13	82	4	—	—	—
Perot (12)	22	44	32	—	—	—
First-time voters (9)	54	34	11	—	—	—
Union households (24)	60	29	9	56	23	22
Nonunion households (76)	46	44	8	42	39	19
Religious Right (16)	26	65	8	—	—	—

*Comparable income categories were used in 1992.
SOURCES: Voter News Service exit polls for 1996; Voter Research and Surveys exit polls for 1992

VOTERS: THE REASONS WHY

	PER CENT VOTING FOR		
	CLINTON	DOLE	PEROT
Which issues mattered most in deciding how you voted?			
Medicare, social security (15%)	67%	26%	6%
Budget deficit (12)	28	52	19
Crime, drugs (7)	41	50	8
Education (12)	78	15	4
Economy, jobs (21)	61	27	10
Taxes (11)	19	73	7
Foreign policy (4)	35	55	8
Is the condition of the economy:			
Excellent (4)	78	18	3
Good (52)	62	31	5
Not so good (36)	34	52	12
Poor (7)	23	50	21
Which candidate quality mattered most in deciding how you voted?			
Cares about people like me (10)	72	17	9
Is honest and trustworthy (20)	9	84	7
Shares my view of government (20)	42	45	10
Stands up for what he believes in (13)	42	40	15
Is in touch with the 1990s (10)	89	8	4
Has a vision for the future (16)	77	13	9
Abortion should be:			
Legal in all cases (25)	70	20	7
Legal in most cases (35)	56	32	11
Illegal in most cases (24)	32	57	10
Illegal in all cases (12)	24	67	8
More important in your vote:			
Issues (58)	70	20	8
Character (37)	18	71	10
Which is closer to your view?			
Government should do more to solve problems (42)	72	19	6
Government does too many things (52)	30	60	9
In the House election, did you vote for:			
The Republican (47)	14	77	7
The Democrat (51)	83	8	7
In general, which is better for the country?			
President and Congress of the same party (55)	57	36	6
President of one party, Congress of other (38)	37	50	11
Opinion of what Clinton wants to do in the next four years:			
Support almost all (25)	93	5	2
Support some (35)	66	22	10
Support only a little (20)	7	73	18
Oppose almost all (17)	4	86	9

SOURCE: Voter News Service exit polls

Patrick J. Buchanan's populist campaign for the Republican presidential nomination, in which he expressed the fear and anger of workers threatened with downsizing. The press took him at his word and wrote all kinds of stories about the deteriorating situation of American workers. There was only one problem. It wasn't true.

Clinton surged into the lead last spring on a strong economic performance and a tide of national optimism. When the President asks, "Are you better off than you were four years ago?" most Americans say yes. Buchanan, who called for economic insurrection, has disappeared. Clinton, who boasts of greater economic security, was reelected. So which candidate got it right?

What about the "character issue"? Another non-story? Not quite. The Nov. 5 exit poll asked, "Do you think Bill Clinton is honest and trustworthy?" Voters said no, 54-42 per cent. "Do you think Clinton has told the truth about Whitewater and other matters under investigation?" Again no, 59-33 per cent. So how in the world did he win?

Voters who said character was more important than issues voted 71 per cent for Dole. Those who said issues were more important than character voted 70 per cent for Clinton. Which was more important to voters? Issues, by 58-37 per cent. Issues trumped character.

Elections are about change. When there's not much interest in change, there's not much interest in the election. Even more so when the outcome is a foregone conclusion.

Clinton established his double-digit lead over Dole in late January, at the time of his State of the Union speech. Nothing much changed in the next nine months. More than 200 public polls of the presidential contest were published this year. The Republican candidate was never ahead in a single one.

For all the complaints about the press covering the election as if it were a horse race, one thing is clear: Voters lose interest if the election is *not* a horse race. You can't fill the stands if everybody knows which horse is going to win.

In the end, Clinton won an unimpressive victory. The voters rewarded him for his economic performance. But they didn't come to trust him, and they didn't give him much of a mandate.

Remember how the campaign began a year ago? There was a lot of excitement about the prospect of Colin L. Powell's running for President. Well it's still there. When the exit poll asked voters how they would have voted if Powell had been the Republican nominee, they went for Powell by 10 points over Clinton. See? Nothing has really changed.

PRIMARY COLOURS: NASTY, BRUTISH AND SHORT?

Godfrey Hodgson

This year's American election campaign has already produced its share of upsets and surprises. But does the primary system skew the national debate on policy towards demagoguery and irrelevant issues?

AMERICA'S FOUR-YEARLY ELECTIONS HAVE COME TO SERVE TWO purposes, not just one. Obviously, the election is a mechanism for choosing a President, a Vice-President, a new House of Representatives, one-third of the United States Senate and thousands of state and local officials as well, right down to the proverbial dog-catcher.

Less obviously, but very significantly, the election process has also come to be the occasion for a diffuse but quite serious and important process of political introspection and debate – almost, indeed, sometimes of national psycho-analysis.

Every four years, in other words, the onset of the presidential campaign is the cue for millions of words to be expended in newspapers and magazines and on television on discussion of the national agenda. Some of the debate may be wise, some foolish. But the debate itself is surely a healthy and profoundly democratic process.

The argument of this article is that primary elections have come to have a significant distorting effect, not only on the process for selecting a presidential candidate, but perhaps even more on that accompanying national debate about issues and policy.

Fading in the fall

Numerous examples over the past thirty years, since John F. Kennedy revived the presidential primary for his own reasons, illustrate this tendency for media coverage of the primaries to distort the national debate. Senator Eugene McCarthy's peace crusade in 1968 is perhaps the best-known. The gap between the Reverend Jesse Jackson's salience in the early months of 1984 and his lapse into obscurity as summer approached is another case in point. That same year, Gary

GODFREY HODGSON is the Director of the Reuters Programme at Green College, Oxford. He is a writer and broadcaster and long-time commentator on American politics.

Hart made much of the running in the early primaries with his 'new ideas', only to fade. Pat Buchanan's success in dictating a right-wing populist agenda and Steve Forbes's advocacy of the 'flat tax' in the early stages of this year's campaign raises serious questions about the effect of the primary system on the US political agenda.

Nowadays the election is not simply reported in the media like the day's stock prices or the night's ball game. In an important sense the media have ceased to reflect political activity that would be taking place anyway. They have become the arena in which the election takes place. This is true of what are called the 'paid' as well as the 'unpaid' media.

Of course, both the candidate selection process and the debate are reported, fully and some would say *ad nauseam*, in the news media. At the same time 'paid media', that is, political advertising and especially television spot commercials, have also come to be vitally important in defining the issues as well as the candidates. Media, paid and unpaid, have become so absolutely central to the strategies of candidates that the traditional model, of media reporting a contest taking place 'out there' somewhere, has come to be beside the point.

Robert Dole ensured nomination on 'Super Tuesday'

Photograph by Ira Wyman/Sygma

Once upon a time

Once upon a time politicians – from Andrew Johnson's 'Swing around the circle' at the dawn of the railroad age to Harry S. Truman's whistle-stop tours in its nostalgic twilight – criss-crossed the country to meet the voters, hoping that the media would report their movements and their words. At the same time they met influential politicos behind closed doors and tried to persuade them, with arguments pitched at every level from the noble to the sordid, to give them their support.

That is not what politicians do now. Candidates and their increasingly 'scientific' pollsters, consultants and advisers plan their whole campaign strategies around the image the media – and that essentially now means television – can give them. Television spot campaigns hammer home messages of soundbite simplicity and intensity, while the candidate tries in photo opportunities, debates and brief clips on the evening news to establish an equally simple but favourable image: relaxed, sexy, reliable, dynamic, or whatever he and his pollsters, consultants and advisers think he needs.

Most primaries are party primaries. (The 'cross-over' primary in California, where registered voters can vote in either party's primaries, is one significant exception, and there are a few others.) The candidate's goal, therefore, is to win, not a majority of the electorate, but a majority of those voting in his party. He is seeking, notionally or schematically, not one more than 50 per cent of the vote, but one more than half of a half, or one more than 25 per cent of the vote.

In practice, this, too, is a 'best case'. For one thing, primary turnouts are usually much lower than turnouts in the general election. For another, there will be several candidates in most primaries. Far less than a quarter of the vote will do.

Media attention focuses heavily on a comparatively limited number of primaries, above all on New Hampshire, a small and in many ways unusually atypical state. A candidate who, like Pat Buchanan this year, wins a narrow majority over the 'front-runner' in two or three of the early primaries, will have gained an advantage it will be hard, and expensive, to overtake.

Great expectations

This year's New Hampshire primary is a good illustration of the multiplier effect of these cumulative distortions. Buchanan defeated Senator Robert Dole there this February by less than 2 per cent of a tiny electorate. (The population of New Hampshire is roughly that of a typical English county.) As a result of this relatively trivial electoral event, Mr Buchanan found himself the temporary 'front-runner'. His marginal victory came close to eliminating Senator Robert Dole from the race. An even smaller number of votes was enough to give former Governor Lamar Alexander of Tennessee equally temporary credibility as the 'moderate' who might 'stop Buchanan'.

There is an even more bizarre consequence of the intense focus of media attention on the New Hampshire primary: sometimes a candidate does not even need to win to benefit from his showing there. It is enough to do better than the pundits predicted.

In 1968, President Lyndon Johnson withdrew from the whole race, in which he had previously been assumed to be the overwhelming favourite, not because he was beaten in New Hampshire by Senator Eugene McCarthy of Minnesota, the peace candidate, but because his win over Senator McCarthy was not sufficiently decisive.

In several more recent cases, where a candidate won, but did not win as easily as newspaper and television experts predicted, his campaign was badly damaged. If this 'expectation factor' is taken into account, the effect of the New Hampshire primary on the outcome of the entire presidential campaign is worrisomely great.

This article is being written early in the primary season, which is in any case 'front-end loaded' by the circumstance that California, the most populous and therefore most electorally powerful state, has chosen to move its primary forward from early June to 26 March. California has done this precisely to make sure that its votes are not wasted in the candidate selection process. They would be if by the time of the California primary a candidate could be sure of the nomination however Californians might vote.

This year, therefore, whether or not you decide that it is nasty or brutish, the primary season will be short. By the end of March, after only six weeks of campaigning, 30 states will have conducted pri-

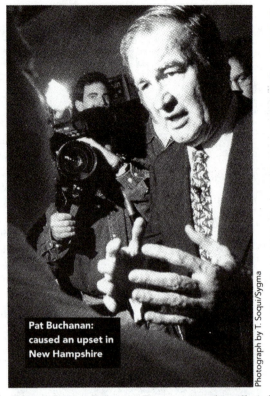

Pat Buchanan: caused an upset in New Hampshire

Photograph by T. Soqui/Sygma

mary elections to decide which candidate their delegates should support at the Republican nominating convention.

There are, of course, Democratic primaries, too; but so far no serious challenge to President Clinton has emerged, so in 1996 the primaries are essentially a Republican event. Altogether 43 states will hold primaries this year, as against a mere 16 when Senator Kennedy chose to enter several primaries to emphasise his nationwide appeal.

Moreover, though no national initiative has been taken to establish regional primaries, in practice the primary season has been largely regionalised. On 5 March, Connecticut, Maine, Massachusetts, Rhode Island and Vermont held what amounted to a New England regional primary without New Hampshire. Just to emphasise its differentness, New York with 102 delegates held its own solitary primary on 7 March.

On Super Tuesday, 12 March, Florida, Mississippi, Oklahoma, Tennessee and Texas went to the polls (with Oregon) for what amounted to a southern regional primary. A week later, four big Midwestern states (Illinois, Michigan, Ohio and Wisconsin) with a total of 229 delegates held a sort of Midwestern primary. Finally, on 26 March, California, Washington and Nevada, with 213 delegates between them, held a West Coast primary of their own. By then it was clear that Senator Dole had won the nomination – barring a miracle.

Clawing back power

A brief historical diversion is necessary to point up some of the ironies of the way the primary process has evolved. The first primary elections were held in the early twentieth century as part of the Progressive movement's determination to claw back political power from the cliques and rings of party bosses who in practice controlled the choice of convention delegates, often in closed 'caucuses' at which only party 'regulars' were welcome.

By 1960, for a variety of reasons, the Progressive zeal had worn thin. Primaries were coming to be seen as an old-fashioned, even a quaint piece of political ritual. In that year, however, John F. Kennedy and his advisers had a political problem, and they saw the primaries as part of the solution. The problem was that until that year it had always been held axiomatic that Roman Catholics, such as Senator Kennedy, were not 'available', that is, electable.

The Kennedy brains trust had the bright idea of putting its man in for a broad swathe of primaries to demonstrate the breadth of his political appeal. It made a special effort in West Virginia, hitherto considered the most Protestant state in the nation. Kennedy's victory over Senator Hubert H. Humphrey of Minnesota, a Protestant, in the West Virginia primary, had a significant effect in persuading media pundits that he could win the nomination.

Inventing Iowa

Sixteen years later, Jimmy Carter of Georgia had a different — indeed, essentially an opposite — problem. A born-again Baptist from southern Georgia, Carter was experiencing difficulties persuading the media and fund-raisers that he could have a national appeal. Certainly things did not look promising in New Hampshire for a candidate with such a strongly sectional flavour, and New Hampshire, then as now, jealously guarded its position as the state with the earliest primary.

Carter's backers, led by Pat Caddell, had the bright idea of using the Iowa county caucuses, held – as luck would have it – before New Hampshire, as a pseudo-primary. They toured these normally placid meetings with their candidate, giving the press and television a splendid opportunity to cover a Southern governor getting acquainted with Midwestern farm folk.

By 1980, however, the number of states using primary elections to choose their candidates for the party nominating conventions had gone up from 18 in 1960 to 31. It has subsequently risen, undoubtedly in large part because of the copious free advertising the New Hampshire primary has given to the entire process, to 43 out of 52 states and territories, including the District of Columbia and Puerto Rico. Arrangements for Guam, American Samoa and the American Virgin Islands had not been decided when this was written.

By the late 1970s there was widespread discontent with the primary system. The principal objection was that it was so long drawn out that it was becoming impossibly expensive for all but the personally wealthiest candidates – or those who had access to massive financing by single-issue or other pressure groups. There was less agreement on what could be done to reform the system.

The two most popular ideas in the reform-minded community of political journalists, academics and (mainly liberal) public interest groups were a national primary, and regional primaries. By degrees and almost by accident, something like a modified regional primary system has come into existence, with the *ancien régime* primacy of New Hampshire grudgingly respected, though Louisiana and Iowa now have caucuses which are reported by the media as a significant pointer to sentiment about the candidates.

The attraction of extremes

The Buchanan campaign points up the second factor. Not only does a handful of votes in a number of small or smallish states have a disproportionate effect on the overall result of the election. The disproportionate importance of this handful of states with their puny totals of voters exaggerates, even more than the system does already, the advantage of appealing to those voters likely to be attracted by extreme positions.

In 1996, the accident of the Louisiana caucuses and the New Hampshire, Delaware and South Carolina primaries being so early, and therefore receiving such heavy media coverage, has undoubtedly helped Pat Buchanan to take maximum electoral advantage of his peculiar populist/authoritarian conservatism, as well as of his strong 'pro-life' position on abortion.

It is not only minority or extremist views on the Right that are favoured by the present system, but minority and extremist positions generally. The Reverend Jesse Jackson, for example, with his strong

> THE LOUDEST SOUND IN THE LAND AFTER THE CONVENTIONS IS THAT OF POLITICIANS WHO TOOK EXTREME POSITIONS TO WIN THEIR PARTIES' NOMINATIONS RUSHING TOWARDS THE CENTRE.

appeal to African-American and Hispanic voters, has always looked likely to prove a far stronger proposition in the primary stage of the campaign than he would be in the general election in November. The loudest sound in the land after the conventions is the sound of the politicians who took extreme positions to win their parties' nomination rushing towards the centre.

Many foreigners, and some Americans, think of the presidential election as lasting for months. It is true that pre-election manoeuvring now preoccupies many politicians, including some Presidents, from almost immediately after the mid-term elections, if not before. But the decisive autumn campaign, the 'general election', as Americans call it, runs for only two months, from Labor Day at the beginning of September to the Tuesday after 1 November.

By that stage, it is too late to initiate elaborate debate about national policy issues. It is usually too late to introduce new issues to the electorate, except in the broadest headline simplicities. To the extent that election year is the time for national debate and reflection, and it is, that time is long past when the two champions approach the final shoot-out.

Irrelevant issues

That phase of the presidential campaign, therefore, which allows general discussion of policy issues, including foreign-policy issues, coincides with the primary campaign. It coincides, that is, with the stage of the process when the premium is on taking bold and, if necessary, extremist positions.

In the primary period, the game is to build coalitions that will take the candidate, not to a majority of the national electorate, but to a string of victories in each of which his actual vote is likely to be far less than 25 per cent of the whole electorate in each of the particular states.

This is not only a recipe for demagoguery. It virtually guarantees that a substantial proportion of media attention and public discussion will focus on issues that are irrelevant to many Americans, and on policies that have a disproportionate appeal to sundry, often quite small, minorities.

Protectionist campaigns by Richard Gephardt (Democrat of Missouri) and Pat Buchanan are examples. While there is a mass of evidence that the great majority of American voters oppose protectionist policies, primary campaigns centring around them have attracted disproportionate media attention.

American politics in the television age are already volatile. In the policy debate that accompanies a presidential election, the new, the different, the extreme, are all likely to secure more attention in the all-powerful media than the tried, the moderate, the unexciting but carefully thought through.

In the end, it is true, the electoral process tends to assert the massive common sense of the American people and to choose moderate and centrist candidates. But in the meantime, policies designed to attract minorities of the electorate will have had more of an airing than they deserve, and will continue to distort the policy debate more and longer than they deserve.

The triumph of the center-right.

GOLDEN MEAN

John B. Judis

Newt Gingrich said that this election could be the most important since 1896—the election that inaugurated a thirty-six-year Republican majority. But it probably won't make the pages of most history books. Like the election of 1984, when Ronald Reagan won in a landslide, but when Democrats retained the House and gained two Senate seats, it reaffirmed the existing balance of political forces in the country. It was a vote against dramatic change and for a continuation of a center-right government.

Many of the basic political positions in Congress haven't changed in twenty years; only the party labels of those espousing them have. Political scientists used to complain that the real antagonists in Congress were not Democrats and Republicans, but a coalition of Northern Democrats and Northeastern and Far Western Republicans, on the one hand, and a coalition of Midwestern Republicans and Southern Democrats on the other. Since the 1960s, the GOP has steadily made inroads in the Democratic deep South and the Democrats have become the majority party in the Northeast and Far West. This election took the process one step further. Republican congressmen were ousted in Maine, Massachusetts, Connecticut, New York, New Jersey, California and Washington, while Republicans won previously Democratic seats in Texas, Oklahoma, Mississippi, Arkansas and Alabama. Republicans are still competitive in the North (look at Maine's two GOP senators), and

Democrats can still win statewide office in the South (look at the Senate results in Louisiana and Georgia), but the Northeast and Far West now tilt Democratic and the deep South and Southwest Republican. And across the country, the parties are roughly at equal strength, as they were in the 1880s, when each was capable of capturing either the White House or Congress.

If a realignment or revolution were to occur, as Gingrich prophesied, the circumstances underlying politics—the relations between regional businesses, between business and labor, between small and large business and between ethnic and social groups—would have to shift significantly. That has not occurred. Instead, American politics has continued to gravitate toward the same position. Former Carter pollster Pat Caddell was the first to define this position as a combination of social liberalism and fiscal conservatism, but it goes beyond purely budgetary stinginess.

From the late '30s, when the New Deal ran aground, through the Nixon administration, there was a center-left standoff on core economic issues between business and its allies, on the one hand, and labor and its allies on the other. This standoff meant that business got tax cuts and generous subsidies but that labor, consumer groups and minorities got job bills, guaranteed health care for senior citizens, increases in Social Security payments and legislation regulating workplace safety. Then the ground shifted. In the first two years of the Carter administration, when Democrats had a "veto-proof majority," business groups were nevertheless able to defeat labor law reform and the establishment of a new Consumer Protection Agency. Business's newfound clout, which reflected labor's decline and the emergence of interest groups like the Business Roundtable, spelled the end of center-left government and the beginning of a center-right regime. While business organizations could not repeal OSHA or privatize Social Security, they could block any new spending or regulatory initiatives along these lines. At the same time, Congress had to heed growing popular majorities in favor of cultural and social reforms that came out of the '60s—from environmental protection to abortion rights and gun control. Support for these issues cut across class lines, but was concentrated among middle- and upper-middle-class Americans, who were likely to respond to direct mail appeals.

When the White House or Congress has tried to defy this economic and social consensus, it has been quickly repudiated. The AFL-CIO and its congressional backers had to give up on labor law reform, and they couldn't even get Congress to pass a striker replacement bill. On the other side, Ronald Reagan had to replace his Secretary of the Interior and director of the Environmental Protection Agency with moderates acceptable to the environmental movement. Reagan was also careful to talk up, but do nothing about, sanctioning school prayer or outlawing abortion. Clinton had to abandon his attempt to expand health services to the working poor and to limit the prerogatives of the health and insurance industries. And Gingrich and the House Republicans had to give up their attempt to gut environmental laws and to raise Medicare premiums while reducing benefits. In this sense, while there have been political twists and turns along the way, government has adhered to a remarkably similar course from 1977 to 1997.

The years that have most clearly defined this course were 1982 to 1984, when Reagan had to rewrite his tax bill and accept a bipartisan fix of Social Security; and 1996, when Clinton and the Republican Congress agreed to the deregulation of the telecommunications industry and to minor changes in health care coverage that didn't threaten the insurance industry. Clinton signed a welfare reform bill, but, unlike his original bill, it did not redistribute income by providing new funds for jobs or training. He signed an immigration bill that deprived illegal and legal immigrants of benefits, but did not police employers who hired illegal immigrants. The one apparent exception was the minimum wage law, which was not pushed by the administration but by the AFL-CIO and its allies in Congress. Clinton and the Republicans agreed to a bill, however, that also contained significant, and in some instances egregious, business subsidies.

Early this summer, it seemed that this election might actually alter the status quo. By shutting down the government, Gingrich and the House Republicans had raised the specter of radical conservatism. It looked like Democrats could run against Gingrich the way they used to run against Herbert Hoover. During the primary, the Christian Coalition, which is anathema to many voters outside the deep South, had increased its visibility within the Republican Party. And in the presidential race, Clinton had a 73-year-old opponent whose own party seemed lukewarm on him and who had opposed unpaid family and medical leave.

Even more important, the AFL-CIO under its new president, John Sweeney, had actively entered the election. In the past, the federation had been content to give money to candidates and send out endorsements to their members, but this time it threw hundreds of staff and $35 million into targeted congressional races. Labor's new strategy threatened, in effect, to create a countervailing force to business predominance over both parties. And labor's first efforts at running ads worked dramatically. It got endangered moderate Republicans like Connecticut's Chris Shays to champion an increase in the minimum wage. If the election had been held in mid-July or so, the Democrats might have regained majorities in both the Senate and the House, and labor and its allies would have wielded considerable clout with these new majorities.

But over the last two months the election turned around. The Republicans in Congress, led by Trent Lott, the new majority leader, worked out an accommodation with Clinton to pass welfare reform, the minimum wage and the Kassebaum-Kennedy health care bills—and then ran on these bipartisan accomplishments. They abandoned the anti-government rhetoric of the 1994 election; and they claimed to be friends of clean air and water. Some candidates such as Minnesota Senate candidate Rudy Boschwitz and Cleveland Representative Martin Hoke said they were closer to the Clinton administration than their Democratic opponents. Even candidates strongly identified with the religious right, such as Louisiana Senate candidate Woody Jenkins or Senator Robert Smith in New Hampshire, rarely mentioned abortion. Ralph Reed and the Christian Coalition handed out their voter guides the Sunday before election, but otherwise kept a low profile. Those candidates who remained most closely tied to the right, such as Jenkins or gubernatorial candidate Ellen Craswell in Washington, still lost, but other Republicans successfully avoided the stigma of either the Gingrich revolution or the Christian Coalition.

The Republican National Committee and the Republican Senate and House campaign committees also took advantage of business support and of a June Supreme Court ruling permitting independent expenditures to mount a furious ad campaign during the last three weeks of the election. RNC Chairman Haley Barbour complained repeatedly about the AFL-CIO pumping $35 million into the campaign, but business groups contributed about $242 million. Roughly two-thirds of this money went to Republican candidates and to the Republican national committees. The Republican committees raised $400 million for this election compared to $250 million for the Democrats. And, in the campaign's last month, they spent it to reverse the tide toward a Democratic Congress.

In the last weeks of October, the National Republican Senate Committee alone spent $10 million in independent expenditures, while the Democratic Senate Campaign Committee spent $1.1 million. The Republican committees spent $500,000 on Wyoming's Senate race, or roughly $1 a vote. They lavished $768,000 on Oregon Senate candidate Gordon Smith, $423,000 on New Hampshire's Senator Smith. They also poured money into Chuck Hagel's race in Nebraska and Dick Zimmer's in New Jersey. Their expenditures were supplemented by business groups who ran their own ads. The American Medical Association laid out $420,000, helping five Republican House candidates, and $129,000 for Republican Senate candidate Susan Collins in Maine. The Democrats who withstood the late onslaught were those who had almost as much cash themselves—like Robert Torricelli in New Jersey. Others, like Kathy Karpan in Wyoming, Ben Nelson in Nebraska or Dick Swett in New Hampshire, had their voices drowned out and their candidacies defined for them. After the Republican Senate committee had inundated the state's inexpensive media outlets with ads saying Karpan was "too liberal for Wyoming," she would meet small children who chanted the phrase at her the way they might repeat a catchy slogan for beer or deodorant.

Of course, the other factor that prevented Democrats from winning Congress was the faltering Clinton campaign. In early October, Clinton appeared on his way to a landslide that could have rivaled Lyndon Johnson's victory over Barry Goldwater in 1964. (Johnson held Goldwater to victories in Arizona and the deep South.) A win that size would have shifted at least four or five Senate seats and at least a dozen more House seats into the Democratic column. But in the second week of October, stories began emerging about DNC fund-raiser John Huang's efforts to woo foreign contributors. These stories were damning in themselves, but they also raised the specter of future investigations that could cripple a second Clinton term.

Dole and Jack Kemp were unable to push the issue effectively—Dole because it raised his own negatives and Kemp because he eschewed any harsh criticism of his opponents. But Ross Perot, who had championed campaign finance reform, gave voice to popular outrage and to the fear of a "Watergate II." Perot played what should have been Kemp's role—the anti-Clinton attack dog. He even described the Clintons as "felons." Though Perot didn't help himself that much—his poll ratings initially rose, then dropped on election eve—his withering attacks, concentrated during the last week, tarred Clinton and helped boost Dole over 40 percent.

As it stands, neither Clinton nor the Republicans in Congress will take office with a clear mandate. Clinton campaigned on his economic record and on a promise of innocuous, incremental reforms such as the extension of unpaid family and medical leave. Congressional Republicans attempted to distance themselves from their Contract with America without proposing a new contract. By the campaign's close, they were even withdrawing their support for Dole's 15 percent tax cut.

Clinton will have trouble getting his own way among Democrats. As a lameduck president, he will have to endure Democrats jockeying for position in 2000. The Republican leadership, meanwhile, will be hamstrung in Congress. Republicans slightly increased their majority in the Senate, but largely by filling seats vacated by conservative Democrats. The remaining Democrats (who are slightly to the left of the previous group) will be able to filibuster any right-wing initiatives. In the House, Gingrich will command a smaller majority, and a quarter to a third of it will be composed of Republicans like John Hostettler in Indiana, Mark Neumann in Wisconsin, or Jon Fox in Pennsylvania who barely defeated Democratic challengers. The right will still be vocal, and the left will have a much louder voice because the AFL-CIO did help knock off nineteen Republicans, but, in both houses, the balance of power will be held by Democrats like Bob Kerrey or Charlie Stenholm and Republicans like Susan Collins or Chris Shays. It will be the center-right in command.

If there is a precedent for 1997, it is probably 1996. Clinton will be able to win Congress's support for incremental social reforms and for pro-business trade initiatives with China and Latin America. The Republicans will probably agree to putting Medicare and Social Security in the hands of a bipartisan commission that will produce proposals that are amenable to the insurance industry, but don't obviously or immediately gouge senior citizens. And they will quarrel over the details of a balanced budget plan, while seeking compromises that avoid achieving a balanced budget during their political lifetime.

There are several things, however, that could upset this placid scenario. First of all, the Clinton administration could be paralyzed by scandal, as the Clintons and the Democratic National Committee face inquiries from both House and Senate committees. Whether the administration will be engulfed by scandal depends on what Independent Prosecutor Kenneth Starr comes up with. Secondly, the GOP leadership, in its eagerness to pay back its business contributors and solidify its fundraising base, could overreach again as it did in 1995 and precipitate an anti-Republican backlash in 1998. And, finally, a recession could halt the rush toward a balanced budget plan and revive the argument within the Democratic Party over government economic intervention. In that case, the Clinton administration and the congressional Democrats could part company, as occurred during the last year of the Carter administration, and the Democrats could find themselves deeply divided as they head into the next elections. But even these possibilities still might not alter the drift of American politics. A political realignment may be in the offing, but it is certainly not in sight.

Demosclerosis

The Disease That's Petrifying American Government

Jonathan Rauch

Jonathan Rauch, a contributing editor of National Journal, *is author of* Demosclerosis: The Silent Killer of American Government, *published by Times Books. Single copies of this book are available from the Democratic Leadership Council.*

In 1991, President Bush appointed Diane Ravitch, a Democrat, to be the Education Department's assistant secretary in charge of research. She had plans and ideas. She got nowhere. Ravitch soon discovered that all but a fraction of the education research budget was assigned, by law, to entrenched recipients with slick lobbyists and protectors in Congress. "The vast bulk is frozen solid," she later said. For instance, a handful of established regional laboratories virtually monopolized a key chunk of the research budget. The laboratories maintained a lobbying group, run by a former aide to a

key member of the House Appropriations Committee, which looked after them in perpetuity.

Ravitch, now a visiting scholar at New York University, managed to kill a single tiny program—one that spent only $8 million or so at its peak. Unable to kill anything old, she had neither the means nor the support to create anything new. She had hoped to create videos for parents and a computerized information network for educators. "But there was no interest group for that," she said.

In the end, Ravitch found there were only two ways to do her job. One method was to shovel money out the door to the established lobbies. Her department's clients would all be happy—but the government's education research program would stagnate. The other method was to try to set new priorities—but that would entail trench warfare against the interest

groups, a masochistic and probably futile exercise. Some choice.

"At first," Ravitch said of her time in Washington, "I thought it was about people really solving problems. But what it's really all about is people protecting their districts and the organizations they're close to. If you don't get the interest groups' support, you can't change anything, but if you change anything, you don't get their support. That's the conundrum.

"At the beginning, I thought I could shape the agency," she continued. "But I couldn't do that. That was already done. My priorities were irrelevant. And that, for me, was a devastating discovery."

Devastating, indeed. Devastating not only for people who work in government but for government itself. Little by little, Washington is turning brittle and rotting, like an intricate machine turning to rust.

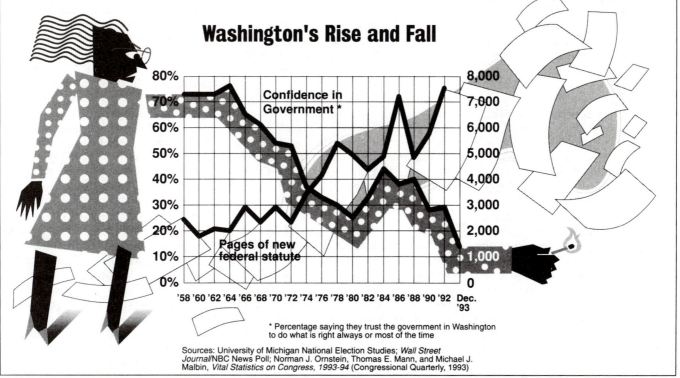

Washington's Rise and Fall

Confidence in Government *

Pages of new federal statute

'58 '60 '62 '64 '66 '68 '70 '72 '74 '76 '78 '80 '82 '84 '86 '88 '90 '92   Dec. '93

* Percentage saying they trust the government in Washington to do what is right always or most of the time

Sources: University of Michigan National Election Studies; *Wall Street Journal*/NBC News Poll; Norman J. Ornstein, Thomas E. Mann, and Michael J. Malbin, *Vital Statistics on Congress, 1993-94* (Congressional Quarterly, 1993)

ILLUSTRATION BY SAM WARD

Most Americans—and most Washingtonians—assume that Washington's problems lie in partisan feuding or political careerism or George Bush or Bill Clinton or whatever. If only it were that easy. What Diane Ravitch ran up against-and what Bill Clinton is running up against, in a bigger way—is a syndrome that I call demosclerosis: government's progressive loss of the ability to adapt.

Demosclerosis is a slow-acting, cumulative disorder that gradually turns government into a living fossil. In principle, it is treatable. But in practice? Unfortunately, the record so far is discouraging. The cure will have to be more radical than anything anyone in power, or the blowhard Ross Perot, has yet suggested.

People aren't mad at Washington for not getting enough done; they're mad because what Washington gets done is failing to solve their problems.

To see what demosclerosis is, a good place to begin is with what it emphatically, though subtly, is not: "grid-lock."

In his first press conference after winning the 1992 election, President-elect Clinton declared that his "clear mandate" was to end the gridlock in Washington. His interpretation mirrored the popular wisdom. Things that needed doing supposedly weren't getting done. In response, a whole lot of legislating and policy-making got done last year; President Clinton won a larger share of congressional votes than has any new President since Eisenhower in 1953.

There's something fishy about the "gridlock" story, however. Consider the chart on page 197. Americans' confidence in the federal government has fallen dramatically during the past 30 years. In 1958, 73 percent said they trusted the government in Washington to do what's right "just about always or most of the time." In December 1993, only 14 percent did. Today, seven of 10 Americans say government creates more problems than it solves; three-fourths say government wastes "a lot" of their tax money; and so on, and on.

Now, here's the curious thing. Over that same period, government has been anything but gridlocked. Far from declining, the level of activity has risen any way you measure it. One typical yardstick is the number of new pages of federal law added each year. As the chart shows, the more pages of new laws the government passed, the more unhappy people were. Whatever soured people on government, it wasn't gridlock.

Objectively speaking, in fact, *gridlock never happened.* In Washington, things always get done—ever more frenetically, indeed. The Bush years saw passage of the sweeping Clean Air Act and other environmental measures, the almost equally sweeping Americans with Disabilities Act, new money for child care, a major highway bill, a major anti-deficit bill (bigger than Clinton's!), at least 10 piecemeal reforms affecting health care and much else. In the civil rights field alone, the "era of gridlock" produced the Civil Rights Act of 1991, the Voting Rights Language Assistance Act, the Civil Liberties Act Amendments of 1992, the Minority Farmers Rights Act, the Japanese-American Redress Entitlement Programs, the anti-redlining provisions of the banking-reform law, the Hate-Crimes Statistics Act, and the aforementioned Americans with Disabilities Act. Overall, the number of laws and regulations enacted under President Bush remained well in line with the post-1970 norm.

Clearly, something is wrong with the standard analysis of Washington's problems. Maybe this:

The gridlock metaphor implies that traffic isn't moving—a static problem. And therein lies the error. Try, instead, a dynamic metaphor. Imagine that your car's front-end alignment went dangerously askew. This isn't a problem of static immobility but of dynamic imbalance—a very different kind of problem. The last thing you'd want to do about it is to drive faster ("get more done"). On the other hand, driving 10 miles an hour is no answer, either. You need to fix your alignment.

This second, dynamic kind of problem is what's wracking government and infuriating the public. People aren't mad at Washington for not getting enough done; they're mad because what Washington gets done is failing to solve their problems. Government's activity level rises, yet its achievement level falls. The wheels spin faster, yet the car shakes, lurches, veers randomly. Why?

Imagine a rocket ship with three thrusters headed for Jupiter. Now imagine that the thrusters are slightly out of balance. At first, you might not notice. After a while, though, the rocket would be a little off course, then a lot off course, then hurtling aimlessly into deep space. To maintain control, you would constantly need to fight the rocket's tendency to drift. And if you didn't fight hard enough, the whole mission would end in disaster.

A modern democracy faces a similar problem. It's difficult for government to do things, but that's as it should be. The founders made the American system change-averse on purpose, which is why we have competing power centers and the Bill of Rights. The trouble is that everything is not *equally* difficult to do. To create a subsidy or program is hard. To reduce an existing subsidy or program is much harder. And to completely eliminate a subsidy or a program is hardest of all.

This imbalance is fundamental to the way democracy works. Inherently, democracy allows people to form groups—lobbies—to seek benefits from the government. Those groups, of course, can do good as well as harm. The problem comes from a side effect of groupism: Once you create a benefit or program, its beneficiaries organize to protect it, and once that happens, getting rid of either the program or the group is almost impossible.

The Clinton Administration's own "reinventing government" report put the problem well. Government, said the report, "knows how to add, but not to subtract." A politician who challenges any existing lobby or program can expect all-out war—whereas a politician who simply adds to the existing pile of programs collects campaign contributions, support back home, and "Honorary Dairyman of the Year" awards.

President Clinton learned this lesson the hard way. During the Bush years, when some members of Congress suggested raising the heavily subsidized fees for grazing on federal land, ranchers' groups spent heavily to defeat them, laid siege to Capitol Hill, and denounced the reformers as "socialists" promoting "cultural genocide." Last year, the Clinton Administration's own proposal to raise land-use fees met with the same warm reception. Western land interests and their friends in the Senate made life so hot for the President that he beat a full retreat in the spring and then was mauled when he tried again in the fall. Eventually, if he tried hard enough, the President could get some of what he wants. But the cost in time, energy, and political capital would be enormous. And that is just for one little subsidy.

I'm not saying all subsidies are bad. Whether the Small Business Administration or rural electric subsidies or grazing subsidies or any other particular program is worthwhile is a matter of opinion. But that hardly matters, because it turns out that what a program actually does, or even how well it works, is irrelevant. Any politician, well-meaning or not, who tries to withdraw *any* group's program or subsidy, with justification or not, gets that group's fist in his face. It happens even when agencies try to re-channel money within an existing program. Even closing a local Agriculture Department office or an underused veterans' hospital is a nightmare.

The result is bizarre: *Government is stuck with almost everything it ever tries.* In 1993, Congress managed to get rid of four programs—most notably the superconducting super collider—and four was rightly considered an exceptional haul (it took Ronald Reagan eight years to kill that many major programs). In the Agriculture Department, President Clinton sought to kill more than 200 small items, worth $160 million. (That may sound like a lot, but in fact it was a routine Presidential request.) Of those items, he bagged only three dozen, together worth $38 million—better than the Bush Administration had done, but still only 1/2000th of the department's budget. In the Education Department, Clinton tried to kill about a dozen programs, most of them, again, items that routinely show up on Presidential hit lists. All but one minuscule item sailed happily on.

In response to complaints that the Administration's "reinventing government" effort recommended only 15 program eliminations, the budget director, Leon Panetta, replied, "I would kiss the ground and thank God if we could eliminate 15."

So here is the fatal imbalance: As hard as it is for the government to adopt programs, adapting or getting rid of them, once the beneficiaries have dug in, is much harder still. As in the case of the unbalanced spaceship, at first this problem may seem minor. For a while, government can just add new things on top of old things. But only for a while.

Another thought experiment. Suppose you were chosen to rescue a dying company But here's the catch: You can't drop a single product, close a single factory or scrap any equipment. You can develop new cars and computers, but you also have to keep all the old cars and computers on the market—tail fins, vacuum tubes, and all. "Impossible!" you say. "No one could revitalize a company under such conditions!" And you're right.

But that's exactly the situation the federal government now faces. The government is like the old Soviet economy, in which old enterprises never shut down, preventing new ones from springing up. The Soviet economy was fairly modern in Stalin's day, but it failed to adapt. The same thing is happening to the U.S. government now.

In the fight against demosclerosis, standard pro-government liberal ideology ("More programs!") is counterproductive, and standard anti-government conservative ideology ("Less government!") is beside the point.

Today, Washington spends five times more in constant dollars than it did in the late 1940s, when it could "afford" the Marshall Plan; it spends three times what it did in John F. Kennedy's day. Yet, for "lack of money," President Clinton's visionary national service plan was scaled down to a pea-sized $1.5 billion over three years, less than one year's cotton subsidy. Of course, this federal "poverty" isn't poverty at all. It's rigidity—alias demosclerosis. With every group fiercely defending every program, government can't reallocate resources. It gets stuck in its past, like a city buried in its own detritus.

An institution can't solve problems if it can't adapt. In a world where almost nothing works the first time, the key to solving problems is to experiment. President Clinton understands this; in his inaugural address, he pledged to "make our government a place for what Franklin Roosevelt called 'bold, persistent experimentation.'" The problem is that in

a demosclerotic society, FDR's brand of experimental government *cannot exist.* When you're stuck with virtually everything you ever try, trial and error is impossible. You can't get rid of your mistakes, your failures, your anachronisms.

Instead, programs and policies and subsidies pile up and work to every end at once. Sometimes they make war on each other, as when turn-of-the-century antitrust law undercuts efforts to encourage strategic business partnerships. The government's farm disaster-relief program and its crop-insurance program work at cross-purposes, yet both are defended and both go on and on. Maladaptive programs create new problems, creating demand for still more programs, leading to still more interest groups and more seizing-up.

Bit by bit, program by program, the government turns dysfunctional. Eventually, it reaches the point of critical failure. That is, it begins to create at least as many problems as it solves. The public believes that government has already reached that point. And the public is probably right.

"OK," say a lot of people, especially old-style Democrats, "let's pass new programs. That will fix it." But it won't. Remember, this is a *dynamic* problem, which is what makes it so insidious. Passing new programs is no solution because in a decade or two, after they're locked in, the new programs will be part of the old problem.

Take health-care reform. If major reforms are adopted, everyone will say, "That's the end of gridlock," and President Clinton will boast that Washington is back in action. But the glow will fade. Hard as it may be to adopt a health program, the much tougher problem will be to *adapt* it after enactment—or, tougher still, to get rid of it and replace it with something better. Lobbies will lock in every favorable provision, ensuring that re-allocating benefits—to say nothing of cutting them or rebuilding the whole program—is a political mare's nest. If lobbies calcify the health program, after a decade or two it will cause at least as many problems as it solves.

In its later stages, demosclerosis becomes weirdly convulsive. As government's flexibility dwindles, Washington scrambles ever more frantically, yet finds success ever more elusive. Enraged, the public turns against government and rails at politicians. But as politicians reply by piling new programs and subsidies on top of old ones, things get worse and the public becomes even angrier. Americans and their government become like the ill-tempered farmer and the arthritic nag. The farmer loads more and more on the nag, the nag becomes weaker and weaker, the angry farmer beats and whips the nag, the battered nag becomes weaker still. That's the chart on page 197.

It's important to understand that "change" is no escape if "change" just means piling programs, subsidies, and laws on top of other programs, subsidies, and laws. On the other hand, the answer also can't be simply to reduce the size of government. The issue isn't how to make government smaller (or larger) but how to make it more *flexible*.

In the fight against demosclerosis, standard pro-government liberal ideology ("More programs!") is counterproductive, and standard anti-government conservative ideology ("Less government!") is beside the point. We need to try something else. But what?

The forces of demosclerosis never just go away. They need to be fought unremittingly with a countervailing force, preferably one that attacks and weakens the lobbies themselves. That force is competition.

What lobbies want out of life is a comfy burrow to call home. They want a subsidy, tax break, or a favorable law or regulation that they can depend on year after year to shelter them from competition for resources. Such shelters take

---

Killing subsidies is, of course, exactly what interest groups exist to prevent. To beat them, it's critical to do the job wholesale, in a package big enough to show a real payoff.

---

many forms and benefit every class of people. Farmers get cash subsidies; Medicare recipients get in-kind benefits; real estate agents get tax loopholes; textile makers get protective tariffs; taxi drivers get medallions that restrict competition.

I'm not saying that all benefits for

everyone should be eliminated or that no programs are justified. I am saying that the true cost of such subsidies is much higher than the dollar figure in the federal budget: As subsidies become nesting places for lobbies and obstacles to adaptation, the ultimate victim is government itself. But if protection strengthens interest groups, competition can weaken them. And it can be harnessed in any number of ways.

• First, *force lobbies to compete with each other.* This turns out to be fairly hard to do. If the cattlemen propose to raise their subsidies by cutting the wheat farmers' benefit checks, they can expect to get the wheat farmers fist in their face. So lobbies seek a detente in which everybody goes along with everybody else's subsidies—and the bill is paid by taxpayers, consumers, or the unborn (that's the budget deficit).

How, then, to force confrontations? One way is to reduce the budget deficit, preferably over time to zero or even to surplus. Entirely apart from the economic benefits, when lobbies can't feed on the future, they must fight over a relatively smaller budget in the present. Meanwhile, when government reduces the deficit, it has to set priorities—a healthy exercise that stimulates adaptation.

Another way to force lobbies to compete is to decentralize. The economist Alice M. Rivlin—now of the Office of Management and Budget—has proposed a scheme in which Washington would cede to the states control of programs in education, job training, economic development, housing, transportation, social services, and others, in exchange for picking up broad social-insurance programs like health care and Social Security. True, states and localities are subject to the forces of demosclerosis, but they have an advantage over Washington: They compete with each other for people and jobs. That gives them less room to shelter lobbies than Washington's vast expanses provide.

• Second, and even more important: *clean out subsidies,* including tax breaks. Get rid of things to make room for things, and do it vigorously and on a broad scale. This weakens lobbies and strengthens government. The sugar lobby's mission is to defend the sugar subsidy. Get rid of the subsidy, and the lobby, while perhaps it won't vanish overnight, loses a lifeline. Moreover, resources pried from groups that captured them decades ago are freed for more pressing

needs. Government gains space to adapt because funds can be used for new ventures.

For years, anti-government conservatives have talked about eliminating programs (though talk is about all they've done). Yet it is government's *friends* who should be scraping off barnacles, for the benefits ultimately flow to government itself. Liberals who never met a program they didn't like are loving government to death. They need to understand that without a determined and thorough housecleaning, government will rot.

Killing subsidies is, of course, exactly what interest groups exist to prevent. To beat them, it's critical to do the job wholesale, in a package big enough to show a real payoff. The model is the 1986 tax-reform bill, which swept away enough tax loopholes to allow major reductions in tax rates—pain rewarded with tangible gain. And the anti-model is the timid budget-plan President Clinton proposed last year. That plan failed to offer a visible payoff, either in the form of a dramatically lower deficit or a dramatically reformed government. Why support pain with nothing to show for it? No wonder no one wanted to vote for Clinton's plan.

• Finally, *expose entrenched interests to economic competition.* Domestically, government should hunt for and get rid of regulations and barriers that shelter specific industries and groups. The competition fostered by school choice, for example, is good for public schools in the long run, but it's bad for public-school employees' lobbies.

Perhaps most important of all, government should expose lobbies to *foreign* competition. Goods, money, and ideas from abroad fuel the innovation that makes ancient lobbies irrelevant and dissolves their political bases. That was one reason why so many groups hated the North American Free Trade Agreement.

NAFTA was good, but GATT, the General Agreement on Tariffs and Trade, is even better. Acting under its auspices, more than 100 countries recently agreed to reduce their trade barriers. Although multilateral trade negotiations are often slow and frustrating, they allow countries to attack *each other's* lobbies. Americans go after the European farm lobby and Europeans go after the U.S. maritime lobby. GATT is political reform in disguise.

Of all the counter-measures in the fight against demosclerosis, foreign competition may offer the best combination of effectiveness and accessibility. We know it helps, and we have the means to pursue it. Above all, foreign competition hammers entrenched lobbies every day. It's a sentinel that never sleeps.

To President Clinton's credit, 1993 brought progress on trade. On other fronts in 1993, however, he kicked away the opportunity for radical reform. Proposing only timid changes in government's structure, he tried to appease rather than confront the lobbies—which, whenever possible, returned the favor by humiliating him.

"He's a get-along, go-along kind of guy, fundamentally," says Rep. Timothy J. Penny, D-Minn., a prominent deficit

The forces of demosclerosis never just go away: The groups keep forming, the dynamic imbalance persists. Though government is in bad enough shape already, it can get worse.

hawk. "He's transitional in that he doesn't so much disagree with the old agenda but he's got a new approach. He's trying to layer the new on top of the old." Instead of trying to reorder the ramshackle, maladaptive mess that government has become, Clinton and Congress tried stacking more things on top of other things—the very strategy that created the mess to begin with. "Ross Perot was a wake-up call," says Penny, "and we hit the snooze button."

That isn't good enough. The forces of demosclerosis never just go away: The groups keep forming, the dynamic imbalance persists. True, hacking away at barnacles is no one's idea of fun. But for a glimpse of the future if Washington continues on its current course, look back at the chart on page 197. Then extend both lines. Though government is in bad enough shape already, make no mistake: It can get worse.

GOING TO EXTREMES, LOSING THE CENTER

W. JOHN MOORE

On the last day of the 1991-92 term, the U.S. Supreme Court issued perhaps its most eagerly anticipated decision of the decade, *Planned Parenthood of Southeastern Pennsylvania v. Casey.*

The Court's opinion created no legal milestone. *Roe v. Wade*, the 1973 ruling establishing a woman's fundamental right to abortion, "should be retained and once again confirmed," the Justices held. But they also said that states could impose restrictions on abortion, including a requirement that minors notify their parents before terminating a pregnancy. In short, the ruling was a compromise—one that most Americans would accept, according to public opinion polls.

Activists on both sides of the abortion debate wasted no time in attacking, though. "Don't be fooled by the Court's smokescreen. What the Court did today is devastating for women," the National Abortion and Reproductive Rights Action League (NARAL) warned on the day of the decision. "Today, the Bush Court took away a woman's fundamental right to choose and invited every politician in America to interfere in what remains of this freedom."

NARAL's bitter opponent, the Chicago-based Americans United for Life, was just as unhappy. The Court has "taken two steps backward and turned a blind eye and a deaf ear to legal protection for children before birth. We are strongly disappointed that a majority of the Supreme Court reaffirmed abortion on demand," the anti-abortion group said in a press release.

The reaction of the two antagonists symbolizes interest-group politics in Washington, where a clash of conservative and liberal agendas has destroyed opportunities for consensus sought by the broader public. Eager to attack, seldom willing to compromise, these partisans disdain moderate solutions.

"You get a polarization of debate generated by elites which ordinary citizens find neither affects their interests nor addresses their concerns," said Thomas E. Mann, director of governmental studies at the Brookings Institution in Washington. "Interest groups have discovered that they can play on fears people have as a way to advance their own agendas."

Across the political spectrum, on a host of issues, interest groups have discovered that nothing rouses the faithful like a simple message denouncing your archenemy as evil incarnate. NARAL attacks Americans United for Life. Earth First! battles the timber industry. The Sierra Club blasts leaders of the "wise use" movement, who in turn demonize Interior Secretary Bruce E. Babbitt. People for the American Way chases the Christian Right across the countryside.

Extremism in the defense of ideology is no vice. Moderation in the pursuit of donor dollars is no virtue.

"Polarized rhetoric and extreme positions help arouse the faithful and stimulate membership and contributions," said William A. Galston, deputy assistant to President Clinton for domestic policy and previously a leading light of the centrist Democratic Leadership Council. "For systemic reasons, there is more short-term mileage to be gotten in narrower-focused intensity than in a broader approach."

But the interest groups' gain comes at a cost. A public seeking solutions in Washington discovers a government held hostage at times by interest-group rhetoric.

MESSY DEMOCRACY

To some experts, the clash of ideas is democracy at work, proof positive of the beauty of pluralistic politics. University of Virginia sociologist James Davison Hunter, in *Culture Wars: The Struggle to Define America* (Basic Books, 1991), wrote that bitter disputes articulate issues at the heart of American culture. "But these differences are often intensified and aggravated by the way they are presented in public," Hunter added.

Campaign managers, political pundits, think-tank impresarios and the news media have helped perpetuate what Mann describes as an "attack on the middle."

Once upon a time, Washington think tanks went about their business quietly, with cadres of analysts using their expertise to influence policy. That kind of intellectual power remains a goal for most think tanks.

But as think tanks proliferate, the need to define an identity that's different from the competition's becomes paramount. The quest for money and attention leads to brasher statements and more-dramatic policy prescriptions, James A. Smith wrote in *The Idea Brokers: Think Tanks and the Rise of the New Policy Elite* (Basic Books, 1991). "When all of this is refracted through a media filter, it creates a perception of polarization," Smith said.

The news media, of course, thrive on conflict. There is CNN's *Crossfire*, a show based on the dubious premise that the truth somehow emerges from liberal and conservative soundbites. "For the media," Mann argues, "the road to truth is in finding two extremes and letting them clash. It is the new definition of fairness."

Hard-hitting attacks on the Clintons have helped The American Spectator and other conservative publications boost their readership.

In his influential book, *Why Americans Hate Politics* (Simon & Schuster Inc., 1991), *Washington Post* political columnist E.J. Dionne Jr. argues that conservatives and liberals have ignored the majority of voters.

"Wracked by contradiction and responsive mainly to the needs of their various constituencies, liberalism and conservatism prevent the nation from settling the questions that most trouble it," Dionne wrote. "On issue after issue, there is consensus where the country should move or at least on what we should be arguing about; liberalism and conservatism make it impossible for that consensus to express itself."

But to succeed, politicians at least must persuade a majority of voters to support them. Washington interest groups are bound by no similar constraints. In fact, many groups are established to represent the viewpoint of a tiny portion of the populace that is absolutely passionate about a single issue—whether it be abortion, guns or the environment.

What an interest group lacks in size, it can make up for with intensity. A group with an ideological agenda can't compromise without losing some of its constituents, who respond to fund-raising letters in part because they agree with the blistering rhetoric and absolutist positions staked out by the group.

"Few people are likely to send money to an organization because of its intense, flaming moderation," said R. Kent Weaver, a senior fellow at Brookings.

"A lot of this rhetoric is directed toward the 5 or 10 per cent of the people on each side who are major contributors," said Burdett Loomis, a political scientist at the University of Kansas (Lawrence).

As a result, Loomis added, interest groups succeed better at stopping perceived threats than in accomplishing legislative victories that may require compromise. The liberal People for the American Way, for example, made its name by leading the opposition to the nomination of Robert H. Bork to the Supreme Court. The group stopped Bork—and its contributions reached the highest level ever the next year.

Interest groups thrive on highlighting the differences between themselves and their foes and obscuring the similarities. The result is political discourse with all the civility of Bosnia. "The politics of bombast," as Brookings's Mann puts it.

The growth of single-issue or cause-oriented interest groups is a relatively recent development. Thirty per cent of such groups have formed since 1975; in 1986, at least 20 per cent of all interest groups and trade associations in Washington were in that category, according to an academic study that year.

Ironically, interest groups grow the fastest when their political prospects look the gloomiest. Consider the Fairfax (Va.)-based National Rifle Association (NRA), long considered the undisputed champion of single-interest groups. Last year, the NRA failed to stop legislation that established a waiting period for handgun purchases; this spring, it suffered another blow when the House passed legislation that would ban assault rifles. But since the May 16 vote, the NRA has signed up 55,000 new members.

Clinton's support for gun control, which was crucial to the defeat of the gun lobby, has become the primary focus of the NRA's membership campaign. "Make no mistake: Bill Clinton is the American gun owner's worst nightmare," the NRA warned in a letter to prospective members last year. What was possibly Clinton's worse sin, according to the NRA? The President even "kissed [gun control advocate] Sarah Brady at rallies."

THANK YOU, MR. WATT

In the early 1980s, the environmental movement found itself confronting a hostile Administration determined to ease regulations on business. But environmental activists soon discovered a silver lining in the person of James G. Watt, President Reagan's Interior Secretary. Watt "was the devil figure for the environmentalists, like Jane Fonda and Teddy Kennedy used to be for the Right," Weaver of Brookings said.

Watt's visage on mailings was a magnet for money and support. The Wilderness Society prepared an eight-pound, two-volume compendium of press clips and critical cartoons in its *Watt Book.*

"In 1982, 95,000 new members joined our ranks largely because of the anti-environmental stance of James Watt," the Sierra Club said in a fund-raising letter a decade ago. The Sierra Club doubled its membership just during Watt's tenure. And membership and contributions kept growing during the 12-year Republican reign—until the election of Clinton and Vice President Albert Gore Jr., a hero among environmentalists. In 1993, the Sierra Club's contributions dipped an estimated 6.8 per cent. *(See chart, next page.)*

Other environmental groups have experienced similar drops in donations. The economic recession was part of the reason. But environmentalists attribute much of the falloff to the Gore factor. "There is this view that because Clinton has Gore on his team that he will do the

Whether the issue is the environment or gun control, interest groups thrive on highlighting differences between themselves and their foes and obscuring the similarities. "Few people are likely to send money to an organization because of its intense, flaming moderation," an analyst says.

HCI "Go To Hell" prospect piece 6/93

right thing on the environment. So contributions to most environmental groups have dropped or remained the same," said Graham Cox, vice president for public affairs at the National Audubon Society in New York City.

Some environmental groups have responded by discovering new enemies. The Sierra Club's latest foes are the partisans of what is called the "wise use" movement, conservative groups opposed to tough environmental restrictions on federal lands.

Environmental groups are not the only organizations that have discovered the downside to winning. After the pro-abortion rights Clinton-Gore team captured the White House, NARAL saw its monthly contributions drop by a third last year and its membership decline by 150,000.

"The worst thing that can happen to an interest group is that you win," said Ronald G. Shaiko, a specialist on interest-group politics at the American University in Washington.

Meanwhile, conservative groups have enjoyed a resurgence. The American Conservative Union now says it has 500,000 members, a fivefold increase since the 1992 election. The increase follows years of decline during the Republican years, acknowledged Jeff Hollingsworth, the group's executive director. With Reagan's election, he said, "conservative activists may have felt that the dream came true."

Now, "the shock of a Clinton-Gore Administration has brought conservatism back to life," Hollingsworth said. If many political analysts argue that Clinton has governed as a centrist, Hollingsworth disagrees. "There's plenty of evidence that Bill Clinton talks moderate and liberals get all the action," he said.

That view certainly sells with conservatives: The President and Hillary Rodham Clinton headline almost every fundraising letter mailed by a conservative organization to a carefully targeted audience. "These people are predisposed to loathing the Clintons," a conservative fund-raising expert conceded.

Opinion magazines with a conservative bent have pummeled the Clintons in

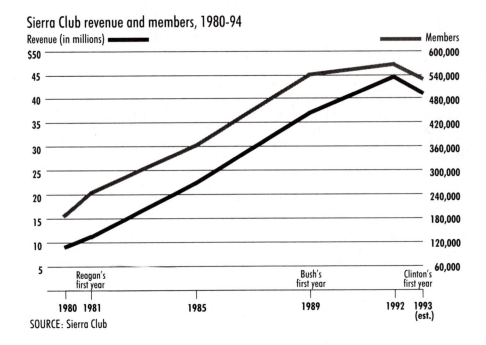

Sierra Club revenue and members, 1980-94

SOURCE: Sierra Club

story after story. Hillary Clinton graces (again) the June cover of *The American Spectator*, drawn as a witch astride a jet airplane. The story, *The Washington Post* said, is "the latest installment in that magazine's crusade to show that Hillary is the Antichrist of American politics." Inside, the subscription come-ons are even tougher.

The strategy works. According to figures compiled by the Audit Bureau of Circulations in Schaumburg, Ill., circulation at *The American Spectator* climbed from 72,468 in 1992 to 128,146 in 1993. Another conservative magazine, the weekly *National Review*, has also flourished in the Clinton year, with its circulation reaching 221,000 in 1993, up from 168,000 in 1992. Meanwhile, the left-wing bible, the *Nation*, saw its circulation drop approximately 5 per cent over the same period.

PRESS CLIPS

The mainstream news media share responsibility for catering to the extremes. Journalists often try to transform every discussion into a debate—

leaving little time to analyze or provide perspective. Even shows for high-brow audiences, such as ABC News's *Nightline* or the Public Broadcasting System's *MacNeil/Lehrer NewsHour*, parade casts of dueling policy wonks. Woe to the analyst, critic or historian interested in context or complexity.

When talk radio pros decided that it was time to provide some balance to right-winger Rush Limbaugh, the man hired was lefty Jim Hightower, former head of the Texas Agriculture Commission—whose views are summed up in his immortal words, "There ain't nothin' in the middle of the road but yellow stripes and dead armadillos."

But the center is also the place to find most Americans, who are often unmoved by ideological concerns and unenthusiastic about interest groups. According to many political scientists, there is grave danger in Washington's basing policy only on pleas from ideological diehards.

"The sum of all interest groups is not the national interest," the American University's Shaiko said. "And it never will be."

Cultivating the Grass Roots To Reap Legislative Benefits

Joel Brinkley

Special to The New York Times

WASHINGTON, Oct. 31—At first glance, the letters looked innocent enough, just a few dozen pieces of mail among the 1,000 or more that most members of Congress receive every week. But as Sean Cavanaugh, a Congressional aide, read through them, it almost seemed as if vipers were slithering out of the envelopes.

Most of the letters were handwritten, some with the trembling script of the elderly, and they cried out with fear and despair: If Congress approved an obscure proposed change in Medicare policy, "then my husband will die."

The aide said he was sickened. After he had read several of the letters, he realized that all were the same.

Lobbyists at Work

"They were just rote language," he said. It was as if someone had advised the writers just what to say. That convinced Mr. Cavanaugh that his boss, Representative Benjamin L. Cardin, was the target of an industry-driven lobbying campaign. And when Mr. Cardin, a Maryland Democrat, had a look he decided "it was a really nasty, terribly misguided campaign," because the proposed change would actually have little effect on patients.

But the most striking thing about the letters, the Congressman said, was that "I never heard from the people who were really behind them."

His experience is not at all unusual because these days that is how lobbyists work. Gone is the time when backslapping, cigar-chomping influence peddlers were the main instruments of Washington lobbying.

"The high-profile access merchant has virtually disappeared," said Mark Cowan, who until last month was head of the Jefferson Group, a prominent lobbying firm.

Over the last several years, lobbyists have been turning away from the direct approach in favor of "grass roots" strategies. The goal is to persuade ordinary voters to serve as their advocates, and the letters that arrived in Mr. Cardin's office last summer were one example.

Using the technologies of this electronic age, lobbyists can now quickly reach and recruit thousands of Americans. Many lawmakers say lobbyists have grown so skillful that their tactics have changed the way Congress works.

"Unfortunately it has caused Congress to govern more by fear and an intense desire for simple, easy answers," said Representative Steve Gunderson, Republican of Wisconsin. "Once that grass-roots constituency has been activated, it's impossible ever to explain how proposals might have been changed," or to correct incorrect perceptions. "So we are forced to take complicated issues and simplify them so we can defend out positions."

Not every member thinks it is fair to blame the lobbyists for this. Senator Carl Levin, Democrat of Michigan, calls that "a cop-out."

"Congress has the responsibility to stand up to that," he says. Blaming lobbyists "is an excuse for a lack of political will."

Technology
Quick Satellites, Reams of Faxes

No matter who is correct, most everyone agrees that the rudimentary grass-roots campaigns of just a few years ago—fill-in-the-blank post cards, and forms torn out of the newspaper—have grown far more sophisticated and effective.

"The genie is really out of the bottle now," said Richard Viguerie, whose direct-mail campaigns for conservative causes started the grass-roots movement in 1965. "It's out, and it ain't ever going back—no matter how hard Congress tries."

To mobilize their members, many trade groups have installed banks of computerized fax machines that can send faxes automatically around the country overnight, instructing each member to ask his employees, customers and others to write or call their congressmen.

The National Association of Manufacturers started a campaign like that last summer that virtually smothered Congress in letters and phone calls opposing President Clinton's proposed energy tax, and as a result the plan was withdrawn.

Other lobbyists now run carefully targeted television advertisements pitching one side of an argument. That approach was used only rarely before now because of the tremendous cost. But once one industry decides it is willing to spend the money, others find they have little choice.

Many of these advertisements end with a toll-free phone number that viewers can call if they find the pitch convincing: New tele-marketing companies answer these calls, and transfer the callers directly to the offices of the appropriate congressmen.

Television Appeals
The American Trucking Association's approach has jumped beyond the fax machine. Until now, the truckers have mobilized their members by sending out hundreds of faxes. The problem was, "some of our members were inundated with so many faxes that they didn't always read them," said Sandy Lynch, an association official.

So this month the truckers began using a new satellite network connecting the Washington headquarters to affiliates in every state. Now, with little notice, Thomas Donohue, president of the association, can appear on television monitors in affiliate offices nationwide and rally his members to action.

To be sure, direct lobbying is not extinct. Washington still has its share of lobbyists from the old school. And many lobbyists still effectively lubricate the system with campaign donations, speaking fees, expense-paid trips and other gifts for lawmakers or their aides.

But even some of the old-style lobbyists are being drawn into the grass-roots movement—like it or not. Thomas H. Boggs Jr. is considered one of Washington's most influential lobbyists. When lawmakers and others talk about lobbyists of the old school, his name comes up first.

He notes that most Washington lobbying involves issues that are small and technical, though lots of money might be involved. For that, Mr. Boggs says, direct lobbying continues to be effective.

"Where these grass-roots campaigns have been used a lot are the big public policy debates," he said. Even then, Mr. Boggs said he still prefers not to use grass-roots strategies "because the costs are really high."

Nonetheless, more and more often now, he finds he has little choice. "In many cases we do it as a defensive measure," because the other side starts it first.

Tactics
Glad-Handing Goes Grass Roots

Even with the change in strategy, many of the fundamental concerns about lobbyists remain the same. Speaking of his profession, one of the city's senior lobbyists, Jerry Jasinowski of the National Association of Manufacturers, warned of one problem. Look out for companies or individuals or trade associations that get a small provision into law to serve the interests of a narrow group. That is dangerous."

There could hardly be a more striking illustration than the six-year legislative history of Medicare Payment policies for two obscure pieces of medical equipment, nebulizers and aspirators. Together they cost the Federal Government about $120 million last year—much of it wasted, in the Government's view.

This was the equipment the patients were writing about in the letters to Mr. Cardin. And the story behind them also illustrates the evolution of lobbying strategy, from direct lobbying to grass-roots campaigns.

Nebulizers administer medicine in aerosol form, usually through a mask. Aspirators are small pumps that suck out the fluid that accumulates in the lungs of patients on respirators. And for more than 20 years, Medicare offered indefinite reimbursement for patients who rented them. The problem was that many patients used them for years, so the Government ended up spending so much on rent that the devices could have been purchased many times over.

In 1987, Congress tried to solve this by establishing a list of equipment that could be rented for only 12 months, after which it had to be purchased. At the time, Thomas Antone was president of the National Association of Medical Equipment Suppliers, the trade group representing the companies that rent and maintain the equipment.

"Senators and congressmen don't know much about this," Mr. Antone observed. And as he recalled, he and the Congressional aides agreed that the new regulation ought to include an exception for equipment that needed frequent or substantial service. That equipment would continue to be rented.

When the bill went to a Senate-House conference committee, Mr. Antone recalls, some conferees decided they wanted the bill's language to include a couple of specific examples of equipment that might require frequent service. And when the bill left the committee, the conferees had cited nebulizers and aspirators.

Mr. Antone says he does not know how that happened. But Charles Spalding, chief of the Medical Services payments branch at the Health Care Finance Administration, said, "The industry proposed it."

Since that time, however, the Government has learned that the devices generally need little if any significant service. And yet, Mr. Spalding said, "some folks with chronic conditions have to pay $30 or $40 a month more or less indefinitely" in copayments to rent a nebulizer or aspirator, even though "a common purchase price for one is $200 or $250."

Last year the Government spent $120 million reimbursing Medicare patients for the rental of just these two devices. But this summer, Congress set out to remove both of them from the frequent servicing category.

'Constant Stream' of Faxes

While the change was still being debated, Deborah Harnsberger, a lobbyist with the equipment suppliers group, said the industry's position was that aspirators should not be removed from the rental list. Some nebulizers could be moved, she added, while some others should not.

And to make that point, she said, "we are using grass roots as part and parcel of what we are doing. A constant stream of faxes and phone calls is going from here to our members."

In the end, the trade group won a partial victory. Congress left it up to the Health and Human Resources Department to decide whether nebulizers and aspirators should be rented or purchased—giving the industry another opportunity to make its case.

At the same time, Corine Parver, president of the lobbying group, disavows the letters to Mr. Cardin.

"We don't engage in that kind of lobbying" using patients, she said, suggesting that it was probably the work of an overzealous affiliate of the trade group who took grass-roots lobbying to an unethical extreme.

The Change
'Super-Lobbyists' On the
Bandwagon

Some lobbyists can point to the moment when their profession began taking its new path: March 3, 1986. That's the day Time magazine published a photo on its cover of the lobbyist and former Reagan aide Michael Deaver in the backseat of his limousine talking on the phone. The headline asked: "Who's this man calling?"

Right away the photo sparked new convulsions of concern about high-power "super-lobbyists."

"That was the line of demarcation," Mr. Cowan says now.

Unfavorable publicity along with changing social and political attitudes and stricter conflict-of-interest

laws began making it more difficult for high-profile lobbyists like Mr. Deaver to be effective. And at about the same time, lobbyists began to notice that labor unions and so-called public interest groups, like Ralph Nader's Public Citizen, were using a different approach.

These groups generally did not have super-lobbyists. So when they wanted to influence policy, they used what they called their "grass-roots"

Presidents on Lobbyists: No Love Lost

"There are two methods of curing the mischiefs of faction, one by removing its causes, two by controlling its effects. By a faction, I understand a number of citizens, whether amounting to a majority or a minority of the whole, who are united and actuated by some common impulse of passion, or of interest, adverse to the rights of other citizens, or to the permanent and aggregate interests of the community."

James Madison,
in the Federalist Papers of the 1780's

"The host of contractors, speculators, stockjobbers and lobby members which haunt the halls of Congress, all desirous to get their arm into the public treasury, are sufficient to alarm every friend of his country. Their progress must be stopped."

James Buchanan,
writing to Franklin Pierce in 1852,
before either man had served as President

"I think that the public ought to know the extraordinary exertions being made by the lobby in Washington" for a pending tariff bill. Washington is so full of lobbyists that "a brick couldn't be thrown without hitting one. It is of serious interest to the country that the people at large should have no lobby and be voiceless in these matters, while great bodies of astute men seek to create an artificial opinion and to overcome the interests of the public for their private profit. It is thoroughly worth the while of the people of this country to take knowledge of this matter. Only public opinion can check and destroy it."

Woodrow Wilson,
speaking at a news conference in 1913

"By virtue of their wealth and freedom from regulation, some lobbies can threaten to or actually unleash almost unlimited television and direct-mail assaults on uncooperative legislators. At the same time they can legally reward those who do their bidding. The lobbies are a growing menace to our system of government."

Jimmy Carter,
from his memoir, 'Keeping Faith'

"Within minutes of the time I conclude my address to Congress Wednesday night, the special interests will be out in force. Those who profited from the status quo will oppose changes we seek—the budget cuts, the revenue increases, the new investment priorities. Every step of the way they'll oppose it. Many have already lined the corridors of power with high-priced lobbyists."

Bill Clinton,
as he announced his economic plan on Feb. 15

networks. This meant getting their members around the country to tell Washington how they felt.

In the mid-1980's, one lobbyist, Jack Bonner, said he and others in his field began to see "that certain groups were doing this very well—unions, environmental groups, consumer groups—while business was doing it rather poorly." Fewer than 5 percent of the Fortune 500 companies were using grass-roots lobbying, Mr. Bonner found. So he and others adopted the practice and began trying to improve on it.

The difference was that corporate lobbyists had more money to throw behind the effort. And with the added resources, they were able to take advantage of the latest technology. As their strategies grow ever more elaborate, some of the original grass-roots lobbyists worry that they can no longer keep up.

"These developing technologies—like computerized grass roots—combined with enormous resources, are overwhelming the system," complained Fred Wertheimer, head of Common Cause, one of the first organizations to use modern grass-roots lobbying. "It gives these organizations special advantage. And it's gotten to the point where the Government is no longer capable of dealing with it."

Defense Lobbyists' Version Of a White Knight

Most lobbyists will quickly acknowledge that their profession still has an unsavory reputation. The public "thinks we are a small group, in Gucci shoes, somehow controlling issues in a way that is at variance with the public interest," Mr. Jasinowski said.

Most lobbyists are not likely to describe themselves as altruistic servants of the public good. But they say the public is unfairly disdainful of them.

"The average person forgets that they have lobbyists too," said Richard H. Kimberly, president of the American League of Lobbyists. "Maybe they go to church. Well, churches lobby. Maybe they are retired. Well, the retired people have a lobby. But instead, when people think of lobbyists they think of organizations like the N.R.A.," the National Rifle Association.

Fair enough, but do any of the corporate and commercial lobbyists that are so often the target of complaint actually perform work they are proud of? Mr. Kimberly said he would try to find a lobbyist who was working on a campaign that the public might admire.

Ten days later, he said he was having a hard time finding anyone willing to step forward. But he did point to Casey Dinges, the lobbyist for the American Society of Civil Engineers.

Mr. Dinges said his organization discovered last fall that the Department of Housing and Urban Development was about to propose a new standard for the construction of mobile homes. After Hurricane Andrew destroyed thousands of trailers in South Florida in August 1992, the Government decided the building standards were inadequate. So Mr. Dinges's organization drafted a detailed new standard and lobbied the Government to adopt it.

"Just because someone lives in a mobile home, why can't they be safe?" Mr. Dinges asked. Besides, he said, when inadequate building standards cause problems, "our members are the ones who have to clean the stuff up."

HUD decided to adopt the engineers' standard; a senior Federal official said the department considered it "rigorous and complete." But as soon as HUD announced its decision, one lobbyist's proud victory became another's desperate battle.

And so the grass roots came into play. The Manufactured Housing Institute, representing mobile home manufacturers, unleashed a furious lobbying campaign to defeat the engineers' proposal. The lobby argued that the engineers' standard would raise trailer prices in some areas by as much as 36 percent. Bruce Savage, spokesman for the group, said: "It may be nice to have a 'safe' home. But if no one is buying them, what's the point?"

When the department asked for public comment on the proposed new standard this summer, the manufacturers "contacted all our members on our grass-roots network," Mr. Savage said. HUD was flooded with a thousand letters of complaints.

The department will not make its final ruling until later this autumn, and so the lobbying continues. But for now, the engineers' proposal is still on the table.

This Mr. Smith Gets His Way in Washington

Federal Express Chief Twists Some Big Arms

NEIL A. LEWIS

WASHINGTON, Oct. 11—As the Senate rushed to adjournment earlier this month, one odd and seemingly inconsequential item stood in the way: the insertion of a few words in a 1923 law regulating railway express companies.

It was not the kind of thing that would ordinarily seize the attention of senators eager to go home barely a month before Election Day. But they stayed in session until the language was enacted, because the beneficiary of the arcane language was the *Federal Express* Corporation, which has become one of the most formidable and successful corporate lobbies in the capital.

Federal Express wanted the language change because it might exempt its operations from the National Labor Relations Act and, as a result, help it resist efforts by unions to organize its workers. Despite passionate speeches by opponents on behalf of organized labor, the company was able to engineer a remarkable legislative victory, prevailing upon the Senate to remain in session two extra days solely to defeat a filibuster by its opponents.

"I was stunned by the breadth and depth of their clout up here," said Senator Russell D. Feingold, a first-term Democrat from Wisconsin who had opposed the change. In the end, Mr. Feingold was one of 31 senators who voted against Federal Express.

Senators say the ingredients in Federal Express's success are straightforward, distinguished from other corporate lobbying by degree and

Table 1

HIRED GUNS

During the first six months of this year, Federal Express spent $1,149,150 on lobbying, $367,000 of which went to outside law firms. Here are the law firms that Federal Express hired and how much each was paid.

Oldsker, Ryan, Phillips & Utrecht	$80,000
The Dutko Group*	60,000
O'Brien Calio	60,000
Cassidy & Associates	42,000
Aun Eppard Associates	40,000
Washington Counsel, P. C.	40,000
Cliff Madison Government Relations*	20,000
Bill Simpson & Associates	15,000
James E. Boland*	10,000

*Worked on Railway Labor Act
Source: *Public Citizen from Senate records*

skillful application: a generous political action committee, the presence of popular former Congressional leaders from both parties on its board, lavish spending on lobbying, and a fleet of corporate jets that ferry dozens of officeholders to political events around the country.

Mr. Feingold said that as he tried to rally support against the Federal

Table 2

POLITICAL CONTRIBUTIONS

The 10 largest corporate political action committees, ranked by contributions in the current election cycle through Aug. 30.

1. United Parcel Service	$1,312,031
2. AT&T	1,074,683
3. Lockheed Martin	759,950
4. Union Pacific	605,790
5. Federal Express	**600,500**
6. Ernst & Young	600,365
7. Philip Morris	595,226
8. Northrop Grumman	584,050
9. Ameritech	550,854
10. RJR Nabisco	495,150

Source: *Citizen Action from Federal Election Committee filings*

Express legislation, he was frequently and fervently rebuffed by colleagues who said they had acquired obligations to the company.

"The sense I got was that this company had made a real strong effort to be friendly and helpful to Congress," Mr. Feingold said.

He would not identify the lawmakers but said that as he approached them about the legislation, he discovered that many just wanted to talk about how Federal Express had helped them. "In these informal conversations, people mentioned that they had flown in a Fedex plane or gotten other favors," he said.

'I know who butters my bread,' one senior Senator reportedly said.

Senator Ernest F. Hollings, a South Carolina Democrat who proposed the amendment to help Federal Express, said he did so because he was grateful to the company for its willingness to use its planes to fly hay to his state during droughts.

But others say lawmakers benefit more directly. Senator Paul Simon, an Illinois Democrat who is retiring this fall, said that in a caucus of the Senate's Democrats just before the recess, one senior senator refused to oppose the company, bluntly telling his colleagues, "I know who butters my bread."

Mr. Simon would not identify the lawmaker except to say he was a longtime member of the Senate.

"I know that I have ridden in their planes several times," said Mr. Simon, who opposed Federal Express on this bill. "But what happened here was just a blatant example of the power of their political efforts. If the John Smith company came along and asked for the same thing, it wouldn't have a prayer."

Federal Express, Tennessee's biggest private employer, makes no apologies either for the merits of the legislation it sought or for its efforts to establish relationships with members of Congress.

"We play the game as fairly and aggressively as we can," said Doyle Cloud, the vice president of regulatory and government affairs for Federal Express. "We have issues constantly in Washington that affect our ability to deliver the services our customers demand as efficiently as possible."

For example, Mr. Cloud said, Federal Express regularly seeks to make clearances through customs easier to increase efficiency. "To do things like that, it's absolutely necessary that we are involved politically as well as regulatorily," he said.

In addition to its cargo fleet, Federal Express maintains four corporate jets that when not used for company trips are made available to members of Congress. Mr. Cloud said that they were used mostly to ferry groups of lawmakers to a fund-raising event and only rarely for an individual lawmaker.

Congressional regulations require that lawmakers using corporate aircraft reimburse the company for the equivalent of first-class air fare, and Mr. Cloud said that was always done. Records maintained publicly by Congress do not show how often members use corporate flights. Federal Express declined to make the company's records available, but Mr. Cloud said that during political seasons, Federal Express might fly a group of lawmakers about once a week.

Two popular former lawmakers, meanwhile, serve on the Federal Express board: George J. Mitchell of Maine, the former Democratic leader of the Senate, and Howard H. Baker Jr., the former Republican leader of the Senate.

The company's political action committee is one of the top five corporate PAC's in the nation. In the 1993–94 election cycle it gave more than $800,000 to 224 candidates for

the House and Senate. According to the Federal Election Commission, it gave $600,500 to candidates in this cycle through August. The company has also donated more than $260,000 this year to the Democratic and Republican parties.

In the first six months of 1996, Federal Express reported spending $1,149,150 to influence legislation, an investment that included the hiring of nine Washington lobbying firms. Typically, a company hires a number of lobbying firms because each one has a relationship with an individual lawmaker who may be important on particular issues.

"The sky's the limit for Federal Express when it wants to get its own customized regulatory protection made into law," said Joan Claybrook, president of Public Citizen, a Washington-based government watchdog group.

During the legislative debate last week, it appeared that the company also used a United States Ambassador to press its case, but the diplomat and company have denied that.

When a lobbyist for organized labor sought to talk to Senator J. Bennett Johnston about the Federal Express issue, Mr. Johnston replied in the presence of several witnesses that he already had made up his mind, because he had just been successfully lobbied on the issue on behalf of Federal Express by James R. Sasser. Mr. Sasser, a former Democratic senator from Tennessee, is the current Ambassador to China and would be prohibited from lobbying on behalf of Federal Express.

Mr. Johnston, a retiring Democrat from Louisiana, said through his spokeswoman that his comment was a "terrible slip of the tongue." The spokeswoman said that Mr. Johnston had just been lobbied by Frederick Smith, the founder and chairman of Federal Express, and that he had meant to use Mr. Smith's name.

The spokeswoman, Audra McCardell, said that Senator Johnston had lunch earlier in the week with Ambassador Sasser and that the Federal Express matter had come up "in chitchat." She said that Mr. Johnston had merely told Mr. Sasser how he was going to vote on the issue. For his part, Mr. Sasser, who was retained as a consultant by Federal Express before his confirmation as an ambassador, said in a telephone interview that he did not lobby Mr. Johnston, although they might have discussed the issue.

Mr. Smith spends considerable time in Washington, where he is regarded as Federal Express's chief advocate. It was Mr. Smith who hit a lobbying home run in 1977 when he persuaded Congress to allow the fledgling company to use full-sized jetliners to carry its cargo, rather than the small planes to which it had been restricted. Mr. Cloud said that was the watershed event that allowed the company to grow to its present dominating position in the industry, with almost $10.3 billion in annual business.

Federal Express has also been able to get other special provisions written into the law. In 1995, for example, Congress gave it an exemption from certain trucking regulations. It has also won exemptions from noise abatement requirements.

The provision that Federal Express successfully sought last week was insertion of the words "express company" in legislation that designates companies that can be organized by unions only under the Railway Labor Act. Under that law, unions are allowed to organize only in national units, rather than locally. Federal Express is fighting efforts by the United Automobile workers to unionize its drivers. Of the 110,000 domestic employees of the company, only its 3,000 pilots are unionized.

Allen Reuther, the U.A.W.'s chief lobbyist, said that the union found it "especially outrageous for the Senate to provide this special interest provision for just one company."

Federal Express and its supporters in the Senate attached the legislative language as a rider to an airport bill that promised dozens of local airport improvements and enhanced security measures. Many lawmakers who usually vote with labor decided the bill had to pass, even with the Federal Express provision.

But the votes of 17 Democrats to help Federal Express by ending a filibuster against the provision—including that of Senator Thomas A. Daschle of South Dakota, the minority leader—angered labor officials, especially John J. Sweeney, president of the A.F.L-C.I.O. Some union leaders said they might withhold future contributions to the Democratic Senate Campaign Committee.

But after Senator Edward M. Kennedy of Massachusetts, who led the filibuster, visited Mr. Sweeney on Thursday with a note of thanks for his support, the tension eased and union officials relented. President Clinton signed the airport measure into law on Wednesday.

RESISTING PRESSURES ON A
FREE PRESS

*As the pendulum swings toward conservatism from
liberalism, it is imperative that all sides of the political spectrum
continue to be represented in the nation's media.*

William H. Rentschler

Mr. Rentschler, publisher of The Rentschler Report, *a national journal of independent opinion, is a three-time winner of the Peter Lisagor Award by the Chicago Headline Club and a five-time Pulitzer Prize nominee.*

WHO, in his own words, is "the poster boy of free speech"? To hear him tell it, in melodious, self-satisfied tones, it is Rush Limbaugh, one of the reigning superstars of talk radio, who also describes himself as "undaunted, undistracted, serving humanity." Through the 600-plus stations that carry his one-sided, egocentric, wildly popular talk show, he proclaims grandly, "This is Rush Limbaugh, with my brain tied behind my back, just to make it fair."

Limbaugh was credited by former Rep. Vin Weber (R.-Minn.), leading the House Republican Orientation Conference for newly elected GOP Congressmen, with being "as responsible as any person" for the November, 1994, landslide.

"No, I'm not running for President," maintains this self-styled paragon of family values. "But I should be." All this might seem ludicrous if it weren't for his enormous influence with rank-and-file, rightward-tilting voters, who otherwise feel themselves voiceless. Meanwhile, there is a sinister element in Limbaugh's message that gravely threatens the credibility of the mainstream media, which generally adhere to the journalistic obligation of presenting both sides of controversial issues, encouraging dissent, and allowing debate to flourish on their pages and TV screens.

This is not the Limbaugh way. He is unapologetically biased, unbalanced, and partisan. Among his weapons are a supercilious sneer and cackle of dismissive laughter, the nasty putdown, and ridicule of the "traditional liberal media" and those "liberal" political figures he fixes in the crosshairs of his lethal verbal assault weapon, especially Pres. Bill Clinton and First Lady Hillary Clinton.

"The Left is never gonna go away. They're arrogant and they hide from people what they really are," he tells his listeners in his confidential, I'm-letting-you-in-on-a-dirty-little-secret tone of voice. "You try to like these people, but it's not easy." He suggests a tactic: "Don't ever mention the names of liberal columnists."

"And I," Limbaugh gloats, "am the liberals' worst nightmare." This is probably so. As the Greek dramatist Sophocles said in 409 B.C., "Everywhere among the race of men, it is the tongue that wins and not the deed."

Journalism is more than a job; it is a calling, a quasi-public service occupation. The duties of the devoted, committed journalist are wide-ranging, exacting, intimidating, and severe. Today, many in the print field veer away from those stringent obligations and seek the greater glory of TV panel spots, celebrity status, and a giant leap forward in compensation.

It wasn't so long ago that a reporter was simply a reporter, who covered his or her assignments factually, fairly, fully, "without fear or favor," as *The New York Times* demanded of its staff. Some of that ethic persists across the entire field of print journalism, and some pursue it rigorously, but it has been diluted by the ever-quickening pace of the rapidly changing world of communications. Despite that accelerating and unsettling trend, most newspapers are run by editors who believe it continues to be their prime duty to give a fair airing to countervailing points of view.

The *Times,* deplored by Limbaugh and his conservative coterie, exemplifies this balance day in, day out. On its Feb. 1, 1995, editorial page, for instance, in the premier position adjacent to the masthead, were two letters that effectively stated diametrically opposing points of view on the critical matter of defense spending. The first letter, from the national vice president of the Air Force Association, made a strong, predictable case for beefed-up military outlays and greater preparedness in the post-Cold War era. The second, written by a Fellow at Harvard's Russian Research Center, stated that the U.S. military budget of $273,000,000,000 in 1993, plus that of its allies, "outstrips sevenfold [the combined] spending of $66,000,000,000 by our potential enemies." He noted that U.S. defense outlays exceed by $39,000,000,000 those of the next nine nations, including France, Great Britain, and Germany. He argued persuasively for shifting some of our defense budget to meet civilian needs and reduce the Federal budget deficit.

The Times' balanced approach follows closely a sound and thoughtful admonition by its publisher, Arthur Hays Sulzberger, in 1948: "Obviously, a man's judgment cannot be better than the information on which he has based it. Give him the truth and he may still go wrong when he has the chance to be right, but give him no news or present him only with distorted and incomplete data . . . and you destroy his whole reasoning processes, and make him something less than a man."

No such balance exists on Limbaugh's "Excellence in Broadcasting" Network. He preaches the gospel according to St. Rush, and most callers seem to agree with his bombastic right-wing propaganda. Limbaugh's tone of certainty destroys the entire reasoning processes of most of his callers. The articulate dissenters are few.

"Discussion in America means dissent," author and cartoonist James Thurber noted in 1961. John F. Kennedy warned in 1959, before his election as president, "Let us not be afraid of debate or dissent—let us encourage it. For if we should ever abandon these basic American traditions . . . what would it profit us to win the whole world when we have lost our soul?"

Limbaugh, free speech's "poster boy," would argue that he is the very manifestation of dissent. However, he is so good at what he does mainly because Limbaugh has no one across the table to challenge on equal terms some of his outrageous ideological assertions. His program is largely a lovefest of like-minded listeners/callers massaging the giant ego of their hero.

What is dangerous to the free flow of conflicting ideas and balanced reporting—so critical to the effective functioning of a free society—is the increasing domination of the print media and air waves by a lavishly financed propaganda campaign that reached its present zenith in the 1994 political races.

Because the Far Right sees the Public Broadcasting System—TV and radio—as a balancing force, and thus threatening to its agenda, Republicans in Congress have set out to disembowel the beast by eliminating or severely restricting its Federal funding. In an ominous opening salvo, Sen. Larry Pressler (R.-S.D.), new chairman of the Commerce Committee, which controls PBS funding, demanded sensitive information on the sex, ethnic and professional backgrounds, and political leanings of the system's employees. He quickly backed off after a firestorm of protest based on invasion of privacy, according to the Associated Press. Total Federal support for all public broadcasting nationwide, AP reported, is $285,000,000, about equal to the cost of one military jet.

The media assault from the right is by no means limited to Limbaugh or the spate of conservative talk shows, including that of Watergate conspirator G. Gordon Liddy, and dozens of local offerings. It is far broader. Consider several examples:

• William F. Buckley's *National Review* and R. Emmett Tyrrell's *American Spectator* trumpet a right-wing agenda without much pretense of fairness and balance. As far as they are concerned, they are right; they know it; and that is all that matters. There is little dissent or debate in their pages.

• The comparatively new National Empowerment Television Network, with a claimed "reach" of 11,000,000 homes, is a venture of longtime professional conservative Paul Weyrich. It provides a forum for House Speaker Newt Gingrich (R.-Ga.) and is being supported by, among others, Michael Huffington, who spent $28,000,000 of his own fortune in barely losing the 1994 senatorial race to Dianne Feinstein (D.-Calif.). The network sponsored an intimate $50,000-a-couple soiree in early February, 1995, at Washington's Hay Adams Hotel honoring Gingrich, who is their featured superstar host and contributor of his views to the network.

• Hillsdale College in Michigan aggressively promotes the conservative agenda in its newsletter, *Imprimis,* with a circulation of 565,000.

Not all so-called conservatives relish the strident message of the movement's present-day leadership. In a July, 1994, interview, Barry Goldwater, the patron saint of modern-day conservatism, former five-term U.S. senator, and 1964 Republican presidential candidate, was asked, "Are you still a conservative?"

"Oh, yeah, of course I am, always will be," he responded. "A lot of so-called conservatives today don't know what the word means. They think I've turned liberal because I believe a woman has a right to an abortion. That's a decision that's up to the pregnant woman, not up to the Pope or some do-gooders or the religious right. . . . One problem today is with these neo-conservatives, the radical right, the religious extremists whose interpretation is very narrow and who want to destroy everybody who doesn't agree with 'em. I see them as betrayers of the fundamental principles of conservatism."

Goldwater was reminded that GOP chairman Haley Barbour, an architect of the 1994 Republican sweep, charges critics of this group with "religious bigotry" and "Christian bashing."

Snorted Goldwater, "That's a crock. He's way the hell off base, dead wrong. That religious bunch is crazy. They're dangerous. They'll destroy the Republican Party. Maybe eventually the Democratic Party, too."

The increasingly powerful organs of the right—print and electronic—contrive to blunt the impact and counter the influence of what conservatives deride as the "liberal media"—especially the nation's largest daily newspapers and a handful of TV superstars—which they believe pose a danger to "their" America. This assault is patently phony, strictly strategic in its intent to undermine public trust in traditional sources of news and opinion. What the conservatives deride as "liberal" are, for the most part, those mainstream daily newspapers that, whatever their editorial positions, attempt to provide some semblance of balance in their

coverage. This above all else infuriates the "Johnny-One-Notes" like Limbaugh, who accept only their own brand of orthodoxy.

In reality, considerably less than a majority of the body politic, they are so sure they, and only they, are right that they feel it is their God-given right, even duty, to suppress, derogate, and ridicule any and all contradictory viewpoints. Their dogmatism and certainty are scary and dangerous to the foundations of a free society. They cluster under the protective banner of the First Amendment, ignoring the fact that it at least implies a sense of responsibility.

Supreme Court Justice Oliver Wendell Holmes, Jr., opined that the First Amendment, at its most basic level, does not give a person the right to "shout fire in a crowded theater." Later, Chief Justice Warren Burger noted dryly that the same principle applies even if the theater is largely empty. With Limbaugh's audience of approximately 25,000,000 comes an unprecedented level of arrogance and mean-minded, destructive rhetoric meant not only to wound, but to destroy perceived foes of the conservative movement.

As a former editor and publisher of community newspapers, I would not suggest the press giants are above reproach—far from it. They can be infuriating and grossly irresponsible at times, as well as shoddy in their attention to high principle. Nor by any means are the TV networks exemplary, as they jostle for ratings and profits by exploiting violence, sex, and all things sensational. Largely gone are the days when the likes of Edward R. Murrow, Chet Huntley, and Walter Cronkite were dominant, rational, even-handed, and widely respected.

Still, there remains among the mainstream media a certain compelling instinct for some measure of fairness. If you or I are slandered on TV, we usually can get our face and view before a camera within hours. If we are attacked in the press, the offending paper probably will carry a rebuttal, apology, or letter to the editor. That won't necessarily undo the damage, but it may assuage the hurt to some degree. That is not generally so with most staunchly conservative media outlets.

In 1994, for example, former Delaware governor and onetime presidential aspirant Pete duPont wrote a "Conservative Manifesto" for *National Review,* where he serves as chairman of the National Review Institute. Included was a section on crime and punishment that was a draconian rehash of failed, counterproductive programs incredibly expensive to taxpayers, a pitch for "tough on crime," but counter to the conservative mission of reduced Federal spending. As a longtime member of the Board of Directors of the National Council on Crime & Delinquency, I responded with a point-by-point rebuttal letter to the editor. I received a gracious response from duPont, but *National Review* adamantly refused to publish my letter.

My experience with *The Wall Street Journal*'s editorial page is similar. The paper often buries input that takes issue with some of editor Robert Bartley's favorite conservative nostrums.

Such, of course, is the prerogative of Buckley and Bartley. However, they express outrage when perceived "liberal" bias creeps into a news story in a major daily, such as *The New York Times, Washington Post, Los Angeles Times, San Francisco Chronicle, Philadelphia Inquirer, St. Louis Post-Dispatch, Atlanta Journal and Constitution, Milwaukee Journal, Minneapolis Star Tribune,* or *Boston Globe.*

They seem to ignore the fact that a sizeable majority of the nation's daily newspapers endorsed Ronald Reagan and George Bush in three consecutive presidential elections. Thus, the blanket "liberal media" charge has a hollow ring when such conservative ideologues as press lords Rupert Murdoch and Conrad Black, Jack Welch of General Electric (owner of NBC), and other deep-pocket owners control so much of the nation's press capacity and airtime. Certainly, the *Chicago Tribune* can't be categorized as "liberal." There are many others that simply don't fit the pejorative term of "liberal press," used relentlessly by the Limbaughs and Buckleys, but they drum it home anyway.

> **❝ What the conservatives deride as 'liberal' are, for the most part, those mainstream daily newspapers that, whatever their editorial positions, attempt to provide some semblance of balance in their coverage. ❞**

What is most worrisome is the carefully orchestrated frontal attack on the mainstream media by a band of zealots whose unabashed aim is to destroy their credibility and influence. The ultimate effect is to sow seeds of doubt in the public mind; to narrow—not broaden—rational national debate, and thus widen the chasm that separates Americans from one another.

"Freedom to differ is not limited to things that do not matter much," Supreme Court Justice Robert H. Jackson said in 1943. "That would be a mere shadow of freedom. The test of its substance is the right to differ as to things that touch the heart of the existing order."

If it is necessary to differ, it is a time to do so in a spirit of civility, reason, and good-will, rather than unbending rancor and arrogant certainty as the urgent issues of these troubled times are debated. Americans must bridge what writer Studs Terkel has called "the great divide" if they are to approach full potential for decency and greatness.

For all its faults, foibles, prejudices, excesses, and its sometimes resort to baser instincts, Americans should thank God for the free press that is denied most of the world's peoples. Neither the press nor other avenues of communications are truly free when they promote—under government fiat or their own free will—rigid conformity, an "official" doctrine, or a "party line." It only occurs when they provide accurate, complete, balanced news and information, which give a citizen, as the *Times'* Sulzberger put it so aptly, "the chance to be right."

We should be thankful, too, that our early leaders had the wisdom and foresight to give us the First Amendment, thus protecting even those who abuse and misuse its protective cloak. It is our duty to be vigilant against every assault on that right so vital to preserving our liberty.

Journalist Max Lerner wrote in 1949: "The problem of freedom in America is that of maintaining a competition of ideas, and you do not achieve that by silencing one brand of idea." What is more important in a free society than safeguarding, continually advancing, and guaranteeing "a competition of ideas"?

Heeding the Call

PAUL STAROBIN

Too many scribes have criticized what they didn't understand, but nowadays, it pays for a journalist to have at least a passing familiarity with the ideals—and mavens— of conservatism. Are media types liberal? Yes, but the times, they are a-changin'.

A tip for job-hunting journalists: Bone up on Adam Smith and put down that volume by John Kenneth Galbraith. If you want to work at a place such as *Time* magazine or *The Wall Street Journal*, you'd better display an open-minded comprehension of the ideas that animate conservatism.

When liberalism held sway in national political life, a knowledge of conservative thinking maybe wasn't so important. But as Bob Dylan might say, the times, they are a-changin'.

"We're interested in what's new and fresh and interesting, and a helluva lot of what's new and fresh and interesting is conservative ideas," Dan Goodgame, *Time*'s Washington bureau chief, said. "We've got to have people who are not just open to that but fascinated by that— eager to report on it," he said, adding that he has rejected applicants who had impressive writing skills but "seemed sure that there were government programmatic solutions to problems and that what the Republicans were talking about wasn't worthy of consideration."

"I have never asked someone how they vote, but I am interested in how they approach problems, whether it's the environment or health care," Alan Murray, chief of *The Wall Street Journal*'s Washington bureau, said. "Do you end up with people who have a tendency to be more sympathetic toward government-oriented solutions and perhaps less aware of, less conscious of, market-oriented solutions? That's something I try to be conscious of."

In the waning days of his presidential campaign, GOP nominee Robert Dole repeatedly accused the national press corps of an inveterate liberal bias. Most journalists, and even many conservative political operatives, discounted the assault as a desperate tactic by a drowning politician.

But while it's a stretch to hold the press responsible for Dole's demise, top Washington news executives widely agree that a liberal bias, often coupled with an ignorance of conservatism, is a real problem for the national press corps—a problem that tends to crop up mostly, often not even consciously, in coverage of policy issues, particularly those with a cultural dimension. And the journalists say it's especially important to address this matter at what may be the dawn of a new era of conservatism, marked by a Republican hold on Congress that is likely to endure at least until the elections in 2000.

Bureau chiefs aren't advocating ideological litmus tests for new hires or affirmative action for conservative-leaning applicants. They stress that many Washington reporters whose personal preferences may lean to the liberal have demonstrated a fair, open-minded attitude toward coverage of conservative policies and politicians. Anyway, plenty of reporters are agnostic sorts, lacking any firm ideological beliefs. Their bosses fret at least as much about attitudinal problems, such as cynicism, that have nothing to do with ideology.

Nevertheless, senior journalists in management slots are worried about the consequences of a Washington press corps with ingrained values and preferences that stand in sharp contrast to the

Staff members at Time objected to this 1994 cover.

nation's at large. And a smug or complacent liberal perspective, they say, is sometimes part of a larger mind-set that includes hostility toward, or a lack of understanding about, the ways of life in big patches of the country.

"I don't want someone who thinks going to church twice a week is aberrant behavior," *Time*'s Goodgame said. "While it may be in Cleveland Park (D.C.) or pick-your-own Washington suburb, it's not in the rest of the country."

Doyle McManus, Washington bureau chief of the *Los Angeles Times,* said his main concern has been a long-standing "cultural gulf" between the public and "disproportionately liberal-Democratic-secular-humanist reporters." Because mainstream news organizations were "out of touch" with "a whole sphere of American society," he said, they were slow to notice such things as the growing influence of the Religious Right in the Republican Party.

"Do I think it would be a good thing to have more reporters with a conservative sensibility?" McManus asked. "You bet."

Not least, greater ideological diversity might curtail such harsh attacks as *Time*'s Dec. 19, 1994, cover featuring an illustration of House Speaker Newt Gingrich, R-Ga., as "Uncle Scrooge." The cover line declared: " 'Tis the season to bash the

poor. But is Newt Gingrich's America really that heartless?" Former managing editor James R. Gaines used the caricature over the objections of *Time* staff members who argued that it unfairly assumed that anyone who wanted to reform welfare was a bad person.

"Gingrich never recovered from the way he was stigmatized immediately after the November 1994 elections," Paul West, the Baltimore *Sun*'s Washington bureau chief, said. "I think he has a legitimate gripe that he was portrayed in a way that planted a negative picture in the public's mind. . . . These things are very complicated, but those portrayals of Gingrich allowed the Democrats and Clinton to demagogue the 'medi-scare' issue" in the 1996 elections, West said.

But now, in a sign that maybe the laws of the free market apply even to the national press corps, journalists at conservative publications are in demand. David Brooks, a senior editor of *The Weekly Standard*, is the target of "a bidding war," a Washington newspaper bureau chief said, and there are other magazine staff members who have caught the eye of bigwig editors elsewhere. What's more, *The Standard*'s editor, Republican guru William Kristol, is a hot property—he recently signed a two-year contract to serve as a political news consultant for ABC News.

Those who welcome ideological diversity as a healthy sign point out that back in the 1970s and '80s, a number of journalists joined big-time news organizations such as *Newsweek* from the ranks of the neoliberal *Washington Monthly* magazine, edited by Charles Peters.

Meanwhile, CBS News recently signed up conservative polemicist Laura Ingraham as a commentator and consultant. Al Ortiz, the network's Washington bureau chief, said, "You want a large news organization, I wouldn't say to reflect the composition of the country, but to have a feel for many of the opinions and views of the country." And these days, "the country is by and large conservative and cautious," he observed. Ingraham is also an analyst for the MSNBC cable news network.

Let's not overstate job prospects for conservatives in top-echelon journalism, however. A Washington editor for a prominent news organization said he would never hire anyone from *The Washington Times,* the aggressively conservative daily. "I find that their bias creeps into their news judgment too often," the editor said.

BLIND SPOTS

It's not just the complaints of Dole (and Gingrich, for that matter) that have put the liberal-bias issue on the map. A survey by the Roper Center for Public Opinion Research Inc. released earlier this year found that 89 per cent of Washington's congressional reporters voted for Bill Clinton in 1992. Moreover, 61 per cent of the reporters identified themselves as either "liberal" or "liberal to moderate," and 62 per cent agreed that their role "is sometimes to suggest potential solutions to social problems."

Quarrel with those numbers if you wish, but surveys going back to 1936 have consistently identified liberalism as the reigning political philosophy of the national press corps. What's changed is that liberalism is less popular with the public, thus widening the ideology gap between the deliverers and the consumers of the news. It's OK for journalists "sometimes to suggest potential solutions to social problems," but the exercise probably works best when the suggesters and the public occupy common philosophical ground. (*See box*, "Liberal at Least Since FDR.")

Moreover, a Roper Center poll in September found that two-thirds of voters disagreed with the statement that the press was providing "unbiased accounts" of the campaign—and among those who perceived an ideological bias, a big majority said it ran in favor of Democrats. Two-thirds of self-identified liberal voters, but only one-third of conservatives, said there was "a balance" to coverage.

"It's horrible," the *Journal*'s Murray said of public distrust of the news media on ideological grounds. "Credibility is what we trade on."

One reason for the distrust, no doubt, is a long-standing, broad-brush effort by conservative media-watchdog activists to portray the mainstream press as a liberal, Democratic organ. Back in the early 1970s, the Nixon White House helped to launch that effort, according to memos recently released by the National Archives. By targeting media celebrities such as Peter Jennings, the urbane ABC News anchor, conservative advocacy groups have found they can raise money just as liberal groups raise funds by painting Gingrich as a devil. *(For more on conservative media-watchdog groups, see box, "There Are Watchdogs and There Are Watchdogs.")*

In fact, political coverage is probably less liberally tinged now than it was, say, 25 years ago, when journalism was enriched by *Doonesbury* types in tune with the countercultural vibes of Woodstock.

These days, the typical Washington journalist is apt to wear subdued business attire and carry a briefcase. For this crowd, "weed" is what you remove from the garden, not what you put into a pipe.

"I rarely detect any bias at *The Washington Post*," *The Weekly Standard*'s Brooks said. National Public Radio? "I used to find them liberal. Now I find their political coverage very straight," Brooks, a regular commentator on the radio network, said.

ABC News certainly doesn't lack ideological diversity. Chief White House correspondent Brit Hume is an out-of-the-closet conservative—"Brit has on occasion pointed things out to us" with respect to how conservatives think, Robin Sproul, the network's Washington bureau chief, said. Consultant Kristol is solicited for story ideas. And, of course, there's the ubiquitous George F. will, a regular on the Sunday talk show *This Week* and on other ABC programs.

Nor is there any shortage of conservative commentary in opinion circles. *The Washington Post* op-ed page features such conservative voices as *Newsweek*'s Robert J. Samuelson, James K. Glassman and syndicated columnists Charles Krauthammer and Robert Novak, in addition to Will. There are fewer liberals writing regularly for *The Post*'s page. And the conservative yakkers on *The McLaughlin Group* sometimes outnumber the liberals ones.

Dole's complaints notwithstanding, few conservatives really believe that liberal media bias was an important factor in his defeat. Asked shortly before the election how many percentage points "liberal media bias" was costing Dole in the polls, Brooks replied, "Probably none."

True, the nonpartisan Center for Media and Public Affairs in Washington found that 50 per cent of major television networks' campaign stories on Clinton were "positive" in tone, compared with 33 per cent of stories on Dole.

But the press jumped all over allegations that Democrats had illegally raised funds from foreign sources. For example, on Oct. 29, the lead segment on the nightly news shows of ABC, CBS and NBC featured the Democratic National Committee's having to back down from its refusal to disclose to the Federal Election Commission a list of contributors. NBC anchor Tom Brokaw warned of this "alarming" development; CBS gave airtime to Republican National Committee chairman Haley Barbour's unproven accusation that Democratic fund raisers were "openly, blatantly, flagrantly violating the law."

The scandal, which the *Los Angeles Times* and other news organizations broke, may well have helped the Republican Party retain its control of Congress and kept Clinton from winning a majority of the vote.

The press was adhering to traditional norms: Just about any whiff of scandal is exciting to journalists; it matters little whether the target is a Republican or a Democrat.

Policy coverage is another matter. In the Washington milieu, editors say, beat reporters too often do not view with sufficient skepticism activist-federal-government approaches to such problems as dirty streams or inadequate health insurance coverage.

Referring to over-all press coverage, not to his own newspaper's, Murray said that "there does seem to be among environmental reporters a certain greenness that's evident in their copy," and "it seems to me that there was a fair amount of sympathy" among Washington reporters for Clinton's 1993 health care reform plan.

Political journalist Ronald Brownstein of the *L.A. Times* said there is a "reflexive" tendency within the press corps to equate spending on government social programs with "compassion."

This can result in portrayals of conservatives as defiant, mean-spirited types. Brooks said a photographer's insistence that he pose for a *New York Times Magazine* picture with his arms folded across his chest upset him because it made him look "smug and menacing." (The photographer, Joseph Pluchino, said, "I just did it because he is a short little guy, and with his arms hanging low, he looks stumpy.")

Editors widely agree that the biggest problem area on the bias front is coverage of social-policy issues—the stuff clus-

tered around the "values" agenda that constitutes the battleground of the nation's "culture wars." This includes abortion, school prayer, affirmative action, welfare reform, standards for educational textbooks, gay rights and the regulation of movies, music and other aspects of popular culture.

Mostly, the bias is of the blind-spot variety—sins of omission, not commission, whether it's a good story that is never pursued, and perhaps not even conceived, or a source never interviewed. "That's where a lot of the bias exists—in not taking seriously enough conservative approaches to governmental or societal problems," *Time*'s Goodgame said. This problem tends to surface in analytical and interpretive reporting, a genre increasingly in vogue in the age of around-the-clock bulletins from cable news services.

Plain ignorance, coupled with mental sloth, can also be a factor—in 1993, after a *Post* national reporter characterized followers of the Religious Right as "largely poor, uneducated and easy to command," the newspaper hastily issued a correction stating that "there is no factual basis for that statement." But the correction was printed following an outcry from Religious Right groups—what's remarkable is that the declaration managed to slip through *The Post*'s editing screen in the first place.

And when the Republicans seized Congress in 1994, many Washington journalists were unfamiliar with pivotal figures in the conservative movement, such as strategist Grover G. Norquist. A bigwig daily newspaper reporter called *National Journal* in a frantic search for information about the libertarian Cato Institute. For too many Washington journalists, the experience was akin to the late anthropologist Margaret Mead's voyage to Samoa. In part, of course, the ignorance reflected the fact that Republicans had been out of power in the House for 40 years—but it also was testimony to the press corps's dearth of conservative-movement acquaintances in town.

Journalists pride themselves on writing about outrages. But what is outrageous to a Washington journalist might not be outrageous to a truck driver in Michigan, and vice versa. Consider this pair of blind-spot examples:

● Clinton's affirmative action policies: In the Oct. 17 presidential debate in San Diego, Clinton bragged, "I've done more to eliminate programs—affirmative action programs—I didn't think were fair and to tighten others up than my predecessors have since affirmative action's been around."

In fact, Clinton's changes to the government's affirmative action policies have been exceedingly modest—he has elimi-

THERE ARE WATCHDOGS AND THERE ARE *WATCHDOGS*

The press needs to guard against a liberal bias, but let's not forget this: For conservative partisans, the bias rap is a handy tool for cultivating grassroots support and trying to block unwelcome coverage.

It's been that way at least since the first Nixon Administration, when Vice President Spiro T. Agnew got great mileage out of his alliterative charge that the press corps consisted of "nattering nabobs of negativism" (a line written by Nixon speechwriter William Safire, now a *New York Times* columnist).

The Nixon White House, in fact, was enmeshed in efforts to promote the activities of conservative media-watchdog groups, including Accuracy in Media (AIM), a Washington-based group founded in 1969 by Reed Irvine, at that time an aide at the Federal Reserve Board.

"I realize that we can't do too much for AIM in the way of money, but don't you think we could recruit top names?" Nixon White House aide Charles W. Colson asked of fellow staff member Peter M. Flanigan in a Jan. 6, 1971, memo recently released by the National Archives. "They really perform yeoman services for us and are gaining in stature and effectiveness," Colson said of AIM.

And on April 11, 1972, Colson told Nixon chief of staff H.R. (Bob) Haldeman of efforts to work with conservative groups to develop a guide for tracking network television news coverage: "We think we're on the verge . . . of having a pretty effective apparatus for discovering bias (as if we needed any help), documenting the case and then making the complaint and generating the publicity desired," Colson wrote.

Irvine, who's still chairman of AIM, said that his group didn't receive funds from the Nixon Administration and that he was unaware of any efforts by the Nixon White House to steer private funds to his group, which is backed by conservative philanthropists.

These days, the lead dog in targeting the press for liberal bias is the Alexandria (Va.)-based Media Research Center, a tax-exempt group run by Brent Bozell, a nephew of conservative guru William F. Buckley Jr. and finance director for Patrick J. Buchanan's 1992 presidential campaign. The center has an annual budget of some $4 million; it has drawn support from conservative sources, including the John M. Olin Foundation and Thomas L. (Dusty) Rhodes, president of *National Review*.

Founded in 1987, Bozell's shop tapes and transcribes the major television networks' morning and evening news shows each day—and then pores through the material looking for anything suggestive of favoritism toward liberals or antagonism toward conservatives. Often, they don't find much—a sensational nonpolitical event, such as an earthquake, can mean a long stretch of thin gruel for the bias monitors. Nevertheless, this has become a crusade, and a career, for a fair number of people. And they are pretty good at soundbites of their own.

"One of the most frightening sentences in the English language is, 'More people get their news from ABC News than any other source,' " said Tim Graham, a former Republican congressional aide who's the associate editor of *MediaWatch*, a newsletter that features such departments as the Janet Cooke award, "to distinguish the most outrageously distorted news story of the month. (Cooke, remember, was the *Washington Post* reporter whose Pulitzer prize-winning story on a young heroin addict turned out to be a fake.)

Are the media really all that demonically liberal? Graham, who conceded in an interview that "certainly it's harder today to lament an exclusion of conservative ideas" in the press, replied: "You have to understand that we are serving an audience of people. . . . I'm not saying we're lying to them," he said of *MediaWatch*'s subscribers, but "when we write that newsletter, it is partly to create that sense of outrage. . . . We have fun with this."

Fun? When Graham last year called CBS News's Washington correspondent Eric Engberg to present him with a Janet Cooke award for a piece on conservative efforts to "defund" the Left, Engberg barked, according to Graham, "I'm watching you like a hawk, you lying little worm."

It's true. "I did call him a lying little worm," Engberg said in an interview, also confirming that he has studied the tax records of Bozell's group and has baited Graham about drawing a low salary. "One of my beats at CBS is what I call the reptile beat—keeping track of political dirty-tricks operators," he said. Engberg, whom CBS colleague Bernard Goldberg once castigated for liberally biased reporting, also made available to *National Journal* the memos he had obtained from the National Archives on the Nixon White House's promotion of conservative media-watchdog activities.

Although groups such as Bozell's are plainly motivated by politics, many editors say that the bias-watch effort can be effective. In response to persistent complaints, news organizations including the *Los Angeles Times* stopped referring to Republican efforts to overhaul medicare as "cuts" and started calling them "reductions in future growth in spending." *Wall Street Journal* Washington bureau chief Alan Murray, who believes that "cuts" is the accurate term, said the watchdogs have "mau-maued" the press.

Tim Graham of Media Research Center's MediaWatch Duke poster models center's send-up of TV anchors.

Meanwhile, broad-brush criticism by watchdog groups has helped spark just the sort of public backlash against the mainstream news media on which the Nixon White House was banking. Shortly before the November elections, a conservative press basher took to the "chat room" of the Media Research Center's World Wide Web site to call for a national boycott of "the basically useless news media."

Agnew must be chuckling in his grave.

nated not "programs" but only one program—a small one at the Pentagon that set aside certain contracts for minority-owned businesses.

Conservatives sharply opposed to affirmative action are infuriated that the President has been taking political credit for such minor changes. But the mainstream press has not been pounding at the door of the Administration to check on how aggressively Clinton has moved, in his words, "to mend" affirmative action. The day after the debate, *The Washington Post* devoted an article to facts stretched by the contestants, but Clinton's affirmative action boast was not mentioned.

And *The Post* has plenty of company. An Administration official familiar with press inquiries on this topic said he was not aware of any reporter's asking whether Clinton had done more than his predecessors to curtail affirmative action. Reporters who see themselves as fierce government watchdogs in this instance look more like napping puppies.

● Wal-Mart's pop-music standards: In this case, a big newspaper seemed outraged by a development that a lot of people may not find outrageous. In a page-one, above-the-fold story on Nov. 12, *The New York Times* reported, as the headline declared, "Wal-Mart's CD Standards Are Changing Pop Music." Noting that Wal-Mart Stores Inc. is the nation's largest seller of pop music, pop/jazz reporter Neil Strauss wrote that the retail chain's "refusal to stock albums with lyrics or cover art that it finds objectionable"—coupled with the alteration of albums by the music industry to meet Wal-Mart's standards—"has long been a frustration for some customers, musicians and record-industry executives."

The piece quoted, in order, a 13-year-old who said he didn't like Wal-Mart's policy; his mother, who said that it was her job, not Wal-Mart's, to regulate her son's listening tastes; and film director Oliver Stone, who darkly warned of "a new form of censorship that's coming into being in this country."

Although *The Times* noted that "not every parent" is opposed to Wal-Mart's policy, there was not a single quotation from any such parent or from anyone else, other than a Wal-Mart spokesman who defended the chain's policy.

There was virtually nothing in the piece, in short, indicating that there probably is a substantial stratum of opinion in America in favor of what critics may view as a free-expression violation but what supporters view as long-overdue steps by American business to implement "family-values" policies.

In the days after the article was published, retiring Sen. Sam Nunn, D-Ga., applauded the Wal-Mart policy—"We as Americans cannot remain cheerfully neutral on fundamental questions of right and wrong," he said—and Religious Right columnist Cal Thomas wrote that "Wal-Mart deserves the support of everyone who is tired of garbage-peddlers masquerading as descendants of the Founding Fathers."

Meanwhile, former federal Judge Robert H. Bork has written a hot best-seller, *Slouching Towards Gomorrah* (No. 3 on *The Times Book Review*'s list the day the newspaper's story on Wal-Mart appeared), that devotes a chapter to "the case for censorship" of such things as "the more degenerate lyrics of rap music." Why

LIBERAL AT LEAST SINCE FDR

OK, what about The Poll—you know, that famous finding that a whopping 89 per cent of Washington's congressional journalists voted for Bill Clinton in 1992?

A lot of scribes insist that number is just way too high. Well, it is high, but it's also in the ballpark of surveys of this sort that go back 60 years.

Here's the deal. For a study on relations between Congress and the press, the Freedom Forum media studies center in Arlington, Va., retained the Roper Center for Public Opinion Research Inc., a respected outfit based at the University of Connecticut (Storrs), to conduct a survey of congressional correspondents.

The Freedom Forum provided the Roper Center with a list of 350-odd reporters covering Congress for mainstream print, television and radio news organizations ranging from the Associated Press to NBC News. Not included were opinion pundits or talk-radio hosts. The Roper Center drew a random sample of 225 journalists from this list, to whom it sent a self-administered questionnaire that included the for-whom-did-you-vote query. (In its published description of the survey, the Freedom Forum erroneously said the questionnaire was sent to "all" Washington-based bureau chiefs and congressional correspondents.)

The Roper Center got back 139 completed questionnaires, on which the 89-per-cent-for-Clinton number is based. George Bush got 7 per cent, Ross Perot got 2 per cent and "other" got 2 per cent. (Among all voters, Clinton got 43 per cent, Bush got 37 per cent and Perot got 19 per cent.) The survey's maximum sampling error for a sample of this size is plus-or-minus 2.8 per cent. In an interview, Kenneth Dautrich, the center's associate director, said, "It was done well. . . . I haven't had to ward off any methodological attacks on the survey."

And it's unlikely there are any significant flaws. Yes, the number for Bush is quite low, but as media analyst S. Robert Lichter noted in a recent article in the now defunct *Forbes Media Critic* journal, "No Republican presidential candidate has polled more than 27 per cent of the votes cast by any sample of prominent journalists since 1960, a period that included landslide victories by Richard Nixon in 1972 and Ronald Reagan in 1984."

The public voted 61 per cent for Nixon and 38 per cent for George McGovern in 1972; the Washington press corps voted 73 per cent for McGovern and 27 per cent for Nixon, according to a joint survey of some 150 Washington correspondents by Harvard University and *The Washington Post*.

Even when liberalism was at its apex among the masses, the national press was more to the left than the public. Back in 1936, 64 per cent of Washington correspondents backed the reelection of Franklin D. Roosevelt, and 6 per cent favored a Socialist Party or Communist Party candidate, according to a survey by sociologist Leo Rosten. A Gallup Organization Inc. poll taken at the same time as the survey found that 50 per cent of the public backed FDR's reelection and 2 per cent favored a left-wing candidate; FDR won with 62 per cent of the vote.

Studies of this sort generally find that the Washington press corps is more liberal than are the news media as a whole. A separate Roper Center survey of 100 editors from some 1,400 daily newspapers across the nation found a vote of 60-22 per cent for Clinton over Bush in 1992, with 4 per cent for Perot. Well, 60 per cent is a lot lower than 89 per cent. No wonder Republicans keep talking about aiming their message "beyond the Beltway."

quote only Stone and not also a Bork, a Ralph Reed or a William J. Bennett?

Blind-spot liberal bias is partly explained by what *Time* magazine's Goodgame called the "experiential bias" in the national press corps—the underparticipation of journalists in the sorts of institutions that traditionally hatch a fair number of conservatives, including the military and the police.

Also, survey research strongly suggests that journalism has traditionally attracted folks of a liberal, social-reformist bent. In America, the anti-establishment tradition of Progressive Era muckrakers has long been a source of romance and inspiration for many wanna-be reporters. David Halberstam spoke for a good many who entered the craft when he wrote, in 1981, that he "believed deeply" that "journalism had a crucial role as the societal conscience of last resort."

But in today's age, a rebellious ethos may be fertile soil for a cadre of conservative-leaning journalists. Many young conservative scribes worked at ideologically tinged college newspapers that were viewed with deep suspicion on campus. These journalists also view themselves as anti-establishment—it's just that they cast their irreverent eye toward such institutions as big government and big labor.

UPTOWN JOURNALISTS

A liberal bent is certainly not the national press corps's only flaw. Many veteran journalists think the most worrisome problem is an insular, urban, upper-class perspective, fostered by the transformation of journalism over the past few decades from a relatively low-paying, low-status craft to a remunerative, high-status profession.

"I do often think, 'What does the media lose by not having in its reporter ranks more people who come from a blue-collar background, more people who come from a rural background?' " said Bruce Drake, managing editor of National Public Radio News and formerly an editor of *The Daily News* in New York City. "That kind of cultural perspective is much more on my mind as a concern than liberal bias is."

On trade issues, economic populists often accuse the mainstream press of having little patience for the argument that free trade can be harmful to working-class communities.

And in a recent *American Lawyer* cover story, Stuart Taylor Jr. said that "class bias," in part, explained "the mainstream media's manifest disdain" for Paula Jones, the Arkansas woman who has sued Clinton for sexual harassment. In 1994, *Newsweek* Washington bureau chief Evan Thomas described Jones on a television talk show as "some sleazy woman with big hair coming out of the trailer parks." He subsequently apologized for this "elitist" remark.

This sort of problem won't be ameliorated by the hiring of journalists from conservative publications such as *The Standard*. Their backgrounds are pretty much the same as those of the folks who work at *The New York Times*—Kristol is a former professor at Harvard University's John F. Kennedy School of Government who grew up in the intellectual salons of Manhattan; Brooks was raised in Greenwich Village and attended the University of Chicago.

These journalists represent, perhaps, a counterelite, but as conservative media critic Terry Eastland said, "Many of these elites have more in common with each other than they think they do." Conservative presidential hopeful Patrick J. Buchanan's angry broadsides against Wall Street and big business in the GOP primaries appalled *The Standard*—"Voters need to be told that things are good," it declared in a March 4 editorial.

Other press critics say the biggest problem with Washington journalism is not elitism or ideological bias but a reflexive cynicism that produces a "gotcha" obsession with scandal and endless scrutiny of the motives of political decision makers. The problem is not that the press is "liberal"—it's that reporters are "cantankerous," White House press secretary Michael D. McCurry said.

Cynicism, which is endemic in journalism, is certainly worth addressing. But the liberal-bias problem (and, for that matter, the elitism problem) is probably more fixable. It couldn't hurt to have greater diversity of all sorts, including the ideological mix, within the ranks of Washington's hard-bitten press crew. And maybe it's high time.

Did You Have a Good Week?

The new unit of political significance

James Fallows

When I read the newspaper at home, I always start with sports. But when I've been away for a while and am going through old papers, I find I can flip right past the sports pages. The close games and league races that are so absorbing when they are happening *right now* are boring once the suspense is gone.

More and more, it's the same with the real news. I'm not talking about covering political campaigns as if they were sporting events. This tendency has existed for decades and is well understood. Rather, I mean a development whereby most of the serious news we get is presented with the same artificial, short-lived intensity as sports. Precisely because we know that sports don't matter in a life-and-death sense, we can happily act for a while as if they did. In a few minutes it will all be over, and soon we'll have some other, equally interesting showdown to watch.

Through May and early June of this year, for example, the United States seemed headed toward a nuclear confrontation with North Korea. Numerous reports said that President Bill Clinton had come to his "testing time" and "moment of truth." Of course, the "day of reckoning," as *The Wall Street Journal*'s political analyst Gerald Seib called it, did not come. I interviewed a South Korean diplomat, in Seoul, just after former President Jimmy Carter's visit, and he described the moment when he knew that the crisis had passed.

"It was when the O. J. Simpson car chase began," he said. "As soon as the American media had O. J. to deal with, you could *feel* the weight of CNN and the American pundits come off our shoulders."

North Korea's nuclear program returned to its natural dimensions, as a serious long-term problem but not one that required a response *right now.* By the time the American opinion machine was ready to deal with an issue other than O. J., the Whitewater hearings were at hand, along with the buildup for an invasion of Haiti. North Korea's nuclear rods, it goes without saying, were still there.

The Clinton years have come across as an endless stream of emergencies, each seeming to demand total attention while it is under way, but many forgettable as soon as they are done.

Zoë Baird. Kimba Wood. Travelgate. The haircut on the LAX tarmac. David Koresh and the Waco siege. Document-shredding at the Rose law firm. The death of Vincent Foster. Webster Hubbell. Barbra Streisand at the White House. The secrecy of the health-care task force. Casualties in Somalia. Criticism of Les Aspin and Warren Christopher. The Administration's fights for its political life over the first budget bill, over NAFTA, over the crime bill, over health reform. The showdown with China over human rights and with Singapore over caning. The latest skirmish in the trade war with Japan. Threats of action against Serbia, Haiti, North Korea, Cuba. Paula Jones. Whitewater recusals. Joshua Steiner and his diary. The disasters in Bosnia and Rwanda.,

This list looks preposterously jumbled, and that is the point of it. Some of the events, in the Balkans and Rwanda, were world tragedies. Others, involving the Branch Davidians and Vincent Foster, were tragic on a smaller scale. Some—including the budget plan, health care, and NAFTA—will play a part in any ac-count of the Clinton years. Others were temporary flaps, including quite a few whose plot lines are difficult to keep straight even now.

Yet every one of these issues, at least for a while, got right-now treatment by the press. We all recognize the signs that an issue has become an Issue: CNN specials, live C-SPAN or NPR hearings coverage, same-day discussion on *Nightline* and *Crossfire*, end-of-the-week wrap-ups on the Washington talk shows.

Journalists claim that they do their jobs by raising questions and looking on skeptically, and that the President and other politicians must do theirs by providing satisfactory answers. This sounds nice. Yet by moving constantly from one emergency to the next, our opinion system has changed the very nature of the political and governmental fight.

For politicians and the public, the struggle is not so much to make or hear convincing arguments. It is to concentrate on anything at all. By the time the Clinton health plan floundered, in August, the conventional wisdom was that the President had waited too long before turning his full attention to it. I wonder why! Hearing about the latest crisis on talk shows and op-ed pages is for the public like living with car alarms in New York: the constant warnings are enough to make you uneasy—but not quite enough to inspire action.

. . .

The right-now atmosphere has had at least two measurable effects, both bad, on the progress of Bill Clinton's Administration. First, it has played a part in the repeated premature obituaries for his presidency issued by the press. In May of last year, when Clinton had served eight percent of a four-year term, Elizabeth Drew was asked on the *McNeil/Lehrer NewsHour* what was at stake in the upcoming House vote on his budget plan. "Nothing less than the Clinton presidency," she replied.

In fairness to her, it was not an overstatement by the standards of the time. Within the month *Time* had published its cover story on "The Incredible Shrinking President," and *Newsweek* had run a cover picture of Clinton with the caption "What's Wrong?" Then David Gergen came to the White House, Clinton was declared to have made a new start, and the obituaries were forgotten—until they were rolled out again later that year and throughout the current one.

Bill Clinton is known to feel that the press is biased against him. Every President since John Kennedy has felt the same way. Maybe, by now, some reporters and columnists do dislike Clinton and his associates. If so, it's a trivial point. The real problem is that so many members of the press are comfortable making overstatements they must know cannot be true.

The other effect has been to add a curious edginess to the public mood. The opinion industry has become a powerful but unacknowledged lobby in behalf of U.S. intervention, for intervention's sake, around the world. On talk shows and TV specials we see a nightmarish sequence of emergencies appearing out of nowhere. Their backgrounds are not explained, and each crowds the others for airtime. The bridge at Gorazde. The Rwandan refugee camps in Zaire. Flotillas from Guantanamo Bay.

The implied message of each of these scenes is "Do something *now!*" The message is conveyed not only by the suffering itself but also by commentators who say that each case is a test of the President's "character" and "decisiveness." Some of the cases may demand immediate American action to relieve suffering. But the game-day mentality of the press has created a general enthusiasm for intervention almost as strong as the post-Vietnam fear of foreign entanglements. The enthusiasm sometimes wears off as an actual commitment nears, as with the intervention in Haiti. But while an Administration is deciding whether and how to get involved, the press chorus is saying, Act now!

▪ ▪ ▪

I keep mentioning the political talk shows because they have been the most important force for turning real news into sports. Some of their effects are obvious. *The McLaughlin Group*, *The Capital Gang*, *Crossfire*, the Sunday-morning talk shows, and the countless local knockoffs of the Washington battling-journalists shows reward reporters for exhibiting all the wrong traits. These talk shows highlight personality rather than work product, opinion and attitude rather than reporting, and prediction—which is less accurate than the bookies' line on games and for which the journalists are less accountable than bookies—instead of analysis of what has actually occurred.

The Fox network and ESPN spend hours each Sunday on the buildup to the day's slate of NFL football games and, when the games are done, dispose of the results in a few minutes. The political talk shows follow the same plan.

Since each of the Washington shows covers more topics than any of the reporters can know about in detail, discussion naturally drifts to the one subject all the reporters do know: the pure mechanics of politics. ("How is Bob Dole likely to respond to this health-reform plan, Cokie?")

But the worst effect of the shows is so profound that it is barely noticed. This is to make the week the fundamental unit of political measurement. The central question on most of the shows is whether the President had a good week or a bad week. Getting a treaty ratified can mean a good week; a Travelgate-style staff shakeup can make a bad week. As in sports, the wins and losses are toted up as if they all had equal weight.

"It is rarely acknowledged, but asking 'Who won the week?' is a political act," Jay Rosen, of New York University, wrote last year in the magazine *Tikkun*. "The question . . . sets a rhythm to politics that permits the media to play timekeeper, umpire and, finally, judge. The question would not occur to an ordinary citizen."

Ordinary citizens, Rosen said, realize that politics concerns values and choices, not simply the up and down of each tactical fight. Will I pay more taxes? What will schools or health care be like? Will the Army have to stay and fight in Haiti or Bosnia? Most journalists recognize these issues, at least in theory. "But in . . . their day-to-day view of the scene," Rosen concluded, they "have accumulated a huge stake in the denial of meaning, the hollowing out of politics into a game of perceptions, to be played inside the media itself." They are, in other words, just playing the game.

The 'New' Media and Politics: What Does the Future Hold?

Doris A. Graber, *University of Illinois at Chicago*

Beyond new technological advances, what makes the 'new' media new? I contend that the chief change brought about by the new media is the empowerment of media users. They now have greater control over incoming and outgoing messages, and their ability to contact literally millions of people has grown exponentially. These changes have sharply increased the need for new communications policies. I also argue that, despite an explosion of available information, the political information diet of average Americans will remain meager.

The Changing Media Landscape

The Growing Information Supply

During the closing decades of the twentieth century, over-the-air networks and cable television systems have multiplied, adding hundreds of broadcasting channels. Satellites carry vast numbers of radio and television programs beamed to customers' backyard satellite dishes. Senders of political messages now have available scores of inexpensive channels for sending customized political messages to diverse

audiences. This is likely to improve the electoral chances of minority candidates and minority parties who can readily tailor their messages to the concerns of selected audiences. The needs and interests of specific audiences, such as groups differing in ethnicity, religious beliefs, or sexual orientation, or groups with special concerns related to their vocations and avocations are more likely to be addressed. Customizing also makes information transmission more effective than when depersonalized news is directed to heterogeneous mass audiences. Computers equipped with modems allow information seekers to gain access to the Internet system, which now carries a huge array of politically relevant messages. Other potentially rich sources for information that computer-literate individuals can tap are electronic mail networks and bulletin boards.

Unfortunately, while a great deal of effort has been devoted to creating new channels for carrying information, attention to the quality and diversity of the political content carried by these channels has lagged. When it comes to serious political information, choices offered by various channels, for the most part, amount to surface,

rather than substance distinctions. Impartial, analytical information about public figures and public policy issues that would improve citizens' ability to appraise the political scene is all-too-scarce. Despite an explosion of politically oriented Home Pages on the World Wide Web, surprisingly little has been added that is genuinely new or that enriches the information supply beyond the offerings of the far smaller circle of 'old' media.

Media User Empowerment

The new media have freed users from the tyranny of the time-clock. Twenty-four-hour news channels and computer news sources now make news available around the clock, rather than at times dictated by media delivery schedules. The rapid spread of home computers has increased the size of audiences who can reach computerized data at times of their choice. Video recorders allow average Americans to preserve particular information packages for use wherever, whenever, and as often as they wish. Eighty-five percent of America's households have at least one video recorder to selectively tape programs or play rented tapes. People can also buy political information

From *PS: Political Science and Politics*, March 1996, pp. 33-36. © 1996 by the American Political Science Association. Reprinted by permission.

stored on audio and video tapes and on CD-ROM.

The new media have also eased the control of professional journalists over the framing and interpretation of the news. Thanks to broadcasts of ongoing events, ready availability of full texts of messages, and interactive talk show broadcasts, people now can watch many happenings in real time, often in their entirety. While the initial choice of events to be broadcast is still reserved for journalists, the second step—editing and framing a story—can now be in news consumers' hands. CNN or C-Span viewers, for example, can make their own interpretations and draw their own conclusions while watching live broadcasts. Subscribers to on-line computer services can download full texts, including pictures, into their home computers. They can edit such information to suit their taste by adding, combining, or deleting data.

For those who like to ask newsmakers their own questions, numerous talk-show programs offer excellent opportunities. Politicians and media audiences like talk shows because most hosts, unlike peevish Washington reporters, allow their guests to present their arguments in their own words and from their own perspectives. Talk shows provide prized opportunities for direct interaction between ordinary folk and political leaders. The candidates' ample use of the talk show format during the 1992 campaign loosened the grip of traditional media over candidate messages. Audiences for talk shows were huge. Bill Clinton's one-hour appearance on *Donahue* was seen by nearly 8 million viewers. Television appearances on Larry King's show were seen by an estimated 2.5 million people. Candidates even appeared on rock-music-oriented MTV where a 1992 candidate forum attracted over 3 million—presumably elusive young American voters in the 18–34 age group. Campaigning on these programs also had a large echo effect. The standard mass media and individual pundits widely reported remarks made during talk shows, thus raising their profile and political significance.

New Political Pressure Tools

Finally, thanks to the new electronic networks, individuals can now inform people worldwide and mobilize them for political action. Individuals and groups eager to spread their political messages no longer depend on media coverage to publicize their appeals. In cyber-

---

While available food for political thought has grown, despite much overlap and redundancy, the appetite for it and the capacity to consume it remain limited. The ceiling for the demand for political information has already been reached for most people.

---

space, a single private citizen can address hundreds of thousands of people via computer from the privacy of his or her home. Additionally, electronic publishing on home computers has vastly boosted the numbers of newsletters that various social, professional, and trade communities can distribute.

By mid-1995, more than 25 million people in the United States— 14% of the adult population—were connected to the Internet; worldwide audiences make the cyberspace community much larger. These numbers have been growing rapidly. However, there is likely to be a growth ceiling because the pool of computer-literate consumers is limited by educational, economic, and technical constraints. Projecting current user figures into the future, based on the demographic characteristics of the computer literate population, it seems unlikely that the majority of Americans will be cyberspace users in the foreseeable future.

The Current Impact of New Media

What difference have the new media made thus far in the political lives of average Americans and what does the future portend? Unfortunately, information transmission capacity has vastly exceeded use. While available food for political thought has grown, despite much overlap and redundancy, the appetite for it and the capacity to consume it remain limited. The ceiling for the demand for political information has already been reached for most people. The interest in talk shows recorded during the 1992 presidential campaign does not represent a major permanent spike in political interest and news consumption. Rather, it reflects a revived appetite for political fare when appealing formats compete with the current disliked offerings.

Unlike talk shows, political information available in cyberspace presents major challenges to the intellectual skills of information consumers. The fact that millions of American adults still are functionally illiterate when it comes to reading printed materials does not bode well for looking to a future when computer literacy will reach 90%. In practice, cyberspace riches are available only to individuals with superior education and financial resources. These are the publics who already participate far more in politics than their less privileged fellow citizens. As technology continues to evolve, the knowledge gap between the information privileged and the information underclass is likely to grow. Since knowledge means power, an information-deprived class is likely to suffer other power deprivations. It cannot readily avail itself of Internet resources that empower interest groups to use the information superhighway to organize and lobby for their causes. Hence the influence of educationally and economically privileged groups on politics, which has always been substantial, may be greatly enhanced. The end result may be a more fragmented polity, making political gridlock more likely.

Reinventing Communications Policy

The multiplication of media, especially the growth of public computer networks, requires a complete rethinking of the scope and purposes of federal regulation of broadcast media. The Communications Act of 1934 was passed because transmission facilities were scarce. Congress wanted to make certain that the limited numbers of available broadcast channels were parceled out equitably and served broad public interests. Printed media were left largely outside the regulatory scheme. The First Amendment to the U.S. Constitution protects their independence from government intrusion. Fifty years later the basic regulatory framework remains intact although its ostensible raison d'être—the scarcity of transmission channels—has largely vanished. Government leaders and industry leaders, aware of the transformation of the communication delivery systems, agree that the 1934 Act must be revised. But there is no agreement on specific plans. Pressures for easing regulations are balanced by pressures to continue and even increase government controls.

Regulatory Options

If the Communications Act of 1934 is put to well-deserved rest, the government has several basic policy options for dealing with the new media system. It can play a hands-off, laissez-faire role, allowing the system to grow according to the push and pull of market forces, with only minor controls to assure that the system operates effectively. Regulation would be limited to safeguards to protect national security, maintain social norms and privacy, and to guard intellectual property rights.

Media channels can also be treated as common carriers, like the telephone or rail and bus lines. Common carrier status makes transmission facilities available to everyone on a first-come, first-served basis. Congress, the FCC and various local governments like the common carrier concept that has been adopted for communications satellites. While court decisions make the power of Congress to impose common carrier features on the communication industry questionable, these decisions do not constrain state and local authorities.

As a third option, the government can confer public trustee status on communication enterprises. This status grants media owners full control over access to their channels, but requires them to meet certain public service obligations. Examples are equal time allotments to proponents and opponents of controversial public policies, or channel time for public and government broadcasts, including broadcasts serving public education, public safety, and medical and social services. The rationale for conferring trustee status on broadcasters lies in the potentially crucial impact that mass media have on American society. Trusteeship status has strong support in the United States and much of the world. Although it runs counter to the basic philosophy on which the American system was built, namely, that communication should be entirely free from government control, it appears to be the frontrunner among the options available as a framework for future communications policy.

Paying the Piper

Whether mass communication facilities are treated like any private enterprise, like a common carrier, or like a trustee, their costs have to be paid. There are several possibilities. The costs can be born by advertisers, by audience payments, by government subsidies, or by various combinations of these funding sources. Currently, advertisers pay the largest share of the nation's mass communication budget, although these costs are passed on to consumers in the form of higher prices. But advertisers' share is shrinking as multiplication of information channels splits audiences into smaller slices that are uneconomical targets for many advertisers.

What seems to be emerging in the new era is a system that is predominantly supported by audience payments. A major social drawback of such a system, which framers of new policies need to consider, is the plight of poor families who cannot afford many of the specialized programs that they need. Inequalities could be reduced through government subsidies but, given budgetary constraints, heavy government subsidies are unlikely. Shortage of public funds also means that the private sector will continue to finance the development of advanced communication networks. The likely consequence is continued emphasis on light entertainment fare that has mass appeal and attracts advertising dollars or user fees, rather than more serious programming.

Hazards in the Information Marketplace

The new technologies have exacerbated a number of serious threats to major public and private interests. The protection of confidential information ranks high on that list. Safeguarding the secrecy of confidential public and private information as well as individual privacy presents major challenges in societies eager to preserve open access to data bases. Despite security codes, astute computer users can assemble scattered bits of information very quickly to gain insights into situations that should remain confidential. Current laws are inadequate to safeguard individual and collective privacy. If they are not revised, the information superhighway may become an Orwellian nightmare where individuals and organizations are exposed to every traveller's inquisitiveness.

The flurry of mergers and acquisitions approved by the government during the 1990s has raised concerns about excessive concentration of control over the public's information supply. Media entrepreneurs who dominate a large share of the information market-place may become mouthpieces for special interests, and financial returns may become their programming lodestar. Many of the megamedia companies involved in these mergers are giant transnational corporations that exercise vast influence over the information tendered to the world's publics. This information shapes important economic and political issues throughout the world. Fortunately, excessive concentration, which leaves the field largely to the giants, has been partly balanced by the lush growth of specialized media, such as local cable television geared to serving particular community interests. Still, current merger policies raise worrisome issues.

Regulations to prevent inappropriate uses of the airways also need to be updated to cope with new problems. Currently, anarchy reigns in the fast-growing web of public and private computer networks that links millions of people around the globe. This state of affairs has allowed crooks to pursue get-rich-quick schemes to defraud the unwary among the hundreds of thousands of people exposed to these messages. Pornography flourishes in places where children can access it readily, while self-appointed censors hunt down messages that they consider offensive and destroy them. However, more effective government rules and regulations to guard against criminal and other antisocial behaviors in cyberspace are not enough. They must be supplemented by a new, more responsible user ethic.

The Outlook for Progress

A look at communication technologies tells us what is possible, but it does not indicate what is likely to happen, particularly in the short run. A number of barriers block the full development of new mass communication technologies. They are political, economic, and social, along with typical patterns of resistance to major innovations

and the tendency to adapt innovations to perpetuate rather than replace old procedures.

In the political arena, partisan and bureaucratic barriers must be surmounted. Many new developments never get off the ground because they are opposed for partisan reasons, or because bureaucracies impose too many regulations to guard against abuses. Frequently, unrealistically high standards are prescribed, raising costs beyond economically feasible levels. The situation is complicated even further when state and local rules are piled on top of federal regulations. Setting requirements for public service and for open-access channels and for service for outlying areas requires controversial political decisions about matters apt to be very expensive. In sparsely populated areas, for example, costs of information services may exceed profits temporarily or permanently. Communication technologies involve large investments; their sudden obsolescence when regulatory agencies approve new technologies may become a crushing financial burden.

Early entrants into a technological field often develop a squatter's mentality about their rights such as access to certain broadcast frequencies or exclusive use of particular technologies. Latecomers to the mass communication field, on the other hand, are eager to reallocate facilities and to introduce even more advanced technologies. If their requests are granted, proven technologies may be sacrificed to new claimants whose prospects for success are uncertain. Meanwhile, technology continues its advance, raising fresh problems that further delay the green light for implementing new systems.

Whatever directions new communications policies take, they will have a profound impact on the directions of American politics generally. Unfortunately, the structure for making communications policy remains fragmented at all government levels and ill-suited to deal with existing problems, to say

nothing of those that must be anticipated. Narrow, short-term issues are addressed, while far-reaching, long-term problems are ignored. Government leaders are unwilling to enter the thickets of communications policy making when so many other battles must be fought. Congress and the Federal Communications Commission (FCC), which oversees the information superhighway, thus far have done little beyond preliminary discussions and studies to cope with the flood of new problems that recent developments have raised. The FCC has not even tackled crucial issues of standardization of technologies so that investments in equipment and training can be kept moderate.

The ultimate prognosis remains clouded. There are bright dreams of high quality diverse information easily available to all travellers on the information superhighway. There are forebodings that the new highway will turn out to be a clone of older routes where the same dreary information cargo makes up most of the freight. And there are nightmares about gridlock, government and private spying on unsuspecting travellers, and propaganda barrages that obscure important facts. Which scenario will emerge? Much hinges on the willingness of industry and government leaders, as well as average citizens, to take control of communications issues to ensure the developments of a sound information system. A do-nothing policy that leaves developments to chance is irresponsible and dangerous.

About the Author

Doris A. Graber is professor of political science at the University of Illinois at Chicago. She has written numerous articles and books on political communication topics including *Verbal Behavior and Politics* (1976), *Processing the News: How People Tame the Information Tide* (1993), *Public Sector Communication: How Organizations Manage Information* (1992), and *Mass Media and American Politics*, 5th ed. (1996). Her forthcoming book, *Virtual Political Reality: Learning About Politics in the Audio-Visual Age*, analyzes the political impact potential of audio-visuals in news broadcasts.

Hillary and us

Rocky relationship with media?
Not really, just no relationship at all

KATHY KIELY AND JANE FULLERTON

Kathy Kiely and Jane Fullerton are reporters in the Washington bureau of the Arkansas Democrat-Gazette.

The scene at the U.S. courthouse in Washington on the chill, January day that Hillary Rodham Clinton testified before the Whitewater grand jury looked like, as one of the shivering, ink-stained wretches standing amidst the inevitable herd outside put it, "O.J. East."

At least 10 television satellite trucks and 27 cameras, along with countless scribes representing newspapers from as far away as Japan, were on hand to record the first lady's brief, innocuous remarks as she entered the building. They were still there more than four hours later to report—Live! in the case of some TV stations—her only slightly less brief, but, if anything, even more innocuous remarks as she exited.

Was ever so much wattage (or, for that matter, so many calories) expended to cover so little news?

It's hard to figure who was made the more miserable by it all: the—according to her own aides—intensely private first lady, for whom the presence of so many cameras and microphones must have seemed a scourge, or the reporters, at least a few of whom ended the day feeling frozen, futile, and nagged by the sense that there must be a better way to protect the public's right to know.

Before all you smug Outside the Beltway-ites start enjoying another good laugh over the mob journalism practiced by your oft-maligned brethren in the Washington press corps, consider our dilemma.

Hillary Clinton is without doubt the most overtly newsy first lady this country ever has had. Yet she's also one of the most elusive, as far as the press is concerned.

There have been lots of presidents' wives before this one who have wielded immense power. Liz Carpenter, who was Lady Bird Johnson's press secretary and who has researched American first ladies, says, "Texas wouldn't be in the union if Julia Tyler [whose husband, John, was the nation's 10th chief executive] hadn't lobbied for it."

Most historians suspect that Woodrow Wilson's second wife, Edith, virtually ran the country when he was enfeebled by a stroke, and we know now that even the assiduously decorative Nancy Reagan oversaw the White House staff and her husband's schedule with an iron hand.

Until now such things have been done in a discreet—or, if you prefer the more sinister view—covert fashion.

To her credit, Hillary Clinton is the first first lady not to sneak around on the American public when it comes to her interests and her influence. Despite the insinuations of her detractors, she is the least Lady Mac-Beth-like of presidential wives. She doesn't coyly play house by day and stealthily plot policy over the First Pillow. From day one of the Clinton administration, she and her husband have made it clear that this first lady is an important player and that she'd have a say over more than what place setting to use at the next state dinner.

In addition, Mrs. Clinton is the first first lady to have been her family's primary breadwinner. Because politicians' finances are something reporters and the public really do have a right to know about—for there is where potential conflict of interest lies—Mrs. Clinton should expect to be subjected to a different kind of scrutiny than any of her predecessors.

Yet despite her ground-breaking role within her husband's administration, Hillary Clinton has broken no new ground in terms of her public accountability.

She clearly believes the press has given the American people a false impression of her. "It's hard to get to know people here simply by watching them or watching them entertain," says Neel Lattimore, a spokesman for Mrs. Clinton. "If you take snapshots of her at any given time, that's what you'll get. But it's a snapshot taken with a cheap camera. We hope reporters will slow down and look at all aspects of her."

But it has been difficult to persuade Hillary Rodham Clinton to sit for a portrait.

Her press relations are not so much rocky as they are non-existent.

In the more than three years since her husband's inauguration, she has had only one news conference—virtually a command performance that was required to explain her controversial dabbling in the futures market.

A veteran White House reporter who not long ago asked a member of Mrs. Clinton's staff when the first lady might hold her next meeting with the press was told: "You'll have to travel with her. She has press conferences when she travels."

Liz Carpenter, who became the first professional news person to work for a first lady when she joined Lady Bird Johnson's staff, was a great believer in using travel to build press relations. In a recent interview,

Carpenter recalled that she organized 47 press trips for Mrs. Johnson, including one in which "85 newswomen—and some newsmen" followed Lady Bird down the Rio Grande in rubber rafts. "I tried to make them fun," Carpenter said of the trips.

It's difficult to imagine anything similar taking place today. Hillary Clinton generally doesn't invite press to travel with her except on foreign trips, prohibitively expensive for all but the flushest news organizations.

For long periods, Mrs. Clinton has remained incommunicado to reporters. She either has been "working on health care policy" or "writing her book" and didn't have time for interviews. Her press staff

> "Yet despite her ground-breaking role within her husband's administration, Hillary Clinton has broken no new ground in terms of her public accountability."

argues that when she broke her latest silence, she made up for it in a big way—giving more than 30 interviews during her two-week book tour.

By giving one blast of, for the most part, 20- to 30-minute interviews after months of not talking at all, the first lady virtually guaranteed she would be asked the same five questions 20 to 30 times.

This gave her plenty of opportunity to polish her answers, but provided the press—and by extension, the American public—with little opportunity to plow new ground, to ask the kind of unexpected question that yields an unrehearsed answer, to learn anything new about this bright, complicated woman who is not only the president's wife but his chief adviser.

Mrs. Clinton's staff complains that the press often treats her superficially. Is this entirely the press' fault? During Mrs. Clinton's book tour, Ellen Warren, a *Chicago Tribune* news reporter with extensive experience covering Washington politics and policy, had her interview request turned

down. The first lady talked to the *Tribune*'s gossip columnist instead.

The contrast with Eleanor Roosevelt couldn't be more stark. Hillary Clinton often cites FDR's first lady as a role model but she has not followed her example of holding regular meetings with the press.

She may be missing a bet. Those who have attended her rare, informal sit-downs with reporters have found Mrs. Clinton to be charming and personable.

Moreover, there are many in the public who are prepared to sympathize with this pioneer of a first lady and the difficulties inherent in the role she is playing. Among the crowd outside the courthouse on the day of Mrs. Clinton's grand jury appearance were a number of well-dressed, middle-aged women.

"Most women—at least those of us who have a few decades on us—know how hard it is to be an assertive woman. And it's still the same for our daughters," says Mandy Wertz, who forsook the comfort of her Arlington home to stand out in the raw mid-winter cold holding up a We-Love-You-Hillary sign the first lady probably couldn't have seen.

Probably no one is more tuned into this potential reservoir of support for Hillary Clinton than the canny Liz Carpenter. "I really feel a sense Hillary is my daughter," Carpenter says. "She's everybody's daughter. She's the young woman who in the '70s walked through the doors that my generation opened."

Here's the irony: So are many of the reporters who cover Washington these days.

Even the most casual survey of the White House briefing room would find many reporters who are, like the first lady, working moms and who must, like the first lady, juggle the demands of a hectic professional life with those of home and family. Or they are married to women who are. (One Sunday during the Persian Gulf War, a male reporter for a major publication that shall remain unidentified had to ask a colleague to cover for him at the White House for a few hours. He had to return home to babysit so his wife could go to work.)

Eleanor Roosevelt, who did so much to promote the careers of the often-ridiculed "news hens" of her day, probably would be delighted by the new generation of Washington reporters—both male and female.

But Hillary Clinton doesn't know them and they really don't know Hillary Clinton.

Wouldn't Eleanor Roosevelt be surprised?

There's history to role of first lady

BY LEWIS L. GOULD

The recent swirl of public controversy about Hillary Rodham Clinton has triggered a renewed journalistic debate about the proper role of presidential wives in American history.

What has received less attention is the part the press itself has played in this century to place the wife of the president in the spotlight. The national debate over Hillary Rodham Clinton arises from her own actions, but the terms of the controversy derive from the historical experience of other first ladies as political celebrities.

Americans are ambivalent about presidential wives. First ladies must perform diverse duties without error and any deviation from perceived standards brings instant criticism. At the same time, the role undergoes constant adjustment as the public's view of women evolves and the presidency itself changes.

In 1902, Edith Kermit Roosevelt hired the first full-time social secretary to manage how Mrs. Roosevelt dealt with the public so the first lady could be an arbiter of good taste and feminine fashion.

Illness kept Helen Taft from fulfilling her dream of being an activist first lady. Ellen Wilson died after only a year and a half in the White House, and Edith Wilson overstepped the implied limits of her position when she screened correspondence and visitors to her sick husband in 1919-20.

Florence Harding had a more feminist emphasis and paid special attention to courting the press about White House activities. Grace Coolidge provided an infusion of glamour and style, making sure the press knew of her extensive patronage for art and culture. Will Rogers called her "chuck plumb full of magnetism" even though her husband prohibited her from making public statements. Lou Henry Hoover was the first presidential wife to speak to radio audiences. She even talked on the record with the newswomen who covered her during public appearances on behalf of the Girl Scouts.

The next major innovations came with Eleanor Roosevelt in 1933. Her news conferences with female reporters, her daily newspaper column, and her frequent public statements made her a national personality in the manner of no previous first lady. Mrs. Roosevelt aroused strong passions from her friends and enemies. The acerbic Westbrook Pegler pursued Eleanor Roosevelt constantly in his newspaper column, and received a flow of "tips" from those who disliked the first lady, including a former White House employee who shared information about Mrs. Roosevelt's "physical life" and the allegations of lesbianism that circulated during the 1930s and '40s.

Bess Truman and Mamie Eisenhower reverted to a more passive form of press relations that suited their dislike of social activism.

Then Jacqueline Kennedy imbued the institution in the early 1960s with glamour and celebrity. With the burgeoning impact of network television and more intense scrutiny of the White House, media attention to the first lady soared. Behind the scenes, it was difficult. Mrs. Kennedy's policy toward reporters, she told an aide, was "minimum information given with maximum politeness." Her term for the female reporters who covered her was "the harpies."

During the next three decades the emphasis on activism reappeared. The first lady's staff looked to the press corps for stories about the social causes that the president's wife sponsored. Lady Bird Johnson's decision to name Liz Carpenter as chief of staff and press secretary marked a crucial step in the bureaucratic evolution of the institution. No longer was the first lady an informal news source.

Pat Nixon was less visible in her public role between 1969 and 1974, but Betty Ford and Rosalynn Carter resumed the activism. Both pushed the boundaries of the institution, and evoked controversy from the public about their willingness to assert themselves on such issues as the Equal Rights Amendment and mental health.

Nancy Reagan's controversial eight years underscored how much the popular expectation of first lady activism had become embedded within the treatment of the news media. Faced with press criticism of her opulent lifestyle during her first year, Mrs. Reagan and her advisers used self-mockery at the 1982 Gridiron Dinner to defuse journalistic attacks and the "Just Say No" campaign against illicit drugs to validate her credentials as a first lady with a real cause. When Mrs. Reagan brought down Donald Regan in 1987, she called up memories of Edith Wilson and comparable indictments from male critics in the press such as William Safire.

Barbara Bush was as adroit with the press as any modern first lady. Despite her dislike and suspicion of the media, as revealed in her diaries, she maintained a level of public approval and applause that often saw her outpacing her husband in the polls. Only at the end of her husband's term did some stirrings occur within the press corps regarding Mrs. Bush's influence at the White House.

For Hillary Rodham Clinton, there was never a honeymoon with the press and now she faces an ordeal of scrutiny and examination unparalleled in the history of presidential wives. The reasons for the difficult relationship between the Clintons and the media defy easy explanation. Some of the tension relates to a press corps permeated with male suspicion of strong, assertive women. On the other side, the Clintons have had a testy relationship with Washington journalists, and the maladroitness and evasiveness of the first lady and her staff have compounded their problems.

First ladies often come to the White House believing the history of the institution is irrelevant to their goals. Reporters covering presidential wives want to know about the history only when the need parallels with contemporary episodes. Neither can escape the experience of the last nine decades.

Lewis L. Gould is Eugene C. Barker Centennial Professor in American History at the University of Texas, where he has taught a course on first ladies since 1982, and is editor of "American First Ladies: Their Lives and Their Legacy."

Products of American Politics

- **Domestic and Economic Policy (Articles 57–63)**
- **Foreign and Defense Policy (Articles 64–66)**

Products refers to the government policies that the American political system produces. The first three units of this book have paved the way for this fourth unit, because the products of American politics are very much the consequences of the rest of the political system. Yet it is not a one-way relationship. Public policies themselves affect the other components of American politics treated in the preceding units of the book.

Dilemmas and difficulties in one policy area often reflect dilemmas and difficulties in others. Indeed, tensions between fundamental viewpoints and values lie at the heart of much public policy making in all spheres: equality vs. freedom, reliance on the public sector vs. reliance on the private sector, collectivism vs. individualism, internationalism vs. isolationism, and so forth. Stating that such conflicts exist hardly resolves them. Nor does everyone agree about which fundamental values or viewpoints are in conflict. Most of us would agree, however, that mere "efficiency" is not all that is at issue in policy making in the American political system.

The health of the American economy is always a prominent policy issue in the American political system. One of the most remarkable consequences of 12 years under Presidents Reagan and Bush was enormous growth in budget deficits and in the national debt. Substantial increases in military spending combined with sizable tax cuts led to annual deficits in the neighborhood of $200 billion during the Reagan presidency (1981–1989). For years many economists said that high rates of inflation and other unwelcome economic consequences were bound to follow. Nevertheless, both inflation and unemployment figures remained within what most observers viewed as tolerable limits, and economic growth continued. During Bush's presidency (1989–1993), problems with the national government's budget and budgetary process continued. Large budget deficits occurred on an annual basis and neither the president nor Congress seemed willing or able to do anything about them. Moreover, the nation's economy had entered a recession by the halfway mark of President Bush's term. Unemployment rates and the nation's overall economic health emerged as serious and prominent public concerns in 1991 after the Persian Gulf War ended. Democratic candidate Bill Clinton emphasized these problems and defeated the incumbent president in November 1992.

As President Clinton began the last year of his first term in office, concerns about economic stagnation and decline in workers' real incomes remained. Moreover, on two occasions in late 1995 and early 1996 nonessential parts of the national government were shut down because Congress and the president had not agreed on relevant budgetary measures for 1996 and beyond. While both sides to the dispute claimed to want to eliminate the budget deficit by the early twenty-first century, they disagreed over how that goal was to be accomplished. In particular, there were differences over what to do about taxes and how to handle social welfare programs such as AFDC (Aid to Families with Dependent Children), Medicaid, and Medicare. In his 1996 reelection campaign, President Clinton maintained that the U.S. economy was once again healthy and that the national government was on the road to a balanced budget. A majority of voters seemed to accept those claims. They returned Clinton to office by a comfortable margin over Republican opponent Bob Dole, while Republicans kept control of both houses of Congress. How and when to balance the national budget will likely remain a much-debated issue during President Clinton's second term.

Domestic public policy usually involves "trade-offs" among competing uses of scarce resources, and during his 1992 campaign Bill Clinton called attention to many such trade-offs in the area of health care. For example, are we as a nation content to spend a greater proportion of our national income on health care than any other industrialized country? If not, are we willing to limit medical spending when that may mean that some sophisticated and sometimes life-saving treatments become less available to middle-class Americans? Do we want to extend medical insurance to those millions of less affluent Americans currently uninsured, even though this might result in higher costs and/or less medical treatment for those who are already insured? As president, Clinton introduced a comprehensive health care reform proposal late in 1993, but neither his plan nor any alternative reform bill was enacted by Congress in the subsequent year. As the 104th Congress was convened under Republican control in 1995, minor reforms seemed possible but by no means certain. Little was done. As the 105th Congress covened in January 1997, the prospects for reform again seemed uncertain.

Other domestic policy areas also involve trade-offs. To what extent should we force the unemployed who are receiving welfare payments to work, and what responsibility should the government take for preparing such citizens for work and ensuring that jobs are available? To what extent should public policy be formulated to redistribute wealth in the United States? Will productivity decline or remain stagnant if public policy fails to maximize profit incentives? How much are cleaner air and other environmental goals worth in terms of economic productivity, unemployment, and so forth? Such trade-offs underlie debate about specific tax policies, social welfare programs, immigration policies, environmental problems, and the like.

For at least 3 decades, the United States and the Soviet Union each had the capacity to end human existence as we know it. Not surprisingly, the threat of nuclear war often dominated discussion of American diplomacy and national security policy making. Yet no nuclear weapons have been exploded in warfare since the United States dropped two atomic bombs on Japan in the closing days of World War II. Since that time, the United States has used conventional forces in a number of military actions— in Korea, Vietnam, Grenada, Panama, and the Persian Gulf area. In 1991 the Soviet Union dissolved into 15 independent republics. This change left the United States as the world's sole remaining superpower and has greatly affected world politics and U.S. foreign policy ever since. Questions about the appropriateness of U.S. intervention in disparate places such as Bosnia-Herzegovina, Somalia, Haiti, and even Russia have been at the forefront of foreign policy concerns since President Clinton assumed office. The threatened proliferation of nuclear weapons in North Korea also posed a difficult problem for the Clinton administration.

The foreign and defense policy process in the United States raises a host of related issues. One of these includes the struggle between legislative and executive branches for control of foreign and defense policy. Conflict between the branches sometimes takes place today in the context of the War Powers Resolution of 1973, which is itself a legacy of the Vietnam War. In 1991 Congress authorized war with Iraq, which was the first time since World War II that there has been explicit and formal congressional approval prior to commencement of military hostilities by the United States. In late 1995 President Clinton committed the United States to sending troops to Bosnia-Herzegovina as part of a multinational peacekeeping force. Despite some opposition in Congress, resolutions supporting the troops were passed. Another issue is the legitimacy of covert action, or at least the degree to which planned covert action by the United States may be kept secret from members of the executive and legislative branches who have responsibilities in the national security area. Finally, there is the recurring question of the relationship between foreign policy and democracy, in particular, how the role of being a superpower in the modern world may undermine some of the essential processes of democracy.

The traditional distinction between domestic and foreign policy is becoming more and more difficult to maintain, since so many contemporary policy decisions seem to have important implications for both the foreign and domestic scenes. The first section contains articles whose primary focus is on domestic and economic policies. The second section treats foreign policy and defense matters. Even so, the distinction is not always clear-cut. President Clinton's emphasis on the connection between domestic and international economic issues in maintaining what he calls national economic security reinforces this point. The North American Free Trade Agreement, passed by Congress at President Clinton's urging in 1993, is an important example of government policy that clearly addresses both domestic and foreign affairs.

Looking Ahead: Challenge Questions

What do you think is the single most important social welfare or economic policy issue facing the American political system today? The single most important national security or diplomatic issue? What do you think ought to be done about them?

What factors increasingly blur the distinction between foreign and domestic policy issues?

How would you compare President Clinton's performance in the areas of social welfare and economic policies with the way he handled national security and diplomatic affairs? What changes has he tried to make in each of these areas?

What policy issues currently viewed as minor matters seem likely to develop into crisis situations?

What do you think is the most significant policy failure of American national government today? The most significant policy success?

What do you think about the idea of devolution, which means giving state and local governments *more* responsibility for policy making and policy implementation and the national government *less*? What reasons are there to expect the state and local governments to do a better—or worse—job than the national government in such areas as welfare and health care benefits for the old and the poor?

Federal Government Mandates

WHY THE STATES ARE COMPLAINING

Martha Derthick

Martha Derthick, formerly director of the Brookings Governmental Studies program, is the Julia Allen Cooper Professor of Government and Foreign Affairs at the University of Virginia. She thanks John Dinan for research assistance.

Hard pressed by recession, state governments have been complaining that Congress keeps passing laws ordering them to undertake expensive new programs—but without providing the money to do so. Complaints about federal mandates are not new. In 1980 New York City Mayor Edward I. Koch wrote bitterly of the "mandate millstone" in an article in *The Public Interest*, giving currency to the term.

The main concern of state officials is political: who will pay the costs of government? But their complaints raise constitutional issues as well. In various ways the Constitution protects the states' existence as governments, having their own elected officials and the power to raise taxes and to enact, enforce, and interpret laws. How far can federal mandates be pushed without infringing on the states' governmental character?

The federal government influences state governments in four main ways—through court decrees, legislative regulations, preemptions, and conditional grants-in-aid. As a quick review will show, all four have grown significantly more coercive in the past half century.

Judicial Decrees

Until the mid-1950s federal courts interpreting the Constitution had habitually told the states what they might *not* do. They had struck down literally hundreds of state laws. But they had refrained from telling states what they *must* do. This changed with school desegregation. In 1955, with *Brown v. Board of Education II*, the Supreme Court gave federal district courts responsibility for entering the orders and decrees to desegregate public schools. The Court's ruling initiated a judicial effort to achieve racial integration with affirmative commands, telling school districts how to construct their attendance zones, where to build schools, where to bus their pupils, and how to assign their teachers.

Once courts and litigants discovered what could be done (or attempted) in the schools, other state institutions, especially prisons and institutions for the mentally ill and retarded, became targets. Nearly all state prison systems now operate under judicial decrees that address overcrowding and other conditions of prison life, and federal judges routinely mandate construction programs and modes of prison administration.

Needless to say, federal judicial mandates come without money, because courts have no way of raising money.

Legislative Regulations

Congress is also a source of affirmative commands to the states. When it imposes taxes and regulations—such as social security payroll taxes, wages-and-hours regulation, and emissions limits—on private parties, it must decide whether to cover state governments as well, for they and their local subdivisions are employers and, in some respects, producers.

For much of the nation's history, Congress did not tax and regulate state governments because it conceived of them as separate, sovereign, and equal. In a leading statement of this constitutional doctrine, the Supreme Court ruled in 1871 (*Collector v. Day*) that a federal income tax could not be levied against a county judge in Massachusetts. An earlier decision of the Court (*Dobbins v. The Commissioners of Erie,* 1842) had settled that the states could not tax the salary of an officer of the United States. Under 19th-century conceptions of federalism, it followed that the federal government could not tax the salaries of officers of the states.

When the Social Security Act of 1935 was passed, states as employers were routinely exempted from paying the payroll tax. Similarly, when the Fair Labor Standards Act of 1938 set maximum hours and minimum wages for industrial employers, no one would have imagined extending such regulation to state and local governments.

Yet as these New Deal measures were being enacted, the doctrine of sovereign immunity that had protected the states was collapsing. The Supreme Court overruled *Collector v. Day* in 1939. Eventually, under the nationalizing impact of the New Deal, Congress began regulating state governments just as if they were private parties. For example, Congress extended wages-and-hours regulation to some state and local employees in 1966, to the rest in 1974. The Supreme Court at first upheld the move, but then, in response to the law of 1974, changed its mind. In 1976 the Court forbade Congress from exercising its commerce power so as to "force directly upon the States its choices as to how essential decisions regarding the conduct of integral governmental functions are to be made" (*National League of Cities v. Usery*). But the stan-

---

 From *The Brookings Review,* Fall 1992, pp. 50-53. © 1992 by the Brookings Institution. Reprinted by permission.

dard proved impractical and was abandoned in 1985 (*Garcia v. San Antonio Metropolitan Transit Authority*). Speaking for the Court, Justice Blackmun wrote that the "political process ensures that laws that unduly burden the States will not be promulgated." The Court seemed to wash its hands of the subject, leaving the states to the mercy of what Justice O'Connor in dissent called Congress's "underdeveloped capacity for self-restraint."

Preemptions

Preemptions are commands to the states to *stop* doing something and let the federal government do it. They are sanctioned by the supremacy clause of the Constitution, which requires that state laws yield to federal ones in case of conflict. Historically, preemptions have been not so much a calculated technique of intergovernmental relations as something that "just happened" as a byproduct of congressional action. It was left to the courts to rule, in response to litigation, whether preemption had taken place.

Recently preemptions have become both more frequent and more explicit. Congress passed more than 90 new preemptive laws in the 1970s and again in the 1980s, more than double the number for any previous decade. Partly because of pressure from the courts to be explicit, Congress now often does declare an intention to preempt. And the states naturally experience such declarations as coercion, even if they are being prevented from doing things rather than commanded to do them.

There is also a modern variant on the use of preemption, called by students of federalism "partial preemption." In the 1970s, as it enacted a new wave of regulation, Congress hit on a way of making use of the states for administration. It would preempt a field—say, occupational health and safety or surface mining or air pollution control—but permit the states to continue to function providing that they adopted standards at least as exacting as those it stipulated. The Supreme Court upheld this technique (*Hodel v. Virginia Surface Mining and Reclamation Association,* 1981).

Technically, the states can refuse the federal government's invitation to serve as administrators of its regulations. But in practice they have responded. "Each State shall . . . adopt . . . a plan which provides for implementation, maintenance, and enforcement" of federal air quality standards, the Clean Air Act says—and each state does. Better to be subordinate governments than empty ones.

Grant-in-Aid Conditions

Federal grant-in-aid conditions addressed to the states have been around at least since the Morrill Act of 1862, which gave the states land—30,000 acres for each member of Congress—to endow colleges in the agricultural and mechanic arts.

In theory, states have always been able to refuse federal grants. In practice, they have generally found them irresistible. And as time passed, states' dependence increased: aid was habit-forming. In 1965 federal highway grants passed $4 billion a year. In 1970

grants for public assistance, including Medicaid, passed $7 billion a year. Altogether federal grants in 1970 amounted to nearly 30 percent of states' own-source revenues. It is absurd to hold, as constitutional doctrine formally does, that such grants can be rejected, and the burden of the accompanying conditions thereby avoided.

Over time, the conditions of grant programs expanded in scope and detail. Successful political movements left their mark on grant programs through conditions that apply to all or most grant programs. The rights revolution of the 1960s and 1970s, for example, left a legacy of anti-discrimination requirements, and the environmental movement a requirement that environmental impact statements be prepared for federally aided projects.

Similarly, conditions have multiplied program by program. Section 402 of Title IV of the Social Security Act of 1935 took 2 brief paragraphs to describe what should be contained in state plans for aid to dependent children. By 1976 section 402 had grown to 9 pages; by 1988, to 27.

Also, Congress in the 1970s began threatening to withhold grants, particularly those for Medicaid and highways, to achieve objectives connected only loosely or not at all to the underlying purpose of the grant. When Congress set a national speed limit of 55 miles per hour in 1974 and a minimum drinking age of 21 in 1984, it did so by threatening to withhold highway grants from states that failed to comply.

Finally, the language of grant-in-aid statutes has become more coercive. Federal law makes some Medicaid services "mandatory" and Congress keeps adding to the list.

From time to time presidents, especially Republicans, have tried to reduce and simplify grant conditions. The revisions that Nixon, Ford, and Reagan achieved, in the form of revenue sharing and block grants, have been modest and, in the case of general revenue sharing, short-lived. Conditioned grants for specific purposes have persisted and always predominated.

Historically, grant-in-aid conditions could be enforced only by administrative action, primarily the threat to withhold the grant. Because withholding was self-defeating, it was not often used. Federal administrators got what compliance they could through negotiation. However, with the rights revolution and the rise of judicial activism, many grant-in-aid conditions became judicially enforceable, particularly in programs of AFDC and education of handicapped children. A whole new set of commands emanated from an awe-inspiring source, the courts.

As grant conditions became more coercive, grants did not keep pace. Grants as a share of states' own-source revenues reached a peak at 32 percent in 1976 and then began to fall.

Do Mandates Matter?

The rise of the affirmative command, occurring subtly and on several different fronts, constitutes a sea-change in federal-state relations. The states have been converted from separate governments into subordinate

Congress is not much inclined to contemplate the deeper issues of federalism and to ask, self-critically, whether or where it should exercise restraint in its use of mandates.

ones, arguably mere "agents" in some programs. In constitutional significance, the change is comparable to the transformation by which the federal government ceased over the course of many years to be a government of limited, specified powers and became free to engage in any domestic activity not prohibited by the Bill of Rights.

That mandates developed only in the past 40 years does not necessarily mean that they are contrary to the Framers' intentions. That depends on which Framers one consults. Today's federalism is what the losing side of 1787 feared, but arguably what the winning side hoped for. Madison, after all, went into the Constitutional Convention saying that the states should be retained because they would be "subordinately useful." That is precisely what they have become. And there is at least a hint in *The Federalist* that affirmative commands would be acceptable. Number 27, written by by the ardently nationalistic Hamilton, anticipated that the federal government would employ the states to administer its laws. It is hard to see how that could have happened in the absence of mandates.

Yet most fundamentally, *The Federalist* saw federalism as a way to safeguard the public against abuses of governmental power and to sustain republicanism, the great central principle of the American regime. As Hamilton argued in number 28, "Power being almost always the rival of power, the general government will at all times stand ready to check the usurpations of the state governments, and these will have the same disposition towards the general government. The people, by throwing themselves into either scale, will infallibly make it preponderate. If their rights are invaded by either, they can make use of the other as the instrument of redress."

Indeed, the institutions of federalism can be used by the people to play different levels of government—and through them different policy choices—off against each other. One sees this happening most vividly in the prolonged contest over abortion policy, in which the federal courts "corrected" the restrictive excesses of state laws in the early 1970s and state legislatures responded by "correcting" the libertarian excesses of *Roe v. Wade*, and so on—in a heated intergovernmental exchange that threatens to be endless because the rival political movements are incapable of compromise.

Today mandates come in so many different forms and with so many different purposes that it is difficult to speak of them as a class. Limited, for the sake of discussion, to those that compel expenditure, they clearly raise important questions about republicanism. Judicial mandates come from a body that is not elected at all; congressional mandates, from a body that is not responsible to the various state electorates. When the federal judiciary commands the states to spend more on prisons and Congress commands them to spend more on Medicaid, they are making decisions that state electorates have no way to review. State officials lose their ability to weigh competing claims on state budgets. Of course, no such weighing is done at the federal level, where mandates are produced in isolation

from one another. Neither the courts nor Congress, framing commands to the states, asks the question, "how much, compared to what?" that is crucial to rational, responsible policymaking. At some point, federal commands to the states may come to implicate the guarantee clause of the Constitution: "The United States shall guarantee to every state in this Union a Republican Form of Government."

Can Mandates Be Curbed?

How strongly state officials oppose mandates may be questioned. Accepting subordination as a fact of life, they have produced scattered complaints but not concerted or doctrinaire opposition. Although the loss of budgetary discretion is a serious problem for governors, it is hard for all 50 of them to get together on anything, much less take a public stand *for* overcrowded prisons or *against* medical care for pregnant women.

Largely devoid of interest in constitutional issues except for its own battles with the president, today's Congress is not much inclined to contemplate the deeper issues of federalism and to ask, self-critically, whether or where it should exercise restraint in its use of mandates. If it can expand the benefits of government while imposing much of the cost on other governments in the system, why not do it?

By contrast, the Supreme Court, habituated to thinking in constitutional terms, and made conservative by a series of Republican appointments, is engaged in a wide-ranging retreat from the use of mandates. In school desegregation, prison administration, and enforcement of grant-in-aid conditions, not to mention voting rights, abortion, and *habeas corpus*, the Court has signaled that it will show more deference to the states. But it is one thing for the Court to practice self-restraint and quite another for it to attempt to restrain Congress. The Court does not lightly challenge a co-equal branch of government, nor has it had much success in the past in devising practical and enduring standards to protect the state governments.

There remains, nonetheless, a strong case for federalism, as Alice Rivlin, for one, has urged in the 1991 Webb Lecture before the National Academy of Public Administration and in *Reviving the American Dream*. As Madison foresaw, the task of governing so vast a country is too formidable for one government alone. It is significant that someone as thoughtful and experienced as Rivlin, whose whole career has been based in Washington and devoted to shaping national policy, should conclude that national uniformity is a liability in some areas of government. She names education and skills training, child care, housing, infrastructure, and economic development as activities that are "likely to succeed only if they are well adapted to local conditions, have strong local support and community participation and are managed by accountable officials who can be voted out if things go badly."

Rivlin's vision of revitalized state government calls, appropriately, for interstate equalization of revenues, to be achieved—and here her proposal becomes radical—by the states' adopting "one or more common

By contrast, the Supreme Court, habituated to thinking in constitutional terms, is engaged in a wide-ranging retreat from the use of mandates.

taxes (same base, same rate) and sharing the proceeds." She suggests a single state corporate income tax or a uniform value-added tax, shared on a per capita basis and substituted for state retail sales taxes. To achieve this, the states would need the "blessing and perhaps the assistance of the federal government."

Indeed. There is no plausible mechanism, formal or informal, by which the 50 states could voluntarily agree on a common tax. It would have to be imposed by Congress in a fresh stroke of centralization—a mandate, if you will—entailing preemption of a particular tax source and dedication of the proceeds to the states, with no conditions attached. The absence of conditions proved not to be politically durable when general revenue sharing was tried in the 1970s. State political leaders might be forgiven if they doubt

whether Congress would be willing to take the heat for imposing a new tax while turning the proceeds over to them.

Perhaps no other of our governing institutions has been subject to so much change and yet so resistant to planned, deliberate reform as federalism. Its history is one of centralization, steady and seemingly irreversible. Yet the case for lodging a large measure of domestic responsibility and discretion with the states and their local subdivisions remains strong. So is the case for the states having governments—republican governments chosen by state electorates and accountable to them, and capable of raising their own revenues and deciding how those revenues should be spent. It is one of the ironies of federalism that deliberate acts of decentralization, such as Rivlin proposes, depend on centralization as a precondition.

The Entitlement Time Bomb

John Attarian

John Attarian is a freelance writer in Ann Arbor, Michigan, who holds a doctorate in economics and has written on deposit insurance, pension insurance, the federal budget deficit, and Social Security.

In recent years, Congress has periodically boiled with efforts to balance the federal budget—and with good reason. Federal spending has exploded out of control, due to spending for entitlement programs like Social Security, Medicare, and Medicaid.

This fiscal mismanagement has already exacted serious economic penalties, according to many analysts, including the General Accounting Office (GAO), the investigative arm of Congress. Moreover, if entitlement spending continues to go unaddressed, they say, America's economic future will be extremely grim.

Federal budget deficits mushroomed from fiscal 1981's $79 billion to sums exceeding $200 billion for most of the 1980s and '90s.

As of 1981, the national debt was $994.3 billion, or 33.5 percent of the gross domestic product (GDP). For the year 2000, it is projected to be $6.18 trillion, or 69.1 percent of GDP—a 522 percent increase in 20 years, while GDP rose only 202 percent. In other words, the federal government is spending and borrowing income far faster than America produces it.

And *entitlement spending*—transfer payments to people declared by law to be "entitled" by reason of income level, age, occupation, and so on to receive them—has been the cause. Major entitlements—such as Social Security, Medicare, Medicaid, government retirement benefits, unemployment compensation, food stamps, and the Earned Income Tax Credit (EITC), which the budget treats as an outlay—now consume over half the annual budget.

Moreover, the dynamics of the budget's components over the past 30 years prove that entitlements are the engine driving the growth in federal spending and deficits (see table).

AN UNSTOPPABLE LOCOMOTIVE?

Entitlement spending has more than doubled as a share of the budget since 1965 and is the largest, fastest-growing sector today. Except for a temporary rise due to Ronald Reagan's defense buildup, the Pentagon's share has fallen since the Vietnam era. Likewise, the share for domestic discretionary spending—domestic spending that must be voted on by Congress, for items like government operations, education, infrastructure repair, and so on—has dropped substantially.

But thanks to chronic large deficits stoked primarily by soaring entitlements, spending for net interest on the national debt has risen steadily.

How did America come to this pass? Briefly, according to political observers, thanks to an ideology of activist government and a prosperity that gave the impression that such activism was easily affordable, many new entitlements—such as Medicare and Medicaid (both enacted in 1965), Supplemental Security Income (1972), and the EITC (1975)—were created in the 1960s and '70s, and existing ones such as Social Security were expanded, with little thought or provision for future costs.

The overwhelming bulk of entitlement spending is for such non-means-tested programs (i.e., those that distribute benefits to all who qualify for them, regardless of income or assets) as federal retirement benefits, Social Security, and Medicare. As of fiscal 1995, non-means-tested programs cost $609.3 billion and were 40.1 percent of total outlays and 77.1 percent of major entitlement spending.

■ *A nation barreling toward bankruptcy:* As more people swell the ranks of America's senior citizens, the fiscal burden of entitlement programs like Social Security and Medicare mounts.

Two programs—Social Security and Medicare—now dominate entitlement spending and the budget as a whole. At $333.3 billion in fiscal 1995, Social Security is the largest single item in the budget. Medicare, costing $156.9 billion, is the fourth-largest, after defense and interest on the debt. Combined, Social Security and Medicare now consume $490.2 billion—almost a third of all federal spending.

By contrast, major means-tested entitlement programs (i.e., programs benefiting only people with lower incomes and assets) cost $181.1 billion and accounted for just 11.9 percent of federal spending in fiscal 1995. Social Security outlays alone are almost twice those for all federal poverty programs.

It follows that focusing on cutting poverty programs will not solve the problem. Whatever welfare's flaws, budget busting is not one of them. The conclusion is inescapable: America's fiscal crisis cannot be resolved without radical reform of Social Security and Medicare.

As is widely known, entitlement outlays are not subject to annual appropriations votes by Congress. Adding entitlements and net interest payments on the national debt (a legal obligation of the government), about two-thirds of federal spending is essentially beyond congressional control.

The data (see next page) also show that entitlement spending is insensitive to the economy's position in the business cycle. It was far higher in 1985, a good year, than in 1975, a recession year. And entitlement outlays for 1995, a good year, far exceed those for 1990, a recession year. This is mostly true even of the one major entitlement responsive to economic fluctuations: unemployment compensation.

In good and bad times alike, the spending valve is now stuck open. In short, thanks to entitlements, America has lost control of federal spending. Hence the plunge into debt.

THE ECONOMIC CONSEQUENCES

Growing far faster than both total outlays and GDP, more than doubling as a share of both in 30 years, entitlements are outstripping the U.S. economy's capacity to finance them. They are also creating a serious drag on American economic performance.

The chronic massive deficits, economists say, are devouring America's seed corn: the savings that finance investment. Over the past 30 years, government deficits have consumed an increasing share of the country's declining national savings. Net national saving—private-sector saving after public-sector deficits are subtracted—averaged 8.1 percent of GDP in the 1960s and 7.2 percent in the 1970s, but only 3.7 percent in the 1980s and a mere 1.7 percent in 1990–93.

Just a tiny sliver of national output, then, is now available for investment to sustain American productivity and living standards in future years.

Another indicator of the growing diversion of moneys from productive investment to deficit finance is the federal government's share of total net borrowing in the credit market. In 1965,

MAJOR ENTITLEMENTS AND THE BUDGET, 1965-1995
(dollar amounts in billions; fiscal years)

ITEM	1965	1970	1975	1980	1985	1990	1995	% Growth
Social Security	17	30	64	117	186	247	333	1,859
Medicare	–	6	12	31	64	96	157	2,517
Medicaid	–	3	3	14	23	41	89	28,667
Federal retirement	3	6	13	27	39	53	66	2,100
Veterans benefits	4	7	13	14	16	16	20	400
Unemployment comp.	2	3	13	17	16	17	21	950
Food and nutrition	–	1	7	13	17	21	34	3,300
Supplemental Security	–	–	4	6	9	12	25	525
EITC	–	–	–	1	1	4	15	1,400
Family support	3	4	5	7	9	12	17	467
Tot. Major Entitlements	**29**	**60**	**134**	**247**	**380**	**519**	**777**	**2,579**
Total as % of outlays	25	31	40	42	40	41	51	104
Total as % of GDP	4	6	9	9	10	10	11	175
Total outlays	118	196	332	591	946	1,253	1,519	1,187
GDP	671	986	1,511	2,645	3,971	5,460	7,005	944
Deficit	1	3	53	74	212	221	164	16,300
National debt	332	381	542	909	1,817	3,206	4,921	1,382
Net interest	9	14	23	53	130	184	232	2,478
... as % of outlays	8	7	7	9	14	15	15	88
DDS*	26	39	67	129	146	183	252	869
... as % of outlays	22	20	20	22	15	15	17	-23
Defense	51	82	88	135	253	300	274	437
... as % of outlays	43	42	27	23	27	24	18	-58

SOURCE: OFFICE OF MANAGEMENT AND BUDGET

* Domestic Discretionary Spending

the government did only 5.8 percent of total borrowing. By 1980, its share of borrowing had hit 21.4 percent. It reached a staggering 55.3 percent in 1991 and 57.5 percent in 1992. This was the real, if unadmitted, cause of the "credit crunch" and recession of the early 1990s: Government borrowing to finance budget deficits was diverting credit from business, the phenomenon known to economists as *crowding out.*

Financing the budget deficit devoured a still-massive 49.3 percent in 1993. As of 1995, the government did 23.9 percent of total net borrowing—a considerably smaller share, to be sure, than earlier in the decade, but still over *four times* as much as the government took in 1965, just before the entitlement explosion began.

Entitlement spending has more than doubled as a share of the budget since 1965 and is the largest, fastest-growing sector today.

In short, public-sector elephantiasis, driven by mushrooming entitlement spending, contributed mightily to the stagnation of productivity and real wages since the early 1970s, and to the recession of the early '90s.

Such has been the performance and economic impact of entitlement spending in the recent past. What of the future?

THE TICKING BOMB

The economic feebleness of the deficit-dominated early 1990s warns that the United States is running the risk of getting caught in a vicious circle of entitlement-fueled spending, deficits, and stagnation. The trap can be described as follows:

● The deficits that finance the spending devour the savings that should be invested to create jobs and productivity growth.

● The resulting stagnation curtails revenue growth and helps drive up entitlement spending, borrowing to cover the entitlement spending, and spending on interest on the borrowing.

● The deficits thus grow from both sides of the ledger, feeding another round of spending, borrowing, and stagnation.

Ominously, according to many economists, the United

States is sitting on a huge, ticking time bomb.

They say that the ongoing health-care cost inflation and the aging of the American population will, if current policies remain unchanged, drive entitlement spending to unsustainably high levels.

The Congressional Budget Office projects that, under current law, entitlement spending, thanks mostly to Medicare and Medicaid spending growth, will be about $1.62 trillion in 2005, or 60.1 percent of total outlays and 14 percent of GDP, and that the budget deficit will be $472 billion.

After 2010—as the baby boomers born between 1945 and 1965 begin to retire and draw Social Security, Medicare, and civil service and military retirement benefits—the outlook gets worse yet. Again assuming no change in current law, the President's Bipartisan Commission on Entitlement Reform projected that, by 2012, entitlement spending plus interest on the national debt will require all federal tax revenue.

And by 2030, the commission said, Medicare, Medicaid, Social Security, and federal retirement programs *alone* will devour all federal revenues. That is, revenues will not suffice to cover all entitlement spending, let alone the rest of the budget.

When the huge baby boom generation retires, the population of Social Security beneficiaries will grow much faster than the population of workers paying taxes to finance their benefits. Tax revenue will no longer suffice to cover benefit costs, and Social Security will have to cash in the government bonds in its "trust funds."

According to the Board of Trustees' actuarial analysis, using pessimistic demographic and economic assumptions, which former Chief Actuary A.

Haeworth Robertson has argued are the most realistic, the Social Security payroll tax will no longer generate a surplus over benefit outlays after 1999. Social Security's Old Age Survivors and Disability Insurance trust funds will be bankrupt in 2016 under the pessimistic assumptions, in 2029 under intermediate ones.

MEDICARE, MEDICAID TEETERING

The crisis will arrive even sooner for Medicare. In 1995, its expenditures exceeded income, and it began draining its Hospital Insurance trust fund. Under both the "low-cost" and intermediate assumptions of Medicare's Board of Trustees, the trust fund will be exhausted in 2001. Under pessimistic ("high-cost") assumptions, exhaustion will occur in 2000.

To obtain money to pay off the Treasury debt from the trust funds, the federal government will have to cut spending elsewhere in the budget, raise taxes, or, most likely, increase borrowing from the public, which will drive budget deficits higher. Assuming that all redemption of

the trust funds' government debt is financed by new borrowing, under the Social Security trustees' pessimistic assumptions, the deficit from Social Security and Medicare *alone* will be $66 billion in fiscal 2000, $175 billion in 2005, $341 billion in 2010, and $686 billion in 2015.

When the funds are totally exhausted, unless Social Security and Medicare benefits are radically cut or their payroll taxes drastically increased, deficits will soar higher yet.

While the demise of Social Security and Medicare certainly constitutes the lion's share of the lurking menace of runaway entitlements, other entitlement programs also have vast potential for trouble:

• The Congressional Budget Office projects that Medicaid outlays will be almost triple their 1995 level in just 10 years, hitting $148 billion in 2000 and $232 billion in 2005.

• The present value of future civil service retirement benefits promised under current law—that is, the amount of money that would have to be invested today to pay for them—is now over $1.1 trillion.

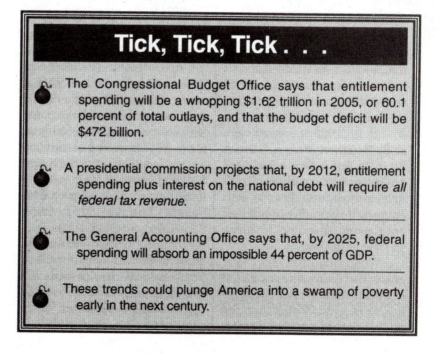

Tick, Tick, Tick . . .

● The Congressional Budget Office says that entitlement spending will be a whopping $1.62 trillion in 2005, or 60.1 percent of total outlays, and that the budget deficit will be $472 billion.

● A presidential commission projects that, by 2012, entitlement spending plus interest on the national debt will require *all federal tax revenue.*

● The General Accounting Office says that, by 2025, federal spending will absorb an impossible 44 percent of GDP.

● These trends could plunge America into a swamp of poverty early in the next century.

Unfortunately, no money has been reserved to cover these future obligations.

● Similarly, unfunded military retirement benefits promised under current law have a present value exceeding $713 billion, and the estimated present value of unfunded veterans' benefits is over $190 billion.

Simply to provide retirement benefits to its own people, then—never mind Social Security and Medicare beneficiaries—the government has committed itself to spending over $2 trillion, but without providing the means to make these commitments good. Even while confronting Social Security and Medicare bankruptcy, the government will have to find money to honor these obligations, too.

All in all, entitlement spending mandated under current law is a recipe for ruinous deficits. Indeed, in 1995, the GAO, using a long-term growth model to simulate the economic impact of future deficits, projected that under current tax and spending policies, by 2025 federal spending will absorb 44 percent of GDP and the budget deficit will exceed 23 percent of GDP. Net interest on the debt would be roughly 30 percent of total federal spending in 2025.

■

The entitlement state has the potential to make America an economic backwater choked with poverty.

■

THE NATION'S SLIDE INTO POVERTY

To finance chronic huge deficits, government borrowing would devour virtually all available credit. The resulting crowding out would make the credit crunch of the early 1990s recession trivial. Businesses would be unable to maintain existing plants and equipment, let alone expand or upgrade them.

America's capital stock would shrink accordingly, as would productivity, output, and employment. The GAO projected that by 2025 investment would disappear, our capital stock would be less than half its 1994 level, and real per-capita GDP would have barely grown since 1994.

With deficits consuming

most domestic savings and foreign lenders unlikely to prop up a bankrupt government, there would be little choice but for the Federal reserve Bank to purchase U.S. government bonds, a practice known as *monetizing* the deficits. When what is essentially one branch of the government finances the rest of the bureaucracy, the country starts to print money at a furious pace, expanding the money supply and risking hyperinflation.

The entitlement state, then, has the potential to make America an economic backwater choked with poverty.

Perhaps even worse than the size of the entitlement time bomb and its potential for devastation, observers say, is the deafness of America's politicians to its ticking. So far, little effort has been made, by either President Clinton or the Republicans in Congress, to confront the entitlements issue, to educate the American people about the need for making deep sacrifices, and to actually undertake those sacrifices.

The country still has some time left, but it is running out fast.

Put an End to

CORPORATE WELFARE

It is time for the Federal government to stop providing special benefits to industries and companies through tax breaks, trade policies, and spending programs.

Stephen Moore and Dean Stansel

The authors are, respectively, director of fiscal policies and a fiscal policy analyst, Cato Institute, Washington, D.C.

SECRETARY OF LABOR Robert Reich was right on target late in 1994 when he identified "Federal aid to dependent corporations" as a major contributor to the budget crisis. He also was correct to challenge Congressional Republicans and Washington think tanks to propose termination of Federal activities that fall into the category of "corporate welfare."

The list of corporate subsidy programs is longer and the dollar expenditures are far greater than most members of Congress and the Clinton Administration suspect. Corporate pork is pervasive. For instance, Congress funds more than 125 programs that subsidize private businesses. Subsidy programs to such businesses cost Federal taxpayers more than $85,000,000,000 annually, and the dollar amount has been growing substantially in recent years. Every major Cabinet department has become a conduit for government funding of private industry.

Within some Cabinet agencies, such as the Departments of Agriculture and Commerce, almost every spending program underwrites private businesses.

The following list includes some of the more egregious taxpayer subsidies to industries and firms:

● Through Sematech, a consortium of very large U.S. computer microchip producers, the Pentagon provides nearly $100,000,000 a year of support to the industry. However, of the more than 200 chip makers in the U.S., only the 14 largest, including Intel and National Semiconductor, receive Federal support from Sematech. Originally designed to help U.S. firms compete against foreign competition, it now subsidizes the largest producers to help fend off smaller domestic competition.

● An estimated 40% of the $1,400,000,000 sugar price support program benefits the largest one percent of sugar farms. The 33 biggest sugar cane plantations each receive more than $1,000,000.

● Through the Rural Electrification Administration and the Federal power marketing administrations, the government provides about $2,000,000,000 in subsidies each year to large and profitable electric utility cooperatives, such as ALLTEL, which had sales of $2,300,000,000 in 1994. Federally subsidized electricity holds down the costs of running ski resorts in Aspen, Colo.; five-star hotels in Hilton Head, S.C.; and gambling casinos in Las Vegas, Nev.

● During 1994, the Forest Service spent $140,000,000 building roads in national forests, thus subsidizing the removal of timber from Federal lands by multi-million-dollar timber companies. Over the past 20 years, the Forest Service has built 340,000 miles of roads—more than eight times the length of the interstate highway system—primarily for the benefit of logging companies.

● The Department of Agriculture Market Promotion Program spends $110,000,000 per year underwriting the cost of advertising American products abroad.

● In 1994, a House of Representatives investigative team discovered that Federal environmental cleanup and defense con-

From *USA Today Magazine*, September 1995, pp. 24-26. © 1995 by the Society for the Advancement of Education. Reprinted by permission.

tractors had been milking taxpayers for millions of dollars in entertainment, recreation, and party expenses. Martin Marietta Corp. charged the Pentagon $263,000 for a Smokey Robinson concert, $20,000 for the purchase of golf balls, and $7,500 for a 1993 office Christmas party. Ecology and Environment, Inc., of Lancaster, N.Y., spent $243,000 of funds designated for environmental cleanup on "employee morale" and $37,000 on tennis lessons, bike races, golf tournaments, and other entertainment.

Congress no longer can afford to ignore the growing scourge of corporate welfare. Any serious attempt to balance the budget will require a strategy for getting businesses off the $85,000,000,000 annual dole.

The Clinton Administration and other proponents of Federal subsidies to the private sector often maintain government support of American business is in the national interest. A multitude of economic, national security, and social arguments are voiced to justify corporate aid. Government support is said to protect industries from failure to preserve high-paying American jobs; subsidize research activities that private industries would not finance themselves; counteract the business subsidies of foreign governments to ensure a "level playing field"; boost high-technology companies whose profitability is vital to American economic success in the 21st century; maintain the viability of "strategic industries" that are essential to national security; finance ventures that otherwise would be considered too risky for private capital markets; and assist socially disadvantaged groups, such as minorities and women, to establish new businesses.

On the surface, that kind of policy may seem to promote America's economic interest. However, there are at least eight reasons such policies are misguided and dangerous.

The Federal government has a disappointing record of picking industrial winners and losers. The function of private capital markets is to direct billions of dollars of capital to industries and firms that offer the highest potential rate of return. The capital markets, in effect, are in the business of selecting corporate winners and losers. The underlying premise of Federal business subsidies is that the government can direct the limited pool of capital funds more effectively than venture capitalists and private money managers can. Decades of experience, though, prove that government agencies have a much less successful track record than private money managers of correctly selecting winners. The average delinquency rate is higher for government loan programs (eight percent) than for commercial lenders (three percent). The Small Business Administration delinquency rates reached over 20% in the early and mid 1980s; the Farmers Home Administration delinquency rate has approached 50%.

Much of what passes today as benign industrial policy is little more than a political payoff to favored industries or businesses.

Corporate welfare is a huge drain on the Federal treasury for little economic benefit. It is supposed to offer a positive long-term economic return for taxpayers, but the evidence shows that government "investments" have a low or negative rate of return. In the late 1960s, the Federal government spent nearly $1,000,000,000 on the Supersonic Transport, which experts in Washington expected would revolutionize air travel. Instead, the project went bankrupt and never flew a single passenger. In the late 1970s, the Federal government expended more than $2,000,000,000 of taxpayer money on the Synthetic Fuels Corporation—a public-private project that Department of Energy officials thought would provide new sources of energy for America. The SFC was closed down in the 1980s, never having produced a single kilowatt of electricity.

Corporate welfare creates an uneven playing field. Business subsidies—often said to be justified because they correct distortions in the marketplace—create huge market distortions of their own. The major effect of corporate subsidies is to divert credit and capital to politically well-connected firms at the expense of their politically less influential competitors. Sematech, for ex-

ample, was launched to promote the U.S. microchip industry over rivals in Japan and Germany. In practice, it has become a cartel of the large U.S. chip producers—such as Intel—that unfairly handicaps the hundreds of smaller American producers. Farm subsidies create another arbitrary distortion. Agricultural price supports are alleged to be critical to the survival of American farmers. The truth is that, of the 400 classified farm commodities, about two dozen receive more than 90% of the assistance funds. Over 80% of the subsidies enrich farmers with a net worth of more than $500,000.

Corporate welfare fosters an incestuous relationship between government and business. Government and politics are inseparable. Much of what passes today as benign industrial policy is little more than a political payoff to favored industries or businesses. Taxpayer dollars that are used to subsidize private firms routinely are returned to Washington in the form of political contributions and lobbying activities to secure even more tax dollars. For instance, the outdated Rural Electrification Administration survives primarily because of the lobbying efforts of the National Rural Electrical Cooperative Association in America. With a $78,000,000 budget, that association is one of the most influential and heavily financed lobbying groups in Washington.

During the 1992 presidential campaign, Vice Pres. Dan Quayle traveled to Michigan to announce a $250,000,000 plan to upgrade the M-1 tank. It just happened to be built by General Dynamics in Sterling Heights, Mich. Before the campaign, the Bush Administration had argued convincingly that, in the post-Cold War era, the more expensive tank was unnecessary.

Many of the top recipients of technology

Hardworking American taxpayers are having their pockets picked by Federal programs that provide hefty handouts for private industry.

research grants awarded by the Clinton Administration were substantial contributors to the Clinton campaign or the Democratic National Committee. For example, eight Fortune 500 firms that were multi-million-dollar award-winners of the Advanced Technology Program or the Technology Reinvestment Project in 1994 also were large Democratic campaign contributors, according to Federal Election Commission data compiled by Common Cause. These included AT&T, Boeing, Chevron, General Electric, McDonnell Douglas, Shell, Texaco, and United Technology. At the very least, such golden handshake programs create an impression that government is for sale.

Corporate welfare is anti-consumer. One of the main effects of many corporate subsidy programs is to raise costs to consumers. Trade restrictions, often sought by politically powerful industries, are estimated to cost consumers $80,000,000,000 a year. The sugar program is estimated to cost consumers several billion dollars a year, according to a U.S. Department of Commerce study that concluded: "Because sugar is an ingredient in many food items, the effect of the sugar program is similar to a regressive sales tax, which hits lower-income families harder than upper-income families."

The most efficient way to promote business in America is to reduce the over-all cost and regulatory burden of government. Corporate welfare is predicated on the misguided notion that the best way to enhance business profitability in America is to do so one firm at a time. A much more effective way to boost the competitiveness and productivity of American industry is to create a level playing field, thus minimizing government interference in the marketplace and substantially reducing tax rates and regulatory burdens. For example, all the Federal government's efforts to promote the big three U.S. automobile companies are insignificant compared with the regulatory burden on that industry, which now adds an estimated $3,000 to the sticker price of a new car. Eliminating just half the business subsidies in the Federal budget would generate enough savings to pay for the entire elimination of the capital gains tax. Clearly, a zero capital gains tax would generate far more jobs and business startups than the scores of targeted business handouts in the Federal budget.

Corporate welfare is anti-capitalist. It converts the American businessman from a capitalist into a lobbyist. Corporate welfare, notes Wall Street financier Theodore J. Forstmann, has led to the creation of the "statist businessman in America." The statist businessman is "a conservator, not a creator; a caretaker, not a risk taker; an argument against capitalism even though he is not a capitalist at all." For instance, the Fanjul family, owner of several large sugar farms in the Florida Everglades, earns an estimated $60,000,000 a year in artificial profits thanks to price supports and import quotas. The Fanjul family is a fierce defender of the sugar program and, in 1992, contributed $350,000 to political campaigns. All of that has a corrosive effect on the American free enterprise system.

Corporate welfare is unconstitutional. The most critical reason government should end corporate subsidy programs is that they lie outside Congress' limited spending authority under the Constitution. Nowhere in the Constitution is Congress granted the authority to spend funds to subsidize the computer industry, enter into joint ventures with automobile companies, or guarantee loans to favored business owners.

Government provides special benefits to individual industries and companies through a vast array of policy levers. The three major business benefits come in the forms of special tax breaks, trade policies, and spending programs.

When Reich protested against "aid to dependent corporations," his criticism was directed toward "special tax benefits for particular industries." The Democratic Leadership Council's Progressive Policy Institute has specified some 30 such "tax subsidies" that led to a loss of $134,000,000,000 in Federal revenues over five years.

Inefficient subsidization —the ethanol example

One of the most inefficient tax subsidies is that for the production of ethanol—a corn-based gasoline substitute. The industry enjoys a tax credit for companies that blend ethanol and an exemption from Federal excise taxes. The tax breaks allegedly are justified on the grounds that they reduce pollution and U.S. dependence on foreign oil. Yet, a U.S. Department of Agriculture study finds that the $500,000,000 subsidy for ethanol "represents an inefficient use of our nation's resources." It concludes, "When all economic costs and benefits are tallied, an ethanol subsidy program is not cost effective." As for the supposed energy conservation and environmental benefits, a study by agricultural economist David Pimental at Cornell University discovered: "About 72% more energy is used to produce a gallon of ethanol than the energy in a gallon of ethanol."

Politics, not economics, is the principal motivation behind the ethanol subsidies. Archer Daniels Midland (ADM), a $10,000,000,000 agribusiness based in Decatur, Ill., produces 70% of the ethanol used in the U.S. An estimated 25% of its sales are of ethanol and corn sweetener (another highly subsidized farm product). ADM and its CEO, Dwayne Andreas, have been among the nation's most generous campaign contributors, with more than $150,000 in lifetime contributions to Sen-

ate Majority Leader Bob Dole alone.

Most targeted tax breaks create similar economic inefficiencies. Nonetheless, we reject the notion that allowing a company to keep its earnings and pay less in taxes somehow is a "subsidy." Furthermore, with the Federal government already collecting $1.3 trillion in revenues each year, we oppose any policy that would give Congress more tax dollars to spend. Research suggests that policies that would bring additional dollars into the Federal treasury would invite higher Congressional spending, not lower budget deficits.

Our recommendation is that Congress abolish all tax deductions, including all the special tax breaks for industries identified by the Progressive Policy Institute, in exchange for lower over-all corporate and personal tax rates on business and personal taxpayers. That could be accomplished through Rep. Dick Armey's (R.-Tex.) flat tax proposal or Rep. Bill Archer's (R.-Tex.) retail sales tax concept. Any such tax policy reform should be made on a revenue-neutral basis or as a net tax cut.

As for trade barriers, according to Benjamin Franklin, "Most of the statutes, or acts, edicts, and placards of parliaments, and states for regulating and directing of trade have been either political blunders or obtained by artful men for private advantage under pretense of public good." In 1991, there were more than 8,000 product tariffs imposed by Washington, all obtained for private advantage under pretense of public good.

By erecting trade barriers, the government rewards one industry at the direct expense of another. For instance, in 1991, prohibitive duties were placed on low-cost Japanese computer parts. The motivation was to save jobs in U.S. factories that make computer circuit boards. However, the decision to keep out foreign parts inflated by almost $1,000 the cost per personal computer manufactured by U.S. companies, such as IBM, Apple, and Compaq. That gave a huge advantage to Japanese computer companies, significantly reduced sales of the U.S. computer firms, and, worst of all,

Because they intermingle government dollars with corporate political clout, business subsidies have a corrupting influence on America's system of democratic government and entrepreneurial capitalism.

thousands of American jobs were *lost*.

Steel import quotas are equally injurious economically to American manufacturers. Trade specialists believe that the inflated steel prices paid by U.S. firms have contributed to the competitive decline of several American industries, including automobiles. The cost to the American economy of steel quotas is estimated at $7,000,000,000 per year.

No one knows precisely the total cost to American consumers of barriers to free trade, but several authoritative sources place the figure at $80,000,000,000 per year. There is virtually no specific U.S. trade restriction for which the economy-wide costs do not exceed the industry-specific benefits. Therefore, Congress immediately should lift all barriers to free trade.

There are at least 125 separate programs providing subsidies to particular industries and firms with a price tag exceeding $85,000,000,000 per year. We recommend the immediate abolition of all such programs.

Because they intermingle government dollars with corporate political clout, business subsidies have a corrupting influence on America's system of democratic government and entrepreneurial capitalism. Despite the conventional orthodoxy in Washington that the nation needs an even closer alliance between business and politics, the truth is that both government and the marketplace would work better if they kept a healthy distance from each other.

It is ironic that at a time when the Federal government is in litigation with Microsoft, perhaps America's most innovative and profitable high-technology corporation in decades, for successfully dominating the software industry, Congress is spending hundreds of millions of dollars trying to prop up the firm's less efficient computer industry rivals. A situation exists whereby Federal regulatory policies increasingly are geared toward punishing success, while Federal corporate welfare policies increasingly reward failure. That is not the way to preserve America's industrial might.

The balanced budget crusade

Robert Eisner

ROBERT EISNER is Kenan Professor of Economics, Emeritus, at Northwestern University and a past president of the American Economic Association.

A "BALANCED budget," no matter that few know what it means, particularly by archaic federal accounting rules, seems to be an American icon. Republicans and President Clinton now both proclaim it as a goal, differing only on timing and the means of achieving it.

The politics of all this seem overwhelming. Republicans think they have an issue to gain the support of most of the 20 million 1992 Perot voters who seem obsessed over the deficit and the debt it creates. Democrats, apparently scared witless that the Republicans are right on the politics, are reduced largely to saying, "Me too, but not your way!"

It has not always been so. In his 1864 annual message to Congress, Abraham Lincoln said:

> The public debt on the first day of July last, as appears by the books of the treasury, amounted to $1,740,690,489.49. Probably, should the war continue for another year, that amount may be increased by not far from five hundred million dollars. Held as it is for the most part, by our own people, it has become a substantial branch of national, though private, property. For obvious reasons, the more nearly this property can be distributed among all the people the better. . . . The great advantage of citizens being creditors as well as debtors, with relation to the public debt, is obvious. Men can readily perceive that they cannot be much oppressed by a debt which they owe themselves.

In 1962, President John F. Kennedy declared, "Obviously deficits are sometimes dangerous—and so are surpluses. . . . What we need is not labels and cliches but more basic discussion of the sophisticated and technical questions involved in keeping a great economic machine moving ahead." And, in 1981, Congressman Jack Kemp stated, "The Republican party no longer worships at the altar of a balanced budget."

Everybody tells the pollster that a balanced budget is good, until it is learned how it might be balanced and whom it will hurt. That many would be hurt is clear. Senate Republicans, in the fall of 1995, put forth proposals that take large bites out of prospective outlays for Medicare, Medicaid, education, research, and countless other programs. House Republicans were generally ready to go their Senate colleagues one better by adding more massive tax cuts, thus necessitating still more draconian cuts in spending.

But it is not just the "special interests" of those directly affected that may be hurt by budget cuts. Slashing productive public investment—in human capital and in physical infrastructure—can have damaging effects on the private economy and our present and future welfare. And, if the loss of purchasing power, whether due to the government giving the public less as it reduces outlays or taking from it more as it raises taxes, depresses the economy or brings us into a recession, the damage will be enormous.

False alarm

By conventional measures, the deficit has, in fact, dramatically decreased, from $290 billion or 4.9 percent of Gross Domestic Product (GDP) in 1992 to $203 billion or 3.1 percent of GDP in 1994 and to $164 billion or 2.3 percent of GDP in 1995. The debt, which increases each year by the amount of the deficit, is no longer growing faster than the nation's income.

If we look at budgets of other leading nations, we find that almost all of them have larger deficits—in proportion to the size of their economies—than we do. Indeed, the Maastricht agreement for the European Economic Union sets a limit on deficits of no more than 3 percent of GDP, a figure that we will be well below this year and, even by conservative (or alarmist?) Congressional Budget Office projections, below this entire century.

If we account for capital outlays the way the federal budget does, we would find that most cities and states frequently, if not chronically, run deficits. And composite balance sheets of American households and businesses would show that both add hugely to their debt every year, which means, by federal accounting rules, that they are running massive deficits, generally greater than that of the federal government. Why then should the federal government balance its budget, particularly if to do so will entail massive sacrifice by such "special interests" as the elderly, the ill, the young, the poor, businessmen, farmers, veterans—indeed, the great bulk of the population?

Most of the simplistic arguments for a balanced budget are without merit. First, we will not go "bankrupt." The deficit contributes not to a national debt owed to other countries but to a federal government debt overwhelmingly owed to its own people in our own currency. A sovereign government can always get or create the money necessary to roll over such a debt or to pay it off.

Second, the deficit and debt are not adding to the burdens of our children. As President Lincoln knew—and it was hardly original with him—for every debtor there is a creditor, and our children will eventually be just as much creditors as debtors. Every savings bond and Treasury bill, note, and bond constituting the debt, except for the minor portion owned by foreigners, will be an asset of our posterity. If we are putting an extra burden on our children, it is not in those pieces of paper, which will in fact be their inheritance of wealth.

Third, our deficits are not causing others to lose confidence in us and, hence, driving down the value of the dollar. We remain the greatest and strongest economy in the world. If a balanced budget "strengthens" the dollar, it will only do so because it slows the economy so that we import less and, hence, supply fewer dollars to the rest of the world.

Fourth, our deficits are not driving up inflation or interest rates. The historical relation between deficits and interest rates is murky indeed. Federal Reserve policy, the state of the economy, and expected inflation are what really matter.

How a balanced budget hurts

What then do analytical economists see as the role of the deficit and its possible effect on the current economy and our future? Conservative economist Robert Barro of Harvard University and his many followers argue for "Ricardian Equivalence," which holds that, as a first approximation, it does not matter whether government expenditures are financed by current taxes or by current borrowing—a deficit. The reasoning is that, if taxes are cut, thus creating a deficit, taxpayers' behavior will not be affected. They will say to themselves that the resulting debt will have to be serviced and/or paid off in the future. Hence, their lower taxes now will be matched by higher taxes later. They will not therefore spend the money they are no longer paying in taxes. They will either set it aside to pay their higher taxes in the future themselves or they will leave the money to their children to pay the taxes.

Most professional economists, however, believe that Ricardian Equivalence is of limited applicability and reject the argument that deficits do not matter. Contradicting Barro's views, most of us apparently feel richer when, other things being equal, we own our share of $3.5 trillion dollars of Treasury obligations than when we don't. And we feel still richer if deficits increase our real holdings of those assets. Hence, we generally spend more on consumption.

If we are already buying everything our economy is capable of producing—we are operating at full employment and full capacity—production of more goods to satisfy our consumption demand can only come at the expense of production of investment goods. We may then put a burden on our children by leaving them less productive because we leave them fewer capital goods. But suppose, as in most of our history except during wartime, we are not producing at full capacity. Then, more spending induced by deficits can, and is likely to, increase consumption and, concomitantly, to increase business investment and production, thus providing for the increased consumption. Far from burdening our children, we are actually aiding them even as we help ourselves.

Further, increased holdings of government debt will induce us to spend more of our incomes only if our holdings have risen in real terms adjusted for inflation and, more fundamentally, have *risen relative to our incomes*. Since the debt held by the public averaged about $3,500 billion in fiscal year 1995, inflation, at the roughly 3 percent of the past year, would mean that holders of that debt suffered a loss in its purchasing power or real value equal to (approximately) 3 percent of $3,500 billion, or some $100 billion. Thus the real increase in the debt, and therefore the real deficit, is only the nominal deficit of $164 billion minus $100 billion, or $64 billion. And, with national income growing at 6 percent per year, the debt would have to grow at more than 6 percent of that $3.5 trillion—a nominal deficit of more than $210 billion or some $50 billion *more* than last year's $164 billion—to cause us to spend a larger proportion of our incomes.

A "balanced budget" would hardly be balanced in a growing economy. It would imply a debt-to-income ratio declining by about 6 percent per year, thus reducing our spending and bringing the risk of recession.

If our concern is that we provide properly for the future, it is absurd to try to balance a budget that makes no distinction between government expenditures for current consumption and government expenditures of an investment nature—for physical infrastructure, basic research and the development of new technology, the education of our children, and the health of our people. We might well wish to balance a current operating budget and restrict our borrowing to net investment, borrowing and investing enough, as a rule of thumb, to have a total deficit that keeps the ratio of debt to national income or GDP constant. But balancing the budget at the expense of our public investment in the future is one way that we really borrow from our children—and never pay them back.

Will a balanced budget drive down interest rates, perhaps abetted by the Federal Reserve, so that we have more private investment? That is a dicey proposition. Lower interest rates tend to encourage investment, particularly in housing, although they also lower the interest income of millions of households. But the loss of $200 billion of purchasing power *each year* is likely to slow the economy so much that private investment, despite the best efforts of the Fed, will be less, not more.

"Supply-side economists" would reduce taxes, particularly marginal tax rates, regardless of their effect on the deficit (although some have claimed that the lower rates will increase taxable income so much that tax revenues would rise, and hence, reduce the deficit).

Some deficit hawks

What are the arguments in favor of balancing the budget, even as it is currently measured? Perhaps the most important one does not really relate to budget balancing at all but to reducing the role of government. Nobel Laureates Milton Friedman of the Hoover Institution and James Buchanan of George Mason University see the discipline of a balanced budget as preventing excessive government spending. Friedman and Buchanan, and many others, believe that in a representative form of government such as ours there are major incentives for our legislators to enact programs that may not even be in the long-term interests of the groups that promote them, much less society as a whole. The public is, however, notoriously reluctant to support higher taxes. If the programs had to be paid for by tax increases, the legislators would not dare to enact them. Economists arguing for a balanced budget on the grounds that it is necessary to reduce the role of government are not therefore arguing for a balanced budget per se. They generally disapprove of raising taxes to balance budgets more than they do of deficits.

"Supply-side economists" would reduce taxes, particularly marginal tax rates, regardless of their effect on the deficit (although some have claimed that the lower rates will increase taxable income so much that tax revenues would rise and, hence, reduce the deficit). The application of their views, along with the military buildup and the recession of 1982–1983, contributed to the large, much decried Reagan deficits. It may well be argued that those deficits, by pumping purchasing power into the economy, were a major factor in the recovery from that recession.

Many economists, including such prominent figures as Charles Schultze of the Brookings Institution, chairman of the Council of Economic Advisers under President Carter, Nobel Laureate Franco Modigliani of MIT, and Benjamin Friedman, chairman of Harvard's Economics Department, argue that deficits crowd out private investment. They claim that deficits reduce the nation's productivity and place a burden on future generations. When it is pointed out that, despite (or because of?) our recent deficits, gross private domestic investment has soared to record heights, both in absolute real terms and as a percentage of GDP, the reply is that this investment has been financed by foreigners. And this, we are told, has its cost: The interest and dividends on this investment will be paid to foreigners over the years ahead.

Budget deficits, by my estimates, do indeed contribute to trade or current account deficits with other nations. Essentially, they do so by raising our GDP and national income, thereby increasing our imports. If balancing the domestic budget were to eliminate those international deficits, they would do so by slowing our own economy. We would buy fewer Toyotas (the variety made in Japan, not Kentucky) but fewer Chryslers and Fords as well. And, further, it must be pointed out, even current account deficits averaging $100 billion a year for the next five years would add only $500 billion to net foreign claims on the United States. At a 4 percent real rate of return, that would cost us $20 billion per year, less than 0.3 percent of our GDP, hardly a burden worth risking a recession over. In the long run, we should expect a lower exchange rate to balance our current accounts, at least to a point where foreign claims become a constant proportion of our GDP.

On the larger question of deficits crowding out the total of all investment, domestic and foreign, the critical issue is how much slack there is in the economy. What Schultze, Modigliani, and Benjamin Friedman apparently have in mind is an economy that, over the long run, is essentially at full employment or, at least, at a level of employment—some call it the "natural rate"—that deficits and aggregate demand cannot generally affect. Increased government demand or consumption demand has no free resources to draw upon. The consequence will be increased inflation. It is not clear why this alone would reduce private investment. But, if the response of the Federal Reserve to the inflation is to increase nominal *and* real interest rates, the result may be expected to be a reduction in real investment and an increased burden on the future.

While changing the level and composition of government expenditures may matter, a balanced budge will do no good or harm to the economy as a whole.

If, however, the economy is at less than full employment, the increased effective demand resulting from a structural deficit will increase total output, carrying increased investment to meet the increased demand for consumer goods. My own research has indicated that this is exactly what is happening. Correctly measured, real structural deficits have been followed by lower unemployment, greater output, and more consumption *and* private investment. They have also been accompanied by more *public* investment. Far from contributing to an increased burden on our future, they have provided for greater well-being for our children and our grandchildren.

Dissident voices

Many economists agree that deficit reduction is desirable in the appropriate circumstances. But they view the current crusade for a balanced budget under current federal accounting rules that do not separate out capital expenditures—let alone a constitutional amendment that would put the economy into a fiscal straight jacket—as misguided and ill-informed. The list of dissidents includes Nobel Laureates (and past presidents of the American Economic Association) Kenneth Arrow of Stanford University, Gérard Debreu of the University of Cali-

fornia, Berkeley, Lawrence Klein of the University of Pennsylvania, Franco Modigliani and Robert M. Solow of MIT, and James Tobin of Yale University. Also included are Moses Abramovitz of Stanford, William Baumol of New York University, Charles P. Kindleberger of MIT, John Kenneth Galbraith of Harvard University, William Vickrey of Columbia University, all past presidents of the American Economic Association, and Hyman Minsky of the Levy Economic Institute, Robert Heilbroner of the New School for Social Research, Peter Bernstein, formerly with Shearson-Lehman, Paul Davidson of the University of Tennessee, and many others. Many have spoken out, but their voices have not broken through.

Some economists think that, while changing the level and composition of government expenditures may matter, a balanced budget will do no good or harm to the economy as a whole. Others think it can do serious harm. Whichever group is right, the sacrifice to attain that "balance" will be as useful as the ancient sacrifices to propitiate pagan gods—or those Western religious crusades of yesteryear.

Ten Essential Observations on Guns in America

James D. Wright

James D. Wright is the Charles and Leo Favrot Professor of Human Relations in the department of Sociology at Tulane University. He has written widely on problems of fire arms and gun control, including two books. His current researches are on the effect of poverty on the urban underclass, alcohol and drug treatment programs for the homeless, and health problems of street children in Latin America.

Talk of "gun control" is very much in the air these days. Emboldened by their successes in getting the Brady Act enacted, the pro-control forces are now striking on a number of fronts: bans on various so-called assault weapons, mandatory gun registration, strict new laws against juvenile acquisition and possession of guns, and on through the list. Much current gun-control activity springs from a recent and generally successful effort to redefine gun violence mainly as a public health issue rather than a criminal justice issue.

Increasingly, the ammunition of the gun control war is data. Pro-control advocates gleefully cite studies that seem to favor their position, of which there is no shortage, and anti-control advocates do likewise. Many of the "facts" of the case are, of course, hotly disputed; so too are their implications and interpretations. Here I should like to discuss ten essential facts about guns in America that are not in dispute—ten fundamental truths that all contestants either do or should agree to—and briefly ponder the implications of each for how the problem of guns and gun violence perhaps should be approached. These facts and their implications derive from some twenty years of research and reflection on the issues.

1. *Half the households in the country own at least one gun.* So far as I have been able to determine, the first question about gun ownership asked of a national probability sample of U.S. adults was posed in 1959; a similar question asking whether anyone in the house-hold owns a gun has since been repeated dozens of times. Over the ensuing thirty-five years, every survey has reported more or less the same result: Just about half of all U.S. households own one or more guns. This is probably not the highest gun ownership percentage among the advanced industrial societies (that honor probably goes to the Swiss), but it qualifies as a very respectable showing. We are, truly, a "gun culture."

Five important implications follow more or less unambiguously from this first essential observation.

The percentage of households owning guns has been effectively constant for nearly four decades; at the same time, the total number of guns in circulation has increased substantially, especially in the last two decades. The evident implication is that the increasing supply of guns has been absorbed by population growth, with newly formed households continuing to arm themselves at the average rate, and by the purchase of additional guns by households already owning one or more of them. In fact there is fairly solid evidence that the average number of guns owned by households owning any has increased from about three in the late 1970s to about four today.

The second implication is thus that many (and conceivably nearly all) of the new guns coming into circulation are being purchased by people who already own guns, as opposed to first-time purchases by households or individuals who previously owned no guns. I think it is also obvious that from the viewpoint of public safety, the transition from N to N + 1 guns is considerably less ominous than the transition from no guns to one gun. If this second implication is correct, it means that *most of the people in the gun shops today buying new guns already own at least one gun*, a useful point to keep in mind when pondering, for example, the alleged "cooling off" function to be served by waiting periods imposed at the point of retail sale.

Furthermore, it is frequently argued by pro-control advocates that the mere presence of guns causes people to do nutty and violent things that they would otherwise never even consider. In the academic literature on "guns as aggression-eliciting stimuli," this is called the "trigger pulls the finger" hypothesis. If there were much substance to this viewpoint, the fact that half of all U.S. households possess a gun would seem to imply that there ought to be a lot more nuttiness "out there" than we actually observe. In the face of widespread alarm about the skyrocketing homicide rate, it is important to remember that the rate is still a relatively small number of homicides (ten to fifteen or so) per hundred thousand people. If half the households own guns and the mere presence of guns incites acts of violence, then one would expect the bodies to be piled three deep, and yet they are not.

Fourth, gun ownership is normative, not deviant, behavior across vast swaths of the social landscape. In certain states and localities, it would be an odd duck indeed who did not own a gun. Surveys in some smaller southern cities, for example, have reported local gun ownership rates in excess of 90 percent.

And finally, to attempt to control crime or violence by controlling the general ownership or use of guns among the public at large is to attempt to control the behaviors of a very small fraction of the population (the criminally or violently inclined fraction) by controlling the behaviors and activities of roughly half the U.S. population. Whatever else might be said about such an approach, it is certainly not very efficient.

2. *There are 200 million guns already in circulation in the United States*, give or take a few tens of millions. It has been said, I think correctly, that firearms are the most commonly owned piece of sporting equipment in the United States, with the exception of pairs of sneakers. In any case, contestants on all sides of the gun debate generally agree that the total number of guns in circulation is on the order of 200 million—nearly one gun for every man, women, and child in the country.

It is not entirely clear how many acts of gun violence occur in any typical year. There are 30–35,000 deaths due to guns each year, perhaps a few hundred thousand nonfatal but injurious firearms accidents, maybe 500,000 or 600,000 chargeable gun crimes (not including crimes of illegal gun possession and carrying), and God knows how many instances in which guns are used to intimidate or prey upon one's fellow human beings. Making generous allowances all around, however, the total number of acts of accidental and intentional gun violence, whether fatal, injurious, or not, cannot be more than a couple of million, at the outside. This implies that the 200 million guns now in circulation would be sufficient to sustain roughly another century of gun violence at the current rates, even assuming that each gun was used once and only once for some nefarious purpose and that all additions to the gun supply were halted permanently and at once. Because of the large number of guns already in circulation, the violence-reductive effects of even fairly Draconian gun-control measures enacted today might well not be felt for decades.

Most of the people in the gun shops today buying new guns already own at least one gun.

Many recent gun-control initiatives, such as the Brady Act, are aimed at the point of retail sale of firearms and are therefore intended to reduce or in some way disrupt the flow of new guns into the domestic market. At the outside, the number of new guns coming onto the market yearly is a few million, which adds but a few percent to the existing supply. If we intend to control gun violence by reducing the availability of firearms to the general public, as many argue we should, then we have to find some workable means to confront or control the vast arsenal of guns already circulating through private hands.

Various "amnesty," "buyback," and "please turn in your guns" measures have been attempted in various jurisdictions all over the country; in one well-publicized effort, teenagers could swap guns for Toys R Us gift certificates. The success of these programs has been measured in units of several dozen or at most a few hundred relinquished firearms; the net effect on the overall supply of guns is far too trivial to even bother calculating.

3. *Most of those 200 million guns are owned for socially innocuous sport and recreational purposes.* Only about a third of the guns presently in circulation are handguns; the remainder are rifles and shotguns. When one asks gun owners why they own guns, various sport and recreational activities dominate the responses—hunting, target shooting, collecting, and the like. Even when the question is restricted to handgun owners, about 40 percent say they own the gun for sport and recreational applications, another 40 percent say they own it for self-protection, and the remaining

20 percent cite their job or occupation as the principal reason for owning a gun.

Thus for the most part, gun ownership is apparently a topic more appropriate to the sociology of leisure than to the criminology or epidemiology of violence. Many pro-control advocates look on the sporting uses of guns as atavistic, barbaric, or just plain silly. But an equally compelling case could be made against golf, which causes men to wear funny clothes, takes them away from their families, and gobbles up a lot of pretty, green, open space that would be better used as public parks. It is, of course, true that golf does not kill 35,000 people a year (although middle-aged men drop dead on the golf course quite regularly), but it is also true that the sport and recreational use of guns does not kill 35,000 people a year. There are fewer than a thousand fatal hunting accidents annually; death from skeet shooting, target practice, and such is uncounted but presumably very small. It is the violent or criminal *abuse* of guns that should concern us, and the vast majority of guns now in circulation will never be used for anything more violent or abusive than killing the furry creatures of the woods and fields.

The sport and recreational use of guns does not kill 35,000 people a year.

Unfortunately, when we seek to control violence by controlling the general ownership and use of firearms among the public at large, it at least *looks* as though we think we have intuited some direct causal connection between drive-by shootings in the inner city and squirrel hunting or skeet shooting in the hinterland. In any case, this is the implication that the nation's squirrel hunters and skeet shooters often draw; frankly, is it any wonder they sometimes come to question the motives, not to mention the sanity, of anyone who would suggest such a thing?

4. *Many guns are also owned for self-defense against crime, and some are indeed used for that purpose; whether they are actually any safer or not, many people certainly seem to feel safer when they have a gun.* There is a fierce debate raging in gun advocacy circles these days over recent findings by Gary Kleck that Americans use guns to protect themselves against crime as often as one or two million times a year, which, if true, is hard to square with the common assumption of pro-control advocates that guns are not an efficacious defense against crime. Whatever the true number of self-defensive uses, about a quarter of all guns owners

and about 40 percent of handgun owners cite defense against crime as the main reason they own a gun, and large percentages of those who give some other main reason will cite self-defense as a secondary reason. Gun owners and gun advocates insist that guns provide real protection, as Kleck's findings suggest; anti-gun advocates insist that the sense of security is more illusory than real.

But practically everything people do to protect themselves against crime provides only the illusion of security in that any such measure can be defeated by a sufficiently clever and motivated criminal. Dogs can be diverted or poisoned, burglar bars can be breached, home alarm systems can be subverted, chains and deadbolt locks can be cut and picked. That sales of all these items have skyrocketed in recent years is further proof—as if further proof were needed—that the fear of crime is real. Most people have also realized, correctly, that the police cannot protect them from crime. So people face the need to protect themselves and many choose to own a gun, along with taking many other measures, for this purpose. Does a society that is manifestly incapable of protecting its citizens from crime and predation really have the right or moral authority to tell people what they may and may not do to protect themselves?

Since a "sense of security" is inherently a psychological trait, it does no good to argue that the sense of security afforded by owning a gun is "just an illusion." Psychological therapy provides an *illusion* of mental wellness even as we remain our former neurotic selves, and it is nonetheless useful. The only sensible response to the argument that guns provide only an illusion of security is, So what?

5. *The bad guys do not get their guns through customary retail channels.* Research on both adult and juvenile felons and offenders has made it obvious that the illicit firearms market is dominated, overwhelmingly, by informal swaps, trades, and purchases among family members, friends, acquaintances, and street and black-market sources. It is a rare criminal indeed who attempts to acquire a gun through a conventional over-the-counter transaction with a normal retail outlet. It is also obvious that many or most of the guns circulating through criminal hands enter the illicit market through theft from legitimate gun owners. (An aside of some possible significance: Large numbers of legitimate gun owners also obtain guns through informal "street" sources.)

As I have already noted, many efforts at gun control pertain to the initial retail sale of weapons, for example, the prohibition against gun purchases by people with felony records or alcohol or drug histories contained in the Gun Control Act of 1968, the national five-day waiting period, or various state and local permit and registration laws. Since felons rarely obtain guns through retail channels, controls imposed at the point of retail sale necessarily miss the vast majority of criminal firearms transactions. It is thus an easy

---

The national five-day waiting period will have no effect on the acquisition of guns by criminals because that is not how the bad guys get their guns in the first place.

---

prediction that the national five-day waiting period will have no effect on the acquisition of guns by criminals because that is not how the bad guys get their guns in the first place.

Having learned (now more than a decade ago) that the criminal acquisition of guns involves informal and intrinsically difficult-to-regulate transfers that are entirely independent of laws concerning registration and permits, average gun owners often conclude (whether rightly or wrongly) that such measures must therefore be intended primarily to keep tabs on them, that registration or permit requirements are "just the first step" toward outright confiscation of all privately held firearms, and that mandated registration of new gun purchases is thus an unwarranted "police state" intrusion on law-abiding citizens' constitutional rights. Reasoning in this vein often seems bizarre or even psychotic to proponents of registration or permit laws, but it is exactly this reasoning that accounts for the white-hot ferocity of the debate over guns in America today.

And similar reasoning applies to the national waiting period: Since it is well known that the bad guys do not generally obtain guns through normal retail channels, waiting periods enforced at the point of retail sale can only be aimed at thwarting the legitimate intentions of the "good guys." What conceivable crime-reductive benefit will a national five-day waiting period give us? If the answer is "probably very little," then the minds of average gun owners are free to speculate on the nefarious and conspiratorial intentions that may be harbored, consciously or not, by those who favor such a thing. The distinction between ill-considered and evil is quickly lost, and the debate over guns in America gets hotter still.

That the illicit gun market is supplied largely through theft from legitimate owners erodes any use-

ful distinction between legitimate and illegitimate guns. Any gun that can be owned legitimately can be stolen from its legal owner and can end up in criminal hands. The effort to find some way to interdict or interfere with the criminal gun market while leaving legitimate owners pretty much alone is therefore bootless. So long as anybody can have a gun, criminals will have them too, and it is useful to remember that there are 200 million guns out there—an average of four of them in every second household.

6. *The bad guys inhabit a violent world; a gun often makes a life-or-death difference to them.* When one asks felons—either adult or juvenile—why they own and carry guns, themes of self-defense, protection, and survival dominate the responses. Very few of the bad guys say they acquire or carry guns for offensive or criminal purposes, although that is obviously how many of them get used. These men live in a very hostile and violent environment, and many of them have come to believe, no doubt correctly, that their ability to survive in that environment depends critically on being adequately armed. Thus the bad guys are highly motivated gun consumers who will not be easily dissuaded from possessing, carrying, and using guns. If sheer survival is the issue, then a gun is a bargain at practically any price. As James Q. Wilson has argued, most of the gun violence problem results from the wrong kinds of people carrying guns at the wrong time and place. The survival motive among the bad guys means exactly that the "wrong kinds of people" will be carrying guns pretty much all the time. The evident implication is that the bad guys have to be disarmed on the street if the rates of gun violence are to decline, and that implies a range of intervention strategies far removed from what gun control advocates have recently urged on the American population.

7. *Everything the bad guys do with their guns is already against the law.* That criminals will generally be indifferent to our laws would seem to follow from the definitions of the terms, but it is a lesson that we have had to relearn time and time again throughout our history. So let me stress an obvious point: Murder is already against the law, yet murderers still murder; armed robbery is against the law, yet robbers still rob. And as a matter of fact, gun acquisition by felons, whether from retail or private sources, is also already illegal, yet felons still acquire guns. Since practically everything the bad guys do with their guns is already against the law, we are entitled to wonder whether there is any new law we can pass that would persuade them to stop doing it. It is more than a little bizarre to assume that people who routinely violate laws against murder, robbery, or assault would somehow find them-

selves compelled to obey gun laws, whatever provisions they might contain.

8. *Demand creates it own supply.* That "demand creates its own supply" is sometimes called the First Law of Economics, and it clearly holds whether the commodity in demand is legal or illegal. So long as a demand exists, there will be profit to be made in satisfying it, and therefore it will be satisfied. In a capitalist economy, it could scarcely be otherwise. So long as people, be they criminals or average citizens, want to own guns, guns will be available for them to own. The vast arsenal of guns already out there exists in the first instance because people who own guns like guns, the activities that guns make possible, and the sense of security that guns provide. "Supply side" approaches to the gun problem are never going to be any more effective than "supply side" approaches to the drug problem, which is to say, not at all. What alcohol and drug prohibition should have taught us (but apparently has not) is that if a demand exists and there is no legal way to satisfy it, then an illegal commerce in the commodity is spawned, and we often end up creating many more problems than we have solved.

Brazil and several European nations manufacture small arms; the Brazilian lines are relatively inexpensive but decent guns. In fundamental respects, the question whether we can disarm the American criminal population amounts to asking whether an organized criminal enterprise that successfully illegally imports hundreds of tons of Colombian cocaine into the U.S. market each year would not find the means to illegally import hundreds of tons of handguns from Brazil. And if this is the case, then it seems more or less self-evident that the supply of firearms to the criminal population will never be reduced by enough to make an appreciable difference.

9. *Guns are neither inherently good nor inherently evil; guns, that is, do not possess teleology.* Benevolence and malevolence inhere in the motives and behaviors of people, not in the technology they possess. Any firearm is neither more nor less than a chunk of machined metal that can be put to a variety of purposes, all involving a small projectile hurtling at high velocity downrange to lodge itself in a target. We can only call this "good" when the target is appropriate and "evil" when it is not; the gun itself is immaterial to this judgment.

Gun-control advocates have a long history of singling out "bad" guns for policy attention. At one time, the emphasis was on small, cheap handguns—"Saturday Night Specials"—which were thought to be inherently "bad" because no legitimate use was thought to exist for them and because they were thought to be

the preferred firearm among criminals. Both these thoughts turned out to be incorrect. Somewhat later, all handguns, regardless of their characteristics, were singled out (as by the National Coalition to Ban Handguns); most recently, the so-called military-style assault weapons are the "bad guns of the month."

From the gun culture's viewpoint, restrictions on the right to "keep and bear arms" amount to the systematic destruction of a valued way of life and are thus a form of cultural genocide.

Singling out certain types of guns for policy attention is almost always justified on the grounds that the type of gun in question "has no legitimate use" or "is designed only to kill." By definition, however, all guns are "designed to kill" (that is, to throw a projectile downrange to lodge in a target), and if one grants the proposition that self-defense against predation and plunder is a legitimate reason to own a gun, then all guns, regardless of their type or characteristics, have at least some potentially "legitimate" application. It seems to me, therefore, that the focus in gun-control circles on certain "bad" guns is fundamentally misplaced. When all is said and done, it is the behavior of people that we should seek to control. Any gun can be used legitimately by law-abiding people to hunt, shoot at targets, or defend themselves against crime; and likewise, any gun can be used by a criminal to prey upon and intimidate other people. Trying to sort firearms into "inherently bad" and "inherently good" categories seems fundamentally silly.

10. *Guns are important elements of our history and culture.* Attempts to control crime by regulating the ownership or use of firearms are attempts to regulate the artifacts and activities of a culture that, in its own way, is as unique as any of the myriad other cultures that comprise the American ethnic mosaic. This is the American gun culture, which remains among the least understood of any of the various subcultural strands that make up modern American society.

There is no question that a gun culture exists, one that amply fulfills any definition of a culture. The best evidence we have on its status as a culture is that the single most important predictor of whether a person owns a gun is whether his or her father owned one, which means that gun owning is a tradition transmitted across generations. Most gun owners report that there were firearms in their homes when they were growing up; this is true even of criminal gun users.

The existence and characteristics of the American gun culture have implications that rarely are appreciated. For one, gun control deals with matters that people feel strongly about, that are integral to their upbringing and their worldview. Gun-control advocates are frequently taken aback by the stridency with which their seemingly modest and sensible proposals are attacked, but from the gun culture's viewpoint, restrictions on the right to "keep and bear arms" amount to the systematic destruction of a valued way of life and are thus a form of cultural genocide.

Guns evoke powerful, emotive imagery that often stands in the way of intelligent debate. To the pro-control point of view, the gun is symbolic of much that is wrong in American culture. It symbolizes violence, aggression, and male dominance, and its use is seen as an acting out of our most regressive and infantile fantasies. To the gun culture's way of thinking, the same gun symbolizes much that is right in the culture.

It symbolizes manliness, self-sufficiency, and independence, and its use is an affirmation of man's relationship to nature and to history. The "Great American Gun War," as Bruce-Briggs has described it, is far more than a contentious debate over crime and the equipment with which it is committed. It is a battle over fundamental and equally legitimate sets of values.

Scholars and criminologists who speculate on the problem of guns, crime, and violence would thus do well to look at things, at least occasionally, from the gun culture's point of view. Hardly any of the 50 million or so American families that own guns have ever harmed anyone with their guns, and virtually none ever intend to. Nearly everything these families will ever do with their firearms is both legal and largely innocuous. When, in the interests of fighting crime, we advocate restrictions on their rights to own guns, we are casting aspersions on their decency, as though we somehow hold them responsible for the crime and violence that plague this nation. It is any wonder they object, often vociferously, to such slander?

Do It Yourself

Washington—and Americans—are at a crossroads between the collective approach to social security and medicare and the corporate trend toward self-reliance. Workers may become more prudent consumers as they assume responsibility for retirement and health care costs, but the disadvantaged may find it difficult to provide for their own needs.

JULIE KOSTERLITZ

Once upon a time, not so very long ago, we were all in it together. With the creation of social security in the wake of the Great Depression, continuing with the spread of company pension and health plans after World War II and climaxing with the passage of medicare in 1965, Americans constructed a public and private social welfare system to provide themselves with greater economic security.

Mostly these were collective arrangements through which working Americans of great and modest means alike pooled their resources for financial protection against often random, but universal, hazards. Chief among these were the risk of illness or injury and the risk of outliving one's savings. Industrial Age substitutes for the extended family, these arrangements have run on cross-subsidies—the healthy supporting the sick, the young shoring up the old and, often, high-wage earners helping those with low wages.

Now, however, that system of social welfare is up for grabs. Pools are breaking apart, and the guarantees are disappearing. In their place are new programs that require individuals to take on the responsibility and risk of providing for their own financial security. "We're coming to a series of turning points, whether we realize it or not," departing Labor Secretary Robert B. Reich said in an interview.

These changes bring the likelihood of more unequal outcomes: Some will undoubtedly improve their lot, while others, just as surely, will face greater hardship.

The old guarantees are vanishing as employers make workers responsible for retirement and health care. Medicare and social security may follow suit.

The transformation is already well under way in the private sector. Employers' traditional pension plans with their guaranteed fixed payments are being supplanted by voluntary, individually owned and controlled, tax-subsidized retirement savings accounts. Earlier this year, Congress approved—as a limited experiment—tax subsidies to medical savings accounts (MSAs), an individualized alternative to traditional employer-sponsored group health insurance. MSAs essentially allow workers to leave the health insurance risk pool, taking their premium contributions with them to help finance their own care.

It may not be long before social security and medicare, traditionally politically insulated from fundamental change, undergo a similar transformation. With the medicare trust fund's costs already outstripping its income, and social security's expected to follow suit in the not-too-distant future, calls are mounting in some quarters for fundamental change: converting social security to a system of private individual savings accounts, and medicare to a system of vouchers to be put toward the cost of private health plans or MSAs.

What's driving these changes? Clearly some economic forces are at work: Slower growth makes it tougher to finance the ever more sophisticated health care and the longer retirements we have come to expect. An increasingly competitive business environment makes employers more cost-conscious about benefits. A growing disparity between incomes makes these programs' egalitarian features an increasing drag on the prospects of the well-to-do. And the changing nature of the labor market makes rewards for long service less enticing to workers and bosses alike. Most workers nowadays don't intend to spend their careers at one job, and employers are reluctant to encourage all of their workers to stay.

Demography hasn't helped either. Longer life expectancies and a rapidly aging population will greatly accelerate the nation's cost of supporting retirement. Rising health care costs compound the problem.

Political attitudes have also changed with time. Increasing public disillusion with government may have its corollary in the rising emphasis on individual responsibility and self-reliance. These attitudes are also encouraged by the powerful business interests that stand to make money on the new "do-it-yourself" arrangements: mutual funds and insurance companies to name two.

Some see a broader cultural shift. "It's part of the fragmentation of America, the breakdown in the idea of community, the ethic that we share some responsibility for each other," said John C. Rother, the director of legislation and public policy for the American Association of Retired Persons, who is on sabbatical from that post to research policy options for the graying of America.

Others of a more libertarian or conservative bent believe that the collective arrangements are bringing about their own demise because they mask the true cost of benefits and fuel overconsumption. "The ability to rely on politics, to plan a life based on political redistribution of income is going away. It's not sustainable," author and former Bush Administration aide James P. Pinkerton said in an interview.

In the boom days after World War II, with employers eager to attract workers and still-ascendant labor unions flexing their muscles, employee benefit plans spread throughout corporate America.

To those critics, a move toward self-provision beats the alternative: more redistribution of wealth and rationing of benefits. David Frum, a Toronto-based senior fellow at the conservative Manhattan Institute, writes in his recent book, *What's Right:* "The right sort of entitlement reform must not only liberate Washington from impossible spending commitments; it must liberate people from the Washington social-welfare system, by moving them toward individual

control of their own pension and health plans."

But to others, this trend signals danger. "The potential problem has to do with what I call 'the secession of the successful,' " Reich said. "You've got to be very careful that we don't simply create back doors through which the wealthier, the healthier and the better-off can simply remove themselves from risk pools, thereby leaving the sicker and the less-well-off facing even higher premiums and fewer ways of making it."

Over the next decade, Congress and the President will be asked to make a basic choice: whether to try to shore up the traditional public and private collective arrangements and their egalitarian ideals or to embrace self-reliance. "The issue here is how much risk we're going to bear societally and how much we're going to put on individuals," Robert D. Reischauer, a Brookings Institution senior fellow and former Congressional Budget Office director, said.

It's the same debate Americans have had with themselves periodically, since at least the days of the New Deal. But such sweeping questions are never answered once and for all: Societies change their institutions to reflect changing circumstances and public preferences.

The public, however, has shown massive ambivalence. In the early 1990s, Americans clamored for guaranteed health care coverage but blanched at the elaborate government orchestration President Clinton proposed. Voters reacted harshly to reports of Republicans' meddling with medicare yet returned them to control both chambers of Congress.

This debate's outcome could depend heavily on how it is framed. "Once you define [the debate as] taking care of themselves as opposed to having government take care of them, you're on a very different slope, in my judgment," Theodore R. Marmor, a professor of public policy and management at Yale University, said.

And they may break down along class lines. "Those who do well in life tend to view the world as a fair place. Their success is indication of hard work and prudent decisions," Reischauer said. "For those on the other end, the world is a slightly unfair place, where external forces relegate them to the bottom."

Americans' ambivalence, memorialized by their recent vote to keep a divided government, guarantees a continuing struggle in Congress on these critical issues.

BENEFIT PLANS STALL

In the boom days after World War II, with employers eager to attract workers and still-ascendant labor unions flexing their muscles, employee benefit plans spread throughout corporate America.

But for at least the past decade, the trend has stalled. The share of the population covered by employer pension plans leveled off around 49 per cent in 1987; the share of the nonelderly with job-related health coverage fell from 69.5 per cent in 1988 to 63.8 per cent in 1995, according to the Employee Benefit Research Institute (EBRI). The institute says this means that in 1995 roughly eight million more nonelderly Americans lacked health insurance than in 1988.

Just as important, however, the character of the benefit arrangements is changing. The traditional pension plan of the postwar era, specially structured to reward long tenure with a company, guaranteed all workers a "defined benefit" for the duration of their retirement—however long that might be. The onus was on employers to come up with the money and to insulate workers from the downside risks of investments.

Starting in the late 1970s, an increasing share of employers began promising to make only a "defined contribution" toward a worker's retirement fund. The onus was still on employers to come up with the contributions, and workers benefited from the investment savvy of the collective pension fund. They were, however, no longer guaranteed a predetermined benefit.

But after 1981, encouraged by a change in Internal Revenue Service regulations, an increasing number of employers moved another step away from the world of guarantees, setting up retirement plans that merely offered workers the opportunity to contribute their own money to tax-deferred retirement savings plans. Known to the public by their tax code nomenclature, 401(k)s, these savings accounts have also acquired another name: "do-it-yourself" plans. With these plans, what workers draw in retirement depends on how much they save (many employers match part of workers' contributions), on their investment savvy and on the vagaries of the stock markets.

The change was, in part, a response to a more competitive business climate. Plans rewarding seniority no longer made sense, Dallas L. Salisbury, president of the EBRI, said. "In an environment where you're reengineering [for efficiency], the last thing you want is a tool that encourages everyone to stay, because the ones it proves most effective in keeping are those with the lowest marketability."

But the change has also both reflected and magnified a growing disparity in wages between the top and bottom earners. The old-style plans typically required everyone to participate, provided some subsidies (both from those who died before collecting benefits and sometimes from shareholders) and set contribution levels that were proportional to salaries. The new plans, with their emphasis on voluntarism, have different sets of incentives and subsidies, which tend to favor those with higher incomes. "The wage gap is being mirrored in a benefits gap," Reich said. "Companies are providing fairly generous compensation packages to top-level executives, not only wage packages and stock-option packages, but also benefit packages of all sorts. The further you go down in the company ranks, the more you see these wages dropping, but also the cost of benefits being shifted to employees or dropped altogether."

Efforts to preserve the egalitarian ideal in retirement plans have stumbled and arguably have even backfired. In 1986 and again in 1993—concerned at the growing drain on the Treasury and anxious to ensure that retirement plans didn't merely become tax shelters for the wealthy—Congress imposed an array of rules designed to curb benefits at the top of the income scale and to assure some measure of parity between high and low-income earners.

But employers argued that the rules were cumbersome and counterproductive and that they discouraged employers from setting up such plans. Congress responded earlier this year by relaxing some of the rules governing the retirement savings plans. *(See NJ, 9/21/96, p. 2003.)*

Before that, however, top corporate executives had already begun circumventing the restrictions by opting out of or supplementing their companies' retirement plans with separate, corporate-subsidized—although somewhat riskier-arrangements for themselves. A recent *New York Times* series documented the rapid rise in the use of these "deferred-compensation" arrangements. Under these arrangements, executives opt to let their companies retain and invest some of their pay—effectively deferring taxes on that money until the executives receive it years later. Unlike 401(k) plans, there are no limits on how much can be put away. Some companies guarantee high interest rates and offer matching contributions on the deferred pay.

These developments don't merely ratify a greater disparity of benefits, they also sever the link between upper-income and lower-income workers. Before the equity-oriented 401(k) rules were liberalized, top executives had a self-interest in seeing that their low-wage counterparts contributed to 401(k) plans. The new rules permit indifference. Similarly, as *The Times* notes, separate deferred-compensation plans for top officials remove the executives' personal stake in the viability or the generosity of the corporate retirement plans for the rank and file.

COSTS SHIFT TO WORKERS

The nature of corporate health care plans is also changing. Already corporate plans are shifting more costs to workers: According to Labor Department data, the share of employers who pay the full freight for workers' health coverage dropped from 74 per cent in 1980 to just 37 per cent in 1993.

The limited introduction of tax-subsidized medical savings accounts could also fundamentally alter the nature of health insurance—doing away with most risk sharing and fragmenting risk pools.

Moreover, some employers appear to be moving—as many in the pension arena already have—away from the guarantee of broad health care benefits over to the lesser guarantee of a fixed-dollar contribution toward the cost of a health plan. Jack A. Meyer, president of the Economic and Social Research Institute in Washington, reports that two private coalitions he works with that bring together small businesses to purchase health care services are on the verge of introducing such a system; several large businesses have also suggested they may move in this direction.

Meyer said the goals, to introduce competition by health plans and cost consciousness by consumers, are appealing. But over time, this could split up the broader risk pool, with the wealthier and those in ill health opting to pay more for privileges such as wider selection of physicians.

The limited introduction of tax-subsidized MSAs could also fundamentally alter the nature of health insurance—doing away with most risk sharing and fragmenting risk pools.

Here's why: MSAs substitute low-deductible plans that have high premiums with high-deductible, or catastrophic illness insurance plans that charge lower premiums. Employers or employees can stash away pre-tax dollars in the savings accounts to help defray costs below the deductible, as well as any uncovered expenses. What they don't use builds up with tax-free interest. Cash can be taken out and spent for other things, but the withdrawn amount is slapped with taxes and a penalty.

Many analysts, including those at the American Academy of Actuaries, believe these plans would be attractive to the healthy (who are unlikely to use up all the cash on medical care) and the wealthy (because they can afford possible out-of-pocket expenses and because their higher tax brackets make tax-free savings more attractive).

MSAs are likely to be unattractive to that small share of the population with chronic illnesses, people who know that they'll require more care and who will spend their own money each year to meet the deductible. They may also scare off low-income people, who are loath to take the risk of having to pay out of pocket for health care. Those people will be left in an increasingly costly risk pool. "You have relatively few people who account for most of [the health insurance] claims," said Anna M. Rappaport, a principal at the Chicago office of William M. Mercer Inc., a New York City-based employee benefits consulting firm. "It's a social question who will pay for them, if not everyone contributes" to the cost of their care.

MSA advocates dispute this analysis, arguing that the plan will have universal appeal and benefit. More important, they argue, it's the best means for controlling costs without having government or health maintenance organizations impose rationing. "Risk pooling distorts incentives for any kind of consumption. When the item consumed is health care, the distortions are the worst," according to John C. Goodman, president of the Dallas-based National Center for Policy Analysis, who came up with the MSA concept in the mid-1980s. "There's going to be draconian rationing unless people set aside funds" for their own care, he said.

It was after a protracted and bitter battle over just such issues that Congress approved the limited version of tax-subsidized MSAs. Among the limitations: Only 750,000 taxpayers working for small businesses or for themselves can set them up. After evaluating the results of the experiment at the turn of the century, Congress will have to vote on whether to expand the MSAs' availability.

Goodman, of course, is betting the plans will prove so popular that Congress will have no choice. "There will be pressure to let more people in," he said.

Ironically, the controversial MSA measure was attached to a broader bill that was intended to shore up the traditional system of pooling risk. The Health Coverage Availability and Affordability Act restricts insurers' ability to deny people coverage because of preexisting conditions and guarantees most workers the right to keep their health insurance when they leave their jobs.

That Congress passed both measures at the same time, despite their conflicting philosophies, is perhaps a reflection of both public ambivalence on the deeper issues and the challenges facing divided government in tackling the issues.

"This society has to make a choice— we'll make it implicitly or explicitly," Reich said. "The choice is whether we try to somehow prop up the private system of social [welfare] or whether we embark upon a new system of [public] social insurance for the middle class or below." A critical problem with the second option, he conceded, is that "we don't have the money."

Still, Reich maintains that it is possible to use the resources of government selectively to plug holes in the private-sector safety net. Case in point: The Clinton Administration's proposal to create a narrow, publicly financed health insurance program for the short-term unemployed—a proposal for which, Reich insists, financing has already been identified.

There is, Reich concedes on reflection, a third alternative: "Sink or swim . . . that is, everyone is on his or her own. That's the direction we're moving in right now."

THE EGALITARIAN IDEAL

It may prove difficult enough, however, just to maintain the public social insurance programs we already have. The question is not whether to cut social security and medicare: Some retrenchment in both programs is a given.

The more nettlesome question is about whether it's possible, or indeed desirable, to preserve the programs' universal and collective nature and their egalitarian ideals.

Last year's dustup between Clinton and the Republican Congress over medicare may have been a preview of the battles

to come. The '96 campaign trail rhetoric notwithstanding, the fight was not exclusively, or even principally, about how much to "cut" (or, in Republican parlance, how much to "slow the growth of") medicare spending. Indeed, Congress's final spending proposal wasn't radically different from the President's.

The deeper differences were over the government's promise of providing equal treatment for the elderly. Republicans billed their plan as an opportunity for medicare beneficiaries to take advantage of health plans that were more diverse and efficient.

Congressional Democrats and the Clinton Administration, however, argued that the GOP plan would have fragmented medicare's broad risk pool, because it provided inadequate safeguards against health plans that use subtle methods to skim off the good health risks, leaving everyone else in an anorexic public program. Democrats argued that it also would have made access to certain types of plans dependent on the ability to pay. "You easily could have gotten risk segmentation and a class-based system," Brookings's Reischauer said.

The political coup de grâce from the Democrats' standpoint is that the GOP measure, which was part of a broader budget reconciliation bill that Clinton vetoed, included a proposal to give medicare patients access to MSAs—a further threat to the medicare risk pool.

But don't think some of the same issues won't be back, and soon. Congress and the President may partially dodge the medicare bullet with smaller fixes to next year's budget that would also push back the date of medicare's rendezvous with bankruptcy, now projected for 2001. But as the baby boomers start retiring, medicare's costs will become so large that most analysts doubt the feasibility of raising taxes to cover them.

"As an abstract philosophical issue, it's hard for people to say, 'We choose not to do social insurance,' " said Gail R. Wilensky, a senior fellow at the nonprofit health foundation Project Hope who ran medicare for two years during the Bush Administration. But faced with vastly higher taxes, she said, "people may be willing to take a second look."

The government may well be forced to choose between two unpalatable alternatives: continuing to offer all beneficiaries an equal, but deteriorating level of care or, following the private employers' lead, limiting its own financial liability and offering beneficiaries a defined contribution toward the cost of care. Patients who could afford to pay extra for better-quality plans would be free to do so, and the rest would have to take what they could get.

Reischauer concedes that sooner or later, fiscal constraints may force the government to abandon medicare's classless character. "It would be impossible not to sacrifice that somewhat under any of the alternatives," he said.

> *The problem isn't merely that there are no painless solutions. It is also that one consequence seems inevitable: the program becomes an increasingly unattractive financial proposition for the well-to-do.*

Although social security's fiscal problems aren't nearly as severe, reform quickly raises some similarly thorny questions.

The problem isn't merely that there are no painless solutions. It is also that, no matter how the pain is distributed— whether taxes are raised, the retirement age extended, or cost-of-living increases reduced—one consequence seems inevitable: The program becomes an increasingly unattractive financial proposition for the well-to-do.

Until recently, despite the program's built-in redistribution to the less-well-off, all recipients got more in benefits than they put in—thanks to rising payroll taxes and to favorable economic and demographic trends.

Already, however, high-income single men who retired in the past decade are projected to receive less in lifetime benefits than they contributed to social security, and other high-income groups will eventually face the same prospect. Cuts in the program only exacerbate the problem. "It becomes a very bad deal for younger workers, and that's especially true at upper-income levels," William J. Beeman, director of economic studies at the corporate-sponsored think tank Committee for Economic Development, said. Low-income workers still get a positive rate of return on their contributions when they retire, he said, but "of course, political pressures are more heavy from middle and upper-income people."

Converting social security to a system of private individual savings accounts might eventually obviate that problem—it would lessen redistribution of income. Fans of this approach contend that because the money can be invested in stocks and bonds, everyone—including low-income elderly people-would get a better return on their money than they do from social security. The rich might benefit disproportionately from the change, they admit, but what does that matter if everyone's better-off?

Social security's defenders don't buy this economic scenario, for a host of reasons. Instead, they argue, many low-income and middle-income retirees would face greater risk of ending up worse-off. *(For more about privatization of social security, see NJ, 12/23/95, p. 3136.)*

But one level below the dizzying technical arguments about how to overhaul social security—and indeed the entire social welfare system—are profound philosophical disagreements about the value of collective action, the pooling of risk and trying to ensure everyone an equitable financial outcome.

"Besides the fiscal problem, there's a growing realization that insuring all the actions anyone takes, takes responsibility away from the individual and causes more irresponsible behavior," David D. Boaz, executive vice president of the libertarian Cato Institute in Washington, said.

Libertarians, Yale professor Marmor countered, imagine that all people have equal capacity to fend for themselves, "to distribute their income over the life cycle and to protect themselves from [financial] risks . . . even when the sources of these risks are largely outside the individuals' control.

"It's the lake Wobegon problem: All the children are above average and all the women are good-looking," he paraphrased.

Boaz agreed that many events in a lifetime are beyond an individual's control. But he argued, "We would be a healthier, stronger, more prosperous people if we act as though we can control all the consequences. Some people will suffer" in such a system, "but over-all suffering will be less than where everyone is guaranteed against the consequences of their actions."

Marmor, however, believes that such a world would reward privilege rather than virtue. "If the world were as genial a place as it is for those who have a good education and scarce skills, rich families or trust funds," he said, U.S. society would not need a cushion. But, he noted, well-off people "are a trivial proportion of the population."

Abolish Income

"Replacing the income tax with a national retail sales tax dramatically will boost savings and

THE FEDERAL income tax system is inherently flawed. It is the biggest impediment to economic growth in the country and represents the worst form of big government intrusion into the lives of its citizens. Each year, it costs Americans more than 5,000,000,000 hours of time to comply with it. The tax code is unfair, riddled with loopholes, and has been changed 31 times in the past 41 years. Moreover, it doesn't work. By its own admission, the Internal Revenue Service fails to collect from nearly 10,000,000 taxpayers, resulting in an estimated $127,000,000,000 in uncollected taxes annually.

I propose scrapping the income tax and cutting back the Internal Revenue Service drastically. Replacing the income tax with a national retail sales tax dramatically will boost savings and investment, which, in turn, will increase wages and create additional jobs. In fact, economist Dale Jorgensen of Harvard University has concluded that, if a consumption tax like the national sales tax had replaced the current system in 1986, the U.S. would have experienced one trillion dollars more in economic growth.

The present level of economic growth provides little help in attempts to balance the budget. With an expanding economy, on the other hand, Americans could achieve higher standards of living and the government can finance necessary programs. In a low-growth economy, there are far too few resources for all competing interests. The economy becomes a zero sum game in which no one gains, except at the expense of another.

This was not always the case. In the century prior to 1970, excluding the Depression years, the economy grew at an annual rate close to four percent. Since the early 1970s, though, the growth rate has slowed to around 2.4%, dropping to an anemic annual rate of just 1.6% in the first half of 1995.

Vigorous economic growth would enable the nation to avoid this zero sum scenario. However, the economy is weighed down by an income tax system that dis-

Sen. Lugar (R.-Ind.) is chairman of the Agriculture, Nutrition, and Forestry Committee.

courages growth by taxing savings and investment at least twice.

I propose to unleash the economy by eliminating the income tax, both personal and corporate, the corresponding capital gains tax, and the estate and gift tax, and replacing them with a broad-based consumption tax on retail goods and services. Any tax proposal must meet six criteria. It has to be friendly to savings and investment, simple, the least intrusive, fair, transparent, and border-adjustable. If we are going to overhaul the tax system—rather than tinker with it—the sales tax best meets these criteria.

The first and most imperative reason for replacing the income tax with a national sales tax is that it would liberate the economy by encouraging savings. For the first time in the modern era, the next generation of Americans may be economically worse off than the previous one. Over the past several years, the average income of families has fallen. They feel trapped in a box with diminishing hope of escaping.

The bottom line is that, as a nation, we do not save enough. Savings are vital because they are the source of investment and productivity gains—supplying the capital for buying a new machine, developing an innovative product or service, or employing an extra worker. According to a 1995 poll, 72% of Americans realize that they are not saving enough for the future. The net national savings rate in the 1990s has been 1.8% of Gross Domestic Product, compared with 8.1% in the 1960s, 7.2% in the 1970s, and 3.7% in the 1980s.

The Japanese save at a rate nine times greater than Americans, and the Germans save five times as much as we do. Today, many people believe that Americans inherently consume beyond their means and can not save enough for the future. Few realize that, prior to World War II—before the income tax system reached its present form—Americans saved a larger portion of their earnings than the Japanese.

A national sales tax would reverse this trend by directly taxing consumption and leaving savings and investment untaxed. Economists agree that a broad-based consumption tax would increase the U.S. sav-

FEDERAL DISPOSAL SITE #1040

ings rate substantially. Economist Laurence Kotlikoff of Boston University estimates that it would more than triple in the first year. The implementation of a national sales tax is expected to create 1,000,000 new jobs over a 10-year period and a three percent rise in wages over that same time. Americans and the economy can not afford to wait any longer.

The second factor in choosing an effective tax system is its simplicity. Under a national sales tax, the burden of complying with the income tax code would be lifted. There would be no records to keep or audits to fear. The money a person makes is his or her own. You don't have to report it. You don't have to hide it. You may decide if you want to save it, invest it, or give it to your children. It is only when you buy something that you pay a tax. Although I

Tax and the IRS

investment, which, in turn, will increase wages and create additional jobs." **by Richard G. Lugar**

applaud the efforts of flat tax advocates to simplify tax forms, nothing could be more simple than no forms at all.

The national sales tax is the least intrusive of the tax proposals. The IRS would be dismantled substantially under the proposal and no longer would look over the shoulders of every American. There would be no audits. Americans would not waste time and effort worrying about record-keeping, deductions, or exemptions that are part of the current tax code. Although the flat tax proposals tax consumption, they do so by giving the income tax a face-lift and leaving the IRS largely intact.

The national sales tax is the fairest. Everyone pays it, including wealthy individuals, criminals, illegal aliens, and others who currently avoid taxation. Wealthy Americans who consume more would pay higher taxes under the national sales tax. Individuals who save and invest their money will pay less. Gone are the loopholes and deductions.

The national sales tax also would tax the underground economy. When criminals and illegal aliens consume the proceeds of their activities, they will pay a tax. Foreign tourists will pay as well. Tax systems that rely on income reporting never will collect any of this revenue.

Of course, the fairness test must consider those with limited means to pay taxes. An integral part of the plan is protection for Americans who need it—senior citizens, the unemployed, and those with low-paying jobs.

One strategy for addressing this situation would exempt a threshold level of goods and services consumed by each American from the Federal sales tax. Each citizen who has a Social Security number would receive this exemption. For example, if the exemption level were $5,000, a family of four would have its first $20,000 of spending exempt from the sales tax. This figure is approximately 33% above the poverty line for a family of four.

Another strategy might be the exemption of items such as housing or medicine. Americans understand and are comfortable with this practice. This is the method the majority of states have chosen and the one advocated by Rep. Bill Archer (R.-Tex.), chairman of the House Ways and Means Committee. In the end, it will be up to this committee and the Finance Committee in the Senate to decide the most desirable path.

The national sales tax is the most transparent of the tax reform proposals. A Federal tax that is evident to everyone would bolster efforts in Congress to achieve prudence in spending. There should be no hidden corporate taxes that are passed on to consumers or withholding mechanisms that mask the amount they pay in taxes. Every year, the public and Congress openly should debate the tax rate necessary for the Federal government to meet its obligations. If average Americans are paying that rate every day, they will make certain that Congress spends public funds wisely.

Finally, exports would benefit from the enactment of a national sales tax. In January, 1995, the U.S. registered one of the largest trade deficits in the nation's history. We must adopt a tax system that encourages exports. Most of our trading partners have tax systems that are border-adjustable. They are able to strip out their tax when exporting their goods. In comparison, the income tax and, for that matter, the flat tax are not border-adjustable. American goods that are sent overseas are taxed twice—once by the income tax and once when reaching their destination. In comparison, since the national sales tax would not be levied on exports, it would level the playing field with our trading partners. Best of all, foreign imports would be taxed when they are consumed in the U.S.

We live in an exciting time when the world is embracing free enterprise. The Uruguay round of GATT significantly lowered the barriers to trade. Congress is opening the telecommunications industry to competition, better enabling individuals and companies to interconnect across the globe. Goods and information are able to flow freely between nations with few obstructions. One of the last remaining barriers between countries is their tax systems. We must face the fact that America is competing with other nations whose tax systems are more friendly to investment than is our income tax.

If we enact a tax system that encourages investment and savings, billions of dollars of investment will flow into the country. During a poll taken by Princeton Economics International, executives of the top 20 Japanese companies stated unanimously that they would bring manufacturing to the U.S. if our country enacted a broad-based retail consumption tax. It makes sense. America has the most stable political system, the best infrastructure, a skilled workforce, and the largest consumer market in the world.

There will be complex transitional issues to address, but, in the end, this country will be stronger and more prosperous. With a national sales tax, America would become a magnet for jobs and investment from around the world. Its economic growth and prosperity would be unsurpassed. Our citizens and economy should not be denied this opportunity any longer.

America's Incoherent Foreign Policy

Morton A. Kaplan

Morton A. Kaplan is Distinguished Service Professor of Political Science Emeritus at the University of Chicago and editor and publisher of THE WORLD & I.

Since the demise of the Cold War—a product in part of President Ronald Reagan's lucid vision—American diplomacy has entered into a state of progressively worsening terminal incoherence. Although the vision that drove Reagan's Cold War policy did not always result in well-conceived implementation, it was matched in conception and success only by the brilliant European policy of the Truman administration, John Foster Dulles' policy of producing a split between the Soviet Union and China by pressure over the offshore islands of Quemoy and Matsu, and Nixon's plan, before Watergate, to end the Vietnam War.

For generations, the United States had to work with extremely unsavory allies, including Stalin and Middle Eastern and Latin American despots, to fend off dangerous foes. With the demise of the Soviet Union, the United States at last has an opportunity to work directly for its positive objectives: human rights and democratic development. Yet it is paying a disproportionate budgetary price for minuscule returns.

The cause is easy to discern. Our foreign-policy and national-security establishments have not the faintest glimmer of how to relate the domestic and international modalities of foreign and military policy to the prior objectives. Like bureaucrats everywhere, they lack nerve and vision.

They are aware that pressure should be put on China in favor of human rights. But they have so disorganized an international security structure that China can play the economic card by awarding a contract to Airbus that should, and would, have gone to Boeing except for the fact that the Europeans have a free NATO ride in Europe while undermining our human-rights goals in Asia and elsewhere for marginal economic ends.

THE PERILS OF SUPERPOWERDOM

Although the United States is no longer the great superpower it was in the immediate aftermath of World War II and is no longer a necessary barrier to a threatening Soviet Union, it is the *only* superpower. Other nations need it more than it needs them. Yet, except for the Gulf war, when the European nations were threatened by Saddam's possible hegemony over Gulf oil, it has rarely secured cooperation for its most important human goals.

Only when our allies understand that the United States will support them *only* if they support us will this condition change. This is not a matter of dictating to them but of making clear that the price of failing to pursue our common human and democratic objectives is the loss of American support. Only when the United States builds international modalities adapted to its major objectives will this condition change.

I shall offer one brief—not necessarily the only or the best—prescription that at least attempts coherence. Step one is to understand that NATO is not a paramount interest of the United States. There is no threat from

Russia. The western Europeans want NATO because of the residual American security guarantee. Unlike pre–World War I Serbia, the Bosnian mess was a human-rights mess, not a national-security mess. And, we are pulling the Europeans out of the mess they got themselves into, at a price that is far too high for us, without anything in return.

Poland and Hungary want to be part of NATO because they want to be part of the West, not part of the East. They also see the American relationship as an ultimate, although not a vital, guarantee. But the threatened extension of NATO to the east is a heavy cross for the democratic forces in Russia. This is not a prudent move.

The eastern European desire to be part of the West could be fully met by becoming part of Europe. This would not be potentially destabilizing to the democratic process in Russia. Europe, Russia, and the United States could offer individual and joint guarantees of the territorial integrity of the eastern European and Baltic states. The residual guarantee Hungary and Poland desire could be met because NATO is pledged to defend Europe. If Europe desires us to remain in NATO, then it should meet our needs as expressed below. There is no requirement for NATO forces to be stationed in eastern Europe.

America is paying too high a price for NATO. European nations need it more than we do, because they lack confidence in their ability to defend their interests with force. We should insist upon an additional modality adapted to our democratic and human-rights aims as the price of our remaining in NATO. Former Vice President Dan Quayle came close to the correct prescription when he called for an organization with specific aims that would include the United

COURTESY OF DEPARTMENT OF DEFENSE

■ *Well-armed for peace:* **President Reagan's policies to rebuild the American military in the 1980s were decisive in destroying communism and safeguarding democracy worldwide.**

States, the western European major powers, Russia, Japan, and China. However, the details of membership were slightly incorrect, as were the tasks he assigned to it.

NEW ORGANIZATION NEEDED

As I have proposed on a number of occasions for more than 10 years, there should be a new organization, the membership of which should include the United States, Europe as a collective entity, Russia (as long as it remains democratic), and Japan, but not China, at least unless and until it becomes democratic. It should have a collective role with respect to the peace, human rights, and democratic

development. In case of threats to the peace, joint intervention need not be required, but there should be an agreement not to pursue conflicting courses—military, diplomatic, or economic—disadvantageous to a state that intervenes in support of the principles of this organization.

Although we could not expect Europe to use force to prevent the occupation of Taiwan by China, it should fully support by economic and diplomatic measures such use of force by the United States. This organization should agree that there should be only one China but that neither force nor the threat of force should be used to unify China. It should agree that Taiwan should join the UN

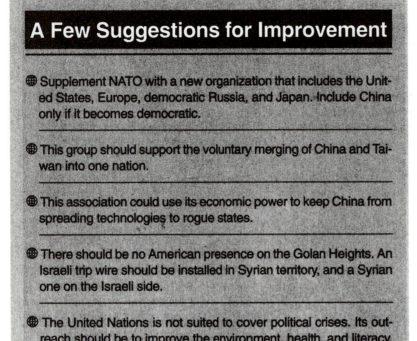

A Few Suggestions for Improvement

⊕ Supplement NATO with a new organization that includes the United States, Europe, democratic Russia, and Japan. Include China only if it becomes democratic.

⊕ This group should support the voluntary merging of China and Taiwan into one nation.

⊕ This association could use its economic power to keep China from spreading technologies to rogue states.

⊕ There should be no American presence on the Golan Heights. An Israeli trip wire should be installed in Syrian territory, and a Syrian one on the Israeli side.

⊕ The United Nations is not suited to cover political crises. Its outreach should be to improve the environment, health, and literacy, to which all its members can make a reasonable contribution.

General Assembly as a government of China but that Taiwan should adopt a constitutional clause including unification under democratic procedures as its ultimate aim.

With respect to China's dissemination of threatening technologies to states with destabilizing aims, this is the organization that should negotiate with China. If it does this jointly, its economic leverage would be overwhelming.

This organization could have played a major role with respect to Syria, although the United States should have been capable of accomplishing this by itself. Instead, we have had the unholy spectacle of our unsuccessful courting of Assad rather than our imposing a reasonable policy on him.

If the following proposal had been forcefully and privately urged by the United States, we likely would not have had the Hezbollah attacks that led to the Israeli attacks in Lebanon. Peres likely still would have remained prime minister while continuing to pursue a peace that had prospects for success because it responded to the security needs of Israel and minimal dignity requirements for a Palestinian entity.

Assad should have been informed that if he did not reach a peace with Lebanon, we would recognize the Golan Heights as part of Israel. Of course, this should have been made conditional on the reasonableness of Israel. Syria should have been promised the entire Heights in return for a peace agreement, the normalization of relations with Israel, and other measures specified below.

There is no need for an American presence on the Heights. An Israeli trip wire could be installed in Syrian territory and a Syrian trip wire in Israeli territory, with zones of demilitarization proportional to the width of the two states. It is not in the American interest to station its forces on the Heights. Furthermore, an American presence would be a disadvantage to Israel because it would impede Israeli retaliation if Syria violated the agreement. Some reasonable arrangements would have to be made for the settlers. And Assad should be forced not only to get rid of the terrorists from Syria and Lebanon but to cut off a few heads in the process.

With respect to human rights, all the members should agree to follow consistent, although not necessarily identical, policies. This organization should also support movements toward democracy, although not by force, unless very brutal regimes were involved. It should have a secretariat that would report yearly on the state of democratic developments and measures to minimize military instabilities in various regions of the world.

It should be obvious that the United Nations is not the best organization for these tasks. It includes too many tyrannies. Furthermore, like the old League of Nations, which had no veto, it accentuates horse-trading and irresponsibility, diffusing authority by allowing too many members to vote that share no responsibility for support or action. It should be limited to more general goals such as environmental, health, literacy, and other issues to which all its members can make a reasonable contribution. There is only one world with respect to these issues.

Whatever defects this program may have, it has a coherence adapted to American values and interests. There may be better programs, but they will not be produced by committees.

PUMPING UP THE PENTAGON

THE DOMESTIC GEOPOLITICS OF MILITARY SPENDING

BY WILLIAM D. HARTUNG

All last year, as the White House and the Congress were debating how far to go in shredding the social safety net by cutting welfare, health care, education, nutrition and scores of other domestic programs in the name of deficit reduction, one agency was repeatedly spared from the budget-cutting ax: the Pentagon. Six years after the fall of the Berlin Wall, the United States is still spending more than $250 billion a year on the military. This is three times the military spending of any other nation on earth, and eighteen times more than the combined military budgets of the so-called "rogue states" (Iran, Iraq, Libya, Syria, North Korea, and Cuba) that the Pentagon claims are its principal potential adversaries in the post-Cold War era.

Not only have President Clinton and the Congress failed to scale back the Pentagon's massive budget overkill, they have actually pushed through a budget that is higher than what Secretary of Defense William Perry asked for. The Clinton Administration's January 1995 military budget proposal was an as-

William D. Hartung is a Senior Research Fellow at the World Policy Institute of the New School for Social Research and the author of And Weapons for All.

tounding $257 billion, a figure roughly comparable to what the United States was spending at the end of the Nixon/Ford administrations, when the U.S.-Soviet arms race was still a going concern. Throughout the spring and summer of 1995, Congress made matters worse by tacking on more than $7 billion to the Pentagon's already enormous request, to pay for big ticket weapons like the B-2 bomber and Star Wars defense systems. The last straw came in December, when President Clinton signed Congress' inflated defense appropriations bill (despite threatening for months to veto it because of the $7 billion in added spending) because he thought it would help him win over key members to support his proposed troop deployment to Bosnia.

Why is the Pentagon getting a free ride when every other program in the budget is on the chopping block? Two key factors explain why this is happening: the U.S. military's misguided post-Cold War defense strategy, and the latest variation on the Pentagon's budgetary weapon of last resort, pork barrel politics. At present, the military budget constitutes the world's largest corporate welfare fund.

MISSION IMPLAUSIBLE

To the extent that there is any logic to the decision to hand over more than a quarter of a trillion dollars per year to the Pentagon, it lies in the U.S. military's current strategy of preparing to fight two major regional conflicts simultaneously. This approach was originally devised under the direction of Colin Powell during his stint as head of the National Security Council in the Bush Administration, and then ratified by the late Les Aspin's "bottom up review" of defense spending during the Clinton Administration's first year.

As Michael Klare makes clear in *Rogue States and Nuclear Outlaws*, the decision to focus on preparations for war with ambitious regional powers like Iraq and North Korea had little to do with any legitimate attempt to reassess America's defense needs. Its real purpose was to conjure up a threat that sounded menacing enough to justify continued high levels of military spending. Maverick Pentagon

From *Dollars and Sense*, May/June 1996, pp. 18-21, 37. © 1996 by *Dollars and Sense*, a progressive economics magazine published six times a year by the Economic Affairs Bureau, Inc. First-year subscriptions cost $18.95 and may be ordered by writing *Dollars and Sense*, One Summer Street, Somerville, MA 02143.

budget analyst Franklin Spinney has asserted that many of his colleagues are well aware that their strategy bears little resemblance to reality, but he argues that that was never the point: "The two-war strategy is just a marketing device to justify a high budget." Merrill McPeak, the retired Air Force Chief of Staff who served in that post from 1991, 1994, reinforced Spinney's point in an interview with *Time* magazine reporter Mark Thompson:

"We should walk away from the two-war strategy. Neither our historical experience nor our common sense leads us to think we need to do this. We've had to fight three major regional contingencies in the past 45 years [Korea, Vietnam, and Iraq]. One comes along every 15 years or so. Two have never come along simultaneously."

If the two-war scenario is just a marketing device, then the Pentagon deserves the salesman of the decade award. Other than a few independent voices like former House Armed Services Committee chairman Ron Dellums (D-CA), hardly anyone with political authority in Washington has dared to question the assumptions underlying the Pentagon's ill-considered new strategic doctrine, for fear of being labeled "soft on defense." It's a lot safer to be "soft on defense contractors," and rake in the contracts and campaign contributions that come with such a stance. And that's exactly what most members of Congress have been doing, particularly the Republican conservatives who are part of Newt Gingrich's so-called "revolution."

THE B-2 BOMBER

The fall and rise of the B-2 bomber is a case study in the workings of the new domestic geopolitics of defense spending. The B-2 — which at over $1 billion per copy is the most expensive aircraft ever built — was originally designed to wage nuclear war against the Soviet Union. The plane's original mission was absurd enough, but now that the Cold War is over and the Soviet Union no longer exists, even the Pentagon and the Air Force have had to admit that the B-2 no longer makes sense.

Yet despite vocal opposition to building more B-2s by everyone from Secretary of Defense William Perry to House Budget Committee Chairman John Kasich (R-OH), Congress still pushed through nearly half a billion dollars in new spending for the aircraft last year. These funds were merely the down payment on what could amount to an additional 20 B-2s, at a cost of more than $30 billion.

The B-2 may not be needed to defend the country, but it is definitely needed to defend the flow of Pentagon dollars to California and other defense-dependent states. The victory of the B-2 in the House of Representatives, which involved beating back two separate amendments aimed at killing the plane, drew upon an unholy alliance of unreconstructed hawks like Robert ("B-2 Bob") Dornan (R-CA) and liberal Democrats like Los Angeles representative Maxine Waters who happen to have B-2 contractors in their districts. The majority of the members of the Congressional Black Caucus joined their colleague Waters in voting for the B-2, as did a number of other prominent liberals who seem to view defense spending as the last truly invulnerable form of federal aid.

Wavering members of Congress had a good deal of help making up their minds on the B-2, in the form of a barrage

Nuclear submarine construction at General Dynamics shipyard in Groton, Connecticut.

of letters from B-2 employees orchestrated by prime contractor Northrop Grumman, and a flurry of glossy television, newspaper, and magazine ads that touted the plane as one of the "right technologies" for "right now." The independent National Security News Service has estimated that a coalition of B-2 contractors spent over $1 million on print advertisements alone in a one-month period prior to the House vote. TV spots on major Sunday talk shows such as ABC's "This Week With David Brinkley" undoubtedly ran into additional hundreds of thousands of dollars, if not millions. Members needing further persuasion could also count on receiving a friendly little reminder note from the Political Action Committee (PAC) of Northrop Grumman or another firm involved in the B-2 project, complete with a generous check.

THERE HAS BEEN A
TREND SINCE THE
END OF THE REAGAN
MILITARY SPENDING
BOOM TOWARD
CONSOLIDATING
DEFENSE
PRODUCTION IN
LESS UNIONIZED,
LOWER COST AREAS
IN THE SOUTH.

These corporate investments apparently paid off: an analysis by the Center for Responsive Politics indicates that the 219 members of the House who voted for the B-2 in June 1995 received an average of $3,285 from major B-2 contractors during 1993/94, nearly three times the average amount received by the 203 members who voted against the plane. After the June vote, Northrop Grumman kept the PAC money flowing, handing out an additional $70,000 over a six week period. More than 70% of these funds went to members who had supported the B-2, with the biggest contributions reserved for members of Congress from California (where most of the production work on the plane is done). Apparently every penny counted: a September resolution by Ron Dellums and John Kasich to strip B-2 funding out of the defense budget came within 6 votes of succeeding.

BRINGING HOME THE BACON

The spending patterns of Northrop Grumman and other top defense firms provide a window onto the shifting politics of defense spending. Historically, defense industry PACs have tried to hedge their bets by funding incumbent members of both parties, reserving their largest contributions for members of key committees such as Armed Services and Appropriations, or for members with a special interest in helping the firm (e.g., because the company has a major plant in the member's state or district). Since the Democrats ran the House of Representatives for four decades prior to the November 1994 elections, they routinely received more defense industry funding than Republicans. That

is, until the fall of 1994, after Newt Gingrich began warning corporate PACs that they would face "the coldest two years in Washington" they had ever seen if they didn't get on the stick and start giving money to Republican challengers.

It took defense firms a few months to respond to Gingrich's message, but they jumped to attention and adopted a strong pro-Republican tilt once the new Republican majority took over the Congress in January 1995. From January through April of 1995, nine top defense contractors donated a total of over $450,000 to members of the House, with more than 77% of it going to Republicans. The top recipients were House Appropriations Committee Chairman Robert Livingston (R-LA), $15,000; B-2 advocate Norman Dicks (D-WA), $10,500; House Majority Leader Dick Armey (R-TX), $9,000; and (surprise!) House Speaker Newt Gingrich, $8,000.

A study of 1995 defense spending votes in the Senate by the Council for a Livable World demonstrates that the pattern of pork barrel politicking that accompanied the B-2 budget battle in the House was far from an isolated instance. Of the $5 billion that the Senate Armed Services Committee added to the Pentagon budget beyond what the Department of Defense had requested, 81% of the added monies were targeted to states represented by Senators who sit on one of the two key defense committees, Armed Services and Defense Appropriations. The members of these panels certainly brought home the bacon. Senator Trent Lott inserted $1.4 billion for an amphibious assault ship to be built by Ingalls Shipbuilding, a major employer in his home state of Mississippi. Senator Christopher Bond (R-MO) benefited from the addition of 12 McDonnell Douglas F/A-18 aircraft that will be built at the company's St. Louis-area facility. And pro-defense Democratic Senator Joseph Lieberman of Connecticut helped steer through $90 million to find three CH-53 "Super Stallion" helicopters for the Marine Corps, aircraft that will be built by the Sikorsky Division of the Connecticut-based defense conglomerate United Technologies.

Other examples of pork barrel spending on defense projects abound. An October 1995 House-Senate conference committee on defense appropriations threw in $20 million for a cyclone coastal patrol boat built in Louisiana, the home state of Republican House Appropriations Committee Chairman Robert Livingston; $34 million more for the Multiple Launch Rocket system, built primarily in Texas and Arkansas; and last but not least, $30 million to build more cluster bombs at the Kansas Army Ammunition Plant in Parsons, Kansas. A Senate aide described the cluster bombs for Kansas as "a Dole item," referring to the role of Senate Majority Leader and Republican presidential candidate Robert Dole in adding the money to the defense bill. Not so coincidentally, Dole's presidential bid has received $5,000 — the maximum allowable by law — from Day and Zimmerman, the Pennsylvania firm that runs the Kansas Army Ammunition plant.

In parallel with this pronounced tendency to shower contracts and political contributions on either Republican or Democratic members of the key defense committees, there has been a trend since the end of the Reagan military spending boom toward consolidating defense production in less unionized, lower cost areas in the South. This trend will probably accelerate under the new Republican majority in the Congress, for the simple fact that most of the key Republican leadership hails from the South or Southwest. And as one defense official put it in an interview with the *Washington Post*, "All politics is local . . . If I'm a defense contractor I'm going to do everything I can to locate in a powerful chairman's district because I have immediate access. Jobs are important on the Hill." Aside from the independent-minded Sen. Mark Hatfield (R-OR), all the powerful chairmen of the key Armed Services and Appropriations panels that deal with defense matters are southern Republicans like Floyd Spence and Strom Thurmond of South Carolina, and Robert Livingston of Louisiana.

The geographic dispersion of the newly formed defense behemoth Lockheed Martin, a product of the March 1995 merger of Lockheed and Martin Marietta, further explains why the industry's march to the south is likely to continue. A majority of the workers at Lockheed Martin's 10,000 strong Marietta, Georgia facility live in Newt Gingrich's district, building everything from C-130 transport planes to P-3C anti-submarine warfare planes to the next generation F-22 stealth fighter plane. Funding for the company's Fort Worth, Texas fighter plane factory is zealously guarded by home state Republican powerhouses: House Majority leader Dick Armey and Senator and erstwhile presidential contender Senator Phil Gramm. And the firm is in the process of providing a $236,000 golden parachute to former Tennessee Governor and self-described "Washington outsider" Lamar Alexander in recognition of his service on the Martin Marietta board of directors in the period leading up to the merger.

WHAT TO DO: CUT THE PENTAGON DOWN TO SIZE

Advocates of higher military spending won most of their budget battles during 1995 with relative ease, but they may yet lose the war. As cuts in health care, welfare, education, and other necessary programs start to be felt in com-

IF PRESIDENT CLINTON
WAS SMART,
HE WOULD SUPPORT
THE PROGRESSIVE
CAUCUS IN ITS
EFFORTS TO CUT THE
PENTAGON BUDGET.

munities throughout the country, the Pentagon's charmed status will come under much harsher public scrutiny.

Even during 1995, there were important victories for supporters of Pentagon spending cuts. In a small but significant gain for fairness, Rep. Bernie Sanders (I-VT) shamed a majority of his colleagues into stripping out $31 million in taxpayer funding that the Pentagon had planned to hand over to Lockheed Martin to help pay lavish bonuses to "truly needy" executives and board members like Lamar Alexander and Norman Augustine who were affected by the company's spring 1995 merger.

The Sanders amendment is just one example of a long list of issues relating to waste, fraud and abuse at the Pentagon that have been raised by the Congressional Progressive Caucus under the leadership of Sanders and Rep. Peter DeFazio (D-OR). Other issues brought to light by the caucus include the Air Force's routine practice of flying generals and cadets around in its own fleet of Lear jets for such critical missions as returning from vacations in Europe or attending football games in Hawaii; setting aside funds to build a third golf course at one particularly favored military base; and spending funds on Star Wars research that could have been used to get thousands of military personnel and their dependents off of Food Stamps.

Like the $900 hammers and the $6,000 toilets seats that finally helped raise public outrage over the Reagan military buildup in the 1980s, the concrete examples of unconscionable waste that have been highlighted by Sanders and DeFazio offer the best hope of sparking a popular backlash against the Pentagon's $260 billion-plus post-Cold War budget. To his credit, DeFazio has also taken a stand against special interest money in defense decisionmaking by being the first lawmaker to sign a pledge organized by Peace Action, the nation's largest national grassroots peace group. Signers commit themselves to accept no funds from any weapons manufacturing company or trade association.

If President Clinton was smart, he would support the Progressive Caucus in its efforts to cut the Pentagon budget, instead of tilting rightward on defense issues every time he needs a favor from the Republican-controlled Congress. Otherwise he will have precious little to distinguish himself on Pentagon budget issues from his Republican opponent in the 1996 campaign, and he will have thrown away an issue that could have brought populist Reagan Democrats and Perotistas back into the Democratic column.

As this article went to press, the Clinton Administration put forward a total military spending proposal of more than $252 billion for Fiscal 1997, a modest inflation-adjusted cut of roughly 6% from the bloated budget that was passed by Congress last year. Republican Congressional hawks like Floyd Spence and Strom Thurmond have already threatened to increase the President's proposal by $10 to $12 billion. Meanwhile, Secretary of Defense William Perry reassured major defense contractors that the re-election of Bill Clinton would be good for their bottom lines. Perry pointed out that the Pentagon plans to increase spending on new weapons systems from $38 billion this year to over $60 billion by the end of this decade. So much for reinventing government.

Whether or not Clinton chooses to act, there must be a grassroots outcry against the unnecessary billions that are being handed to the Pentagon and its contracting network at the expense of already underfunded domestic needs. Otherwise, the Department of Defense will continue to live off the fat of the land while necessary public investments in the health, welfare, and employment of the majority of Americans go begging for funds. We can't afford to let that happen.

Resources: Rogue States and Nuclear Outlaws: America's Search for a New Foreign Policy, Michael Klare, 1995; "Our Overstuffed Armed Forces," Lawrence J. Korb, *Foreign Affairs*, November/December 1995; "Ready for What? — The Phantom Readiness Crisis," *The Defense Monitor*, Center for Defense Information, June 1995; "Why the Pentagon Gets a Free Ride," Mark Thompson, *Time*, June 5, 1995; Nancy Watzman and Sheila Krumholz, *The Best Defense: Will Campaign Contributions Protect the Industry?*, Center for Responsive Politics, July 12, 1995.

Editor's note: This article is an adapted and updated version of William D. Hartung, "Notes from the Underground: An Outsider's Guide to the Defense Budget Debate," which appeared in the Fall 1995 edition of the *World Policy Journal*, available from the World Policy Institute at the New School, 65 Fifth Ave., Suite 413, New York, NY, 10003, tel. 212-229-5808.

For information on what you can do: Peace Action, 1819 H St. NW, Suite 660, Washington, DC 20036-3606, tel. 202-862-9740.

Consider this paradox: The cold war is over and, despite the fact that the Soviet Union is no more, the Pentagon budget is slated to increase over the next seven years. Meanwhile, however, we are virtually defenseless against what Senator Sam Nunn calls our "number one security concern"—small nuclear weapons in the hands of extremists or rogue nations.

The current defense posture of the United States is the Maginot line of the late twentieth century. Like that fortified border France built to defend against Germany after World War I, ours is a huge investment designed to fight the last generation's battles. (The Maginot line was, of course, skirted with ease by Hitler's blitzkrieg.)

DETERRENCE IS DEAD, BUT WE CAN KILL THE NUCLEAR THREAT

GAR ALPEROVITZ, KAI BIRD & THAD WILLIAMSON

BUY THE NUKES

ILLUSTRATED BY RANDALL ENOS

America is a nation uniquely protected from invasion by two oceanic moats. But it remains vulnerable to nuclear weapons. Many are relatively small, easy to produce, cheap and easy to deliver. With the end of the cold war, they present a threat to the United States that is growing, not diminishing. The Pentagon's budget, however, deals with the new threat almost as an after-thought. Instead, it seeks to fight wars in all parts of the globe and hold on to nuclear weapons of various sizes and shapes.

In the wake of the World Trade Center and Oklahoma City

taining a nuclear arsenal. In today's era—characterized by grow-ing technical and political imponderables—the notion that we can continue to rely on nuclear deterrence for real security seems ridiculously naïve. Indeed, the deterrence theory collapses en-tirely in the event of a terrorist act. How and where could we re-taliate? Moreover, nuclear weapons now play a role unfavorable to the United States even within Washington's own narrow terms of reference. In June 1992 the late Les Aspin, then chairman of the House Armed Services Committee, observed: "A world

SO LONG AS VAST NUMBERS OF NUCLEAR DEVICES AND UNSECURED FISSILE MATERIALS EXIST, PROSPECTS FOR PREVENTING DI-VERSION REMAIN DUBIOUS. FORMER ASSISTANT SECRETARY OF DEFENSE GRAHAM ALLISON OBSERVES THAT NUCLEAR DEVICES CAN BE SHIPPED IN PIECES 'SMALL AND LIGHT ENOUGH TO GO BY FEDERAL EXPRESS, U.P.S. OR EVEN THE U.S. POSTAL SERVICE.'

bombings, it is no longer difficult to imagine a determined ter-rorist group getting its hands on a crude nuclear device. Given the large number of nuclear weapons scattered around the globe—and the Russian mafia's exploitation of ever greater eco-nomic insecurity in the former Soviet Union—the ingredients for instruments of mass destruction can all too easily be smug-gled out of current inventories. In August 1994 German police recovered almost a pound of plutonium at the Munich airport; in December 1994 Czech police seized more than six pounds of highly enriched uranium from the back seat of a car in Prague. In February 1995 Russian Interior Minister Viktor Yerin reported that he was investigating some thirty cases in which radioactive materials had been stolen from Russian nuclear facilities.

It would be tragically simple to hide a nuclear weapon aboard a freighter bound for New York or San Francisco harbor. Con-sider also the vast expanse of the American-Canadian border and the number of immigrants who illegally cross over from Mexico every day. Former Assistant Secretary of Defense Gra-ham Allison, now director of Harvard's Center for Science and International Affairs, observes that a "criminal or terrorist group could even ship a weapon into the United States in pieces small and light enough to go by Federal Express, U.P.S. or even the U.S. postal service."

Under the START II treaty, now awaiting ratification here and in Russia, the United States will reduce its strategic warheads from roughly 8,000 today to 3,500 by the year 2003. But after tactical weapons are added in, there will still be nearly 12,000 nuclear weapons outside the U.S. arsenal. By the end of the 1990s some 100 metric tons of plutonium are expected to be extracted from obsolete U.S. and Russian weap-ons. So long as vast numbers of nuclear devices and unsecured fissile materials exist, prospects for preventing diversion to other countries or organizations will remain dubious.

During the cold war, proponents of nuclear weapons could cite the deterrent value of such arms to argue in favor of main-

without nuclear weapons would not be disadvantageous to the United States. In fact, a world without nuclear weapons would actually be better. Nuclear weapons are still the big equalizer, but now the United States is not the equalizer but the equalizee."

In cold, hard, realistic terms, nuclear weapons are the bul-wark of our Maginot line. Not only are such weapons increas-ingly useless; in maintaining them the United States encourages other nations to build and hold them "for their own protection" as well—thereby increasing the very threat U.S. policy seeks to contain. Even so ardent a cold warrior as Paul Nitze agrees that we "might reasonably contemplate making nuclear weapons largely obsolete for the most practical and fundamental strate-gic missions."

The obsolescence of nuclear weapons, as a usable means of warfare or as a deterrent, is slowly being recognized within the national security establishment; but largely unaddressed is the question of what to do. If we want real security—rather than the mere trappings of it—it is time for a radical refocusing of resources, for putting our money where the true problem lies. There is an obvious solution: The United States should buy up nuclear weapons throughout the globe and then dismantle them. Along with reducing the U.S. nuclear arsenal, this should be the top pri-ority of U.S. national security policy.

Washington has, in fact, been nibbling away at buying nu-clear security: In 1993 it gave $59 million to Belarus to dis-mantle its small arsenal; in 1994 it paid Kazakhstan an undisclosed amount estimated at $20-30 million in compensa-tion for the removal of some 600 kilograms of weapons-grade uranium; and also in 1994 it offered Ukraine some $900 million in economic assistance after it renounced nuclear weapons. The United States has appropriated a total of $1.6 billion over the past five years to help the former Soviet republics disarm and safeguard nuclear materials. There is also a $12 billion, twenty-year agreement under way to buy 500 tons of weapons-grade uranium from Russia.

The Clinton Administration has used the promise of improved economic ties to rein in North Korea's nuclear weapons effort as well. In October 1994 the United States agreed to help Pyong-yang build two "safe" nuclear energy reactors in return for a freeze of its weapons program. A State Department official de-

Gar Alperovitz is the author of The Decision to Use the Atomic Bomb *(Knopf). Kai Bird is the author of* The Chairman: John J. McCloy/The Making of the American Establishment *(Simon and Schuster). Thad Williamson is research associate at the National Center for Economic and Security Alternatives.*

4. PRODUCTS: Foreign and Defense Policy

scribed the overall approach as "Walk softly and carry a big carrot." The problem is, the carrots offered have been disproportionately tiny in comparison with the urgency of the issue—and puny in relation to most items in the Pentagon's weapons budget. Fifteen months after the agreement with North Korea, implementation of the plan remains slow and international inspectors have not had complete access to all nuclear facilities. Although there has been recent forward motion, the parties are still struggling over details of the aid program. Also, Congressional Republicans have threatened to slash by 40 percent the $23 mil-

could also offer enormous sums of money as rewards to individuals who report on cheating or inform on proliferators and nuclear smugglers. (Criteria for who qualifies would undoubtedly involve difficult choices, but in the end the priority must obviously be the maintenance of U.S. nuclear security.)

If $25 billion off the top of the military budget is not enough, then we could go to $50 billion. This sum would buy an impressive amount of hardware, nuclear and even non-nuclear, including chemical and biological. The total combined military budgets of non-allied countries, other than those of the former Soviet Union,

THE PENTAGON HAS BEEN PLAYING PENNY ANTE IN THE LIFE-AND-DEATH POKER GAME CONCERNING THE ONLY REAL DIRECT THREAT TO AMERICAN SECURITY. WE COULD BUY OUT—EVEN AT THE INFLATED VALUE OF, SAY, $5 MILLION APIECE—ALL THE WARHEADS REMAINING WORLDWIDE AFTER IMPLEMENTATION OF THE START II TREATY, AND STILL HAVE MONEY LEFT OVER.

lion the United States is supposed to contribute to the incentive package. The purchase of Russian uranium has dragged because the United States Enrichment Corporation, a semi-private entity created by Congress to buy up highly enriched uranium, has encountered difficulties with private uranium interests, which fear world prices will ultimately suffer under the program. (Even if the plan is successful, Russia will still have a stockpile estimated at 700 tons of weapons-grade uranium.) Ukraine's leaders recently warned that without further assistance they may have to suspend their nuclear-weapons dismantling program.

Total U.S. spending on nuclear-war prevention in fiscal 1995 amounted to roughly $2.2 billion, less than 1 percent of the Pentagon budget. This includes assistance to the former Soviet republics for dismantling weapons and safeguarding materials; the costs of disassembling U.S. nuclear weapons; and support for nonproliferation research, the negotiation and implementation of arms control and nonproliferation agreements, and the International Atomic Energy Agency. The $27 billion spent maintaining our own nuclear posture is almost thirteen times this figure. U.S. military analysts have observed that spending money to cut down what remains of the former Soviet nuclear threat is a highly efficient defense strategy. For the right price it would be possible to purchase and dispose of or safeguard a very high percentage of the world's existing nuclear supplies—and also to make sure that new production is curtailed.

In fiscal 1996 nearly $265 billion is scheduled to be spent for national security through traditional "defense" programs—almost as much as the rest of the world combined spends on defense, and roughly three times more than any other single nation. Suppose instead the United States peeled off $25 billion—the cost of about a dozen B-2 bombers—from the top of this huge budget to see what else it could buy. Since the military expenditures of most other nations are relatively small—and their domestic needs large—there is no question that this country could purchase a great deal. We

that possess or have sought nuclear weapons—including Syria, North Korea, Libya, Iran, Iraq, Algeria, China, India and Pakistan—is estimated to be approximately $32 billion.

For $100 billion we could not only buy out the annual operating budgets of the entire military establishments of the above nine nations, we could also buy (even at the inflated value of, say, $5 million apiece) all the warheads that will remain worldwide after implementation of the START II treaty—and still have money left over.

If this sounds outrageously expensive, note that a kitty of $25 billion per year for ten years would produce $250 billion. If we took $50 billion from the defense budget to buy down other nuclear powers for ten years running, there would be $500 billion to spend. In either case, the totals are enough to buy out most of the world's significant military and nuclear threats—and to fund an aggressive strategy for safeguarding and removing surplus plutonium and highly enriched uranium from the former Soviet Union.

Variations on this basic theme are obviously possible—and alternative scenarios involving different mixes of build-down and buyout can be developed. (Graham Allison, for instance, has suggested an overall program in the $30 billion range, with Europe and Japan paying two-thirds of the cost.) If the buyout package is properly designed, like the Marshall Plan it could stimulate the U.S. economy at the same time that it helps restructure and build trading-partner economies around the world. A serious effort would obviously also require the United States to take the lead with other major powers simultaneously to reduce radically their own arsenals—else others cannot be expected to take the effort seriously.

The central point is that even as the Pentagon spends hundreds of billions to hold on to ever more useless missiles and bombers, and prepare for increasingly unlikely wars abroad, it has been playing penny ante in the life-and-death poker game concerning the only real direct threat to American security. It is time to confront our modern nuclear Maginot line—before it gives way to a blitzkrieg that would make Oklahoma City look like child's play.

Index

Credits/Acknowledgments

Cover design by Charles Vitelli

1. Foundations of American Politics
Facing overview—National Archives photo. 51—Illustration by Frederick H. Carlson/F. Carlson Illustration. 70—Illustration by Stephen D. Kroeger.

2. Structures of American Politics
Facing overview—Library of Congress photo by McPheeters & Krouier.

3. Process of American Politics
Facing overview—AP/Wide World photo by Ron Edmonds. 218—National Journal photo by Richard A. Bloom.

4. Products of American Politics
Facing overview—U.S. Air Force photo by Sergeant Bob Simons. 237—The World & I photo.

ANNUAL EDITIONS ARTICLE REVIEW FORM

■ NAME: _____ DATE: _____

■ TITLE AND NUMBER OF ARTICLE: _____

■ BRIEFLY STATE THE MAIN IDEA OF THIS ARTICLE: _____

_____

■ LIST THREE IMPORTANT FACTS THAT THE AUTHOR USES TO SUPPORT THE MAIN IDEA:

_____

_____

_____

_____

■ WHAT INFORMATION OR IDEAS DISCUSSED IN THIS ARTICLE ARE ALSO DISCUSSED IN YOUR TEXTBOOK OR OTHER READINGS THAT YOU HAVE DONE? LIST THE TEXTBOOK CHAPTERS AND PAGE NUMBERS:

_____

_____

_____

_____

_____

■ LIST ANY EXAMPLES OF BIAS OR FAULTY REASONING THAT YOU FOUND IN THE ARTICLE:

_____

_____

_____

_____

■ LIST ANY NEW TERMS/CONCEPTS THAT WERE DISCUSSED IN THE ARTICLE, AND WRITE A SHORT DEFINITION:

_____

_____

_____

_____

*Your instructor may require you to use this ANNUAL EDITIONS Article Review Form in any number of ways: for articles that are assigned, for extra credit, as a tool to assist in developing assigned papers, or simply for your own reference. Even if it is not required, we encourage you to photocopy and use this page; you will find that reflecting on the articles will greatly enhance the information from your text.

We Want Your Advice

ANNUAL EDITIONS revisions depend on two major opinion sources: one is our Advisory Board, listed in the front of this volume, which works with us in scanning the thousands of articles published in the public press each year; the other is you—the person actually using the book. Please help us and the users of the next edition by completing the prepaid article rating form on this page and returning it to us. Thank you for your help!

ANNUAL EDITIONS: AMERICAN GOVERNMENT 97/98
Article Rating Form

Here is an opportunity for you to have direct input into the next revision of this volume. We would like you to rate each of the 66 articles listed below, using the following scale:

1. **Excellent: should definitely be retained**
2. **Above average: should probably be retained**
3. **Below average: should probably be deleted**
4. **Poor: should definitely be deleted**

Your ratings will play a vital part in the next revision. So please mail this prepaid form to us just as soon as you complete it.
Thanks for your help!

Rating	Article	Rating	Article
	1. The Declaration of Independence, 1776		35. In Whose Court?
	2. The Constitution of the United States, 1787		36. Still Trying to Reinvent Government
	3. The Size and Variety of the Union as a Check on Faction		37. Government *Can* Work
	4. Checks and Balances		38. You Can't Fix It If You Don't Raise the Hood
	5. The Judiciary		39. Uncle Sam's Corporate Lawyers
	6. The Empty Symbolism of American Politics		40. Why Americans Don't Vote
	7. What Will Rogers Could Teach the Age of Limbaugh		41. What If We Held an Election and Nobody Came?
	8. The Selfish Decade		42. The Politics of Money
	9. A Civics Lesson		43. The Dirtiest Election Ever
	10. The Spiral of Inequality		44. Bill's Big Backers
	11. You Say You Want a Devolution		45. Small Change
	12. The Last Taboo		46. Primary Colours: Nasty, Brutish and Short?
	13. Can Democratic Government Survive?		47. Golden Mean
	14. The Paradox of Integration		48. Demosclerosis
	15. Our Bodies, Our Souls		49. Going to Extremes, Losing the Center
	16. Race and the Constitution		50. Cultivating the Grass Roots to Reap Legislative Benefits
	17. The Bill of Rights and the Supreme Court: A Foreigner's View		51. This Mr. Smith Gets His Way In Washington: Federal Express Chief Twists Some Big Arms
	18. Racial Gerrymandering		52. Resisting Pressures on a Free Press
	19. Rule by Law		53. Heeding the Call
	20. Let Us Pray		54. Did You Have a Good Week?
	21. Do We Ask Too Much of Presidents?		55. The 'New' Media and Politics: What Does the Future Hold?
	22. The Separated System		56. Hillary and Us: Rocky Relationship with Media? Not Really, Just No Relationship at All
	23. Is the President a Waffler?		57. Federal Government Mandates: Why the States Are Complaining
	24. An Agenda at Risk?		58. The Entitlement Time Bomb
	25. Rush to Judgment: Picking Presidents		59. Put an End to Corporate Welfare
	26. Will Clinton Sing Second-Term Blues?		60. The Balanced Budget Crusade
	27. Imperial Congress		61. Ten Essential Observations on Guns in America
	28. *Too Representative Government*		62. Do It Yourself
	29. The "Outside" Role: A Leadership Challenge		63. Abolish Income Tax and the IRS
	30. It's Not *Mr. Smith Goes to Washington*		64. America's Incoherent Foreign Policy
	31. What Am I? A Potted Plant?		65. Pumping Up the Pentagon: The Domestic Geopolitics of Military Spending
	32. A Conservative Case for Judicial Activism		66. Buy the Nukes
	33. The Rehnquist Reins		
	34. Illiberal Court		

(Continued on next page)

ABOUT YOU

Name _____ Date _____

Are you a teacher? ❑ Or a student? ❑

Your school name _____

Department _____

Address _____

City _____ State _____ Zip _____

School telephone # _____

YOUR COMMENTS ARE IMPORTANT TO US !

Please fill in the following information:

For which course did you use this book? _____

Did you use a text with this *ANNUAL EDITION*? ❑ yes ❑ no

What was the title of the text? _____

What are your general reactions to the *Annual Editions* concept?

Have you read any particular articles recently that you think should be included in the next edition?

Are there any articles you feel should be replaced in the next edition? Why?

Are there any World Wide Web sites you feel should be included in the next edition? Please annotate.

May we contact you for editorial input?

May we quote your comments?

**No Postage
Necessary
if Mailed
in the
United States**

ANNUAL EDITIONS: AMERICAN GOVERNMENT 97/98

BUSINESS REPLY MAIL

First Class   Permit No. 84   Guilford, CT

Postage will be paid by addressee

Dushkin/McGraw·Hill
Sluice Dock
Guilford, Connecticut 06437